ACCOUNTING FOR MANAGERS AND INVESTORS

MICHAEL H. GRANOF
Graduate School of Business
University of Texas at Austin

PRENTICE-HALL, INC., Englewood Cliffs, New Jersey 07632

Library of Congress Cataloging in Publication Data

GRANOF, MICHAEL H.
    Accounting for managers and investors.

    Includes index.
    1. Accounting. I. Title.
HF5635.G7718 1983   657   82-16598
ISBN 0-13-002725-1

Editorial/production supervision
    and interior design: LINDA C. MASON
Cover design: WANDA LUBELSKA
Manufacturing buyer: RAY KEATING

Printed in the United States of America
10   9   8   7   6   5   4   3

ISBN 0-13-002725-1

Prentice-Hall International, Inc., *London*
Prentice-Hall of Australia Pty. Limited, *Sydney*
Editora Prentice-Hall do Brasil, Ltda., *Rio de Janeiro*
Prentice-Hall Canada Inc., *Toronto*
Prentice-Hall of India Private Limited, *New Delhi*
Prentice-Hall of Japan, Inc., *Tokyo*
Prentice-Hall of Southeast Asia Pte. Ltd., *Singapore*
Whitehall Books Limited, *Wellington, New Zealand*

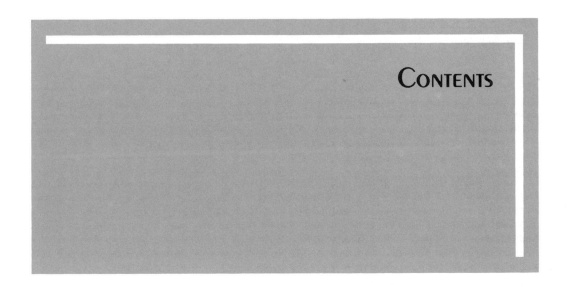

Contents

Preface

This book is intended as an introduction to accounting and financial reporting. Its objective is to provide an understanding of the principles and practices of accounting in a way that captures the discipline's rigor, intellectual richness, and dynamism. It is entitled *Accounting for Managers and Investors* primarily because managers and investors are two large and easily identifiable groups which prepare and use accounting information. The subject matter is equally relevant to others whose professional or personal interests will require them to make decisions that will have financial consequences.

Accounting for Managers and Investors has been written as a basic text for introductory courses that encompass topics in both financial and managerial accounting. The material on financial accounting has been drawn extensively from *Financial Accounting: Principles and Issues*, by this author. But much of it has been recast so as to stress the managerial implications of financial reporting practices. Efforts have been made, for example, to point out managerial actions that will have an impact on reported earnings that will be counter to their effect on the firm's true economic interest.

This text is distinguished from other introductory texts by the great emphasis which it places upon the choices among principles and practices that the accounting profession, as well as individual accountants and managers, must make. Accounting summarizes financial events of the past and projects the consequences of decisions that will affect the future. A financial history or forecast—like those of politics and economics—can be presented in a number of different ways. The optimum manner depends very much on the decisions that it is intended to facilitate and the information preferences of the parties that will rely on it. Seldom, if ever, is there a single "correct" version of a financial statement.

An underlying premise of this book is that anyone who uses or prepares financial statements must develop the ability to understand the essence of economic events and to evaluate the alternatives by which they can be described. The text does, of course, present "generally accepted accounting principles"—those established by official rule-making authorities and widely accepted by managers and accountants. It endeavors to explain why they, as opposed to other possible conventions, have been accepted. But it also evaluates alternatives.

The alternatives are focused upon for several reasons, all of which are indicative of the level of understanding and types of skills that this text seeks to promote. First, an understanding of alternative practices leads to an appreciation of the rationale for, as well as the deficiencies of, the prescribed practices. Indeed, several generally accepted conventions make little sense except when compared with the other possibilities.

Second, the principles on which particular reports are based may not be appropriate for purposes other than for which they were designed. Managers and investors must be aware of their limitations and be able to compensate for them.

Third, accounting is a powerful weapon in negotiations and other forms of advocacy proceedings. Managers must be able to present financial data in a way that best serves the interests that they represent. At the same time, they must have sufficient understanding of accounting principles to call into question the financial data presented by the opposition. This is not to imply that they engage in fraud or deceit. Quite the contrary, it is merely to stress that accounting reports and the principles on which they are based should not be considered inviolate. They are subject to challenge and change by the parties using them.

Fourth, companies have considerable discretion over amounts reported in their financial statements. In making comparisons among firms, analysts must be able to distinguish between differences of economic substance and those attributable merely to accounting practices.

Fifth, current accounting conventions are as immutable only as the composition of the present rule-making boards. Managers and investors may be directly affected by changes in accounting principles and need the skills to evaluate them and determine their implications for the firms with which they are concerned.

Admittedly the focus upon alternatives adds a measure of complexity to the study of accounting. But it does no service to students of accounting to shelter them from reality by pretending that current conventions are the only conventions. Controversy is not something of which accountants should be ashamed. Challenge and change are the signs of a vibrant profession, one endeavoring to adapt to new economic conditions and commercial practices.

Compared with other introductions to accounting, this text cannot be described as "procedural." It is an inadequate source of reference for an aspiring bookkeeper or businessman who wants to set up an accounting system for a small enterprise. It does not, however, slight the double-entry system of accounts. Almost three chapters are devoted to the double-entry structure of accounts, the accounting cycle, and routine bookkeeping procedures. Many concepts and issues throughout this text are explained in terms of journal entries. The double-entry system is a model of order and logic. It is the basis of modern accounting practice as well as theory and it is unmatched as a pedogogical vehicle for understanding virtually all accounting issues.

This volume is divided into two parts. The first pertains to financial accounting; the second to managerial accounting. As explained in the text, this distinction between the two is not nearly so sharp as the organization of the book might suggest. The separation was made because most accounting instructors prefer to deal with topics conventionally classified as managerial accounting apart from those thought of as financial accounting. For the most part, the managerial chapters are free-standing and can easily be integrated into the financial section.

The problem material that accompanies each chapter is intended to be instructive and challenging. Very few problems are of the type for which a solution can be developed by merely changing the numbers of an illustration found in the body of the chapter. Many serve to highlight accounting issues. They are designed to draw attention to the rationale for, or limitations of, a particular accounting practice. Numerous problems are inspired by actual annual reports or news items that have appeared in the financial press.

Each chapter is accompanied by an exercise for review and self-study. It is intended to solidify the student's understanding of an important concept by breaking it down into a series of simple leading questions.

I am most appreciative of the constructive comments of the following professors who reviewed the draft of this text: Shahid L. Ansari (New York University); Thomas G. Evans (University of South Carolina); Sanford C. Gunn (State University of New York at Buffalo); and Mahmood A. Qureshi (California State University, Northridge).

I also wish to express gratitude toward Alex and Irwin Jarett who provided the illustrations of computer graphics included in Chapter 22.

M. H. G.
Austin, Texas

INTRODUCTION 1

ACCOUNTING: A DYNAMIC DISCIPLINE

Accounting involves the collection, summarization and reporting of financial data. It is a dynamic discipline, in which new principles and procedures are constantly evolving. The objective of this text is to provide its readers—presumably current and future managers and investors—with the knowledge and skills necessary to take full advantage of accounting information. They should be able to use it in planning, controlling and evaluating the activities of the organizations as well as in making personal and corporate investment decisions. They should be aware not only of the wealth of information that financial reports can provide, but equally important, be cognizant of their limitations. They should, at the very least, be able to know when to consult accounting specialists and to ask the right questions of them.

The theme of this book is that there are few accounting principles or techniques that are "correct" and unassailable. Accounting aims to provide information that facilitates the decisions that managers and investors, among others, have the responsibility to make. What is most correct is generally what is most useful. It is essential that a manager or investor who relies on accounting reports understand not only why they have been prepared as they have, but also what are the possible alternatives.

OBJECTIVES OF ACCOUNTING

Accounting is concerned with the description of economic events, with the measurement of economic values, and with the determination of periodic changes in such values. It aims to provide information that serves several broad purposes. Among them are:

1. *Allocating the scarce resources of our society.* Under any form of economic arrangement, be it capitalism or socialism, decisions as to where capital should be invested are made on the basis of information contained in financial statements. In a free enterprise system, private investors make determinations as to the stock of companies they purchase largely on the basis of data contained in periodic reports of earnings. Bankers and other suppliers of funds study financial reports before making loan decisions. Government agencies decide whom to tax and whom to subsidize on the basis of financial reports. The decisions of labor unions as to how much of a wage increase to seek are strongly influenced by reports of profit or loss.

2. *Managing and directing the resources within an organization.* Managers of profit and nonprofit entities alike rely upon accounting information to assure that they maintain effective control over both their human and material resources and to make certain that within their organizations they allocate such resources to the products, subunits, or functions where they can be most productive.

3. *Reporting on the custodianship of resources under the command of individuals or organizations.* Individuals, acting either as investors or merely as citizens, entrust resources to professional managers and governmental officials. They expect such managers or officials to provide them with periodic reports by which their performance in office can be evaluated.

Focus on Future

Accounting focuses on the *measurement and communication* of a wide range of financial data. Accountants provide the information required to make decisions as to where to allocate financial resources, and once such decisions are made they provide the data necessary to effectively control such resources. Periodically, as the management process is being carried out, accountants "report the score"—they provide information by which the results of prior decisions can be evaluated.

Viewed from a slightly different perspective, accounting aims to enable managers, investors, creditors, and other users of financial statements to determine the future earning power of an enterprise. Decisions made today can affect only the future, not the past. Those who seek information from financial statements are primarily concerned with how well the enterprise will perform in the years to come rather than those gone by. Will the enterprise be able to satisfy its obligations to those to whom it is indebted? Will it be able to meet the wage demands of its employees? Will it be able to provide adequate returns to its owners?

What will occur in the future, however, can best be predicted by what has taken place in the past. The competence of management in administering the enterprise in the years to come can most readily be forecast by examining the record of prior years. The ability of a firm to generate revenues in years ahead depends in large measure on resources acquired in periods behind. Accounting, while it necessarily reports on events of the past, does so to facilitate decisions that will affect the future.

FINANCIAL VERSUS MANAGEMENT ACCOUNTING

A distinction is conventionally made between *financial* accounting and *management* accounting. Financial accounting is concerned with reports to parties external to the organization. Management accounting pertains to financial data to be used within the organization.

Financial accounting focuses primarily on providing information to *investors* and *potential investors.* Other groups of users such as creditors, regulatory agencies, or employees, may also of course be able to obtain a wealth of vital information from the accounting reports. But over the years, in circumstances in which the information needs of user groups have been in conflict, the demands of investors have been given priority. In reporting to outsiders, organizations must adhere to "generally accepted" accounting principles. These principles represent a combination of pronouncements by rule-making authorities and long-standing traditions. They help to assure that the reports are comparable to those of other organizations, that they are consistent over time, and that they are not deliberately false or misleading.

Management accounting serves the information requirement of insiders—directors, managers, and employees. It provides the information needed to establish the objectives of the organization, to develop the strategies and plans to fulfill those objectives, to administer and control the day-to-day activities of the organization, and to evaluate periodically the success that the organization is having in fulfilling its objectives. When it issues reports to insiders, an organization need not satisfy externally imposed standards or adhere to specified accounting principles. The number, frequency, and content of reports can be determined at the discretion of management.

Part I of this text deals with topics that are usually considered within the realm of financial accounting; Part II with those in the area of management accounting. The boundaries between the two are not, however, nearly as distinct as may be implied by the organization of this book. It is important for a manager to be as facile with financial accounting as with management accounting. Most transactions in which a firm might engage have both managerial and financial accounting ramifications. The means of deciding, for example, whether a firm should replace an old machine with a new one is conventionally considered an issue of management accounting. The manner in which the event is reported in the financial statements—an important factor to be taken into account in making the decision—is a topic of financial accounting.

THEME OF BOOK

A theme of the book is that there are very few accounting principles which are not subject to challenge. It is essential that the manager understand not only how accounting is currently practiced and why it is so practiced but also, and most significantly, which are the possible alternatives.

Accountants are concerned with the description of economic events, with the *measurement* of economic values, and with the determination of periodic changes in such economic values. A brief example can be used to demonstrate the difficulty of establishing precise rules of measurement that can be unanimously agreed upon. The illustration involves concepts and terminology that will be defined or explained in subsequent chapters; a layman's understanding of them should suffice, however, to appreciate why a number of basic accounting issues remain unresolved.

Example

Chemco, Inc., was organized on January 1, 1983. On that date the company sold to individual investors shares of common stock for $1 million cash. The objective of the company was to purchase a liquid solvent from a chemical company and to resell and deliver it to industrial customers. Upon its formation the company purchased storage tanks, delivery trucks, and other equipment at a total cost of $1 million. The useful life of such *fixed assets* was estimated as 10 years.

The following additional events took place during the company's first year of operations:

1. The company purchased 4 million gallons of solvent at a total cost of $2.4 million (an average cost of $.60 per gallon).
2. The company sold 3.6 million gallons of solvent at a price of $.70 per gallon. Total sales revenue was, therefore, $2.52 million and at the end of the year the firm had in inventory (i.e., goods available for sale) the 400,000 gallons that had not yet been sold.
3. Total operating costs for the year, including labor, advertising, selling, and administrative costs, were $200,000.

income—a measure of "better-offness"

The question at issue is how much profit did the firm earn during its first year of operations. Income, or profit, is a measure of change in "well-being." How much "better off" was the firm at the end of the year than it was at the beginning?

Profit is commonly computed by deducting from sales or other revenues the expenses incurred in the production of such revenues. Thus, for the first year of operations:

Sales revenue for the year was $2.52 million. Cost of the solvent *purchased* (at an *average* price of $.60 per gallon) was $2.4 million, but of the 4 million gallons purchased only 3.6 million gallons, or 90 percent of those purchased, were actually sold. Hence, the cost of the solvent actually sold was 90 percent of $2.4 million, or $2,160,000. Cost of the remaining 400,000 gallons that were being held in inventory awaiting sale cannot be considered an expense of the first year of operations since the solvent has not yet been used and can be assumed to retain its original value.

Operating expenses of the period were $200,000. In addition, the company purchased fixed assets—tanks, trucks, and equipment—at a cost of $1 million. But the entire purchase price of such fixed assets cannot be considered to be an expense only of the first year of operations. The assets have a 10-year life; they will serve to benefit 10 accounting periods. The cost must be spread over, or *allocated* to, each of the 10 periods. Hence, *depreciation* for the period was $1 million ÷ 10 = $100,000.

The implication of the "bottom line" of the income statement is that Chemco, Inc., and collectively its stockholders were $60,000 better off at the end of the first year of operations than they were at the beginning. The computation of net income was governed by "generally accepted accounting principles" —those currently followed by the large majority of accountants and their clients.

Sales revenue (3.6 million gal @ $.70 per gal)		$2,520,000
Less: Costs applicable to revenues:		
Cost of goods sold (3.6 million gal @ $.60 per gal)	$2,160,000	
Other operating expenses	200,000	
Depreciation ($1 million ÷ 10 years)	100,000	2,460,000
Income		$ 60,000

But is the company really $60,000 better off at the end of the year than it was at the beginning? Consider some alternative approaches to determining the income of the company.

Should Increases in Market Values of Assets be Recognized?

Suppose that the "going" or "market" price for the fixed assets which the company had purchased on January 1 for $1 million had, by year end, increased to $1,150,000. Should $150,000 be added to the revenues ("revenue from appreciation of fixed assets") to reflect the increase in value (thus increasing income to $210,000)? Or should the increase in market value be ignored? Under conventional accounting procedures (for reasons to be indicated shortly) the increase in the value of the fixed assets *would not*, in fact, be reported in financial reports to be made available to stockholders, creditors, or the general public. But many accountants argue that conventional procedures should be modified so that gains from appreciation are given recognition in accounting reports.

Which Solvent should be Assumed to have been Sold First?

Suppose also that, of the 4 million gallons of solvent that were purchased at a total cost of $2.4 million, the first 3.6 million were purchased at a price of $.59 per gallon (a total cost of $2,124,000) and the last 400,000 gallons were purchased at a price of $.69 per gallon (a total cost of $276,000). Should the cost of the 3.6 million gallons sold be computed using the *weighted average* price of solvent purchased during the year ($.60, as in the earlier computation), or should it be assumed that the solvent that was purchased

first was sold first? If the latter assumption is made, then the cost of goods sold would not be $2,160,000 as previously calculated. Instead it would be 3.6 million gallons times $.59 per gallon: $2,124,000. Since the cost of goods sold would then be $36,000 less than before, income would be $36,000 greater: $96,000.

Alternatively, since all solvent purchased was mixed together in the same tank, is it less logical to assume that the solvent purchased *last* was sold first? Cost of goods sold would then be 400,000 times $.69 per gallon + 3.2 million times $.59 per gallon— a total of $2,164,000 (as compared with $2,160,000)—and income would be $4,000 *less* than that originally computed. Conventional practice would permit the company to make any one of the three assumptions regarding the flow of costs; it could assume that the goods sold were purchased at an "average" price, the first price, or the last price.

Can Inflation be Ignored?

Suppose additionally that in the course of the company's first year of operations inflation was a major problem in the country and that the general consumer price level increased by 10 percent. Was the income of the company still $60,000? Were the shareholders of the company really $60,000 better off at the end of the accounting period than they were at the beginning? When they initially purchased the common sock of Chemco, Inc., they surrendered $1 million of purchasing power. If after one year they were able to sell the stock for $1,060,000—original investment plus the "income" of the period—they would clearly be worse off at the end of period than they were at the beginning, for it would take $1.1 million to purchase the goods and services that previously could have been obtained for $1 million. Should the financial statements of the company take into account the loss of purchasing power? Traditional practice would not incorporate gains or losses in purchasing power into the determination of income. But many accountants believe that they are as essential to a comprehensive evaluation of company performance as the more direct revenues and expenses. In fact, authoritative pronouncements presently require that corporations above a specified size provide supplementary data on the impact that inflation has had on earnings.

The objective of this oversimplified example is to dispel at the very beginning of this text any notion that the study of accounting is merely a matter of learning to apply

directly with the decisions it is designed to facilitate. Unfortunately, what is relevant for one group of financial statement users may not be relevant for another. As a result there is no such thing as "all-purpose" financial statements. Data that may be useful for one type of decision may be useless—or highly misleading—for another. What might be useful to an investor might mislead a manager. A brief example may illustrate this conflict.

Example

The MNO Company manufactures a single product in a plant that it rents. In a given year it produces and sells to its regular customers 1,000 units at a cost of $300 per unit, determined as follows:

Fixed costs (those that are unaffected by changes in number of units produced): rent, executive salaries, heat, power, administrative costs, etc.	$100,000
Variable costs (those that change in proportion to number of units produced): labor and materials ($200 per unit produced × 1,000 units)	200,000
Total costs	$300,000
Number of units produced and sold	÷ 1,000 units
Cost per unit	$ 300

existing rules and procedures. Unfortunately, there are few definitive answers to questions asked of accountants. The discipline of accounting is alive with issues that are currently—and likely to remain forever—unresolved.

STANDARDS AND NONSTANDARDS

Relevancy

If information provided by the accountant is to be useful, then, above all, it must be *relevant*—it must bear upon or be associated

The plant is not currently operating at capacity. The federal government has offered to buy 500 units of the product at a price of $250 each. If the company were to accept the offer, its sales to its regular customers would remain unchanged. Should the company sign the contract to sell to the government, even though the selling price is below "cost?"

From the standpoint of an executive of the company, the *relevant* cost to be considered would be $200 per unit, rather than the $300 previously computed. The fixed costs of $100,000 will, of course, remain unchanged whether or not the company accepts the offer of the government. The only additional costs the company would have to incur are the variable costs. If the company accepted the offer of the government, it would earn additional revenue of 500 units times $250 per unit—$125,000—and incur additional costs of 500 units times $200—$100,000. Thus, it would be $25,000 better off by accepting the offer.

If the company accepted the offer, then the average cost of each unit produced would be $267:

Fixed costs: rent, executive salaries, heat, power, administrative costs, etc.	$100,000
Variable costs: $200 per unit produced × 1,500 units (the new level of production)	300,000
Total costs	$400,000
Number of units produced	÷ 1,500
Average cost per unit	$ 267

The average cost per unit would be the relevant cost for the determination of overall income to be reported to investors. But for a management decision as to whether or not to accept the offer of the government, the relevant cost would be the *incremental* or *marginal* cost—the cost of producing the additional units required for the government contract.

Objectivity

Accounting information should, ideally, be *objective* and *verifiable*. Qualified individuals working independently of one another should be able, upon examination of the same data or records, to derive similar measures or reach similar conclusions. Insofar as possible information contained in financial reports should not depend on the subjective judgments of the individual accountant who prepared it.

Herein lies a catch. Information that is most objective may not be relevant to many decisions, and that which is most relevant may not be objective. A few illustrations will serve to highlight the conflict.

1. Should a corporation report land at *historical cost* or *fair market value*? The most objective amount would be *historical cost*—that which the company paid for the land. Such amount is readily verifiable. But of what relevance is it? The company may have bought such land decades ago, and the historical cost provides no indication of what it can be sold for today. Yet any amount other than historical cost—e.g., present market value—would necessarily involve estimates or appraisals and hence be less objective. *Conventional accounting reports are based on historical costs.* Increases in market values are *not*, as a rule, given accounting recognition. Some accountants maintain, however, that assets should be carried at the amounts for which they could be sold. Their position will be evaluated in the course of the chapters that follow.

2. Should a firm's statement of annual income reflect as earned revenue the potential selling price of goods that the company has produced but not yet sold? Or, alternatively, should the firm defer recognition of such revenue until it has actually sold the items, or even until it has actually collected the full selling price in cash? Income is often said to result from the entire process of production and sale, and since the firm is *usually* able to

sell what it produces, financial statements in which income has been reported as soon as goods have been produced would be most relevant for most decisions. But such statements would be considerably less objective than those in which profit recognition is delayed until the goods have been formally sold—and hence a firm sales price has been established—or until cash has actually been collected and the full amount to be received is known with certainty.

3. Should a company's income statement include as current pension expenses, only amounts actually paid to retired workers or amounts that will eventually have to be paid to present employees as well? A company provides its employees with retirement benefits. The liability for the pensions is incurred during the productive years of the employees. The actual cash payment, however, does not have to be made until an employee retires and the actual amount to be paid may depend on the number of years the employee survives after his retirement. Such amount cannot be determined with certainty until after the employee dies. Should the company report an estimate of the pension expense as the employee "earns" the right to his pension (the most relevant time), or should it wait until it actually disburses the cash (when the expense can be objectively determined)?

One of the central themes of this text is that a great many accounting issues can be attributable to the conflict between the objectives of relevance and objectivity. Accountants are continually faced with situations in which they must trade the realization of one goal for that of the other.

Uniformity

Accounting practices should be uniform both within and among corporations or other organizations. Ideally, financial reports

of one enterprise should be readily comparable with those of another. In practice, the goal of comparability has not yet been achieved. Such failure can be ascribed to at least two causes. First, until recently both the professional accounting societies and the government agencies responsible for establishing accounting principles and maintaining accounting standards have allowed individual companies a relatively free hand in selecting among alternative accounting practices. Even today, for example, some firms within the same industry will assume that goods purchased first are sold first, while others will assume that goods purchased last are sold first. Second, the task of prescribing uniform principles that would be appropriate for all companies—or even those within a specific industry—is one that is easier to write about than to accomplish. In the last several decades the range and complexity of business transactions have increased enormously. Accounting procedures designed to account for one type of transaction may be highly inappropriate for a slightly different transaction or even an identical transaction that takes place under slightly differing circumstances. For example, a dividend check received by a company that owns a 1 percent interest in the firm that declared the dividend could justifiably be accounted for differently from one received by a company that owns a 99 percent interest in the same firm; the latter company is likely to control the dividend policy of the firm whereas the former is not.

Consistency

For a reader to compare performance in one period with that in another, financial statements must be based on accounting practices that are consistent over time. Thus, although different firms may make differing assumptions pertaining to the flow of goods, the same firm would ordinarily be expected to base its financial reports on the same assumptions from one year to the next. "A foolish consistency," Emerson pointed out, however, "is the hobgoblin of little minds." In an era of a rapidly changing business environment, accounting practice must necessarily change also. Hence, over a number of years, some degree of consistency must be sacrificed in order for accounting to achieve its other objectives.

Nonstandards

Laymen place far greater faith in financial statements than is generally warranted. It is essential, therefore, that the limitations of financial statements be clearly understood.

not accurate

Financial statements are *not accurate* (i.e., precise). This is as true if amounts are carried out to the penny as if they are rounded off to the hundreds or, in the case of many published reports, to the thousands of dollars. Accounting statements are necessarily based on estimates; estimates are inherently inaccurate. In an earlier example it was indicated that the useful life of the fixed assets purchased was 10 years. However, is it possible to predict with any degree of precision how long an asset, such as a truck, will last? Why not 9 years, or even 15? If in the example useful life were estimated to be 8 years instead of 10, then depreciation charges would have increased from $100,000 per year to $125,000. Net income would have decreased from $60,000 to $35,000—a reduction of over 41 percent!

not sole measure of performance

Financial data *cannot be used as the sole measure of managerial accomplishment.* Financial statements of private enterprises generally focus on *profit* or *income.* But profit is by no means a comprehensive measure of performance. Profit tells only a small part of the annual story of a business. Profit for a period of one year can readily be manipulated in order to make an enterprise "look good." To the extent that a manager knows that he will be evaluated on the basis of income for a given single year he can readily increase *reported* profit by postponing maintenance and nonessential repairs, cutting back on advertising and research and development costs, and reducing the quality of products or services. The negative impact of such actions is unlikely to be reflected in reported profits until subsequent years.

But profit, even over a longer period of time, may be only a poor indication of management performance. Profit, after all, can be influenced by factors over which a manager has little control. In the 1970s, for example, some oil companies reported unusually high earnings. Yet because of the sudden increase in worldwide oil prices those years, the managers of a number of individual oil companies would have had to have been throughly incompetent not to have led their firms to record earnings. At the same time, managers in firms which were unable to obtain needed petroleum supplies, except at extraordinarily high costs, may have suffered declines in income which could not practically have been avoided. As long as profits are influenced to a considerable extent by forces beyond management control (and such forces do not exert equal pressures on all firms alike—not even those within a given industry) net income by itself may be an inappropriate criterion for management evaluation.

Moreover, managers have goals in addition to that of maximizing profit. (Indeed, some writers have suggested that executives in major corporations do not even attempt to maximize profits; instead they seek to achieve "satisfactory" levels of earnings.) Many managers would include among their goals improving the environment surrounding company plants; increasing the economic, social, physical, and mental well-being of employees; and increasing the number of minority employees on the corporate payroll. Accountants do not purport that the extent to which such objectives have been achieved is given recognition in conventional financial statements.

not neutral

Financial statements are *not neutral*. It is often said that accounting information must be unbiased—that accountants should be disinterested umpires who "call 'em like they see 'em." Accountants may indeed attempt to use an unbiased measuring device when reporting on economic events. But value judgments enter into the measurement process as accountants determine *what* to measure. Accountants measure income as conventionally defined: revenues less expenses. But they include in their measurements only *selected* revenues and expenses. They do not, for example, include in their financial reports costs of "externalities," such as water or air pollution, employee injuries, or discriminatory hiring practices. Similarly, they fail to give recognition to the benefits received by their efforts to clean up the environment, improve community welfare, and eliminate safety hazards. Indeed several firms, on an experimental basis, have prepared "social" income statements and balance sheets which are based on nonconventional judgments as to what revenues and costs should be measured and reported upon.

not designed to minimize taxes

The primary criterion by which the adequacy of financial statements should be judged is *not* whether they minimize the tax liability of the reporting business entity. In the course of this text, numerous alternative accounting procedures will be presented and evaluated. The merits of the alternatives will normally be considered in terms of their objectivity and their relevance to the users of the financial information. Sometimes, unfortunately, a company's choice among alternatives is motivated primarily by income tax considerations, and as a consequence its financial reports are both less objective and less useful to stockholders and potential investors than they might otherwise be.

That is not to say that managers and accountants should not carry out a firm's activities so as to pay the least amount of taxes legally permissible. Judge Learned Hand has pointed out:

> Over and over again courts have said that there is nothing sinister in so arranging one's affairs as to keep taxes as low as possible. Everyone does so, rich and poor; and all do right, for nobody owes any public duty to pay more than the law demands.

But accounting reports filed with the Internal Revenue Service are not generally relevant for decisions that investors, creditors, employees, or managers must make. Taxable income as reported to the Internal Revenue Service is computed in accord with specific provisions of the tax codes and regulations. Such provisions are *not* necessarily consistent with "generally accepted" accounting principles. In general (though with a number of exceptions) a company is permitted to follow differing accounting principles in determining taxable income than in calculating income to be reported to the general public. Some companies do, in fact, maintain supplementary accounting records or even "sets of books." Such a practice is neither illegal nor unethical; it is simply reflective of different information needs of different decision makers.

DISTINGUISHING BETWEEN AN ECONOMIC EVENT AND THE DESCRIPTION OF IT

Managers as well as other users of financial reports must be on the alert to distinguish between economic events and the description of them. An economic event might leave an entity better or worse off than it was previously. The manner in which the event is described may make it *appear* as if the entity is better or worse off, but in fact has no direct effect on its actual well-being.

Suppose, for example, that the Boeing Corporation in 1983 receives orders for 100 of its new series 300 jets. In 1984 the company produces the jets; in 1985 it completes the jets and delivers them to its customers. Some accountants would urge that the revenue from the sale be recognized at the time the order (uncancelable) is received. Others would suggest that revenue be recognized as the planes are being produced. Still others would urge that recognition be delayed until the jets are actually completed and delivered. As will be seen in later chapters, persuasive arguments can be made in favor of each position. Regardless, however, of how and when the company elects to *report* the transaction, the receipt of the order is an important substantive economic event. It is one that investors will certainly take into consideration in evaluating corporate prospects. If the company recognizes sales revenue at the time the order is received, then the company may *appear* to be economically better off than if it delays recognition but the accounting description, by itself, would not make the company any better off.

In some circumstances, parties external to the organization base decisions affecting the company on the descriptions of transactions as they are contained in the financial reports. Taxing authorities, for example, may assess corporate income taxes on income as *reported* in the financial statements. Banks or other lenders may place restrictions on the payments of dividends that depend on reported income. In those circumstances, the manner in which a transaction is described will influence events (the assessment of taxes, the granting of credit, or the payment of dividends) which are events of economic substance and which do affect the well-being of the company. But even then, it is not the financial reports that make the company better or worse off; it is the way they are interpreted and used.

ACCOUNTING ALTERNATIVES—DO THEY MAKE A DIFFERENCE IN STOCK PRICES?

Financial information plays a major role in the allocation of capital in our economy. The price of a firm's common stock is to a great extent a function of *anticipated* profits. Since investors wish to maximize the returns on their investments, they are willing to pay more for the stock of a firm with a brighter rather than a dimmer future. The higher the market price of a firm's common stock relative to earnings, the greater its capability to obtain equity financing.

Reported earnings of the past are often viewed as the primary predictor of earnings of the future. In this text we shall demonstrate repeatedly that over a limited number of years a firm can increase the income figures reported to the public simply by selecting judiciously among accounting alternatives. One might hypothesize, therefore, that the market price of the stock of a firm that *reports* higher earnings than others as a consequence of adopting more liberal accounting principles and policies would also be relatively higher than those of its more conservative counterparts. If the hypothesis is correct, then the capital markets would have been "fooled" by accounting information, and a measure of inefficiency would thereby have been introduced in the free market system.

There is a substantial body of literature to suggest, however, that the capital markets as a whole are not so fooled—that, in fact, investors give consideration to differences in accounting practices and adjust accordingly. Assume, for example, that the common stocks of firms in a specific industry were being traded, on average, at a price that was equal to 10 times annual earnings. If a company reported earnings of $5 per share, its common stock could be expected to sell for $50 per share. If it reported earnings of $4 per share, its stock could be expected to sell for $40 per share. But suppose that a company reported earnings of $5 per share because, relative to other firms in the industry, it adhered to more liberal accounting principles. Otherwise it would have reported earnings of only $4 per share. Would its stock still be traded at $50 per share? According to a number of studies, it is likely that the common stock would be sold for only $40 per share.

The studies are encouraging in that they support the contention that investors, as a group, are sufficiently sophisticated to distinguish among various accounting practices and to look beyond the "bottom line" of the income statement. Moreover, they suggest that the accounting profession need not be so concerned about mandating specific practices as was once generally believed. Regardless of alternative selected, investors will make the adjustments necessary to make earnings of one company comparable with those of others.

Obviously, however, investors can make the necessary adjustments only if they have available the requisite information—the details of the underlying transactions—to do so. If, therefore, the studies suggest that the accounting profession need not be especially concerned about specifying particular accounting practices, they also imply that the profession need be very concerned about making certain that corporations disclose enough about their operations and financial position to enable investors to evaluate the results of transactions in a manner other than the one selected by the corporation.

The studies in no way suggest that *individual* investors properly interpret financial statements. They deal exclusively with *investors as a group*. Individual investors, as well as managers, creditors, labor union officials, and other users of financial statements, must still bear the burden of carefully analyzing the financial statements and evaluating the impact of alternative accounting practices.

THE ACCOUNTING PROFESSION

A Brief Background

Accountants are employed by *public* accounting firms, corporations, and private business enterprises as well as by government and other nonprofit organizations. The term *accountants* is often used to designate persons who provide a wide range of services—from clerks who perform routine clerical functions to corporate vice-presidents who make major financial decisions.

The public accountant who has satisfied various state-imposed education and experience requirements and has demonstrated technical competence on a nationally administered examination is recognized as a *certified public accountant* (CPA). In most states a CPA must have earned a bachelor's degree; must have completed a specified number of courses in accounting and related disciplines such as business law, finance, and economics; and must have been employed as an independent auditor, under the supervision of another CPA, for at least one to three years.

Although modern accounting can trace its roots to 1494, when an Italian monk named Fr. Luca Paciolo described a "double-entry" accounting procedure that forms the basis for accounting practice today, public accounting as a profession is relatively new. The development of the profession was spurred primarily by new forms of economic activity associated with the Industrial Revolution. Many of the significant developments in the early stages of the profession's growth can be traced to Great Britain. By the latter half of the eighteenth century, small associations of professional accountants began to develop. In the early part of the twentieth century, the momentum for growth and innovation shifted to the United States. Since 1900, the number of public accountants in the United States has grown exponentially.

Ask a layman what certified public accountants do, and he is more than likely to refer immediately to income taxes. In truth, CPAs are associated with three primary functions: auditing, management advisory services, and tax services. It is the auditing function that is unique to, and most characteristic of, the public accounting profession.

Auditing and Financial Reporting

The purpose of the audit function is to lend credibility to financial reports. Persons who rely upon such reports want assurance that they "present fairly" the results of the economic activities that they purport to describe.

Regulatory agencies such as the Securities and Exchange Commission and the New York Stock Exchange require that publicly held corporations under their jurisdiction have an *independent* party—a CPA —*attest* to, or vouch for, the fairness of the financial statements the companies issue to their stockholders. Similarly, banks, insurance companies, and other investors and lenders of funds also demand that financial statements on which they intend to rely be audited or attested to by CPAs.

Although the CPA firm is *not* assigned the responsibility of preparing external financial reports—*corporate management* is so charged—its influence over them is predominant. The CPA firm does not, of course, verify each of the transactions underlying the financial statements. In a large corporation the number of transactions in a year would make that an impossible task. The firm does, however, review the accounting systems used to accumulate and summarize the underlying data, tests a substantial number of transactions (especially those involving large dollar amounts), and, most importantly, makes certain that the financial statements have been prepared in conformity with generally accepted accounting principles. The end product of the independent CPA's examination is the auditor's report or opinion on the financial statements. Typically, it might appear as shown in Exhibit 1-1. Alternatively, if the auditors have been unable to obtain sufficient evidential matter on which to base

EXHIBIT 1-1

─── ACCOUNTANTS' REPORT ───

**Deloitte
Haskins Sells**
CERTIFIED PUBLIC ACCOUNTANTS

1114 Avenue of the Americas
New York 10036

General Motors Corporation, its Directors and Stockholders: February 8, 1982

We have examined the Consolidated Balance Sheet of General Motors Corporation and consolidated subsidiaries as of December 31, 1981 and 1980 and the related Statements of Consolidated Income and Changes in Consolidated Financial Position for each of the three years in the period ended December 31, 1981. Our examinations were made in accordance with generally accepted auditing standards and, accordingly, included such tests of the accounting records and such other auditing procedures as we considered necessary in the circumstances.

In our opinion, these financial statements present fairly the financial position of the companies at December 31, 1981 and 1980 and the results of their operations and the changes in their financial position for each of the three years in the period ended December 31, 1981, in conformity with generally accepted accounting principles applied on a consistent basis.

Deloitte Haskins & Sells

---

an opinion, or if they take exception to the information as presented, they might disclaim an opinion, qualify their opinion, or even express an "adverse" opinion—i.e., "In our opinion the aforementioned consolidated financial statements *do not* fairly present the financial position. . . ."

CPA firms range in size from those with a single practitioner to those with over 1,200 partners and several thousand in professional staff. Over 85 percent of the audits of the 2,600 companies that are listed on U.S. Stock exchanges are audited by the eight largest CPA firms, a group often referred to as "the Big Eight." Owing to their size and the importance of their clients to the economy, these eight firms have had a preeminent impact on the practice of accounting and the establishment of accounting principles in the United States.

In recent years the accounting profession has been severely criticized for its alleged failure to conscientiously fulfill its audit responsibilities. To a great extent such criticism has been the result of a number of corporate bankruptcies, frauds, and illegal or unethical practices. It has been charged that

the financial reports of the companies were false and misleading in that they failed to reveal deteriorating financial conditions, misappropriations of funds by high-level corporate officials, or illegal payments to foreign officials. In many of the cases, the auditors were accused of either allowing their clients to employ inappropriate accounting principles or misapplying acceptable accounting principles. In a number of widely publicized cases, auditors have been successfully sued by stockholders who suffered losses attributable to their reliance upon the financial reports, and in other cases auditors have been charged with criminal fraud for actions associated with statements that were allegedly false and misleading. Typically in these cases the financial reports in question were said to have artificially inflated company earnings and correspondingly overstated the values of assets or understated the values of liabilities. A key objective of this text is to explore the difficulties faced by management and auditors in selecting among and applying "generally accepted accounting principles" and to highlight resulting limitations of financial reports.

Tax Services

For many corporations the effective tax rate on income, taking into account federal income taxes as well as state and local taxes, is over 50 percent. For individuals the tax rate on income over a specified amount may be as high as 80 percent. It is critical that managers give careful consideration to the tax implications of their decisions. Indeed, it is essential that they calculate the tax impact before entering into a transaction, while they still have an opportunity to alter its terms in a way such that the tax burden can be minimized. Accountants provide tax services both as members of internal tax staffs and as outside advisors. Of course, they prepare tax returns as mandated by statute. Their more important function, however, is counseling management *in advance* of a business undertaking, as to how their firm's tax liability can be reduced.

Management Advisory Services

Most CPAs serve as financial advisors to their clients. Large CPA firms have separate management consulting divisions which provide a wide range of services to both industry and government. Although most consulting engagements are directly related to the accounting and reporting systems of their clients (a large number, for example, involve installation of data processing equipment), some are in such diverse fields as marketing, pensions and insurance, and production management. Smaller CPA firms often provide day-to-day business advice to their clients; some establish the accounting systems used by their clients and maintain a close watch over them to make certain that they are operating as planned.

In recent years the consulting activities of many firms, especially the larger ones, have come under fire for being incompatible with the primary function of CPAs, that of attesting to financial reports. Critics assert that CPAs who provide consulting services cannot be sufficiently independent of their clients to provide unbiased audit services. They question, for example, whether a CPA firm which has advised a client on means of increasing income, and has seen such advice followed *unsuccessfully*, could be sufficiently objective in auditing the financial reports that reflect the results of its own poor advice. CPAs respond that they have developed professional guidelines which minimize the possibility of bias and that the benefits of consulting services to their clients—and hence to society—far outweigh the risk of diminished independence.

Accountants in Industry

Accountants who are employed by business enterprises commonly serve in a staff capacity. They provide advice and service to virtually all units of the organization. The industrial accountants of today are likely to be responsible for maintaining financial records. In all probability, however, they will do much more. They will be key members of the management team, counseling on a wide range of corporate activities. The chief accountant of a company is often known as the *controller*. The following list is suggestive of the functions that are carried out by a controller's department:

Long-range and strategic financial planning
Data processing and information processing
Tax planning and administration
Budgeting
Reporting to stockholders and government agencies
Financial performance evaluation

The distinction between a controller and a *treasurer* varies from firm to firm, but in general the treasurer is concerned with relations between the company and its stockholders, bankers, and other creditors as well as with the administration of the firm's investments and insurance policies.

Many accountants in industry serve as *internal auditors*. Corporate internal audit departments have traditionally been responsible for verifying the accuracy and reliability of internal accounting reports and records. Today, they still perform that function. Their role has expanded, however, to include reviews of the efficiency and effectiveness of all corporate operating and management systems. In many firms they function as a team of internal management consultants.

The *National Association of Accountants* is the leading professional association of industrial accountants. Through a related organization, the *Institute of Management Accounting*, the association recognizes as *Certified Management Accountants* (CMAs) members of the profession who pass a rigorous examination and satisfy specified experience and educational requirements.

Accountants in Nonprofit Organizations

Government and other nonprofit (or, more properly, not for profit) organizations are unconcerned with the computation of net income; they are interested in public service, not profit. Yet financial budgets, accounting controls, and quantitative measures of performance are as necessary in nonprofit as in profit-making organizations. Unfortunately, many nonprofit organizations have been slow in realizing the importance of adequate accounting systems and reports. Today, however, they are attempting to make rapid reforms in the area of financial management,

and as a result job opportunities in such organizations are abundant.

Nonprofit accounting is an especially challenging field. Administrators of nonprofit organizations require the same types of information as their counterparts in private industry to carry out effectively the functions of management. On a day-to-day basis, problems of planning, controlling, and evaluating performance in nonprofit organizations are remarkably similar to those in industry. The manager of a government-owned electric power company must make the same types of decisions as does one in a private utility. Supervisors of motor pools, mail rooms, clerical departments, and maintenance staffs in government are equally as concerned with reducing costs and increasing output as are those who hold similar positions in private industry.

Accounting in the public sector can be distinguished from that in the private sector by the absence of profit as a primary measure of organizational performance. In the private sector, accountants focus on profit as an indicator of how much better off a company is at the end of an accounting period than it was at the start. In the public sector, managers are not interested in how much better off an organization is; instead they are concerned with how much service or benefit it has provided to the community in relation to costs incurred. Unfortunately, such benefits and costs may be exceedingly difficult to identify, let alone measure.

Suppose, for example, that a state official requested information to determine which of two school districts, each of which received the same amount of funds, was more effectively managed. What data should the accountant provide? There are numerous possibilities: number of students attending schools, number of graduates, number of graduates who were able to find jobs, average reading level of students at various grade levels, average change in reading level over a period of several years, etc. None of the measures, either individually or cumulatively, is likely to be a satisfactory indicator of administrative performance. Accountants, experienced in the art of measurement, can play a major role in helping organizations to more clearly define their objectives and appraise the progress they have made in achieving them.

The U.S. General Accounting Office (GAO), the "watchdog of Congress," as well as state and local audit agencies are actively engaged in evaluating the efficiency and effectiveness of governmental programs. The GAO, the staff of which is composed largely of persons with accounting backgrounds, has recently issued reports that are seemingly unrelated to accounting. Among the titles are "Problems of the Upward Bound Program in Preparing Disadvantaged Students for a Postsecondary Education," "Issues Related to Foreign Sources of Oil for the United States," and "More Intensive Reforestation and Timber Stand Improvement Programs Could Help Meet Timber Demand."

Generally Accepted Accounting Principles

What are "generally accepted accounting principles?" Who decides what is, and what should be, generally accepted? To a large extent what is generally accepted is what has been done over a large number of years. Hence, tradition and widespread use are major determinants of what is generally accepted.

rule-making authorities

But in an effort to make practice more uniform, as well as to eliminate obvious abuses in financial reporting, the accounting profession, private industry, and government have created specific organizations to promulgate accounting principles and standards. Two such groups are the *Financial Accounting Standards Board* (FASB) and the *Securities and Exchange Commission* (SEC).

The Financial Accounting Standards Board began operations in 1973. The board consists of seven full-time members, who are drawn from industry, the accounting profession, and government. Its function is to develop accounting principles. The board is appointed by an independent board of trustees, whose members, in turn, are nominated by the American Institute of Certified Public Accountants (AICPA) as well as by several other private organizations concerned with financial reporting. As problems in financial reporting come to its attention, the board, with the assistance of a full-time research staff, considers the possible means of resolving them. After a lengthy process during which it issues preliminary proposals and receives comments from interested parties, it issues "Statements of Financial Accounting Standards." Such statements must be adhered to by all CPAs in their determination of whether the financial reports of their clients are in conformity with generally accepted accounting principles.

Prior to the formation of the Financial Accounting Standards Board, the task of developing accounting principles was assigned to the *Accounting Principles Board* (APB), which was a board appointed by the AICPA. During its life span of 14 years (1959 to 1973) the APB issued 31 "opinions" which accountants are required to follow. The board was dissolved and replaced by the FASB primarily as the result of criticism that it was too slow in reacting to reported abuses; that its members, many of whom were partners of large CPA firms, were overly influenced by pressures brought by their clients; and that its research capability was inadequate.

The authority of the Securities and Exchange Commission to regulate financial reporting derives from the Securities Act of 1933, the Securities Exchange Act of 1934, and the Public Utility Holding Company Act of 1935. In past years, the SEC, an independent agency of the federal government, has elected to allow responsibility for the establishment of accounting principles to rest in the private sector, specifically with the AICPA and the FASB. In the face of criticism that the authoritative organizations in the private sector have been insufficiently sensitive to the interests of the public at large, the SEC has, in recent years, played an active role in the promulgation of accounting principles. The pronouncements of the SEC are issued either as amendments to *Regulation S-X*, a document that prescribes the form and content of financial reports to be submitted to the SEC, or as *Accounting Series Releases*, statements that indicate the current positions of the agency on matters of financial reporting. Seldom are the pronouncements of the SEC in direct conflict with those of the FASB, but the FASB takes appropriate note of the views of the SEC in formulating its own statements of accounting principles.

political influences

Neither the FASB nor other rule-making authorities have been able to establish accounting principles in a manner as orderly, logical, and rational as they or their constituents would like. Accounting, regrettably, lacks the theoretical underpinnings of such disciplines as mathematics or physics. There are no axioms or postulates from which operational guidelines can be derived. The preferability of one principle as opposed to another is often in the eye of the beholder.

The interests of the various parties that will be affected by a particular accounting principle may be in conflict. A new principle that would likely enable large oil companies to report higher earnings may, because their mix of activities differs, cause smaller firms in the same industry to report lower earnings.

As the FASB considers potential pronouncements it invites comments from concerned parties. On occasion, intense pressures have been brought to bear on the Board to take a particular stance. Inasmuch as the Board does not operate in a political vacuum, it must weigh carefully the views of groups that will be affected by its rulings. Moreover, individual members of the Board do not always see eye to eye on controversial issues. As a consequence, pronouncements of the Board may be as much a product of compromise and reconciliation of conflicting views as of logic and consistency.

SUMMARY

The primary purpose of this introductory chapter has been to dispel any notion that an understanding of accounting involves little more than a familiarity with the more widely adhered-to practices and procedures. The chapter has placed considerable emphasis on the limitations of accounting reports: they are not based on universally accepted principles; they are not "accurate," since they are a function of numerous estimates and judgmental determinations; they cannot be used as the sole measure of managerial accomplishment; they are not neutral; they cannot always serve as a basis for comparing financial position or income of one company with that of another. The decision to stress the negative was made at some risk; a student may be misled into questioning whether the efforts required to understand such a seemingly limited discipline are commensurate with the benefits to be derived.

The intent of the approach was to emphasize the dynamic nature of accounting. Accounting information serves a variety of functions and is used by parties with different interests and goals. As a consequence, there can never be any single "correct" means of reporting upon an economic event or quantifying an economic value. The principles upon which a particular accounting report is based must necessarily represent compromises among the various objectives (sometimes conflicting) of financial reporting. The balance among objectives that is appropriate for one company at a particular time may be inappropriate either for a different company or for the same company at some other time.

In Chapter 2 we shall present an overview of financial reports and shall examine the underlying structure upon which the discipline of accounting is built.

QUESTIONS FOR REVIEW AND DISCUSSION

1. On January 15, 1983, the controller (the chief accounting officer) of the Highland Hills Corp. reported to the president that company income for the previous year was $1.5 million. Two months later, after conducting an examination of the company's books and records, Scott and Co., Certified Public Accountants, determined that the company had earned only $900,000. Upon receiving the report of the CPAs, the president declared that he was going either to fire the controller or to engage a new CPA firm. "One of the two," he commented, "must be either dishonest or incompetent." Do you agree?

2. The financial vice-president of a corporation recently urged that all amounts in the firm's annual report to stockholders be "rounded" to the nearest thousand dollars. "It is misleading," he said, "to give stockholders a report in which all figures are carried out to the last penny." Explain what the financial vice-president most likely had in mind by his comment.

3. The Mid-Western Gas and Electric Co. recently submitted statements of income to stockholders, to the Internal Revenue Service, and to the Federal Power Commission. In no two of the reports was net income the same, even though the period covered by the reports was identical. Release of all three reports was approved by the firm's certified public accountants. How is it possible for all three reports to be "correct"?

4. In preparing a financial statement to accompany his loan application to a local bank, Glen Ellison was uncertain as to whether he should report his home as having a value of $25,000 or $115,000. Ellison purchased his house 25 years ago at a price of $25,000; similar homes in his neighborhood have recently been sold for between $100,000 and $125,000. Which amount do you think would be more useful to the bank? Which amount is more objective?

5. The accounting reports of one company are unlikely to be readily comparable with those of another. Why has it not been considered feasible to develop a set of accounting rules by which all companies must abide?

6. "A corporation's annual report to stockholders, if correctly prepared, is an unbiased indicator of its performance during the period covered by the report." Do you agree?

7. In the early stages of the development of the accounting profession, independent auditors would "certify" to the "accuracy" of a company's financial statements. Today, independent certified public accountants express an "opinion" that the company's financial statements "present fairly" the firm's financial position and results of its operations. Why do you suppose CPAs are reluctant to "certify" to the "accuracy" of a company's financial statements?

8. What role does the Financial Accounting Standards Board play in the development of accounting standards? What role does the Securities and Exchange Commission play?

9. What three primary services do CPA firms render to their clients? Why are such services sometimes thought to be in conflict with one another?

10. James Wood is concerned about his prospects for reelection as mayor of the town of Wippakinetta. Mayor Wood had promised the citizens of Wippakinetta that as long as he was in charge of fiscal affairs, the town would never run a deficit—i.e., that expenditures would never exceed revenues. Yet in 1983 the town did, in fact, report a deficit of $900,000. The deficit was attributable entirely to the fleet of nine buses purchased by the city. The city purchased and paid for the nine buses in November 1983. At the time the city ordered the buses it had met all requirements for a federal transportation grant for the full cost of the vehicles. As the result of a bureaucratic snarl, payment of the grant was delayed until the following year.

The city accounting system requires that revenues be recognized only upon actual receipt of cash and that expenses be recorded upon cash payment.

a. What deficiencies do you see in Wippakinetta's accounting system? What revisions would you suggest?

b. Suppose alternatively that the city did not receive a federal grant to pay for the buses. It is the policy of the city to pay cash (not to borrow) for transportation vehicles and equipment. The useful life of the buses is approximately five years. In those years in which new buses must be acquired reported municipal expenditures are substantially greater than in those years in which they need not. As a consequence, some citizens believe that the operating efficiency of the city is less in the years in which buses are replaced than in others. Do you believe that the city is really less efficient by virtue of its acquisition of new buses? How might the financial reporting practices of the city be changed so as to reduce the confusion on the part of some of its citizens?

11. Critics of traditional financial accounting have asserted that financial reports are biased in that they fail to account for certain "social" benefits provided and costs incurred. They recommend that corporations prepare and distribute a "socioeconomic operating statement." The statement might take the following form:

Social benefits		
Improvement in the environment	$xxxx	
Minority hiring program	xxxx	
Day-care center	xxxx	
Staff services donated to hospitals	xxxx	$xxxx
Social costs		
Damage to the environment	$xxxx	
Work-related injuries and illness	xxxx	
Failure to install recommended safety equipment	xxxx	xxxx
Social surplus (deficit) for the year		$xxxx

Comment on the proposed financial report in terms of the dual accounting goals of relevancy and objectivity.

PROBLEMS

1. There is no such thing as "correct" cost. Alternative computations of cost facilitate different types of decisions.

Artcraft, Inc., manufactures costume jewelry rings. The firm has three employees, each of whom earns $10,000 per year. It rents its plant and equipment at a cost of $10,000. Materials used in the production of the rings cost $4 per ring.

The company has been manufacturing 5,000 rings per year. It has sold them for $15 each.

The company was recently approached by the manager of a large department store. He offered to purchase 1,000 rings at a cost of $7 per ring. If the company were to accept the offer, its other sales would be unaffected. Since the company has not been operating at capacity, it would not have to add additional employees, space or equipment.

a. Determine the average cost of a ring at an operating level of 5,000 rings.

b. Determine the average cost of a ring if the offer of the department store were to be accepted and the company were to increase volume to 6,000 rings per year.

c. If you were an executive of Artcraft, Inc., would you recommend that the company accept the offer? Determine income at the present operating level and again at the new operating level if the company were to accept the offer.

d. What is the *relevant* cost to be considered in making the decision whether to accept the offer?

2. Financial statements are based on estimates. The impact of the estimates on reported earnings may be substantial.

TransAmerica Airlines owns and operates 10 passenger jet planes. Each plane had cost the Airlines $6 million. The company's income statement for 1983 reported the following:

Revenue from passenger fares		$30,000,000
Operating expenses		
(including salaries,		
maintenance cost,		
terminal expenses,		
etc.)	$22,000,000	
Depreciation		
of planes	5,000,000	27,000,000
Income		
before taxes		$3,000,000

Each plane has an estimated useful life of 12 years. The $5 million depreciation charge was calculated by dividing the cost of each plane ($6 million) by its useful life (12 years). The result ($500,000) was multiplied by the number of planes owned (10).

a. Suppose that the useful life of each plane was 8 years rather than 12 years. Determine income before taxes for 1983. By what percent is income less than that computed above?

b. Suppose that the useful life of each plane was 15 years. Determine income before taxes for 1983. By what percent is income greater than that originally computed?

c. It is sometimes said that accountants must be concerned that financial statements are accurate

to the penny. Based on your computations, do you agree?

3. It is not always obvious when a company is "better off" by virtue of its production and sales efforts.

The Quick-Cut Lawnmower Co. began operations in January 1983. In its first month of operations the company manufactured 200 lawnmowers at a cost of $60 each. Although it completed all 200 mowers by the end of the month, it had not yet sold any of the mowers.

In February the company produced 300 mowers. It sold and delivered to customers both the 200 mowers manufactured in January and the 300 mowers manufactured in February. Selling price of the mowers was $100 each.

a. Determine income for January and for February.

b. Assume instead that on January 2 the company signed a noncancellable contract to sell 500 mowers at $100 each to a major chain of department stores. The contract called for delivery in February. The company completed but did not deliver 200 of the mowers by January 31. It completed the remainder and delivered all 500 by February 28. Determine income for each of the two months.

4. The most relevant information may not always be the most objective.

The president and sole owner of the Blue Mountain Brewery asked a CPA firm to audit (i.e., to express its opinion on the fairness of) the financial statements of his company. The audited financial statements had been requested by a local bank in order to facilitate review of the company's application for a loan.

The controller of the company, who had actually prepared the statements, included among the firm's assets "Land—$3,000,000." According to the controller, the land was reported at a value of $3 million since the company had recently received offers of approximately that amount from several potential purchasers.

After reviewing the land account, the CPA firm told the president that it could not express the usual "unqualified" opinion on the financial statements as long as land was stated at $3 million. Instead, it would have to express an "adverse" opinion (i.e., "the financial statements do *not* fairly present . . .") unless the land were valued at

$150,000, the amount the company had actually paid for it.

The president was dumbfounded. The land, he told the CPA, was purchased in 1921 and was located in the downtown section of a major city.

a. At what amount do you think the land should be recorded? Explain. Which amount is likely to be the more relevant to the local banker? Which amount is the more objective?

b. Which amount should be reported if the statements are to be prepared in accord with "generally accepted accounting principles."

5. *Sometimes it is easy to assign specific costs to specific items sold; sometimes it is more difficult. Choice of method used to determine cost affects the determination of reported income.*

The De Kalp Used Car Co. purchased four cars in the month of June and sold three cars. Purchase prices and sale prices are as follows:

	Purchase Price	Sale Price
Car 1	$600	$1,000
Car 2	700	1,100
Car 3	800	1,200
Car 4	900	—

The Natural Foods Grocery Store purchased 300 pounds of sugar in the month of June and sold 200 pounds. The sugar is not prepackaged. Instead, as the sugar is purchased it is added to a single barrel; as it is sold, it is scooped out and given to the customer in a paper bag. During June 100 pounds of sugar were purchased on each of three separate dates. Purchase prices, in sequence, were $.60, $.70, and $.80 per pound. All sugar was sold at $1.00 per pound.

Determine the income of the two merchants for the month of June. (Ignore other costs not indicated.)

Are there other assumptions that you might have made regarding the cost of the goods actually sold? Would income remain the same?

6. *Accounting reports that are suitable for making a long-term investment decision may not be appropriate for deciding whether to discontinue a product line.*

John Williams sells greeting cards. Operating out of a garage that he rents for $1,000 per year, he purchases greeting cards from a wholesaler and distributes them door to door. In 1982 he sold 1,000 boxes of cards at $3 per box. The cost of the cards from the wholesaler was $1 per box.

In 1983 Williams decided to expand his product line to include candy. In that year he sold 300 boxes of candy for $5 per box. The candy cost him $4 per box. By making efficient use of his garage, he found that he was able to store his inventory of cards in one-half the garage; thus he could use the other half for his candy. His sales of cards neither benefited nor suffered as the result of the new product. Sales in 1983 were the same as in 1982.

At the conclusion of 1983 Williams had to decide whether to continue selling candy or to return to selling cards only. His friend, Fulton, an occasional accountant, prepared the following report for him:

Sales of candy (300 boxes @ $5)		$1,500
Less costs:		
Cost of candy sold		
(300 boxes @ $4)	$1,200	
Rent ($\frac{1}{2}$ of $1,000)	500	1,700
Net loss on sale of candy		($ 200)

On the basis of the report Williams decided to abandon his line of candy.

a. Do you think he made the correct decision? Explain.

b. Prepare a report comparing the total earnings of Williams in 1982 with those in 1983. How do you reconcile the apparent contradiction between your report and that of Fulton?

7. *Higher reported earnings for a particular year can sometimes be achieved by actions that do not serve the long-run interests of the enterprise.*

Don Watson, president of a construction corporation, was concerned about the poor performance of his company in the first 11 months of the year. If the company continued at its present pace, reported profits for the year would be down $20,000 from those of the previous year. Thinking of ways to increase reported earnings, the president hit upon what he considered to be an ingenious scheme: Two years earlier the company had purchased a crane at a cost of $100,000. Since the crane was now 2 years old and had an estimated useful life of 10 years, it was currently reported on the company's books at eight-tenths of $100,000: $80,000. Prices of cranes had increased substantially in the last 2 years, and the crane could be sold for $120,000. The president suggested that the company sell the crane for $120,000 and thereby realize a gain on the sale of $40,000 ($120,000 less the book value of $80,000). Of course, the company would have to buy a new crane—and new cranes were currently selling for $160,000—but the cost of the new crane could be spread out over its useful life of 10 years. In future years, the president realized, "depreciation" charges would increase from $10,000 on the old crane ($100,000 divided by 10) to $16,000 on the new ($160,000 divided by 10), but in the current year, the company would report a gain of $40,000. Hence reported income would go from $20,000 less than that in the previous year to $20,000 greater.

a. The scheme of the president is, in fact, consistent with generally accepted accounting principles. Do you think, however, that the company would really be $40,000 better off if it sold the old crane and purchased a new one than if it held on to the old one? Comment.

b. Would the scheme of the president be in the best interest of the stockholders "in the long run?"

c. Assume that generally accepted accounting principles requires that "fixed assets," such as the crane, be reported on corporate books at the price at which it could currently be sold— i.e., $120,000. Would the scheme of the president accomplish its desired results? Why do you suppose generally accepted accounting principles do not require that such assets be valued at the prices at which they could be sold?

OVERVIEW 2 of FINANCIAL STATEMENTS

Organizations, both profit and nonprofit, report on their financial position and performance by means of two basic financial statements, the *balance sheet* and the *income statement*.* Because of inherent limitations in the balance sheet and income statement, these two basic statements are supplemented by a third statement, the *statement of changes in financial position* and by footnotes which explain and amplify the reported numerical data. Many reports contain a fourth statement, the *statement of changes in retained earnings*, although this statement is often combined with the income statement.

The concepts that underline the preparation of the basic statements are those that underlie the discipline of accounting. They are, in general, as applicable to reports to be issued to stockholders and other "outsider" groups as to those intended for use by parties within the organization. Part I of this text is directed primarily to the principles upon which financial reports are constructed. Even though some of the issues raised in Part I are applicable only to "external" financial reports, they are nonetheless of immediate concern to managers of all of specialties. Managers, after all, must be cognizant of how the results of their actions will be described to outsiders and will affect the calculation of net income.

THE BALANCE SHEET

The balance sheet reports the status of the enterprise at a *specific point in time*. It describes the enterprise *as of* the close of business on a specific date. In contrast, the income statement reports the history of a business for a period of time, e.g.,

---

* Nonprofit, including government organizations, do not, strictly speaking, earn income. They do not, therefore, prepare *income statements*. They do, however, prepare statements which have similar characteristics, even though they may bear different titles. Common among the titles are *statement of operations* and *statement of revenues and expenditures*.

EXHIBIT 2-1

The Austin Company
Balance Sheet as of June 30, 1983

Assets		*Liabilities and Owners' Equity*	
Cash	$ 15,000	Liabilities	
Accounts receivable	80,000	Accounts payable	$ 90,000
Merchandise inventory	60,000	Wages payable	20,000
Equipment	110,000	Bonds payable	250,000
Buildings	330,000		
Patents and copyrights	25,000	Total liabilities	$360,000
		Owners' equity	260,000
Total assets	$620,000	Total equities	$620,000

income for the month of June, income for the year ended December 31, 1983.

Assets

The balance sheet, or *statement of financial position* (as it is less frequently but more descriptively called), indicates the financial resources (assets) available to the firm to carry out its economic activities as well as the claims against such resources. These resources may be either *tangible* (of a physical nature) such as buildings, equipment, land, and motor vehicles or *intangible* (characterized by legal rights) such as amounts owned by customers (accounts receivable), patents, and bank deposits. They represent *future* benefits or service potentials.

Equities

The claims against the enterprise are referred to as *equities* (meaning "rights to or claims against"). There are two primary categories of equities: *liabilities* and *owners' equity*.

Liabilities are the claims against the business by creditors. They are amounts to be paid in the *future*. They include amounts owed to employees, suppliers, banks, bond-holders, and government agencies. Owners' equity represents the "residual" interests of the owners. It includes the amounts that they contributed to the business either at the time of formation or when additional funds were needed for expansion as well as the earnings accumulated over the years. Owners' equity may be viewed as the resources that would be left over for the owners if the business were to be dissolved and all the creditors were to be paid.

1. *Assets:* Probable future economic benefits obtained or controlled by a particular entity as a result of past transactions or events.
2. *Liabilities:* Probable future sacrifices of economic benefits arising from present obligations of a particular entity to transfer assets or provide services to other entities in the future as a result of past transactions or events.
3. *Owners' equity:* The residual interest in the assets of an entity that remains after deducting its liabilities; the interests of the owners of a business enterprise.*

An abbreviated balance sheet is indicated in Exhibit 2-1.

* Based on definitions of the Financial Accounting Standards Board in *Elements of Financial Statements of Business Enterprises*, Statement of Financial Accounting Concepts No. 3, December 1980.

Accounting Equation

As illustrated, the equities, i.e., the claims against the assets, including the residual interest of the owners, *must* be equal to the assets themselves. Thus, in general form,

$$\text{Assets} = \text{Claims against the assets}$$

or

$$\text{Assets} = \text{Equities}$$

In a slightly more specific form,

$$\text{Assets} = \text{Claims of outsiders} + \text{Claims of owners}$$

or

$$\text{Assets} = \text{Liabilities} + \text{Owners' equity}$$

In Exhibit 2-1,

$$\$620,000 = \$360,000 + \$260,000$$

The basic accounting equation, assets = liabilities + owners' equity, serves as the foundation for the *double-entry* record-keeping process on which modern accounting is based. Any *transaction* (financial event) which increases (decreases) the left-hand side of the equation (assets) must, by definition of the terms of the equation, increase (decrease) the right side of the equation (the claims against such assets) by an identical amount.

Consider, for example, several transactions in which an enterprise might engage as shown on page 29. The titles beneath the amounts indicate the specific accounts (types of assets or equities) that would be affected.

Events Which Affect Owners' Equity

The basic accounting equation can be expressed in a slightly altered form:

$$\text{Assets} - \text{Liabilities} = \text{Owners' equity}$$

This equation is equivalent to the one previously illustrated, but the latter expression, by isolating owners' equity on one side of the equation, focuses more directly on the interests of the owners of the business. As a general rule the equity of the owners will increase as the result of two types of events:

1. The owners make a direct contribution to the firm. Such contribution is almost always made in return for the right to share in the profits of the firm. If the firm is a corporation, evidence of an ownership interest is provided by a stock certificate indicating the number of "shares" of stock owned. If the firm is a partnership, then the partnership agreement indicates the proportionate interest in the enterprise of each of the owners.

2. The firm earns income. The net assets (assets less liabilities) of the firm will be greater than they were previously; hence the residual interest of the owners will also be greater.

Conversely, the equity of the owners will decrease as the result of two opposite types of events:

1. The owners make withdrawals from the firm. The firm pays out a portion of its assets to the owners. In a corporation, such withdrawals are known as *dividends*. The effect is to reduce the assets of the firm and to reduce the remaining equity of the owners— that is, to reduce the size of the asset pool in which the owners are entitled to share.

2. The company incurs a loss. The net assets (assets less liabilities) of the firm are reduced; hence the residual interest of the owners is also reduced.

THE INCOME STATEMENT

The accounting equation and the balance sheet indicate net assets (assets less liabilities) and the owners' claims against such net assets at a given *point* in time. The income statement, on the other hand, indicates changes in owners' equity (and thus changes in net assets) over a given *period* of time resulting from the operations of the business, *excluding* contributions or withdrawals on the part of the owners. (Such changes are indicated in the statement of changes in owners' equity.) The income statement indicates the revenues of the period and the expenses incurred in earning such revenues.

Revenues

Revenues are the inflows of cash or other assets attributable to the goods or services provided by the enterprise. Most commonly, revenues result from the sale of the company's product or service, but they could also result from interest earned on loans to outsiders, dividends received on shares of stock of other companies, royalties earned on patents or licenses, or rent earned from properties owned.

Expenses

Expenses are the outflows of cash or other assets attributable to the profit-directed activities of an enterprise. Expenses are a measure of the effort exerted on the part of the enterprise in its attempt to "realize" (to obtain) revenues.

An income statement, in condensed form, is illustrated in Exhibit 2-2.

Stocks Versus Flows

Contrast the manner in which the date appears on the income statement with the way it does on the balance sheet. The income statement is *for the year ended* June 30, 1983—it describes what has happened over a one-year period. The balance sheet is *as of* June 30, 1983—it describes the business as of a particular moment in time.

The relationship between the balance sheet and the income statement can be explained with reference to a household bathtub filled with water. The water in the bathtub is comparable to the owners' equity—or, alternatively, to the net assets (assets less liabilities)—of the firm. In describing the level of water in the tub one could say that at a given moment the tub contains x gallons of water. Similarly, one could describe a firm as having a particular level of net assets. Indeed, the balance sheet of a firm does exactly that. It indicates, and describes, the level of assets, of liabilities, and of the difference between the two—owners' equity.

Suppose, however, that water is entering the tub through the faucets and at the same time it is leaving through the drain. It would still be possible—and indeed necessary if comprehensive information is to be pre-

EXHIBIT 2-2

The Austin Company
Income Statement for the Year Ended June 30, 1983

Revenue from sales			$120,000
Cost of merchandise sold	$70,000		
Wages and salaries	15,000		
Advertising	3,000		
Rent	4,000	$92,000	
Taxes		12,000	104,000
Net income			$ 16,000

sented—to describe the level of water in the tub. One could say, for example, that at 11:03 p.m. there were 10 gallons of water in the tub. But such information would hardly constitute a very complete description of activity in the tub. Also needed would be a description of the rate at which the water level is rising or falling. More complete information might be as follows: Water is entering the tub at the *rate* of 3 gallons per

	Assets	=	Liabilities	+	Owners' Equity
Owners contribute $100,000 cash to form a business. (*The owners have an interest of $100,000 in the assets.*)	+$100,000 (cash)	=			+$100,000 (contribution of owners)
The new firm borrows $50,000 from a bank. (*The lender has a claim of $50,000 against the assets of the firm.*)	+$50,000 (cash)	=	+$50,000 (notes payable)		
The firm purchases equipment for $10,000, giving a note for the full amount. (*The seller of equipment has a claim of $10,000 against the assets.*)	+$10,000 (equipment)	=	+$10,000 (notes payable)		
The firm purchases supplies for $8,000 cash. (*Some transactions may affect only one side of the equation.*)	+$8,000 (supplies) −$8,000 (cash)				
The firm repays $3,000 of the amount it borrowed from the bank. (*The claim of the lender against the assets of the firm is reduced by $3,000.*)	−$3,000 (cash)	=	−$3,000 (notes payable)		
The firm purchases merchandise inventory for $15,000; it pays $5,000 cash and receives the remaining $10,000 of goods "on account." (*One transaction may affect more than two accounts; note that the liability account affected is referred to as "accounts payable" rather than "notes payable" since no formal written note was presented to the supplier.*)	+$15,000 (merchandise inventory) −$5,000 (cash)	=	+$10,000 (accounts payable)		
The firm sells merchandise which originally cost $15,000 for $20,000 cash. (*As the result of this transaction the firm has "earned" $5,000. The firm gave up assets of $15,000 in exchange for those of $20,000. As a result, the claims of the owners against the business are $5,000 greater than they were previously. The owners' equity account affected is commonly referred to as retained earnings when the enterprise is a corporation or as owners' capital, e.g., J. Smith, capital, if the firm is a partnership or proprietorship.*)	+$20,000 (cash) −$15,000 (merchandise inventory)	=		+	$5,000 (retained earnings)

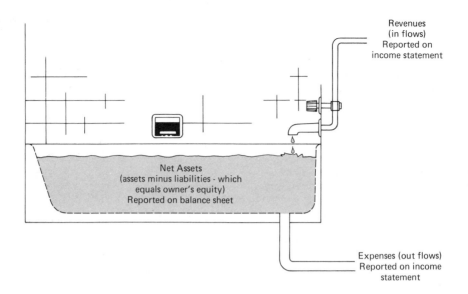

Revenues
(in flows)
Reported on
income statement

Net Assets
(assets minus liabilities - which
equals owner's equity)
Reported on balance sheet

Expenses (out flows)
Reported on income
statement

minute; it is leaving at the rate of 2 gallons per minute; hence it is rising at the *rate* of 1 gallon per minute.

So also with the firm. Information is required as to the rate at which the equity of the owners is increasing or decreasing. The water entering the tub might be compared to revenues; the water leaving, to expenses; and the difference between the two, to income. Thus it might be said that assets are entering the firm at the *rate* of $3 million per year (i.e., revenues for the year are $3 million), that assets are leaving the firm at the *rate* of $2 million per year (i.e., expenses for the year are $2 million), and that the change in net assets (owners' equity) for the year is $1 million (i.e., income for the year is $1 million).

If the amount of water in the bathtub at 11:03 p.m. were 10 gallons and it were increasing at the rate of 1 gallon per minute, then the amount at the end of the minute would be 11 gallons. The beginning amount plus the net amount added during the period would equal the ending amount.

So too with the firm. If the owners' equity at January 1, 1983, were $10 million and income for the year were $1 million, then owners' equity at the end of the year would be $11 million.

Balance Sheet Describes Position as of a Point in Time

The balance sheet indicates the equity that the owners have in the firm at any given *point* in time. Such point of time is usually the end of a month or the end of a year. The balance sheet also indicates the assets and the liabilities which result in the particular level of owners' equity.

Income Statement Indicates Rate over a Period of Time

The income statement indicates the *rate* at which the equity of the owners is changing. It reveals the revenues, the expenses, and the resultant income for the period. Assuming that no assets or liabilities entered or left the firm from other sources (e.g., the owners neither contributed nor withdrew assets), then owners' equity at the beginning of the period per the balance sheet sheet plus income for the period (per the income statement) must equal owners' equity at the end of the period (per the new balance sheet):

Owners' equity, beginning of period

$+(-)$ Income (or loss) for the period

$+(-)$ Additional contributions (or withdrawals) of owners during the period

$=$ Owners' equity, end of period

The owners' equity of the Austin Company as of June 30, 1983, was $260,000. If during the following year, that ending June 30, 1984, the company had income of $25,000 and paid dividends of (i.e., the owners withdrew) $19,000, then owners' equity as of June 30, 1984, would be $266,000:

$$\frac{\text{Owners' Equity}}{\text{6/30/83}} + \frac{\text{Income}}{\$25,000} - \frac{\text{Dividends}}{\$19,000}$$
$$\frac{\$260,000}{\$260,000}$$

$$= \frac{\text{Owners' Equity}}{\text{6/30/84}}$$
$$\frac{\$266,000}{}$$

THE BALANCE SHEET—A MORE DETAILED EXAMINATION

Exhibits 2-3 through 2-6 illustrate the financial statements of the Mercury Truck Manufacturing Corporation for the year 1983. The balance sheet in Exhibit 2-3 is divided not only into the major categories of assets, liabilities, and owners' (stockholders') equity but several subcategories or accounts as well.

Current Assets

Current assets include cash and such other assets that will either be transformed into cash or will be sold or consumed within one year or within the *normal operating cycle* of business if longer than one year. For most businesses the normal operating cycle is one year, but for some (such as those in the tobacco or distilling industries in which the products must be stored for a period of several years) it may be a longer period. *Cash* includes not only currency but bank deposits as well. When it is said that a company disburses "cash" there is no necessary implication that it is making a payment in currency. The term could (and most commonly does) apply to payments by check.

Marketable securities include shares of stock and other securities held by the firm as short-term investments. Such securities are ordinarily reported at original cost, unless there has been a drop in the price at which they are selling in the open market; in such case they are reported at the (lower) market value. Primarily because of the accountant's tendency to be conservative in asset valuation and revenue realization, increases in market value are almost never given accounting recognition, however,

Accounts receivable—the amounts due from customers—represent those amounts that can be expected to be collected within the normal operating cycle (those that cannot are included among noncurrent assets). Deducted from accounts receivable is an *allowance for doubtful accounts*—an estimate of the amounts owed to the company that will be uncollectible. Thus, the net amount of accounts receivable represents not the total amount owed to the firm but only the amount that it estimates will actually be collectible.

Inventories include both items available for sale to customers and raw materials, parts, and supplies to be used in production. Inventories are ordinarily reported at original cost of either purchase or production, but in the event that the cost of replacing such items has declined, then the inventories may

EXHIBIT 2-3

Mercury Truck Manufacturing Corp.
Statement of Position as of December 31, 1983

Assets

Current assets			
Cash			$ 1,042,954
Marketable securities			380,000
Accounts receivable	$9,083,414		
Less allowance for doubtful accounts	100,000		8,983,414
Inventories			10,958,103
Prepaid expenses			331,115
Total current assets			$21,695,586
Noncurrent assets			
Property, plant, and equipment			
Land			$ 918,649
Buildings	$4,805,401		
Less accumulated depreciation	1,207,021		3,598,380
Machinery and equipment	$9,835,027		
Less accumulated depreciation	2,414,042		7,420,985
Net property, plant, and equipment			$11,938,014
Investment and other assets			
Investment in subsidiary			$ 6,244,395
Notes receivable			3,682,487
Unamortized organization costs			1,000
Patents and trademarks			34,000
Total investment and other assets			$ 9,961,882
Total noncurrent assets			$21,899,896
Total assets			$43,595,482

Liabilities and Stockholders' Equity

Current liabilities	
Accounts payable	$ 5,515,469
Notes payable	4,152,249
Salaries and wages payable	1,938,795
Taxes payable	1,662,171
Interest payable	82,157
Total current liabilities	$13,350,841
Noncurrent liabilities	
Advances from customers	$ 87,218
Notes payable	3,057,679
Bonds payable	10,048,075
Total noncurrent liabilities	$13,192,972
Total liabilities	$26,543,813
Stockholders' equity	
Preferred stock ($100 par value)	$ 96,655
Common stock ($1 par value, 625,773 shares issued and outstanding)	625,773
Retained earnings	16,329,241
Total stockholders' equity	$17,051,669
Total liabilities and stockholders' equity	$43,595,482

be "written down" to reflect the decline in value. As with marketable securities, increases in value are not ordinarily given similar accounting recognition.

Prepaid expenses represent services or rights to services purchased but not yet consumed. As they are consumed they will be "charged off" as actual expenses. A firm might, for example, purchase a one-year insurance policy for $120 ($10 per month). At the time of purchase it would record the policy as a current asset, prepaid insurance— $120. Each month it would reduce the asset by one-twelfth of the original amount ($10) and would charge insurance expense with the same amount. Thus, after eight months, the balance in the prepaid insurance account would be only $40 (four months remaining times $10 per month). Other common prepaid expense accounts are prepaid interest, prepaid advertising, and prepaid rent. Prepaid expenses are one type of *deferred charge*— outlays made in one period to benefit future periods.

Noncurrent Assets

Noncurrent assets are those assets that *cannot* be expected to be sold or consumed within a normal operating cycle of the business. Noncurrent assets are usually considered to be *long-lived* assets, and plant assets in particular are often referred to as *fixed* assets.

Property, plant, and equipment are recorded on the balance sheet at original cost. Deducted from each of the assets, other than land, is *accumulated depreciation*—an allowance to reflect the fact that the assets are being "consumed" over time, by wear and tear as well as by technological obsolescence.

Depreciation is the process of allocating (spreading) the cost of an asset over its useful life. Depreciation on each individual asset or group of similar assets is computed separately, and the total amount accumulated is a function of the original cost, age, and expected useful life of the asset. No depreciation is provided for land since it is not consumed over time and seldom declines in utility.

Investments and other assets include amounts owed to the company by outsiders that are not due for at least one year and amounts that the company has invested in other companies. If, for example, a company owns 30 percent of another company, such interest would ordinarily be included among investments and other assets. An interest in another company, however, may be classified as either a current or a noncurrent asset. The decision as to how the interest should be classified depends to a large extent on the *intent* of the company's management. If it intends to maintain its interest for a relatively long period of time and views ownership as a long-term investment, then the amounts owned should be classified as a noncurrent asset. If, on the other hand, the company purchases the interest with the intention of selling it as soon as additional cash might be needed (e.g., if it purchases a few hundred shares of General Motors' stock as a temporary investment with no intention of exercising significant control over the company), then the amount owned should be classified as a current asset.

Deferred charges such as prepaid expenses may also be included among noncurrent assets. If, for example, a company purchased an insurance policy or a license that had more than a one-year life, then the percentage of original cost representing the unexpired portion of such insurance policy or license would be included among noncurrent assets.

Some deferred charges represent outlays that will benefit future accounting periods but for which both the number of such periods and the value of the benefits are exceedingly difficult to measure. Consider the costs incurred to organize a corporation: the legal fees required to draw up the documents of incorporation, the costs of printing the shares of stock to be issued, and the fees paid to the state upon filing for a corporate charter. Such costs—like those of buildings and equipment—were incurred to benefit the business over a long period of time. Just as income of a single year of operations would be understated if the entire cost of a building were charged as an expense at the time it was purchased, income would also be distorted if the costs of organizing the corporation were charged off in a single year. As a result, organizational costs are frequently reported as assets of the company, and each year a portion of such costs are *amortized* (i.e., "depreciated") and charged off as an expense.

Deferred charges representing benefits which will accrue to the firm over a long period of time in the future are often a source of confusion to stockholders. Deferred charges, unlike most other assets, are intangible and frequently have no market value. Amounts spent as organizational costs, for example, cannot readily be transferred to any other business entity; they cannot be sold to outsiders. How, then, can such amounts be considered assets?

The question must be answered in terms of the nature of all assets. Assets can be interpreted as future services to be received in money or benefits convertible into money. They can be viewed as "bundles of services" available for use or sale by a particular entity. The determination of service potential is made with respect to the business entity issuing the financial reports—not with respect to the world at large.

In accordance with currently employed practices of valuation (alternative practices will be discussed in subsequent chapters), assets are measured and recorded at the time they are acquired at the price paid for them. As their service potential declines over time (e.g., as the assets are consumed), the reported value is reduced *proportionately* through the process of depreciation or amortization. If one-third of the services has been consumed, then the asset is reported at two-thirds its original cost. As long as the asset is not intended for sale to outsiders, market value seldom enters into the determination of the amount at which an asset is reported. Indeed, an automobile owned by a business might be reported at an amount either greater or less than the price at which similar used cars are being traded.

The outlay for organizational costs will benefit many accounting periods. To the extent that it has "future service potential"— the corporation would not exist without it—it can properly be considered an asset. Even though it may have no value to outsiders, it should still be reported on the balance sheet at initial cost less that fraction of cost representing services already consumed.

Current Liabilities

Liabilities are also categorized as either current or noncurrent. *Current liabilities* are those expected to be satisfied out of current assets (or through the creation of other current liabilities) or to be satisfied within a relatively short period of time, usually one year. Most common categories of current liabilities are amounts owed to employees for wages and salaries; to suppliers for services, supplies, and raw materials purchased (conventionally called trade accounts, or simply *accounts payable*); to the government for taxes (taxes payable); and to banks or other lenders for amounts borrowed (notes payable) and for interest on such amounts (interest payable) that is payable within one year.

Noncurrent Liabilities

Noncurrent liabilities include all other amounts owed. They include long-term (for a period greater than one year) notes as well as bonds. Bonds are similar to long-term notes but differ in that the promise to pay is usually included in a more formal legal instrument and in that the term of the loan is often longer. The same bond or note may be classified as both a current and a noncurrent liability. The portion that is due within one year would be considered current; the portion due beyond one year would be noncurrent.

Just as amounts that a company pays in advance to receive goods or services in the future are considered to be assets of the company, so too are amounts that others pay to the company for goods and services to be provided by the company considered to be liabilities of the company. Suppose, for example, that TWA sells a ticket for a trip the traveler intends to take a month after purchase. At the time of sale the airline receives an asset (cash or accounts receivable) equal to the price of the ticket. At the time of sale it incurs an obligation to provide services (i.e., one airline trip) to the customer. To be sure, the obligation is not a liability in the usual sense, in that the airline has no monetary debt outstanding to the customer. But it is an obligation nonetheless. Such amounts are reported among the liabilities and may be labeled as appropriate: "advances from customers," "revenues received but not yet earned," or, less descriptively but more generally, *deferred credits*. They are classified as current if the obligation is

likely to be satisfied within one year; otherwise they are classified as noncurrent.

"Nonassets and Nonliabilities"

Not all amounts that a firm will have to pay to others if it continues in business are recorded as liabilities, nor are all amounts that it can be expected to receive recorded as assets. If a firm signs a three-year contract with a new president, for example, and promises to pay him $200,000 per year, the firm may be legally liable for the full $600,000 as long as the new president is willing to provide the required services. The firm would not, however, record the full amount as a liability. Only as the president "earns" his salary—i.e., as he performs his side of the bargain—would the firm record as a liability amounts earned but not paid. Similarly accounted for is a transaction in which a firm borrows $1,000 from a bank at a 12 percent rate of interest and gives the bank a one-year note. At the end of the one-year period, the firm will owe the bank $1,120—the principal of $1,000 plus interest of $120. At the time the note is signed, however, the only liability that would be recorded is the $1,000 actually borrowed. Each month, as the company has use of the borrowed funds, an additional $10 interest for one month will be recorded as a liability. The bank, for its part, would record as an asset a note for $1,000. It, too, would recognize an asset "interest receivable," only as it *earns* the interest revenue with the passage of time.

In general, assets and liabilities arising out of "executory" contracts (those contingent upon the mutual performance of the two sides to the contract) are recorded only to the extent that one of the parties has fulfilled its contractual obligations. The reason for such limited accounting recognition of assets and liabilities will become considerably clearer as the relationship between balance sheet and income statement accounts is discussed more fully in subsequent chapters.

Owners' Equity

The stockholders' equity section of the corporate balance sheet is divided into at least two main subsections. The first indicates the *capital contributed by shareholders*— either at the time the corporation was formed or when additional shares of stock were issued in the course of the corporation's existence. Corporations may issue several different types of stock.

Common stock generally gives its owners the right to vote for members of the corporation's board of directors as well as on numerous other corporate matters and the right to share in corporate profits whenever dividends are declared by the board of directors.

Preferred stock, on the other hand, generally does *not* carry voting rights, but it does ordinarily guarantee the owner that he will receive dividends of at least a minimum amount each year. The dividend rate is fixed at the time the stock is issued.

Often shares of both common and preferred stock are arbitrarily assigned a *par* or *stated* value (e.g., $100 per share). Such values have some legal, but little economic, significance, and shares are commonly issued for amounts above or below these arbitrarily assigned values. Amounts that the company receives above the par values of the shares are categorized as *additional paid-in capital* or *capital in excess of par* and those below as a *discount* on the shares issued.

The second subsection, *retained earnings*, indicates the accumulated earnings of the business. Retained earnings will be com-

mented on in greater detail later in this chapter.

If the firm is not a corporation, that is, if it is a *sole proprietorship* (a firm owned by a single individual) or a *partnership* (a firm owned by two or more parties), then the owners' equity section of the balance sheet may take a somewhat different form. Since such enterprises do not issue stock and are not bound by many of the legal restrictions that apply to firms that do, it is generally most useful to readers of the financial reports to indicate the entire equity of each of the owners in a separate account. The owners' equity section of the Mercury Truck Manufacturing Corp., if it were owned by two partners, W. King and F. Prince, might appear as follows:

Partners' capital	
W. King, capital	$ 9,525,347
F. Prince, capital	7,526,322
Total partners' capital	$17,051,669

THE INCOME STATEMENT—A CLOSER LOOK

Statements of income are presented in a variety of formats, but virtually all are based on the fundamental relationship

$$\text{Revenues} - \text{Expenses} = \text{Net income}$$

Although the income statement illustrated in Exhibit 2-4 is that of a manufacturing corporation, there are no costs of either labor or raw materials listed among the expenses. The company would, of course, maintain separate accounts for labor, materials and other factors of production, but to avoid inundating the reader with detail such costs are grouped together in one account, *cost of goods sold*. Cost of goods sold may not represent the actual costs of labor, material,

EXHIBIT 2-4

Mercury Truck Manufacturing Corp.
Statement of Income for the Year Ended December 31, 1983

Revenues		
Sales		$32,904,468
Rents received from equipment leased		3,464,491
Miscellaneous revenues		1,209,975
Total revenues		$37,578,934
Expenses		
Cost of goods sold		28,691,473
Selling and administrative expenses		2,319,231
Depreciation expense		1,704,621
Property taxes and other taxes not based on income		823,347
Interest expense		1,221,896
Total expenses		$34,760,568
Income before taxes and extraordinary items		2,818,366
Taxes on income		1,245,000
Income after taxes, but before extraordinary items		$ 1,573,366
Extraordinary gain—amount received upon settlement of litigation	$576,923	
Less applicable taxes	276,923	300,000
Net income		$ 1,873,366
Earnings per share of common stock		$ 2.99

and other factors to production incurred during the reporting period. Adjustment must be made for those costs applicable to goods that may have been produced but not yet sold (i.e., retained in inventory) and those goods that have been sold but were produced in prior periods.

Extraordinary Gains and Losses

Occasionally firms engage in transactions or are affected by events that are highly unusual and are unlikely to be repeated. Examples of such events might be losses from natural disasters or from governmental expropriation of a company's plant in another country. Unless such gains or losses are segregated from income derived from the normal operations of the firm, the income statement will not serve as a meaningful instrument of comparison among financial performances of various years. Moreover, the income of the year in which such events or transactions occurred will provide little insight into earnings potential for the future. As a consequence, such *extraordinary items*— those which are *exceptional in nature and infrequent in occurrence*—are reported separately in the income statement. And since these events are likely to have a major impact on the income taxes of the firm, the applicable taxes are also reported separately.

EXHIBIT 2-5

Mercury Truck Manufacturing Corp.
Statement of Retained Earnings
for the Year Ended December 31, 1983

Balance at January 1, 1983		$15,223,060
Net income for 1983		1,873,366
		$17,096,426
Less dividends declared		
Preferred stock ($10 per share		
on 1,000 shares outstanding)	$ 10,000	
Common stock ($1.21 per share		
on 625,773 shares outstanding)	757,185	767,185
Balance at December 31, 1983		$16,329,241

THE STATEMENT OF RETAINED EARNINGS

The statement of retained earnings (Exhibit 2-5) serves as the link between the income statement and the balance sheet. The basic accounting equation can readily be expanded as follows:

$$\text{Assets} - \text{Liabilities} = \overbrace{\begin{array}{l}\text{Capital contributed by owners} \\ + \text{ Retained earnings}\end{array}}^{\text{Owners' equity}}$$

Retained earnings represent the sum of the earnings of the accounting periods that the company has been in existence less the amounts paid as dividends to stockholders. The retained earnings per the balance sheet at the beginning of the period (which of course must be identical to those at the end of the previous period), plus the income for that period per the income statement, less any dividends declared during the period, equals the retained earnings at the end of the period:

Retained earnings, balance at beginning of year

+ Income − Dividends declared

Retained earnings, balance at end of year

Retained Earnings Contrasted with Assets

The statement of retained earnings, by indicating both dividends declared during the year and the income for the year, provides a reconciliation of the retained earnings at the beginning of the year with those at the end.

Retained earnings, it cannot be overemphasized, *do not* represent tangible resources of the firm. Earnings *per se* cannot be distributed to stockholders; earnings cannot be used to purchase goods or services. Only cash or other assets are generally accepted in exchange for other goods or services. Retained earnings represent nothing more than *claims* against the assets of the enterprise—the claims of the owners attributable to the income earned by the firm over the course of one or more years. Although assets must be equal to the claims against those assets (claims of owners as well as creditors), *there is generally no specific relationship between particular assets and particular claims.* The existence of retained earnings, for example, in no way implies the availability of free cash.

Dividends

Dividends are distributions of the assets of the enterprise to its owners. The asset distributed most often is cash, but it could, in fact, be any asset of the firm. As the assets of the firm are reduced upon distribution to the owners, so also are the claims of the owners against such assets. Assume, for example, that several individuals contribute a total of $1,000 to form a corporation. During the first year of operations the firm earns $200. Its position, at the end of the first year, as indicated by the accounting equation might appear as follows:

Assets = Liabilities + Capital contributed by owners + Retained earnings

$1,200 = $0 + $1,000 + $200

If the firm declared and paid a dividend of $100, then the position of the company after the $100 in assets had been distributed would appear as

Assets = Liabilities + Capital contributed by owners + Retained earnings

$1,100 = $0 + $1,000 + $100

The statement of retained earnings is not included in the financial reports of all corporations. Some companies indicate the dividends distributed to shareholders directly beneath the net income figure on the income statement and omit the reconciliation between beginning-of-year and end-of-year retained earnings. Others include the reconciliation as an addendum to the income statement. Moreover, if during the year there are significant changes in any of the other owners' equity accounts (e.g., if additional amounts of stock are sold), then the statement of changes in retained earnings is sometimes expanded to include such changes and re-titled "statement of changes in owners' equity."

THE STATEMENT OF CHANGES IN FINANCIAL POSITION

The statement of changes in financial position has only recently (1971, per a decision of the Accounting Principles Board) become a required component of published corporate reports, equal in status to the balance sheet and the income statement. The statement of changes in financial position is illustrated in Exhibit 2-6.

The statement of changes in financial position is most commonly used to indicate changes during the year in the companies' *working capital* position. Working capital, often used interchangeably with the term *funds*, refers to the difference between the *current assets* (cash, accounts receivable, inventory, etc.) and the *current liabilities* (wages payable, accounts payable, etc.) of the firm. The working capital position of a company is an indication of its *liquidity*—its ability to meet current debts as they come due. Current assets, other than prepaid expenses, can normally be expected to be transformed into cash within a year. They can thereby be used to satisfy the firm's current liabilities, which, by definition, will come due within a year. Prepaid expenses make unnecessary the cash disbursements which might otherwise have to be made.

Profitability versus Liquidity

The statement of changes in financial position indicates both the sources and applications of working capital—how a

EXHIBIT 2-6

Mercury Truck Manufacturing Corp.
Statement of Changes in Financial Position
for the Year Ended December 31, 1983

Sources of working capital		
Operations		
Net earnings	$1,873,366	
Add: Operating expenses deducted in the determination of net earnings that did not require the use of working capital	1,704,621	$3,577,987
Issue of common stock		4,960,519
Amounts borrowed from bank		1,000,000
Total sources of working capital		$9,538,506
Applications of working capital		
Cash dividends paid to stockholders		$ 754,986
Purchases of property, plant, and equipment (less disposals)		3,011,819
Increases in investments and other assets		254,735
Portion of long-term debt reclassified as a current liability		2,307,656
Total applications of working capital		$6,329,196
Net increase in working capital for the year		$3,209,310

company acquired working capital and what it did with it. Its importance can readily be illustrated by a question relating to an extreme situation: Is it possible for a company to be profitable (as reported on its income statement) and still be bankrupt because of a deficiency of liquid assets? The answer, of course, is a resounding, and all too frequent, yes.

Consider the case, for example, of a small electronics company. Encouraged by the great demand for its products and the resultant high profits, it decides to expand its operations. It applies all available cash toward the purchase of new manufacturing equipment and, in addition, borrows heavily to finance the expansion. Orders continue to increase as anticipated, but there are substantial delays between the dates an order is received, when the product is manufactured, and when the cash is collected. In the mean-

time, obligations which the firm incurs come due, leaving the company with insufficient cash, or assets which could readily be transformed into cash, to meet its current debts. Creditors, who may themselves be caught in a "cash squeeze," may be unable or unwilling to give the company additional time to generate the necessary cash to meet its obligations. Consequently, the firm may have to default on its debts and be placed under the financial supervision of a court-appointed trustee of bankruptcy.

The income statement is a severely deficient indicator of a firm's ability to generate cash to pay bills, finance expansion, or pay dividends, since transactions may be recorded as revenues and expenses long before or after they result in inflows or outflows of cash or other components of working capital. The purchase of an item of equipment may result in a cash outflow in the year in which it is purchased, but it would not result in an expense on the income statement of the same amount. Rather, the purchase price would be charged as an expense (i.e., depreciated) over the useful life of the equipment. To remedy the deficiencies of the income statement in this regard, the statement of changes in financial position has been made an integral part of the financial report. By focusing on changes in both cash and other accounts which are either "near" cash (other current assets) or which will require the disbursement of cash in the near future (current liabilities), the statement of changes in financial position is able to describe an additional aspect of the firm's financial health.

There are considerable variations among firms in both the format and the substance of the statement of changes in financial position. Some firms elect to report changes in working capital. Others, however, choose to indicate changes in cash or cash plus selected other current assets, such as accounts receivable or marketable securities that can most readily be transformed into cash. The statement of changes in financial position will be discussed in detail in Chapter 14.

FOOTNOTES

The basic financial statements, no matter how detailed and conscientiously prepared, can never capture all elements of an organization's financial position or changes in well-being. Footnotes serve to fill in some of the gaps left by the basic statements. Examples of the types of disclosures that should be made in footnotes are:

1. Accounting policies adopted by the company. This information enables an analyst to recognize and make adjustment for differences among firms in reported results of operations and financial position arising solely from the use of alternative accounting methods.

2. Additional detail and support for amounts reported in the body of the financial statements. This type of disclosure gives recognition to the needs of different parties for varying levels of data aggregation.

3. Pending legal actions. The outcome of litigation, both civil and criminal, in which a firm is involved, may have a pervasive and far-reaching impact on its financial well-being.

4. Breakdown of earnings and assets by business segment. Insofar as a firm engages in more than one line of business, the separation of financial data by industry (or groups of related industries) facilitates the evaluation of past performance and prospects for the future.

MEASURES OF FINANCIAL PERFORMANCE AND HEALTH

The performance of a business over a period of time as well as its well-being as of any particular point in time can never be evaluated by examining any single dollar amount that is reported in the firm's financial statements. Net income, by itself, for example, tells nothing about how well a company has employed the resources within its command. A large company may have several times the earnings of a smaller company, yet relative to size the performance of the smaller firm may have been better.

Financial performance and fiscal health can best be described by ratios which relate one aspect of a firm's performance or status to another. Some of these ratios are, either by convention or requirement, reported in the body of the financial statements or in the accompanying supplementary data. Others must be calculated by the party engaged in the evaluation.

It is important that investors, creditors, managers, and accountants be familiar with the most widely used of the financial ratios.

The ratios can serve as the basis for evaluating not only a business as a whole, but also its component units and the activities in which it engages. They can warn of fiscal stress. They can point to companies or components of companies to which (or away from which) resources should be directed. Moreover, it is essential that managers be aware of the criteria that outsiders will employ in evaluating their company in order that they can consider the impact on those criteria of any actions that they take. It is equally crucial that independent auditors be knowledgeable of the criteria because some managers may be motivated to select from accounting alternatives those principles that have few meritorious characterics other than their ability to improve the financial ratios.

Ratios themselves, however, must never be evaluated in a vacuum. What are important are trends over time and comparisons with firms in the same or related industries. Should a key ratio or series of ratios increase or decrease from one year to the next, it may be a sign of either financial deterioration or improvement.

There are no fixed minimum or maximum values below which a ratio should not fall or above which it should not rise. But whenever the ratio of a particular firm is substantially out of line with those common in the industry, the analyst should be alert to either potential financial difficulty or unusual financial strength. Normal ranges for most ratios and percentages vary considerably from industry to industry. Some industries, electric utilities for example, require large amounts of invested capital in order to support their operations. Other industries, supermarkets for instance, require relatively small amounts of permanent capital. As a consequence, supermarkets can be expected to have a much higher ratio of net income to total invested capital (return on investment) than would electric utilities. Supermarkets, on the other hand, tend to earn a relatively small profit on each dollar of sales since the *markup* on grocery products is relatively small. By contrast, once the physical facilities have been acquired, the cost of generating electricity is relatively low. Thus, electric utilities would generally have a much higher ratio of net income to sales revenue (return on sales) than would supermarkets. Industry norms for a number of key indicators can be obtained from publications of industry trade associations or of financial service bureaus such as Dun and Bradstreet or Standard & Poor's.

The ratios that are to be described in this chapter are among the most fundamental of performance indicators. Other ratios will be discussed throughout the text in the sections pertaining to the accounts or activities on which the ratios focus.

Earnings per share

Earnings per share (EPS) is reported in the financial statements directly beneath net income. It is computed by dividing net income by the average number of shares outstanding during the period (with adjustment for additional shares that the company may have to issue in the future.)* Earnings per share allows individual stockholders to determine their interests in total corporate earnings by multiplying EPS by number of shares owned. It facilitates comparisons of performance among years in which a greater or lesser number of shares may have been outstanding.

Per its statement of income (Exhibit 2-4), Mercury Truck Manufacturing Corp. had net income after taxes in 1983 of $1,873,366.

---

* Owing in part to the required adjustment for the additional shares, the computation of earnings per share can be quite complex. The computation of EPS will be refined and discussed in greater detail in Chapter 12.

Per its statement of position (Exhibit 2-3) it had outstanding on December 31, 1983, 625,773 shares of common stock. Earnings per share for 1983 (based on number of shares outstanding on December 31, 1983, rather than average number of shares outstanding during the year) was, therefore, $2.99:

$$\text{Earnings per share} = \frac{\text{Net income}}{\text{Shares of common stock outstanding}}$$

$$= \frac{\$1,873,366}{625,773} = \$2.99$$

Price/Earnings Ratio

A short analytical step from earnings per share is the *price/earnings* ratio. The price/earnings (P/E) ratio compares earnings per share with the price per share at which the common stock of the company is being traded on the open market.

The importance of the P/E ratio to investors is indicated by its being incorporated in the daily stock market tables of the *Wall Street Journal* as well as many other financial periodicals. Suppose that as of December 31, 1983, the market price per share of Mercury Truck Manufacturing Corp. was $21\frac{1}{4}$ (i.e., $21.25). The price/earnings ratio would be approximately 7.1 to 1.

Price/earnings ratio

$$= \frac{\text{Market price per share of common stock}}{\text{Earnings per share}}$$

$$= \frac{\$21.25}{\$\ 2.99} = 7.1 \text{ to } 1$$

Return on Investment

The measure of corporate performance that is generally considered most relevant to both managers and investors is *return on investment*. Return on investment relates the

earnings of the enterprise to the resources provided by its owners. The resources provided by the owners are measured by their equity—which, of course, is equivalent to net assets (i.e., assets less liabilities). Thus,

$$\text{Return on investment (ROI)} = \frac{\text{Net income}}{\text{Owners' equity}}$$

The balance sheet of Mercury Truck Manufacturing Corp. indicates that the total investment of stockholders at the end of 1983 was $17,051,669. This amount includes the direct contributions of stockholders plus the earnings over the years that have been retained in the business. The statement of income reveals that earnings for the year were $1,873,366. Hence, return on investment was 11 percent:

$$\text{Return on investment} = \frac{\$1,873,366}{\$17,051,699} = 11\%$$

An alternative means of computing return on investment which tailors the percentage specifically to the information requirements of managers, as opposed to external parties, will be discussed in Chapter 16*.

Current Ratio

Another widely used measure of financial health is the *current ratio*. The current ratio provides an insight into the ability of the enterprise to meet its short-term debts. As such it is especially meaningful to parties considering whether to extend credit to the firm. The current ratio compares current assets to current liabilities; that is, it relates cash and the assets that are most likely to be transformed into cash within a single business

* Preferably, owners' equity should be computed by calculating the average owners' equity during the year. Such refinement, as well as others to be discussed in Chapter 16, is ignored for the sake of simplicity at this stage of the text.

cycle to the debts that will fall due within that period.

$$\text{Current ratio} = \frac{\text{Current assets}}{\text{Current liabilities}}$$

The current ratio of Mercury Truck Manufacturing Corp. is 1.6 to 1:

$$\text{Current ratio} = \frac{\$21,695,586}{\$13,350,841} = 1.6:1$$

Importance of Comparisons

Financial statements provide an insight into a company's past operating performance and future earnings potential that is perhaps unmatched by that which could be obtained from any other sources. But the picture presented has meaning only when viewed from the proper perspective. Managers, investors, and other users of the statements must be able to examine the financial data with reference to financial position and results of operations of both previous years and of other companies in the same or related industries. No set of dollar amounts, ratios, or other indicators of financial health have meaning in and of themselves. They are of significance only when compared with similar indicators of the same company in other years and of other companies in the same or related industries. Toward this end, corporate annual reports should include complete financial statements for the year immediately prior to that being reported upon as well as summary information for a period of 5 to 10 years.

Financial statements are often "rounded" to the nearest thousand or even million dollars. The practice of rounding serves to highlight the imprecision of financial statements; they are necessarily based on a number of estimates and judgmental determinations. Although such estimates and judgmental determinations unquestionably permit a degree of subjectivity to enter into the financial statements, and perhaps make them less comparable with those of other firms, they serve at the same time to make them more relevant for most decisions that they will be used to facilitate.

SUMMARY

In this chapter we have presented an overview of the three primary financial statements—the balance sheet (statement of financial position), the income statement, and the statement of changes in financial position—as well as a secondary statement, the statement of changes in retained earnings. The chapter was intended to familiarize the reader with the purposes of each statement, with its underlying nature, with its basic format, and with the terminology conventionally employed.

The key to accounting as it is currently practiced is the fundamental accounting equation: assets − liabilities = owners' equity. This equation serves as the basis for analyzing and recording all accounting events. In the following chapter we shall illustrate in greater detail the means by which transactions are given accounting recognition.

EXERCISE FOR REVIEW AND SELF-TESTING

(The solutions to this exercise—and similar exercises in other chapters—will be found following the last problem in the chapter.)

1. A group of entrepreneurs form a corporation. They contribute to the enterprise $100,000 cash. To provide evidence of their investment, the corporation issues to them 10,000 shares of common stock, assigning to each share a par value of $10.

a. What are the total assets of the corporation immediately after it has been formed?

b. What are the total equities of the corporation? That is, what are the total claims of the owners against these assets?

2. The corporation borrows $50,000 from a bank.

a. What are the total assets of the corporation now?

b. What are the total claims against these assets? Of these total claims (equities), how much are claims of outsiders (liabilities); how much are claims of the owners?

3. The company acquires an automobile for $10,000 cash.

a. What are the total assets of the corporation?

b. What are the corporation's liabilities; its owners' equity?

4. The company acquires 300 units of inventory at a cost of $5 per unit. The purchase is made "on account," with the firm promising to pay for the goods within 30 days.

a. What are the total assets of the corporation now?

b. What are the corporation's liabilities; its owners' equity?

5. The firm sells 100 of the units of inventory for $7 per unit. The purchasers pay cash.

a. What are the total assets of the corporation?

b. What are the corporation's liabilities; its owners' equity?

6. By how much has the equity of the owners increased since they made their initial contribution of cash? How much "better off" is the corporation (and thus its owners) since the owners made such contribution? What was the "income" of the corporation during the period in which the transactions took place?

QUESTIONS FOR REVIEW AND DISCUSSION

1. Explain why the balance sheet of a firm might be dated "*As of* December 31, 1983," but the income statement dated "*For the Year Ended* December 31, 1983."

2. What is meant by owners' equity? Why is owners' equity not necessarily indicative of the amount of cash that would be returned to the owners if the assets of a business were to be sold and the creditors paid the amounts owed to them?

3. A bookkeeper recently totaled up the recorded assets of a firm and found that they came to $1,398,576. The total liabilities came to $600,000 and the total owners' equity to $800,000. Are such totals possible in the context of the double-entry bookkeeping process if no error has been made? Suppose instead that assets were equal to liabilities plus owners' equity. Do such totals assure that no accounting errors have been made?

4. Which of the following events would usually be accorded accounting recognition on the books of General Electric Co.?

1. The firm signs a three-year contract with its union.

2. The firm issues 1,000 additional shares of common stock.

3. An officer of General Electric sells on the open market 3,000 shares of company stock from his personal holdings.

4. The passage of another year has reduced the remaining useful life of plant and equipment.

5. The wholesale price of copper wire has *increased*. General Electric Co. has 100,000 feet of copper wire in inventory.

6. The wholesale price of copper wire has *decreased*. General Electric Co. has 100,000 feet of copper wire in inventory.

5. Included among a firm's noncurrent assets are "unamortized corporate organizational costs, $25,000." What is meant by such an asset? Is it possible to sell such an asset? If not, why is it considered an asset?

6. The same firm has recorded among its current liabilities "advances from customers, $3,000." Why is such amount a liability? What impact did receipt of the $3,000 have on the accounting equation?

7. A company reported substantial earnings for the last several years, yet it is about to file for bankruptcy. How is such a situation possible?

8. A firm recently received a check from a customer for $10,000, yet it did not record such amount as "revenue." What are two possible reasons why cash received is not revenue?

9. A firm recently purchased equipment for $80,000 yet did not record an expense. Why not? Will the amount paid ever be reported as an expense? When?

10. What is meant by a *current asset?* How is it possible that shares of the common stock of XYZ Company owned by one company may be recorded as a current asset but those owned by another may be recorded as a noncurrent asset?

11. What is meant by *preferred stock?* What preferences do preferred stockholders have over common stockholders? What rights do common stockholders have that preferred stockholders generally do not have?

12. What are *extraordinary items?* Why are they reported on the income statement apart from ordinary operating revenues and expenses?

13. Is it possible for a firm to have a substantial balance in retained earnings and still be unable to declare a cash dividend? Why?

PROBLEMS

1. Balance sheet accounts indicate the value assigned to resources or obligations as of a particular point in time. Income statement accounts provide information on inflows and outflows of resources during a particular period of time.

Some accounts are conventionally reported on the balance sheet; others are reported on the income statement. For each of the accounts indicated below, specify whether it would ordinarily be reported on the income statement or on the balance sheet.
1. Sales revenue
2. Accounts receivable
3. Insurance expense
4. Prepaid insurance
5. Inventories
6. Cost of goods sold
7. Depreciation expense
8. Accumulated depreciation
9. Interest expense
10. Notes payable
11. Retained earnings
12. Investment in subsidiary

2. All transactions serve to increase or decrease the balances in some combination of asset, liability and owners' equity accounts.

For each of the following transactions, indicate whether assets (A), liabilities (L) or owners' equity (OE) would increase (+) or decrease (−). The first transaction is illustrated for you.
1. A corporation issues common stock in exchange for cash. (A+ ; OE+)
2. It issues preferred stock in exchange for a building.
3. It purchases inventory, giving the seller a 30-day note for the amount of the merchandise.
4. It collects from a customer the amount the customer owed on goods purchased several months earlier.
5. It exchanges shares of preferred stock for shares of common stock.
6. It repays bondholders by issuing to them shares of common stock.
7. It declares and pays a dividend to stockholders, thereby distributing assets of the company (cash) to the owners.
8. It returns to a manufacturer defective merchandise for credit on its account.
9. It receives from a customer defective merchandise and reduces the balance owed by the customer. The merchandise had been sold at a profit. The goods returned have no value.

3. Assets must equal liabilities plus owners' equity.

The balances that follow were taken from the December 31, 1983, balance sheet of a corporation. Arrange a sheet of paper into three columns, each corresponding to a term in the accounting equation:

Assets = Liabilities + Owners' Equity

Place each of the balances in the appropriate column. Total each of the columns to make certain that the equation is in balance.

Marketable securities	$ 20,000
Common stock	100,000
Buildings and equipment	300,000
Bonds payable	250,000
Accounts receivable	90,000
Prepaid rent	15,000

statement and a balance sheet. Derive the amount of retained earnings.

5. *Owners' equity equals assets minus liabilities. Owners' equity is affected by income (or loss), capital contributions, and capital withdrawals (dividends).*

Fill in the missing amounts. Assume that there

	(a)	(b)	(c)
Assets, December 31, 1983	$100,000	$50,000	?
Liabilities, December 31, 1983	25,000	10,000	$20,000
Owners' equity, *January* 1, 1983	60,000	?	80,000
Income, 1983	80,000	8,000	5,000
Dividends paid, 1983	?	4,000	10,000

Preferred stock	50,000
Inventories	80,000
Taxes payable	25,000
Advances from customers	3,000
Accounts payable	17,000
Interest payable	8,000
Organization costs	12,000
Retained earning	64,000

4. *Retained earnings may be derived from other balance sheet accounts.*

From the following accounts, taken from the books and records of the Finch Company on December 31, 1983, prepare both an income

Cash	$15,000
Accounts payable	12,000
Building and equipment	90,000
Cost of goods sold	60,000
Notes payable	5,000
Wages and salaries payable	3,000
Preferred stock	20,000
Common stock	50,000
Marketable securities	18,000
Inventory	22,000
Sales revenue	88,000
Tax expense	3,000
Taxes payable	1,000
Rent expense	4,000
Prepaid rent	1,000
Retained earnings	?

were no capital contributions by owners during 1983. (*Hint:* First compute owners' equity as of December 31, 1983.)

6. *Corporate performance may be evaluated by relating income to the investment of the owners, which may be expressed in terms of "book" or "market" values.*

Hoover Company, the manufacturer of vacuum cleaners, had, as of December 31, 1979, $491,091,068 in assets and $263,376,708 in liabilities. Net income for 1979 was $39,263,333. The common stock of the company, which is traded "over the counter," closed on December 31, 1979, at $12\frac{3}{4}$. There were 12,114,995 shares of common stock outstanding.

a. Compute the return on the stockholders' equity (ROI).

b. Compute the price/earnings ratio. Compute also the reciprocal of the price/earnings ratio (i.e., earnings/price) and express it as a percentage.

7. *Account titles generally provide an indication of whether the account represents a "stock" (and is thereby reported on the balance sheet) or a "flow" (and is thereby reported on the income statement).*

From the following account balances, taken from the books and records of the Julie Company as of December 31, 1983, prepare an income statement and a balance sheet. Title and date the statements as appropriate, and, insofar as the information permits, separate assets and liabilities into current and noncurrent classifications.

Cash	$18,000
A. Julie, capital	51,600
Sales	75,000
Cost of goods sold	52,000
Prepaid insurance	1,000
Advances from customers	3,000
Patents	8,000
Depreciation expense	2,500
Insurance expense	2,000
Interest revenue	500
Interest expense	900
Prepaid interest	200
Interest payable	600
Accounts receivable	10,000
Inventory	9,000
Rent expense	6,000
Advertising expense	5,000
Notes payable (due in three years)	8,000
Buildings and equipment	26,000
Notes receivable	10,000
Accounts payable	19,000

8. *In the absence of additional contributions by owners, owners' equity is increased by earnings and decreased by dividends and losses.*

The Gail Company was organized as a partnership on January 2, 1983. Each of its two owners contributed $10,000 in cash to start the business. After one year of operations the company had on hand the following assets: cash, $18,000; accounts receivable, $3,000; inventory available for sale, $10,000; furniture and fixtures, $25,000.

The company owed suppliers (i.e., accounts payable) $8,000 and had notes outstanding to a bank (due in 1987) of $16,000.

a. Prepare a balance sheet as of December 31, 1983.

b. Assuming that the owners neither made additional contributions of capital to the business nor made any withdrawals, compute income for 1983.

c. Assume instead that during the year the owners withdrew $4,000 from the business. Compute income for 1983.

9. *The beginning balance in an account plus increases and minus decreases in that account during a period equals the ending balance.*

The table following is a condensed balance sheet of the Withington Corporation as of December 31, 1983. On a sheet of paper, copy the account titles

Withington Corporation

	Balance 12/31/83	Transaction 1	2	3	4	5	6	Balance 1/31/84
Cash	$ 40,000							
Accounts receivable	25,000							
Inventory	57,000	+8,000						
Prepaid rent	2,000							
Equipment	85,000							
Building	200,000							
	$409,000							
Accounts payable	$ 19,000	+8,000						
Wages payable	4,000							
Notes payable	38,000							
Bonds payable	150,000							
Common stock	45,000							
Retained earnings	153,000							
	$409,000							

and the initial balances. Leave room for seven additional columns of figures. Label six of the columns Transaction 1, 2, 3, etc., and the seventh column "Balance, 1/31/84."

The following six transactions took place in January. Indicate the effect that each would have on the balance sheet. Summarize the effects of the six transactions on the December 31, 1983, balance by adding across the rows and indicating the new balance in the column marked "Balance, 1/31/84."

1. The company purchases inventory on account, $8,000. (Transaction 1 is done for you.)
2. The company purchases equipment for $12,000, giving the seller a two-year note.
3. The company pays its employees the $4,000 owed.
4. The company declares and pays a dividend of $20,000.
5. The company reaches an agreement with its bondholders. In exchange for their bonds, they agree to accept shares of common stock that have a market value of $150,000.
6. The company collects $5,000 that was owed by its customers.

10. The balance sheet is nothing more than a detailed expression of the accounting equation.

Arrange a sheet of paper into three columns, each corresponding to a term in the accounting equation:

$$Assets = Liabilities + Owners' Equity$$

Indicate the impact that each of the following transactions would have on the accounting equation. Suggest titles for the specific accounts that would be affected.

1. Whitman and Farrel form a corporation. The corporation issues 1,000 shares of common stock and sells 500 shares to each of the founders for $3 per share.
2. The corporation borrows $3,000 from a bank, giving the bank a one-year note.
3. The corporation purchases furniture and fixtures for $5,000. The company pays $1,000 cash and gives a six-month note for the balance.
4. The corporation rents a building. It pays, in advance, the first month's rent of $700.

5. The corporation purchases office supplies for $400 cash.
6. The corporation purchases inventory for future sale to customers for $1,200 cash.

Compute the "balance" in each of the accounts. Summarize the balances in the form of a balance sheet.

11. Working capital (current assets less current liabilities) in adequate amounts provides assurance that a firm is able to meet its obligations as they come due. It is important that all transactions be analyzed in terms of their impact upon working capital.

For each of the transactions described, indicate the effect that it will have upon current assets, current liabilities, and working capital. State whether current assets, current liabilities, and working capital will increase, decrease, or remain the same, and specify the accounts that will be affected. Indicate also any accounts, other than current assets or current liabilities, that will be affected. Transaction 1 is done for you as an illustration.

1. A company purchases equipment for $7,000 cash.
2. It borrows $3,000 and issues a 60-day note.
3. It borrows $5,000 and issues a three-year note.
4. It purchases inventory for $1,000 and promises to pay within 30 days.
5. It purchases inventory for $600 cash.
6. It purchases a building for $100,000 and issues 10-year bonds for the same amount.
7. It repays a five-year note for $1,790.
8. It sells, for $100, goods carried in inventory that were recorded at their original cost of $80. The purchaser agrees to pay within 60 days. (Analyze this transaction in two steps: the increase in the asset received, and the decrease in the asset surrendered.)
9. It sells, for $600 cash, land that it had recorded on its books for the same amount.
10. It records first-year depreciation on a building that originally cost $100,000 and that has a 20-year life. (That is, the company determines that one-twentieth of the services to be provided by the building have already been consumed.)

Transaction Number	Current Assets	Current Liabilities	Working Capital	Other Accounts
1	Cash − $7,000	No effect	− $7,000	Equipment + $7,000

12. *Retained earnings must not be associated with cash or any other specific assets.*

As of December 31, 1983, the balance sheet of the Morgan Motors Co. appeared as follows (thousands of dollars):

Cash	$ 85,000
Other current assets	75,000
Other assets, including buildings, land, and equipment	670,000
Total assets	$830,000
Liabilities	$220,000
Common stock (10,000,000 issued and outstanding)	10,000
Retained earnings	600,000
Total equities	$830,000

In 1983 the company had earnings of $40 million. Since there were 10 million shares of common stock outstanding (par value per share, $1.00) earnings per share were $4. In 1983 the company declared no dividends since the directors claimed funds were needed for expansion.

Shortly after the close of the year, the president of the company received a letter from a stockholder protesting the company's refusal to declare a dividend. The letter said in part,

When I studied accounting "retained earnings" were called "surplus." No amount of name changing can obscure the fact that the company has $600 million available for distribution to stockholders.

a. How would you respond to the angry stockholder? Does the company have $600 million available for distribution to stockholders?

b. Suppose the company did decide to declare a dividend of $60 per share ($600 million). What effect would such dividend likely have on corporate operations?

c. Does the balance sheet provide assurance that the company could, in fact, declare a dividend of $60 per share even if it wanted to? Why?

d. Suppose that instead of earnings of $40 million the company had a loss of $10 million. The company nevertheless declared a dividend of $2.00 per share. A disgruntled stockholder questioned the decision and wrote to the president:

Dividends are supposed to be distributions of earnings. How is it possible to pay a dividend in a year in which there were no earnings?

How would you respond to his question?

13. *Alternative borrowing arrangements have different effects upon the current ratio.*

The balance sheet of the First Corporation as of December 31, 1983 appears on the following page.

a. Compute the current ratio as of December 31, 1983.

b. Suppose that the company were to borrow an additional $50,000 and give the bank a six-month note. How would that affect the current ratio?

c. Suppose instead that the company were to borrow $50,000 and give a note payable in full at the end of two years. How would that affect the current ratio?

d. Suppose instead that the company were to issue bonds for $200,000 and use the proceeds to purchase a new plant? How would that affect the current ratio?

14. *Alternative financing arrangements may have substantially different effects on the accounting equation as well as on earnings per share.*

The following information relates to the Emerson Corp.:

Total assets, 12/31/83	$10,000,000
Total liabilities, 12/31/83	2,000,000
Total owners' equity, 12/31/83	8,000,000
Net income 1983	1,000,000
Number of shares of common stock outstanding	100,000

a. Determine earnings per share for 1983.

First Corporation
Balance Sheet
December 31, 1983

Assets		*Liabilities and Owners' Equity*	
Current assets		Current liabilities	
Cash	$ 10,000	Accounts payable	$ 30,000
Accounts receivable	20,000	Notes payable	20,000
Note receivable	50,000		
Marketable securities	15,000		$ 50,000
Inventories	5,000		
		Noncurrent liabilities	
	$100,000	Bonds payable	$100,000
Noncurrent assets		Owners' equity	
Plant and equipment	$120,000	Common stock	$200,000
Land	70,000	Retained earnings	20,000
Investment in			
subsidiaries	80,000		$220,000
	$270,000		
		Total liabilities and	
Total assets	$370,000	owners' equity	$370,000

b. The Emerson Corp. is currently negotiating to purchase a new manufacturing facility. The present owners of the plant are asking $2,000,000 for the facility. Emerson Corp. estimates that the increased capacity of the new plant would add $300,000 annually to its income. But in order to purchase the plant it would have to borrow the $2,000,000. It estimates that it could issue long-term bonds at an annual interest rate of 11 per cent (i.e., $220,000 per year).

  1. If the company were to purchase the plant and borrow the necessary funds, what effect would the purchase (excluding effects on earnings) have on "the accounting equation"?
  2. What effect would it have on earnings per share (assuming that income would otherwise have been the same as in 1983)? Ignore income tax considerations.

c. Assume instead that Emerson is considering an alternative means of purchasing the new plant. Instead of offering the present owners of the plane $2,000,000 in cash, it would offer them common stock of the Emerson Corp. that has a present market value of $2,000,000. The common stock of the Emerson Corp. is currently being traded on a major stock exchange at $100 per share. The Emerson Corp. would issue 20,000 new shares of common stock. Obviously, the company would no longer have to issue the bonds.

  1. What effect would the alternative purchase plan have on the accounting equation?
  2. If you were a present stockholder of Emerson Corp. concerned primarily with earnings per share, would you prefer the original purchase plan or the alternative proposal? Why?

15. The balance sheet is closely related to the income statement.

The balance sheets and income statements of the Ames Corp. for the years ending December 31, 1982 through 1985, are indicated in the table following. Also indicated are dividends paid during those years. Some critical figures, however, have been omitted. You are to provide the missing figures. The Ames Corp. began operations on January 1, 1982.

	1982	1983	1984	1985
	Balance Sheet			
Assets				
Cash	$100	$200	$?	$300
Accounts receivable	200	100	300	100
Inventory	350	?	100	100
Building and equipment	600	900	800	400
Liabilities and owners' equity				
Accounts payable	$200	$100	$200	$300
Notes payable	?	600	300	100
Common stock	200	200	200	300
Retained earnings	100	400	?	?
	Income Statement			
Sales	$?	$1,000	$?	$1,200
Cost of goods sold and other operating expenses	500	?	600	?
Net income	?	?	400	300
Dividends paid	$ 0	$ 150	$200	$?

16. *Not all financial events give rise to assets or liabilities. Sometimes, assets or liabilities resulting from contractual arrangements are recognized only upon the performance of either of the parties to the contract.*

Indicate the nature (i.e., descriptive account title) of the assets and liabilities (if any) that would receive accounting recognition on the books of the Utica Company as a result of the following events or transactions:

1. The Utica Co. employs six men to perform routine maintenance work at a rate of $5 per hour. The men work a total of 200 hours. They have not yet been paid.
2. The company signs a three-year contract with a security company. The company will provide guard service for the company at a cost of $200 per month.
3. The security company performs one month's services as promised.
4. The company orders machinery and equipment at a cost of $10,000.
5. The machinery and equipment previously ordered is received and installed as agreed upon by the manufacturer.
6. A customer orders 300 units of the company's product at a price of $2 per unit.

7. Utica Co. ships the merchandise previously ordered.
8. Utica Co. borrows $40,000 at an interest rate of 10 percent per year. The company gives the bank a four-year note.
9. One year elapses, and the company has paid the bank neither principal nor interest on the note.
10. The company guarantees to repair any defective products. During the year it sells 10,000 units of product. It estimates from previous experience that 5 percent of such units will be returned for repair work. It estimates also that the cost of such repairs will be $1 per unit.

17. *The statement of changes in financial position accounts for the increase or decrease in working capital (current assets minus current liabilities) during a period.*

The balance sheets following are of the Todd Company as of December 31, 1982 and 1983. Also provided is information pertaining to financial events that took place during 1983.

Additional information:

1. The company had income in 1983 of $37,000. Working capital provided by operations was actually $52,000, since $15,000 of the expenses

deducted from revenues did not involve an outlay of current assets or an increase in current liabilities—i.e., depreciation expense involved a reduction in buildings and equipment (a noncurrent asset).

2. The company purchased equipment (for cash) at a cost of $35,000.
3. The company sold a parcel of land that had cost $10,000 for $10,000 (cash).
4. The company borrowed from the bank an additional $15,000 and agreed to repay the entire loan in five years.
5. Owners of the company made cash withdrawals totaling $12,000.

Required:

a. Compute working capital as of December 31, 1982.

b. Compute working capital as of December 31, 1983.
c. Compute the increase or decrease in working capital during the year 1983.
d. Based on the additional information, prepare a statement of changes in financial position in which you account for all increases (sources of) and decreases (applications of) in working capital. Be certain that the net increase or decrease in working capital is equal to the amount computed in part c. Use the following format.

Sources of working capital:

Applications of working capital:

Net increase (decrease) in working capital for the year:

Todd Company
Statement of Position

	December 31, 1982	December 31, 1983
Assets		
Current assets		
Cash	$ 30,000	$ 20,000
Accounts receivable	40,000	70,000
Inventory	39,000	44,000
Prepaid rent	5,000	5,000
	$114,000	$139,000
Noncurrent assets		
Land	$ 50,000	$ 40,000
Building	160,000	150,000
Equipment	15,000	45,000
	$225,000	$235,000
Total assets	$339,000	$374,000
Liabilities and owners' equity		
Current liabilities		
Accounts payable	$ 71,000	$ 68,000
Wages payable	5,000	4,000
Interest payable	3,000	2,000
	$ 79,000	$ 74,000
Noncurrent liabilities		
Notes payable	$ 60,000	$ 75,000
Owners' equity	200,000	225,000
Total liabilities and owners' equity	$339,000	$374,000

18. *Some transactions affect the composition of net assets (assets less liabilities) without affecting the level of net assets. Others serve to increase or decrease the level of net assets—and thereby result in an increase or decrease in owners' equity.*

Arrange a sheet of paper into three columns, each corresponding to a term in the accounting equation. Indicate the impact that each of the following transactions would have on the accounting equation. Suggest titles for each of the specific accounts that would be affected.

1. Petrified Products, Inc., purchases furniture and fixtures for $30,000, giving a five-year note.
2. The company purchases "on account" merchandise inventory for $15,000.
3. The firm, realizing that it had purchased an excessive amount of furniture, sells a portion of it. It sells for $3,000 cash furniture that had initially cost $3,000.
4. The firm sells an additional amount of furniture. It sells for $5,000 cash furniture that had initially cost $2,000. (Has the "level" of net assets increased as the result of this transaction?)
5. The firm sells for $800 "on account" merchandise inventory that had been purchased for $600.
6. The firm purchases supplies for $300 on account.
7. The firm uses supplies that had originally cost $200.
8. The firm collects $600 of the amount owed to it by customers.
9. The firm pays one month's rent in advance, $400.

10. At the end of one month, the firm wishes to give accounting recognition to the fact that it had occupied the rented premises for the one month paid for in advance.

19. *Information about income, dividends, and new shares issued can be derived from the shareholders' investment section of the balance sheet.*

The following is taken from the owners' equity section of the balance sheet of Fruehauf Corporation, a manufacturer of trucks and automobile parts and equipment:

	December 31, 1979	December 31, 1978
Common stock, par value $1.00 share		
Authorized 40,000,000 shares		
Issued 12,839,166 and 12,749,128 shares		
at December 31, 1979, and 1978, respectively	$ 12,839,166	$ 12,749,128
Additional paid-in capital	226,807,615	225,144,160
Earnings retained for use in the business	301,611,199	241,679,609
Cost of 630,883 shares of common stock held		
in treasury (deduction)	(15,678,303)	(15,678,303)
Total shareholders' investment	$525,579,677	$463,894,594

The firm's common stock is traded on the New York Stock Exchange. The company reported earnings in 1979 of $88,692,990.

a. What was the total amount of dividends that the company declared in 1979?
b. How many additional shares of common stock did the firm issue in 1979?
c. What was the average amount per share for which the additional shares were issued? (*Hint:* Consider changes in *both* the common stock, par value and the additional paid-in capital accounts.)
d. How many shares of stock were issued *and* outstanding as of December 31, 1979? (Shares of stock that a company holds in its treasury are not considered to be outstanding.)
e. What was the approximate amount of earnings per share in 1979? For convenience base the computation on number of shares outstanding on December 31, 1979, rather than average number of shares outstanding during the year.

20. *The following three problems require a careful look at a set of actual financial statements.*

White Consolidated Industries, Inc., headquartered in Cleveland, Ohio, is a diversified, international manufacturer and marketer of major home appliances and industrial equipment and machinery. Its home appliances are sold under the brand names Frigidaire, Gibson, Kelvinator, and White-Westinghouse. The balance sheet and income statement shown on page 56 appeared in its 1979 annual report.

a. Explain, as best you can from the information provided, the reason for the improvement in earnings in 1979 over 1978.

b. Did each major group of costs increase in proportion to the increase in sales revenue?

c. How do you account for the fact that income before extraordinary item increased by a greater percentage than net income *per common share* before extraordinary item?

d. What percentage of income (before extraordinary item) did the firm pay in taxes in 1979?

e. The extraordinary item represents a refund in income taxes owing to a settlement with the Internal Revenue Service. The amount in dispute resulted from a transaction that took place in 1971. What justification can there be for treating the refund as an "extraordinary item" as opposed to including it in "other income—net"?

21. Refer to the financial statements of White Consolidated Industries, Inc., as presented in problem 20.

a. Compare the ability of the company to meet its current obligations as they come due in 1979 with that in 1978. Why might the current ratio have declined between December 31, 1978, and 1979 even though reported income was substantially greater in 1979 than in 1978?

White Consolidated Industries, Inc., and Subsidiaries
Consolidated Statements of Income

	Year Ended December 31	
	1979	1978
Net sales	$2,010,114,000	$1,655,979,000
Other income—net	9,588,000	9,309,000
	2,019,702,000	1,665,288,000
Costs and expenses		
Cost of products sold	1,657,748,000	1,363,339,000
Selling, general and administrative expenses	214,318,000	170,564,000
Interest	31,064,000	30,216,000
	1,903,130,000	1,564,119,000
Income before income taxes and extraordinary item	116,572,000	101,169,000
Income taxes	53,650,000	46,651,000
Income before extraordinary item	62,922,000	54,518,000
Extraordinary item	12,783,000	—
Net income	$ 75,705,000	$ 54,518,000
Net income per common share		
Based on average shares outstanding:		
Before extraordinary item	$4.87	$4.33
Extraordinary item	1.08	—
Net income	$5.95	$4.33

White Consolidated Industries, Inc., and Subsidiaries
Consolidated Balance Sheets

Assets	December 31, 1979	December 31, 1978
Current assets		
Cash	$ 18,242,000	$ 20,116,000
Income tax claim receivable	16,061,000	—
Trade receivables (less allowances of $7,615,000 in 1979 and $6,458,000 in 1978)	275,300,000	250,419,000
Inventories	484,386,000	395,149,000
Prepaid expenses and other current assets	3,551,000	3,935,000
Total current assets	797,540,000	669,619,000
Investments and other assets		
Investments in foreign companies and other assets	9,634,000	8,314,000
Excess of cost over purchased net assets	17,087,000	17,087,000
	26,721,000	25,401,000
Property, plant, and equipment		
Land	11,147,000	11,294,000
Buildings	172,279,000	157,130,000
Machinery and equipment	361,918,000	328,614,000
	545,344,000	497,038,000
Less allowances for depreciation and amortization	208,500,000	196,918,000
	336,844,000	300,120,000
	$1,161,105,000	$995,140,000

Liabilities and Equity	December 31, 1979	December 31, 1978
Current liabilities		
Trade accounts payable	$ 143,603,000	$ 92,922,000
Accrued payroll, payroll taxes and amounts withheld from employees	38,438,000	31,009,000
Other payables and accruals	137,562,000	111,349,000
Accrued and deferred income taxes	3,941,000	1,555,000
Current maturities of long-term debt and redeemable preferred stock	14,339,000	11,131,000
Total current liabilities	337,883,000	247,966,000
Long-term debt	272,505,000	252,496,000
Convertible subordinated debentures	5,196,000	47,279,000
Deferred income taxes	20,673,000	18,650,000
Long-term warranties, pensions, and other liabilities	52,736,000	48,961,000
Redeemable preferred stock	67,059,000	72,168,000
Common stockholders' equity		
Common stock—par value $1 a share: Authorized 50,000,000 shares; Issued 13,696,091 shares at December 31, 1979 and 11,850,660 shares at December 31, 1978	13,696,000	11,850,000
Other capital	139,994,000	99,379,000
Retained income	257,492,000	202,520,000
	411,182,000	313,749,000
Less cost of 436,500 shares of common stock in treasury	6,129,000	6,129,000
	405,053,000	307,620,000
	$1,161,105,000	$995,140,000

b. Compare the return on the investment of stockholders in 1979 with that in 1978?

c. Did the firm issue additional shares of common stock in 1979? How can you tell?

d. Did the firm declare dividends in 1979? What was the probable amount? How can you tell?

e. Suppose that the price at which the common stock of the firm was traded was $17 on December 31, 1978, and $24 on December 31, 1979. What were the price/earnings ratios (excluding the extraordinary item) as of those dates? How would the increase in the market price of the shares be reflected in the financial reports of the firm?

f. Based on number of shares of common stock outstanding and the market price per share ($24) on December 31, 1979, what was the total value of the shares outstanding? What was the total value of the equity of the common stockholders per the firm's balance sheet? Why are the two amounts not the same?

22. The following is the statement of changes in financial position for White Consolidated Industries, Inc., as it appeared in the firm's 1979 annual report. Several amounts, however, have been omitted. Refer to the income statement and balance sheet of the company as they appear in problem 20. Fill in the missing amounts.

SOLUTIONS TO EXERCISE FOR REVIEW AND SELF-TESTING

1. a. Assets = $100,000
   b. Equities = $100,000

2. a. Assets = 150,000
   b. Total equities = $150,000; those of owners = $100,000; those of outsiders = $50,000

3. a. Assets = $150,000 (This transaction serves to decrease "cash" and increase "fixed assets"—i.e., the automobile.)
   b. Liabilities = $50,000; owners' equity = $100,000

4. a. Assets = $151,500
   b. Liabilities = $51,500; owners' equity = $100,000

White Consolidated Industries, Inc., and Subsidiaries
Consolidated Statements of Changes in Financial Position

	Year Ended December 31	
	1979	1978
Source of funds		
From operations		
Income before extraordinary item	$ a	$ 54,518,000
Items not affecting working capital		
Depreciation and amortization	27,131,000	24,244,000
Noncurrent deferred income taxes and reserves	5,798,000	3,815,000
Other	(539,000)	(581,000)
Totals from operations before extraordinary item	95,312,000	81,996,000
Extraordinary item	b	—
Totals from operations	108,095,000	81,996,000
Proceeds from long-term debt	33,064,000	26,043,000
Sales and retirements of property, plant, and equipment—net	3,246,000	4,833,000
Proceeds from stock options and conversions of debentures	41,802,000	846,000
	186,207,000	113,718,000

| | Year Ended December 31 | |
	1979	1978
Application of funds		
Additions to property, plant, and equipment	67,101,000	36,633,000
Cash dividends paid	d	19,134,000
Reductions of long-term debt	13,055,000	20,995,000
Reductions of debentures	42,083,000	739,000
Preferred stock redemptions	4,450,000	3,489,000
Other changes	781,000	789,000
Increase in working capital	$ c	$ 31,939,000
Changes in the components of working capital are summarized as follows:		
Increase (decrease) in current assets		
Cash	$ e	$ 579,000
Income tax claim receivable	16,061,000	—
Trade receivables	24,881,000	40,352,000
Inventories	f	12,036,000
Prepaid expenses and other current assets	(384,000)	(933,000)
(Increase) decrease in current liabilities		
Trade accounts payable		1,926,000
Accrued payroll, payroll taxes, and amounts withheld from employees	(7,429,000)	(3,886,000)
Other payables and accruals	g	(18,254,000)
Accrued and deferred income taxes	(2,386,000)	1,317,000
Current maturities of long-term debt and redeemable preferred stock	(3,208,000)	(1,198,000)
Increase in working capital	$ 38,004,000	$ 31,939,000

5. a. Assets = $151,700 ($151,500 per above, plus $700 cash received upon sale, minus $500 of goods surrendered.)

   b. Liabilities = $51,500; owners' equity = $100,200 (The "level" of assets increased by $200 as a consequence of the sale of 100 units. Liabilities remained unchanged but the equity of the owners must have increased by $200.)

6. Owners' equity has increased by $200; income of the corporation was $200.

THE 3 RECORDING PROCESS

The accounting system is a model of logic and order. This chapter will serve to introduce the *accounting cycle*—the procedures that lead from the initial recognition of a financial event to the preparation of financial statements. Its objective is to provide an understanding of the relationships among the various accounts that appear on the financial statements. In particular, it seeks to demonstrate the tie between the income statement and the balance sheet.

The accounting cycle will be described in terms of conventional books and records. In firms in which the accounting system is computerized, the books and records may not take the physical forms suggested by the descriptions in this chapter. Data may be scattered throughout an electronic data bank rather than recorded in neat columns in a journal or ledger. Nevertheless, the underlying principles, the structure of accounts and the final products (the financial statements) are virtually the same, irrespective of whether the system is maintained manually or electronically.

LEDGER ACCOUNTS

The basic accounting equation—assets = liabilities + owners' equity—or the slightly expanded equation—assets = liabilities + capital contributed by owners + retained earnings—serves as the basis for all accounting transactions. Conceivably, all financial events that affect a business and are deemed worthy of accounting recognition could be recorded in a single ledger (or book of accounts), derived from the basic equation. Changes in assets would be indicated on the left-hand side of the page; changes in liabilities or owners' equity would be indicated on the right.

CDE Company
"General Ledger"

Assets		Liabilities and Owners' Equity	
1. Cash (asset +)	+ $25,000	**1.** Common stock (owners' equity +)	+ $25,000
2. Furniture and fixtures (asset +)	+ 10,000	**2.** Accounts payable (liability +)	+ 10,000
3. Merchandise (asset +) ⎰+ 7,000			
Cash (asset −) ⎱− 7,000			
4. Cash (asset −)	− 5,000	**4.** Accounts payable (liability −)	− 5,000
	$30,000		$30,000

Example

1. The CDE Company issues capital stock for $25,000 cash. (An asset, *cash, is increased;* owners' equity, *common stock, is increased.*)

2. The company purchases furniture and fixtures for $10,000 on account. (An asset, *furniture and fixtures, is increased;* a liability, *accounts payable, is increased.*)

3. The company purchases merchandise for $7,000 cash. (An asset, *merchandise, is increased;* an asset, *cash, is decreased.*)

4. The company pays $5,000 of the amount it owes on account. (An asset, *cash, is decreased;* a liability, *accounts payable, is decreased.*)

The ledger indicates that after the fourth transaction the firm has assets of $30,000 and liabilities and owners' equity of the same amount. The ledger reveals that the accounts are "in balance" (they would have to be unless an error was made), and it indicates the total assets and the total liabilities and owners' equity. But by itself it provides little information that would be useful to either management or owners. Since each side of the ledger page combines changes in a great variety of accounts, the balance in any particular account is not readily available. To find the amount of cash on hand, for example, it would be necessary to search the entire page (or entire book insofar as there were numerous transactions) for all entries affecting cash. How much more convenient it would be if a separate page were provided for each account. Thus,

CDE Company
General Ledger

Cash

(1)	25,000	**(3)**	7,000
		(4)	5,000

Furniture and fixtures

(2)	10,000	

Merchandise

(3)	7,000	

Accounts payable

(4)	5,000	**(2)**	10,000

Common stock

	(1)	25,000

In the illustration each of the "T"'s represents a separate page in the ledger or book of accounts. Thus, there is a separate page or "T account" for cash, furniture and fixtures, accounts payable, etc.

An increase in an *asset* account is recorded on the *left* side of the ledger page or T account; a *decrease* in an asset account is recorded on the *right* side.

Conversely, an *increase* in a *liability* or *owners' equity* account is recorded on the *right* side of the ledger page or T account; a *decrease* in a *liability or owners' equity* account is recorded on the *left* side.

The balance in an account at any particular time can be determined by subtracting the amounts recorded on one side from those recorded on the other. The convention of recording increases in assets on the left side of the account and increases in liabilities and owners' equity on the right may be related directly to the accounting equation (assets = liabilities + owners' equity) in which assets appear to the left of the equal sign and liabilities and owners' equity to the right.

DEBITS AND CREDITS

In accounting terminology, any entry to the left side of an account is referred to as a debit and any entry to the right side as a credit. The term *charge* is often used interchangeably with *debit*.

Debits are used to signify *increases in assets* or *decreases in liabilities or owners' equity*.

Credits are used to represent *decreases in assets* or *increases in liabilities or owner's equity*.

If a company purchases merchandise for cash, the accountant would *debit* the merchandise account and *credit* the cash account. It would ordinarily be expected that at any given time the asset accounts would show a *debit* balance (that is, the entries on the left side of the account would exceed in dollar amount those on the right) and the liabilities and owners' equity accounts would show a *credit* balance.

Debits and credits are often a source of confusion to an individual who has had dealings with either a bank or a department store. Should a person deposit funds in the bank, the bank would ordinarily *credit* his account. Should he withdraw funds or be charged for services, the bank might send him a *debit* (debt) memo. Similarly, when a person returns merchandise to a store, the store credits his account; it advises him that his liability to the store has been reduced. Does it not appear that *credits* are associated with increases in assets and *debits* with increases in liabilities? Bear in mind, however, that both the bank and the department store maintain their records from their own points of view, not those of their customers. Thus, when a customer deposits money in the bank, the liability of the bank to the customer is increased. Hence, the bank *credits* his account on its books. (If the customer maintained a set of books, then he would *debit* his account, "cash in bank," to reflect the debt of the bank to him.) Similarly, when the department store accepts returned merchandise from a customer the accounts receivable of the store have been decreased; thus the store *credits* the account on its books that represents the amount owed by the customer.

JOURNAL ENTRIES

Each T account represents a separate page in a book of accounts. Such a book is often referred to as a *general ledger*. Since a transaction normally affects two or more accounts, each transaction necessitates entries on two or more pages. No one page will contain a complete record of the transaction; at best it will indicate only one-half of the transaction. To maintain a comprehensive history of all transactions that affect the various accounts, firms conventionally maintain a *journal*—a book which serves as the source of many of the entries to the various accounts. The purchase of merchandise for ($7,000) necessitates that a debit entry be made in the merchandise account and a credit entry be made in the cash account. The journal is a convenient place to indicate both accounts affected by the transaction. At the time of purchase, the firm would record the following in the journal:

Debit: Merchandise $7,000
Credit: Cash $7,000

The words "debit" and "credit" are conventionally omitted from the entry. Debits are distinquished from credits by the placement of the account title and the amounts. The account to be debited is placed along the left-hand margin, and that to be credited is indented slightly. Similarly, the amount to be debited is shown slightly to the left of that to be credited. A brief explanation is often indicated beneath the entry, and the entry is numbered or lettered to facilitate referencing. Thus,

(1)

Merchandise $7,000
  Cash $7,000
To record the purchase of merchandise.

The amounts indicated in the journal would be posted to or recorded in the appropriate ledger account either at the time the transaction is recorded in the journal or, if more convenient, after a number of transactions have been recorded.

Some simple transactions can be used to illustrate the relationship between entries in the journal and those in the various ledger accounts. In this and in several subsequent examples the nature of the account (asset, liability, owners' equity) and whether it has increased ($+$) or decreased ($-$) will sometimes be indicated in parentheses next to each journal entry. B. Heller, an electronics specialist, decides to establish a microcomputer repair service. He signs a lease on a store.

1. He takes $50,000 of his personal funds and deposits them in a checking account in the name of "Heller Computer Service."

2. He purchases tools and test equipment for $25,000. He gives a two-year note for the full amount.

3. He purchases parts for $15,000. He pays $10,000 cash and receives 30-days' credit for the balance.

4. He pays rent in advance for the first three months, $1,000 per month.

Required Journal Entries
(1)
Cash in bank (asset$+$) $50,000
  B. Heller, invested
    capital (owners' equity$+$) $50,000
To record the initial contribution of cash.

(2)
Tools and equipment
  (asset$+$) $25,000
        Notes payable (liability$+$) $25,000
To record the purchase of tools and equipment.

(3)
Parts inventory (asset$+$) $15,000
    Cash (asset$-$) $10,000
    Accounts payable (liability$+$) $ 5,000
To record the purchase of the parts. (Note that a journal entry can combine more than one debit or credit. The account "notes payable" is used to record a liability when a written note is given by the borrower.

When short-term trade credit is accepted, the liability is recorded as an "account payable.")

(4)

Prepaid rent (asset +) $3,000
   Cash (asset −) $3,000

To record the rent paid in advance. ("Prepaid rent" represents the right to use the store for three months. It is a current asset—one that will be "written off" or *amortized* as it expires over the three-month period.)

The journal entries would be *posted* to the various ledger accounts:

$50,000 minus the sum of $10,000 and $3,000—$37,000.

The balance sheet separates current from noncurrent assets and liabilities (Exhibit 3-1). In the exhibit, the note payable is classified as a noncurrent liability since it will not be due for over one year. Similarly, the tools and equipment are classified as noncurrent assets, because they are expected to have a useful life greater than one year. Prepaid rent, the parts inventory, and the cash in bank are all expected either to be used up or to "turn over" (be replaced by like assets) within a

	Assets				Liabilities and Owners' Equity	

	Cash in bank			Accounts payable		B. Heller, invested capital
(1)	50,000	(3) 10,000		(3) 5,000	(1)	50,000
		(4) 3,000				

	Tools and equipment		Notes payable
(2)	25,000	(2)	25,000

	Parts inventory
(3)	15,000

	Prepaid rent
(4)	3,000

If it were decided to prepare a balance sheet after the four transactions had been journalized and posted, then it would be necessary to determine and summarize the balances in each amount. The balance in each account can readily be calculated by subtracting the total credits from the total debits. Thus, the balance in the cash in bank account is

one-year period, so they are classified as current assets.

An additional exhibit may serve to illustrate the accounting treatment afforded other types of financial events. The Universal Sales Corporation is organized on June 1, 1983. The events listed in Exhibit 3-2 occur during the first month of operation:

EXHIBIT 3-1

Heller Computer Service
Balance Sheet as of December 31, 1983

Assets			Liabilities and Owners' Equity		
Current assets			Current liabilities		
Cash in bank	$37,000		accounts payable	$ 5,000	
Parts inventory	15,000		Noncurrent liabilities		
Prepaid rent	3,000	$55,000	Notes payable	25,000	$30,000
Noncurrent assets			Owners' equity		
Tools and			B. Heller,		
equipment		25,000	invested capital		50,000
			Total liabilities and		
Total assets		$80,000	owners' equity		$80,000

EXHIBIT 3-2

Date

6/1 The company issues 10,000 shares of stock to its two cofounders for a price of $50 per share, which is received in cash.

(1)

Cash (asset+)	$500,000	
Common shares (owners' equity+)		$500,000

To record the sale of common stock.

6/1 The firm issues $100,000 of long-term bonds, payable on June 1, 2013, with interest payable semiannually at a rate of 9% per annum.

(2)

Cash (asset+)	$100,000	
Bonds payable (liability+)		$100,000

To record the issue of long-term bonds.
(The liability only for the principal, not the interest, is recorded at this time.)

6/2 The company purchases a building for $300,000. It gives a down payment of $100,000 and a 10-year note for the balance.

(3)

Building (asset+)	$300,000	
Cash (asset−)		$100,000
Notes payable (liability+)		200,000

To record the purchase of the building.

6/3 The company purchases equipment for $100,000 and incurs installation and transportation costs of $20,000. The equipment is purchased "on sale." The salesman informs the purchaser that it normally sells for $130,000.

(4)

Equipment (asset+)	$120,000	
Cash (asset−)		$120,000

To record the purchase of equipment.
The installation and transportation costs are assumed to be necessary to bring the equipment to a *serviceable* condition; hence they are added to the cost of the equipment. The alleged discount of $30,000 is ignored. Except in highly unusual circumstances, an asset is recorded at the amount which is actually to be paid as long as the transaction is "at arm's length"—that is, between two independent parties. Such amount represents the fair market values of the assets both received and surrendered by the purchaser.)

EXHIBIT 3-2 *(continued)*

Date

6/27 The firm decides to rent-out a portion of its building. The company acquires a lessee, and a five-year lease is signed. Rent is to be $1,000 per month, and three months' rent is paid in advance. Occupancy is to begin July 1.

(5)

Cash (asset +)	$3,000	
Rent received in advance (liability +)		$3,000

To record three months' rent received in advance.
(The company has received the cash. It is still obligated to provide services to the lessee. "Rent received in advance" can be viewed as "value of rental services yet to be furnished.")

6/28 The company receives an invoice (a bill) from its attorneys—$5,000—for services performed in connection with drawing the corporate charter and issuing common stock.

amorting in capitalization of organization, NLT 20 yrs

(6)

Organization costs (asset +)	$5,000	
Accounts payable (liability +)		$5,000

To record the costs of organizing the corporation.
(The organization costs, like the cost of equipment and the prepaid rent, were incurred in order to benefit future accounting periods. Although they are "intangible"—they cannot be seen or felt—they are nevertheless *assets* of the company. Accounts payable, rather than cash, has been credited because the company has not yet paid the invoice.)

6/28 The company hires J. Pringle as president. The two parties sign a two-year employment contract requiring the firm to compensate Pringle at a salary of $35,000 per year.

No entry is required.
Although the firm seemingly has incurred a liability of $70,000, the president has not yet performed any services for the company. As indicated previously, accountants generally record liabilities resulting from contracts only to the extent that services have been performed or cash has been paid. Thus, after Pringle has been employed for one month, the company will, at that time, record a liability of one-twelfth of $35,000, or $2,917.

6/28 The company purchases merchandise for $60,000. The company is granted a "trade discount" (one available to all commercial customers) of 10%.

(7)

Merchandise inventory (asset +)	$54,000	
Accounts payable (liability +)		$54,000

To record the purchase of merchandise.
(The firm will be required to pay $54,000; that is, the "fair market" value of both the goods received and the consideration to be paid.)

6/28 The firm purchases 100 shares of General Motors stock as a temporary investment. Cost per share is $61.

(8)

Marketable securities (asset +)	$6,100	
Cash (asset −)		$6,100

To record the purchase of 100 shares of General Motors stock.

6/29 The company pays $5,000 of the amount it owes to its supplier.

(9)

Accounts payable (liability −)	$5,000	
Cash (asset −)		$5,000

To record the payment to the supplier.

EXHIBIT 3-2 (*continued*)

Date

6/29 The company returns merchandise that is defective to the supplier. The merchandise cost $7,000 after taking into account the discount. The supplier gives the company credit for the merchandise returned.

(10)

Accounts payable (liability −)	$7,000	
Merchandise inventory (asset −)		$7,000

To record the return of merchandise.

6/30 The company learns through *The Wall Street Journal* that the market price of its General Motors stock has increased to $64 per share.

No entry is necessary.
Increases in the market value of assets generally are not recorded—in large measure because of the accountant's preference toward conservative expressions of value.

6/30 The market price of the General Motors stock declines to $61 per share. The company sells 50 shares.

(11)

Cash (asset +)	$3,050	
Marketable securities (asset −)		$3,050

To record the sale of 50 shares of General Motors stock.
(The stock was sold at original cost; hence there was no gain or loss on the sale.)

As before, the journal entries must be posted to ledger or T accounts so that the balances in the accounts can be summarized in a statement of position (Exhibit 3-3). To facilitate the process of summarizing the end-of-period balances, double lines have been drawn beneath the recorded debits and credits. The difference between the sums of the debits and credits has been indicated on the appropriate side of the T account. This amount represents not only the balance at the close of one accounting period but also the balance at the beginning of the next accounting period. For example, if $374,950 is the cash balance at the end of June 1983, it must also be the balance at the beginning of July 1983. Thus, the same account—the same ledger sheet—that was used in June could also be used in July. The entries for the latter year would simply be recorded beneath the end-of-old-year (beginning-of-new-year) balances.

REVENUES AND EXPENSES

Up to this point in the chapter, the illustrated transactions, with few exceptions, involved only exchanges among asset and liability accounts. Goods or services were received in exchange for other assets or for the firm's promise to pay in the future. Increases or decreases in liability accounts were offset by concurrent increases or decreases in asset accounts. As a result, the level of *net* assets—that is, assets less liabilities (which is equal, by definition, to owners' equity)—remained the same. To refer back to the bathtub analogy used in the previous chapter, the level of water in the tub never changed as a consequence of the transactions illustrated. The only time owners' equity did change was when owners made their initial investment in the business.

Since the differences between assets and liabilities stayed constant once the owners

EXHIBIT 3-3

	Assets					Liabilities and Owners' Equity		

Cash

(1)	500,000	(3)	100,000
(2)	100,000	(4)	120,000
(5)	3,000	(8)	6,100
(11)	3,050	(9)	5,000
	374,950		

Accounts payable

(9)	5,000	(6)	5,000
(10)	7,000	(7)	54,000
			47,000

Organization costs

(6)	5,000
	5,000

Bonds payable

		(2)	100,000
			100,000

Equipment

(4)	120,000
	120,000

Rent received in advance

		(5)	3,000
			3,000

Merchandise inventory

(7)	54,000	(10)	7,000
	47,000		

Notes payable

		(3)	200,000
			200,000

Building

(3)	300,000
	300,000

Common shares

		(1)	500,000
			500,000

Marketable securities

(8)	6,100	(11)	3,050
	3,050		

EXHIBIT 3-3 *(continued)*

Universal Sales Corporation
Balance Sheet as of June 30, 1983

Assets			*Liabilities and Owners' Equity*		
Current assets			Current liabilities		
Cash	$374,950		Accounts payable	$ 47,000	
Marketable securities	3,050		Rent received in advance	3,000	$ 50,000
Merchandise inventory	47,000	$425,000			
			Noncurrent liabilities		
Noncurrent assets			Notes payable	$200,000	
Building	$300,000		Bonds payable	100,000	300,000
Equipment	120,000				
Organization costs	5,000	425,000	Total liabilities		$350,000
			Owners' equity		
			Common shares— 10,000 shares issued and outstanding		500,000
			Total liabilities and owners' equity		
Total assets	$850,000		equity		$850,000

made their initial contribution to form their companies, the subsequent transactions could not possibly have left them any better or worse off than they were at the very start of business. There were no inflows or outflows of net assets to the business, no revenues, and no expenses and hence no profits or earnings that could be retained in the business.

How does the firm record those transactions that do, in fact, result in increases or decreases in the equity of its owners? Assuming that the firm has not previously incurred losses which have reduced the equity of the owners below their original contribution, any transaction in which assets received or liabilities reduced are greater than assets surrendered or liabilities incurred must increase the earnings being retained by the firm. Take, for example, a merchandise transaction. A firm sells for $100 goods that it had previously purchased for $70. The firm receives an asset of $100; it surrenders an asset of $70. Assets have increased by $30, so the owners of the business are $30 better off than they were previously. Income as the result of the transaction is $30, and hence retained earnings must have increased by $30.

To view the transaction in two steps: The receipt of cash resulted in an increase of $100 in both cash and retained earnings. An appropriate journal entry would be

(1)

| Cash (asset +) | $100 | |
| Retained earnings (owner's equity +) | | $100 |

The transfer of goods to the new owners resulted in a decrease in both merchandise and retained earnings:

(2)

Retained earnings
(owners' equity −) $70
    Merchandise inventory
      (asset −) $70

Cash		Retained earnings		
(1) 100		**(2)** 70	**(1)**	100

Merchandise		
Previous balance xxx	**(2)**	70

As a consequence of the transaction, it can be said that the firm had *revenues* of $100 and *expenses* of $70.

Revenues: Inflows or other enhancements of assets of an entity or settlements of its liabilities during a period from delivering or producing goods, rendering services, or other activities that constitute the entity's ongoing major or central operations.

Expenses: Outflows or other using up of assets or incurrences of liabilities during a period from delivering or producing goods, rendering services, or carrying out other activities that constitute the entity's ongoing major or central operations.

Income: The excess of revenues over expenses; the change in equity (net assets) of an entity during a period from transactions and other events and circumstances from nonowner sources. It includes all changes in equity during a period except those resulting from investments by owners and distributions to owners.*

A series of simple transactions can further illustrate the relationships among revenues, expenses, and retained earnings.

An entrepreneur establishes Booksellers, Inc., to sell books door to door. The firm issues 1,500 shares of common stock (par value $1) in exchange for $15,000 cash.

(1)

Cash (asset +) $15,000
    Common stock
      (owner's equity +) $15,000
To record the issuance of common stock.

The firm purchases advertising circulars at a cost of $500, paid in cash. A firm's assets and the claims (by owner) against the assets increase.

(2)

Advertising circulars
    (asset +) $500
      Cash (asset −) $500
To record purchase of advertising circulars.
This transaction involves only an exchange of one asset for another. It affects neither the level of net assets (assets minus liabilities) nor the equity of the owner.

The firm distributes the circulars.

---

* Based on definitions of the Financial Accounting Standards Board in *Elements of Financial Statements of Business Enterprises*, Statement of Financial Accounting Concepts No. 3, December 1980. The Board distinguishes between revenues and expenses and gains and losses. The latter are increases and decreases respectively in equity (net assets) resulting from the peripheral or incidental transactions of an entity rather than its primary activities. For simplicity the distinction is not generally made in this text; gains and losses are included among revenues and expenses.

(3)

Retained earnings
  (owner's equity – ;
  advertising expense) $500
        Advertising circulars (asset –) $500

To record the distribution of advertising circulars. This transaction results in a reduction in an asset without an offsetting decrease in another asset or an increase in a liability. Therefore, it serves to reduce the equity of the owner (i.e., retained earnings).

The firm leases an office and pays one month's rent in advance, $600.

(4)

Prepaid rent (asset +) $600
    Cash (asset –) $600

To record payment of rent in advance. An asset, prepaid rent, is received in exchange for another asset, cash.

The firm gives accounting recognition to the use of the office for one month.

(5)

Retained earnings (owner's
  equity – ; rent expense) $600
    Prepaid rent (asset –) $600

To record occupancy of office for one month. The level of net assets is reduced; hence the equity of the owner is reduced.

The firm purchases an automobile for $12,000 cash. It estimates the useful life of the car to be two years (24 months).

(6)

Automobile (asset +) $12,000
    Cash (asset –) $12,000

To record purchase of the automobile. One asset is exchanged for another.

The firm gives recognition to the use of the auto for one month.

(7)

Retained earnings
  (owner's equity – ;
  depreciation expense) $500
    Automobile (Asset –) $500

To record the use (depreciation) of the automobile for one month. The asset was expected to provide services for 24 months. One-twenty-fourth of its service potential has now been consumed. The equity of the owner has correspondingly been reduced by the value of the services consumed. (It is conventional for an "allowance for depreciation" rather than the asset itself to be credited for the amount of depreciation charged, but an explanation of such "contra accounts" will be deferred to the next chapter.)

The firm purchases for sale to customers 400 books at $5 per book.

(8)

Merchandise inventory
  (asset +) $2,000
    Cash (asset –) $2,000

To record purchase of merchandise inventory. Once again, one asset is exchanged for another.

The firm sells the 400 books for $10 each.

(9)

Cash (asset +) $4,000
    Retained earnings (owner's
    equity + ; sales revenues) $4,000

To record sale of books. As a consequence of this first part of the sales transaction—that in which recognition is given to the revenues earned—the assets of the firm are increased; so too is the equity of the owner.

(10)

Retained earnings (owner's
  equity – ; cost of goods
  sold) $2,000
    Merchandise inventory
    (asset –) $2,000

To record the cost of books sold. As a result of the second part of the transaction—that in which recognition is given to the cost of the merchandise sold—an asset is reduced; so too is the equity of the owner. The entire transaction (entries **9** and **10**) leaves the firm with $2,000 of additional assets and its owner with $2,000 of additional claims against the assets.

The firm incurs utility costs of $200 and pays them in cash.

(11)

Retained earnings (owners' equity − ; utility expense)	$200	
Cash (Asset −)		$200

To record utility costs. Each of the previous expenses have been recorded in two steps. First, an asset (i.e., advertising circulars, prepaid rent, automobile, merchandise inventory) was acquired; then it was consumed. An initial entry involved an exchange of one asset for another; a second involved a reduction in an asset and a corresponding reduction in retained earnings. This transaction, however, was recorded in a single step. Conceptually, this transaction is not different from the others. For *bookkeeping convenience*— motivated in large measure by the brief interval between the moment when electricity, gas, or water is received by a firm and when it is actually consumed—the cost of the utility services was never placed even temporarily in a "storage" (asset) account. Instead, the assets of the firm, as well as the equity of the owner, were presumed to have been reduced at the time the utility costs were first given accounting recognition.

The journal entries can be posted to T accounts. To highlight the impact of the transactions on the equity of the owner, a brief explanation is included beside each of the entries to the retained earnings account.

At the conclusion of the first month of operations, the position of the company can be reported as shown in Exhibit 3-4.

Because retained earnings are now $200, it is apparent that the equity of the entrepreneur has increased by that amount and that the earnings of the one-month period were also $200. The firm is $200 "better off" at the end of the first month than it was at the beginning. Income for the period is therefore $200.

If the owners of a business make no withdrawals from their firm, then income can be determined by subtracting retained earnings at the beginning of the period from those at the end. But both owners and managers of a business need far more information than income alone. They need to know *how* that income was derived: What were the sources of revenue? What were the expenses? A statement of income can readily be derived from the entries in the retained earnings account (Exhibit 3-5).

Suppose, however, that there were not six entries that affected retained earnings but that instead there were several hundred. At the end of the accounting period they would have to be classified into a small number of

EXHIBIT 3-5

Booksellers, Inc. Statement of Income for the First Month of Operation		
Sales revenue		$4,000
Less: Expenses		
Cost of goods sold	$2,000	
Advertising	500	
Rent	600	
Depreciation	500	
Utilities	200	3,800
Income		$ 200

EXHIBIT 3-4

Assets				Liabilities and Owners' Equity		

Cash

(1)	15,000	**(2)**	500
(9)	4,000	**(4)**	600
		(6)	12,000
		(8)	2,000
		(11)	200
	3,700		

Common stock

	(1)	15,000
		15,000

Advertising circulars

(2)	500	**(3)**	500

Retained earnings

Advertising expense	**(3)**	500	**(9)**	Sales revenue	4,000
Rent expense	**(5)**	600			
Depreciation expense	**(7)**	500			
Cost of goods sold	**(10)**	2,000			
Utility expense	**(11)**	200			200

Prepaid rent

(4)	600	**(5)**	600

Automobile

(6)	12,000	**(7)**	500
	11,500		

Merchandise inventory

(8)	2,000	**(10)**	2,000

Booksellers, Inc.
Balance Sheet as of the End of the First Month

Assets		Liabilities and Owners' Equity	
Cash	$ 3,700	Common stock	$15,000
Automobile	11,500	Retained earnings	200
Total assets	$15,200	Total equities	$15,200

revenue and expense categories so that they could be summarized into a meaningful statement of income. Would it not make more sense to divide the retained earnings account into several subaccounts, each of which would represent a particular type of revenue or expense (Exhibit 3-6)?

The retained earnings subaccounts would have but one purpose. They would be used to accumulate data necessary to prepare the periodic statements of income. As soon as the last business day of an accounting period was complete and all entries to subaccounts had been made, the balances in those accounts would be transferred to the overall retained earnings account. The subaccounts could be viewed as serving a very temporary function. They would be used to accumulate, by category, the revenues earned and the expenses incurred for one accounting period only. Seldom do users of financial statements demand knowledge of total revenues and

EXHIBIT 3-6   Retained Earnings Subaccounts

Retained Earnings		=	Retained Earnings	
Advertising **(3)** 500 expense	**(9)** Sales revenue 4,000		Advertising expense	Sales revenue
Rent expense **(5)** 600			**(3)** 500	**(9)** 4,000
Depreciation **(7)** 500 expense				
Cost of **(10)** 2,000 goods sold			Rent expense	
Utility **(11)** 200 expense			**(5)** 600	
			Depreciation expense	
			(7) 500	
			Cost of goods sold	
			(10) 2,000	
			Utility expense	
			(11) 200	

expenses, by category, since the inception of the company, because such information would bear upon few decisions that they are required to make. Instead they want the information on a period-by-period basis. As a result, each subaccount—the revenue and expense accounts—would be terminated—closed—at the end of each accounting period. New revenue and expense accounts would be established for the next accounting period.

Returning to the accounts of Booksellers, Inc., the revised journal entries (including only those that affected retained earnings) would appear as

(3)

Advertising expense	$500	
Advertising circulars		$500

To record the distribution of advertising circulars.

(5)

Rent expense	$600	
Prepaid rent		$600

To record occupancy of office for one month.

(7)

Depreciation expense	$500	
Automobile		$500

To record the use (depreciation) of the automobile for one month.

(9)

Cash	$4,000	
Sales revenue		$4,000

To record sales of books.

(10)

Cost of goods sold	$2,000	
Merchandise inventory		$2,000

To record the cost of the books sold.

(11)

Utility expense	$200	
Cash		$200

To record utility costs.

CLOSING ENTRIES

At the end of the accounting period the balances in the revenue and expense accounts would be transferred to the overall retained earnings account. Normally, revenue accounts would have a credit balance; expense accounts would have a debit balance.

The transfer can be made by two simple journal entries (Exhibit 3-7). First, a journal entry is made in which each revenue account is debited with an amount equal to the balance in the account, and retained earnings is credited with the total of such amounts. Second, a similar journal entry is made in which each expense account is credited with the balance in the account and retained earnings is debited. If the company had a profit, then the net effect of the two entries would be to increase the balance in retained earnings, and if a loss, then to decrease the balance.

After the closing entries have been made and posted to the individual revenue and expense accounts, the balances in those accounts must be zero. The company would then be ready to open new revenue and expense accounts (subaccounts of retained earnings) to accumulate data for the statement of income for the following accounting period.

It must be emphasized that only the revenue and expense accounts need be "closed" at year end. The balance in the Booksellers, Inc., *cash* account was $3,700 at the end of the first month of operations. It will necessarily be $3,700 at the beginning of the second month. Asset and liability accounts describe the position of a business at a given point of time. Revenue and expense accounts describe inflows and outflows per a given period of time (a week, a month, a year). Once that period of time has elapsed, new accounts must be established to meter the flows of the next accounting period.

EXHIBIT 3-7

Entries to "Close" Revenue and Expense Accounts

Closing Entry 1

Sales revenue	$4,000	
Retained earnings		$4,000

To close revenue account

Closing Entry 2

Retained earnings	$3,800	
Cost of goods sold		$2,000
Advertising expense		500
Rent expense		600
Depreciation expense		500
Utility expense		200

To close expense accounts

Advertising expense

(3)	500	500→

Sales revenue

←4,000	(9)	4,000

Rent expense

(5)	600	600→

←*Closing Entry 2*

Depreciation expense

(7)	500	500→

←*Closing Entry 1*

Cost of goods sold

(10)	2,000	2,000→

Utility expense

(11)	200	200→

Retained earnings

→3,800	4,000←

OVERVIEW: REVENUES AND EXPENSES ARE SUBACCOUNTS OF RETAINED EARNINGS

The reader should take special note of the approach to revenues and expenses taken in the previous illustration. At the start of the example, whenever there was a transaction that resulted in an increase or decrease in the *level* of net assets, the retained earnings account was either debited or credited. Subsequently, however, the entries were revised. Instead of a debit or credit being made directly to retained earnings, it was made to a revenue or expense account. Then, at the end of the accounting period, the balances in the various revenue and expense accounts were transferred, via a closing entry, to retained earnings.

This approach was taken to emphasize the relationship between revenue and expense accounts and retained earnings. Revenue and expense accounts are but temporary "subaccounts" of retained earnings, the "parent" account. At the conclusion of an accounting period they are closed out and their balances are transferred to the parent account. The impact, therefore, of an entry to a revenue or expense account is an increase or decrease in retained earnings and thus in the equity of the owners.

THE COMPLETE ACCOUNTING CYCLE DEMONSTRATED

To demonstrate the complete accounting cycle for an accounting period, we shall assume that Daniel's Den, Inc., a restaurant and night club, has been in business for one month. Its financial position as of June 30, 1983, is described by a balance sheet prepared as of that date (Exhibit 3-8).

Most firms complete an accounting cycle once a year. That is, once a year they close

their books, prepare a complete set of financial statements, and open new revenue and expense accounts. There is no conceptual reason, however, why a firm cannot complete an accounting cycle more frequently than once a year. For purposes of illustration it may be assumed that Daniel's Den, Inc., closes its books at the end of each month.

It is clear from the owners' equity section that the company is organized as a corporation, since only corporations and not partnerships or proprietorships have stockholders.

Impact of Dividends on Retained Earnings

It is also obvious from the owners' equity section that the corporation earned a profit during its first month of operations. This is indicated by the positive balance in the retained earnings account. There is, however, no way to be sure *how much* profit was earned during the first month. The firm earned at least $8,720, but it may have earned considerably more than that. If the company decided to distribute the earnings to its shareholders in the form of a cash dividend, then the balance in the retained earnings account would be equal to the first-month earnings of the company less the dividends paid to stockholders. In paying the dividends to stockholders the firm would have made the following (or a similar) journal entry:

Retained earnings
(owners' equity –)   xxxxx
    Cash (asset –)   xxxxx
To record the declaration and payment of a dividend.

The distribution of the cash would have reduced both the assets and the retained earnings.

EXHIBIT 3-8

Daniel's Den, Inc.
Statement of Position at June 30, 1983

Assets		
Current assets		
Cash in bank	$26,120	
Inventory of beverages	12,000	
Inventory of food	1,200	
Inventory of supplies	6,000	
Prepaid rent	5,600	$ 50,920
Noncurrent assets		
Furniture and fixtures	$23,600	
Kitchen equipment	47,200	70,800
Total assets		$121,720
Liabilities and owners' equity		
Current liabilities		
Accounts payable		$ 15,000
Noncurrent liabilities		
Notes payable		30,000
Total liabilities		$ 45,000
Owners' equity		
Common stock		$ 68,000
Retained earnings		8,720
Total owners' equity		$ 76,720
Total liabilities and owners' equity		$121,720

Recording Transactions

Assume that the events reported in Exhibit 3-9 take place during the month of July 1983. Many of the transactions are summaries of several individual transactions—for example, the sales indicated were by no means made to a single customer in a single evening.

Taking a Preclosing Trial Balance

After the journal entries have been posted to the individual accounts (See Exhibit 3-10), it is possible to take a *trial balance* of the accounts. A trial balance is nothing more than a complete listing of the balances in each of the accounts. Naturally, the total debit balances must be exactly equal to the total credit balances. If they are not, an error has been made, and the accountant or bookkeeper must review the individual accounts and retrace each of the postings back to the journal entries.

Unfortunately, the equality of total debit balances to total credit balances is only a necessary condition for the accounts to be in order; it is by no means a sufficient condition. For even if in the trial balance total debit balances are equal to total credit balances, the financial records may still be in error. Transactions may have been recorded using incorrect dollar amounts or may not have been recorded at all; journal entries may have been posted to improper ledger accounts.

EXHIBIT 3-9   *Record of Transactions*

1. The club purchases glassware and other supplies on account for $2,000.

(1)

Inventory of supplies	$2,000	
Accounts payable		$2,000

To record the purchase, on account, of supplies.

2. Advertising costs for the month amount to $5,200. As of the end of the month, the bill for the advertising has not yet been paid.

(2)

Advertising expense	$5,200	
Accounts payable		$5,200

To record advertising costs.

3. Utilities expense for the month amounts to $600. The entire amount is paid in cash.

(3)

Utility expense	$600	
Cash		$600

To record the cost of utilities.

4. The club pays the salaries of bartenders, waiters, and kitchen employees—a total of $16,000.

(4)

Salary expense	$16,000	
Cash		$16,000

To record the cost of employee salaries.

5. The club purchases, for inventory, beverages (cost $16,000) and food (cost $4,000). The purchases are made "on account."

(5)

Inventory of beverages	$16,000	
Inventory of food	4,000	
Accounts payable		$20,000

To record the purchase, on account, of beverages and food.

6. The club makes payments of $18,000 to creditors from whom it had purchased goods or services on account.

(6)

Accounts payable	$18,000	
Cash		$18,000

To record payments to suppliers and other creditors.

7. Sales of beverages for the month total $60,000; those of food $12,000.

(7)

Cash	$72,000	
Sales revenue, food		$12,000
Sales revenue, beverages		$60,000

To record sales of food and drink.

8. The club rents its premises for $2,800 per month. Upon signing the lease on June 1, the company paid three months' rent in advance. The amount paid was recorded in an asset account, prepaid rent. No rent payments were made during the month of July, but the firm must give accounting recognition to the use of the premises.

(8)

Rent expense	$2,800	
Prepaid rent		$2,800

To record the cost of rent for the month of July and the corresponding reduction of the asset, prepaid rent.

9. The note payable indicated on the June 30 balance sheet bears interest at the rate of 12% per year. Interest is payable monthly but at the month's end the company had not yet made its July payment. The firm must give accounting recognition to the expense of using borrowed funds for one month.

(9)

Interest expense	$300	
Interest payable		$300

To record the cost of using borrowed funds for the month of July: one-twelfth of 12% of $30,000.

EXHIBIT 3-9 *(continued)*

10. The club estimates that both the furniture and fixtures and the kitchen equipment have a useful life of 5 years (60 months). The furniture and fixtures originally cost $24,000; the kitchen equipment cost $48,000 (the difference between original cost and the amount shown on the balance sheet represents depreciation recorded for the first month of operation). The firm must give accounting recognition to the pro rata cost of the equipment for one month.

(10a)

Depreciation expense	$400	
Furniture and fixtures		$400

(10b)

Depreciation expense	$800	
Kitchen equipment		$800

To record depreciation (one-sixtieth of original cost) for the month of July.
(The entries could, of course, have been combined into one.)

11. An inventory taken at the month's end indicates the following balances of beverages, food, and supplies on hand:

Beverages	$4,000
Food	400
Supplies	3,600

Since the accounts indicate the balances on hand at the beginning of the month and the purchases during the month (see entries **1** and **5**), the amounts sold or used during the month can readily be derived (assuming, of course, no theft or other misuse) using the procedure that follows:

(11)

Cost of beverages sold (expense)	$24,000	
Cost of food sold (expense)	4,800	
Cost of supplies used (expense)	4,400	
Inventory of beverages		$24,000
Inventory of food		4,800
Inventory of supplies		4,400

To record the cost of the sale or use of beverages, food, and supplies and to reduce the balance in the beverage, food, and supplies inventory accounts to those indicated by the physical count.

	Beverages	Food	Supplies
Balance on hand, July 1	$12,000	$1,200	$6,000
Add: Purchases in July	16,000	4,000	2,000
Amounts available for sale or use	$28,000	$5,200	$8,000
Less: Balance on hand, July 31	4,000	400	3,600
Amount sold or used in July	$24,000	$4,800	$4,400

A trial balance may be taken at any time. One taken before the closing entries (those which transfer the balances in the revenue and expense accounts to retained earnings) are made is referred to as a *preclosing* trial balance (see Exhibit 3-11); one taken after the closing entries have been made is called a *postclosing* trial balance.

By identifying the revenue and expense accounts from a preclosing trial balance, a statement of income may be prepared (Exhibit 3-12).

Closing Entries

The preclosing trial balance could also be used to prepare a balance sheet except for the fact that one account would not be current. *The balance in the retained earnings account would represent that of the previous period.*

EXHIBIT 3-10

Preclosing Ledger Accounts

| | Assets | | Liabilities | | Owners' Equity *(Including Revenues and Expenses of the Period)* |

Assets

Cash in bank

Bal. 7/1	26,120	(3)	600
(7)	72,000	(4)	16,000
		(6)	18,000
Bal. 8/1	63,520		

Inventory of supplies

Bal. 7/1	6,000	(11)	4,400
(1)	2,000		
Bal. 8/1	3,600		

Furniture and fixtures

| Bal. 7/1 | 23,600 | (10a) | 400 |
| Bal. 8/1 | 23,200 | | |

Inventory of food

Bal. 7/1	1,200	(11)	4,800
(5)	4,000		
Bal. 8/1	400		

Inventory of beverages

Bal. 7/1	12,000	(11)	24,000
(5)	16,000		
Bal. 8/1	4,000		

Liabilities

Accounts payable

(6)	18,000	Bal. 7/1	15,000
		(1)	2,000
		(2)	5,200
		(5)	20,000
		Bal. 8/1	24,200

Notes payable

| | | Bal. 7/1 | 30,000 |
| | | Bal. 8/1 | 30,000 |

Interest payable

| | | (9) | 300 |
| | | Bal. 8/1 | 300 |

Owners' Equity *(Including Revenues and Expenses of the Period)*

Common stock

| | | Bal. 7/1 | 68,000 |
| | | Bal. 8/1 | 68,000 |

Retained earnings

| | | Bal. 7/1 | 8,720 |

Sales revenue, beverages

| | | (7) | 60,000 |

Sales revenue, food

| | | (7) | 12,000 |

Advertising expense

| (2) | 5,200 | | |

Salary expense

| (4) | 16,000 | | |

EXHIBIT 3-10 (*continued*)

Preclosing Ledger Accounts

	Assets			Liabilities	Owners' Equity (*Including Revenues and Expenses of the Period*)

Kitchen equipment

Bal. 7/1	47,200	(10b)	800
Bal. 8/1	46,400		

Prepaid rent

Bal. 7/1	5,600	(8)	2,800
Bal. 8/1	2,800		

Utility expense

(3)	600

Rent expense

(8)	2,800

Depreciation expense

(10a)	400
(10b)	800
	1,200

Interest expense

(9)	300

Cost of beverages sold

(11)	24,000

Cost of food sold

(11)	4,800

Cost of supplies used

(11)	4,400

EXHIBIT 3-11

Daniel's Den, Inc.
Preclosing Trial Balance as of July 31, 1983

	Debit Balances	Credit Balances
Cash in bank	$ 63,520	
Inventory of beverages	4,000	
Inventory of food	400	
Inventory of supplies	3,600	
Prepaid rent	2,800	
Furniture and fixtures	23,200	
Kitchen equipment	46,400	
Accounts payable		$ 24,200
Interest payable		300
Notes payable		30,000
Capital received from stockholders		68,000
Retained earnings		8,720
Sales revenue, beverages		60,000
Sales revenue, food		12,000
Advertising expense	5,200	
Utility expense	600	
Salary expense	16,000	
Rent expense	2,800	
Depreciation expense	1,200	
Interest expense	300	
Cost of beverages sold	24,000	
Cost of food sold	4,800	
Cost of supplies used	4,400	
	$203,220	$203,220

EXHIBIT 3-12

Daniel's Den, Inc.
Statement of Income for the Month Ending July 31, 1983

Revenues		
From sales of beverages	$60,000	
From sales of food	12,000	$72,000
Expenses		
Advertising expense	5,200	
Utility expense	600	
Salary expense	16,000	
Depreciation expense	1,200	
Rent expense	2,800	
Interest expense	300	
Cost of beverages sold	24,000	
Cost of food sold	4,800	
Cost of supplies used	4,400	59,300
Net income		$12,700

EXHIBIT 3-13

Closing Entry 1

Sales revenue, beverages	$60,000	
Sales revenue, food	12,000	
Retained earnings		$72,000

To close revenue accounts.

Closing Entry 2

Retained earnings	$59,300	
Advertising expense		$ 5,200
Utility expense		600
Salary expense		16,000
Depreciation expense		1,200
Rent expense		2,800
Interest expense		300
Cost of beverages sold		24,000
Cost of food sold		4,800
Cost of supplies used		4,400

To close expense accounts.

Until the closing entries have been made, earnings of the current period would not have been added to retained earnings.

It makes sense, therefore, first to make the closing entries and then to prepare the balance sheet from the postclosing trial balance. The postclosing trial balance would give effect to the closing entries and would therefore exclude revenue and expense accounts. It would include only those accounts required to prepare the balance sheet.

The entries necessary to close the revenue and expense accounts (Exhibit 3-13) can also be prepared from the data contained in the preclosing trial balance.

Once the closing entries have been made and posted to the appropriate ledger accounts (only those affected by the closing entries are shown in Exhibit 3-14), then the balances in all revenue and expense accounts would be zero. Their balances would have been transferred to retained earnings. In this example, $72,000 of revenues (per closing entry 1) and $59,300 of expenses (per closing entry 2) have

been transferred. The net amount of the transfer is $12,700—income for the period.

Taking a Postclosing Trial Balance

A postclosing trial balance can be taken from the remaining accounts, those that have not been closed (Exhibit 3-15). These would be the owners' equity accounts—including retained earnings account, which have been adjusted by the closing entries—as well as the asset and liability accounts.

The postclosing trial balance includes only balance sheet accounts. The income statement accounts have been closed to retained earnings. They have been "zeroed" out, ready to meter the flows of the next accounting period. By contrast, the balances that remain and are reported in the postclosing trial balance will be carried forward to serve as the opening balances of the accounting period that follows. By properly classifying each of the accounts in the postclosing trial balance into groups of assets (current and noncurrent), liabilities (current and noncurrent), and equities, a balance sheet (also called a statement of position; see Exhibit 3-16) can be prepared. Once this has been done the recording process has completed a full cycle: a new accounting year can now begin.

SUMMARY

The accounting equation, assets = liabilities + owners' equity, serves as the basis for recording all transactions worthy of accounting recognition and for maintaining the basic books of account. The fundamental accounting cycle may be summarized in eight steps:

1. Transactions are recorded in journals in the form of journal entries.

EXHIBIT 3-14

Selected Ledger Accounts
(Postclosing—Revenues, Expenses, and Retained Earnings)

	Rent expense				Depreciation expense	
(8)	2,800	(C2)	2,800	(10a)	400	(C2)	1,200
				(10b)	800		

	Interest expense				Advertising expense	
(9)	300	(C2)	300	(2)	5,200	(C2)	5,200

	Utility expense				Salary expense	
(3)	600	(C2)	600	(4)	16,000	(C2)	16,000

	Cost of beverages sold				Cost of food sold	
(11)	24,000	(C2)	24,000	(11)	4,800	(C2)	4,800

	Cost of supplies used				Sales revenue, beverages	
(11)	4,400	(C2)	4,400	(C1)	60,000	(7)	60,000

	Retained earnings				Sales revenue, food	
(C2)	59,300	Bal. 7/1	8,720	(C1)	12,000	(7)	12,000
		(C1)	72,000				
		Bal. 8/1	21,420				

2. The component parts of the journal entries (the individual debits and credits) are posted to (recorded in) appropriate ledger accounts.

3. At the end of the accounting period the balance in each ledger account is determined by computing the difference between the total debit entries and the total credit entries (taking into account the opening balance).

4. The balances in the various accounts are summarized in the form of a preclosing trial

EXHIBIT 3-15

Daniel's Den, Inc.
Postclosing Trial Balance as of July 31, 1983

	Debit Balances	Credit Balances
Cash in bank	$ 63,520	
Inventory of beverages	4,000	
Inventory of food	400	
Inventory of supplies	3,600	
Prepaid rent	2,800	
Furniture and fixtures	23,200	
Kitchen equipment	46,400	
Accounts payable		$ 24,200
Interest payable		300
Notes payable		30,000
Common stock		68,000
Retained earnings		21,420
	$143,920	$143,920

EXHIBIT 3-16

Daniel's Den, Inc.
Statement of Position as of July 31, 1983

Assets		
Current assets		
Cash in bank	$63,520	
Inventory of beverages	4,000	
Inventory of food	400	
Inventory of supplies	3,600	
Prepaid rent	2,800	$ 74,320
Noncurrent assets		
Furniture and fixtures	23,200	
Kitchen equipment	46,400	69,600
Total assets		$143,920
Liabilities and Owners' equity		
Current liabilities		
Accounts payable	$24,200	
Interest payable	300	$ 24,500
Noncurrent liabilities		
Notes payable		30,000
Total liabilities		$ 54,500
Owners' equity		
Common stock		$ 68,000
Retained earnings		21,420
Total owners' equity		$ 89,420
Total liabilities and owners' equity		$143,920

balance. The sum of the accounts that have debit balances must equal the sum of the accounts with credit balances; otherwise an error has been made.

5. Based on the balances in the revenue and expense accounts of the preclosing trial balance, an income statement is prepared.

6. Journal entries are made to "close" the revenue and expense accounts—that is, to transfer the balances in those accounts to retained earnings.

7. Once the closing entries have been made, the revenue and expense accounts would have zero balances. The balances in the remaining accounts are summarized in the form of a postclosing trial balance.

8. Based on the postclosing trial balance, a balance sheet is prepared.

In Chapter 4, the explanation of the accounting cycle will be expanded to take into account additional types of transactions and financial events.

EXERCISE FOR REVIEW AND SELF-TESTING

1. A trucking service company purchases, on account, 1,000 gallons of gasoline at $1.80 per gallon. Indicate the effect of the transaction on each of the terms of the basic accounting equation, expressed as assets − liabilities = owners' equity.

2. The company uses 200 of those gallons. Determine the effect on each of the terms of the accounting equation.

3. The firm provides delivery services for a customer and bills the customer $2,000. Determine the effect on each of the terms of the accounting equation.

4. Compute the net effect of the events described on owners' equity (and, more specifically, on retained earnings).

5. Prepare journal entries to record the purchase and use of the 200 gallons of gasoline and the provision of delivery services. Rather than debiting or crediting retained earnings directly, make use of appropriate revenue or expense accounts.

6. Assume that these were the only transactions having an effect on revenue and expense accounts. Prepare two additional journal entries to "close" the accounts.

7. Determine the net effect on retained earnings of the journal entries that you have made. Is it consistent with your response to part 4?

8. Determine the amounts by which each of the asset and liability accounts increased as a result of your journal entries. Does the increase in net assets equal the change in retained earnings?

9. Should the asset and liability accounts also be "closed" to a parent account? If not, why not?

QUESTIONS FOR REVIEW AND DISCUSSION

1. What is a debit? What is a credit?

2. How do you account for the fact that when a customer returns merchandise to a department store he is given *credit*—an increase in a liability or a decrease in an asset—on his account when it would appear as if his liability to the store has been decreased?

3. "All accounting transactions can be recorded directly to balance sheet accounts. There is no reason to maintain income statement accounts." Do you agree? Explain.

4. What is the purpose of *closing entries*? Why must revenue and expense accounts have a zero balance at the start of each accounting period? Why aren't balance sheet accounts "closed" at the end of each accounting period?

5. If, prior to the end of an accounting period (before closing entries have been made), one

were to take a trial balance of all *balance sheet* accounts (assets, liabilities, owners' equity), the debits would probably not equal the credits. Why not?

6. What differences, if any, are there in accounting for corporations as opposed to partnerships or proprietorships (single-owner businesses)?

7. The retained earnings account is generally one of the least active on the balance sheet. What types of transactions or financial events require an entry directly to the retained earnings account?

8. A company purchases merchandise listed in a catalog at a price of $50,000. The company is allowed a discount of 20 percent ($10,000) but incurs shipping costs of $2,000, taxes and duties of $500, and insurance of $750. At what value should the goods be recorded on the books of the company? What general rule governs the values at which assets, such as merchandise inventory or plant equipment, should be initially recorded?

9. (1) If at the end of an accounting period the trial balance is not in balance (the debits do not equal the credits), then an accounting error has been made. (2) If at the end of an accounting period the trial balance is in balance, then an accounting error has not been made. Do you agree with either or both of these statements? Explain.

10. What accounting recognition would be given to each of the following financial events on the books of International Electric Co.?
    1. International Electric Co. owns 3,000 shares of Ford Motor Co. common stock. In the course of a year, the market price of the stock increases from $50 per share to $60.
    2. International Electric Co. has outstanding 20,000 shares of its own common stock. In the course of a year, the market price of the stock increases from $45 per share to $50.
    3. William Barefield sells 100 shares of International Electric Co. to Jill Abelson for $45 per share.

PROBLEMS

1. Financial accounting requires an understanding of only nine basic types of transactions.

An accounting transaction, when analyzed in terms of the basic accounting equation, can have only nine possible effects, summarized as follows. Analyze each of the financial events listed, and indicate by letter which of the nine effects is best described. Base your answer on the assumption that each transaction is being entered directly into position statement accounts (i.e., bypassing the income statement), but indicate which of the transactions would, in fact, ordinarily be reported on the income statement.
1. Collection of an account receivable.
2. Purchase of merchandise on account.
3. Sale of merchandise on account.
4. Recognition of the cost of goods that have been sold.
5. Declaration (but not payment) of a dividend.
6. Payment of a dividend that had been previously declared.
7. Recognition of one year's depreciation on a company-owned truck.
8. Payment of one month's rent on a truck that the company leases from a "rent-a-truck" agency.
9. Issuance of 1,000 shares of the company's own common stock in exchange for forgiveness on a $100,000 note payable.
10. Exchange of 1,000 shares of common stock for 2,000 shares of preferred stock.
    a. Asset +; asset −.
    b. Asset +; liability +.
    c. Asset +; stockholders' equity +.
    d. Asset −; liability −.
    e. Asset −; stockholders' equity −.
    f. Liability +; liability −.
    g. Liability −; stockholders' equity +.
    h. Liability +; stockholders' equity −.
    i. Stockholders' equity +; stockholders' equity −.

2. A familiarity with the "mechanics" of accounting can serve to facilitate an understanding of its underlying concepts, principles and issues.

Complete the following table by specifying whether each of the accounts would ordinarily be

	A debit *would serve to increase/decrease the account*	A credit *would serve to increase/decrease the account*
1. Cash	increase	decrease
2. Interest payable		
3. Interest receivable		
4. Interest revenue		
5. Interest expense		
6. Marketable securities		
7. Common stock		
8. Retained earnings		

increased or decreased by a debit and a credit. The first one is done for you as an an example above.

3. *A preclosing trial balance summarizes the balances in all ledger accounts; only some of the accounts, however, are affected by year-end closing entries.*

Indicated in the table is the December 31, 1983, *preclosing* trial balance of the Boston Company. Prepare required year-end closing entries. What was the company's income for the year?

	Debits	Credits
Cash	$10,000	
Accounts receivable	12,000	
Inventory	5,000	
Supplies	1,000	
Prepaid rent	800	
Accounts payable		$ 3,000
Accrued interest payable		200
Notes payable		2,000
Common stock		1,000
Retained earnings		23,600
Sales revenue		48,000
Cost of goods sold	35,000	
Supplies expense	4,000	
Rent expense	9,600	
Interest expense	400	
	$77,800	$77,800

4. *Not all of the financial events described in this problem require financial recognition, but those that do affect only balance sheet accounts.*

Prepare journal entries (as necessary) to reflect the following financial events pertaining to the Edinburg Corporation in the month of June 1983.

1. The company issues $300,000 in long-term bonds. The bonds provide for the payment of interest twice each year at an annual rate of 8 percent. The bonds are payable 10 years from date of issue.

2. The company purchases a new typewriter. Normal selling price of the typewriter is $400, but because the machine is on sale, the company pays only $320, all in cash.

3. The company signs a contract with the Watch-dog Security Service to receive guard service for the period July 1, 1983, to June 30, 1984. The contract calls for payment of $2,000 per month, payable 15 days after the close of the month in which the service is provided.

4. The firm receives a check for $5,000 from one of its customers for payment on merchandise that was delivered in January. The amount owed is included among the company's accounts receivable.

5. The firm purchases 100 shares of Exxon common stock for $84 per share as a short-term investment.

6. The *Wall Street Journal* reports that the price of Exxon stock has increased to $88 per share.

7. The company purchases manufacturing equipment for $86,000. The company pays cash of $20,000 and gives a three-year note for the balance. In addition, the company incurs

costs (paid in cash) of $2,000 to install the equipment.

8. The company issues 10,000 shares of its common stock for $12 per share. The common stock has a par value of $10 per share.
9. The company pays $600 rent on its office space. The rent is applicable to the month of May and had previously been recorded as a liability, "accrued rent payable."
10. The company returns to the manufacturer raw materials that it deems defective. The company had been billed $900 for such materials and had recorded the amount as a liability.

5. *Revenues and expenses result in an increase or decrease in net assets (assets minus liabilities) as well as in owners' equity.*

If the basic accounting equation is expressed in the form assets − liabilities = owners' equity, then which of the following transactions serve to increase or decrease the right side (owners' equity) of the equation? Which transactions would represent revenues or expenses as opposed to only changes in asset and liability accounts?

1. A firm purchases fuel oil for cash.
2. It purchases fuel oil on account.
3. It uses the fuel oil previously purchased.
4. It pays for the fuel oil previously purchased on account.
5. It receives and pays the electric bill; no previous accounting recognition has been given to electric costs.
6. It provides services for a customer and bills him.
7. It collects the amount previously billed.
8. It borrows an amount from a bank.
9. It repays the amount borrowed.
10. It gives accounting recognition to interest on the amount borrowed and makes the interest payment.

6. *Transactions that affect only asset and liability accounts must be distinguished from those that involve revenue and expense accounts.*

Prepare journal entries to reflect the following transactions. Be certain to indicate the nature of each account affected.

1. A company purchases supplies for $500 cash.
2. The company uses $300 of the supplies.

3. The company purchases merchandise for $3,000 on account.
4. The company pays $1,500 of the $3,000 owed to suppliers.
5. The company sells for $4,000, on account, merchandise that had initially cost $3,000. (Two entries are required.)
6. The company collects $4,000 from its customers.
7. It borrows $10,000 at 6 percent annual interest.
8. The company pays one year's interest.
9. The company purchases for cash a machine for $6,000. The machine has an estimated useful life of three years.
10. The company gives accounting recognition to the use of the machine for one year.

7. *Balance sheet accounts for the end of one year can be derived from data pertaining to the following year.*

The following data pertain to Fowler, Inc. (in millions):

	1983	1982
Assets, December 31	$2,000	$?
Liabilities, December 31	900	?
Common stock outstanding, December 31	500	500
Retained earnings, December 31	600	?
Revenues	1,100	1,000
Expenses	800	700
Dividends	200	200

The expenses for 1983 include $300 million which have not yet been paid as of December 31. Other than this amount, there were no changes in liabilities during 1983.

a. Prepare in summary form the entries to close the revenues and expense accounts of 1983.
b. Determine the missing amounts for 1982.

8. *From the perspective of a bank, customer deposits are liabilities; mortgage loans are assets.*

The following is the 173rd semiannual financial Statement of Farm & Home Savings Association of Nevada, Missouri (000s omitted):

Consolidated Balance Sheet at
December 31, 1980

Assets	
Cash and securities	$ 130,810
First mortgage loans	1,981,427
Other loans	21,777
Stock in Federal Home Loan Bank of Des Moines	16,750
Accounts and notes receivable, and other assets	37,858
Office buildings and equipment	36,653
Real estate purchases for development	32,910
Real estate	3,263
Total assets	$2,261,448
Liabilities and retained earnings	
Savings accounts	$1,834,271
Advances from Federal Home Loan Bank	240,468
Borrowers' tax and insurance reserve	11,909
Other liabilities	56,965
Deferred income	8,745
Retained earnings	109,090
Total liabilities and retained earnings	$2,261,448

Prepare journal entries to record the following transactions:

1. A depositor adds $500 to a savings account.
2. The bank makes a mortgage loan of $120,000 on a residential home.
3. A borrower makes a monthly mortgage payment of $620, comprising the following:

Interest	$450
Repayment of loan balance	30
Addition to tax and insurance reserve	140

(Credit interest directly to retained earnings.)

4. The Association borrows $250,000 from the Federal Home Loan Bank.
5. The Association purchases for $150,000 additional stock in the Federal Home Loan Bank of Des Moines.

9. *When a firm returns merchandise, it receives "credit" on its account.*

Prepare journal entries to reflect the following events on the books of both Wholesale, Inc., and Retail, Inc.

1. Wholesale, Inc., sells, for $5,000 on account to Retail, Inc., merchandise that had cost Wholesale, Inc., $4,000.

2. Upon discovering that some of the merchandise did not meet its specifications, Retail, Inc., returns it to Wholesale, Inc. The returned merchandise had been sold to Retail for $1,000 and had cost Wholesale $800.

3. Retail, Inc., pays the balance due on its account.

10. *A balance sheet prepared from a preclosing trial balance will not balance.*

The preclosing trial balance of Frost, Inc., as of December 31, 1983, is as follows:

	Debits	Credits
Cash	$ 3,000	
Accounts receivable	5,000	
Other assets	12,000	
Accounts payable		$ 5,000
Other liabilities		2,000
Capital contributed by stockholders		4,000
Retained earnings		6,000
Sales revenue		25,000
Cost of goods sold	18,000	
Other expenses	4,000	
	$42,000	$42,000

a. If, from the trial balance, you were to prepare an income statement and a balance sheet, which accounts would have to be adjusted? Why?

b. Prepare an income statement.

c. Make the necessary closing entries.

d. Prepare a balance sheet, taking into account the effect of the closing entries.

11. The basic accounting can be expanded so as to highlight the relationships among the various balance sheet accounts and revenues, expenses, and dividends.

Arrange a piece of paper in columns with the following headings, each of which corresponds to a term in the accounting equation:

Assets = Liabilities + Contributed capital

+ Retained earnings, 1/1 + Revenues

− Expenses − Dividends

a. Indicate the effect of each of the following events or other items of information on the accounting equation.
   1. As of 1/1 a firm reported assets of $200,000, liabilities of $100,000, contributed capital of $10,000, and retained earnings of $90,000.
   2. The firm purchased merchandise, on account, for $80,000.
   3. It issued additional common stock for $40,000 cash.
   4. It borrowed $10,000.
   5. It made sales of $98,000, all of which were for cash.
   6. The cost of merchandise sold was $50,000.
   7. It incurred interest costs, which were paid in cash, of $7,000.
   8. Taxes assessed for the period, payable the following period, were $11,000.
   9. It declared and paid dividends of $4,000.

b. Determine, by summing the columns, the financial position of the firm at the end of the accounting period as well as the revenues, expenses, and dividends of the period.

c. Compute income for the period.

d. Determine the end-of-period balance in retained earnings assuming that the balance as of 1/1 is adjusted to give effect to the revenues, expenses, and dividends of the period.

12. Owners' equity increases whenever net assets
(assets minus liabilities) increase, and decreases whenever net assets decrease.

Indicate the effect (if any) that each of the several transactions described would have on owners' equity (after closing entries have been made):
1. The firm sold for $100 merchandise that had cost $80.
2. The firm purchased merchandise for $2,000.
3. The firm purchased a truck for $12,000 cash.
4. The firm purchased and used $300 of supplies.
5. The firm paid its advertising agency $600 for ads that had been run (and had been given accounting recognition) the previous month.
6. The firm received $750 in dividends on 1,000 shares of XYZ Co. stock that it owns.
7. The firm paid $45 interest on $1,000 that it had previously borrowed from a local bank.

13. Because of the logical relationships inherent in an accounting system, lost data can be reconstructed.

Given the following data about a company over a period of three years, determine the missing amounts.

	1983	1984	1985
Retained earnings, 1/1	$1,000	$5,000	$?
Revenues for the year	8,000	?	?
Expenses for the year	?	5,000	8,000
Income for the year	6,000	?	4,000
Dividends declared during the year	?	2,000	3,000
Retained earnings, 12/31	5,000	7,000	?

14. Entries to revenue and expense accounts can be viewed as entries to retained earnings.

Assume that a company maintains only four accounts: (1) assets, (2) liabilities, (3) invested capital, and (4) retained earnings. The following transactions occurred during its first month of operations:
1. The owners of the company contributed a total of $100,000 to establish the business.
2. The company issued bonds for $50,000; that is, it borrowed $50,000.
3. The company purchased equipment, $60,000, giving the seller a note for the full amount.
4. The company purchased merchandise for cash, $40,000.

5. The company had sales of $30,000. Cash sales were $25,000, and those on account, $5,000.
6. The company paid $2,000 rent for the current month.
7. The company paid one month's interest on the bonds, $250.
8. The company recognized one month's depreciation on the equipment purchased. The estimated useful life of the equipment is 60 months.
9. The company paid insurance premiums for two months—the current month and the following month—$300 per month.
10. The company collected $2,000 of the accounts receivable from customers.
11. The company learned that $500 of the amount owed by customers would not be collectible owing to the bankruptcy of one customer.
12. The company determined that of the merchandise purchased $22,000 remained on hand, unsold, at the end of the month.
    a. Establish T accounts for each of the four accounts. Prepare a journal entry to record each of the transactions, and post the entries to the appropriate T accounts. Compute end-of-month balances in each account.
    b. Determine income for the month.
    c. Suppose that the company had paid a dividend of $2,000 to its owners. How would that affect the balance in the retained earnings account? How would it affect income for the month?

15. *Some errors affect only the income statement or the balance sheet; those that affect both are generally more serious.*

A bookkeeper made several errors as described below. For each, indicate whether, for the period in which they were made, they would cause a misstatement, of (1) the balance sheet only, (2) the income statement only, or (3) both the balance sheet and the income statement.

1. Failed to record a sale of $300, on account, to a customer.
2. Failed to record the collection of $200 owed by a customer for a purchase he had made several weeks earlier.
3. Incorrectly recorded the issuance of 1,000 shares of common stock at $2 per share; made the following journal entry:

Cash	$2,000	
Marketable securities		$2,000

4. Recorded the purchase of a new carburetor for a company-owned vehicle as an addition to fixed assets rather than as a repair.
5. Recorded funds given to a salesman to entertain customers as a miscellaneous expense rather than a sales expense.
6. Failed to record the purchase of a new truck.
7. Failed to record depreciation on a company-owned car.
8. Incorrectly counted merchandise inventory on hand at year end.
9. Failed to record repayment of the company's loan from a bank.
10. Failed to record payment of interest on the same loan.

16. *A balance sheet may not balance until a certain key account has been updated.*

Arrange a sheet of paper as indicated in the table on page 93. Leave room for additional accounts that might be required. The first column indicates balances as of January 1.

a. Record the effect of the transactions described, all of which occurred in the month of January, in columns 2 and 3. Indicate the month-end balances in the accounts in columns 4 through 7 as appropriate. Record the total of each column.

1. Sales for the month, all on credit, were $70,000.
2. Collections from customers totaled $80,000.
3. Purchases of merchandise intended for sale were $45,000. All purchases were "on account."
4. Goods on hand at the month's end totaled $5,000.
5. Other operating expenses were $15,000. They were paid in cash.
6. Depreciation expense, in addition to other operating expenses, was based on an estimated useful life of five years (60 months) for all fixed assets (Assume fixed assets were all purchased on 1/1.)

Account	Balance 1/1	Transactions in January		Income Statement for January		Balance Sheet 1/31	
		Dr.	Cr.	Dr.	Cr.	Dr.	Cr.
Cash	$20,000						
Accounts receivable	50,000						
Merchandise inventory	15,000						
Fixed assets	60,000						
Accounts payable	30,000						
Notes payable	25,000						
Common stock	2,000						
Retained earnings	88,000						

b. Why doesn't the balance sheet balance after all transactions have been posted?

c. Prepare a journal entry to close accounts as necessary.

17. Most firms close their books once a year. Financial statements, however, can be prepared at any time and for any time period. The balance sheet and the income statement may be derived from a preclosing rather than a postclosing trial balance. Retained earnings, however, must be adjusted for the income or loss of the period.

Typewriter Rental Service, Inc., began operations on January 1, 1983. During its first month of operations, the following events took place:

1. The company issued 200 shares of common stock at $100 per share.

2. The company rented a store for $200 per month. It paid the first month's rent.

3. The company purchased 20 typewriters at a price of $500 each. The company paid cash of $4,000 and promised to pay the balance within 60 days.

4. The company purchased, on account, supplies for $500.

5. The company rented the typewriters. Total revenues for the month were $800. Of this amount $200 was collected in cash.

6. The company paid $150 cash to cover other operating expenses.

7. A count at month end indicated that $450 of supplies remained on hand.

8. At month end the company gave accounting recognition to the depreciation of 1 month on its typewriters. The useful life of the typewriters is estimated at 36 months.

a. Prepare journal entries to recognize the above transactions.

b. Post the journal entries to T accounts.

c. Prepare a preclosing trial balance.

d. Prepare an income statement and a statement of position (balance sheet).

18. Retained earnings may be affected not only by revenues, expenses, and dividends but by "extraordinary" gains, losses, and prior period adjustments as well. In evaluating extraordinary gains, losses, and prior period adjustments, first consider their impact upon assets and liabilities. The effect on retained earnings should then become relatively clear.

The Bastrop Co. had a balance in retained earnings as of January 1, 1983, of $2.5 million. The following financial events, which affected the company, occurred in 1983.

1. The firm had operating revenues of $3.8 million and operating expenses of $2.6 million.

2. The company suffered an extraordinary loss, not included in operating expenses, of $600,000, attributable to the expropriation of foreign properties.

3. In January 1983 the company paid dividends of $3 per share on 100,000 shares of common stock outstanding. The dividend had been declared in December 1982 and had been properly accounted for at that time.

4. The market price of the company's common stock was $60 per share on January 1, 1983. On December 31, 1983, it was $55 per share.

5. In June 1983 the company issued 10,000 additional shares of common stock. The stock had a par value of $1 per share and was issued at a price of $58 per share.

6. During 1983 the firm discovered that it had failed in 1982 to charge depreciation on one of its assets. The amount of depreciation that should have been charged was $60,000. The company corrected the error in 1983 by making a "prior period adjustment" (i.e., reducing income of 1982).

7. In December 1983 the company declared a common stock dividend of $4 per share on 110,000 shares outstanding and a preferred stock dividend of $1 per share on 200,000 shares outstanding.
   a. Indicate the impact of each event on *retained* earnings.
   b. Determine the December 31, 1983, balance in retained earnings.

19. It is essential to distinguish between sales revenues and cash collections.

This case is based on an actual incident.

Boscoble Auto Parts began operations in mid-1982. According to records maintained by the proprietor, sales for 1983, the first full year of operation, were $98,000. The company made sales both for cash and credit. At the end of each day, the proprietor recorded the day's "sales" in a book he called the "sales journal." The single figure recorded each day was the sum of the sales for cash, the sales for credit, and the subsequent cash collections on previous sales for credit.

Per supplementary records, which may assumed to be correct, at the beginning of 1983 the company had accounts receivable from customers of $8,000; at the end of 1983 the amounts receivable from customers had increased to $10,000. During 1983, $22,000 had been collected from customers who had made purchases on credit.

On December 31, 1983, a count of the parts on hand revealed that the company had an inventory of parts that cost $25,000. A count on December 31, 1982, revealed an inventory of $15,000. During 1983 the company had purchased from suppliers parts that cost a total of $65,000. Other cash operating expenses for the year were $23,000.

In an effort to assist the proprietor, the Small Business Administration has engaged you as a consultant to evaluate the firm's record-keeping system.

a. What was the primary deficiency in the firm's accounting system? How could it be eliminated? What entry in a journal should the proprietor make each time (1) a cash sale is made; (2) a credit sale is made; (3) cash is collected on a previously recorded credit sale.

b. Determine first total cash sales and then total credit sales. By how much were 1983 sales overstated? The firm paid sales taxes to the state based on the amount recorded in the sales journal. The sales tax rate is 5 percent. How much of a refund from the state should the proprietor request?

c. What was the cost of goods actually sold in 1983?

d. What was the correct income (loss) during 1983?

20. This problem serves to review the accounting cycle.

Upon receiving a gift of $4,000, J. Keats decides to enter the copy business. During the first month of operations, the following events took place:

1. Keats places the entire $4,000 in a bank account in the name of "Fast-Copy Co."

2. He signs a three-year lease on a store. Rent is to be at the rate of $400 per month. Keats pays three months' rent at the time he signs the lease, $400 for the current month and $800 in advance.

3. He purchases furniture and fixtures for $1,500. He pays $500 at the time of purchase and promises to pay the balance within 60 days.

4. He signs a rental agreement with a manufacturer of copy equipment. The agreement stipulates that Keats will pay $200 per month plus $.02 for each copy made.

5. He places advertisements in the local newspapers. The cost of the ads is $600, payable in cash.

6. He purchases paper and other supplies for $800 on account.
7. He makes his first copies for customers. He sells 30,000 copies at $.05 each. Customers pay cash for all copies.
8. He takes an end-of-month inventory and finds $200 of supplies on hand.
9. He withdraws $200 from the business to meet personal expenses.
10. He pays the amount due the manufacturer of the copy equipment for the first month's operations.
11. He gives accounting recognition to the use of the furniture and fixtures for one month. The furniture and fixtures have an estimated useful life of five years.
    a. Prepare journal entries to record the transactions of the first month of operations.
    b. Post them to T accounts.
    c. Prepare an income statement for the month.
    d. Prepare any closing entries that would be necessary *if* the books were to be closed at the end of the month (ordinarily books would be closed only at the end of a full accounting period, usually one year).
    e. Prepare a statement of position (a balance sheet).

21. *This problem serves not only to review the accounting cycle but also to highlight a key deficiency of income as a measure of financial strength.*

The stockholders of Regal Gifts, Inc., were extremely gratified to receive an income statement from management. It revealed that in its first year of operations, the company, which operates a gift shop, had earnings that far exceeded original expectations. Two months after receipt of the income statement, the company was forced to declare bankruptcy. The following information summarizes the major financial events of the company's first year of operations:
1. Stockholders purchased 1,000 shares of common stock at a price of $100 per share.
2. The company leased a store in a shopping center. Monthly rent was $1,000. During the year rent payments of $12,000 were made.
3. The company purchased furniture and fixtures for the store at a cost of $30,000. The company paid cash of $20,000 and gave a one-year note

for the balance. The estimated useful life of the furniture and fixtures is 10 years.
4. In the course of the year the company purchased at a cost of $240,000 merchandise intended for sale. The company paid $210,000 cash for the merchandise; as of year end the balance was owed.
5. The company had sales of $240,000. Sales were made for both cash and credit. As of year end, the company had outstanding receivables from customers of $40,000.
6. The company paid salaries of $40,000.
7. The company incurred and paid other operating costs of $15,000.
8. As of year end, the company had $90,000 of merchandise still on hand.
    a. Prepare journal entries to reflect the financial events of the company's first year of operations.
    b. Prepare an income statement and a balance sheet.
    c. Prepare an analysis of the cash account. Indicate the sources of cash and how it was used.
    d. Explain why the company may have been forced to declare bankruptcy.

SOLUTIONS TO EXERCISE FOR REVIEW AND SELF-TESTING

1. Assets (fuel inventory) would increase by $1,800. Liabilities (accounts payable) would increase by $1,800.
   Owners' equity would not change.
2. Assets (fuel inventory) would decrease by $360. Liabilities would not change.
   Owners' equity would decrease by $360.
3. Assets (accounts receivable) would increase by $2,000.
   Liabilities would not change.
   Owners' equity would increase by $2,000.
4. Owners' equity (in this case retained earnings) would increase by $1,640 ($2,000 − 360).
5. Fuel inventory (asset+) $1,800
   Accounts payable (liability+) $1,800
   To record purchase of fuel.

Fuel expense (owners' equity −) $360
  Fuel inventory (asset −) $360
To record use of fuel.
Accounts receivable (asset +) $2,000
  Delivery revenue (owners' equity +) $2,000
To record delivery services provided.

6. Retained earnings
    (owners' equity −) $360
      Fuel expense (owners' equity +) $360
  To close expense account.
  Delivery revenue
    (owners' equity −) $2,000
      Retained earnings
      (owner's equity +) $2,000
  To close revenue account.

7. The net effect of the journal entries is to increase retained earnings by $1,640, an amount equal to that determined in item 4.

8. Increase in assets
    Fuel inventory
      ($1,800 − $360) $1,440
    Accounts receivable   2,000 $3,440

   Less increase in liability:
     Accounts payable   1,800
       Increase in net assets $1,640

9. The increase in net assets is equal to the increase in retained earnings.

   No. There is no need to transfer the balances in asset and liability accounts to "parent" accounts. Moreover, the balances at the end of an accounting period must remain for the start of the next accounting period. Unlike revenue and expense accounts, asset and liability accounts do not have to be "zeroed out" to accumulate new information each accounting period.

ACCRUING 4
REVENUES
AND EXPENSES

The primary purpose of this chapter is to examine the accrual basis of accounting and to explore its implications for both managers and investors. The accrual basis of accounting is the method whereby revenues and expenses are recognized at the time that they have their primary *economic* impact, *not necessarily when cash is received or disbursed.* Revenues are assigned to the accounting period in which a *critical event*, such as the rendering of services or the sale of goods, takes place. Costs are charged as expenses in the period in which the organization benefits from them. In commercial organizations, costs are incurred in order to generate revenues. Thus, to the extent practical costs are *matched* to the revenues to which they are related.

DEFICIENCIES OF CASH BASIS

The preeminence of the accrual method can be appreciated when it is compared to the cash method. Cash basis accounting views as the critical economic event the collection or disbursement of cash. Revenues attributable to the sale of goods or the provision of services are considered to be *realized* (given accounting recognition) at the time that cash is collected from customers. Costs are charged as expenses only as actual payment is made for goods or services acquired.

The cash basis of accounting is deficient because it focuses on activities—the receipt or disbursement of cash—which by themselves have relatively little economic significance and which can be easily manipulated by management. When a firm acquires goods or services, the timing of payment is often discretionary. If a firm acquires goods near the end of one period, it can delay recording an expense simply by waiting until the start of the next period to write a check. The City of New York, for example, which had been on a cash basis of accounting, once delayed until July, the start of a new fiscal year, paying school-teachers their June salaries, which are traditionally paid at month end. The City postponed recognition of the expenditure to the next fiscal year and was able thereby to give the appearance of having reduced its operating deficit.

The distorting effects of the cash basis are most pronounced when a cash disbursement is intended to benefit a large number of accounting periods. If a firm were to acquire for cash equipment that was expected to be used for several years, then the entire expense would be reported in the year of purchase. The revenues generated by the goods produced by the machine would be given recognition, however, over the life of the machine.

ADVANTAGES OF THE ACCRUAL BASIS

Under the accrual concept, revenues are *realized* when there is evidence that the firm is economically better off owing to its production and sales activities. The criteria for recognizing revenues will be discussed in the next chapter.

Costs are charged as expenses in the same period as the revenues to which they relate are recognized. Insofar as it is impractical to relate specific costs to specific revenues, then the costs are charged as expenses in the period in which the goods are consumed or the services provided. Costs which are intended to provide future benefits are *capitalized*—i.e., recorded as assets (bundles of "prepaid" expenses)—until such time as the benefits are actually realized. At the time office supplies are purchased, their cost is stored in an asset account, "supplies inventory." It is recorded as an expense only as the supplies are consumed. The supplies could be consumed either before or after they are actually paid for.

Similarly, the cost of services provided by an office clerk is generally recorded as an expense during the period in which the firm benefits from his services even though a paycheck may be drawn in a subsequent (or even a previous) accounting period.

Accrual accounting is as advantageous to managers as it is to investors. Both groups use financial reports to assess organizational performance of the past in order to predict and make plans for the future. Accrual accounting, inasmuch as it reports on inflows and outflows of all types of resources, not exclusively cash, generally provides a superior match of efforts to accomplishments.

Several series of events and the appropriate journal entries can be used to illustrate the accrual concept and highlight the distinction between flows of *resources* and flows of *cash*.

Example 1   Supplies

A company purchases supplies but does not pay for them until after they are consumed:

(a)

12/17/83
Supplies inventory (asset +) $300
  Accounts payable (liability +) $300
To record the purchase of $300 of supplies on account. (No expense is charged.)

(b)

2/5/84
Supplies expense (expense +) $200
  Supplies inventory (asset −) $200
To record the use of $200 of the supplies previously purchased.

(c)

3/2/84
Accounts payable (liability −) $300
    Cash (asset −) $300
To record payment of the $300 owed for the supplies. (No expense is charged.)

The expense is charged when the supplies are *consumed*—not when the supplies are received or when they are paid for. The *use* of the supplies is the critical economic event.

Occasionally, a term such as *supplies* is used to refer to both an asset, "supplies in inventory," and an expense, "supplies expense." Accountants allow themselves considerable flexibility in the titles by which they describe accounts. To avoid confusion, however, titles that clearly indicate the nature of the account should always be employed.

Example 2 Salaries

A company benefits from the services of salaried employees in one accounting period but does not pay them until the next.

Salaries are paid each Tuesday for the week ending the previous Friday.

(a)

12/30/83 (Friday)
Salaries expense
    (expense +) $14,000
      Accrued salaries payable
      (liability +) $14,000
To record one week's salaries.

(b)

1/3/84 (Tuesday)
Accrued salaries
    payable (liability −) $14,000
      Cash (asset −) $14,000

To record payment of $14,000 owed for salaries.

The expense is charged in the accounting period in which the work is performed—regardless of when cash payment is actually made.

Example 3 Sales (Advances)

A firm receives payment in advance for merchandise that it will sell (deliver) to a customer in a subsequent accounting period.

The significant event in a sales transaction is most frequently (though not necessarily) considered to be the transfer of goods (and title) to the customer. It is at the time of transfer, therefore, that both sales revenue and the related cost of the goods sold should be recognized.

(a)

12/15/83
Cash (asset +) $25,000
    Advances from customers
    (liability +) $25,000
To record advance payment from a customer for merchandise to be delivered in the following period.

(b)

2/20/84
Advances from
    customers (liability −) $25,000
      Sales revenue (revenue +) $25,000

(c)

2/20/84
Cost of goods sold
    (expense +) $18,000
      Merchandise inventory
      (asset −) $18,000
To record the cost of the goods delivered to the customer as part of the sales transaction recorded in entry (b).

Example 4 Sales (On Account)

A company sells merchandise in one period but receives payment in a subsequent period.

(a)

12/20/83
Accounts receivable
   (asset +) $46,000
     Sales revenue (revenue +) $46,000
To record the sale of merchandise to a customer.

(b)

12/20/83
Cost of goods sold
   (expense +) $33,000
     Merchandise inventory
       (asset −) $33,000
To record the cost of the goods delivered to the customer as part of the sales transaction recorded in entry (a).

(c)

3/11/84
Cash (asset +) $46,000
     Accounts receivable
       (asset −) $46,000
To record the receipt of the amount previously billed.

As in the previous example, both revenue and the related expense are recorded at the time the merchandise is delivered to the customer—not when the cash payment is received.

Example 5 Dividends

A company declares (announces its intention to pay) a dividend in one accounting period but does not pay it until the next period. For example, on November 28, 1983, a company declares a dividend of $1.00 per share payable to stockholders on January 15 of the following year; there are 50,000 shares of stock outstanding.

(a)

11/28/83
Dividends (cannot
   properly be classified
   as revenue, expense,
   asset, or liability;
   they represent a
   reduction of owners'
   equity owing to a
   distribution of assets
   to stockholders) $50,000
     Dividends payable
       (liability +) $50,000
To record the declaration of the dividend.

(b)

1/15/84
Dividends payable
   (liability −) $50,000
     Cash (asset −) $50,000
To record the payment of the dividend.

On December 31, 1983, when year-end financial statements are prepared the "dividends" account (like revenue and expense accounts) would be "closed" to retained earnings:

12/31/83
Retained earnings $50,000
   Dividends $50,000

As a consequence, the dividend will have its critical impact on the financial statements (i.e., will result in the decrease of owners' equity) in the year in which it is declared, rather than when it is actually paid. It is upon declaration of the dividend that the company establishes its obligation to distribute assets to stockholders.

PERIODIC ADJUSTING ENTRIES

Adjusting for Continuous Processes

Some expenses are incurred and some revenues are earned on a continuous basis. Buildings, for example, depreciate over time. Rent, insurance, and interest expenses are also incurred as a function of time. Similarly, electricity and heating costs are often incurred without interruption. Revenues, such as interest revenue, rent revenue, and insurance premium revenue (from the standpoint of an insurance company), are also continuously being earned. To the extent that the accrual concept requires that accounting recognition be given to expenses as they are incurred and to revenues as they are earned, a firm's bookkeeper would have to be making entries around the clock to keep the accounting records current.

Although the accrual concept need not be adhered to with a vengeance, it is important that the financial records be updated periodically, and it is essential, if misleading reports are not to be presented, that an enterprise give recognition to ongoing revenues and expenses whenever financial reports are to be issued. In practice, it is common for firms to make updating journal entries monthly, quarterly, or, at a minimum, annually.

Several *updating* entries are indicated in the examples that follow. Common to all is that the credits to revenues or the debits to expenses are made regardless of whether or not there has been a receipt or disbursement of cash.

Example 1   Interest

On January 1 a firm borrows $3,000 for two months at an annual rate of interest of 12 percent.

1/1/83

Cash (asset+)	$3,000	
Notes payable (liability +)		$3,000

To record the receipt of cash and the corresponding liability.

1/31/83

Interest expense (expense+)	$30	
Accrued interest payable (liability +)		$30

To record both interest expense for one month and the corresponding liability. The term "accrued" is frequently used to reflect the fact that the related expense or revenue has been earned or incurred but the asset or liability is not yet contractually receivable or due.

2/28/83

Interest expense (expense+)	$30	
Accrued interest payable (liability+)		$30

To record the interest expense for the second month.

2/28/83

Accrued interest payable (liability−)	$ 60	
Notes payable (liability−)	3,000	
Cash (asset−)		$3,060

To record the subsequent payment of both the interest and the principal due.

In this example *interest expense* was debited at the end of each month—and the liability to make the required payments was credited—to give accounting recognition to the continuous accrual of the cost of using borrowed funds.

2/28/83	Interest expense (expense +)	$ 30	
	Accrued interest payable (liability −)	30	
	Notes payable (liability −)	3,000	
	Cash (asset −)		$3,060

To record payment of note and related interest.

The two entries of 2/28 could have readily been combined as above.

Example 2 Rent

On June 15 Left Bank Properties, Inc., leases a residential house to a tenant. Rent is $400 per month, and the lease is for a one-year period beginning July 1. One month's rent is paid in advance. Subsequent payments are to be made each month.

6/15/83

| Cash (asset +) | $400 | |
| Unearned rent (liability +) | | $400 |

To record both the receipt of one month's rent in advance and the corresponding "liability"— in this instance a "deferred credit" or obligation to provide services to the tenant. "Unearned rent" is similar to "advances from customers."

7/31/83

| Unearned rent (liability −) | $400 | |
| Rent revenue (revenue +) | | $400 |

To give accounting recognition to both the revenue earned in July and the satisfaction of the related liability.

8/31/83

| Rent receivable (asset +) | $400 | |
| Rent revenue (revenue +) | | $400 |

To give accounting recognition to the revenue earned in August. (Assume that the tenant has failed to make the required payment for August.)

9/31/83

Cash (asset +)	$1,200	
Rent receivable (asset −)		$400
Rent revenue (revenue +)		400
Unearned rent (liability +)		400

To record $1,200 cash received from tenant. The amount received represents rent for August, which was due the previous month; rent for September, which is currently due; and rent for October, paid in advance.

Example 3 Depreciation

On January 2, 1983, a firm purchases a bookkeeping machine for $10,000. The estimated useful life of the machine is five years, after which it will have negligible scrap or resale value:

1/2/83

| Office equipment (asset +) | $10,000 | |
| Cash (asset −) | | $10,000 |

To record the purchase of the machine.

12/31/83

| Depreciation expense (expense +) | $2,000 | |
| Office equipment— accumulated depreciation (contra asset +) | | $2,000 |

To record depreciation for the first year. An identical entry would be made at the end of each of the following four years.

Contra Accounts

In Example 3, it was necessary, at the end of the first accounting period, to give accounting recognition to the fact that the "bundle of future services" represented by the asset, office equipment, had been depleted by one year's use. The credit in the journal entry was not made directly to "office equipment"; instead it was made to "office equipment—accumulated depreciation." The latter account is known as a *contra* (meaning against or opposite) or *offset* account, and its balance is always reported directly beneath that of the account with which it is associated. If the contra account is associated with an asset account, then the asset account would always have a debit balance, and the contra account would always have a credit balance. The asset account would indicate the original cost of the equipment; the contra account would indicate the expired portion of the cost. The difference between the two would reflect the unexpired cost (i.e., its *book value*). At the end of the *second* year of operation, the office equipment and the related contra account would appear as follows:

Office equipment

1/1/83	10,000		

Office equipment, accumulated depreciation

		12/31/83	2,000
		12/31/84	2,000

The two accounts would be reported on the balance sheet as follows:

Office equipment	$10,000	
Less: Accumulated depreciation	4,000	$6,000

The periodic credits could have been made directly to the office equipment account. Use of the contra account, however, provides additional information: the original cost of the equipment as well as the portion of the cost that has expired to date.

Should the assets be removed from the books, it would also be necessary to remove the related accumulated depreciation from the contra account. Assume, for example, that immediately after the second year the office equipment described above was sold for $7,000. The book value at the time of sale was $6,000—the original cost of $10,000 less accumulated depreciation of $4,000. Hence there was a gain on the sale of $1,000. The following journal entry would therefore be appropriate:

Cash (asset +)	$7,000	
Office equipment—accumulated depreciation (contra asset −)	4,000	
Office equipment (asset −)		$10,000
Gain on sale of equipment (revenue +)		1,000

To record the sale of office equipment

The expression "allowance for" depreciation is often used in place of "accumulated" depreciation.

Three Means of Accounting for an Expense

Periodically, additional adjustments to the financial records must be made. These adjustments stem primarily from the willingness of business enterprises and their accountants to permit out-of-date information to remain in the accounts in order to obtain a measure of bookkeeping convenience. There is no harm in such practice—as long as necessary adjustments are made prior to the preparation of financial statements derived from the accounts.

Suppose that at the beginning of an accounting period a company has on hand $1,000 in supplies. During the accounting period the company purchases for cash $4,000 of supplies and consumes $2,000. The correct ending balance in the supplies account would therefore be $3,000; supplies expense for the period would be $2,000 (the amount consumed):

Balance, supplies inventory, 1/1	$1,000	
Purchases, 1/1–12/31	4,000	$5,000
Supplies used (expense), 1/1–12/31		2,000
Balance, supplies inventory, 12/31		$3,000

perpetual method—no year-end adjustment required

The most direct means of accounting for supplies would be to increase the supplies inventory account each time supplies were purchased and to decrease the account each time supplies were withdrawn and presumably used. Thus,

(a)

Various Dates

Supplies inventory	$4,000	
Cash		$4,000

To record the purchase of supplies. (If the $4,000 of supplies represents the sum of several purchases, then similar journal entries would be made for each purchase.)

(b)

Various Dates

Supplies expense	$2,000	
Supplies inventory		$2,000

To record the use of $2,000 of supplies.

At the end of the year the accounts would appear as follows:

Supplies inventory

Bal. 1/1	1,000	**(b)** var. dates	2,000
(a) var. dates	4,000		
	3,000		

Supplies expense

(b) var. dates	2,000	

Cash

Bal. 1/1	xxx	**(a)** var. dates	4,000

The accounts correctly reflect the fact that ending inventory is $3,000 and supplies expense for the period was $2,000. No adjusting entries are required. It is necessary only to "close" the supplies expense account. But insofar as supplies are withdrawn in small amounts at frequent intervals, record keeping in the course of the year may tend to become burdensome since a separate entry must be made for each purchase and each withdrawal.

periodic method—asset account overstated

Alternatively, a company can avoid making an accounting entry each time supplies are *withdrawn* from the storeroom. Instead of recording both the purchase and the use of supplies, it would record only the purchase. In the course of the year, the supplies inventory account would only be debited—never credited. At the end of the year, however, the firm would take a *physical inventory* (count) to determine the actual amount of supplies on hand. The company would assume that all supplies purchased plus those on hand at the beginning of the year must have been used during the year if they are not physically present at the conclusion of the year. It would adjust the accounts by crediting inventory with the amount required to reduce supplies inventory to reflect the inventory actually on hand and by debiting supplies expense with the same amount—the amount presumably used during the year. Thus,

(a)
Various Dates
Supplies inventory $4,000
     Cash $4,000
To record the purchase of supplies throughout the year.

At the end of the year, prior to the physical inventory count, the accounts would show the following:

Supplies inventory

Bal. 1/1	1,000		
(a) var. dates	4,000		

Supplies expense		Cash	
		xxx	(a) var. 4,000
			dates

If a physical count at year end reveals supplies on hand of $3,000, then $2,000 of supplies ($5,000 per the accounts less $3,000 on hand) must have been consumed. The appropriate adjusting journal entry would be

(b)
12/31 Supplies expense $2,000
              Supplies inventory $2,000
To adjust the accounts at year end to reflect the physical count of supplies.

Supplies inventory

Bal. 1/1	1,000	(b) 12/31	2,000
(a) var. dates	4,000		
	3,000		

Supplies expense

(b) 12/31	2,000		

Once the adjusting entries have been posted, the account balances would be identical to those derived from the procedure illustrated previously. The former approach is often referred to as a *perpetual* method, since the inventory account is always reflective of the actual quantity on hand, and the latter approach as a *periodic* method, since periodic counts are necessary to bring the inventory account up to date.

periodic method—expense account overstated

The same results could be obtained by a third procedure, which is also widely used. A company, instead of charging (debiting) all purchases of supplies to supplies inventory, could charge them to supplies expense. Then, as it would do if it followed the second procedure, it would take a year-end count of supplies on hand. To adjust the inventory account to reflect the actual inventory on hand, the balance in the supplies inventory account (which would represent supplies on hand at the *beginning* of the year) would be debited (increased) *or* credited (decreased) with the amount required to bring it up or down to the quantity indicated by the physical count. The corresponding credit or debit would be made to supplies expense. If more supplies were purchased than were actually used, then the amount in the supplies expense account would have to be reduced (credited); if more were used than purchased (i.e., beginning inventory reduced), then supplies expense would have to be increased (debited).

(a)

Various Dates
> Supplies expense $4,000
> > Cash $4,000

To record the *purchase* of supplies.

At the end of the year, prior to adjusting entries, the accounts would appear as follows:

Supplies inventory

Bal. 1/1	1,000	

Supplies expense

(a) var. dates	4,000	

Cash

	(a) var. dates	4,000
xxx		

If the physical count at year end revealed that $3,000 of supplies were on hand, then supplies inventory would be understated by $2,000. Correspondingly, supplies expense would be overstated by that same amount. The required adjusting entry would therefore be

(b)

12/31   Supplies inventory $2,000
> > Supplies expense $2,000

To adjust the inventory and expense accounts for the excess of the physical count over the balance in the inventory account.

Supplies inventory

Bal. 1/1	1,000	
(b) 12/31	2,000	
	3,000	

Supplies expense

(a) var. dates	4,000	(b) 12/31	2,000

The adjusted balances would, of course, be in accord with those derived by the other two methods.

significance of alternatives

The three methods are of significance for two primary reasons. First, they are illustrative of the flexibility of the double-entry system. Identical events can be accounted for in a variety of ways. If a firm deems it too inconvenient or costly to keep its books and records perpetually up to date—that is, to record immediately every financial event that is worthy of accounting recognition—it can readily make periodic adjustments whenever current information is needed.

Second, the three methods are demonstrative of the intrinsic relationships between balance sheet and income statement accounts. For almost all income statement (*flow*) accounts there are corresponding balance sheet (*storage*) accounts. Among the expenses, cost of goods sold is related to inventory; interest expense is related to either prepaid interest (an asset) or accrued interest payable (a liability). Depreciation is related to fixed assets such as buildings or equipment. Similarly, among the revenues, sales revenue is related to either accounts receivable or to "unearned" or "deferred" revenue (e.g., airline tickets sold but services not yet provided); rent revenue is related to either rent receivable or to "unearned" rent (i.e., rent received in advance).

A Warning

In making either updating or adjusting entries, neophyte accountants are often unsure of the accounts to be adjusted. Although it may be obvious that one account must be corrected, they are unsure of the corresponding half of the entry. There is a temptation, in the face of uncertainty, to debit or credit either "cash" or "retained earnings." In fact, neither is likely to be affected by periodic adjustments. "Cash" needs to be debited or credited only upon the actual receipt or disbursement of cash. Indeed, unless the student can actually envision a transfer of cash—by check, in currency, or by notification of credits or charges by the bank—he can be reasonably certain that it is not "cash" that should be debited or credited. Similarly, retained earnings in the ordinary course of

business are affected directly by only two types of events: the declaration of a dividend and the posting of year-end closing entries. Most updating or adjusting entries affect either an asset or liability account and its related revenue or expense account.

YEAR-END ADJUSTMENTS— AN EXAMPLE

Exhibit 4-1 indicates the December 31, 1983 trial balance of the Altoona Appliance Company, a retail store, before year-end adjustments have been made. Available to the accountant in charge of preparing annual financial statements is the additional information described below which requires accounting recognition.

Unexpired Insurance

The prepaid insurance indicated on the trial balance represents the unexpired portion of a three-year policy purchased in 1982. No insurance expense ($2,000 per year) has yet been charged for 1983.

	(a)	
Insurance expense	$2,000	
Prepaid insurance		$2,000

To record the expiration of one-third of a three-year policy.

Depreciation

The company charges depreciation semi-annually, June 30 and December 31. The building, which originally cost $45,000, is being depreciated over a 30-year period; furniture and fixtures, which originally cost $4,700, are being depreciated over a 10-year period. Depreciation charges for a full year

EXHIBIT 4-1

Altoona Appliance Company
Trial Balance
December 31, 1983

	Debits	Credits
Cash	$ 10,500	
Accounts receivable	43,750	
Allowance for		
uncollectible accounts		$ 4,500
Merchandise inventory	65,200	
Prepaid insurance	4,000	
Supplies inventory	500	
Land	10,000	
Building	45,000	
Accumulated depreciation,		
building		11,000
Furniture and fixtures	4,700	
Accumulated depreciation,		
furniture and fixtures		1,410
Notes receivable	2,000	
Accounts payable		18,200
Sales taxes payable		200
Advances from customers		500
Common stock		25,000
Retained earnings		87,365
Sales revenue		330,200
Gain on sale of furniture		
and fixtures		1,200
Cost of goods sold	217,900	
Wages and salaries	56,700	
Delivery and shipping		
charges	3,350	
Depreciation expense	1,285	
Property taxes	180	
Supplies expense	940	
Other expenses	3,570	
Income taxes	10,000	
	$479,575	$479,575

would be $1,500 and $470, respectively—for a half-year, $750 and $235.*

* The amount to be charged for the second half of the year is less than that charged for the first ($1,285 per "depreciation expense" on the trial balance). As indicated by the account "gain on sale of furniture and fixtures," some fixed assets must have been sold during the year.

(b)

Depreciation expense	$985	
Accumulated deprecia-		
tion, building		$750
Accumulated depreciation,		
furniture and fixtures		$235

To record depreciation for one-half year.

Interest Earned

The note receivable, $2,000, is a one-year note and was received from a customer on November 1, 1983. The note bears a rate of interest of 12 percent. Interest is payable at the expiration of the note. Accounting recognition must, however, be given to interest earned in the two months in 1983 during which the company held the note. Interest earned would be two-twelfths of 12 percent of $2,000—$40.

(c)

Accrued interest receivable	$40	
Interest revenue		$40

To record the interest earned but not yet collected.

Property Taxes

The company makes property tax payments once a year, on January 31. Total taxes payable on January 31, 1984 will be $2,280. Accounting recognition must be given to that portion—eleven-twelfths—of the total amount payable applicable to the current year. Tax expense for 1983, to be added to the expense applicable to January 1983 which was recorded when the previous tax bill was paid, is, therefore, $2,090.

(d)

Property taxes (expense)	$2,090	
Accrued property taxes		
payable		$2,090

To record the portion of property taxes due in 1984 applicable to 1983.

Supplies

A physical count indicated supplies on hand of $300. Supplies purchased during the year were charged entirely to supplies expense. The supplies inventory account must be credited by $200 to reflect the difference between the current balance in the account ($500 per the trial balance) and actual supplies in stock.

(e)

Supplies expense	$200	
Supplies inventory		$200

To adjust the accounts to reflect the physical count of supplies on hand.

Wages and Salaries

The company pays its employees every two weeks. At year end employees had worked four days for which they will not be paid until the first payday of the new year. Wages and salaries applicable to the four-day period totaled $1,090.

(f)

Wages and salaries (expense)	$1,090	
Accrued wages and salaries payable		$1,090

To record wages and salaries earned by employees but not yet paid.

Inventory Shortage

The company maintains its merchandise inventory on a *perpetual* basis. Each time an item is sold an entry is made in which merchandise inventory is reduced by the cost of the item sold, and cost of goods sold is charged for the same amount. Thus, at year end, the amount recorded in the accounts should be in agreement with that actually on hand. However, an actual count of merchandise on hand revealed an unexplained shortage of $600. The shortage, of course, requires accounting recognition.

(g)

Inventory shortage (expense)	$600	
Merchandise inventory		$600

To adjust the accounts to reflect the physical count of merchandise on hand.

Income Taxes

Based on a preliminary computation, income taxes (both state and federal) for the year will total $15,500. To date, the company has, in compliance with the law, made payments, based on quarterly reports of earnings, of $10,000. The company now estimates that additional payments of $5,500 will be required. Although such payments need not be made until March 15, 1984, they represent an expense of the current year, 1983.

(h)

Income taxes (expense)	$5,500	
Accrued income taxes payable		$5,500

To record additional income tax expense based on preliminary computation.

Exhibit 4-2 depicts the affected accounts of the company after the above transactions have been posted. Exhibit 4-3 depicts a trial balance derived from the adjusted accounts; Exhibit 4-4 illustrates the income statement and balance sheet developed from the adjusted trial balance. Notice, however, that the retained earnings indicated on the balance

EXHIBIT 4-2

General Ledger Accounts (Only Those Affected by Adjusting Entries)

Accrued interest receivable				Prepaid insurance			
(c)	40			Bal.	4,000	**(a)**	2,000
	(40)				(2,000)		

Supplies inventory				Merchandise inventory			
Bal.	500	**(e)**	200	Bal.	65,200	**(g)**	600
	(300)				(64,600)		

Accumulated depreciation, building				Accumulated depreciation, furniture and fixtures			
		Bal.	11,000			Bal.	1,410
		(b)	750			**(b)**	235
		(11,750)				(1,645)	

Accrued wages and salaries payable				Accrued income taxes payable			
		(f)	1,090			**(h)**	5,500
		(1,090)				(5,500)	

Accrued property taxes payable				Interest revenue			
		(d)	2,090			**(c)**	40
		(2,090)				(40)	

Inventory shortage expense				Income taxes expense			
(g)	600			**(h)**	10,000		
					5,500		
	(600)				(15,500)		

EXHIBIT 4-2 (*continued*)

Insurance expense			Depreciation expense		
(a)	2,000		Bal.	1,285	
	2,000		**(b)**	985	
				(2,270)	

Property taxes expense			Supplies expense		
Bal.	180		Bal.	940	
(d)	2,090		**(e)**	200	
	(2,270)			(1,140)	

Wages and salaries expense		
Bal.	56,700	
(f)	1,090	
	(57,790)	

EXHIBIT 4-3

Altoona Appliance Company
Adjusted Trial Balance
December 31, 1983

	Debits	Credits	(continued)	Debits	Credits
Cash	$ 10,500		Accrued wages and		
Accounts receivable	43,750		salaries payable		1,090
Allowance for			Accrued income taxes		
uncollectible accounts		$ 4,500	payable		5,500
Accured interest receivable	40		Common stock		25,000
Merchandise inventory	64,600		Retained earnings		87,365
Prepaid insurance	2,000		Sales revenue		330,200
Supplies inventory	300		Interest revenue		40
Land	10,000		Gain on sale of furniture		
Building	45,000		and fixtures		1,200
Accumulated depreciation,			Cost of goods sold	217,900	
building		11,750	Wages and salaries expense	57,790	
Furniture and fixtures	4,700		Delivery shipping charges	3,350	
Accumulated depreciation,			Depreciation expense	2,270	
furniture and fixtures		1,645	Property taxes	2,270	
Notes receivable	2,000		Supplies expense	1,140	
Accounts payable		18,200	Insurance expense	2,000	
Sales taxes payable		200	Inventory shortage	600	
Advances from customers		500	Income taxes expense	15,500	
Accrued property taxes			Other expenses	3,570	
payable		2,090		$489,280	$489,280

EXHIBIT 4-4

Altoona Appliance Company
Income Statement
for the Year Ended December 31, 1983

Revenues		
Sales	$330,200	
Interest	40	
Gain on sale of furniture and fixtures	1,200	
Total revenue		$331,440
Expenses		
Cost of goods sold	217,900	
Wages and salaries expense	57,790	
Delivery and shipping charges	3,350	
Depreciation expense	2,270	
Property tax expense	2,270	
Supplies expense	1,140	
Insurance expense	2,000	
Inventory shortage expense	600	
Other expenses	3,570	
Total expenses		290,890
Income before taxes		$ 40,550
Income taxes		15,500
Net income		$ 25,050

Altoona Appliance Company
Balance Sheet December 31, 1983

Assets

Current assets		
Cash		$ 10,500
Accounts receivable	$43,750	
Less: Allowance for bad debts	4,500	39,250
Accrued interest receivable		40
Merchandise inventory		64,600
Supplies inventory		300
Prepaid insurance		2,000
Total current assets		$116,690
Noncurrent assets		
Land		$ 10,000
Building	$45,000	
Less: Accumulated depreciation	11,750	33,250
Furniture and fixtures	4,700	
Less: Accumulated depreciation	1,645	3,055
Notes receivable		2,000
Total noncurrent assets		$ 48,305
Total assets		$164,995

Liabilities and Stockholders' Equity

Current liabilities		
Accounts payable		$ 18,200
Sales tax payable		200
Advances from customers		500
Accrued property taxes payable		2,090
Accrued wages and salaries payable		1,090
Accrued income taxes payable		5,500
Total liabilities		$ 27,580
Stockholders' equity		
Common stock		$ 25,000
Retained earnings		112,415
Total stockholders' equity		$137,415
Total liabilities and stockholders' equity		$164,995

sheet are those per the adjusted trial balance *plus* income for the year. Until the closing entries are prepared and posted, the balance in the retained earnings account indicates only the beginning balance.

The closing entries (Exhibit 4-5) transfer amounts in the revenue and expense accounts to their *parent* account, retained earnings. Conceptually, they cannot be made until after the income statement has been prepared; otherwise the balances in all revenue and expense accounts would be zero. In this illustration, however, we have taken the liberty of neglecting to prepare a post-closing trial balance. We have instead prepared both the income statement and the balance sheet from the preclosing adjusted trial balance. But as required to assure that the balance sheet is, in fact, in balance we have added to retained earnings the income for the year.

A postclosing trial balance—one struck after the closing entries had been posted—would, of course, be composed entirely of balance sheet accounts.

ERRORS AND OMISSIONS

Organizations do, unfortunately, make errors. An examination of some common types of errors and their impact on financial reports provides additional insight into the accounting process.

Some errors are readily detectable. If an entry to a journal is made in which the debits do not equal the credits, or if incorrect amounts are posted to the ledger accounts, then when a trial balance is struck the sum of the general ledger debits may not equal the sum of the credits.

Other errors, most particularly those related to updating or adjusting entries, are less readily detectable and are likely to impact upon both balance sheet and income statement accounts. Many such errors are, however, *self-correcting* over time. They will automatically be eliminated either upon the liquidation of the offending asset or liability or when other routine adjustments to the accounts are made. Unfortunately, though, the errors may affect the financial reports of one or more intervening accounting periods, and for parties who relied upon the erroneous statements all that ends well may not, in fact, *be* well.

Consider a firm that maintains its inventory records on a periodic basis. The firm physically counts merchandise on hand at the end of each fiscal year. During the year it maintains accurate records of all purchases. In determining the cost of goods sold for the year, it computes goods available for sale (beginning inventory plus purchases during the year) and subtracts goods that remained unsold at the end of the year (ending inventory). If beginning inventory were $3,000,

EXHIBIT 4-5

Closing Entries		
Sales revenue	$330,200	
Gain on sale of furniture and fixtures	1,200	
Interest revenue	40	
Retained earnings		$331,440
To close the revenue accounts.		
Retained earnings	$306,390	
Cost of goods sold		$217,900
Wages and salaries		57,790
Delivery and shipping charges		3,350
Depreciation		2,270
Property taxes		2,270
Supplies expense		1,140
Other expenses		3,570
Income taxes		15,500
Inventory shortage		600
Insurance expense		2,000
To close the expense accounts.		

purchases were $30,000, and ending inventory were $6,000, then cost of goods sold during the year would be $27,000:

Beginning inventory	$ 3,000	
Purchases	30,000	$33,000
Ending inventory		(6,000)
Cost of goods sold		$27,000

If in the following year, purchases were $35,000 and ending inventory were $2,000, then cost of goods sold would be $39,000:

Beginning inventory (same as ending inventory of previous year)	$ 6,000	
Purchases	35,000	$41,000
Ending inventory		2,000
Cost of goods sold		$39,000

Suppose, however, that at the end of the first year the firm miscounted its inventory. Instead of $6,000, the firm counted goods on hand of $5,000. As a result of the miscount, cost of goods sold during the first year would have been reported as $28,000—*overstated* by $1,000. In the second year, the *beginning inventory* would have been understated by $1,000. As a result, cost of goods sold for the second year (assuming a correct count at the end of the second year) would have been reported at $38,000—*understated* by $1,000:

period combined but incorrectly stated for each of the two individual periods. Both current assets (inventory) and retained earnings would be in error after the first year, but correct after the second.

Consider also a firm that received a two-year, $1,000 note in June 1983. The note carried an interest rate of 14 percent. Interest was receivable annually each June; the principal, in its entirety, was due from the borrower at the expiration of the note in June 1985.

If the firm made proper adjusting entries, then revenue from the note would be $70 in 1983 (six months' interest), $140 in 1984 (one year's interest), and $70 in 1985 (six months' interest)—regardless of when cash payments were received. Suppose, however, that the firm neglected to "accrue" interest at the end of 1983 and instead recognized revenue only upon the receipt of cash. For the year ended 1983, revenues, current assets (accrued interest receivable), and retained earnings each would be understated by $70. For the year ended 1984, revenues would be correctly stated, as the firm would have recorded $140 interest revenue upon the receipt of the cash interest payment. However, since the cash payment represented interest for the period June 1983 to June 1984, current assets, and thus retained earnings, would still be understated by $70—the interest for the period June 1984 to December 1984. For the year

	Year 1		Year 2	
Beginning inventory	$ 3,000		$ 5,000	
Purchases	30,000	$33,000	35,000	$40,000
Ending inventory		(5,000)		(2,000)
Cost of goods sold		$28,000		$38,000

Cost of goods sold—and thus income—would be correctly stated for the two-year

ended 1985, however, revenues would be *overstated* by $70, as the entire cash interest payment of $140 would be recorded as revenue. Current assets (accrued interest receivable would be zero), however, would now be correctly stated; so, too, would retained earnings.

Although in the *long run* many errors may be self-correcting, a primary purpose of accounting is to report changes in the welfare of an enterprise in the course of specific, relatively short periods of time. Firms are not permitted the luxury of allowing the passage of the years to compensate for their errors and omissions.

COST OF GOODS SOLD

It has been previously pointed out that, in accordance with the accrual concept, costs are *capitalized* as assets until the intended benefits are actually realized. In a business enterprise costs are incurred in order to generate revenues. Hence, costs should be recognized as expenses at the same time that the benefits that they produce are recognized as revenues. In other words, costs should be *matched* with revenues.

In a retail sales operation the major cost incurred in the generation of revenue is that of the goods to be sold. As the goods to be sold are received, their cost is *stored* in an asset account, "merchandise inventory." Only when they are actually sold, and when sales revenue is recognized, is the cost of the goods sold charged as an expense. At the time of sale (or if a periodic inventory method is followed, then at least in the period of sale) the following entry is made:

Cost of goods sold (expense)   xxxx
    Merchandise inventory (asset)   xxxx

It follows that in a manufacturing operation all costs of producing the goods intended for sale should also be stored as assets until the goods are actually sold. This means that not only should costs of raw materials be capitalized as assets, but so too must costs of labor, maintenance, machines used (i.e., depreciation), and all other costs that can readily be identified with the production process.

When raw materials are purchased, their cost is charged initially to an asset account, "raw materials." As they are placed in production, their cost is transferred to "work in process," another asset account, and when the goods are completed their cost is transferred to "finished goods," also an asset account.

This is also true of labor costs. Although labor, unlike raw materials, cannot be physically stored, the *cost* of labor, like the cost of raw materials, *can* be stored in an asset *account*. Labor costs are conventionally recorded initially in an asset account, "labor," and then transferred immediately (since labor cannot be physically stored) to "work in process." The labor account, although perhaps unnecessary since the costs are transferred immediately to work in process, is ordinarily maintained inasmuch as it facilitates cost control by providing management with a record of labor costs incurred.

So also with other manufacturing costs. Even that portion of manufacturing equipment considered to be consumed in the accounting period must be capitalized as part of the cost of the goods produced. The equipment serves to benefit the periods in which the goods that it has been used to produce are actually sold. Costs of using up the equipment (i.e., depreciation) must be added to work in process (an asset account) and thereby included in the cost of the finished goods. They will be charged as an expense (as part of cost of goods sold) when the finished goods are actually sold.

The manufacturing cycle is depicted graphically in Exhibit 4-6. The key point that the exhibit illustrates is that cost of goods sold represents a conglomerate of several different types of costs. All such costs, even those of services that contribute to the value of the product but that cannot be physically stored (labor and utility costs, for example) are accumulated and retained in asset accounts (such as factory labor, work in process, and finished goods) until the time of sale. Upon sale, when the goods are transferred to a customer, an asset account (finished goods) is reduced (credited) by the cost to manufacture the goods sold and an expense (cost of goods sold) is increased (debited).

The principles and issues relating to manufacturing costs will be dealt with at length in Part II of this text.

PRODUCT VERSUS PERIOD COSTS

Principle of Matching

Central to modern accounting is the *principle of matching*. Insofar as practical all costs should be associated with particular revenues and recorded as expenses in the same periods in which the related revenues are given accounting recognition. Costs that are associated with revenues to be recognized in the future are to be maintained in asset

EXHIBIT 4-6

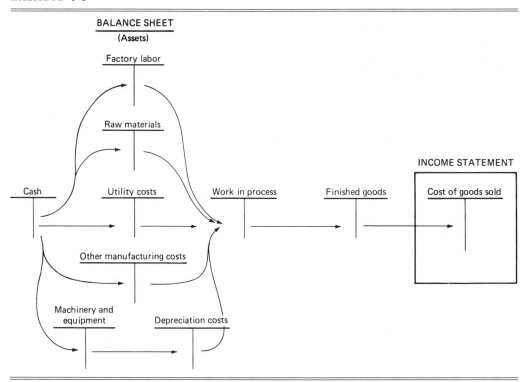

accounts until such time as recognition is accorded the revenues and the costs can properly be charged as expenses.

Expenses have been defined as the goods or services consumed in the creation of revenues. Indeed, *all* expenses are incurred in the hope of generating revenues. If the objective of determining periodic income is to be best served, then all costs incurred by the firm should be capitalized as assets—i.e., charged initially to "work in process" or otherwise added to the cost of goods held in inventory—and recorded as expenses only as the goods are actually sold. Costs of borrowing necessary funds (interest), administering the home office, and selling the products contribute as much to the generation of revenue as those of manufacturing products. Logically, such costs should also be added to the cost of goods manufactured.

In practice, however, many types of costs are not capitalized as assets. Instead they are charged as expenses in the period in which they are incurred, regardless of when the products are sold. The logical inconsistency of capitalizing some costs but not others has by no means been lost upon accountants. They have yielded to practical exigencies, however. It is simply too difficult to associate meaningfully—to match—certain expenses with specific revenues.

Consider, for example, costs of administration—the salaries of officers, secretaries, computer operators, and accountants; the fees paid to outside attorneys and auditors; the costs of renting office space and equipment. If a firm manufactured numerous types of products, it would be difficult, to say the least, to *allocate* such costs to specific products. Or consider sales costs. A salesman might make numerous calls on customers before he receives an order. Is it possible, in any meaningful way, to associate costs of the unsuccessful calls with specific revenues to be generated in the future? Or take interest costs. Funds borrowed benefit the entire company. Can the costs of borrowing be reasonably identified with sales of specific products?

Conventions

In an effort to reduce the need to make knotty allocation decisions, accountants have adopted certain conventions as to which types of costs should be added to the cost of the product and which should be charged off as expenses in the period in which they are incurred. These conventions apply only to reports intended for external parties. They need not be applied to internal financial reports. Although there is by no means universal agreement on the conventions, as a general rule, *direct* manufacturing costs, such as factory labor and raw materials, are always charged to the product (i.e., included in "work in process"). So are several types of *indirect* costs such as depreciation on manufacturing equipment, factory utility costs, rent on the factory building, and salaries of employees who are directly concerned with manufacturing operations. On the other hand, costs of selling, advertising and promotion, interest, employee health and recreational facilities, most taxes, and most other administrative costs are ordinarily considered to be *period* costs, which are charged as expenses as incurred.

The widely followed conventions do not, by any means, eliminate the need to allocate common costs to specific products. *Factory overhead* costs (those which cannot readily be identified with specific products), such as supervision, utilities, maintenance, and rent, must still be assigned on the basis of the best judgment of accountants. And, as a consequence of the conventions, seemingly similar types of costs are sometimes accorded different accounting treatment. Depreciation on tables or chairs in a factory is considered to be a product cost; that on table or chairs in the home office is considered to be a period cost; salaries of accounting clerks who are concerned specifically with factory-related accounts are included among product costs; those of accounting clerks who deal with other types of accounts are included as period costs.

Impact on Financial Statements

In evaluating whether to include a specific cost as a product or a period cost, one relevant question must always be raised: What would be the impact on both the income statement and the balance sheet of alternative classifications?

If within a given accounting period the enterprise sells the *same* number of goods that it produces (assuming no change in per unit costs from one period to the next), then it makes no difference whether a cost is classified as a product or a period cost. Suppose, for example, the salary of an accounting clerk were $12,000 in a given year. During the year the firm produces and sells 12,000 units. If the salary were considered a period cost, then $12,000 would be reported as an expense among "administrative" expenses; if it were considered a product cost, then $12,000 would first be capitalized as "work in process," then transferred to "finished goods inventory" and finally reported as an expense, in the same period, "cost of goods sold."

If the enterprise sells *fewer* goods than it produces, then reported expenses would be *greater* if the costs were categorized as period costs than if they were treated as product costs. Assume the same firm produces 12,000 units but sells only 10,000 units. If the $12,000 salary of the accounting clerk were classified as a period cost, then the full $12,000 would be charged off as an expense. If, however, it were classified as a product cost, then $1 ($12,000 divided by the number of units produced) would be added to the cost of each unit produced. Since 10,000 units were sold, only $10,000 would be included among costs of goods sold. The remaining $2,000 would be *stored* on the balance sheet, included in "finished goods inventory." Hence current assets, specifically inventory, would be $2,000 greater than if the salary were accounted for as a period cost.

If the enterprise sells more goods than it produces, then the reverse would be true. Reported expenses would be less if certain costs were treated as period rather than as product costs. Assume that in the following year the firm produces 12,000 units but sells 14,000 units, taking the additional 2,000 units from inventory. If the accounting clerk's salary were treated as a period cost, then, as previously, the $12,000 would be reported as an expense. But if it were treated as a product cost, $14,000 of salary costs would be charged off as expense—$1 per unit produced and sold in the current period (12,000 units) plus $1 per unit of the goods sold in the current period but produced in the previous period (2,000 units).

BASIC BOOKS OF ACCOUNT

The basic accounting information processing system is simple and straightforward. Relatively few books and records need be maintained or prepared—regardless of the size of the business enterprise and irrespective of whether the system will be manually or electronically maintained.

If the enterprise maintains a computerized accounting system, the journals or ledgers may not take the precise form to be illustrated. They would, however, serve the same function and be designed to accommodate the same information.

The fundamental means of giving accounting recognition to financial events or transactions is the journal entry. Journal entries, as their name implies, are transcribed in journals. Journals are nothing more than books appropriately designed to facilitate two-sided entries of the type illustrated throughout the text. Journal entries are ordinarily prepared from source documents, such as invoices (bills), payment vouchers (internal documents authorizing disbursements), receiving or shipping reports, remittance advices (documents indicating the receipt of cash), and credit memoranda (documents authorizing that a customer be given credit for merchandise damaged or

accounts are maintained. General ledger accounts are represented in this text by T accounts. Posting involves nothing more than transcribing the entries from the journals to the appropriate accounts.

Special Journals

Although conceptually there is need for only a single or *general* journal in which to record transactions, in practice, most firms find that record keeping is facilitated by several supplementary, often called special, journals. Since a firm may enter into numerous transactions which affect identical accounts, it is relatively easy to combine such transactions into a single journal entry and periodically make but one entry to the accounts affected. Supplementary journals enable the firm to do just that. Most firms, for example, maintain a sales journal. The sales journal may be designed as follows:

Sales Journal

Date	Purchaser	Sales (Cr)	Cash (Dr)	Accounts Receivable (Dr)

returned, or special allowances or discounts to which he may be entitled).

Journal entries are *posted* to the *general ledger*, a book in which the current status of all balance sheet and income statement

As each sale is made, the accounting clerk enters the name of the customer to whom the sale was made; the amount of the sale in the column "Sales (Credit)"; the amount of cash received, if any, in the column "Cash

(Debit)"; and the difference between the amount of sale and the amount of cash received in the column "Accounts Receivable (Debit)." At the end of each month, the columns would be totaled. Then either the following entry would be made in the general journal or the amounts would be posted directly to the appropriate general ledger accounts:

Cash	xxxx	
Accounts receivable	xxxx	
Sales		xxxx

Similarly, a firm might maintain a *cash receipts book* and a *cash disbursements book*, both of which are also supplementary journals. One column would indicate the amount of cash received or disbursed; other columns would be reserved for the accounts that would most frequently represent the corresponding side of the journal entry. As with the sales journal, the columns would be periodically totaled and either a single summary entry would be made in the general journal or the totals would be posted directly to the general ledger accounts affected.

Subsidiary Ledgers

A firm almost always finds it necessary to keep records of each customer from whom it holds a receivable, each fixed asset owned, and each supplier to whom it is indebted. But it would obviously necessitate a general ledger of massive proportions if separate accounts were maintained for each customer, supplier, or fixed asset. Instead, most firms maintain, in the general ledger, *control accounts* that summarize the numerous individual accounts. Control accounts might be maintained for accounts receivable, accounts payable, and fixed assets, among others. The individual accounts would be maintained in *subsidiary ledgers*. The subsidiary ledger could be a book or a file of cards, one page or card for each subsidiary account. Obviously the sum of the balances in a subsidiary ledger must equal the balance in the general ledger control account for which the subsidiary ledger provides support. Each time an entry is made to the general ledger control account, one or more entries which sum to the amount debited or credited to the control account must be made to the subsidiary accounts.

Suppose, for example, that in the course of a month a firm makes sales, all on account, to a number of different customers. In the general ledger the firm would debit accounts receivable for the total amount of the sales. In the accounts receivable subsidiary ledger, the firm would debit the individual accounts of the various customers for the amount of each sale. As the customers paid the balance in their accounts, the firm would credit accounts receivable in the general ledger for the total amount collected within a period and credit the individual accounts for the amount of each remittance.

SUMMARY

The primary purpose of this chapter has been to explain the accrual concept and to demonstrate some of its many ramifications for accounting practice. The accrual concept requires that transactions and other financial events be accorded accounting recognition at the time they have their primary economic impact, not necessarily when cash is received or disbursed. Revenues are assigned to the periods in which they are earned. Costs are matched to the revenues that they serve to generate and are charged as expenses in the periods in which accounting recognition is given to the revenues.

The services associated with a cost may be both acquired and paid for in periods other than those in which the revenues to which they must be matched are given accounting recognition. The services provided by supplies, for example, may be acquired (purchased) in one period, consumed in a second, and paid for in a third. The double-entry accounting system allows for costs that will benefit future periods to be *stored* in asset accounts and charged as expenses only as the revenues with which they are associated are recognized. Similarly, the obligation for the payment may be maintained in a liability account until such time as the required cash disbursement is actually made.

In order that a measure of bookkeeping convenience may be achieved, accounting records are not always kept up to date. Sometimes, as in the case of supplies, it is more convenient to record the use of supplies periodically rather than each time supplies are consumed. Or, as in the case of rent or interest revenue, the benefits received accrue over time; it would be physically impractical to update the books on an around-the-clock basis. As a consequence, firms must periodically bring the records to a current status by means of updating and adjusting entries.

The manner in which costs are accounted for in a manufacturing operation is another manifestation of the accrual concept and the related principle of matching. All manufacturing costs are maintained in asset accounts (e.g., raw materials, labor, work in process, finished goods) until that period in which they can properly be matched to revenues from the sale of the product and charged as expenses (cost of goods sold).

Conventionally, not all costs are matched directly with specific revenues. The relationships between some costs and revenues are sufficiently indirect that accountants have surrendered to practical exigencies and make no attempt to match certain costs with particular revenues. These costs, often referred to as *period* costs, are charged as expenses in the periods in which they are incurred, regardless of the amount of revenues recognized in that particular period.

A secondary objective of this chapter has been to provide an overview of the major types of books and records maintained by most business enterprises. Firms conventionally maintain two basic books of account: the general journal and the general ledger. Transactions are recorded in the general journal; they are then posted to the accounts that they affect, which are maintained in the general ledger. To facilitate the processing of large numbers of transactions and the maintenance of large numbers of accounts, most firms employ additional journals and ledgers to support and supplement entries in the general journals and ledgers. These are referred to as specialized or subsidiary journals and ledgers.

In the following chapter we shall expand upon the accrual concept and consider the issue of the most appropriate means of recognizing revenue.

EXERCISE FOR REVIEW AND SELF-TESTING

Global Real Estate leases an office building to a corporate tenant for $300,000 per month. As of January 1, 1983, the tenant had paid two months' rent in advance. The firm included among its liabilities "Unearned rent, $600,000."

1. Assuming that the tenant occupied the apartment for 12 months in 1983, how much rent revenue should the firm recognize during the year? Does it matter how much cash the firm collected from the tenant?

2. Prepare a journal entry that the firm should make at the end of January assuming that it received from the tenant no cash during the month.

3. Suppose instead that during 1983 Global Real Estate received a total of $2,400,000 from its tenant. Each time cash was collected, the firm made an entry in the following form:

Cash   xxx
    Rent revenue   xxx

It made no other entries with respect to rent.
   a. How much rent revenue should properly have been recognized during the year? By how much is rent revenue understated?
   b. At year end, what should be the balance in "Unearned rent"?
   c. What should be the balance in "Rent receivable"?
   d. Prepare a journal entry to adjust and update the accounts.

4. The firm contracted with a maintenance company to perform cleaning services at an annual cost of $120,000. At year end, what amounts should the firm report in its income statement account, "Cleaning expense" and its related balance sheet account, either "Cleaning costs payable" or "Prepaid cleaning costs" if it actually made cash payments of
   1. $ 80,000
   2. $140,000

The maintenance company performed its services throughout the entire year.

5. What generalizations can be made with respect to the relationship among services provided or received, revenue or expense accounts, asset or liability accounts, and cash received or disbursed?

QUESTIONS FOR REVIEW AND DISCUSSION

1. What is meant by the accrual method of accounting? How does it differ from the cash method?

2. Why does the accrual method provide greater insight into organizational performance than does the cash method?

3. What are adjusting entries? Why are they necessary?

4. What are *contra accounts?* Why are they used? Where are they reported on the balance sheet?

5. A company charges all purchases of merchandise intended for sale to "cost of goods sold." Is such practice acceptable? What year-end adjusting entry would be necessary to "correct" the accounts?

6. A bookkeeper incorrectly charges a prepayment of January 1983 rent made on December 28, 1982, to "rent expense." What would be the impact of such error on the financial statements of the year ended December 1982 and that ended December 1983?

7. A manager of a manufacturing company noticed that the account "labor cost" was included in the general ledger among the asset accounts. In view of the fact that he was unable to visually inspect labor costs he wondered how they could possibly be considered to be an asset. How would you answer him?

8. What is meant by the *matching principle?* If a company were to recognize revenue upon the collection of cash from the customer rather than upon the delivery of goods, when would you recommend that the cost of the goods sold be charged as an expense?

9. Distinguish between product costs and period costs. How would you defend the position of accountants who claim that depreciation can sometimes be considered a product cost and sometimes a period cost?

10. Suppose that in a particular accounting period a company sells the same number of goods that it produces. Would it make any difference insofar as net income is concerned if depreciation on office equipment used in the factory were considered a product or a period cost? What if the company sells only a portion of the goods that it produces?

11. Give an example of a subsidiary ledger. Why do companies maintain subsidiary ledgers rather than include all accounts in the general ledger?

12. What is meant by a specialized journal? Give examples of several commonly used specialized

journals. Why do companies maintain specialized journals?

13. An accountant attempted to prepare both an income statement and a balance sheet from an adjusted trial balance. Closing entries had not yet been made. He was unable, however, to get his balance sheet to balance. Assets exceed liabilities plus owners' equity by an amount exactly equal to income for the year. Which account is most likely in error? Why?

PROBLEMS

1. Expenses must be given accounting recognition even if invoices have not yet been received.

As you are getting ready to prepare year-end financial statements you learn that your company has not yet received invoices (bills) for services it received in December. The company estimates that in January it will receive invoices as follows:

From the telephone company	$130
From the gas and electric company	327
From the outside maintenance service	100

a. Prepare any journal entries that you would consider necessary.

b. Suppose you failed to make such journal entries. What effect would such failure have on income of the year, income of the following year, and current liabilities?

2. All costs must be divided between the income statement and the balance sheet.

A firm made the following payments during its first year of operation:

For rent	$12,000
For interest	8,000
For advertising	3,000
For manufacturing products	96,000

The firm's accountant has determined that the following amounts should properly be reported as expenses:

Rent expense	$10,000
Interest expense	7,000
Advertising expense	6,000
Cost of goods sold	80,000

Determine the amounts that should be reported in balance sheet accounts that correspond to each of the reported expenses.

3. Costs may be accounted for in three ways.

The December 31, 1983, balance sheet of a company reported accrued interest payable of $3,000 in connection with bonds outstanding of $100,000. Interest, at a rate of 12 percent, is payable semiannually on April 1 and October 1.

Prepare all required journal entries for the next year, including year-end adjusting entries, assuming that cash payments are made when due, if alternatively

1. The company makes appropriate *accrual* entries every three months.
2. The company debits "interest expense" with the full amount of each cash payment.
3. The company debits "accrued interest payable" with the full amount of each cash payment.

4. Alternative accounting practices can lead to the same results as long as proper end-of-year adjustments are made.

Three companies each account for insurance costs differently. Each began the year with a balance of $400 in prepaid insurance costs, which represented two months of insurance remaining on a one-year policy. Upon the expiration of the policy, each renewed for another year, paying $3,600 in cash. The general ledgers of the three companies reported the following balances as of year end, prior to adjustment:

	Company A	Company B	Company C
Prepaid insurance	$ 400	$4,000	$ 600
Insurance expense	3,600	0	3,400

a. Explain how each of the companies accounts for insurance costs.
b. Determine the "correct" amounts that should be reported as "Prepaid insurance" and "Insurance expense."
c. Prepare the adjusting entries, if any, that should be made by each of the firms.

5. *Cost of goods sold is a conglomerate of all costs associated with the manufacture of a product. Convention often determines whether a particular type of cost is to be considered as being associated with the manufacture of a product or with the other activities engaged in by a firm:*

During March a company incurred the following costs, all of which were related directly to the manufacture of its product:

Raw materials	$100,000
Factory labor	200,000
Utility costs for factory	4,000
Depreciation on factory equipment	10,000
Rent on factory building	50,000

The company started and completed 10,000 units of product. There was no opening inventory.
a. How much cost should have been added during the month to "Work in process"?
b. How much cost should have been transferred to "Finished goods"?
c. Assume that the company sold 8,000 units. What amount should it report as "Cost of goods sold"? What amount as "Finished goods inventory"?
d. Assume that at the end of the month the company discovered that it had failed to record the wages of two secretaries. One was employed in the office of the factory, the other in the office of the marketing department. Each was paid $1,500. Comment on how the omission would affect cost of goods sold and finished goods inventory.

6. *Consider the relationship, if any, between revenue earned and cash collected.*

A company holds from a customer a note receivable of $100,000. Interest is payable each month at a rate of 12 percent per year ($1,000 per month). For each of the following independent situations indicate the amounts that the firm should

report on its December 31, 1983 financial statements for (1) interest revenue, (2) interest receivable, and (3) unearned interest.
1. The balance in interest receivable as of January 1, 1983, was $2,000. The company collects $12,000 in interest payments.
2. The balance in interest receivable as of January 1, 1983, was $2,000. The company collects $14,000 in interest payments.
3. The balance in interest receivable as of January 1, 1983, was $2,000. The company collects $15,000 in interest payments.
4. The balance in unearned interest (interest paid by the borrower in advance) as of January 1, 1983, was $3,000. The company collects $9,000 in interest payments.
5. The balance in unearned interest as of January 1, 1983, was $3,000. The company collects $8,000 in interest payments.

7. *Costs must be matched with revenues.*

During the first three years of its existence, Bravo Company's manufacturing costs, end-of-year inventories, and sales were as follows:

Year	Manufacturing Costs	End-of-Year Inventories	Sales
1	$80,000	$ 80,000	None
2	90,000	130,000	$ 60,000
3	30,000	None	250,000

Ignoring all other costs and revenues, determine the income of Bravo Company for each of the three years.

8. *The significant economic (and therefore accounting) event is the declaration of a dividend, not the payment. Which event will serve to reduce retained earnings?*

On December 13, 1983, the board of directors of a company declared a dividend of $.75 per share of common stock. The dividend will be payable on January 18, 1984, to the "stockholders of record" (i.e., to those who owned the stock on a particular date) of January 10, 1984. The company has 100,000 shares of common stock outstanding.
a. Prepare an appropriate journal entry to record the declaration of the dividend.

b. Prepare an appropriate closing entry as of December 31, 1983.

c. Prepare an appropriate journal entry to record payment of the dividend.

9. *Does choice of accounting method affect total reported earnings over the life of an enterprise?*

Suppose that a company was organized on January 1, 1983. In each of the next 10 years it had sales of $100,000; the costs of the goods sold were $80,000 per year. In each year, the company collected in cash 75 percent of the sales of that year plus 25 percent of the sales of the previous year. Similarly, in each year the company paid in cash 75 percent of the costs incurred in that year plus 25 percent of the costs incurred in the previous year. The company ceased operations at the end of year 10. It remained in business in year 11 only to collect outstanding receivables and to liquidate remaining debts.

a. Assuming that the company maintained its accounts on an *accrual* basis, compute total income for the 11-year period. Determine income for each of the 11 individual years.

b. Assume instead that the company maintained its accounts on a cash basis—i.e., recognized revenues and expenses as cash was received or disbursed. Determine total income for the 11-year period as well as income for each of the 11 individual years.

10. *This exercise reviews the basic entries required to account for depreciable assets.*

Prepare journal entries to record the following events:

1. A company purchases two trucks, each for $15,000 cash. The estimated useful life of a truck is five years, after which it has negligible scrap or resale value.

2. The company records first-year depreciation on the trucks.

3. At the beginning of the second year, the company sells one of the trucks for $13,000 cash.

4. The company records second-year depreciation on the remaining truck.

5. At the beginning of the third year, the company sells the second truck for $8,000 cash.

11. *Should a dance studio recognize revenue when it signs a contract and collects cash or when it provides its services? Which is the more significant economic event?*

Foxtrot Dance Studio offers customers a "One-Year Learn to Dance Special." Customers pay $120 at the time they sign a contract and are entitled to four lessons per month for one year.

In November, 10 customers signed contracts and paid "tuition" for the series of lessons. In December, each of the customers took four lessons.

a. Prepare a journal entry to record the sales of the contracts and the collection of the cash. Assume that revenue is to be recognized only as customers actually take their lessons.

b. Prepare any entries that would be appropriate when the customers took their first four lessons in December. (Ignore expenses incurred in connection with the lessons.)

c. Prepare any *closing* entries that might be necessary on December 31.

d. Suppose that the salesmen of the firm are entitled to sales commissions based on the dollar amount of contracts signed. From the perspective of a sales manager, which is the more significant economic event—the signing of a contract, the collection of cash, or the providing of lessons? Comment on why different means of recognizing revenues or expenses are appropriate for financial statements that will be used for different purposes (e.g., evaluating the performance of salesmen as opposed to evaluating the performance of the organization as a whole).

12. *Firms do not have to give instantaneous accounting recognition to all economic events (including the passage of time), but prior to preparing financial statements they must bring the books up to date.*

In each of the following *independent* situations, prepare any necessary journal entries that would be required either to adjust a company's books or to bring them up to date in order to prepare year-end (December 31) financial statements. Assume that closing entries have not yet been made.

1. Property taxes, which amount to $15,000 annually, are payable on the last day of the city's fiscal year, which ends April 30. No property tax accruals have yet been made.

2. Employees are paid each Monday for wages earned during the previous week. December

31 falls on a Wednesday. Weekly payroll (for a five-day work week) is $3,000.

3. As heating oil was purchased it was debited to "fuel expense." As of the end of the year, heating oil which had cost $300 was still on hand.

4. On March 1, the company purchased a one-year fire insurance policy at a cost of $3,600 paid in cash. The entire cost of the policy was charged to "insurance expense."

5. The company is on a periodic inventory basis. After taking year-end inventory and making appropriate adjustments to its accounts it discovered that $400 of inventory was incorrectly omitted from the count.

6. The company is on a periodic inventory basis. After taking year-end inventory and making appropriate adjustments to its accounts it discovered that goods which had cost $1,000 had just recently been purchased. No accounting recognition, however, had been given to either the purchase or the corresponding liability for payment. (Note that since the adjustment to the accounts resulting from the physical inventory count had already been made, the inventory account is *properly* stated.

7. The company ran an advertisement in the December 30th edition of the local newspaper. The company has not yet received a bill for such advertisement or given it any other accounting recognition. The cost of the advertisement was $250.

8. The company is on a periodic inventory basis. After taking year-end inventory and making appropriate adjustments to its accounts it discovered that a purchase of equipment was incorrectly debited to "inventory" rather than to "equipment." The cost of the equipment was $2,100. (The *physical* count was correctly taken; hence the inventory account is correctly stated.)

9. On June 1 the company borrowed $10,000 from a bank. It paid the entire interest for one year ($1,200) in advance at the time it signed the note. The advance payment of interest was properly recorded, but no entries pertaining to the interest have been made since the date of payment.

10. On November 1 customers placed orders for merchandise with a selling price of $15,900. The customers paid in advance, and their payment was properly recorded. The goods were delivered on December 29, but no accounting recognition has been given to the delivery. The company uses a periodic inventory method, and the goods were not included in the December 31 inventory count. (Hence, both inventory and cost of goods sold are correctly stated.)

13. Incorrect journal entries can subsequently be corrected.

As management was about to prepare year-end financial statements, the journal entries indicated below, which were made by an inexperienced bookkeeper, came to its attention. You are to make the journal entries that would be required to correct the errors. (*Hint:* First determine the entry that should have been made; then determine the most efficient means of eliminating the incorrect, and adding the correct, amounts.)

1. A customer made a payment to reduce the balance in his account.

Cash	$7,500	
Sales revenue		$7,500

2. The company sold for $3,000 a machine that had originally cost $4,000 when purchased three years earlier. Accumulated depreciation on the asset amounted to $2,000.

Cash	$3,000	
Sales revenue		$3,000

3. In January the company paid rent for the previous December. Before preparing the year-end financial statements as of December 31 the company had correctly accrued rent for December.

Rent expense	$5,000	
Cash		$5,000

4. The company charged depreciation of one year on equipment that had cost $6,000 and had a useful life of three years with no salvage value.

Allowance for depreciation	$2,000	
Depreciation expense		$2,000

5. The company paid a bill received from its advertising agency for an ad that it had run the

previous year. The company had properly accounted for the ad at the time it was run.

Advertising expense $6,750
    Cash $6,750

6. The company paid $13,000 to Cooks Flight Service for repairs to its corporate jet. It had given no previous accounting recognition to the repair costs.

Fixed assets, airplane $13,000
    Accounts receivable $13,000

14. *The effects of classifying a cost as a product rather than a period cost will depend upon the relationship between number of units produced and number of units sold.*

Management of a corporation is uncertain as to whether certain administrative, transportation, and depreciation costs should be classified as *product* or *period* costs. Such costs average approximately $120,000 per year. It asks your advice as to the significance over the next two years of its decision. Labor and material costs are estimated at $6 per unit. Selling price of the product is $10 per unit.

a. Suppose that in both year 1 and year 2 the company expects to produce and sell 40,000 units per year. What would be the resultant differences in (1) income, (2) ending inventory, and (3) retained earnings for (or after) each of the two years if the company classified the costs as period rather than product costs?

b. Suppose instead that the company expected in year 1 to produce 40,000 units but sell only 30,000 units and in year 2 to produce 30,000 units and sell 40,000 units. What would be the resultant differences in (1) income, (2) ending inventory, and (3) retained earnings for (or after) each of the two years if the company classified the costs as period rather than product costs?

15. *Many companies charge (debit) an account called "Purchases" for all acquisitions of merchandise inventory (instead of debiting "Merchandise inventory"). This practice is acceptable but requires that an adjusting entry be made at year end to eliminate the balance in the purchases account.*

Examination of a company's general ledger as of the end of the year reveals the following account balances (both debit balances) pertaining to merchandise inventory:

    Inventory $100,000
    Purchases   600,000

Upon inquiry, you learn that the balance in inventory represents that at the *beginning* of the year. No entries were made to that account during the year. All purchases during the year were debited to "Purchases." You also learn that a physical count at the end of the year revealed goods on hand of $60,000.

What adjusting entry would you propose assuming that you want to eliminate the balance in the purchases account, to have the inventory account reflect the correct balance of goods on hand at year end, and to have a cost of goods sold account reveal the cost of merchandise sold during the year?

16. *A company can report a profit yet still experience a reduction in cash.*

Comparative balance sheets for House of Clothes, a chain of sportswear shops, for the years 1983 and 1984 are presented in the table following. Also presented is an income statement for 1984. All sales were recorded initially as charge sales. All purchases of merchandise were made "on account."

a. Compute the amount of cash collections made in 1984 as a result of either current year or prior year sales. Be sure to relate sales to accounts receivable (that is, accounts receivable, 12/31/83 + sales − cash collections = accounts receivable, 12/31/84).

b. Compute the amount of cash disbursed in connection with each of the expenses. Be especially careful in computing cash expended, if any, in connection with purchases of inventory and with depreciation. (*Hint:* Compute first the amount of goods actually purchased.) Be sure to relate each expense to a corresponding asset or liability account (e.g., rent expense to prepaid rent; cost of goods sold to inventory).

c. Does the difference between cash received and cash disbursed equal the difference between cash on hand at the beginning of 1984 and cash on hand at the end? (If not, review your computations.)

House of Clothes
Balance Sheet
(in thousands)

	12/31/83		12/31/84	
Cash		$ 4,000		$ 3,800
Accounts receivable		28,000		44,000
Prepaid rent		1,000		—
Inventory		17,000		14,000
Fixed assets	$20,000		$20,000	
Less: Accumulated depreciation	4,000	16,000	8,000	12,000
Total assets		$66,000		$73,800
Accounts payable		$ 2,000		$ 4,000
Accrued salaries payable		3,500		1,000
Accrued interest payable		200		100
Accrued rent payable		—		2,000
Notes payable		4,800		4,800
Common stock		10,000		10,000
Retained earnings		45,500		51,900
Total liabilities and owner's equity		$66,000		$73,800

d. Comment on why net income cannot be used as a measure of cash received or disbursed.

Income Statement
for the Year Ended 12/31/84
(in thousands)

Sales		$220,000
Cost of goods sold		130,000
Gross margin		$ 90,000
Other expenses:		
Salaries	$67,000	
Interest	600	
Rent	12,000	
Depreciation	4,000	83,600
Net income		$ 6,400

17. *Under conventional accounting practices, the greater the number of units produced, the less the cost per unit—and the less the reported cost of goods sold.*

The Prettyman Doll Co. requires $2 of raw materials and $4 of factory labor to produce each doll. In addition the company estimates that depreciation costs on the factory building and equipment as well as other *fixed* factory costs total $40,000 per year. ("Fixed" factory costs, although considered product costs, do not vary with number of units produced. They would be the same regardless of whether the company produced 10,000 or 50,000 dolls per year.) Sales price per doll is $10.

a. In both 1983 and 1984 the company produced 20,000 dolls and sold 20,000 dolls. Compute the manufacturing cost per doll. Determine also gross margin (sales less cost of goods sold) for each of the two periods.

b. Assume instead that in 1983 the company produced 30,000 dolls but sold 20,000 dolls; in 1984 the company produced 10,000 dolls and sold 20,000 dolls. Determine the manufacturing cost per doll in each of the two years. Compute the amount that should be reported as "finished goods inventory" at the end of 1983. Determine also the gross margin for each of the two years.

c. Suppose the company planned to issue additional capital stock in January 1984. The company controller thought it important that the firm impress potential purchasers with a significant growth in earnings. Based on the above analysis, what steps might company management have taken in 1983 to give the *appearance* of improved performance?

18. *This is a challenging exercise that requires an understanding of the flow of costs in a manufacturing operation.*

The following table gives information taken from the ledger accounts of the Wright Manufacturing Co. The figures reported are the total amounts debited or credited to the various accounts during a year. The figures do *not* represent ending balances and do *not* include beginning balances. Some amounts have been omitted. Based on your knowledge of the accounting flow in a manufacturing operation, you are to fill in the missing amounts. That is, you are to determine which accounts are normally associated with debits or credits to other accounts. (For example, by knowing the amount *credited* to accounts payable, you can determine the amount *debited* to raw materials inventory.) No closing entries have yet been made.

	Debits	Credits
Allowance for depreciation (factory)	$ 0	$ 17,000
Depreciation cost (factory)	?	?
Raw materials inventory	?	95,000
Factory labor cost	107,000	107,000
Work in process	?	?
Finished goods	212,000	?
Cost of goods sold	197,000	0
Factory wages payable	105,000	?
Accounts payable[a]	85,000	110,000

[a] Includes only amounts owed in connection with purchases of raw materials.

19. *Ability to evaluate the effect of errors on the income statement and the balance sheet is persuasive evidence of understanding the double-entry bookkeeping system.*

On December 31, at the end of the 1982 annual accounting period, a firm made the following errors:
1. It failed to record $9,000 of accrued salaries.
2. A portion of the company's warehouse was rented on December 1, 1982 at $15,000 per month to a tenant who paid its December, January, and February rents in advance. The

firm did not make an adjustment for the unearned rent on December 31, which had been credited on receipt to the "rent revenue" account.
3. Through an oversight the firm failed to record $24,500 of depreciation on store equipment. The equipment had a useful life of an additional five years. Depreciation was properly recorded in 1983, and no equipment was sold in 1983.
4. The firm failed to accrue one-half year's interest on a note receivable. The $1,000 note was received on July 1, 1981, and was due on June 30, 1983. Interest was at the rate of 6 percent per year, payable each year on June 30.
5. The firm made an error in adding the amounts on the year-end inventory sheets which caused a $7,500 understatement in the merchandise inventory. (Inventory on December 31, 1983, was properly stated.)
6. On January 2, 1982, the company purchased a two-year fire insurance policy for $8,000. It charged the entire amount to "insurance expense."
7. On December 31, 1982, the company declared a dividend of $600,000 payable on January 15, 1983. The bookkeeper failed to record the declaration.
8. The company owned 1,000 shares of General Motors common stock. On December 20, the company received notification from Gooder and Co., the firm's stockbroker, that General Motors had declared and paid a dividend of $1.20 per share. Since Gooder and Co. holds in its own name the shares owned by the company, it credited the company's account for $1,200. The bookkeeper first recorded the dividend in January 1983 when the cash was forwarded to the company.

Under the assumption that none of the errors was explicitly discovered and corrected in 1983 but that some of the errors would automatically be corrected if normal accounting procedures were followed, indicate the effect of each error on the financial statements. In each case, indicate the amount of the overstatement or understatement the error would cause in the assets, liabilities, owners' equity, revenues, expenses, and net income. If the error would have no effect on an item, then so state. The first one is done for you as an example:

	1982 Income Statement			December 31, 1982 Balance Sheet			1983 Income Statement		
Error	Revenues	Expense	Net income	Assets	Liabilities	Owners' equity	Revenues	Expense	Net income
1	None	Under $9,000	Over $9,000	None	Under $9,000	Over $9,000	None	Over $9,000	Under $9,000

20. *This problem provides a review of the accounting cycle from unadjusted trial balance to financial statements.*

The following table gives the unadjusted trial balance of the Coronet Company as of December 31, 1983, as well as selected other information.

The Coronet Company
Unadjusted Trial Balance
12/31/83

Cash	$ 3,000	
Accounts receivable	5,000	
Merchandise inventory	155,000	
Prepaid rent	1,500	
Furniture and fixtures	15,000	
Accumulated depreciation		$ 6,000
Accounts payable		9,000
Notes payable		6,000
Sales revenue		220,000
Selling expenses	55,000	
General expenses	18,000	
Interest expense	800	
Tax expense	3,500	
Capital received from stockholders		6,000
Retained earnings		9,800
	$256,800	$256,800

Other information:

1. Interest on the note, at a rate of 12 percent, is due semiannually, April 30 and October 31.
2. Useful life of the furniture and fixtures is five years with no salvage value. No depreciation has yet been recorded for the year.
3. The company employs a periodic inventory system. A physical count at year end indicates merchandise on hand of $24,000.

4. The company last paid its rent on December 1. Such payment was intended to cover the month of December. (Rent expense is included among "general expense." The payment was properly recorded.)
5. On December 31, the board of directors declared a cash dividend, payable January 12, of $4,000.
6. $700 of advertising costs were incorrectly charged to "general expenses" rather than "selling expenses."
7. Estimated taxes for the year are $8,500. Of these only $3,500 have yet been paid.
   a. Prepare all necessary updating and adjusting entries.
   b. Post such entries to T accounts.
   c. Prepare a year-end income statement, balance sheet, and statement of changes in retained earnings.

21. *The accounting cycle in manufacturing firms is no different from that in other types of enterprises, but it is especially important that period costs be distinguished from product costs.*

The Highbridge Products Co. began operations on January 1, 1983. The following events took place in January:

1. On January 2 the owners of the company contributed $25,000 in cash to start the business.
2. The company borrowed $10,000 from a local bank. It agreed to make annual interest payments at a rate of 12 percent and to repay the loan in its entirety at the end of three years.
3. The company rented manufacturing and office space. It paid three months' rent in advance. Rent is $400 per month.
4. The company purchased manufacturing equip-

ment at a cost of $35,000 and office furniture and equipment at a cost of $4,800. Both purchases were made on account.

5. The firm purchased raw materials at a cost of $7,000 cash. Of these, raw materials that cost $6,000 were placed in production (added to work in process).

6. The firm hired and paid in cash factory workers, $6,000, and office workers, $1,500. The costs of the factory wages were added to work in process; the costs of the office workers were considered to be period costs and thereby charged directly to an expense account.

7. Factory maintenance costs incurred during the month were $450; factory utility costs were $600. Neither costs have yet been paid. Both were added to work in process.

8. The company recorded depreciation for the month: manufacturing equipment, $1,000; office equipment and furniture, $100. The depreciation costs on the manufacturing equipment were added to work in process; those on the office equipment and furniture were considered to be period costs and charged directly to an expense account.

9. The company gave recognition to interest and rent costs for the month (see events 2 and 3 and determine the appropriate charge for one month). Seventy-five percent of the rent costs were allocated to the factory and added to work in process. The remaining portion of the rent costs, as well as the entire amount of the interest costs, were considered period costs.

10. The company completed, and transferred from work in process to finished goods inventory, goods that had cost $14,000 to manufacture.

11. The company sold for $20,000 (on account) goods that had cost $13,000 to manufacture.

12. Selling and other administrative costs paid in cash were $1,000.
    a. Prepare journal entries to reflect the events that took place in January.
    b. Post the journal entries to T accounts.
    c. Prepare a month-end income statement and balance sheet.

22. *This problem is designed to illustrate a year-end work sheet, a device useful for the preparation of reports from an unadjusted trial balance.*

The end-of-year *unadjusted* trial balance of the Columbia Flying Service is indicated below. The following additional information has come to your attention:

1. Instructor salaries for the last week of the month have not yet been recorded. They will be payable the first week of the new year. Salaries for the one week are $13,500.

2. In the course of the previous two weeks, lessons were given that had been paid for in advance. The amount charged for the lessons was $6,500.

3. No depreciation has been recorded in 1983. The useful life of the planes is estimated at 10 years (no salvage value) and that of the equipment at 7 years (also no salvage value).

4. Rent for December, $1,000, has not yet been paid.

5. The company purchases a one-year insurance policy each year which takes effect on July 1. The entire cost of the current year's policy has been charged to "insurance expense." The 12/31/83 balance in "prepaid insurance" is also that on 1/1/83. No entries to the account have been made during the year.

6. Interest on the $60,000 note outstanding is payable twice each year, April 1 and October 1. The annual rate of interest is 8 percent. The note was issued on April 1, 1983; the amount of interest expense represents the first interest payment, which was made on October 1.

7. A physical count of parts on hand indicated an unexplained shortage of parts that had cost $2,000. No adjustment to inventory has yet been made.

8. All purchases of supplies are charged (debited) to "supplies expense." The balance in "supplies inventory" represents supplies on hand at the beginning of the year. A physical count on December 31, 1983, indicated supplies currently on hand of $4,000.

9. On December 30, the company flew a charter for which it has not yet billed the customer and which it has not yet recorded in the accounts. The customer will be charged $6,800.

10. Based on preliminary computations, the firm estimates that income taxes for the year will be $22,000.

a. Prepare all journal entries that would be necessary to adjust and bring the accounts up to date. (Add any additional account titles that you believe to be necessary.)

b. On a 10-column sheet of accounting paper, copy the trial balance that follows: Leave an additional six or seven lines between the last account balance and the totals to accommodate accounts to be added by the adjusting entries. Use two columns for the account titles and two for the unadjusted account balances. Label the next two columns "Adjustments" (debits and credits), the next two "Income statement" (debits and credits), and the last two "Balance sheet" (debits and credits).

Columbia Flying Service
Unadjusted Trial Balance
December 31, 1983

Cash	$ 37,500	
Accounts receivable	45,000	
Supplies inventory	2,000	
Parts inventory	24,000	
Equipment	42,000	
Equipment, accumulated depreciation		$ 6,000
Planes	216,000	
Planes, accumulated depreciation		71,000
Prepaid insurance	15,000	
Accounts payable		8,000
Lessons paid for but not yet given		28,000
Notes payable		60,000
Common stock		10,000
Retained earnings		78,100
Revenues from lessons		895,000
Revenues from charters		156,000
Salaries	623,000	
Fuel expense	189,000	
Maintenance expense	51,000	
Supplies expense	6,000	
Insurance expense	34,000	
Advertising expense	13,000	
Rent expense	11,000	
Interest expense	2,400	
Licenses and fees	1,200	
	$1,312,100	$1,312,100

c. Instead of posting the journal entries to T accounts, post them to the appropriate accounts in the column "Adjustments." When you have finished posting the entries, sum the two columns and make certain that the totals of debits and credits are equal.

d. Add (or subtract, as required) across the columns, and indicate the total of each account in the appropriate column under the income statement or balance sheet. Take care. Remember that credits have to be subtracted from debits. Make certain that amounts are transferred to the proper column; it is easy to make an error.

e. Add each of the four income statement and balance sheet columns. The difference between the debit and credit columns of the income statement should be the net income for the year. The difference between the debit and credit columns of the balance sheet should also be the income for the year. If the two differences are not equal, then an error has been made. Why shouldn't the balance sheet balance; i.e., why shouldn't the debits of the balance sheet equal the credits? Look carefully at the balance indicated for retained earnings. Is such balance the before or after "closing balance"? Does it include income of the current year?

f. From the work sheet, prepare in good form both an income statement and a balance sheet. Remember that retained earnings have to be adjusted to take into account income for the current year.

SOLUTIONS TO EXERCISE FOR REVIEW AND SELF-TESTING

1. $3,600,000 (12 months × $300,000 per month), regardless, of how much cash was actually collected.

2. Unearned rent $300,000
       Rent revenue $300,000
   To recognize rent revenue in January.

3. a. $3,600,000 (12 months × $300,000 per month) should have been recognized in rent revenue. Rent revenue is understated by $1,200,000

($3,600,000 minus the $2,400,000 of revenue actually recognized).

b. The balance in "Unearned rent" should be zero: the tenant is no longer "ahead" in rent payments.

c. The balance in "Rent receivable" should be $600,000. The firm began the year "owing" the tenant $600,000 in services; it earned $3,600,000 and was entitled to $3,000,000 from the tenant. It collected, however, only $2,400,000; it is owed the remaining $600,000.

d. Unearned rent $600,000
   Rent receivable   600,000
       Rent revenue $1,200,000

To adjust the year-end rent accounts.

4. $120,000 should be reported as "Cleaning expense" regardless of the amount of cash paid.
   1. $40,000 should be reported as a liability, "Cleaning costs payable."
   2. $20,000 should be reported as an asset, "Prepaid cleaning costs."

5. The reported revenue or expense depends upon the value of the services provided or received, regardless of the amount of cash received or paid. The difference between the value of the services provided or received and the amount of cash received would be added to or subtracted from a related asset or liability account.

REVENUES 5
AND EXPENSES

ACCOUNTING CHOICES IN PERSPECTIVE

In this and subsequent chapters alternative means of accounting for economic events shall be presented and examined. The aim of accounting is to provide information about the financial activities of an organization to, among others, owners, investors, creditors, managers, taxing authorities, regulatory agencies, and employees. Different users have different information requirements. The accounting principle or procedure that results in information that is most useful to one type of user may not necessarily be that which best satisfies the information demands of others. The following list of purposes to which accounting information is put is suggestive of why different principles or procedures may better serve the information requirements of some users than others.

✓ 1. Internal control over, and measurement of, cash flows. Some organizations, particularly small single proprietorships, want only the bookkeeping benefits of the double-entry accounting system so that errors can be reduced and control over assets established. The only measurement of performance with which they are concerned is the extent to which cash receipts exceed cash disbursements. For organizations of this type, the cash, rather than the accrual basis of accounting may be most appropriate.

✓ 2. Determination of income tax obligations. The Internal Revenue service permits—sometimes even requires—firms to prepare their tax returns in accord with regulations that are at variance with generally accepted accounting principles as set forth by the Financial Accounting Standards Board or the Securities and Exchange Commission.

✓3. Providing information for specific decisions. Organizations are sometimes required to provide information to a specific user for a specific purpose. For example, a firm may be asked to provide data to an insurance company regarding earnings lost as a consequence of a fire, to a bank as part of a credit review or to a potential customer who wants assurance that the company has the financial wherewithal to fulfill an order. Such statements need not—and sometimes should not—be prepared in accordance with generally accepted accounting principles. They can be prepared in accord with principles that provide the most useful information to those who will use them. Whereas generally accepted accounting principles, for instance, dictate that inventories be stated at the amount paid for them, an insurance company might request that the reports take into account the amount that would have to be paid to replace them.

✓4. Reporting on managerial stewardship. Parties, both internal and external to an organization, require information as to how well managers have carried out their duties. The type of information that best facilitates an evaluation depends very much on the subject and the purpose of the evaluation. Insofar, for example, as the ability of a manager or management team to reduce costs is under review, the report should focus on costs that are within their control. Costs that are the results of prior decisions (e.g., previous acquisition of equipment) or depend on actions taken by others (the assignment of a share of property taxes to a particular division) should be excluded from the analysis or set forth separately. By contrast, investors usually want to determine the overall performance of management in increasing corporate profitability; the type of review that they carry out generally requires that all flows of resources, regardless of the extent to which present individual officers made the initial decision to acquire or expend them, be taken into account.

✓5. Assessing the ability of an organization to generate sufficient cash to meet its obligations and provide a return to its owners in order to make investment and credit decisions. Both investors and creditors want assurance that they will receive a return on any funds provided to an organization. They hope to receive a greater amount of cash than they contributed.

The financial reports of corporations that are filed with the SEC and distributed to stockholders are intended to provide information that is useful in making rational decisions as to whether resources should be committed to the firm. The principles and guidelines established by the rule-making authorities are intended to assure that this function of financial reporting is adequately fulfilled. The rule-making authorities center attention on this function because, unlike other groups of users (such as managers and taxing authorities) potential investors and creditors generally do not have the authority or financial influence to prescribe the information they want and must rely on the information that management communicates to them.

The group of investors and creditors to which external financial reports is targeted is broad and diverse. Not only do individual investors and creditors make different types of decisions, but the models and criteria that they use are not the same. The principles and practices directed by the rule-making authorities represent choices and compromises among competing demands for information. One key to successful investment and credit analysis is the ability to discern the limitations of the principles for the decision at hand and to overcome them by making proper adjustments.

STATEMENT OF THE PROBLEM

The Earnings Process

In the previous chapter it was emphasized that revenues should be *realized* (accorded accounting recognition and considered to result in an increase in net assets) when *earned*, not necessarily when the related cash is received. Omitted, however, was a discussion of when revenues should be considered to be "earned."

Recall the essence of the definition of revenues:

> The inflow of assets into the firm as a result of production or delivery of goods or the rendering of services.

In the illustrations up to this point in the text, revenues have been recognized either with the passage of time (when earned as rent or interest) or when goods or services have been delivered to the customer (when earned in connection with sales transactions). Relatively few types of revenues can appropriately be considered to be earned with the passage of time, since relatively few types of goods or services are provided uniformly over time. Moreover, recognition of revenue at the time that goods or services are delivered to the customer may, for many types of business transactions, result in financial statements that are misleading to both management and investors. Consider, for example, two situations.

> Company A produces aircraft carriers under contract to the U.S. government. On January 2, 1983, the company signed a contract to produce one carrier at a sales price of $800 million. During 1983 and 1984 the company constructed the carrier. In 1985 it delivered the vessel to the government. Cost of producing the carrier was $600 million.

If Company A were to report revenue at the time of sale (when the carrier was de-livered to the government), then it would report zero revenue in both 1983 and 1984, the years of construction prior to delivery. In 1985, when the carrier was delivered, it would report $800 million in revenue. Costs of production would be *capitalized* and remain in asset accounts until charged as an expense in the period in which the revenue was recognized. Hence, ignoring certain *period* costs, the company would report expenses of zero in 1983 and 1984 and of $600 million in 1985. Income would be zero in 1983 and 1984, and $200 million in 1985. Managers or investors who rely upon earnings of the past as a guide to those of the future could easily be misled, after two successive years bereft of profits, into predicting an equally dismal future. In 1985, however, the company seemed to experience a remarkable upturn.

But was the company really $200 million better off in 1985 than in either 1983 or 1984? If revenue is recognized only at time of sale, then do the financial statements really give a meaningful picture of the results of the company's economic activity in each of the three years? Would not an investor have received more relevant and useful information if income of the company had been matched more closely to its productive effort?

> Company B sells furniture on the *installment* plan. Customers make a small down payment and have up to three years to pay the balance of the purchase price. The company sells to poor credit risks. As a consequence, it is unable to make meaningful estimates of the amount it will be able to collect and exerts far more effort (in both time and cost) in collecting its accounts than in making the initial sales. In 1983 the company had "sales" of $1,000,000 but collected only $200,000 in cash. The cost of the merchandise sold was $400,000. Other operating costs were $150,000.

If Company B were to report revenues at the time of sale, then in 1983 it would report revenues of $1,000,000, cost of goods sold of $400,000, and other operating expenses of $150,000—income of $450,000.

But how much confidence could a stockholder place in the reported income? Of the $1,000,000, of reported revenues, only $200,000 has been collected in cash. How much of the remaining $800,000 will be collected is uncertain and cannot readily be estimated. Moreover, although the company has sold and delivered the merchandise to its customers, a major part of its economic effort—the collection of its accounts—has yet to be exerted. Can it really be said, therefore, that the company is $450,000 better off at the end of 1983 than it was at the beginning? Might not the interests of investors be better served if recognition of the sales revenue were deferred until ultimate collection became more certain and a greater portion of economic activity had been exerted?

Need for Periodic Reports

The problem of determining when and how much revenue has, in fact, been earned exists only because managers, investors and other users of financial information insist on receiving *periodic* reports of income. If they were content to receive a single report of profit or loss *after* the enterprise had completed its operations and was ready to return to stockholders their original investment plus any accumulated earnings, then determination of income would be a simple matter: Subtract from the total amount either available or already distributed to stockholders the amount of their total contributions to the firm. The difference would be income over the life of the enterprise. Indeed, in the sixteenth and seventeenth centuries, companies

were frequently formed with an expected useful life of only a few years—perhaps to carry out a specific mission, such as the charter of a ship for a single voyage. Investors in such companies were satisfied to wait until the companies were liquidated to get reports of their earnings.

Most companies today have indeterminate lives, and both owners and managers demand periodic reports of economic progress. Since many transactions are not completed in the same accounting period in which they are started, accountants are forced to make determinations of when and how much revenue should be assigned to specific periods.

IMPACT UPON RELATED ACCOUNTS

Expenses

The issue of revenue realization does not, of course, have an impact solely upon revenue accounts. Directly affected also are both expense accounts and, equally significantly, balance sheet accounts. As pointed out previously, the question of when to recognize *expenses* is inherently tied to that of when to recognize revenues. To the extent that specific costs can be associated with the revenues that they generate, they are *matched* to and charged as expenses in the *same accounting period* in which recognition is given to the revenues. Costs that cannot be directly associated with specific revenues are considered *period* costs and are charged as incurred. Insofar as costs *can* be matched to specific revenues, they may be charged as expenses in an accounting period either before or after they have actually been incurred. In the previous chapter, for example, it was emphasized that costs of production may be incurred in one period but not be reported as expenses (cost of goods sold) until a later period, when the goods are actually sold.

Many situations occur, however, in which costs should properly be reported as expenses in a period earlier than that in which they are incurred. Suppose a company sells and delivers manufacturing equipment. The company guarantees to provide maintenance service on the machines for one year after sale. The cost of providing the maintenance service is a cost that can be directly associated with the revenue generated by the sale of the equipment. It follows, therefore, that it should be *matched* with the sales revenue and charged as an expense (even if an estimate of the actual cost has to be made) in the same accounting period as that in which the related revenue is recognized. The journal entries required to implement this matching approach will be illustrated later in this chapter.

Balance Sheet Accounts

The valuation of assets, liabilities, and owners' equity is also related to the recog-

nition of revenue. Revenue has been defined as an inflow of cash or other assets attributable to the goods or services provided by the firm. When recognition is given to revenue, so also it must be given to the resultant increase in assets or decrease in liabilities. Indeed, recognition of revenue is equivalent to the recognition of an increase of owners' equity (i.e., in retained earnings). An increase of owners' equity must be accompanied by an increase in assets or a decrease in liabilities.

Exhibit 5-1 illustrates the operating cycle of a typical business. The enterprise starts with an asset, generally cash, and continuously transforms it into other assets—first to materials, equipment, and labor and then to work in process, to finished goods, to accounts receivable, and eventually back to cash. If the company earns a profit, then ending cash is greater than beginning cash. The critical question facing the firm is at which point in the production cycle should the increase in the "size" of the asset package

EXHIBIT 5-1

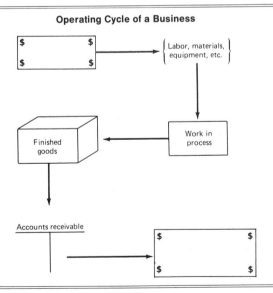

Operating Cycle of a Business

be recognized; at what point in time is the enterprise "better off" than it was before; what should be the *critical event* that triggers recognition of revenue?

Most commonly, especially in a manufacturing or retail operation, the firm recognizes the increase in the value of the assets at time of sale—when goods or services are delivered to customers. By selecting that point as the critical event, however, it is implicitly ignoring the value of the entire production cycle up to that point. It is asserting that all previous transactions involved nothing more than exchanges of assets and liabilities of equal magnitude—that the level of net assets remained unchanged. It is also implying that all subsequent transactions (e.g., collection of cash, fulfillment of warranty obligations, etc.) will also involve nothing more than exchanges of assets and liabilities of equal magnitude and that such exchanges will have no effect on the new level of net assets.

Point of sale is a *convenient* point to recognize revenue for *most* businesses; it is clearly unsuitable for *all* businesses. It is inappropriate in situations in which delivery of goods provides little assurance that the amount owed by the customer will be collectible. Recognition of revenue upon sale may be equally inappropriate where the enterprise has completed a significant portion of its economic activity and eventual collection of cash from a known customer is certain long before the goods are actually delivered to him.

GUIDELINES FOR REVENUE RECOGNITION

There are, unfortunately, no pervasive principles as to when revenue should be recognized. At least four criteria, however, are cited in the accounting literature and have been generally adhered to in practice. Revenue should be recognized as soon as

1. The firm has exerted a substantial portion of its production and sales effort;
2. The revenue can be objectively measured;
3. The major portion of costs have been incurred, and the remaining costs can be estimated with reasonable reliability and precision; and
4. Eventual collection of a substantial portion of cash can reasonably be assured; an estimate can be made of the portion of cash that will prove to be uncollectible.

RECOGNITION AT TIME OF SALE

For most manufacturing and retail concerns, the four criteria of revenue recognition are first satisfied at the point of sale. At that time the firm has exerted a major portion of its economic activity, including its sales efforts. A firm price has been established. Most of the costs have been incurred, even though there might be additional costs, such as those pertaining to product warranties, guaranteed maintenance, and collection of receivables, that might have to be incurred in the future. Collection of cash usually can reasonably be assured, although the firm may have to estimate and make allowances for merchandise that will be returned and customers who will default on their accounts.

RECOGNITION DURING PRODUCTION

For some firms, especially those which provide goods or services under long-term contracts, the dual accounting objectives of providing information that is both relevant and objective can best be served by recognizing revenue as production takes place rather than waiting until point of delivery. Recognition of revenue during the entire production process enables firms to avoid the erratic—and often misleading—pattern of income that may result from point of delivery revenue recognition (as was illustrated earlier in the aircraft carrier example).

Percentage of Completion Method

A widely used means of recognizing revenue throughout the entire production process is known as the *percentage of completion method*. On any given contract, the proportion of total contract price to be recognized as revenue in each accounting period is the percentage of the total project completed during that period. If 20 percent of the project is completed in a particular year, then 20 percent of the expected total revenue from the project would be recognized.

The percentage of completion or any other production-oriented means of revenue recognition is appropriate only when total costs of completing the project can be estimated with reasonable reliability and precision, the contract price is fixed and certain to be collected (as is often the case when the contract is with a government agency or major corporation), and there can be no question about the ability of the firm to complete the project and to have it accepted by the customer.

Another example of a situation in which revenue could be recognized in the course of production would be that in which a management consulting firm undertakes to advise a client on the installation of a new accounting system. Assuming that the consulting firm bills its client on the basis of number of hours of service rendered, then each of the four criteria would be reasonably satisfied as the consulting engagement progresses.

RECOGNITION AT COMPLETION OF PRODUCTION

For those companies that face ready markets and stable prices for their products, the four basic criteria can often be satisfied at the completion of the production process. Prior to 1972, the U.S. government guaranteed to purchase all gold offered to it at a price of $35 per ounce. From the standpoint of a gold mining company, as soon as its production process was complete, its revenue could be objectively determined; it would have few remaining expenses (e.g., storage and transportation), all of which could be readily estimated; and sale of product and collectibility of cash would be assured. Not only would the accounting interests of objectivity and relevance be best served by recognizing revenue as soon as the mining process was complete, but delay of recognition until actual sale would, by valuing gold at its cost to acquire rather than at the amount at which it was certain to be sold, understate the assets of the company.

Few situations today are as well defined as that of the pre-1972 gold mining company inasmuch as the U.S. government presently purchases gold only as needed and at market prices. Nevertheless, recognition of revenue at completion of the productive process is appropriate for those concerns which have negligible marketing costs, face stable prices, and can readily sell all goods that they produce; they can reasonably satisfy the four criteria of revenue recognition at such time.

RECOGNITION UPON COLLECTION OF CASH

In some situations, the four criteria will not be satisfied until the production and sale processes are complete *and* cash has been collected. In those cases it is necessary to delay recognition of revenue until cash is actually in hand. In the previous installment-sales illustration, for example, the company sold to customers whose credit ratings were poor and from whom the company had no assurance that it would be able to collect its accounts receivable. Prudence dictates that no revenue be recognized until the company is certain that its customer receivables can be transformed into cash.

Obviously every company takes a risk when it sells on credit. In most situations, however, the extent of bad-debt losses can reasonably be estimated at time of sale. Only when such losses cannot be estimated would the interests of the users of financial statements be best served by delaying the recognition of revenue. If recognition were delayed, the related assets would be reported at their cost to produce or acquire rather than at the amount that the firm will eventually realize when it actually collects the cash.

Installment Method

The cash collection or *installment* basis of revenue recognition is not widely used today to account for routine merchandise sales—not even those in which the customer pays "on time" or on the "installment plan"—since it is generally possible to make reasonable estimates of credit losses. It is, however, widely used to account for certain types of real estate or other property transactions in which the collectibility of the receivable held by the seller is questionable. A builder, for example, might sell a recently constructed shopping center to a group of investors. The builder accepts from the investors a note for a portion of the selling price with the understanding that the investors will be able to make payments on the note only insofar as they are able to rent the stores in the shopping center. If there is uncertainty as to whether

sufficient space in the shopping center can be rented to enable the investors to make payments on their note, the builder would delay recognition of revenue on the sale of the property until cash is actually in hand.

Relevance and Objectivity

In evaluating the alternative means of revenue recognition to account for specific types of transactions, it is helpful to keep in mind the standards of reporting set forth in Chapter 1. Accounting information must be both *relevant* and *objective*. The cash basis of revenue recognition generally provides the most objective or verifiable information. By the time revenue is recognized, eventual realization is virtually certain as cash is already in hand. The methods which recognize revenue at an earlier stage in the earning process are less objective since doubts may remain as to whether cash will in fact be collected, but insofar as they provide a better indication of a company's economic effort and the rewards that will *most probably* accrue from the effort, they may result in reports that more readily facilitate financial decisions.

ANALYSIS OF TRANSACTIONS

The impact of the alternative bases of revenue recognition on revenues and expenses as well as on assets and liabilities can readily be seen when transactions are analyzed in journal entry form. The journal entry is an expression of the principles previously set forth. The journal entry process may sometimes appear a bit tricky, but it can be simplified if a few guidelines are kept in mind.

1. In those periods in which revenue is to be recognized (and *only* in such periods) a revenue account must be credited. Since recognition of revenue implies an enhancement of net assets, a corresponding debit

must be made to an asset or liability account.

2. In the periods in which revenue is recognized (and *only* in such periods) an expense account must be debited to give recognition to the related costs. The proportion of total expected costs that is charged as an expense in any particular period would be equal to the proportion of total anticipated revenues that is recognized in that period. Since recognition of expenses implies a reduction in net assets, a corresponding credit must be made to either an asset or a liability account. (This guideline gives effect to the *matching* principle, which holds that expenses must be matched with the revenues with which they can be associated.)

3. In all periods in which revenue is *not* recognized, transactions involve *only* exchanges of assets and liabilities; hence, only asset and liability accounts should be debited or credited.

Some examples will serve to illustrate these guidelines.

Example 1   Recognition of Revenue at Time of Sale—Warranty Obligation Outstanding

The Orange Equipment Co., in 1983, purchases equipment (intended for resale) for $50,000 cash. In 1984 it sells the equipment for $80,000 on account, giving the buyer a one-year warranty against defects. The company estimates that its cost of making repairs under the warranty will be $5,000. In 1985 the company collects the full sales price from the purchaser and incurs $5,000 in repair costs prior to the expiration of the warranty.

1983
(a)

Merchandise inventory		
(asset +)	$50,000	
Cash (asset −)		$50,000

To record the purchase of the equipment.

One asset has been exchanged for another.

1984
(b)

Accounts receivable		
(asset +)	$80,000	
Sales revenue (revenue +)		$80,000

To record the sale of the equipment.

Revenue is recognized at point of sale.

(c)

Cost of goods sold		
(expense +)	$50,000	
Warranty expense		
(expense +)	5,000	
Merchandise inventory		
(asset −)		$50,000
Warranty liability		
(liability +)		5,000

To record the expenses associated with the revenue recognized.

Every expense associated with the revenue must be recognized. The warranty expense charged and the warranty liability credited represent an *estimate* of costs to be incurred in the future. Since such costs can be directly related to the sales revenue, they must be recorded in the same accounting period in which the revenue is recorded.

1985
(d)

Cash (asset +)	$80,000	
Accounts receivable		
(asset −)		$80,000

To record customer payment.

(e)

Warranty liability		
(liability −)	$ 5,000	
Cash (asset −)		$ 5,000

To record costs incurred to fulfill the warranty obligations.

The costs incurred to make repairs required under the warranty are *charged* (debited) against the liability that was established at the time the costs were charged as expenses. No additional revenues or expenses are recognized when repairs are actually made. The level of net assets remains the same. In the event that the original estimate of warranty costs proves to be incorrect, then an adjustment can be made as soon as the error becomes known. Thus, if costs were greater than $5,000, the additional amount would be charged as an expense when incurred. If less, then at the expiration of the warranty, the warranty liability account would be debited (decreased) and the warranty expense account credited (decreased) for the difference. (The credit to the warranty expense account will have the effect of reducing warranty expenses in a year subsequent to that in which the initial sale was made.)

Example 2   Recognition of Revenue during Production

The construction of the aircraft carrier described earlier can be used to illustrate the approach to recognizing revenue in which the amount of revenue recognized in any given period depends on the percentage of the entire project completed in that period. Company A contracts to build a carrier at a price of $800 million. It estimates that total construction costs will be $600 million. In 1983 it begins construction and incurs $120 million in costs; in 1984 it incurs $300 million, and in 1985 it incurs $180 million and completes the project. In 1985 the company collects the full contract price from the government.*

---

* The example is oversimplified for purposes of illustration. In practice, the government would probably make periodic cash payments to the contractor during construction of the vessel. The timing of the cash collections, however, would have no impact upon the timing of the revenue recognition.

1983

(a)

Construction in progress at cost (asset +)	$120,000,000
Cash (asset −)	$120,000,000

To record costs incurred in construction of the carrier.

This entry summarizes the effect of a number of entries, which would be made as construction progresses, involving various labor, material, and overhead accounts.

(b)

Construction in progress at contract value (asset +)	$160,000,000
Revenue from construction (revenue +)	$160,000,000

To record revenue based on percentage of completion.

(c)

Expenses relating to revenue from construction (expense +)	$120,000,000
Construction in progress at cost (asset −)	$120,000,000

To record expenses pertaining to construction.

The company has completed 20 percent of the project (percentage of completion in this example is assumed to be equal to the proportion of estimated total costs already incurred). It is therefore appropriate to recognize 20 percent of *both* estimated revenues and expenses. It will report revenues of $160 million, expenses of $120 million, and income of $40 million. The combined effect of entries (b) and (c) is to increase the value of the construction in progress (an asset) by the amount of the income recognized. An asset ("Construction in progress at contract value") is increased by the amount of revenue recognized. Another asset ("Construction in progress at cost") is reduced by the amount of expense charged. As a consequence, construction in progress is now recorded at sales value, whereas, until entries (b) and (c) were made, it was recorded at cost.

The entries for 1984 are similar to those for 1983

1984

(d)

Construction in progress at		
cost (asset +)	$300,000,000	
Cash (asset −)		$300,000,000

To record costs incurred in construction of the carrier.

(e)

Construction in progress at contract		
value (asset +)	$400,000,000	
Revenue from construction		
(revenue +)		$400,000,000

To record revenue based on percentage of completion.

(f)

Expenses relating to revenue		
from construction		
(expense +)	$300,000,000	
Construction in progress at		
cost (asset −)		$300,000,000

To record expenses pertaining to construction.

In 1984 an additional 50 percent of construction is completed; hence it is necessary to recognize 50 percent of *both* total revenues and total estimated expenses. The company will report revenues of $400 million, expenses of $300 million, and income of $100 million. By the conclusion of 1984 the firm will have reported income, for the two-year period combined, of $140 million: 70 percent of total expected income of $200 million. The work in progress will be stated at $560 million, which is $140 million more than its actual cost of $420 million.

1985

The entries for 1985 correspond to those of the preceding years; additional entries are required, however, to record the completion and delivery of the ship and the subsequent collection of cash.

(g)

Construction in progress at		
cost (asset +)	$180,000,000	
Cash (asset −)		$180,000,000

To record the cost incurred in the construction of the carrier.

(h)

Construction in progress at contract		
value (asset +)	$240,000,000	
Revenue from construction		
(revenue +)		$240,000,000

To record revenue based on percentage of completion.

(i)

Expenses relating to revenue		
from construction		
(expense +)	$180,000,000	
Construction in progress at		
cost (asset −)		$180,000,000

To record expenses pertaining to construction.

These entries are identical in form to those made in 1983 and 1984.

(j)

Completed ship at contract

value (asset+) $800,000,000

    Construction in

      progress at contract

      value (asset−) $800,000,000

To record completion of the carrier.

This entry simply reclassifies the asset.

(k)

Accounts receivable

  (asset+) $800,000,000

    Completed ship at contract

      value (asset−) $800,000,000

To record delivery of the ship.

The completed ship is delivered. The purchaser is now indebted to the company for the contract price of the ship.

(l)

Cash (asset+) $800,000,000

    Accounts receivable

      (asset−) $800,000,000

To record the collection of cash.

The cash has now been collected; the manufacturing cycle is now complete.

In 1985, the company will report revenues of $240 million, expenses of $180 million, and income of $60 million. The entries are summarized in Exhibit 5-2. Upon completion of the ship the company will have expended $600 million in cash to construct a ship which will be valued on its books at $800 million. Over the three-year period it will have recognized revenues of $800 million, expenses of $600 million, and income of $200 million.

Example 3 Recognition of Revenue at Completion of Production

In 1983 New York Instruments Co. receives an order from an electronics manufacturer to produce 10,000 units of a part used in the production of television sets. The purchaser agrees to pay $10 a unit for the part, but under the terms of the contract the seller is to store and retain title to the goods until they are needed by the purchaser. Payment is to be made upon delivery of the goods. Cost of producing the part is $6 per unit. New York Instruments elects to recognize revenue upon completion of production. At that time the four criteria are satisfied; revenue can be objectively measured, all major costs have been incurred (storage costs are considered to be negligible), the major part of productive effort has been exerted, and collection of cash is virtually certain.

Assume that the firm begins production of the parts in 1983 and completes and delivers the parts in 1984. Each of the following entries summarizes several individual entries that would be made as costs are incurred and the groups of units are completed and delivered.

During Production—1983, 1984

(a)

Work in process

  (asset+) $60,000

    Cash (asset−) $60,000

To record costs of production.

One asset is exchanged for another. (In practice costs would be charged first to manufacturing accounts, such as labor and raw materials. They would then be transferred to work in process.)

EXHIBIT 5-2

Recognition of Revenue during Production

Cash

Bal. 1/1/83		xxx	**(a)** 120,000,000	1983
(1) 1985	800,000,000		**(d)** 300,000,000	1984
			(g) 180,000,000	1985

(200,000,000)

Construction in progress at cost

(a) 1983	120,000,000	**(c)** 120,000,000	1983
(d) 1984	300,000,000	**(f)** 300,000,000	1984
(g) 1985	180,000,000	**(i)** 180,000,000	1985

(0)

Construction in progress at contract value

(b) 1983	160,000,000	**(j)** 800,000,000	1985
(e) 1984	400,000,000		
(h) 1985	240,000,000		

(0)

Completed ship at contract value

| **(j)** 1985 | 800,000,000 | **(k)** 800,000,000 | 1985 |

(0)

Accounts receivable

| **(k)** 1985 | 800,000,000 | **(l)** 800,000,000 | 1985 |

(0)

Revenue from construction[a]

		(b) 160,000,000	1983
		(e) 400,000,000	1984
		(h) 240,000,000	1985

(800,000,000)

Expenses relating to revenue from construction[a]

(c) 1983	120,000,000		
(f) 1984	300,000,000		
(i) 1985	180,000,000		

(600,000,000)

[a] To be *closed* to retained earnings at the end of each year.

At Completion of Production—1984
(b)

Finished goods at cost
(asset+) $60,000
    Work in process
    (asset−) $60,000
To record completion of goods produced.

Costs are transferred from one asset account to another.

(c)

Finished goods at
market value
(asset+) $100,000
    Manufacturing
    revenue
    (revenue+) $100,000
To recognize revenue upon completion of goods manufactured.

(d)

Cost of goods manu-
factured (expense+) $60,000
    Finished goods at
    cost (asset−) $60,000
To record the expense pertaining to the manufacture of the goods.

Revenues and expenses are given accounting recognition.

The pattern of entries is similar to that in Example 2. At the time revenue is recognized, related expenses are also recognized. The realization of revenue is accompanied by an increase in the carrying value of the goods produced—i.e., the recorded value of the finished goods increases from cost to market value, the amount of the increase being the income earned on the transaction.

At Time of Delivery—1984
(e)

Accounts receivable
(asset+) $100,000
    Finished goods
    at market value
    (asset−) $100,000
To record the delivery of goods.

The finished products, an asset, are exchanged for a receivable, also an asset.

As in the previous examples, events in periods other than those in which revenues and expenses are recognized involve only exchanges among assets and liabilities.

Example 4   Recognition of Revenue upon Collection of Cash (the Installment Basis)

In 1983 a company sells a parcel of land to a developer for $200,000. The original cost of the land to the company was $150,000. Under the terms of the sales contract, the seller is to receive 5 percent of the selling price at time of closing and transfer of title, 60 percent at the end of 1984, and the remaining 35 percent at the end of 1985. Because the company views ultimate collectibility as being highly uncertain, it has decided to recognize revenue only upon actual receipt of cash.*

The pattern of entries to be followed in this example is consistent with that established in the previous illustrations. A distinguishing feature of this example, however, is that the company physically surrenders the property sold *prior* to the time that it recognizes revenues and expenses. Inasmuch as

---

* In this example, recognition of revenue upon receipt of cash would be consistent with AICPA pronouncements contained in an industry audit guide, *Accounting for Profit Recognition on Sales of Real Estate.*

expenses are associated with reductions in assets, the firm must retain an *accounting* interest in the property sold equal to the portion of the original cost of the land not yet charged as an expense (cost of land sold).

At Time of Sale and Collection of First Payment—1983

(a)

Accounting interest in land sold (asset +)	$150,000	
Land (asset −)		$150,000

To record the sale of the land and transfer of title to purchaser.

The purpose of this entry is simply to reclassify the property sold—to distinguish between land to which the company actually holds title and that in which it has merely an accounting interest.

(b)

Cash (asset +)	$10,000	
Revenue from sale of land (revenue +)		$10,000

To record collection of 5 percent of the selling price and to recognize 5 percent of the revenue.

(c)

Cost of land sold (expense +)	$7,500	
Accounting interest in land sold (asset −)		$7,500

To record 5 percent of expenses applicable to the sale of land. (The original cost of the land to the company was $150,000; 5 percent of $150,000 = $7,500.)

The latter two entries recognize a portion of the total revenue to be realized on the sale and an identical portion of the related expense.

At Time of Collection of Second Payment—1984

(d)

Cash (asset +)	$120,000	
Revenue from sale of land (revenue +)		$120,000

To record collection of 60 percent of the selling price and to recognize 60 percent of the revenue.

(e)

Cost of land sold (expense +)	$90,000	
Accounting interest in land sold (asset −)		$90,000

To record 60 percent of the expense applicable to the sale of the land.

At Time of Collection of Third Payment—1985

(f)

Cash (asset +)	$70,000	
Revenue from sale of land (revenue +)		$70,000

To record collection of 35 percent of the selling price and to recognize the remaining 35 percent of the revenue.

(g)

Cost of Land sold (expense +)	$52,500	
Accounting interest in land sold (asset −)		$52,500

To record 35 percent of the expense applicable to the sale of the land.

By the time the final payment has been made, the company will have recorded revenues of $200,000, expenses of $150,000, and income of $50,000. It will report on the balance sheet an increase in cash of $200,000 and a decrease in land of $150,000.

Although the journal entries illustrated lead to a "correct" statement of both income and assets, they are deficient in that the amount due from the customer—i.e., an account receivable—is never incorporated into the accounts. This deficiency results from the nature of the revenue recognition process. Sales revenue is recorded only upon the receipt of cash; hence the increase in assets associated with recognition of revenue can be reflected only upon the receipt of cash. The deficiency can readily be remedied, however, by establishing two related accounts, "accounts receivable" and "accounts receivable—contra." When a contract is first signed, the following entry could be made:

Accounts receivable
  (asset) $200,000
      Accounts receivable—
        contra (asset, contra) $200,000

Then as each payment of cash is received, the entry would be "reversed":

Accounts receivable—
  contra $10,000
      Accounts receivable $10,000

The balance in the two accounts, both of which are balance sheet accounts, will always *net* to zero. The accounts will, however, provide a measure of control over amounts due from customers and indicate the anticipated cash collections.

REVENUE RECOGNITION—SELECTED INDUSTRY PROBLEMS

The criteria for revenue recognition cannot always be easily applied. The illustrations that follow are designed to demonstrate the difficulties of implementation. To a large extent, decisions as to the timing of revenue recognition are left to the good judgment of corporate managers and their accountants. As a consequence, companies in similar industries or even in the same industry have frequently drawn different conclusions as to the most appropriate basis of revenue recognition.

The rule-making bodies of the accounting profession, the Financial Accounting Standards Board and its predecessor, the Accounting Principles Board, have issued a number of pronouncements and industry audit guides which have done much to narrow the alternatives available to companies in similar industries. Nonetheless, differences in practice are still widespread and are likely to remain so in the foreseeable future.

Shipping Industry

In the shipping industry a period of several weeks or months may elapse between the period that cargo is first loaded on board a ship and that when the ship reaches its final destination and the cargo is unloaded. Both selling effort and collection of cash often take place prior to the voyage, but a large portion of expenses is incurred and effort is exerted in the course, and at the conclusion, of the voyage. Therefore, it is by no means clear whether revenue should be recognized at the beginning of, during, or at the end of the voyage. Practice varies considerably within the industry. Compare the following footnotes from the annual reports of three publicly owned shipping companies:

Revenue from vessel operations is recognized *upon unloading* inbound cargoes (terminated voyage basis).
          —Lykes Corp., 12/31/77

Revenue from vessels time-chartered to others is recorded on a pro rata basis *over the period of the charter.*
          —Trans Union Corporation, 12/31/79

Transportation revenues and related voyage expenses are generally recognized at the *commencement of a voyage.*

—R. J. Reynolds Industries, Inc., 12/31/79

Which practice is "correct"? There are neither persuasive answers nor authoritative guidelines.

Trading Stamp Industry

In the trading stamp industry, a company such as Sperry and Hutchinson (S & H Green Stamps), sells stamps to retailers. The retailers distribute the stamps to their customers. The customers save the stamps and after a period of time, perhaps several months, redeem them for merchandise at outlets operated by the trading stamp company. The trading stamp company bills the retailers for the stamps at the time they are delivered.

Should the trading stamp company recognize revenue upon delivery of the stamps to a retailer or should it delay recognition until the stamps are actually redeemed? On the one hand, it is clear that the earning process is not complete until the customers exchange their stamps for merchandise. Only at that time can the company be certain of the number of stamps to be redeemed and the ultimate cost of the merchandise distributed. On the other hand, by the time the company delivers the stamps to the retailer it has completed what it views as the most significant part of its operations—it has convinced the retailer to purchase the stamps. And because of its large volume of business, it can make highly reliable estimates of the percentage of stamps to be redeemed and the cost of the merchandise to be distributed.

The following footnote to the 1979 financial statements of Sperry and Hutchinson indicates how, in fact, the company accounts for its trading stamps:

The company records stamp service revenue and provides for cost of redemptions at the time stamps are furnished to licensees. The liability for stamp redemptions is adjusted each year based upon current operating experience and the cost of merchandise and related redemption service expenses required to redeem 95% of the outstanding stamps issued prior to 1979 and 90% of the outstanding stamps issued thereafter.

TIMING OF EXPENSES

In the course of this chapter it has been emphasized that costs should be charged as expenses in the same period in which the revenues to which they are related are recognized. Net income should be determined by subtracting from revenues the expenses which were incurred to generate the revenues. Indeed, insofar as possible, expenses and revenues should be reported as if a cause and effect relationship exists between them. Regrettably, a cause and effect relationship is not always readily apparent.

As pointed out in the previous chapter, factory costs that can be directly associated with the manufacture of specific products are *capitalized* as assets and charged as expenses in the period in which the goods manufactured are sold. But other costs, such as sales and administrative costs, cannot easily be associated with specific sales and, therefore, out of practical necessity, are charged off in the period in which they are incurred.

There are many additional types of costs for which cause and effect relationships with specific revenues are also unclear. For these costs, accountants may do their best to match them with appropriate revenues, but in the absence of specific rules set forth by authoritative professional or governmental bodies, the determination as to when the costs should be charged as expenses must, in large measure, rest with the judgment of the individual company. As a result, similar types of costs are often accorded dissimilar treatment by firms even within a single industry.

Insurance Industry

Consider, for example, costs incurred by life insurance firms. When a firm writes a policy, it will receive premiums—and therefore recognize revenue from premiums—over the life of the policy. In the period in which it first issues the policy, however, it incurs certain one-time "acquisition" costs, involving commissions, underwriting, and marketing. Should these costs be charged as expenses entirely in the year incurred, or should they be spread out over a number of years? Compare the practices of two leading companies:

> Premiums are recognized as income over the premium paying period of the policy and expenses, including acquisition costs such as commissions in connection with acquiring new business, *are charged to operations as incurred.*
> —Prudential Insurance Company of America, 12/31/79

> Costs of acquiring new life insurance business . . . *have been deferred and are being amortized in proportion to premium revenue recognized.*
> —Transamerica Corporation, 12/31/78

Retailing Industry

Similarly, consider costs, such as those of site selection, rent, stocking the shelves, and advertising, incurred by a retailer prior to the opening of a new store. With the revenues of which accounting periods should such costs be associated? Should they be charged

off as incurred (in a period in which the store might generate zero revenues), in the period in which the store opens, or in several periods subsequent to the opening of the store? Compare the manner in which costs are accounted for by three firms in the retail industry:

> Store preopening costs are charged to expense *in the year incurred.*
> —F. W. Woolworth & Co., 1/31/80

> Expenses associated with the opening of new stores are written off *in the year of store opening.*
> —J. C. Penney Company, Inc., 1/26/80

> Preopening expenses of . . . department stores are deferred and charged to operations over a three-year period.
> —Food Fair Stores, Inc., 7/31/77

REVENUE AND EXPENSE RECOGNITION—AN OVERVIEW

The issue of when to recognize revenues and expenses is pervasive in accounting. It is intrinsically related to virtually all other accounting questions.

In the remaining chapters a great deal of attention will be directed to questions of asset and liability valuation. But answers to questions of valuation must always be viewed with an eye toward their effects on revenues and expenses. After all, income can be defined as the change in net assets between two points in time. To take but a few examples: The question of whether a firm should report marketable securities, such as shares of General Motors stock, at the price the firm paid for them, or the price at which they are currently being sold is also an issue of revenue recognition—that is, should the company recognize gains or losses from market price changes as the value of the stock increases or decreases over time, or should it delay recognition until it actually sells the shares?

The question of whether inventories should be reported at cost to produce them or the price at which they will eventually be sold can also be expressed in terms of whether revenue should be recognized at point of sale or at various points throughout the production process. Disputes over whether or not a firm should assign values to seemingly worthless assets such as "organizational costs," "deferred store opening costs," or "deferred research and development costs" are also conflicts over when such costs should properly be charged off as expenses. It is vital, therefore, that every accounting question be analyzed in terms of its effect on *both* the income statement *and* the balance sheet.

KEY ACCOUNTING CONCEPTS

In the remainder of this chapter we shall consider some key accounting concepts which have been implied in the text but which, up to this point, have not been specifically discussed.

Exchange Prices

There is widespread agreement among parties concerned with accounting that, when first recorded, assets or liabilities should be measured by the *exchange* prices at which the transactions take place. That is, assets and liabilities should be valued with respect to the goods, the services, or the monetary consideration received or surrendered by the two parties to the transaction.

Unfortunately, even the relatively simple guidelines pertaining to the initial recording of assets and liabilities present problems of implementation. Many transactions involve more than a simple exchange of cash for goods or services. Many business transactions involve an element of barter. Goods or services are exchanged for other goods or services rather than for cash alone. In such transactions, accountants must look to the *fair value* of the consideration surrendered—that is, to the amount of money that would have been received had the goods or services been exchanged for cash alone.

The fair values of assets exchanged, however, are not always readily determinable. At what amount, for example, should a new car be recorded when purchased in exchange for cash plus an old car? The automobile salesman may well offer the purchaser a *trade-in allowance* on his old car.

But in the retail automobile industry, trade-in allowances are often significantly higher than true fair market value. Moreover, the *sticker* price on the new car may be an equally unreliable indicator of the true fair market value of the new car. The exchange price at which the new car should be recorded must, therefore, be *estimated;* either the fair market value of the old car or the new car must be appraised by the best means available—e.g., by reference to books of used car prices or by comparison of prices at which similar new cars were sold.

On a grander scale, corporations often purchase entire companies or segments of businesses in exchange for nonmonetary assets. Frequently the consideration is the common stock of the purchaser or of another company owned by the purchaser. Since the value of the stock may not be readily apparent, especially if it is not traded on a major stock exchange, the amounts at which the acquired assets are initially recorded may have to be based on the best estimates of corporate managers, accountants, or independent appraisers.

Arm's-Length Transactions

The exchange prices at which assets and liabilities are first recorded are generally assumed to be the results of *arm's-length* transactions—those between independent parties. Initial measurement of assets and liabilities is especially difficult when an exchange transaction is at less than arm's length—that is, where the two parties are related to one another. It is not unusual for owners of a corporation to sell assets to the corporation itself. For example, a *closely held* corporation (one in which all outstanding shares of common stock are held by a small number of stockholders) might purchase land, buildings, equipment, or other assets from one of its shareholders. There is certainly nothing illegal or unethical about such transactions. But because the prices at which the exchanges take place do not result from negotiations among *independent* parties, they cannot be relied upon to provide fair market values at which the assets should be recorded.

Corporations may also engage in transactions with their subsidiaries—those other corporations in which they own controlling interests. In fact, a subsidiary may have been acquired for the very purpose of being either a supplier of raw materials or a sales outlet for its finished goods. Since the prices at which goods are transferred between parent and subsidiary may be established arbitrarily by parent corporation management, they are inappropriate measures of true economic value. To the extent that the dollar amounts involved in such exchanges are material, the financial statements of both parent and subsidiary should be suspect. Indeed, revenues and expenses, as well as assets and liabilities, would be based on internally determined prices. It is, in large measure, for this reason that corporations combine the individual financial reports of related companies into single *consolidated* reports. In effect, the accountant defines the accounting entity as the sum of the two or more legal entities (the individual corporations). For reporting purposes, transfers among the related corporations are treated no differently from those among different departments of a single corporation. The values of assets and liabilities are based on the exchange transactions involving the *accounting entity* (the consolidated group of companies) and unrelated outsiders.

Accounting values are ordinarily based on monetary transactions with independent parties. Those assets and liabilities which are the result of nonmonetary exchanges, in which the value of the consideration surrendered cannot objectively be determined or in which the exchange price is not arrived at as a consequence of arm's-length bargaining, should be the subject of careful scrutiny on the part of managers, financial analysts or other users of financial reports.

Monetary Unit

Financial statements report the results of economic activity in terms of money. In the United States, the dollar is the conventional unit of measurement. But there is no agreement among accountants that the dollar, or, more specifically, the "unadjusted" dollar, *should* be the unit of measurement.

Financial statements combine and report the results of economic measurements taken over a number of years. For example, on the balance sheet assets purchased in previous years are combined with assets purchased in the current year. An asset of $2 million—land, for example—might be composed of one parcel of land purchased 10 years ago for $1 million and another purchased in the current year, also for $1 million. But, in fact, the measuring unit, i.e., the dollar, of 10 years ago is in no way comparable to that of today. As a consequence of continuous economic inflation, the dollar of today is "worth" considerably less than that of 10 years ago. The $1 million parcel of land purchased 10 years ago cost far more in terms of economic sacrifice than did that purchased today. Adding together current dollars with dollars of 10 years ago would be similar to adding together yards of 36 inches and those of 40 inches.

The accountant's basic unit of measure, the dollar, is, unfortunately, like the elastic yard—it is constantly changing in size.

Conventional accounting reports fail to recognize the continual changes in the value of the dollar. Accounting statements are implicitly based on the assumption—a patently invalid assumption—that the dollar retains a constant value over time. Current dollars are readily combined with or compared to those of previous years with no adjustments made to take into account the impact of inflation.

Recall, for example, the question raised in Chapter 1. The net assets, as conventionally measured, of Chemco, Inc., increased during a year from $1 million to $1.06 million. Its reported income was, therefore, $60,000. As a consequence of inflation, however, it required $1.1 million in assets at year end to acquire goods and services that would have cost only $1 million at the beginning of the year. Was the company really $60,000 better off at the end of the year than it was at the beginning? Is $60,000 a fair measure of its income for the year?

The failure to take into account increases in the general level of prices and in the resultant changes in the basic measuring unit necessarily limits the usefulness of financial reports. Accountants are, of course, cognizant of the limitations. But, they have been unable to agree either upon the most appropriate means of remedying the deficiencies or upon whether proposed measures would avoid introducing additional, and perhaps more seriously, distortions into the financial reports. The issue of "price-level adjustments" is discussed in greater depth in Chapter 15.

The Going Concern

Another widely accepted concept is that once assets have been initially recorded they should thereafter be valued on the assumption that the firm is a *going concern*—one that will continue in operation indefinitely. The concept of the going concern relates directly to an earlier discussion of the nature of assets. It was pointed out that assets are conventionally measured with respect to the particular firm reporting them—not with respect to the general marketplace. Thus, certain assets, "organizational costs," for example, can be expected to have value to the firm on whose books they are recorded, even though they are not readily marketable. The going-concern concept implies that the firm will survive at least long enough to realize the benefits of its recorded assets.

The corollary to the going-concern concept is that when there is evidence that a firm will be unable to survive, its assets should be reported at their *liquidation* values—the amounts that could be realized if the firm were to be dissolved and its assets put up for sale. Thus, if a firm is expected to be dissolved, perhaps as the result of bankruptcy proceedings, the conventional balance sheet would be inappropriate; instead, a balance sheet that indicates net realizable values should be prepared.

In recent years public accountants' interest in the going-concern concept has focused largely on the issue of the point at which the public needs to be warned that the survival of a firm is in serious question.

In practice, the going-concern concept is seldom abandoned in financial statements until a firm is actually involved in legal proceedings leading to liquidation. Independent auditors do, however, have a means by which to warn readers that the assumption of indefinite existence on which the financial statements of a firm are based *may not be* valid. Instead of issuing its usual "clean" opinion, which states that the financial statements "present fairly" the firm's financial position and results of operations, the auditors will set forth the reasons for their doubts about the ability of the company to survive. They will assert only that the statements present fairly *subject to* successful resolution of the matters impinging upon its continued existence. Auditors' reservations normally stem from uncertainties as to whether a firm will be able to obtain adequate financing or essential orders for its goods or services. A "qualified" opinion, however, can only enhance the firm's financial difficulties and may even be something of a "self-fulfilling prophecy." After all, few companies are willing to lend funds to, or contract with, a firm whose survival is in doubt. If auditors issue a going-concern warning before one is really necessary, they run the risk of intensifying the financial problems of their client. If they delay beyond the point at which liquidation is likely, then they will have been a party to the issuance of misleading financial statements—those based on an invalid assumption of continued existence.

Conservatism

Conservatism is widely regarded as one of the pervasive attitudes which underlie finan-

cial reports. Conservatism, as it relates to accounting, means that it is generally preferable that any possible errors in measurement be in the direction of understatement rather than overstatement of net income and net assets. In matters of doubt the recognition of favorable events should be delayed and that of unfavorable occurrences should be hastened. The concept of conservatism has been accorded formal recognition by the Accounting Principles Board, not as a full-fledged accounting principle, but rather as a "modifying convention."

Conservatism has its roots in the uncertainty which pervades all accounting measurements. It has been widely held that the interests of investors and creditors would be more adversely affected by overstatements of assets and profits than by understatements. More harm would accrue to them from an unforeseen or unreported loss than from an unanticipated gain. Moreover, it sometimes has been asserted that corporate managers are inherently optimistic. It is the role of the accountant to contain their optimism and to make certain that it does not spill over onto the company's financial statements.

The convention of conservatism must be applied judiciously. Insofar as accounting measurements are taken from a perspective of pessimism, they may easily be distorted. And to the extent that similar transactions (those which happen to result in gains rather than losses) are accounted for differently, the resultant financial statements may be internally inconsistent.

Moreover, understatement of earnings in one period may lead to overstatement in a subsequent period. It is not unheard of for newly appointed management teams to practice conservatism to an extreme. The new managers attempt to delay recognition of revenues to future periods and to charge costs of the future as current expenses.

Such actions, of course, reduce earnings in the year that the new management group takes over—a poor showing that can be blamed on the previous managers. But they also serve to increase earnings of the future over what they might normally be by adding revenues that should properly have been recognized in the past and eliminating expenses that should not have been previously charged. This type of manipulation—sometimes referred to as taking a "big bath"—does as much to destroy the credibility of corporations and their accountants as the use of execessively liberal accounting methods.

SUMMARY

Revenues should be realized when earned; costs should be charged as expenses at the time the revenues to which they are related are realized. This chapter has addressed the questions of when revenues should be considered to be earned and how costs can most meaningfully be related to specific revenues. In this chapter we have not attempted to provide answers; indeed there are no definitive answers. Instead we have explored the nature of the problems and set forth general guidelines for their resolution.

Revenues are commonly recognized (considered to result in an increase in net assets) at time of sale. They may also be recognized, however, during the process of production, at the completion of the process, or upon collection of the cash owing to the sale. As a rule, revenue should be recognized as soon as

1. The firm has exerted a substantial portion of its production and sales effort;
2. The revenue can be objectively measured;

3. The major portion of costs has been incurred, and the remaining costs can be estimated with reasonable reliability and precision; and
4. Eventual collection of a substantial portion of cash can reasonably be assured; an estimate can be made of that portion of cash that will prove to be uncollectible.

Expenses should be matched with and charged against the revenues that they serve to generate. Often, however, a clearly defined cause and effect relationship is not apparent. In the absence of such a relationship the determination of which expenses should be matched to which revenues must be based, in large measure, on the good judgment of managers and their accountants.

In general, if an enterprise is neither expanding nor contracting, then total reported revenues as well as expenses would be the same without regard to which specific policies of revenue and expense recognition the firm adhered. If, however, as is most commonly the situation, the firm is either increasing or decreasing the volume of its operations, then the impact of alternative practices on reported earnings may be substantial.

Issues of revenue and expense recognition must never be viewed in isolation from those of asset and liability valuation. They are intrinsically related. Any determination that affects reported income must necessarily affect a related balance sheet account. Questions of asset valuation will be addressed directly, however, in Chapter 6.

This chapter has also served to describe and identify the implications of several key concepts that underlie financial statements. Among the concepts discussed were those of exchange prices, arm's-length transactions, monetary units, the going concern, and conservatism.

EXERCISE FOR REVIEW
AND SELF-TESTING

Surfside Construction Co. contracts with the city of Portland to construct five municipal swimming pools. Contract price is $1 million ($200,000 per pool); estimated total cost of construction is $800,000 ($160,000 per pool). The contract requires that the pools be turned over to the city when all five have been completed and that payment be made at that time.

Surfside elects to recognize revenue on a percentage of completion basis, with percentage of completion being measured in terms of number of units completed.

1. In 1983 Surfside incurs $500,000 in construction costs and completes two pools. The cost of each of the completed pools was as estimated, $160,000.
   a. Prepare a journal entry to record the costs incurred.
   b. Inasmuch as Surfside completes two pools, determine the percentage of total revenues that should be recognized. Determine the dollar amount of revenue that should be recognized.
   c. Based on the percentage of revenue recognized, determine the percentage and dollar amount of estimated costs that should be recognized as expenses.
   d. If revenues on the two completed pools have been recognized, then at what value (cost or contract) must the pools be carried on the books?
   e. If the costs of constructing the two pools are to be recognized as expenses, then what asset must be reduced (in an amount equal to the expenses)?
   f. Prepare two journal entries to recognize the revenues and the related expenses.
2. In 1984 Surfside incurs the $300,000 in estimated additional costs and completes the remaining three pools.
   a. Following the pattern established in the previous section, prepare journal entries to record the costs incurred and to give recognition to revenues and expenses. Do total

revenues recognized over the two-year period equal the contract price? Do total expenses equal the estimated costs?
   b. In 1984 Surfside delivered the completed pools to the city and gave accounting recognition to the amount owed by the city. Prepare the appropriate journal entry.

QUESTIONS FOR REVIEW
AND DISCUSSION

1. It is sometimes pointed out that over the life of an enterprise it matters little on what basis revenues and expenses are recognized; it is only because investors and others demand periodic reports of performance that problems of revenue and expense recognition arise. Do you agree? Explain.
2. As soon as it is determined when revenues should be recognized, it should be a simple matter to determine when expenses should be recognized; match the expenses to the revenues which they generated. If this is true, how do you account for the different accounting treatment that similar companies accord to expenses even though they may employ identical methods of revenue recognition?
3. "If financial statements are to be truly objective, then it is inappropriate to recognize revenue on a transaction until the seller has cash in hand; recognition of revenue at any point prior to collection of cash necessarily involves estimates of the amount of cash that will actually be collected." Do you agree?
4. The Evergreen Forest Co. raises trees intended for sale as Christmas trees. Trees are sold approximately five years after they have been planted. What special problems of income determination does the company face if it is to prepare annual financial statements?
5. What criteria as to when revenue should be recognized are widely followed in practice?
6. The Retail Furniture Co. is 100 percent owned by Furniture Manufacturers, Inc. Retail pur-

chases its entire stock of merchandise from its parent company. Retail recently sought a loan from a local bank; the bank requested that Retail submit financial statements that were audited by an independent CPA. Retail has asked you to perform the audit. You would *not* be permitted to audit also the books and records of Furniture Manufacturers, Inc. Assuming that you were fully qualified to perform the audit, what reservations might you have about accepting the engagement? What special problems of income determination are you likely to face?

7. The Jamison Co. has suffered substantial losses in each of the past three years. The company is heavily in debt, and it appears unlikely that the company will be able to meet its obligations as they come due. After auditing the financial statements you are convinced that they "have been prepared in accordance with generally accepted accounting principles consistently applied." The statements clearly disclose the losses of the current and prior years and indicate all outstanding obligations. What additional warnings pertaining to the basis on which the financial statements were prepared would you consider giving the stockholders or potential investors or creditors? What special problems of reporting face companies whose survival is in question?

8. The Crescent Co. engaged in only one transaction in the current year. It sold for $150,000 land which it had purchased eight years earlier for $100,000. The increase in fair market price of the land could be attributed entirely to the impact of inflation—i.e., goods and services which cost $1.00 eight years ago would cost $1.50 today. How much income should the company report for the current year? How much "better off" was the company at the end of the year than it was at the beginning?

9. Accounting statements are said to be conservative. What is meant by conservatism as the concept is applied to financial reports? How does the accountant justify his conservatism? What problems might such conservatism create?

10. The question of revenue and expense recognition is inherently intertwined with that of asset and liability valuation. Explain.

PROBLEMS

1. *This exercise compares the effects of alternative bases of revenue recognition on earnings of a particular period as well as on earnings over the life of a project.*

The Anderson Construction Company agreed to construct six playgrounds for the City of Webster. Total contract price was $1.2 million. Total estimated costs were $960,000.

The following schedule indicates for the three-year period during which construction took place the number of units completed, the actual costs incurred, and the amount of cash received from the City of Webster.

	Year		
	1	2	3
Units completed	1	2	3
Costs incurred	$480,000	$288,000	$192,000
Cash collected	240,000	360,000	600,000

a. Determine revenues, expenses, and income for each of the three years under each of the following alternatives:
  1. Revenue recognized on the basis of the percentage of the project completed. (Percentage of costs incurred indicates degree of completion.)
  2. Revenue recognized as soon as each playground is completed.
  3. Revenue recognized upon the collection of cash.
b. Are total earnings the same over the life of the project?

2. *Under the percentage of completion method, the percentage of total estimated costs recognized as expenses must equal the percentage of total contract value recognized as revenues in any particular year.*

On January 3, 1982, Eastern Electric Co. contracted with United Power Company to produce generating equipment. Estimated cost of the equipment was $2,400,000; contract price was $2,800,000. Eastern Electric recognizes revenue on such contracts on a percentage of completion basis.

In 1982, Eastern Electric incurred $1,800,000 in costs on the project; in 1983, it incurred the remaining $600,000. In 1982 it received from United Power $800,000 in cash (which may be accounted for as an advance payment), and in 1983 it received the additional $2,000,000.

a. Prepare a journal entry to recognize the costs incurred (added to work in process) in 1982. Assume that they were paid in cash.

b. Determine the percentage of revenues and expenses that should be recognized in 1982.

c. Prepare journal entries to recognize the revenues and expenses in 1982.

d. Prepare a journal entry to recognize the cash collected in 1982.

e. Prepare similar journal entries, plus any additional journal entries required to recognize completion of the equipment and delivery to customer in 1983.

3. *Accounting practice does not always conform to accounting theory.*

The following statement of accounting policy was included in the annual report of Santa Fe Industries (December 31, 1976).

Revenues from rail operations are recognized in income upon completion of service. Expenses relating to shipments for which service has not been completed are charged to income and not deferred.

a. Why might such policy be considered objectionable? What "principle" does it violate?

b. How do you suspect the controller of Santa Fe Industries would defend the policy?

4. *It is sometimes necessary to recognize costs as expenses before they have actually been incurred.*

On December 31, 1982, the Valentine Roofing Co. reported among its liabilities the following balance:

Liability for roof guarantees $4,000

During 1983 Valentine constructed roofs for which it billed customers $300,000. It estimates that, on average, it incurs repair costs, under its two-year guarantee, of 2 percent of the initial contract price of its roofs. In 1983 the company actually incurred repair costs of $7,500, which were applicable to roofs constructed both in 1983 and in prior years.

a. Analyze both the liability and expense accounts pertaining to roof repairs in journal entry and T account forms for the year 1983.

b. How can a company justify charging repair expenses *before* they are actually incurred, based only on an *estimate* of what actual costs will be?

5. *Costs of fulfilling warranty obligations must be matched to the revenues with which they are associated.*

In 1980 the Gerard Company sold for cash 20 printing presses at a price of $100,000 each. The presses cost $80,000 to manufacture. The company guaranteed each press for a period of two years starting from the date of sale. The company estimated that the costs of making repairs as required by the guarantee would be approximately 2 percent of sales.

Actual expenditures for repairs of presses sold in 1980 were as follows: 1980, $14,000; 1981, $19,000; 1982, $12,000.

Prepare journal entries to record the sale of the presses and the subsequent repair costs.

6. *If revenue from the sale of an asset is to be associated with the collection of cash, so too must the cost of the asset sold.*

The Walton Company sells a parcel of land for $150,000. Terms of the contract require that the buyer make a down payment of $30,000 at the time the agreement is signed and pay the remaining balance in two installments at the end of each of the next two years. In addition, the contract requires the buyer to pay interest at a rate of 8 percent on the balance outstanding at the time of each of the two installment payments.

Walton Company had purchased the land for $90,000.

Determine the revenues and expenses that the company should report upon each of the cash collections assuming that it elects to recognize revenues on an installment (cash collection) basis.

7. *Changing conditions require changes in accounting practices.*

The following statement appeared in the footnotes to the financial statements of Macmillan Publishing Company, Inc.

> In 1975, the Company changed its definition of the unit of sale for the domestic home study business from the entire contract amount to each individual cash payment, which is generally made when the lesson is delivered. Changing industry regulations affecting refund and cancellation policies and changing patterns of payment were proving to have such unpredictable effects on ultimate contract collectibility that the continued use of prior historical patterns to establish allowances for cancellations and doubtful accounts could have caused serious distortions in the matching of revenues and costs.

a. Which of the two definitions of unit of sale would result in the more "conservative" practice of revenue recognition.

b. Assume that in a particular month a customer contracts to take a home study course consisting of 20 lessons. Total contract price for the entire course is $500. The customer remits $25 for the first lesson.

1. If the unit of sale is considered to be the entire contract and the entire amount of revenue is to be recognized at time of sale), prepare one entry to recognize the signing of the contract and another to recognize the delivery of the first lesson and the collection of cash. Ignore the costs applicable to the revenues.

2. If the unit of sale is considered to be each individual cash payment, prepare an entry to recognize the delivery of the first lesson and the collection of cash. Is it necessary to record the signing of the contract?

8. *Under the completion of production method expenses are matched with revenues upon their recognition.*

Lawncare, Inc., sells to Jaymart Stores lawnmowers that are specially manufactured for sale under a Jaymart brand name. A recent contract requires Lawncare to produce and deliver to Jaymart 1,000 mowers at a price of $150 per unit. Lawncare estimates that its manufacturing costs will be $100 per unit.

a. Lawncare recognizes revenues and expenses on a completion of production basis inasmuch as sale and collection are assured when production is completed. Prepare journal entries to reflect the following events.

1. In a particular month Lawncare incurs $90,000 in production costs, all of which are added to work in process. All costs are paid in cash.

2. It completes 400 units and transfers them to finished goods inventory. The costs of the finished mowers were as estimated, $100 each. Lawncare gives accounting recognition to the associated revenues, expenses, and increase in the carrying value of the inventory.

3. It delivers to Jaymart 300 mowers and bills Jaymart for the items delivered.

b. Lawncare also manufactures lawnmowers under its own brand name for sale to department stores and lawn specialty shops. Sales to these stores are not made under any special contractual arrangements. Goods are shipped as ordered. Do you think that Lawncare should use the completion of production method to recognize revenue on these sales? Would the firm be consistent if it used another method?

9. *On what basis should a manufacturer of custom products recognize revenue?*

The Harrison Co. manufactures television sets for sale to Save-More Discount Stores. Save-More sells the sets under its own brand name. In 1980 Harrison Co. signed a contract to deliver to Save-More 30,000 sets at a price of $100 per set over the next three years. By the end of 1980 Harrison had not yet delivered any sets to Save-More but had 10,000 sets 90 percent complete. In 1981 Harrison completed and delivered to Save-More 23,000 sets—the 10,000 sets started in the previous year plus 13,000 sets started in 1981. In 1982 Harrison completed and delivered the remaining 7,000 sets.

Each set cost Harrison $75 to manufacture. As agreed upon in the contract, Save-More made cash payments of $1 million to Harrison in each of the three years.

a. Determine revenues, expenses, and income for each of the three years if revenue were to be recognized (1) in the course of production, (2) at time of delivery, (3) at time of cash collection. Are total revenues, expenses, and income the same under each of the three methods?

b. Which basis of revenue recognition do you think results in the most objective and relevant determination of corporate performance?

10. *Consider the problems of matching revenues and expenses in a mining company.*

The Fordham Mining Co. has a contract with the American Lead Co. The terms of the agreement provide that American Lead Co. will purchase at a price of $500 per ton all lead which Fordham Mining Co. is willing to sell.

Fordham Mining has determined that costs of mining lead average $400 per ton. Transportation costs to the plant of American Lead add an additional $50 per ton to the cost. In 1982 Fordham Mining Co. mined 10,000 tons of lead, shipped 9,000 tons to American, and collected payment for 6,000 tons. In 1983 it mined 12,000 tons, shipped 11,000 tons, and collected payment for 13,000 tons.

Fordham Mining Co. recognizes revenue as soon as it removes the lead from the ground.

a. Prepare journal entries to reflect operations of Fordham Mining for 1982 and 1983. Assume all costs were paid in cash as incurred.

b. Prepare income statements and balance sheets for 1982 and 1983. Assume that the company's only asset at the start of 1982 was $5 million cash.

c. There is some question as to whether the transportation costs should be charged as an expense in the year in which the lead is mined and the revenue is recognized or in the year in which the lead is shipped and the costs actually incurred. Indicate the impact of the alternative that you did not select on both the income statement and the balance sheet.

11. *On what basis should revenues from membership fees be recognized?*

The Beautiful Person Health Club charges members an annual $240 membership fee. The fee, which is payable in advance, entitles the member to visit the club as many times as he wishes.

Selected membership data for the three-month period January to March 1980 are indicated in the table following:

	Jan.	Feb.	March
Number of new memberships sold	20	30	10
Number of renewals	50	20	10
Number of expirations (including members who renewed)	50	40	10
Total number of active members at end of month	600	610	620

Members who renew their contracts must also pay the $240 annual fee in advance of their membership year.

Monthly costs of operating the health facilities are approximately as follows:

Rent	$ 1,000
Salaries	5,000
Advertising and promotion	3,000
Depreciation and other operating costs	1,500
	$10,500

The company controller and an independent CPA disagree over the basis on which revenue should be recognized. The CPA argues that since members can use the facilities over a 12-month period, revenue from each member should be spread over a 12-month period (i.e., $20 per month per member). The controller, on the other hand, asserts that the entire membership fee should be recognized in the month the member either joins or renews. A major portion of corporate effort, he argues, is exerted *before* and at the time a new member actually joins the club. He points out that the company spends over $3,000 per month in direct advertising and promotion costs, and, in addition, a significant portion of the time of several club employees (whose salaries are included in the $5,000 of salary costs) is directed to promoting new memberships and processing both new applications and renewals.

a. Determine for the three-month period, for which data are provided, the monthly income that would result from adopting each of the two positions.

b. Which position do you favor for external financial reporting purposes?

c. Is a compromise between the two positions possible? Would such a compromise be consistent with what you believe to be sound principles of financial reporting?

d. Suppose that you were the president of the firm. Why might you prefer to receive internal reports that reflect as revenue the full amount of a membership fee in the month that the member either joins or renews?

12. *The impact of alternative accounting practices on income as well as retained earnings (and thus on assets and liabilities) must be evaluated.*

Waterloo Construction Co. begins operations in 1979. The company constructs bridges. Each bridge takes three years to complete, and construction is spread evenly over the three-year period. The contract price of each bridge is $3 million. In the period between 1979 and 1983 the firm begins construction of one bridge at the start of each year. Each bridge is completed after three years; for example, that started in 1979 is completed in 1981.

a. Assume that the firm recognizes revenue only upon the completion of a bridge. Determine annual revenues for the period 1981 to 1983.

b. Assume that the firm recognizes revenue on a percentage of completion basis (one-third of the revenue on each bridge is recognized each year). Determine annual revenues for the period 1981 to 1983.

c. Is there a difference in reported revenues?

d. Determine the balance in retained earnings that the firm would report at the end of 1983 under each of the two methods. Be sure to take into account any revenues that would have been recognized in 1979 and 1980. Assume that no dividends have been declared; ignore expenses related to the revenues.

e. Suppose that starting in 1984 the firm begins construction on two bridges each year. Determine annual revenues for the years 1984 to 1986.

f. Under what circumstances does choice of accounting method have an impact upon reported revenues?

13. *Under what circumstances does choice of basis for recognizing expenditures make a difference?*

It was pointed out in this chapter that there are at least three methods by which retail chain stores charge off costs, such as those of site selection, rent,

payroll, etc., incurred *prior* to the opening of a new store. Preopening costs may be

1. Charged as expense in the year incurred.
2. Charged as expense in the year a new store is opened.
3. Charged as expense over a 36-month period from the date the new store is opened.

Assume that the preopening costs of a large chain average $60,000 per store. Stores are opened on January 1, and all preopening costs are incurred during the prior year.

Prepare a table indicating the amount of preopening costs to be charged as expenses in each year of the period from 1980 through 1982 using each of the three alternative methods.

a. Assume that the company opened three stores each year from 1980 through 1982.

b. Assume alternatively that the company opened one store in 1978, two in 1979, three in 1980, four in 1981, five in 1982, and six in 1983.

14. *The effect on income of using a convenient, but theoretically unacceptable, method of accounting may be immaterial; the effect on assets and retained earnings may be substantially greater.*

Midstate Utility Company does not recognize revenue at the time it delivers electricity to customers. Instead, it recognizes revenue as it bills its customers for the electricity used. The company ordinarily bills customers on the 15th of each month for electricity that they had used in the previous month.

As of December 31, 1982, the company had delivered electricity for which it would bill customers, on January 15, 1983, for $86,000. As of December 31, 1983, the company had delivered electricity for which it would bill customers, on January 15, 1984, for $90,000.

In response to a suggestion by its CPA firm that the company adjust its books at the end of each year to take into account the unbilled revenues, the company controller argued that the adjustments would have but an "immaterial" impact on the financial statements. In 1983 the company had revenues of $1.1 million and income before taxes of $140,000. The company reported current assets of $170,000 and retained earnings of $830,000.

Suppose that the company consistently followed the practice of recognizing revenue in the year in which electricity was delivered rather than that in which it was billed.

a. Compute the impact of the alternative procedure, in both absolute and percentage amounts, on revenues and profits of 1983 (ignore income taxes).

b. Compute the impact on current assets and retained earnings at the end of 1983.

c. Prepare any journal entries necessary to adjust the accounts on December 31, 1983, so that revenue is recognized at the time electricity is delivered rather than when it is billed.

15. *The journal entries associated with the percentage of completion method serve to highlight the relationships among revenue recognition, expense recognition, and asset valuation.*

The Moshulu Construction Co. contracts with the Pelham Corporation to construct an office building. The contract price is $50 million. The Moshulu Co. estimates that the building will cost $40 million and will take three years to complete. The contract calls for the Pelham Corporation to make cash advances of $10 million during each of the first two years of construction and to make a final payment of $30 million upon completion of the building; these cash advances are to be accounted for on the books of Moshulu Co. as a liability until the project is completed.

The company elects to recognize revenue on the percentage of completion basis. Actual expenditures over the three-year period are as follows:

1981	$10,000,000
1982	25,000,000
1983	5,000,000

a. Prepare journal entries to account for the project over the three-year period. Assume that all costs are paid in cash as incurred.

b. Prepare an income statement and a balance sheet for each of the three years. Assume that at the start of the project the only asset of the company is cash of $20 million.

16. *How should revenues and expenses in the shipping industry be recognized?*

The Cromwell Co. was organized on June 1, 1982, for the specific purpose of chartering a ship

to undertake a three-month, 10,000-mile voyage. On June 1, the founders of the company contributed $600,000 to the company in exchange for common stock. On the same day, the company paid the entire $600,000 to the owners of a ship for the right to use it for a period of three months.

During the three-month period the chartered ship made several stops.

Indicated in the table following are the number of miles traveled and the amount of cargo, in terms of dollar billings to customers, that the firm loaded and unloaded. (For example, in June the company loaded cargo for which it billed customers $500,000. During that same month it unloaded $300,000 of that same cargo.)

	Loaded	Unloaded	Number of Miles Traveled
June	$ 500,000	$ 300,000	4,000
July	300,000	100,000	2,500
August	200,000	600,000	3,500
	$1,000,000	$1,000,000	10,000

Operating and administrative expenses, in addition to the charter fee, were $100,000 per month (to be accounted for as a period cost).

The Cromwell Co. was liquidated on August 31, 1982. At that time all expenses had been paid and all bills collected.

a. Determine the income of the company over its three-month life.

b. Determine the income of the company during *each* of the three months. Make alternative decisions as to the methods used to recognize revenues and charge expenses. Assume that revenues are recognized (1) when cargo is loaded and (2) when cargo is unloaded. Assume that the $600,000 is charged as an expense (1) evenly over the three-month period and (2) in proportion to the number of miles traveled.

c. Which methods are preferable? Why?

d. The Cromwell Co. was unable to estimate, *in advance*, the total revenues to be earned during the voyage. If it could, is there another basis, preferable to the other two, by which the $600,000 in charter *costs* might be allocated?

17. *In the advertising industry different firms use different methods to account for costs of developing advertising campaigns for clients.*

The Edward Grant Advertising Agency began operations in January 1980. In 1980 as well as in 1981 the agency billed clients for $800,000. The cost of placing its clients' ads in the media was $720,000 each year. Other operating costs were $40,000. In addition, in 1980 the agency undertook special marketing studies for one of its clients. The studies pertain to advertisements which were actually run in 1981. The cost of such studies was $30,000.

a. Assuming that the company had no assets or liabilities at the time it began operations, that all charges to clients were collected in the year billed, and that all costs were paid in the year incurred, prepare income statements and balance sheets for both 1980 and 1981 under each of two additional assumptions:
  1. The cost of the special studies was charged as an expense in the year in which they were undertaken.
  2. The cost of the special studies was charged as an expense in the year in which the ads with which they were associated were run.
b. Which of the assumptions results in the better matching of costs with revenues?
c. Suppose that the special studies were undertaken in an effort to *obtain* a client. As of the end of 1980, the client had still not agreed to shift its account to Edward Grant. Do you think it would be appropriate to reflect the cost of the special studies as an asset?

18. *Income, as determined for one purpose, may not be appropriate for another.*

Tom Ogden celebrated Christmas 1982 by purchasing a new car. In his first year as sales manager of the newly formed industrial equipment division of the Shakespeare Manufacturing Co., Ogden and his sales force had generated $750,000 in noncancelable orders for equipment.

Ogden's employment contract provided that he receive an annual bonus equal to 3 percent of his division's profits. He was aware that costs of manufacturing the equipment were approximately 60 percent of sales prices and that the company had budgeted $200,000 for administrative and all other operating costs. He could afford to splurge on a new car since, according to his rough calculations, his bonus would total at least $3,000.

In mid-January, Ogden received a bonus check for $1,200. Stunned, but confident that a clerical error had been made, he placed an urgent call to the company controller. The controller informed him that no error had been made. Although costs were in line with those budgeted, reported sales were only $600,000.

The equipment produced by Shakespeare is special-purpose polishing equipment. Since it must be custom-made, customers must normally wait for delivery at least two months from date of order.

a. Demonstrate how the amount of the bonus was calculated by *both* Ogden and the company controller. What is the most likely explanation of the difference in their sales figures?
b. The company president has asked for your recommendations with respect to the bonus plan. Assuming that the objective of the company is to give reasonably prompt recognition to the accomplishments of its sales manager, on what basis do you think revenue should be recognized for the purpose of computing sales manager's bonus? Do you think the company should use the same basis for reporting to shareholders? Explain.

19. *How should a computer software company, in the face of uncertainty as to whether its productive efforts will provide returns, recognize revenues and expenses?*

The University Systems Co. developed a series of computer programs designed to simplify the "back office" operations of stock brokerage firms. All costs of developing the programs have been charged to expense accounts as incurred. Although the programs can readily be applied to the operations of all firms in the industry, certain features of the programs must be custom-designed to meet the specific requirements of each customer. It is generally possible to estimate with reasonable reliability the costs of developing the custom features.

In January 1982 analysts of University Systems made a preliminary study of the "back office" operations of Conrad, Roy, Atwood, Smith, and Harris (CRASH), a leading brokerage firm. University Systems hoped that as a result of the study it could demonstrate the savings in costs and increases in efficiency that its programs could bring about and that it could thereby sell its programs to CRASH. It was agreed that the entire costs of the preliminary study would be borne by University Systems; CRASH was under no obligation to either purchase the programs or pay for the preliminary study. Cost of the preliminary study was $10,000.

The preliminary study was successful; on February 2, 1982, CRASH placed an order with University Systems for its series of programs; the contract price was $150,000.

During February and March, University Systems developed the custom features of the program for CRASH. Costs incurred in February were $8,000, and in March, $12,000. These costs were equal to amounts previously estimated.

On March 15, 1982, University Systems delivered the completed series of programs to CRASH, and they were reviewed and accepted by CRASH management.

On April 4, 1982, University Systems received a check for $50,000 plus a two-year, 8 percent note for the balance.

a. Prepare journal entries to record the events described above.

b. Prepare comparative income statements for the months ending January 31, February 28, March 31, and April 30.

c. In a short paragraph, justify your choice of basis of revenue and expense recognition. Indicate any assumptions that you may have made.

SOLUTIONS TO EXERCISE FOR REVIEW AND SELF-TESTING

1. a. Construction in
      process $500,000
          Cash (or accounts
              payable) $500,000
To record construction costs incurred.

b. The percentage of total revenues to be recognized equals 40 percent (two-fifths); 40 percent of $1 million is $400,000.

c. The percentage of total expenses to be recognized must also equal 40 percent; 40 percent of $800,000 is $320,000.

d. Completed pools must be carried at contract value—$400,000.

e. Construction in process must be reduced by $320,000.

f. Completed pools at
      contract value $400,000
          Revenue from
              construction $400,000
To record revenue from construction.
Expenses relating to
      revenue from
      construction $320,000
          Construction in process $320,000
To record expenses relating to revenues.

2. a. Construction in
      process $300,000
          Cash (or accounts
              payable) $300,000
To record construction costs incurred.
Completed pools at
      contract value $600,000
          Revenue from
              construction $600,000
To record revenue from construction.
Expenses relating to
      revenue from
      construction $480,000
          Construction in process $480,000
To record expenses relating to revenues.

b. Accounts
      receivable $1,000,000
          Completed pools at
              contract value $1,000,000
To record delivery of pools to the city.

Valuation of Assets; 6 Cash and Marketable Securities

PART I: VALUATION OF ASSETS

The next several chapters will be directed primarily to questions of asset and liability valuation—that is, to the problems of determining the most meaningful amounts to be assigned to the various balance sheet accounts. This chapter will be given over to both an overview of the valuation process and to consideration of two specific assets, cash and marketable securities.

Although accountants have been unable to derive a definition of an asset upon which there has been general agreement, almost all proposed definitions stress the notion that assets represent rights to future services or economic benefits. The question facing the accountant is what value—what quantitative measure—should be assigned to the potential services or benefits. (Such question is, of course, directly related to that discussed in the previous chapter: When should increases or decreases in the value of net assets—those associated with revenues and expenses—be accorded accounting recognition?)

The leading objective of this chapter is to provide insight into the nature of *value*. *Value*, as it is used in accounting, can have at least three distinctive meanings:

1. An *assigned* or calculated numerical quantity; as in mathematics, the quantity or amount for which a symbol stands
2. The *worth* of something sold or exchanged; the worth of a thing in money or goods at a certain time; its fair market price
3. Worth in *usefulness* or importance to its *possessor:* utility or merit

The accounting profession has not yet reached a consensus on criteria of valuation. In fact, in accord with generally accepted accounting principles, assets are stated at amounts reflective of each of the three definitions of value.

From the perspective of managers and investors, the distinctions among the three concepts of value are crucial. The "value" assigned to an asset on a financial statement may not—indeed is *unlikely*—to be indicative of the amount for which the asset could be sold or of its ultimate worth to the party owning or using it. As a consequence, decisions that will maximize the reported value of assets may not always maximize their true economic worth and may be counter to the financial well-being of a firm and its investors.

HISTORICAL COST

The first definition, that value is nothing more than an assigned or calculated numerical quantity, implies that value need have nothing to do with inherent worth; it is simply a numerical quantity assigned on a basis that is, presumably, logical and orderly. It is, in fact, this first meaning that is most consistent with current accounting practice.

Financial statements are *cost based*. Assets are initially recorded at the amounts paid for them. Subsequent to date of purchase, assets are, in general (some exceptions will be pointed out later in this chapter), reported at either initial cost or depreciated cost. Depreciated cost is initial cost less that portion of initial cost (often indicated in a contra account) representing the services of the asset already utilized. Land is an example of an asset that is reported at initial cost; plant and equipment are examples of assets that are reported at depreciated cost.

Except at the date assets are purchased, the cost-based amounts reported on a firm's balance sheet do not represent (unless by coincidence) the prices at which they can be either purchased or sold. The reported amounts can be viewed as approximations of neither the fair market value nor the worth of the services which the assets will provide.

They designate nothing more than initial cost less that portion of initial cost already absorbed as an expense.

Amounts Objective

Why do accountants "value" assets at amounts that have nothing to do with either market value or inherent worth? The justification for this practice is two-fold. First, amounts reported on the balance sheet are thought of as being relatively objective. The amount at which an asset is initially recorded is established by an exchange transaction among independent parties; it is an amount that can be readily verified. Thereafter, the initial recorded amount is reduced in a systematic and orderly manner. Once useful life has been determined (and some additional assumptions, to be discussed in later chapters, are made pertaining to the method of depreciation to be used), the computation of book value is straightforward. It is unaffected by fluctuations in the market price of either the asset itself or the goods to the production of which the asset contributes.

Consistent with Principle of Matching

Second, and perhaps more significant, historical cost valuations are consistent with the concepts of income determination discussed in the previous chapter. The cost of an asset is generally charged as an expense as the services associated with the asset are actually provided. That portion of cost that has not yet been charged off as an expense represents the remaining services to be provided and as such must be accorded accounting recognition. The balance sheet is the means of accounting for the unexpired costs of assets. It may be viewed as a statement of *residuals*—costs which have not yet been charged off as expenses and must, resultantly, be carried forward to future accounting periods. The balance sheet (in conjunction with the income statement) provides a measure of accountability over the *initial costs* of assets purchased. It is not purported to indicate the market value of a firm's assets.

Not Useful for Investor and Manager Decisions

To managers as well as investors, who are called upon to make decisions that will affect the future, not the past, historical costs are of little significance. There are virtually no decisions for which historical costs are necessary or even useful.* Assets, by definition, provide benefits that will be realized in the future. The historical cost of an asset provides no insight into the resources that could be derived by either retaining or selling the asset. It provides no basis on which to assess cash flows that the asset will generate in the future or to evaluate the efficiency of management in using the asset.

MARKET VALUES

If, instead, accountants were to accept the second definition of value—the worth of a thing in money or goods at a certain time—then they would most logically look to the market place to determine the amount at which an asset should be reported. They would value assets at their market prices on the date of the balance sheet.

---

* Historical costs are, of course, necessary to make decisions that must, by statute or policy, be based on them. The tax laws, for example, require that the gain on sale of an asset be calculated as the difference between selling price and historical cost. Banks sometimes insist (unwisely in the view of many accountants and lending specialists) that in order to be eligible for a loan, a borrower must maintain a ratio of assets (stated at historical cost) to liabilities that exceeds a specified amount.

Numerous arguments have been advanced for a market price approach to asset valuation. Proponents assert that a balance sheet in which all assets were reported at current values would provide investors and managers with information that would be far more relevant to the decisions that they must make. Current value not only provides an indication of either the price at which an asset might be sold or that which would have to be paid to replace it but may also be used to determine the asset's *opportunity cost*—the amount that might be earned if the asset were sold and the proceeds used in the best alternative capacity.

Input Value Versus Output Value

The market value of an asset can be interpreted as either a current *output price* or a current *input cost*. The two are not necessarily the same, and strong support for using one or the other can be found in the accounting literature. The current output price of an asset ordinarily represents its *net realizable value*—the amount at which it can be sold less any costs that must be incurred to bring it to a salable condition. The current input cost represents the price that would have to be paid to obtain the same asset or its equivalent. From the standpoint of a manufacturing concern the current output price of goods which it had produced and were ready for sale would be the price at which the goods could be sold. The current input cost would be that of manufacturing the goods. The difference between the two would normally be the manufacturer's margin of profit.

Despite its obvious appeal, there are significant disadvantages to the current value approach to reporting assets. The reported value of an asset would be determined apart from its utility to its particular owner. An asset would be valued at its current market price regardless of whether the firm intends to sell it immediately or to continue using it for several additional years. Technological advances may cause the replacement cost of a piece of equipment to decline substantially. But such advances may not necessarily reduce the utility of that equipment to its owner. Moreover, if output values (selling prices) were used, assets such as nonsalable specialized equipment or intangible assets such as organizational costs, deferred start-up and preoperating costs would not be considered to be assets at all; they would be assigned values corresponding to the prices at which they could be sold—zero.

Market Values in Practice

Even though conventional accounting is primarily cost based, in selected situations firms do report assets at market values. In general, whenever revenue is recognized prior to the point of sale, the related asset is reported at either the amount that is expected to be realized or some fraction thereof. For example, when revenue is recognized upon completion of production (e.g., upon the removal of a precious mineral from the ground) the completed products are valued at their anticipated selling price—a current output price. To avoid the distortions in income that would result from delaying recognition of revenue until point of sale, firms are forced to make estimates of the amount of revenue that will actually be realized. The best indication of the amount to be actually realized is a fixed contract price, or in the absence of such a price, the current market price of the commodity intended for sale.

Lower of Cost or Market Rule

The concern of accountants with conservatism also leads them to report current values whenever the market price of an asset intended for sale falls below its acquisition cost. Following the rule of *lower of cost or market*, the accountant compares the historical cost of an asset—that which the company paid to either purchase or produce it—with what it would cost to *replace* it (a current *input* cost). If the market—the replacement—price is less than the historical cost, then the asset is *written down* to the market price and the corresponding loss recognized on the income statement. The lower of cost or market rule is applied only to assets, primarily inventories and marketable securities, that the firm actually expects to sell in the normal course of business. It is grounded on the assumption that financial statements would be misleading if assets were valued at prices higher than those for which the company expects to sell them. The rule is not ordinarily applied to assets, such as plant and equipment, that are not intended for resale. The lower of cost or market rule will be examined in greater detail in Chapter 8 in connection with a discussion of inventories.

FASB Statement No. 33 requires that firms which are greater than a specified size provide information in notes to their financial statements on the replacement cost of their assets. Such firms must also indicate what income would have been had it been determined on the basis of replacement values rather than historical costs.

VALUE TO USER

The third definition expresses value in terms of worth in usefulness or importance to the individual possessor. It suggests that the value of an asset be determined with respect to the particular party that owns it.

This third concept of value is of utmost concern to managers and investors as it underlies virtually all decision models pertaining to assets. Moreover, it is of interest to all persons involved with business and economics because the factors that contribute to the worth of an asset to a particular individual or firm provide insight into the nature of both assets and market prices.

Value to individual owners has not, in the past, been the common basis for stating assets in general-purpose financial reports. In large measure this is because of the difficulty of assessing the future benefits that assets will provide. However, to an increasing extent accountants are now taking into account the worth of the services to be rendered by the asset in determining how it should be reported. This is particularly true when there is available neither an exchange transaction nor a market price that can serve as the basis for valuation.

The economic benefits associated with an asset ordinarily take the form of cash receipts. An individual invests the common stock of a corporation in anticipation of cash receipts greater than the cash disbursement required by the initial purchase. The cash receipts will be derived from periodic cash dividends paid by the company, from the proceeds resulting from the sale of the stock, or from both. Similarly, a manufacturer purchases a machine with the expectation that it will contribute to the production of goods which when sold will generate cash receipts. The value of an asset to its owner is, therefore, the value of the net cash receipts that the asset is expected to generate. The task of the accountant or manager is, first, to identify and measure the cash receipts—an obviously difficult task considering that most assets result in cash receipts only when used in conjunction with other assets and that in a world of uncertainty future sales and costs cannot be readily estimated. And, second, it is to determine the present value of those cash receipts.

Although it might appear as if the value of expected cash receipts is simply the sum of all anticipated receipts, an analysis of some fundamental concepts of compound interest will demonstrate that this is not so. Since cash may be placed in interest-bearing bank accounts or used to acquire securities that will provide a periodic return, it has a value in time. Funds to be received in years hence are of less value than those to be received at present.

COMPOUND INTEREST AND VALUE OF CASH RECEIPTS

Future Value

Suppose that an individual deposited $1 in a savings bank. The bank pays interest at the rate of 6 percent per year. Interest is *compounded* (computed) annually at the end of each year. To how much would the deposit have grown at the end of one year?

The accumulated value of the deposit at the end of one year would be $1 \times 1.06 = \$1.06$.

In more general terms,

$$F_n = P(1 + r)^n$$

where F_n represents the final accumulation of the initial investment after n interest periods

P represents the initial investment or deposit

r indicates the rate of interest

As indicated in Exhibit 6-1, after two years the initial deposit would have accumulated to $1.12—the $1.06 on deposit at the beginning of the second year times 1.06. After three years it would have accumulated to $1.19—the $1.12 on deposit at the beginning of the third year again times 1.06.

EXHIBIT 6-1

Future Value of $1 Invested Today—6% Return
(rounded to nearest cent)

Year

0	1	2	3	4	5	6

$1.00 → $1.06 → $1.12 → $1.19 → $1.26 → $1.34 → $1.42

Employing the general formula (and rounding to the nearest cent),

At the end of two years:

$$F = P(1 + r)^n$$

$$F = \$1(1 + .06)^2 = \$1.12$$

At the end of three years:

$$F = P(1 + r)^n$$

$$F = \$1(1 + .06)^3 = \$1.19$$

At the end of six years:

$$F = P(1 + r)^n$$

$$F = \$1(1 + .06)^6 = \$1.42$$

If an amount other than $1 were deposited, then the accumulated amount could be computed simply by substituting that amount for P in the basic formula. Thus $200 deposited in a bank at a rate of 6 percent would grow to $200 times $(1.06)^6$—$283.70 at the end of six years.

To facilitate computations of compound interest, series of tables have been developed and are readily available in almost all accounting textbooks as well as numerous books of financial tables. Moreover, many business calculators are programmed with time value of money routines. Table 1 in the Appendix of this volume indicates the amounts to which $1 will accumulate at various interest rates and at the end of different accounting periods. The number at the intersection of the 6 percent column and the 6 periods row indicates that $1 would accumulate to $1.4185. $200 would accumulate to $200 times that amount—$200 × 1.4185 = $283.70.

Several examples may serve to illustrate the concept of future value.

Example 1

A company sells a parcel of land for $50,000. The purchaser requests to be allowed to delay payment for a period of three years. The company agrees to accept a note from the purchaser for $50,000 plus interest at an annual rate of 8 percent. What amount would the purchaser be required to pay at the end of three years?

As indicated in Table 1 (8 percent column, 3 periods row), $1 will grow to $1.2597. Hence, $50,000 will grow to $50,000 times $1.2597—$62,985. The purchaser would be required to pay $62,985.

Example 2

An individual deposits $30,000 in a savings bank certificate of deposit. The bank pays interest at an annual rate of 12 percent *compounded semiannually*. To what amount will the deposit accumulate at the end of 10 years?

If interest is compounded semiannually and the *annual* rate of interest is 12 percent, then interest is computed *twice* each year at 6 percent—*one-half* the annual rate. (Interest is almost always stated at an *annual* rate even when compounded semiannually or quarterly.) Each interest period would be 6 months, rather than a year, so that over a 10-year span there would be 20 interest periods. Table 1 indicates that at an interest rate of 6 percent $1 will accumulate to $3.2071 after 20 periods. Hence, $30,000 will accumulate to $30,000 times 3.2071—$96,213. As a general rule, whenever interest is compounded semiannually, the interest rate must be halved and the number of years doubled.

Example 3

A corporation invests $10,000 and expects to earn a return of 8 percent compounded annually for the next 60 years. To how much will the $10,000 accumulate over the 60-year period?

Table 1 does not indicate accumulations for 60 years. However, the table does indicate that $1 invested at 8 percent for 50 years would accumulate to $46.9016. Over 50 years $10,000 would accumulate to $469,016. The table also indicates that $1 invested at 8 percent for 10 years would accumulate to $2.1589. If at the end of 50 years $469,016 were invested for an additional 10 years, it would increase in value to $2.1589 times $469,016–$1,012,558.

Example 4

A corporation reached an agreement to sell a warehouse. The purchaser agreed to pay $800,000 for the warehouse but wanted to delay payment for four years. The corporation, however, was in immediate need of cash and agreed to accept a lesser amount if payment were made at time of sale. The corporation estimated that it would otherwise have to borrow the needed funds at a rate of 15 percent. What amount should the corporation be willing to accept if cash payment were made at the time of sale rather than delayed for four years?

The question can be stated in an alternative form. What amount if invested today at an interest rate of 15 percent would accumulate to $800,000 in four years? From Table 1, it may be seen that $1 invested today would increase to $1.7490. Hence, some amount (x) times 1.7490 would increase to $800,000:

$$1.7490x = \$800,000$$

Solving for x (i.e., dividing $800,000 by 1.7490) indicates that amount to be $457,404. Thus, the company would be equally well off if it accepted payment of $457,404 today as it would be if it waited four years to receive the full $800,000. In other words, $457,404 deposited in a bank today at a 15 percent annual interest rate would increase in value to $800,000 after four years.

Present Value

As implied in Example 4, it is frequently necessary to compute the *present value* of a sum of money to be received in the future. That is, one may want to know the amount which if invested today at a certain rate of return would be the equivalent of a fixed amount to be received in a specific number of years hence.

In simple terms, an example can be formulated as follows. If a bank pays interest at the rate of 6 percent annually, how much cash would an individual have to deposit today in order to have that amount accumulate *to* $1 one year from now? Example 4 illustrated one means of computation. In more general terms, the present value of a future sum can be calculated by rearranging the basic equation for future value—$F_n = P(1 + r)^n$. Thus,

$$P = F_n \frac{1}{(1 + r)^n}$$

where F_n represents the final accumulation of the initial investment after n years

r indicates the rate of interest (which when used in connection with present value computations is often referred to as a *discount* rate, since a future payment will be *discounted* to a present value)

P indicates the required initial deposit or investment

$$P = \$1 \frac{1}{(1 + .06)^1} = \$.94$$

The present value of $1 to be received two years in the future would be

$$P = F_n \frac{1}{(1 + r)^n}; \quad P = \$1 \frac{1}{(1 + .06)^2} = \$.89$$

The present value of $1 to be received six years in the future would be

$$P = F_n \frac{1}{(1 + r)^n}; \quad P = \$1 \frac{1}{(1 + .06)^6} = \$.71$$

In other words, as illustrated in Exhibit 6-2, $.71 invested today at 6 percent interest compounded annually would increase to $1 at the end of six years.

As with future value, if an amount other than $1 were to be received, then the present value of such amount could be determined

EXHIBIT 6-2

Present Values of $1 to Be Received in the Future—6% Return (rounded to nearest cent)

			Year			
0	1	2	3	4	5	6
$.94 ← $1						
.89 ←	$1					
.84 ←		$1				
.79 ←			$1			
.75 ←				$1		
.71 ←						$1

by substituting that amount for F. Thus, if an individual wanted to receive $200 six years from the present, then the amount he would have to invest today at 6 percent interest would be

$$P = \$200 \frac{1}{(1.06)^6} = \$141$$

Table 2 in the Appendix indicates the present value of $1 for various discount rates and time periods. The present value of $1 to be received six years from today discounted at the rate of 6 percent would be $.7050. The present value of $200 would be $200 times .7050—$141.

Concepts of present value are demonstrated in the examples that follow.

Example 1

Assume the same facts as in Example 4 of the previous section. A corporation agreed to sell a warehouse. The purchaser was willing to pay $800,000 four years hence or some lesser amount at time of sale. Assuming that the corporation would have to borrow the needed funds at a rate of 15 percent, what equivalent amount should it be willing to accept if payment were made at time of sale?

Per Table 2, the present value of $1 to be received in four years, at an annual rate of 15 percent, is $.5718. The present value of $800,000 is $800,000 × .5718—$457,440. Save for a $36 rounding difference, the result is identical to that computed in the earlier illustration.

Example 2

A man wishes to give his nephew a gift of the cost of a college education. The nephew will enter college in six years. It is estimated that when he enters college, tuition and other charges will be approximately $40,000 for a degree program. The gift will be placed in a certificate of deposit, which pays interest at an annual rate of 16 percent, compounded *quarterly*. What size gift is required if the full $40,000 is to be available to the nephew at the start of his college career?

Since interest is compounded *quarterly*, the question to be answered is as follows: What is the present value of $40,000 to be received *24* (4 times six years) periods away if discounted at a rate of 4 percent per period? Per Table 2, the present value of $1 to be received 24 periods in the future, discounted at a rate of 4 percent, is $.3901. The present value of $40,000 is, therefore, $40,000 times .3901—$15,604. (*Check:* Per Table 1, the future value of $1 to be received in 24 periods if invested at a rate of 4 percent is $2.5633. $15,604 times $2.5633 is, with allowance for rounding error, $40,000.)

Future Value of an Annuity

Commercial transactions frequently involve not just a single deposit or future payment but rather a series of equal payments spaced evenly apart. For example, a company interested in saving for a particular long-range goal would be concerned with the amount that it would be required to deposit during each of a certain number of years to attain that goal. A series of *equal* payments at fixed intervals is known as an *annuity*. An annuity in which the payments are made or received at the *end* of each period is known as an *ordinary annuity* or an *annuity in arrears*. One in which the payments are made or received at the *beginning* of each period is known as an *annuity due* or an *annuity in advance*. Unless otherwise indicated, the examples in this chapter will be based on the assumption that payments are made or received at the *end* of each period. (Annuity tables in the Appendix contain interest factors for ordinary annuities.)

Suppose that at the *end* of each of four years a person deposits $1 in a savings account. The account pays interest at the rate of 6 percent per year, compounded annually. How much will be available for withdrawal at the end of the fourth year?

As shown in Exhibit 6-3, the $1 deposited at the end of the first period will accumulate interest for a total of three years. As indicated

EXHIBIT 6-3

Future Value of $1 Invested at the End of Each of Four Periods—6% Return (rounded to nearest cent)

	Year			
	1	2	3	4
	$1.00 →	$1.06 →	$1.12 →	$1.19
		$1.00 →	1.06 →	1.12
			1.00 →	1.06
				1.00
Amount available for withdrawal	$1.00	$2.06	$3.18	$4.37

in Table 1, it will increase in value to $1.19. The deposit at the end of the second year will grow to $1.12, and that at the end of the third year will grow to $1.06. The payment made at the end of the fourth year will not yet have earned any interest. As revealed in the diagram, the series of four $1 payments will be worth $4.37 at the end of the fourth year.

The mathematical expression for the future value (F) of a series of payments of a fixed amount (A) compounded at an interest rate (r) over a given number of years (n) is

$$F = A\left[\frac{(1 + r)^n - 1}{r}\right]$$

The value at the end of four years of $1 deposited at the end of each of four years compounded at an annual rate of 6 percent is

$$F = \$1\left[\frac{(1 + .06)^4 - 1}{.06}\right] = \$4.37$$

Table 3 in the Appendix indicates the future values of annuities of $1 for various rates of return. The next three examples illustrate the concept of an annuity.

Example 1

A corporation has agreed to deposit 10 percent of an employee's salary into a retirement fund. The fund will be invested in stocks and bonds that will provide a return of 8 percent annually. How much will be available to the employee upon his retirement in 20 years assuming that the employee earns $30,000 per year?

The future value of an annuity of $1 per year compounded at a rate of 8 percent per year for 20 years is $45.7620. Hence, the future value of an annuity of $3,000 (10 percent of $30,000) is $3,000 times 45.7620—$137,286.

Example 2

An individual invests $1,000 every three months in securities that yield 20 percent per year compounded quarterly. To how much will his investments accumulate at the end of 15 years (60 quarters)?

Table 3 does not specifically indicate values for 60 periods. However, per Table 3, $1,000 deposited at the end of each of 50 periods and compounded at a rate of 5 percent per *quarter* will accumulate to $1,000 times 209.3480—$209,348. At the end of 50 quarters, therefore, the individual will have $209,348 invested in securities. Per Table 1, that sum will increase to $209,348 times 1.6289—$341,007—by the end of the 10 additional quarters. The $1,000 deposited at the end of quarters 51 through 60—an ordinary annuity for 10 periods—will accumulate, per Table 3, to $1,000 times 12.5779—$12,578. The total amount that will have accumulated over the 15-year (60 quarter) period is the sum of the two amounts, $341,007 and $12,578–$353,585.

Example 3

A municipality has an obligation to repay $200,000 in bonds upon their maturity in 20 years. The municipality wishes to make annual cash payments to a fund to assure that when the bonds are due it will have the necessary cash on hand. The municipality intends to invest the fund in securities that will yield a return of 8 percent, compounded annually.

$200,000 represents the future value of an annuity. That is, some amount (x) deposited annually to return 8 percent will accumulate at the end of 20 years to $200,000. From Table 3, it can be seen that $1 invested annually would accumulate in 20 years to $45.7620. Therefore, some amount (x) times

45.7620 would accumulate to $200,000:

$$45.7620x = \$200,000$$

$$x = \frac{\$200,000}{45.7620}$$

$$= \$4,370$$

If deposited annually into a fund which earns a return of 8 percent, $4,370 would accumulate to $200,000 in 20 years.

Present Value of an Annuity

Just as it is sometimes necessary to know the present value of a single payment to be received sometime in the future, so also there is sometimes interest in the present value of a stream of payments. An investor or creditor may wish to know the amount to be received today that would be the equivalent of a stream of payments to be received in the future.

The present value, discounted at 6 percent, of $1 to be received at the end of each of the future four periods is depicted diagramatically in Exhibit 6-4. The present value of the stream of receipts, $3.46, is nothing more than the sum of the present values of the individual receipts. The present values of the

EXHIBIT 6-4

Present Value of $1 to Be Received at the End of Each of Four Periods—6% Return (rounded to the nearest cent)

Year

0	1	2	3	4

$ .94 ← $1
  .89 ←——— $1
  .84 ←——————— $1
  .79 ←——————————— $1
$3.46

individual receipts, which are indicated in the left-hand column, could be taken directly from Table 2.

The mathematical formula for the present value (P_A) of an annuity of A dollars per period compounded at a rate of r for n periods is

$$P_A = A\left[\frac{1 - (1 + r)^{-n}}{r}\right]$$

The present value of an annuity of $1 per period for four periods compounded at a rate of 6 percent is

$$P_A = \$1\left[\frac{1 - (1 + .06)^{-4}}{.06}\right] = \$3.46$$

Table 4 in the Appendix indicates the present values of annuities in arrears (i.e., payments received at the *end* of each period) at various rates of return. Each amount in Table 4 is simply the sum, up to that period, of the amounts in Table 2.

The application of the concept of the present value of an annuity is demonstrated in the examples that follow.

Example 1

An individual wishes to give his daughter a gift of a sum of money, such that if she deposits the sum in a bank she would be able to withdraw $8,000 at the end of each of four years in order to meet her college expenses. The bank pays interest at the rate of 5 percent per year compounded annually. What is the single amount that the individual should give his daughter that would be the equivalent of four annual payments of $8,000 each.

The present value of an annuity of $1 per year for four years compounded at a rate of 5 percent is, per Table 4, $3.5460. The present value of an annuity of $8,000 is $8,000 times 3.5460—$28,368.

The result can be verified as follows:

Initial deposit	$28,368
First-year earnings (5%)	1,418
Balance at end of first year before withdrawal	$29,786
First-year withdrawal	(8,000)
Balance at end of first year	$21,786
Second-year earnings (5%)	1,089
Balance at end of second year before withdrawal	$22,875
Second-year withdrawal	(8,000)
Balance at end of second year	$14,875
Third-year earnings (5%)	744
Balance at end of third year before withdrawal	15,619
Third-year withdrawal	(8,000)
Balance at end of third year	$ 7,619
Fourth-year earnings (5%)	381
Balance at end of fourth year before withdrawal	$ 8,000
Fourth-year withdrawal	(8,000)
Balance at end of fourth year	$ 0

Example 2

A corporation has a choice; it can either lease its new plant at an annual rental fee of $30,000 for 20 years or it can purchase it. Assuming that the company estimates that it could earn 14 percent annually on any funds not invested in the plant, what would be the equivalent cost of purchasing the plant? Assume also that the plant would have no value at the end of 20 years.

The present value of a stream of payments of $1 per year, compounded at a rate of 14 percent, for 20 years, is, per Table 4, $6.6231. The present value of a stream of payments of $30,000 is $30,000 times 6.6231—$198,693. The company would be equally well off renting the plant for $30,000 per year or purchasing it for $198,693 (ignoring, of course, both tax and risk factors).

Example 3

A corporation issues a security (e.g., a bond) that contains the following provision: The corporation agrees to pay the purchaser $20,000 every 6 months for 20 years and make an additional single lump-sum payment of $500,000 at the end of the 20-year period. How much would an investor be willing to pay for such a security assuming that if he did not purchase the security he could, alternatively, invest the funds in other securities which would provide an annual return of 10 percent compounded semiannually?

The company promises to pay an annuity of $20,000 per period for *40* six-month periods. The present value of such an annuity when discounted at a rate of *5* percent (the *semiannual* alternative rate of return) is, with reference to Table 4,

$$\$20,000 \times 17.1591 = \$343,182$$

The present value of a single payment of $500,000, 40 periods hence, discounted at a semiannual rate of 5 percent is, with reference to Table 2,

$$\$500,000 \times .1420 = \$71,000$$

The present value of the stream of payments *and* the single lump-sum payment is, therefore, $343,182 plus $71,000—$414,182. This is the amount the investor would be willing to pay. Similar examples will be alluded to again in Chapter 10; they help explain why a bond with a certain face value (e.g., $500,000) might sell in the open market at a greater or lesser amount (e.g., $414,182).

Example 4

A company wishes to contribute an amount to a pension fund such that each employee will have an annual income of $24,000 upon retirement. The firm's consulting actuary estimates that an average employee will survive 15 years after his retirement and will be employed 20 years prior to his retirement. The company anticipates that it will be able to obtain a return of 12 percent per year on contributions to the fund. How much should the company contribute each year, per employee, to the pension fund?

Upon the retirement of an employee, the company must have in its pension fund an amount equivalent to a stream of payments of $24,000 for 15 years. Per Table 4, the present value of a stream of payments of $1 per year, for 15 years, discounted at a rate of 12 percent is $6.8109. The present value of the stream of $24,000 is $24,000 times 6.8109—$163,461.

The company must, therefore, make equal annual payments of such amount that the accumulated value of the payments after 20 years (the expected number of years an employee will work prior to his retirement) will be $163,461. According to Table 3, a stream of payments of $1, invested to yield a return of 12 percent, will accumulate to $72.0524 after 20 years. Hence, some amount (x) times 72.0524 will accumulate to $163,461.

$$72.0524x = \$163,461$$

$$x = 2,269$$

The firm would have to make 20 annual payments of $2,269 in order to be able to withdraw $24,000 per year for 15 years.

DISCOUNTED CASH FLOW AS A MEANS OF DETERMINING THE VALUE OF ASSETS

The procedures described in the preceding section in which a stream of future cash flows is *discounted* back to the present can be employed to determine the value to a particular firm of either individual assets or groups of assets.

Example

A firm is contemplating the purchase of new equipment. The company has determined that a new machine will enable it to reduce out-of-pocket production costs, after taxes, by $8,000 per year. If the machine will have a useful life of five years and the firm demands that it obtain a return of at least 10 percent per year on all invested funds, what is the maximum amount it would be willing to pay for the machine?

The present value of the stream of equal cash savings is (per Table 4) 3.7908 times $8,000—$30,326. The company would be willing to pay no more than that amount for the new machine.

SUMMARY OF PART I

In accord with conventional financial reporting, the value assigned to an asset is ordinarily based on its historical cost—the amount paid to acquire it, less that portion of initial cost representing the services of the asset already consumed (i.e., allowance for depreciation or amortization). Such amount is relatively objective and is consistent with the concept of income determination by which the cost of an asset is charged as an expense as the services associated with it are actually used. The portion of the cost that represents the services that have not yet been consumed is carried forward to future accounting periods and is reported on the balance sheet.

Alternatively, even though not generally done, an asset could be stated on the balance sheet at its market value. Market value could either be an output price (that at which the asset could be sold) or an input cost (that which would have to be paid to replace the asset). The market value of an asset is usually more relevant than its historical cost for most decisions that readers of financial statements have to make, since it is reasonably indicative of the economic sacrifice being made by the enterprise by holding and using the asset rather than selling it. But market value fails to take into account the utility of an asset to its particular user (e.g., the value of prior year models of equipment may be greater to a company than the market price would indicate). Moreover, the general use of market values (particularly output values) may be inconsistent with the concept that costs should be charged as expenses in the periods associated with the benefits that they provide. Start-up or organizational costs, for example, may not be considered to be assets at all, since they cannot readily be sold in the open market. The entire amounts of the costs would be charged as expenses in the periods in which they were incurred.

The value of an asset could also be stated in terms of its utility to a specific user. The worth of an asset to a particular user may be defined as the present value of the anticipated cash receipts with which it is associated. The present value of the cash receipts must take into account the "time value of money"—the fact that a dollar received today is worth considerably more than one to be received in the distant future. Determination of the present value of cash flows requires an understanding of the fundamental concepts of compound interest—hence the extended discussion of that topic in this chapter. It is often impractical, however, to determine the present value of a particular asset, since individual assets are not generally associated with specific cash receipts. Thus, conventional financial statements seldom express asset values in terms of worth to the individual possessor. Nevertheless, an understand-

ing of the concepts of present values of cash flows provides an appreciation of the underlying forces that determine the market values of assets and is the key to making rational decisions as to whether to purchase and sell assets. Asset acquisition strategies will be discussed in the section of this text devoted to managerial accounting.

In Part II of this chapter, as well as in the next several chapters, we shall deal with problems of valuing specific assets, such as cash, marketable securities, accounts receivable, inventories, and plant and equipment.

PART II: CASH AND MARKETABLE SECURITIES

CASH

Cash is ordinarily reported at its face value. Cash includes currency on hand and funds on deposit in banks that are subject to immediate and unconditional withdrawal (i.e., amounts in checking accounts). It does not in a strict sense include amounts that may be subject to withdrawal restrictions, such as funds in the form of savings accounts, which may technically require advance notification for withdrawal, or certificates of deposit, although in practice the distinction between the two is not often made. Most companies maintain several general ledger accounts for cash; in statements made available to the public, however, most cash balances are summarized into a single figure.

There are several characteristics of cash that make it of distinctive concern to a manager or accountant. Cash is the most liquid of all assets and is the common medium of exchange in our society. As such, it must be the subject of especially tight safeguards and controls. As a general rule, for example, the number of persons handling currency should be kept to a minimum, all currency should be deposited in a bank as soon as feasible, and accounting recognition should be given immediately to all cash receipts via a cash register tape or a manual listing. The responsibility for particular cash funds should be assigned to particular individuals, and whenever possible, in order to better assure that the payments are made to the parties for whom they are intended, disbursements should be made by check rather than with currency.

Cash is the accepted medium of paying bills and satisfying obligations. It is essential that a firm have an adequate amount of cash available to meet its debts as they come due and to make the day-to-day payments required of any operating enterprise. Management, as well as financial analysts and creditors, must, therefore, be continually alert to whether the firm's available cash—or assets that can readily be turned into cash—is sufficient to meet foreseeable needs.

Unproductive Asset

Cash, however, is basically an unproductive asset. Cash on hand or on deposit in a checking account earns little or no interest. Insofar as there is any degree of inflation in the economy, cash continually loses its purchasing power. Unlike many other assets, it produces no services or return to its owner. As a consequence, it is to the advantage of a firm to keep as little cash as possible either on hand or in checking accounts. Cash that is needed for a *safety reserve* or is being held for future purchase of other assets, distribution to shareholders, or payment of outstanding obligations should be invested temporarily in common stocks, short-term government notes, certificates of deposit, or other dividend- or interest-bearing securities.

Cash on Hand; Imprest Basis

Cash on hand includes customer receipts that have not yet been deposited, currency necessary to conduct routine business, and *petty cash*. Petty cash represents small amounts of cash maintained to meet disbursements of insufficient size to justify the time and inconvenience of writing a check. Petty cash funds are frequently accounted for on an *imprest* basis. That is, the general ledger balance of petty cash will always reflect a fixed amount, $100, for example. At any given time the fund itself should contain either cash or payment receipts for that amount. Periodically the fund is restored to its original amount by a transfer from general cash, and at that time accounting recognition is given to the particular expenses that had been incurred. The following journal entry might be made to restore $70 to the petty cash fund:

Postage expense	$30	
Entertainment expense	40	
Cash in bank		$70

To replenish petty cash fund.

Cash in Bank

The balance of cash indicated by a firm's general ledger is unlikely to be that actually available for withdrawal at a particular point in time. Conventional practice dictates that a firm reduce the general ledger cash balance at the time that it writes a check. However, a period of several days or even weeks may elapse before such check reaches and clears the firm's bank. During that period, the balance per the records of the bank will be greater than the balance in the books of the firm by the amount of the check. Similarly, a firm may record deposits at the time it mails them to its bank or places them in a night-deposit box. The bank will credit the firm's account only when it actually receives the deposit. As a consequence, the amount of cash that a firm reports may be either greater or less than that actually available for withdrawal per the records of the bank. Periodically, upon receiving a statement of its account from the bank, the firm must *reconcile* its balance with that of the bank—that is, it must add to the balance per its own books the sum of any checks that are still outstanding and subtract from such balance any deposits *in transit*. The adjusted balance (plus or minus any other *reconciling items* such as customer checks returned by the bank for insufficient funds but not yet recorded by the firm) should be in agreement with the balance reported by the bank. An example of a bank reconciliation is provided in Exhibit 6-5.

EXHIBIT 6-5

Bank Reconciliation ABC Company			
Balance per bank statement, 12/31/82			$16,160.30
Add:			
Deposits in transit		$12,176.25	
December bank service charge not yet recorded on books		10.00	
N.S.F. check[a]		236.17	12,422.42
			$28,582.72
Subtract:			
Outstanding checks			
#367	$ 126.69		
392	24.00		
393	6,200.00		
394	125.00		
395	81.50		
396	5.00	$ 6,562.19	
Note collected by bank but not yet recorded on books		2,000.00	8,562.19
Balance per company books, 12/31/82			$20,020.53

[a] An N.S.F. check is one returned by the bank marked "not sufficient funds." Ordinarily, a bank gives a company credit on its books for all checks deposited. Subsequently, when it learns that it is unable to collect the full amount of a particular check because the person who drew the check has insufficient funds in his account, the bank would return the check to the depositor (the company) and debit its account. The N.S.F. check will be a reconciling item until the company records the return of the check.

Although a student could readily memorize those items that are conventionally added and those which are subtracted in the reconciliation, a more sensible approach is to pose three simple questions with respect to each item in question: That is,

1. Who "knows" about the item? On whose books—the bank's or the depositor's—has it been recorded?
2. What impact has the item had on the books in which it has been recorded? Has it increased or decreased the balance relative to that on the books on which it has not been recorded?

3. Does such amount have to be added to or subtracted from the balance of the bank so that the balance per the bank will be in agreement with the balance per the books?

In this example the books of the bank reflect a balance of $16,160.30, and those of the company, $20,020.53.

1. The company made a deposit of $12,176.25 that has been recorded on the books of the company but not yet on those of the bank. The company knows of the deposit; the bank does not. The balance of the bank by virtue of the deposit, is $12,176.25 less than that of the company. To reconcile the two balances, $12,176.25 must be *added* to the balance of the bank.

2. The bank has deducted and recorded a $10.00 service charge. The bank knows of the service charge; the company does not. The balance of the bank is thereby $10.00 less than that of the company. To effect the reconciliation, $10.00 must be *added* to the balance of the bank.

3. The bank subtracted $236.17 from the balance of the company when it found that it could not collect a customer check for that amount. The bank knows of the deduction; the company does not. The balance of the bank is $236.17 less than that of the company. To reconcile the two balances, $236.17 must be *added* to the balance of the bank.

4. The company has written a number of checks which have not yet *cleared* the bank. The company knows of the checks and has reduced its balance at the time it wrote the checks. The bank does not know of the checks and will not learn about them until after they are deposited by the recipients. The balance of the bank is thus greater than that of the company in the amount of the outstanding checks, $6,562.19. That amount must be *subtracted* from the balance of the bank in order to bring the two balances into agreement.

5. The bank collected the proceeds of a customer note for the company and has given the company credit for it. The bank knows of the collection, but the company does not; it has not yet recorded the receipt of the cash on its own books. The balance of the bank is thereby $2,000.00 greater than that of the company. The $2,000.00 must be *subtracted* from the balance of the bank.

The reconciliation to this point has served to account for and to explain the differences between the cash balance as reported by the bank and that indicated on the books of the company. But it has also indicated that as of the date of reconciliation, December 31, 1982, the books of the company were in error. They were in error not because of any avoidable mistakes or carelessness on the part of the company accountants or bookkeepers, but only because they were not up to date. They had not taken into account those transactions which the bank knew about and recorded but which, as of the date of reconciliation, the company did not know about and had not recorded. If financial statements are to be prepared as of the date of reconciliation, then it is necessary to adjust the books and records of the company to take into account those items which should have been recorded as of the reconciliation date but which were not. Such items would involve those transactions which the bank knew about but which the company did not. In the illustration, they would include the service charge of $10.00, the N.S.F. check of $236.17, and the $2,000.00 note collected by the bank. The following entry would give effect to the adjustment:

Cash	$1,753.83	
Bank service charge (expense)	10.00	
Accounts receivable	236.17	
Notes receivable		$2,000.00

To give effect to adjustments indicated by bank reconciliation. (Accounts receivable has been debited by the amount of the N.S.F. check since the person who wrote the check is now indebted to the company for the amount of such check.)

Classification of Cash

Cash is ordinarily classified as a current asset. In a sense cash is the ultimate current asset in that current assets are defined as those that will be converted into cash within the operating cycle of a business. Nevertheless, there are exceptions. Cash should properly be considered a current asset only when there are no restrictions—either those imposed by contract or by management intent—upon its use as a medium of exchange within a single operating cycle. Suppose, for example, that a company is required by terms of a bond agreement to maintain a *sinking fund* for the retirement of debt that will mature in 10 years. A sinking fund consists of cash or other assets segregated in the accounts in order to repay an outstanding debt when it comes due. All such assets, although normally considered current, when set aside in sinking fund should be classified on the balance sheet as *noncurrent* assets since management has earmarked them for a specific, noncurrent, purpose. The intent of management should be the key criterion for classification.

MARKETABLE SECURITIES

In an effort to obtain a return on what would otherwise be temporarily idle cash, many corporations use such cash to purchase stocks, bonds, or commercial paper (short-term certificates of debt). Temporary investments are ordinarily grouped together in the current asset section of the statement of position under the heading "marketable securities." Marketable securities are distinguished from other corporate investments by corporate intent. The firm ordinarily expects to hold such securities for a relatively short period of time, until a need for cash arises, and does not anticipate exercising any significant degree of control over the company whose shares it may own. If the company has other intentions with respect to the securities, they should ordinarily be classified as "long-term investments," a noncurrent asset.

As with most other assets, marketable securities are reported on the balance sheet at their original cost. However, because the company is likely to sell them in the near future, the current market value is disclosed parenthetically on the face of the statement. Thus,

Cash	$ 80,000
Marketable securities (current market value, $350,000)	335,000

Gains and losses on the sale of individual securities are ordinarily recognized at the time of sale. No recognition is given to fluctuations in market value. Assume, for example, that a company had purchased 100 shares of IBM at $220 per share. The stock would be reported on the statement of position at $22,000. Should the company sell the stock for $250 per share, it would record the sale as follows:

Cash	$25,000	
Marketable securities		$22,000
Gain on sale of marketable securities		3,000

To record sale of marketable securities.

Revenue from dividends or interest on marketable securities is ordinarily recognized upon receipt. Thus, had IBM declared and paid a dividend of $4 per share before the company had sold it, the following entry would have been appropriate:

Cash	$400	
Dividend revenue		$400

To record receipt of dividend.

The one critical exception to the general rule that marketable securities be reported at historical cost is that where the market price of the entire portfolio is less than cost, the carrying value of the securities should be reduced to the market value, and a corresponding loss should be recognized. The exception represents an application of the guidelines of conservatism. Unfavorable events should be accorded accounting recognition at the earliest possible time.

This "lower of cost or market" rule according to a pronouncement of the FASB need not be applied to individual securities; it may be applied to all currently marketable securities taken as a group. Assume, for example, a firm has a portfolio consisting of 100 shares of each of two stocks. Both had been purchased at a cost of $100 per share. The original cost of the portfolio is therefore $20,000. As of year end, the market price of stock A had increased to $110 per share; that of stock B had declined to $80:

	Original Cost	Market Value	Lower of Cost or Market
Stock A	$10,000	$11,000	$10,000
Stock B	10,000	8,000	8,000
	$20,000	$19,000	$18,000

If the lower of cost or market rule were applied on an item-by-item basis, then the portfolio would be written down to $18,000. If applied on a portfolio basis, as recommended by the FASB, then it need be written down to only $19,000. The following entry (or one similar) would be in order:

Decline in market value of marketable securities (expense +)	$1,000	
Marketable securities (asset −)		$1,000

To record decline in market value of marketable securities.

The portfolio basis tends to be less conservative than the item-by-item basis inasmuch as it allows increases in the market value of some securities to offset decreases in the market value of others.

VALUATION OF MARKETABLE SECURITIES—A PROPOSED ALTERNATIVE

The current practice of generally reporting marketable securities at original cost is consistent with that followed in reporting other assets. Some critics, however, maintain that two important characteristics of marketable securities justify an alternative approach. First, the current market value of marketable securities (at any particular point in time) can ordinarily be objectively determined. This is especially true of securities that are widely traded since current prices are readily available either in newspapers or special brokerage service reports. Second, there is always an available market in which to sell the securities. Unlike fixed assets or inventories, marketable securities can be disposed of at the market price by a single telephone call to a stockbroker. As a consequence of these two characteristics, critics of current practice assert that the dual accounting goals of providing information that is both relevant and objective can most effectively be served by valuing securities on the balance sheet at market value rather than at historical costs.

The critics also focus attention on the impact of historical costs on the income statement. Gains or losses from holding a security are given accounting recognition only when the security is actually sold. In an accounting sense, at least, management is neither credited nor censured for holding a security as it increases or decreases in market value until the period of sale. The period of sale may be one subsequent to the one in which the increase or decrease in value actually took place.

To the extent that it has in its portfolio one or more securities that have increased in value since they were purchased, management can readily manipulate reported earnings. If management wishes to improve earnings of the current period, it simply sells those securities that have appreciated in value. If, on the other hand, it wishes to give the earnings of the following year a boost, it delays the sale until then. It is questionable, given the ease by which it can be done, that the sale of a security is of greater economic significance than the changes in its market value while it is being held.

The problem of reporting marketable securities is of special concern to industries, such as mutual funds and insurance, in which all or a sizable portion of assets consist of marketable securities. In those industries it is vital that an investor be concerned with any *unrealized* gains or losses (those representing changes in the market price of securities not yet sold). As a consequence, firms in such industries either already give effect to unrealized gains or losses on both the balance sheet and the income statement or otherwise make prominent disclosure in footnotes.

Although the issue of cost versus market value can readily be highlighted in a discussion of marketable securities, it is one that bears upon all assets and liabilities. It will be alluded to again in several subsequent chapters.

SUMMARY OF PART II

In Part II of this chapter we have dealt with problems of accounting for and reporting cash and marketable securities, both of which are ordinarily classified as current assets.

Cash includes currency on hand as well as demand deposits in banks. It is the most liquid of all assets and is the common medium of exchange in our society. As such it must be the subject of especially tight safeguards and controls.

Cash, although generally classified as a current asset, should properly be grouped with the noncurrent assets in those situations in which it is subject to restrictions upon its withdrawal, regardless of whether the restrictions are imposed by contract or set by management itself.

Marketable securities include those securities which a firm holds as temporary investments. The key issue with respect to marketable securities pertains to the value at which they should be reported on the balance sheet and the point at which increases or decreases in value should be recognized on the income statement. Conventionally, marketable securities are reported at cost. Increases or decreases in market value are recognized only upon the sale of a security. An exception is made, however, when the market value of an entire portfolio is less than its cost. In accord with the "lower of cost or market" rule, the portfolio is written down to its overall market value. Alternatively, however, many accountants argue that all changes in the market values of securities should be given accounting recognition and all gains or losses, both *realized* and *unrealized*, should be reflected immediately in enterprise earnings.

EXERCISE FOR REVIEW AND SELF-TESTING

Try to complete this exercise without using the interest tables in the Appendix.

Assume that today is January 1, 1982. Further assume that the prevailing rate of interest paid by banks on deposits is 8 percent, compounded annually.

1. *Future value of a single amount*. A corporation deposits $100,000 in a bank today.
   a. How much will it have in its account on December 31, 1982?
   b. How much will it have in its account on December 31, 1983?
   c. How much will it have in its account on December 31, 1984?

2. *Future value of an annuity*. A corporation deposits $1000,000 in a bank on December 31, 1982.
   a. How much will it have in its account on December 31, 1982, immediately after making the deposit?
   b. It makes another deposit of $100,000 on December 31, 1983. How much will it have in its account after making the deposit?
   c. It makes yet another deposit of $100,000 on December 31, 1984. How much will it have in its account after making the third deposit?

3. *Present value of a single amount*. A corporation wants to be able to withdraw from its account $100,000 on December 31, 1982.
   a. How much should it deposit today?
   b. Assume instead that it wants to be able to withdraw $100,000 on December 31, 1983. How much should it deposit today?
   c. Assume alternatively that it wants to be able to withdraw $100,000 on December 31, 1984. How much should it deposit today?

4. *Present value of an annuity*. A corporation wants to be able to withdraw from its account $100,000 on December 31, 1982, $100,000 on December 31, 1983, *and* $100,000 on December 31, 1984.
   a. How much should it deposit today?

QUESTIONS FOR REVIEW AND DISCUSSION

1. What is meant by *value* as the term is used in connection with assets reported on the conventional balance sheet?

2. The balance sheet, it is often asserted, provides little indication of a company's inherent worth.

Instead, it is nothing more than a compilation of *residuals*. Do you agree?

3. Historical cost values of assets are of little relevance to most decisions faced by management, creditors, or investors. Why, then, do accountants resist efforts to convert to a market value-oriented balance sheet?

4. Market values can be interpreted as either *input* or *output* prices. What is the distinction between the two? Give an example of each.

5. What are the economic benefits associated with an asset? How can they be quantified?

6. Current assets are defined as those which are reasonably expected to be *realized in cash*, sold, or consumed during the normal operating cycle of the business. Yet cash itself is not always classified as a current asset. Why is this so?

7. The owner of a small corporation was recently advised by his CPA that he "has too much cash sitting in his checking account." The company had a checking account balance of $100,000, and the CPA told the owner that the account was costing the company "about $10,000 per year." The owner of the corporation insisted that this could not be so; the money was deposited in a "no-charge" checking account. What do you think the CPA had in mind when he made his comment?

8. The general managers of two of a large firm's subsidiaries each reported operating earnings in 1982, excluding income from the sale of marketable securities, of $100,000. The manager of company A also indicated that on January 5, 1982, his subsidiary purchased but had not yet sold 1,000 shares of United Mining Co. common stock at $15 per share. On December 31, 1982, United Mining was traded at $45 per share. By contrast, the manager of company B revealed that his subsidiary purchased 1,000 shares of United Mining Co. common stock on April 18, at $35 per share and had sold them on November 25 at $38 per share.

   If conventional accounting principles are adhered to, which subsidiary would report the higher income? Excluding all other factors than those discussed above, which subsidiary do you think had the superior performance in 1982?

PROBLEMS

1. *The next several problems are intended to facilitate understanding of the four basic concepts of compound interest.*

Assuming an interest rate of 8 percent compounded annually, $300,000 is

a. The present value of what amount to be received in five years?

b. The value in five years of what amount deposited in a bank today?

c. The present value of an annuity of what amount to be received over the next five years.

d. The value in five years of an annuity of what amount deposited in a bank at the end of each of the next five years?

2. The board of directors of a printing company decided that the company should take advantage of an unusually successful year to place in a reserve fund an amount of cash sufficient to enable it to purchase a new printing press in six years. The company determines that the new press would cost $200,000 and that funds could be invested in securities that would provide a return of 8 percent, compounded annually.

a. How much should the company place in the fund?

b. Suppose that the return would be compounded quarterly. How much should the company place in the fund?

3. In anticipation of the need to purchase new equipment, a corporation decided to set aside in a special fund $40,000 each year.

a. If the amount in the fund could be invested in securities that provide an after-tax return of 5 percent per year, how much would the company have available in eight years?

b. Assume instead that the company knew that it would require $500,000 to replace the equipment at the end of eight years. How much should it contribute to the fund each year, assuming an annual return of 5 percent?

4. A corporation wishes to provide a research grant to a university such that the university can withdraw $10,000 at the end of each of the next three years. The university will deposit the amount

received in an account that earns interest at the rate of 5 percent per year. How much should the corporation give the university? Prepare a schedule in which you indicate the balance in the account at the end of the three years.

5. On the day of a child's birth, the parents deposit $1,000 in a savings bank. The bank pays interest at the rate of 6 percent per year, compounded annually.

a. How much will be on deposit by the time the child enters college on her eighteenth birthday?

b. Assume instead that the interest at an annual rate of 6 percent is compounded semiannually. To how much will the original deposit increase in 18 years?

6. A corporation borrows $5,000 from a bank. Principal and interest are payable at the end of five years.

a. What will be the amount of the corporation's payment assuming that the bank charges interest at a rate of 10 percent and compounds the interest annually?

b. What will be the amount of the corporation's payment if interest at an annual rate of 10 percent is compounded semiannually?

7. You deposit a fixed amount in a bank. How long will it take for your funds to double if the bank pays interest at a rate of

a. 4 percent compounded annually?

b. 8 percent compounded annually?

c. 8 percent compounded semiannually?

d. 8 percent compounded quarterly?

8. A company wishes to establish a pension plan for its president. The company wants to assure the president or his survivors an income of $40,000 per year for 20 years after his retirement. The president has 15 years to work before he retires. If the company can earn 7 percent per year on the pension fund, how much should it contribute during each working year of the president?

9. *Effective interest rates can be adjusted in a number of different ways.*

Series EE U.S. savings bonds differ from conventional government or corporate *coupon* bonds in that they do not have attached to them coupons that can periodically be redeemed for interest payments. Instead, they carry a face value of a fixed amount, e.g., $25, $50, or $100. The purchaser buys the bonds at a discount. For example, he might pay $75 for a $100 bond that will mature in 10 years. The difference between what he pays for the bond and its face value represents the interest for the entire period during which the bond is outstanding. Upon maturity the purchaser will present the bond to the government and receive its full face value. The government can readily adjust the effective interest rate that it pays by varying either the initial selling price of the bond or the number of years the purchaser must hold the bond before he can redeem it.

a. Suppose the government sells a $100 face value bond for $75 and establishes a holding period of 10 years. What is the approximate effective rate of interest (assume that interest is compounded annually)?

b. Suppose instead that the government wishes to establish an effective rate of 8 percent and a holding period of 10 years. At what price should it sell the bond?

c. If the government wishes to establish an effective rate of 8 percent and a price of $75, how long a holding period should it require?

10. *Truth-in-lending laws are designed to eliminate the type of deception suggested by this problem.*

The Helping Hand Loan Co. placed an advertisement in a local newspaper that read in part, "Borrow up to $10,000 for 5 years at our low, low rate of interest of 6 percent per year." When a customer went to the loan company to borrow the $10,000, he was told that total interest on the five-year loan would be $3,000. That is, $600 per year (6 percent of $10,000) for five years. Company practice, he was told, requires that interest be paid in full at the time a loan is made and be deducted from the amount given to the customer. Thus, the customer was given only $7,000. The loan was to be repaid in five annual installments of $2,000.

Do you think that the ad was misleading? What was the actual amount loaned to the customer? Determine what you consider to be the "true" rate of interest.

11. *Rates of discount determine firms' preferences as to alternative financing arrangements.*

Company A is presently negotiating with company B to purchase a parcel of land. Three alternative sets of terms are under consideration:
1. Company A will pay $400,000 at time of sale.
2. Company A will pay $50,000 at time of sale and give company B a note for $500,000 that matures in five years.
3. Company A will make five annual payments of $100,000 each commencing one year from the date of sale.

Company A can obtain an after-tax return of 7 percent per year on any funds that it has available for investment; company B can obtain a return of 9 percent. Both firms use discount rates to evaluate potential investments that are equal to the rates of return that they can obtain.

Rank the three sets of terms as you would expect them to be preferred by each of the two companies.

12. *Rental charges can be established so that lease arrangements are, in economic substance, equivalent to sales.*

At the request of several of its customers, a heavy equipment manufacturer has decided to give them the option of leasing or buying its products. The company expects a rate of return of 12 percent on all investments. The useful life of its equipment is eight years. Each lessee (i.e., customer) will pay all operating costs including taxes, insurance, and maintenance.

a. The company establishes an annual rental charge of $12,000. What would be the sale price that would leave the company equally well off as if it had leased the equipment for the entire useful life of the equipment?

b. The company establishes a price for the equipment of $75,000. What annual rental charge would leave the company as well off as if it had sold the equipment?

13. *Businesses, as well as individuals, should at least once a month compare the cash balance per a bank statement with that per their own records, account for all differences, and adjust their books as required. The next two problems are exercises in preparing bank reconciliations.*

On December 31, 1982, the general ledger of the Lincoln Company indicated that the cash balance in the firm's checking account at the First National

Bank was $108,753. A statement received from the bank, however, indicated that the balance in the account was $145,974. Investigation revealed the following:

1. The company had drawn checks totaling $53,186, which had not been paid by the bank.
2. The company made a deposit on the evening of December 31 of $26,102. This deposit was included by the bank in its business of January 2, 1983.
3. On December 10, the company had deposited a check given to it by a customer for $103. On December 31, the bank returned the check to the company marked N.S.F. (not sufficient funds in customer's account). The company had given no accounting recognition to the return of the check.
4. The bank debited the account of the company for a monthly service charge of $10. The company had not yet recorded the charge.
5. On December 31, the bank collected a customer note of $10,250 for the company. The company did not receive notification of the collection until January 4.

Prepare a schedule that reconciles the balance per the general ledger with that per the bank statement.

14. The general ledger of the McGuire Corp. indicated cash in bank of $3,822.81 as of December 31, 1983. A statement from the bank, as of the same date, indicated cash in bank of $5,666,00.

As of December 31, the company had outstanding checks of $1,800.00.

On December 29, it mailed a deposit of $465.81 to the bank. As of year end it had not yet been received.

On December 31, the bank collected for the company a note from a customer. As of year end the bank had not yet notified the company. The amount of the note was $500.

On December 18, the company made a deposit in the amount of $423.50. The bank recorded it as $432.50.

a. Prepare a schedule in which you account for the difference between the balance per the company books and that per the bank statement.
b. Determine the amount of cash in bank that should be reported on the firm's end-of-year financial statements. Prepare a journal entry to adjust the present balance.

15. Not all economic events associated with marketable securities are given accounting recognition.

Prepare journal entries (as necessary) to record the following transactions and events on the books of the APO Company, a firm whose fiscal year ends on December 31:

8/20/82 The APO Company purchases as a temporary investment 100 shares of Schaeffer Chemical Co. common stock at the price of $12 per share.

8/31/82 *The Wall Street Journal* reports that Schaeffer Chemical Co. common stock *closed* the previous day at $13\frac{1}{2}$.

9/30/82 The board of directors of Schaeffer Chemical declares a quarterly dividend of $.15 per share.

10/20/82 APO Company receives a dividend check in the amount of $15.

12/31/82 A telephone call to a stockholder reveals that Schaeffer Chemical Co. common stock *closed* at $4\frac{1}{2}$.

1/11/83 APO company sells 50 shares of Schaeffer Chemical at $5\frac{1}{4}$.

During 1982 the company owned no other marketable securities.

16. Alternative bases of asset valuation affect both earnings and assets.

In 1982, 47th Street Diamond Mart acquired a gem for resale. The cost of the jewel to the firm was $1,000. By the end of 1982, the firm would have had to pay $1,200 to acquire a stone of comparable size and quality, and it could have sold the stone to a retail customer, for $1,500. However, it was certain that if it would wait an additional year to sell the jewel, it could do so for $1,800.

a. Indicate the amount at which the firm should report the gem on its balance sheet of December 31, 1982 if it elects to wait one year to sell it, assuming each of the following bases of valuation:
1. Historical cost

2. Market value (input price)
3. Market value (output price)
4. Value to user (the firm determines the present value of expected cash receipts using a discount rate of 7 percent)

b. Indicate the amount of any gain associated with the stone that the firm would report in 1982, assuming each of the bases indicated.

17. *The lower of cost or market rule can be applied on two different bases, each having a different effect on both assets and earnings.*

The table following gives the marketable securities (all common stocks) owned by the Colorado Co. on December 31, 1982. All securities were purchased within the previous 12 months. Also shown are the original purchase prices and the current market prices.

Securities	Number of Shares	Purchase Price	Current Market Price
Amer. Can	100	$35\frac{1}{4}$	40
Cerro	200	$14\frac{1}{2}$	10
Fuqua	100	6	16
GAC Corp.	50	$5\frac{1}{2}$	2
IBM	20	250	240

a. Prepare a schedule indicating the lower of cost or market value of each security.
b. Prepare a journal entry to apply the lower of cost or market rule.
   1. Assume the rule is to be applied on an individual security basis.
   2. Assume the rule is to be applied on a portfolio basis (as recommended by the FASB).
c. Which basis is likely to be more conservative in that it results in lower asset values? Which minimizes the inconsistency of recognizing decreases in market values but not increases?

18. *Do earnings as computed in accord with established conventions always provide the best measure of economic performance?*

At the start of 1982 a corporation had in its portfolio of marketable securities 100 shares of each of stocks A, B, and C. Acquisition cost per share and unit market prices as of the end of 1982

and 1983 were as follows:

	Acquisition Cost	Market Price	
		12/31/82	12/31/83
Security A	$100	$150	$80
Security B	50	80	70
Security C	60	90	63

During 1982 the company engaged in no securities transactions. During 1983 it sold 100 shares of security C for $65 per share.

a. Determine reported earnings related to securities for 1982 and 1983. Be sure to take into account the lower of cost or market rule applied on a portfolio basis.
b. Do you think that reported earnings is an appropriate measure of economic performance? Why?

19. *Measures of performance based on amounts reported in the income statement may be misleading.*

On January 1, 1982 the Grey Corporation acquired 100 shares of common stock of company A and 100 shares of company B. Price per share of both securities was $200.

During 1982 companies A and B declared dividends of $16 and $12 per share, respectively. As of December 31, 1982, the market price of the stock of company A was $210 per share; that of company B was $230 per share.

a. Determine return on investment of each security based on the dollar amounts that would be reported on the firm's balance sheet and income statement.
b. Determine return on investment taking into account any "unrealized" gains or losses. Use *average* market value as the denominator.
c. Which security do you think was the better investment? Which basis for calculating return on investment do you think provides the better measure of economic performance? Why do you suppose that the market values of marketable securities must be disclosed in financial reports?

20. *The basis of asset valuation determines the basis for revenue recognition.*

During 1982 in its first year of operations, the Mann Company purchased, for $60 per unit, 1,000 units of a product. Of these it sold 800 units at a price of $100 per unit. On December 31, 1982, the company was notified by its supplier that in the following year the wholesale cost per unit would be increased to $70 per unit. As a consequence of the increase, Mann Company determined that the retail price would increase to $120 per unit.

Ignoring other revenues and expenses, determine the ending inventory balance, and compute income assuming that ending inventories are to be valued at

1. Historical cost (generally accepted basis).
2. A current market *input* price (a proposed alternative).
3. A current market *output* price (another proposed alternative).

In computing income, distinguish between revenue from the actual sale of product and yet to be realized gains from *holding* the product in inventory. Remember that any recorded increases in the value of the inventory must also be reflected in the determination of income (and, more specifically, of revenue).

21. *This problem describes a common banking arrangement, whereby a borrower is required to maintain a* compensating balance *with a lending institution. It suggests an accounting issue associated with the arrangement.*

Indicated as follows are year-end balances from selected general ledger accounts of the Jefferson Co.:

Cash, First State Bank	$ 50,000
Note payable, First State Bank	500,000
Interest (expense)	70,000

The interest represents borrowing charges for one year on the note payable to First State Bank. Per terms of the loan agreement, the company will maintain in a special interest-free account an amount equal to 10 percent of any loans outstanding to the First State Bank.

The controller of the Jefferson Co. has proposed to include the following comment among the footnotes to its published financial statements. "As of December 31, 1982, the company was indebted to the First State Bank for $500,000. The note to the bank matures in 1986. The company pays interest at the prime rate of 14 percent per year."

The controller indicated that he intends to classify the cash in the special interest-free account with First State Bank as a current asset.

a. Inasmuch as the note payable with which the special interest-free account is associated will be classified as a noncurrent liability, do you think that the compensating cash balance should be classified as a current asset?

b. How much money did the company really borrow from the bank; how much did it have available for use?

c. How much interest did it pay each year? What was the effective interest rate paid?

22. *Present value techniques can be used to determine the value of a business.*

The general ledger of the Odessa Co. reflected, in summary form, the following balances (there were no material liabilities):

Current assets (accounts receivable, inventory, etc.)	$ 40,000
Equipment	80,000
Building	120,000
Land	60,000

The Geneva Company purchased the company for a total of $400,000 (cash). Immediately after purchase an independent appraiser estimated the value of the individual assets as follows:

Current assets	$ 40,000
Equipment	100,000
Building	160,000
Land	100,000

a. Prepare a journal entry to record the acquisition on the books of the Geneva Company.

b. Assume instead that the Geneva Company is willing to pay for the Odessa Company an amount such that its return on investment will be 10 percent per year. Geneva estimates that the earnings (net cash inflow) of Odessa will be $50,000 for the first five years following the acquisition and $40,000 for an indefinite period thereafter.

1. How much would the Geneva Company be willing to invest in order to receive a net cash inflow of $40,000 per year for an infinite number of years? (*Hint:* Of what amount is $40,000 10 percent?)

2. How much would it be willing to invest in order to receive a net cash inflow of $10,000 (the "bonus" earnings) for a period of five years? (*Hint:* What is the present value of an annuity of $10,000 discounted at 10 percent?)
3. How much would it be willing to pay for the Odessa Company?

SOLUTIONS TO EXERCISE FOR REVIEW AND SELF-TESTING

1. a. $100,000 × 1.08 = $108,000.
   b. $108,000 × 1.08 = $116,640.
   c. $116,640 × 1.08 = $125,971.
   Verify your answers by referring to Table 1, future value of $1.

2. a. $100,000.
   b. $100,000 + ($100,000 × 1.08) = $208,000.
   c. $100,000 + ($208,000 × 1.08) = $324,640.
   Verify your answers by referring to Table 3, future value of an annuity of $1 in arrears.

3. a. $100,000 ÷ 1.08 = $92,593.
   b. $ 92,593 ÷ 1.08 = $85,734.
   c. $ 85,734 ÷ 1.08 = $79,383.
   Verify your answers by referring to Table 2, present value of $1.

4. a. It should deposit the sum of the amounts determined in part c:

   $92,593 + $85,734 + $79,383 = $257,710.

   Verify your answer by referring to Table 4, present value of an annuity of $1 in arrears.

RECEIVABLES 7
AND PAYABLES

This chapter will focus on accounts and notes receivable and payable. It will also include a brief section on accounting for payroll transactions.

Definition

Receivables represent claims, usually stated in terms of a fixed number of dollars, arising from sale of goods, performance of services, lending of funds, or from some other type of transaction which establishes a relationship whereby one party is indebted to another. Claims which result from the sale of goods or services and which are neither supported by a written note nor secured by specific collateral (i.e., the creditor has no rights to specific assets in case the debtor fails to pay) are categorized as *accounts receivable*. They are distinguished from amounts backed by written notes (which may or may not arise out of a sales transaction) called *notes receivable* and those arising out of a myriad of other day-to-day business activities, such as *deposits receivable* (e.g., amounts to be received upon return of containers), *amounts due from officers* (perhaps as a consequence of loans), *dividends receivable*, *rent receivable*, and *interest receivable*. Accounts receivable do not ordinarily require payment of interest; notes receivable usually do.

Payables represent the corresponding obligations on the part of the recipient of the goods or services. Many of the questions pertaining to the valuation of payables are mirror images of those relating to receivables. The discussion in this chapter will center largely around receivables, with the expectation that, as appropriate, the reader can generalize to payables.

Receivables and payables that mature within one year (or one operating cycle of the business if it is greater than one year) are classified as current assets or liabilities. Those that mature in a longer period are classified as noncurrent.

Significance

The manner in which receivables are accounted for and reported is of concern to managers and investors for a number of reasons. First, receivables are assets and it is important that the amounts at which they are stated reflect the ultimate benefits they will provide to their holder. Second, issues relating to receivables are fundamental to those of income determination and, thus, performance measurement. Receivables, particularly accounts receivable, often arise out of sales or other revenue-generating transactions. They may be written off as "bad-debt" expenses. The question of when to recognize increases or decreases in receivables may be viewed alternatively as when to recognize revenues or expenses.

Third, receivables, like cash, are often unproductive assets. They may provide either no return or a return less than could be earned on other types of assets. It is generally to the advantage of a firm to collect its non- or low-interest-bearing accounts as soon as possible and to minimize the resources "tied up" in them.

Correspondingly, the concern of investors and managers with *payables* is that the obligations are fairly presented, that the expenses with which they are associated are recorded in an appropriate accounting period, that payment is made when the liability is due, and that the firm avails itself of all discounts for prompt payment.

RECEIVABLES—AN OVERVIEW

The amount at which a receivable should be reported in the financial statements of an enterprise is by no means obvious. Although the dollar amount of a receivable may be clearly evident from the terms of the sale or other agreement which establishes the receivable, not all receivables will prove to be collectible. One of the major causes of corporate bankruptcy is the failure to transform outstanding receivables into cash, and, not surprisingly, a considerable number of legal actions against CPA firms have resulted from alleged overstatements of the amount of recorded receivables that eventually would be collected. Moreover, the face amount of a receivable is not necessarily indicative of its *economic value*. Occasionally, the face amount of a receivable may include an element of *interest*, which, as will be demonstrated later in this chapter, serves to overstate the value of the receivable.

The basic journal entries to establish and to relieve a receivable account are straightforward. Upon the sale of goods and services for $100, for example, the appropriate journal entry would be

Accounts receivable	$100	
Sales revenue		$100

To record the sale of goods and services.

And upon subsequent receipt of customer payment,

Cash	$100	
Accounts receivable		$100

To record the collection of cash.

Variations in the terms of sales and the nature of the transactions resulting in the creation of the receivable necessitate considerable modification in the basic entries in order to accommodate specific circumstances.

UNCOLLECTIBLE ACCOUNTS RECEIVABLE

Direct Write-Off Method

There are two ways of accounting for uncollectible accounts receivable. The first, and *less preferable*, is the *direct write-off* method.

As soon as it becomes obvious that an account receivable is uncollectible, it is *written off*, and a *bad-debt expense* is charged. Upon learning, for example, that a customer from whom it held a receivable of $100 is likely to default on his obligation, a company might give accounting recognition to its loss with the following journal entry:

Bad-debt expense	$100	
Accounts receivable		$100

To write off an uncollectible account.

Concurrently, the firm would also credit the account of the individual customer in the accounts receivable subsidiary ledger. The accounts receivable subsidiary ledger is nothing more than a book or file of the amount owed by each customer. Each element of the file is maintained as a mini general ledger account for a specific customer, with debits indicating additional debts incurred by the customer and credits signifying payments made by him. The sum of the balances due from all customers should, at all times, be equal to the balance in the accounts receivable ledger account (often called the accounts receivable *control* account). Otherwise, an error has been made. In other words, the accounts receivable subsidiary ledger provides the support—or the detail—for the general ledger account.

Allowance Method

The direct write-off method, however, is inconsistent with the matching concepts discussed in Chapter 5; it may lead to an overstatement of *both* income of the period of sale and accounts receivable in the period of sale as well as in the subsequent periods. The *allowance* method overcomes these deficiencies.

Consider, for example, a company in the retail furniture industry. To attract business, the company grants credit to relatively poor credit risks. The policy results in extensive losses on uncollectible accounts, but management is nevertheless satisfied with the policy since it generates increased sales volume which more than offsets the losses. Based on several years' experience, management estimates that for every dollar of credit sales 10 cents will be uncollectible. The company vigorously pursues its delinquent debtors and writes off accounts only after it has made every reasonable attempt at recovery. Few accounts are written off before at least a year has elapsed since a customer has made a payment.

Under the circumstances, it would hardly be appropriate for the company to include among its assets the entire balance of accounts receivable. After all, only a portion of such balance is likely to prove collectible. Similarly, and equally significantly, if in 1983 the company had $500,000 in credit sales, it would not be justified in reporting revenues of $500,000 without making allowance for the fact that only $450,000 (90 percent of $500,000) would, in all probability, be fully realized. The individual accounts related to the sales in 1983 would not be written off for at least one or two years subsequent to 1983. But such losses would be the result of decisions—the decisions to sell to customers who prove to be unworthy of credit—made in 1983. Such losses would relate directly to sales made in 1983; they should be matched, therefore, with revenues of 1983.

There are, however, two obstacles to assigning credit losses to the year in which the sales take place. First, the amount of the loss cannot be known with certainty until several years subsequent to the sales. Normally, however, such amount can be estimated with reasonable accuracy. Based on the past collection experience of the company—or on that of other firms in similar industries—it is possible to predict the approximate amount of receivables that will prove to be uncollectible. The inability to make precise estimates of the anticipated losses can hardly be a justification for making no estimate at all. For even the roughest of estimates is likely to be more accurate than no estimate at all—the equivalent of a prediction of zero credit losses.

Second, even though a firm may be able to predict with reasonable precision the overall percentage of bad debts, it certainly is unable to forecast the *specific* accounts that will be uncollectible. After all, if it knew in advance that a particular individual would be unable to pay his debts, it would never have sold to him in the first place. If a company were to recognize bad debts as expenses and correspondingly reduce its accounts receivable balance, then which subsidiary ledger accounts would it credit? Since the sum of the balances of the subsidiary ledger accounts must equal the balance in the accounts receivable control account—i.e., the general ledger balance—the firm cannot reduce the balance in the control account without, at the same time, reducing the balances in the accounts of specific customers.

A firm can circumvent this second obstacle by establishing a *contra account*, "accounts receivable—allowance for uncollectibles." The contra account will normally have a credit balance (the opposite of the accounts receivable balance) and will always be associated with and reported directly beneath its *parent* account, accounts or notes receivable. To give accounting recognition to the fact that the full amount of the balance of accounts receivable is unlikely to be collected, the firm, instead of reducing or crediting accounts receivable directly, will credit "accounts receivable—allowance for uncollectibles."

To illustrate the procedure, continue the assumption that a firm in 1983 made $500,000 in credit sales. At year end the firm estimates that $50,000 of the outstanding balance will prove to be uncollectible. The following adjusting entry would be appropriate to give accounting recognition to its estimate:

(a)

Sales—uncollectibles (or bad-debt expense)*	$50,000	
Accounts receivable, allowance for uncollectibles		$50,000

To establish an allowance for uncollectibles.

The relevant T-accounts would appear as follows:

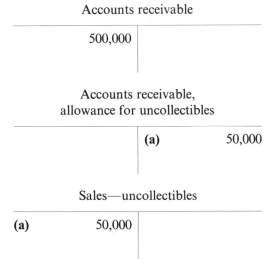

* Many, perhaps even most, companies debit "bad-debt expense" and report the amount among the other expenses. Other firms debit "sales—uncollectibles" and show the account as a reduction of revenues. This author prefers the latter approach. The firm has not incurred an expense. Instead, anticipated revenue has been lost; the firm will realize less than the full amount for which it billed customers.

On the balance sheet accounts receivable (assuming none of the $500,000 has yet been collected) and its related contra account would be reported as

Accounts receivable	$500,000	
Less: Allowance for uncollectibles	50,000	$450,000

As soon as the company is aware that a specific account cannot be collected it is then able to credit the accounts receivable control account as well as the specific accounts receivable subsidiary ledger account. Since the allowance for uncollectibles had been established for the very purpose of accommodating future bad debts, the offsetting debit would be made to the allowance for uncollectibles contra account.

Assume that in 1983 accounts totaling $7,000 are determined to be uncollectible. The appropriate entry would be

(b)

Accounts receivable, allowance for uncollectibles	$7,000	
Accounts receivable		$7,000

To write off specific accounts.

At the same time, the specific accounts to be written off would be credited in the accounts receivable subsidiary ledger. It is important to note that at the time specific accounts are written off *no entry is made to "sales—uncollectibles" or to "bad-debt expense." The effect of the uncollectible accounts on income would already have been recognized in the year the sales were made.* Hence, no further entries to revenue or expense accounts are justified. Moreover, the entry to write off the specific accounts has no effect on current assets or working capital. The *net* accounts receivable

(accounts receivable less allowance for uncollectibles) remains unchanged by the entry because both the parent account and the related contra account have been reduced by identical amounts.

METHODS OF ESTIMATING UNCOLLECTIBLES

There are two widely used methods of determining the charge (debit) to be made each accounting period to "sales—uncollectibles" and the corresponding amount to be added to the allowance for uncollectibles. The first is that illustrated above. Based on the collection experience of the company, an estimate is made of the percentage of *sales* (preferably taking into account only those made on credit) that will prove uncollectible. Each year, as long as the percentage remains stable, the same percentage is applied to the credit sales of the period, and the resultant amount is added to the allowance.

Alternatively, some firms compute the amount to be added to the allowance with specific reference to the accounts receivable outstanding at the end of the period. Such firms prepare what is known as the *aging schedule*. An aging schedule indicates what its name implies—the "age" of each account receivable. That is, it reveals the status of the various accounts—are they current, up to 30 days past due, up to 60 days past due, etc.? An aging schedule is illustrated in Exhibit 7-1.

Based on the aging schedule, the firm estimates the dollar amount of accounts that will be uncollectible. Such amount is indicative of the *total* balance required in the allowance for uncollectibles account.

As a rule, the longer an account is outstanding—the longer a debtor goes without

EXHIBIT 7-1

Aging Schedule as of 12/31/83

Customer Name	Total Balance	Current	No. of Days Past Due 0–30	31–30	61–60	Over 90
J. Faulkner	$ 93,478	$ 93,478				
F. Fitzgerald	60,250	26,139	$ 29,000	$ 5,111		
M. Higgins	100,000	75,000	25,000			
A. Hawthorne	8,222					$8,222
G. Brown	11,650				$11,650	
C. Ryder	92,811	29,206	33,930	26,000	3,675	
D. Deming	37,220		37,220			
G. Hawkins	110,100	110,100				
F. Cohen	116,277	116,277				
	$630,008	$450,200	$125,150	$31,111	$15,325	$8,222

paying—the less likely it is that the account will be collectible. Thus, a considerably greater proportion of accounts that are 120 days past due than those that are current will in all probability be uncollectible. A larger percentage of the balance of accounts 120 days past due must be added to the allowance for uncollectibles than for accounts that are current. The following summary based on the aging schedule in Exhibit 7-1 reveals the total balance required in the allowance for bad debts:

Summary of Accounts Receivable as of 12/31/83

Number of Days Past Due	Amount	Percent Likely to Be Uncollectible	Required Provision
0 (current)	$450,200	2%	$ 9,004
1–30	125,150	8	10,012
31–60	31,111	12	3,733
61–90	15,325	20	3,065
Over 90	8,222	50	4,111
	$630,008		$ 29,925

The total required provision less the balance that is currently in the account is the amount that must be added to the account. Suppose, for example, that the balance in the allowance for bad debts as of December 31 is $7,000. The amount that must be added is $22,925 ($29,925 less $7,000):

Sales—uncollectibles	$22,925	
Allowance for uncollectibles		$22,925

To increase the balance in the allowance account to the required level.

The key distinction between the two methods is that under the percentage of sales method the annual addition is determined by multiplying credit sales by a preestablished percentage. The amount of the addition is thereby computed independently of the existing balance in the allowance for uncollectibles account. Under the aging schedule method the annual addition is determined by first estimating the **required** balance in the allowance for uncollectibles account (as revealed by the aging schedule) and then subtracting from such required balance the actual balance in the account.

Which of the methods of determining the amount to be added to the allowance for uncollectibles—the percentage of sales or the aging schedule—is preferable? Insofar as the firm's estimates of either the percentage of sales to be uncollected or the percentages of the various groups of past due accounts are accurate, and uncollectible accounts are written off on a regular basis each year, then both methods will result in approximately equal credits to the allowance and charges to earnings over time. If, however, write offs tend to follow an irregular pattern with few accounts being written off in good years and many accounts being written off in bad years, then the two methods may have differing impacts on earnings. The percentage of sales method will result in a constant percent of sales being charged to "sales—uncollectibles" regardless of the number of accounts written off in a particular year. The amount of the charge will be a function of sales volume, not of the number of accounts written off. The aging schedule approach, on the other hand, will usually result in a more erratic charge to bad-debt expense. The amount of the charge will be highly responsive to the number and size of the accounts written off. To the extent that it is desirable to match the "cost" of the bad debts to the sales to which they are applicable, then the percentage of sales methods is preferable. However, oftentimes a firm may misestimate the percentage of sales and as a result the balance in the allowance for bad debts becomes either inadequately low or unnecessarily high. Neither method, therefore, is necessarily preferable. The optimum approach may be to use both methods in conjunction with one another— to make an initial estimate of the charge to "sales—uncollectibles" by taking a percentage of credit sales and then to test the adequacy of the allowance for bad debts by preparing an aging schedule.

SALES RETURNS

Sales returns involve considerations similar to those of bad debts. Insofar as goods that have been sold are expected to be returned in a subsequent accounting period, accounting recognition must be given in the period in which they are sold. Financial statements which fail to take into account goods to be subsequently returned and refunds to be given to customers would clearly overstate revenues and, hence, earnings. But as with allowances for bad debts, the necessary accounting entries must reflect the fact that until returns are actually made, the accountant has no way of knowing either the exact amount of such returns or the specific customers who will make such returns.

The accountant must follow an approach similar to that in recording bad debts. He must first make an estimate of anticipated returns (based, perhaps, on previous experience) and then establish an allowance for such returns.

Assume that at year end a firm estimates that merchandise that was sold for $10,000 will be returned in the following year. An appropriate journal entry would be

(a)

Sales—returns	$10,000	
Accounts receivable—		
allowance for returns		$10,000

To record the estimate of sales returns.

Both of the accounts involved in the entry are *contra accounts*. "Sales—returns" would be reported on the income statement as a reduction of sales. "Accounts receivable—allowance for returns" would be reported on the balance sheet as an additional reduction of accounts receivable along with the allowance for uncollectibles.

If the merchandise to be returned can be resold, then it is necessary also to give effect to the fact that expense, i.e., cost of goods sold, in addition to revenues and sales, have been overstated in the year of sale. Assume that the merchandise to be returned had an original cost of $8,000. The required entry to record the anticipated return would be

(b)

Merchandise to be returned (asset)	$8,000	
Cost of goods sold (expense)		$8,000

To record the cost of goods to be returned.

When the merchandise is actually returned, only balance sheet accounts need to be adjusted; the impact on revenues and expenses would have been accounted for in the year of sale:

(c)

Accounts receivable—Allowance for returns (asset; contra)	$10,000	
Accounts receivable (asset)		$10,000

To give the customer credit for merchandise returned.

(d)

Merchandise inventory (asset)	$8,000	
Merchandise to be returned (asset)		$8,000

To record the receipt of returned merchandise.

If the merchandise returned cannot be resold and has no value, then entries **b** and **d** need not be made.

The journal entries pertaining to sales returns are illustrated in this section not because they are especially difficult or unusual, but because they provide another example of the importance of assigning expenses to the accounting period in which their related revenues were recognized. In many industries sales returns, no matter how accounted for, would have but an immaterial impact on earnings. But in some, their effect may be substantial. In the book publishing industry, for instance, it is a common practice to guarantee retailers the right to return unsold merchandise. If a publisher were to recognize revenue at the time that books were shipped to retailers (perhaps a premature point in light of the return policy) without giving effect to the books that it will have to accept back, then both income and assets (accounts receivable) would be significantly overstated.

CASH DISCOUNTS

Frequently, a seller will offer a customer a discount for prompt payment. A company may, for example, sell under terms 2/10, n/30. The total amount is due within 30 days; however, if payment is made within 10 days, the customer is entitled to a discount of 2 percent. In economic substance it is difficult to view such terms as representing a true discount; a more acceptable interpretation is that the customer is subject to a penalty if he fails to make prompt payment. Suppose that a customer buys merchandise with a *stated* price of $100. If he pays on the thirtieth day following purchase rather than on the tenth day, then he has the use of his funds for an additional 20 days. The use of such funds will have cost him $2 for each $98 of merchandise purchased. His effective interest cost will be at an annual rate of approximately 37 percent—360 days/20 days × $2/$98. Only a company with a severely impaired credit rating would be willing to pay such an extraordinarily high rate. An unbiased observer might suspect, therefore, that the merchandise sold had a fair market value not of the stated sales price of $100 but rather of the stated sales price less the discount, $98.

The proper accounting for cash discounts is *not* one of the critical issues facing the business community. It is of interest to accounting students primarily because it provides another example of the importance of accounting for substance over form.

Both purchasers and sellers account for cash discounts in either of two basic ways: the net method or the gross method. The *net* method requires that both purchases and

sales be recorded at the fair market value of the goods traded—that is, sales price *less* the discount—and that payments in excess of the discounted price be recorded separately as a penalty for late payment or as a financing cost. The *gross* method permits purchases and sales to be recorded at the stated price, subject to later adjustment. A simple example can be used to compare the two approaches from the perspective of the purchaser.

Example

A company purchases on terms 2/10, n/30 merchandise that has a sales price of $100,000:

Net Method			Gross Method		
Inventory	$98,000		Inventory	$100,000	
Accounts payable		$98,000	Accounts payable		$100,000

To record the purchase of merchandise.

It pays within the discount period:

Net Method			Gross Method		
Accounts payable	$98,000		Accounts payable	$100,000	
Cash		$98,000	Cash		$98,000
			Purchase discounts		2,000

To record the purchase of merchandise.

Or, alternatively, it fails to pay within the discount period:

Net Method			Gross Method		
Accounts payable	$98,000		Accounts payable	$100,000	
Purchase discounts lost (expense)	2,000		Cash		$100,000
Cash		$100,000			

To record payment after the discount period.

EXHIBIT 7-2

Typical Promissory Note

Acct. No.   NAME

Austin, Texas, _____ 19 ____

NO. _____		$ _____	
Date	Int.	Principal	Balance

ON DEMAND, or if no demand is made, then _____ after date, without grace, for value received, I, we, and each of us, as principals, promise to pay to the order of **THE AMERICAN NATIONAL BANK OF AUSTIN** at its banking house in the City of Austin, Travis County, Texas, the sum of

_____ DOLLARS,

with interest theron at the rate of _____ percent per annum from _____ until maturity, and if not then paid, at the rate of 10% per annum until paid.

    In the event of default in the payment of this note, when due, or in performance of any agreement contained in the security agreement securing payment hereof, or in the event the holder deems itself insecure, then the holder of this note shall have the option, without demand or notice, to declare the principal and interest at once due and payable and to exercise any and all other rights or remedies provided in this note and in the security agreement, if any, including the right to set off against this note and all other liabilities of the undersigned to the holder, all money or other property in its possession held for or owed to the undersigned.

    Each maker, surety, endorser, and guarantor of this note hereby waives presentment for payment or acceptance, notice of non-payment or dishonor, protest, notice of protest, and diligence in the collection hereof or in filing suit hereon and agrees that liability for the payment hereof shall not be affected or impaired by any release of or change in the security, if any, or by any extension in the time for payment; and further agrees to pay all costs and expenses of collection incurred by the holder, and if this note is placed in the hands of an attorney for collection after maturity, or is collected by legal proceedings of any kind, to pay a reasonable attorney's fee, which shall not in any event be less than 10% of the unpaid principal and interest, or the sum of $50.00, whichever is the greater, and shall bear interest at the rate of 10% per annum from the date of its accrual.

    Payment of this note is secured by all money or other property of the undersigned now or at any time hereafter in the possession of the holder in any capacity and also by

AB50-607-01 (1/72)

Address: _____   Name: _____

Due: _____ Phone No. _____

The essential difference between the two methods is that under the gross method inventory is overstated because it is recorded at gross amount payable, which exceeds the fair market value by the amount of discount. As a consequence, upon sale of the goods, cost of goods sold is also overstated. The distortions in the gross method can, of course, be eliminated by an appropriate year-end adjustment, which in effect, serves to convert the gross method to the net method.*

Advantage of Net Method

The net method makes a contribution to management control that the gross method does not. The net method results in a charge to the expense account, purchase discounts

---

* The adjustment would be a credit in the amount of the discount to "Merchandise inventory" (or "Cost of goods sold" to the extent that the merchandise has been resold) and a debit either to "Purchase discounts" (if the discount were taken) or to "Purchase discounts lost" (if the discount were lost).

---

lost, whenever the firm fails to avail itself of the discounts. Management is thereby made explicitly aware of the cost of its negligence in, or policy of, not paying on time. The gross method, by contrast, "buries" the penalty charge in inventory and it is eventually reflected in cost of goods sold.

The entries recording the sales and subsequent collection from the standpoint of the seller would correspond to those of the purchaser. The gross method would result in the overstatement of both sales and accounts receivable.

PROMISSORY NOTES

When a firm extends credit beyond a short period of time (two or three months) or makes a loan, it usually requests formal written documentation of the borrower's obligation to make timely payment. The legal instrument which provides such documentation is known as a *promissory note*. A typical promissory note is illustrated in Exhibit 7-2.

A promissory note, unlike an account receivable, generally provides that the maker (the borrower) of the note agrees to pay a fee, known as interest, for the right to use the funds provided. The promissory note is a legally binding contract. It would specify the following:

The parties involved in the contract—the payor, who is the person or organization that agrees to make the payment, and the payee, who is the person or organization to whom the money is owed (sometimes a note may be drawn to *bearer*—that is, payment is to be made to whomever presents the note to the maker);

The date the note was issued and the date payment is due (some notes state that payment is due in a specific number of days from the date it was issued);

The *principal* of the note (the amount of credit being extended), often referred to as the *face value* of the note;

The rate of interest;

Any collateral or property that the borrower either pledges or surrenders as security for the note;

Interest on a note is expressed in terms of an annual percentage rate. The formula for translating the percentage rate into the actual dollar amount is

$$\text{Interest} = \text{Principal} \times \text{Rate}$$

$$\times \frac{\text{Days of loan}}{\text{Total days in one year}} *$$

If, for example, a company issues a note for $100,000 that bears interest at a rate of 8 percent and is payable in 90 days, the actual interest that it will be required to pay can be computed as

$$\$100,000 \times .08 \times \frac{90}{360} = \$2,000$$

Notes are reported on the balance sheet at their principal or face amount. This convention is a source of confusion to many students since the total obligation of the maker is not only the principal but the interest as well. In the above illustration, for example, the total amount to be paid after 90 days is $100,000 plus $2,000 interest. Yet the note would be recorded on the balance sheet at only $100,000. The logic beyond the convention becomes apparent, however, when the impact of notes and interest on the balance sheet is viewed in conjunction with that on the income statement. Interest is a charge imposed on a borrower for the use of funds over a period of time. From the standpoint of the borrower, therefore, the interest cannot be considered an expense—and hence not a liability—until it has actually used the borrowed funds over a period of time. Over the passage of time, the borrower will recognize the expense associated with the use of funds—interest expense—and at the same time the liability—accrued interest payable. Similarly, the lender will periodically recognize the earnings attributable to the funds that it has provided the debtor and concurrently acknowledge the creation of an asset, interest receivable.

A brief example may make the relationship between income and balance sheet accounts somewhat more clear.

Example

On June 1, Echo Co. informs Foxtrot Corp. that it will be unable to make payment on its open account, which on that date has a balance of $20,000. Echo requests that Foxtrot accept instead a 60-day note that will

---

* To facilitate computations, it is common practice in financial circles to assume that a year has 360 days.

bear interest at the rate of 6 percent. Foxtrot agrees.

Upon accepting the note on June 1, Foxtrot Corp. would make the following entry to record the exchange of an account receivable (which does not bear interest and is unsupported by a formal legal instrument) for an interest-bearing note receivable:

Notes receivable $20,000
    Accounts receivable $20,000
To record acceptance of the note.

Thereafter, with the passage of time Foxtrot Corp. must account for the revenue that it is earning on the note which it holds. Most companies, considering the clerical costs of making frequent journal entries, update their accounts quarterly or at best monthly. Assuming that Foxtrot Corp. updates its accounts monthly, the following entry would be appropriate on June 30:

Accrued interest receivable $100
    Interest revenue $100
To record monthly interest revenue from the the note.

The $100 represents interest for a period of 30 days computed as

$$\$20,000 \times .06 \times \frac{30}{360} = \$100$$

Both 6 percent and 12 percent interest rates are especially easy to work with—6 percent represents monthly interest charges of $\frac{1}{2}$ percent, and 12 percent represents monthly charges of 1 percent.

On July 30, the note would fall due. Assuming that both the note and the interest are paid in full, two entries are required to record collection. The first is identical to that made on June 30; it recognizes the interest earned during the one-month period since

interest revenue was previously recorded:

Accrued interest receivable $100
    Interest revenue $100
To record monthly interest revenue from the note.

The balance in the accrued interest receivable account now stands at $200 and that in the notes receivable account at the original $20,000. Upon collection of both interest and principal, the appropriate entry would be

Cash $20,200
    Accrued interest
      receivable $ 200
    Notes receivable   20,000
To record the collection of the note and interest. (Note that this entry has no effect on revenues or expenses).

From the standpoint of the payor—the maker of the note—the journal entries would be a mirror image of those of the payee.

NOTES WITH INTEREST INCLUDED IN FACE VALUE

Frequently a note will not specifically indicate a rate of interest. Instead, the face value of the note will include not only the amount originally borrowed but also the applicable interest charges as well. A borrower, for example, may give to a bank or other creditor a note for $1,000 in exchange for a 90-day loan. The bank, however, would not give the borrower the full $1,000. Instead, if the going interest rate for that type of loan were 12 percent, it would give the borrower only $970.87. If the annual rate of interest is 12 percent, then the interest on a loan of $970.87 for 90 days would be

$$\$970.87 \times .12 \times \frac{90}{360} = \$29.13$$

The interest of $29.13, plus the principal of $970.87, exactly equals the face value of the note, $1,000.

Regardless of the manner in which the terms of the loan are stated, the difference between the amount actually received by the borrower and the amount that it must eventually repay at the maturity of the note represents the cost of borrowing—i.e., interest. In the present example, the actual amount of the loan as well as the interest could have been readily calculated as follows:

Let x = the actual amount of the loan

If interest is to be at an annual rate of 12 percent, then interest for the 90-day period, approximately $\frac{1}{4}$ year, would be a total of 3 percent of the actual amount of the loan. The total amount to be repaid is the actual amount of the loan, x, plus the interest, $.03x$. The total amount to be repaid has been established (the face amount of the note) at $1,000. Hence,

$$\$1,000 = x + .03x \qquad \text{or}$$

$$\$1,000 = 1.03x \qquad \text{or}$$

$$x = \frac{\$1,000}{1.03} = \$970.87$$

The interest must be the difference between the face amount of the note and the amount actually borrowed: $1,000 minus $970.87, or $29.13. Interest for each 30-day period is therefore $9.71.

When the amount actually loaned is less than the face amount of the note—that is, when the face amount includes both principal and interest—the note is known as a *discount* note and the interest rate as a *discount rate.* The journal entries required to record *discount* notes and the associated interest charges are similar to those for conventional interest-earning instruments.

Assume, for example, that on July 1 a lending institution accepted a three-month note of $1,000 discounted in exchange for an actual cash loan of $970.87. The entry to record the loan would be

Notes receivable,		
face value	$1,000.00	
Cash		$970.87
Notes receivable,		
discount (asset		
contra account)		29.13

To record acceptance of the note.

The overall effect of the entry is to record the asset, notes receivable, at the amount actually loaned. "Notes receivable, discount" is a contra account associated with the account, "Notes receivable, face value." If a balance sheet were to be drawn up immediately after the loan was made, the relevant accounts would be reported on the balance sheet (among current assets) as

Notes receivable,		
face value	$1,000.00	
Less: Discount		
on notes	29.13	$970.87

As with conventional interest-bearing notes, interest must periodically be taken into account. On July 31, the appropriate entry would be (making the simplifying assumptions that one-third of the overall interest charges will be recorded during each of the three months regardless of the actual number of days in the month)

Notes receivable, discount	$9.71	
Interest revenue		$9.71

To record interest on the note for one month.

The effect of such entry is to recognize the interest revenue and also to increase the value of the note (by decreasing the value of the contra account) by the amount of revenue recognized. The entry is similar to that which would have been made had the note been one with a stated interest rate. The main difference is that with the discount note the recognition of the interest results in the net increase of an asset, notes receivable, whereas with the interest-bearing note it results in the increase of a different asset, interest receivable.

The entry made for the month of July would also be made on August 31 and on September 30 to give recognition to the interest revenue earned during each month.

On September 30, when the note is paid, the balance in the "notes receivable, discount" account would have been reduced to zero. Collection of the note could be recorded as follows:

Cash	$1,000.00	
Notes receivable,		
face value		$1,000.00

To record collection of the note.

If the period of the loan were greater than one year, present value techniques such as those described in Chapter 6, could be conveniently used to determine the amount to be advanced to the borrower.

Example

A finance company makes a loan to a customer on a discount basis. The company accepts from the customer a two-year note for $5,000. The actual cash advanced is determined on the basis of a 12 percent annual rate of interest.

Per Table 2 in the appendix, the present value of $5,000 discounted at a rate of 12 percent for two years is

$$\$5,000 \times .7972 = \$3,986$$

The finance company would advance the customer $3,986 and record the loan as follows:

Notes receivable	$5,000	
Notes receivable,		
discount		$1,014
Cash		3,986

To record the loan to the customer.

Interest revenue for the first year would be 12 percent of the *net* balance of the outstanding customer obligation, that is, 12 percent of $3,986—$478. An appropriate journal entry after the note has been outstanding for one year would be

Notes receivable, discount	$478	
Interest revenue		$478

To record interest for the first year.

Since the customer did not actually remit an interest payment, the effective balance of its obligation would increase after the first year by $478. The increase in the effective balance is accounted for by a decrease in the discount. After the first year, the note would be reported as follows:

Notes receivable	$5,000	
Less: Discount on notes	536	$4,464

Interest for the second year would be based on the effective customer obligation at the end of the first year. Thus, it would be 12 percent of $4,465—$536. The entry at the end of the second year to record both interest revenue and collection of the full $5,000 would be

Cash	$5,000	
Notes receivable, discount	536	
Notes receivable		$5,000
Interest revenue		536

To record second-year interest and collection of the note.

The interest revenue on a discount note would increase from year to year, corresponding to an increase in the effective obligation of the customer. Interest must be paid not only on the original amount borrowed but on any unsatisfied obligations for interest as well. (If the loan is for a relatively short period of time—less than one year—the "interest on the interest" is usually ignored because it would be immaterial.)

NON-INTEREST-BEARING NOTES

Occasionally, a firm will appear to sell on especially generous terms of credit. In fact, sometimes the terms seem so generous that they raise serious doubts as to whether the goods are really worth the price at which they were sold.

Assume, for example, that a company sells for $100,000 equipment that it no longer needs. The company accepts from its customer a five-year "interest-free" note for the full sales price. As emphasized in Chapter 6, $100,000 to be received in five years is worth considerably less than the same amount to be received today. Indeed, per Table 2, the present value of a single payment of $100,000 five years hence, discounted at a rate of 8 percent, is

$$\$100,000 \times .6806 = \$68,060$$

Importance of Recognizing Substance over Form

It is hardly reasonable to expect a company to provide an interest-free loan to a customer for five years. A more credible interpretation of the transaction is that interest charges are included in the $100,000 selling price. If the prevailing rate for similar types of loans is 8 percent, the facts suggest that the "true" selling price of the equipment is $68,060. The difference ($31,940) between such amount and the stated selling price of $100,000 represents interest on a five-year loan of $68,060.

If firms are to be concerned with the substance rather than the form of transactions, they must divide the $100,000 into its component parts. They must account separately for the sales price and the interest. They must *impute* interest of $31,940. If the equipment had been recorded on the books of the seller at $50,000, then the following entry would be appropriate:

Notes receivable	$100,000	
Equipment		$50,000
Notes receivable, discount		31,940
Gain on sale of equipment		18,060

To record the sale of the equipment.

During each year that the note was outstanding, the company would accrue interest on the effective balance of the "loan"—the note receivable less the unamortized portion of the discount. Thus, to record interest after one year,

Notes receivable, discount	$5,445	
Interest revenue		$5,445

To record interest for one year on a note of $68,060 at a rate of 8 percent.

And after the second year,

Notes receivable, discount	$5,880	
Interest revenue		$5,880

To record interest for one year on a note of $73,505 at a rate of 8 percent ($73,505 represents the face value of the note less unamortized discount of $26,495).

Over the life of the note, the firm will recognize earnings on the transaction of $50,000—$100,000 received in cash less the recorded value of the equipment of $50,000—regardless of how the $100,000 is divided between "true" sales price and interest. If the transaction were accounted for in accordance with its form (selling price of $100,000), then a gain of $50,000 would be realized at time of sale. If accounted for in accordance with substance (selling price of $68,060), then a gain of only $18,060 would be recognized in the year of sale. The remaining $31,940 would be recognized as interest and taken into income over the five-year period of the note.

From the standpoint of the purchaser of the equipment if the entire $100,000 is assigned to the cost of the equipment, then that amount would be subject to depreciation and recognized as an expense over the remaining useful life of the equipment—perhaps 10 years. If, however, the interest of $31,940 were taken into account, then only $68,060 would be assigned to the cost of the equipment and expensed as depreciation over its useful life. The interest, $31,940, would be charged as an expense over the five-year period of the note. The manner in which the transaction is accounted for has no effect on *total* earnings of either the purchaser or the seller; it does, however, have a significant impact on the timing and classification of such earnings.

INDUSTRY EXAMPLE: RETAIL LAND SALES COMPANIES

The issue of imputed interest is especially important with respect to *retail land sales* companies. Retail land sales companies purchase large tracts of land and subdivide them into small parcels for sale to consumers. They plan communities; install streets, sewers, and utilities; and sometimes construct *amenities* such as golf courses, club houses, motels, and restaurants. Often, they engage in extensive promotional efforts (e.g., free dinners or trips to the site) and frequently they direct their sales efforts at those who are interested in either retirement or vacation homes. Retail land sales companies seldom accept interest-free notes. Sometimes, however, they charge relatively low rates of interest. For example, they might charge a purchaser 12 percent interest annually at a time when the *prime rate* (that charged by banks to their most select customers) is 16 percent and the firms' own cost of borrowing is 19 percent.

Until recently, it was standard procedure in the industry to record sales at the face value of the note received. Such practice, however, was criticized on the ground that it overstated sales revenue and understated interest revenue. Since sales revenue is recognized at the time a sales contract is signed and interest revenue is recognized over the term of the note, the effect was to speed up recognition of revenue and, according to critics, to overstate earnings in the year of the sale. Considering that the notes were often for 10 years and that the difference between the rate actually charged and that normally charged for "loans" of similar types may have been as much as 10 percent, the difference in first-year revenues on a sale of $10,000 could be almost $3,500. To eliminate the possibility of such overstatements in earnings, the Accounting Principles Board prescribed that the required payments on notes receivable that bear unreasonably low rates of interest must be *discounted* by the *prevailing* rate for similar types of credit instruments and that a portion of the stated sales price of the land be accounted for as interest rather than sales revenue.*

Example

New Mexico Land Co. sells parcels of land for $10,000. Purchasers must pay $1,000 down and can give a 10-year note, which

* *Accounting for Retail Land Sales.* American Institute of Certified Public Accountants, 1972.

bears interest at a rate of 4 percent for the $9,000 balance. The note must be paid in 10 annual installments of $1,110. ($1,110 is the annual payment required to repay a loan of $9,000 in equal installments if interest is charged at a rate of 4 percent per year.)

If the company's customers had attempted to borrow the funds from a traditional lending institution, they would have had to pay the prevailing interest rate of 12 percent.

The present value of the consideration—that is, the "true" selling price of the land—can be determined by discounting *all* required payments (both principal and interest) by the *effective* rate of interest, in this example 12 percent:

Present value of $1,000 down payment	$1,000
Present value of 10 annual payments of $1,110 discounted at a rate of 12 percent: Per Table 4, $1,110 × 5.6502	6,272
Present value of all payments	$7,272

As a consequence, the firm would recognize sales revenue of only $7,272. $7,272 represents the worth at time of sale of all the payments to be received by the company. The difference between that amount and $10,000 represents interest revenue and must be reported as such over the 10-year period that the note is outstanding.

RECEIVABLES AND REVENUE IN PRACTICE: THE FRANCHISE INDUSTRY

The relationship between receivables and revenues cannot be overemphasized. The accounting practices of the franchise industry highlight some of the key issues pertaining to the realization of revenue and the valuation of receivables.

Franchisors sell to individual businessmen (franchisees) the right to operate a specific kind of business, to use the name of the franchisor and to provide goods or services associated with the franchisor. Companies such as McDonald's and Holiday Inn are among the best known franchisors, and their establishments appear to have become permanent additions to the American landscape. But hundreds of other franchise operations, often imitators of the well-known firms, make brief appearances on the American scene before fading into oblivion and often bankruptcy.

The revenue of a franchisor ordinarily comes from several sources. First, the franchisor sells franchises to the parties who will operate them. The franchisor receives a small down payment and accepts from the franchisee long-term notes. Second, it generally receives royalties based on the sales volume of the franchisee. Third, it sometimes sells to the franchisee all or a portion of the product that will be sold to the public (e.g., the seasonings for fried chicken).

The source of revenue that presents the most difficult accounting problems is the first—that from the sale of the franchise. Commonly, the franchisor and franchisee will enter into a contractual arrangement many months prior to the time that the franchisee is ready to begin operations. During the intervening period and sometimes for a period subsequent to opening, the franchisor is required to provide services (advertising and management training, for example) to the franchisee. The question arises as to the point at which the revenue from the sale should be recognized and the related receivable should be recorded as an asset. Consistent with the principle that revenue should be related to productive effort, it could be recognized at the time the contract is signed, when the outlet first commences operations, or in the one or more periods in which various services are performed.

The issue of revenue recognition is compounded, however, by the fact that firms in the industry tend to face a high rate of default on notes received from the franchisees. The collectibility of the notes is directly dependent on the success of the individual franchisees. The franchisor can expect payment only insofar as the operations of a franchisee generate sufficient cash to meet its obligations as they come due.

Because eventual collection of cash cannot always be reasonably assured, it has sometimes been suggested that revenue be recognized only as the notes are actually collected; that is, on the cash collection or installment basis. Such approach would eliminate the possibility that the assets of the franchisor are overstated by the amounts that will prove uncollectible; it would make certain that revenue is not prematurely realized. But it would also be inconsistent with the general accounting practice of recognizing revenue when a transaction is substantially completed (and, as necessary, making appropriate provisions for uncollectible accounts). The installment method of accounting is ordinarily reserved for those exceptional cases where there is no reasonable basis for estimating the degree of collectibility of outstanding receivables.

Since the mid-1960s there has been an appreciable growth in the franchise industry. Firms have followed a variety of different accounting practices, and there have been allegations that some firms adopted policies which overstated both earnings and assets. In 1973, to assure greater uniformity of practice, a committee of the American Institute of Certified Public Accountants set forth guidelines for the recognition of revenue.* The committee recommended that revenue from the sale of a franchise should be delayed until the franchisor has substantially performed all of the initial services set forth in the sales agreement. It pointed out that because of a variety of practices in the industry there can be no one specific condition or event that can serve as the sole criterion for recognition of revenue. Substantial performance may occur at different times for different franchisors. Nevertheless, the committee indicated that "conservatism justifies the presumption that *commencement of operations by the franchisee* is the earliest point at which substantial performance has occurred." As a rule, the committee urged, revenue should therefore be recognized at the time that the franchisee starts its operations.

The committee took cognizance of the unusual risks of collection faced by some franchisors. But it recommended that the cash collection basis of revenue recognition be reserved for those exceptional cases where no reasonable basis of estimating the degree of collectibility exists. It urged that companies establish adequate allowances for uncollectible accounts and periodically review such allowances to make certain that they are sufficient in the light of changed conditions.

PAYROLL TRANSACTIONS

Although payroll transactions present few conceptual considerations that have not already been dealt with, they are worthy of discussion because they are of concern to virtually all profit and nonprofit organizations and are sometimes of major magnitude.

* *Accounting for Franchise Fee Revenue.* American Institute of Certified Public Accountants, 1973.

The accounting for payroll transactions is characterized by the fact that the wage or salary expense pertaining to an individual employee may be considerably *greater* than the amount indicated by his wage or salary rate but that the amount actually paid to the employee may be considerably *less* than that indicated by his wage rate. The business firm must pay payroll taxes that are specifically levied on the employer and, commonly, must provide for *fringe benefits* in addition to regular wage and salary payments. Moreover, the employer must withhold from each employee's wages and salary the employee's share of payroll taxes as well as amounts for other designated purposes. Amounts withheld from the employee ordinarily represent a liability of the employer; they must be remitted either to the government or to a specific fund.

Example

An employee is paid at the rate of $2,000 per month. From his salary must be withheld (either by law or by employee election) the following: federal income taxes (according to a schedule published by the Internal Revenue Service)—$355; Federal Insurance Contribution Act deductions (abbreviated FICA and commonly referred to as *Social Security* payments)—7 percent of gross salary—$140; Blue Cross/Blue Shield contribution—$84 per month; savings bond plan—$18 per month. As a consequence of the deductions *take-home* pay of the employee would be $1,403.

In addition, the employer incurs the following voluntary or statutory charges: employer share of FICA contributions—7 percent of gross salary—$140; contribution to company pension fund—8 percent of gross salary—$160; state and federal un-employment insurance taxes—3 percent of gross salary—$60.

The following entry would be appropriate on the payroll date:

Salaries (expense)	$2,000	
FICA expense, employer's share	140	
Unemployment insurance (expense)	60	
Pension expense	160	
Salaries payable		$1,403
Liability for income taxes withheld		355
Liability for FICA (both employee and employer share)		280
Liability for Blue Cross/Blue Shield		84
Liability for savings bonds		18
Liability for pensions		160
Liability for unemployment insurance		60

To record payroll

When cash payments are made to the employee or to the appropriate funds or government agencies, the various liability accounts would be debited; cash would be credited.

If employees are granted periodic vacations, then the expense of their salaries during the vacations should be allocated to those accounting periods in which they are actually performing their services. If, in the above example, the employee were granted a one-month annual vacation, then the $2,000 that he would be paid while on vacation should be charged as an expense during the 11 months in which he worked. The accrual of vacation pay could be effected by the following additional entry each month:

Vacation pay (expense) $182
    Provision for vacation
        pay (liability) $182

To accrue vacation pay—one-eleventh of monthly salary

When the employee takes his vacation—by which time the balance in the provision for vacation pay account should be approximately $2,000—the following entry (which, for simplicity, omits consideration of payroll withholdings and other deductions) would be in order:

Provision for vacation pay $2,000
    Salaries payable $2,000

To record the amount due the employee for vacation pay.

It is particularly important for organizations to spread the costs of vacation pay over the productive periods of their employees if they prepare quarterly or semiannual financial reports in addition to annual reports. If they neglect to *accrue* vacation pay, then cost of operations in the summer months may appear to be considerably higher than in other months. Such increase in operations cost is attributable to the fact that most employees take their vacations in the summer when substitute workers must be hired or production reduced.

RATIOS

This section will be directed to two ratios that are useful in the control and evaluation of accounts receivable.

Accounts Receivable Turnover

Accounts receivable turnover is an *activity ratio. Activity ratios* measure the effectiveness of management in utilizing specific resources under its command. Activity ratios are often referred to as *turnover* ratios. They relate specific asset accounts to sales or to some other revenue or expense accounts with which they are logically associated.

Accounts receivable turnover is the number of times that sales of a year exceeds average accounts receivable. It is computed by dividing sales by average accounts receivable:

$$\text{Accounts receivable turnover} = \frac{\text{Sales}}{\text{Average accounts receivable}}$$

The greater the number of times that accounts receivable turnover, the smaller the amount of funds that the company has "tied up" in accounts receivable and the greater the amount of funds that it can invest in other assets.

The balance sheet and income statement of Fruehauf Corporation, a manufacturer of truck-trailers and auto parts are shown in Exhibit 7-3. In 1980, Fruehauf had sales of $1,878,746,434. As of January 1, 1980, it held accounts receivable of $294,592,981; as of December 31, $244,233,702. Average accounts receivable were thus $269,413,341 [($294,592,981 + $244,233,702)/2].

$$\text{Accounts receivable turnover} = \frac{\$1,878,746,434}{\$269,413,341}$$
$$= 7.0 \text{ times}$$

Ideally, average receivables should be based on 12 individual months rather than beginning- and end-of-year values. Otherwise, the average may be distorted by seasonal fluctuations. Indeed, many companies intentionally choose to end their fiscal years when business activities are at their slowest.

The same relationship can be expressed in an alternative form, *number of days' sales in accounts receivable.* Assuming that all sales were made on account, then on average Fruehauf made $5,218,740 in sales per day:

$$\text{Average sales per day} = \frac{\text{Total sales}}{365}$$

$$= \frac{\$1,878,746,434}{365}$$

$$= \$5,147,251$$

The number of days' sales in accounts receivable may be determined by dividing accounts receivable as of *any particular day* by average sales per day:

Number of days' sales in accounts receivable

$$= \frac{\text{Accounts receivable}}{\text{Average sales per day}}$$

Number of days' sales in accounts receivable as of December 31, 1980

$$= \frac{\$244,233,702}{\$5,147,251} = 47.4 \text{ days}$$

Expressed in another way, based on average sales it takes 47.4 days for the company to collect its accounts receivable. Should the collection period increase from one year to the next, or should it be greater than the number of days in the payment period specified in the company's terms of sales, then there would be reason to investigate whether the firm is experiencing difficulty in collecting from its customers.

Quick Ratio

Liquidity ratios measure the ability of a firm to meet its obligations as they mature.

As indicated in Chapter 2, the primary measure of liquidity is the *current* ratio. The current ratio compares current assets with current liabilities. The higher the ratio of current assets to current liabilities, the less likely the company will be to default on its obligations. Current assets, however, commonly provide either no direct return to the company or a return smaller than could be obtained if funds were invested in long-term securities. Insofar as the current ratio is high, therefore, the company may be incurring an *opportunity cost*—it could be losing revenue by tying up funds in current assets rather than by taking advantage of other financial opportunities.

A test of liquidity more severe than the current ratio is the *quick ratio*. The quick ratio matches cash, marketable securities, and accounts receivable to current liabilities. It provides an indication of the ability of the company to satisfy its obligations without taking into account both inventories, which are less readily transformed into cash than other current assets, and prepaid expenses, which save the company from having to disburse cash in the future but which are not themselves transformed into cash. The ratio of Fruehauf Corporation as of December 31, 1980 is .82 to 1.

Both the current and quick ratios are of special concern to short-term creditors, those

$$\text{Quick ratio} = \frac{\text{Cash} + \text{Marketable securities} + \text{Current receivables}}{\text{Current liabilities}}$$

$$= \frac{\$41,527,022 + \$16,922,342 + \$261,055,297 + \$14,100,000}{\$409,103,170}$$

$$= .82$$

EXHIBIT 7-3

CONSOLIDATED STATEMENTS OF NET EARNINGS
Fruehauf Corporation and Consolidated Subsidiaries

	Year ended December 31		
REVENUES:	**1980**	1979	1978
Commercial sales...	**$1,878,746,434**	$2,291,098,390	$2,097,619,422
Leased equipment rentals.................................	**73,894,850**	71,049,490	58,891,250
Defense sales...	**129,106,392**	89,198,605	88,002,392
Sales and Rentals	**$2,081,747,676**	$2,451,346,485	$2,244,513,064
Earnings before taxes on income of Fruehauf Finance Company......	**28,720,485**	28,272,043	23,887,019
Finance revenue...	**5,670,309**	6,720,516	6,728,798
License revenue and equity in earnings of unconsolidated foreign affiliates...	**8,519,216**	7,954,963	9,089,998
Miscellaneous...	**14,449,710**	11,765,282	(13,517,499)
	$2,139,107,396	$2,506,059,289	$2,270,701,380
COSTS AND EXPENSES:			
Cost of sales, other than items below........................	**$1,688,619,307**	$1,959,455,804	$1,779,613,243
Selling and administrative expense...........................	**165,441,724**	182,584,164	162,157,993
Depreciation..	**79,499,923**	75,971,210	69,151,246
Taxes — other than income.................................	**70,360,878**	75,937,479	61,525,456
Interest, including $30,830,682 in 1980, $27,705,029 in 1979 and $19,129,762 in 1978 to Fruehauf Finance Company.............	**81,872,552**	73,917,642	54,577,095
	$2,085,794,384	$2,367,866,299	$2,127,025,033
Earnings before Taxes on Income	$ **53,313,012**	$ 138,192,990	$ 143,676,347
Taxes on Income (Note D)..................................	**21,100,000**	49,500,000	67,000,000
Net Earnings	$ **32,213,012**	$ 88,692,990	$ 76,676,347
Earnings Per Share of Common Stock — based on average number of shares outstanding:			
Primary...	**$2.63**	$7.28	$6.34
Fully diluted — reflects conversion of debentures................	**$2.50**	$6.74	$5.86

See notes to financial statements.

who are concerned about the firm's ability to meet its obligations within a period of one year. Both, however, should be viewed with considerable care. They are ratios that can readily be manipulated by management. For example, by paying off short-term loans just prior to year end (and subsequently reborrowing at the start of the next year), management may be able to increase its year-end current and quick ratios. It is important to bear in mind that an identical change in both current assets and current liabilities will, in

EXHIBIT 7-3 (continued)

CONSOLIDATED BALANCE SHEETS
Fruehauf Corporation and Consolidated Subsidiaries

ASSETS		December 31, 1980		December 31, 1979
CURRENT ASSETS:				
Cash	$	41,527,022	$	56,669,110
Money market investments – at cost.		16,922,342		857,000
Trade receivables:				
Accounts receivable	$	244,233,702	$	294,592,981
Installment contracts		23,821,595		19,825,547
	$	268,055,297	$	314,418,528
Less allowance for doubtful accounts		7,000,000		7,000,000
	$	261,055,297	$	307,418,528
Refundable income taxes		14,100,000		11,100,000
Inventories		306,725,942		306,198,122
Prepaid expenses		10,876,975		11,436,500
Total Current Assets	$	651,207,578	$	693,679,260
EQUIPMENT LEASED TO CUSTOMERS				
At cost, less accumulated depreciation of $118,951,434 and $112,791,990 at December 31, 1980 and 1979, respectively	$	236,218,391	$	234,529,190
INVESTMENTS AND OTHER ASSETS:				
Investment in Fruehauf Finance Company				
At equity in net assets	$	196,248,139	$	180,527,654
Less amount payable, net of deferred finance revenue – secured by pledge of rentals on equipment leased to customers		(97,759,545)		(121,258,044)
	$	98,488,594	$	59,269,610
Investments in and amounts due from other affiliated companies not consolidated		26,736,540		34,503,678
Other accounts and investments		40,513,294		39,876,607
Total Investments and Other Assets	$	165,738,428	$	133,649,895
PROPERTY, PLANT AND EQUIPMENT				
Land	$	32,091,257	$	31,910,645
Buildings		217,077,964		200,059,541
Machinery and equipment		490,762,128		438,311,495
	$	739,931,349	$	670,281,681
Less accumulated depreciation		268,108,925		232,162,888
Total Property, Plant and Equipment	$	471,822,424	$	438,118,793
	$1,524,986,821		$1,499,977,138	

EXHIBIT 7-3 (continued)

LIABILITIES AND SHAREHOLDERS' EQUITY		December 31, 1980	December 31, 1979
CURRENT LIABILITIES:			
Notes payable to banks (foreign subsidiaries only)	. . . .	$ 31,497,128	$ 24,937,378
Current portion of long-term debt	. . . .	24,530,275	33,075,438
Accounts payable		242,302,759	241,471,461
Employee compensation and benefits		80,210,831	74,079,776
Taxes – other than income		24,148,759	26,875,217
Interest		6,413,418	7,623,347
	Total Current Liabilities	$ 409,103,170	$ 408,062,617
DEFERRED INCOME TAXES		118,162,760	100,172,320
OTHER LIABILITIES		74,209,491	77,087,006
LONG-TERM DEBT AND CAPITALIZED LEASE OBLIGATIONS (including amounts due to Fruehauf Finance Company, secured by transportation equipment, of $52,027,024 and $49,308,734 at December 31, 1980 and 1979, respectively)		394,400,675	389,075,518
SHAREHOLDERS' EQUITY (Note H):			
Common Stock, par value $1 a share: Authorized 40,000,000 shares Issued 12,251,106 and 12,208,283 shares at December 31, 1980 and 1979, respectively		$ 12,251,106	$ 12,208,283
Additional paid-in capital		216,425,069	215,662,883
Retained earnings	. . . .	300,434,550	297,708,511
	Total Shareholders' Equity	$ 529,110,725	$ 525,579,677
Commitments and Contingent Liabilities	. . . .		
		$1,524,986,821	$1,499,977,138

fact, alter the two ratios. If, for example, a firm had current assets of $400,000 and current liabilities of $200,000 and subsequently repaid an outstanding current obligation of $100,000, its current ratio would increase from 2:1 prior to repayment to 3:1 after repayment. The practice of taking deliberate steps to inflate the current and quick ratios is known as *window dressing*.

At the same time, an increase in the current and quick ratios may be symptomatic of financial deterioration rather than improvement. The numerator of the quick ratio includes accounts receivable; that of the current ratio includes accounts receivable as well as inventories. Suppose that a firm's inventory balance is increasing because of an inability to sell its product and its accounts receivable balance is increasing because of a failure to collect outstanding debts. Both the current and the quick ratios would also increase, even though the financial condition of the firm is weakening. This increase points to the danger of focusing on individual rather than groups of relationships. If, for example, ratios of sales to inventory and sales to accounts receivable were computed then the pathological build-up of receivables and inventory would become apparent. It would readily be observed that both balances were increasing at the same time that sales were decreasing.

SUMMARY

Three main ideas pervaded the discussion of receivables and payables:

1. Questions of the amounts at which receivables and payables should be stated are directly related to those of when revenues and expenses should be recognized.

If an enterprise grants credit to its customers, it is doubtful that all of its receivables will be transformed into cash. "Losses" on bad debts are an expected deduction from revenues. They should be charged as a reduction of sales (or an expense) in the same accounting period in which the related sales are made. Correspondingly, accounts receivable should be reduced by the amount likely to prove uncollectible.

Similarly, both sales and receivables should be reduced by the amount of expected returns, allowances and discounts of which customers may avail themselves. They should be reduced also by interest included in the face of the receivable but not yet earned. Notes receivable, for example, often include

in the stated value an element of interest to be earned during the period over which the notes will be held.

2. The substance of a transaction must take precedence over its form. Accountants and managers must look to the economic rather than the stated values of goods or services exchanged. It is not unusual, for example, for firms to allow customers to delay payments for months or even years and make no explicit charges for interest. Money, however, has a time value, and the right to use funds for an extended period of time is not granted casually. Whenever the sales price of an item is *inflated* by unspecified interest charges, the firm must impute a fair rate of interest and account for the revenue from the sale of the item apart from the revenue from the interest.

3. Proper accounting for receivables and payables is dependent on the good judgment of both managers and accountants. The "correct" value of receivables can never be known with certainty. It is dependent on the number of customers that fail to fulfill their payment obligations, the amount of goods returned, and the amount of cash discounts taken. In determining the amount to report as a receivable as well as the amount of revenue to be considered realized, such amounts must necessarily be estimated. Accounts receivable and the related revenues can never be viewed as being "accurately" presented—only "fairly" presented.

EXERCISE FOR REVIEW AND SELF-TESTING

The LJG Company sells a unit of equipment to a customer for $1,000. The customer is permitted to defer payment for one year, but is to be charged interest at a rate of 4 percent. The company accepts a note from the customer for principal of $1,000 plus interest of $40—a total of $1,040.

In fact, the prevailing rate of interest—the rate normally charged similar customers in similar circumstances—is 12 percent, and the company often sells its equipment for less than $1,000.

1. Determine the fair market value of the equipment, taking into account the prevailing rate of interest. What is the present value of the note (both principal and interest) to the company?

2. Prepare a journal entry to record the sale of the equipment. Be sure that the amount of revenue recognized reflects the value of the consideration received. Any difference between the face amount of the note and the amount of revenue recognized should be classified as "Notes receivable, discount."

3. After one year the company collects the entire $1,040 from the customer. Prepare a journal entry to record the collection of the note and to recognize interest revenue for the year. Be sure that the amount of interest revenue recognized reflects the "true" (prevailing) rate of interest.

4. The firm estimates that of the total sales for the year for which notes were accepted, $7,000 will prove to be uncollectible. Prepare a journal entry to add that amount to "Notes receivable, allowance for uncollectibles."

5. A review of notes on hand indicates that $2,500 are presently uncollectible. Prepare a journal entry to write off the notes against the allowance provided.

QUESTIONS FOR REVIEW AND DISCUSSION

1. Why is it preferable for a firm to maintain an allowance for uncollectible accounts rather than simply to write off bad accounts as soon as it is known which specific accounts will be uncollectible?

2. On December 29 a company purchases for $100,000 merchandise intended for resale. The company is granted a 5 percent discount for paying cash within 10 days of purchase. The company records the purchase using the gross method. As of year end the company has not yet paid for the goods purchased but has resold half of them. The company intends to

pay within the specified discount period. Assuming that no adjustment to the accounts has been made, in what way is it likely that the financial statements as of year end are misstated?

3. A company borrows $1,000 for one year at the prevailing interest rate of 6 percent. The note issued to the lender promises payment of $1,000 plus interest of $60 after one year. Upon borrowing the funds the company recorded a liability for $1,060. Do you agree with such accounting treatment? Explain.

4. A finance company loaned an individual $1,000 on a discount basis. The actual cash given to the borrower was only $940; interest was taken out in advance. At the time of the loan the company recorded its receivable at $1,000, reduced its cash by $940, and recognized revenue of $60. Do you agree with such practice? How would you record the loan? Explain.

5. A retail store places the following ad in the paper: "Complete Room of Furniture; $1,000; no money down; take up to 2 years to pay; no interest or finance charges." During a particular month the firm sold 10 sets of the advertised furniture. The company recorded sales of $10,000. If you were the firm's independent CPA, what reservations would you have about the reported sales?

6. A firm acquires a building at a cost of $200,000 but gives the seller a five-year interest-free note for the entire amount. Assuming that the firm would otherwise have had to borrow the funds at a rate of interest of 10 percent compounded annually, at what amount should the building be recorded? What would be the impact of failing to take into account *imputed* interest on reported earnings of the years during which the note is outstanding as well as on those of the remaining years of the useful life of the building?

7. After operating successfully in a single city, the owners of Big Top Ice Cream Parlors decide to sell franchises to individual businessmen in other cities. Within one year they sign contracts and receive down payments for 20

franchises. The total sales price of each franchise is $50,000. The required down payment is a small fraction of total sales price. During the first year only 5 outlets are actually opened. The company reported revenues from sale of franchises of $1 million. What warnings would you give an investor with respect to first-year earnings?

8. The supervisor of a large clerical department in a government agency has determined that efficiency in his department always seems to drop during the summer months. He determines efficiency by dividing total payroll costs by the number of documents processed. Total payroll costs include amounts paid to employees on vacation. The department charges all salaries—both those of workers actually on the job and those on vacation—as an expense in the month paid. Why do you suspect efficiency appears to be low during the summer months? What improvements to the accounting system might you recommend?

9. A finance company charges customers 12 percent interest on all balances outstanding. The company continues to accrue interest revenue on outstanding loans (that is, it debits interest receivable and credits interest revenue) even though loan payments might be past due. Only when it writes off a loan does it cease to accrue interest. What dangers are suggested by such practice?

10. The *quick ratio* of a firm has increased substantially from one year to the next. The treasurer of the firm cites the increase as evidence of improved financial health. Why can an increase in the quick ratio be as much of a sign of financial deterioration as of improved financial health? What other ratio or relationship would you look to for insight as to the significance of the increase.

PROBLEMS

1. Compute simple and compound interest.

In each of the following situations, determine the interest revenue that a firm should recognize.

1. It holds for 180 days a $3,000 note that earns interest at an annual rate of 8 percent.
2. It holds for 30 days a $10,000 note that earns interest at an annual rate of 6 percent.
3. It holds for 400 days a $1,000 note that earns interest at an annual rate of 12 percent (interest is not to be charged on interest accrued at the end of the first year).
4. It holds for five years a $5,000 note that earns interest at a rate of 7 percent compounded annually.

2. This is a simple exercise in accounting for uncollectibles.

The trial balance of the Elton Co. indicated the following:

Sales	$486,000
Accounts receivable	63,000
Allowance for uncollectibles	11,000

In the current year, bad-debt expense had not yet been recorded.

The firm estimates that approximately 5 percent of sales will prove to be uncollectible. A review of accounts receivable reveals that $21,500 of accounts presently on the books are unlikely to be collected and should therefore be written off.

Prepare any entries that you believe are necessary in light of the facts as presented.

3. The stated price of merchandise is not always the "true" price.

A firm sells merchandise for a supposed price of $1,000, but sometimes grants unusually generous terms of credit. Prevailing rates of interest are 10 percent. Determine the amount most indicative of "true" selling price of the merchandise if the buyer
a. pays $1,000 cash today.
b. pays $1,000 cash one year from today.
c. pays $1,000 cash plus interest at 6 percent (that is, $1,060) one year from today.
d. pays $500 six months from today and $500 one year from today.

4. Compute the amount of discount notes.

A bank makes a loan to a customer on a discount basis. Determine the amount that should be advanced to the customer in each of the following situations, assuming that the face amount of the note is $10,000 and the rate of discount is 12 percent per year.

1. The period of the loan is 1 year.
2. The period of the loan is 60 days.
3. The period of the loan is 4 years.

5. *Neither the entries to write off accounts receivable nor to restore accounts that were previously written off have a direct impact upon earnings.*

Transactions involving accounts receivable and related accounts of Warner's Department Store for 1982 and 1983 can be summarized as follows:

	1982	1983
Credit sales	$3,000,000	$3,000,000
Cash collections on accounts receivable	2,800,000	3,100,000
Accounts deemed uncollectible and written off	30,000	65,000

The firm estimates that 2 percent of annual credit sales will prove uncollectible.

Included in the $3.1 million of cash collections in 1983 are $3,000 from customers whose accounts had been written off in 1982. The balances in the accounts when they were written off totaled $8,000. It is the policy of the company to restore in their entirety accounts previously written off upon collection of a partial payment from a customer, since a partial payment is often an indication that payment of the remaining balance will be forthcoming. (To restore an account it is necessary only to "reverse" the entry made to write it off.)

a. Prepare journal entries to record the activity reported above.
b. Compare the impact of credit losses on reported earnings of 1982 with those of 1983.
c. Comment briefly on how your answer to part b would differ if the amount to be added to the allowance for doubtful accounts were based on an aging schedule instead of a flat percentage of sales.

6. *The means of accounting for cash discounts may not be the critical issue of our time, but they point up the importance of recognizing substance rather than form.*

Indiana Industrial Supplies reported accounts receivable of $1 million as of December 31, 1982. Of that amount $800,000 represents sales of the final 20 days of the year. The company allows its customers to take a cash discount of 4 percent of sales price on all merchandise paid for within 20 days.

The company has consistently accounted for cash discounts by the *gross* method. Annual sales and year-end balances in accounts receivable have remained generally constant over the last several years. Approximately 90 percent of customers take advantage of the cash discount. Comment on whether the firm's sales and accounts receivable are likely to be fairly presented at year end. Indicate the amount of any possible over- or understatement.

7. *The gross method of accounting for cash discounts may not reflect the fair market value of goods traded.*

The Grimm Co. purchases all of its merchandise from the Anderson Co. Terms of sale are 1/15, n/30. In the month of December the following transactions took place:

12/2 Grimm purchased $80,000 of merchandise on account.

12/10 Grimm remitted payment for the goods purchased.

12/12 Grimm purchased $50,000 of merchandise on account.

12/31 Grimm remitted payment for the goods purchased.

a. Record the transactions on the books of the Grimm Co. using first the net method and then the gross method.
b. Record the transactions on the books of the Anderson Co. using first the net method and then the gross method. The entries from the standpoint of the seller were not illustrated in the text. They correspond closely to those of the purchaser, however.
c. Assuming that no additional adjustments were made to the accounts and that none of the merchandise acquired by Grimm has yet been sold, comment on any distortions of the accounts that might result from use of the gross method.

Suppose that Grimm had sold all or part of the merchandise that it had acquired. What accounts might be misstated? What information, useful for management control, is highlighted by the net method but obscured by the gross method?

8. *Reported wage expense is generally greater than the amounts actually disbursed to employees.*

Wellman Manufacturing Co. has 100 hourly employees, each of whom worked 40 hours in a given week and was paid $6.50 per hour.

Total federal income taxes which the company was required to withhold for the week were $3,900.

The current Social Security (FICA) rate applicable to both employer and employee is 6 percent.

The company is required to pay 3 percent of gross wages into the State Unemployment Insurance Fund.

The company has a matching pension plan. Employees contribute 5 percent of their wages; the company contributes an equal amount.

The firm is required by union contract to withhold from each employee union dues of $2.50 per week.

Twenty employees have elected to join the savings bond program. The cost of a savings bond, $18, is withdrawn from wages each week and used to purchase a government savings bond.

The company pays medical insurance for each employee. The cost is $8 per week per employee.

a. Prepare a journal entry to record the weekly payroll.
b. Prepare a journal entry to record disbursement of all required payments to the various government agencies, insurance companies, pension funds, etc.

9. *The impact of an accounting change on the balance sheet may be substantially greater than on the income statement. An event may have a significant impact on the interim statements but no effect on the annual statements.*

The Sonora Co. has an annual payroll of approximately $2,000,000. Such amount does *not* include $120,000 paid to employees on vacation. The company does not *accrue* vacation pay; it charges it to expense as employees take their vacations. The controller has rejected the suggestions of the company's independent CPA that vacation pay be recognized on a week-by-week basis; he claims that such recognition would have no effect on the financial statements; it would only increase clerical costs.

The payroll of the company has remained constant for a number of years. Employees are entitled to three weeks vacation each year based on work performed in the previous fiscal year, and such vacations must be taken during July and August. Employees receive their regular wages while on vacation, and all employees must be replaced by temporary employees at the same wage rate. The company's fiscal year ends June 30.

a. Is the controller correct in his assertion that accrual of vacation pay would have no impact on the financial statements? Estimate the impact of a change in policy on both the income statement and the balance sheet.
b. Suppose the firm were to issue *interim* financial statements on December 31 for the six months ending on that date. What would be the impact of accruing vacation pay on the income statement and the balance sheet?

10. *Vacations are not to be accounted for casually—as one company found out.*

The following is an excerpt from the annual report of Eastern Airlines, Inc.

Subsequent to the issuance of the financial statements included in the 1976 Annual Report to Stockholders, the Staff of the Securities and Exchange Commision ("SEC" or "Commission"), reviewed a Registration Statement on Form S-1 filed by the company in March 1977. As a result of this review, the Staff of the SEC requested the company to change its accounting practice with respect to vacation liability, the effect of which was that the company recorded, effective January 1, 1975, a liability of approximately $35 million for earned vacation benefits, notwithstanding the CAB's deferral of implementation of such change and the company's disclosure of this matter in filings with the SEC and annual reports to stockholders. Although the company and its independent accountants continue to believe the accounting practice followed by the company was appropriate in the circumstances, the company agreed, after conferences with the Staff and consideration by the full Commission, to restate its financial statements to give effect to the accounting treatment requested by the SEC.

The cumulative effect of the accounting change, as of January 1, 1975, is shown as a one-time noncash charge against 1975 income in the amount of $35 million. The change also increased the loss before the cumulative effect of the change in 1975 by $4 million ($0.21 per share) and reduced net income in 1976 by $1 million ($0.05 per share).

a. Indicate the entry that the firm most likely made in 1975 to record the $35 million liability for earned vacation benefits.

b. Indicate the entry (omitting numbers) that the company will now make each time an employee takes a vacation. How does this entry differ from that which would have been made prior to 1975?

11. In some industries it is critical that allowances be made for anticipated returns of merchandise sold.

Division Products had gross sales in 1983 (its first year of operations) of $4 million and in 1984 of $6 million. As of December 31, 1983, the company had accounts receivable of $2 million and as of December 31, 1984, $3 million. The business of the company is highly seasonal; most of its sales are made in the last three months of the year.

The company follows standard practice in its industry. It permits the retailers with whom it deals to return for full credit any merchandise that they are unable to sell within a reasonable period of time. In January 1984, the company accepted for return merchandise which it had sold for $400,000. None of the merchandise had yet been paid for by the retailers. A return rate of 10 percent of sales is typical for the industry.

The firm's cost of goods sold is approximately 60 percent of selling price. In financial statements prepared for internal use only (and not in accord with generally accepted accounting principles of reporting to the general public), the firm gives accounting recognition to merchandise returned only when it is actually received; it establishes no year-end allowances.

a. Determine for both 1983 and 1984 the difference in income and assets that would result if the company were to adhere to generally accepted accounting principles and establish an allowance for returned merchandise. Assume that all goods returned could be resold at standard prices.

b. Suppose that the company were in a business, such as toys, in which it is extremely difficult to predict the rate of return from pre-Christmas sales. What warnings would you give to a potential investor or creditor who is likely to rely upon the company's financial statements?

c. How can companies in highly seasonal industries, such as toys, minimize the risk of misestimating sales returns? Why do you suppose that many department stores report on the basis of a fiscal year ending July 31?

12. In the long run, though not in any particular year, bad debts based on an aging schedule should be equal to those based on dollar volume of credit sales.

The Melrose Co. began operations in January 1980. The schedule below indicates credit sales and

(000s Omitted)
End-of-Year Balance in Accounts Receivable

| Year | Credit Sales | Total | Current | No. of Days Past Due | | |
				1–30	31–60	Over 60
1980	$12,000	$1,080	$ 800	$100	$150	$ 30
1981	14,000	1,500	1,100	300	50	50
1982	16,000	1,600	900	400	200	100
1983	18,000	1,820	1,280	220	200	120

end-of-year balances in accounts receivable for 1980 through 1983. The end-of-year balances are broken down by the "age" of the receivables.

The company estimates that approximately 5 percent of all credit sales will prove to be uncollectible. It has also determined that of its accounts receivable balance at any date the following percentages will likely be uncollectible:

Current	15%
1–30 days past due	40
31–60 days past due	50
Over 60 days past due	60

The balance in the "allowance for uncollectibles" account was zero prior to the adjustment at the end of 1980. Actual write-offs of accounts receivable were as follows:

1980	260
1981	580
1982	815
1983	893

a. Determine bad-debt expense for each of the four years assuming first that the company bases its addition to the allowance for uncollectibles on credit sales and alternatively on a schedule of *aged* accounts receivables. Bear in mind that when the sales method is used the bad-debt expense is determined directly. When the aged accounts receivable method is used it is necessary to first determine the required balance in the allowance for uncollectibles account.

b. Compare total bad-debt expense over the combined four-year period under each of the two methods. (They should be the same in this example.) Which method results in the more erratic pattern of bad-debt expense in this particular example? Why?

13. *Interest on troublesome loans should not be accrued.*

The following comment was included in the notes to the financial statements of the Equitable Life Mortgage and Realty Investors:

Non-Accrual of Interest. When it is not reasonable to expect that interest income will be received, its recognition is discon-

tinued. At that point, interest accrued but not received is reversed and no further interest is accrued until it is evident that principal and interest will be collected.

a. Why should the company "reverse" interest accrued but not yet received?

b. What is the most likely journal entry made to effect the reversal?

14. *The effective rate of interest on discount loans may be substantially higher than the stated rate.*

The Confidential Loan Co. placed an advertisement in a local newspaper. It read, in part, "Borrow up to $15,000. Take up to 3 Years to Repay. Low, Low, 6% Interest Rate."

Upon visiting the loan company you learn that on a three-year, 6 percent loan of $15,000, interest of $2,700 ($900 per year) is taken out in advance; you would receive only $12,300 cash. You would be required to repay the loan in three annual installments of $5,000.

Indicate the main points that you might make in a letter to the local consumer protection commission. Be sure to specify the approximate effective rate of interest charged by the company.

15. *This problem illustrates a borrowing arrangement that, although not specifically discussed in the text, represents an application of the principles which were described.*

Sometimes a firm will "discount" with a bank an interest-bearing note that it has received from a customer. The bank will advance the firm the amount to be received from the customer, less interest charges for the number of days until the note matures. When the note matures, the customer will make payment to the firm and the firm will transfer the amount received to the bank.

Suppose a firm receives a one-year note from a customer in the amount of $1,000. The note bears interest at the rate of 8 percent. Immediately upon receipt of the note, the firm discounts it with a bank. The bank, however, accepts notes only at a discount rate of 10 percent.

a. Upon the maturity of the note, how much will the customer be required to remit to the firm?

b. What is the amount that the bank will be willing

to advance to the firm based on its discount rate of 10 percent?

16. *This problem provides an illustration (based on an actual annual report) of a firm whose allowance for uncollectibles was inadequate to cover loan losses.*

The annual report of First Dallas Corporation contained the following comment and table regarding its provision for loan losses:

One of the most significant factors adversely affecting 1981 results was the $126.5 million provision for loan losses, up from $118.5 million in 1980. Net loan charge-offs were $145.8 million, exceeding the provision for loan losses by $19.3 million.

	1981	1980
Balance, beginning of period	$121,352	$ 95,766
Additions (deductions)		
Loans charged-off	(153,688)	(95,583)
Recoveries	7,874	2,669
Net charge-offs	$(145,814)	$(92,914)
Provisions charged to operating expenses	126,500	118,500
Balance, end of period	$102,038	$121,352

a. Prepare journal entries to reflect the activity in the account, "Provision for loan losses" in 1981. (Recoveries are accounted for by reversing the entry that was made to write off the loans.)
b. Based only on the limited information provided, do you think that the balance in the account as of the end of 1981 will be adequate to cover losses on loans to be incurred in the future? Explain.

17. *Even banks and finance companies face difficult questions of revenue recognition.*

Sunrise Finance Co. loaned a customer $10,000 for two years on a discount basis. The customer was to repay $5,000 at the end of each year. The rate of discount (the *effective* rate of interest) was 12 percent.
a. How much cash would the company actually advance the customer? Prepare a journal entry to record the loan and the receipt by the company of a note for $10,000.
b. How much revenue should the company recognize during the first year of the loan? Prepare a journal entry to record receipt of the first payment of $5,000. At what value will the note be reported (net of discount) after the first year? How much revenue should the company recognize during the second year?
c. Many bankers and managers of finance companies assert that a portion—perhaps 15 percent—of the total revenue to be earned over the two-year period should be recognized at the time the loan is made, without waiting for interest to accrue with the passage of time. Given the costs of obtaining customers (advertising) and processing loan applications, why do you suspect they feel as they do?

18. *In the real estate industry it is not uncommon for the selling price of property to include an element of interest.*

The Lincoln Co. purchased a building from the Polk Co. The stated selling price of the building was $100,000. Polk Co. agreed to accept from the Lincoln Co. an *interest-free* note, which was payable in full five years from the date the transaction was closed.

The building has an estimated useful life of 20 years and zero salvage value after that period. At time of sale it had been recorded on the books of the Polk Co. at $40,000. Had Lincoln Co. been required to pay cash for the building, it would have had to borrow the funds from a bank at an annual rate of interest of 10 percent.
a. Prepare a journal entry to record the purchase of the building on the books of the Lincoln Co. Be certain that the entry recognizes "substance over form."
b. Prepare any journal entries that would be required after the first year of ownership to recognize both interest expense and depreciation.
c. Determine the difference on Lincoln Co. earnings of the first year that would result from taking into account, as opposed to ignoring, the *imputed* interest.
d. Determine the difference in Polk Co. earnings of both the first year and second year that would result from taking into account the *imputed*

interest. What would be the total difference in earnings in years 1 through 5? (You should not have to compute earnings in each of the five years to answer this question.)

19. *Determination of the real value of a business acquired by another may be complex.*

The following note appeared in the 1973 financial report of United Brands Company:

On December 31, 1973, the Company sold its 83% interest in Baskin-Robbins Ice Cream Company to J. Lyons & Company Limited, a British food company, for a total of $37,600,000 including $30,300,000 in notes. The notes bear interest at 4% per annum and mature in 3 equal annual installments of $10,100,000 commencing on December 31, 1974. The notes have been recorded in the financial statements at an imputed interest rate of 12%.

a. Determine the present value, discounted at 12 percent, of *all* payments (both principal and interest) that United Brands will receive over the three-year period. Be sure to determine the interest payments as 4 percent of the outstanding balance of the notes at the time of each payment.

b. Prepare a journal entry to record the sale of the 83 percent interest in Baskin-Robbins. Assume that the 83 percent interest had been valued on the books of United Brands at $20 million. To simplify the journal entry and subsequent computation of interest, record the present value of the expected principal and interest payments to be received in a single account, "notes receivable."

c. Prepare an entry to record the first receipt of principal and interest. Be sure to base the computation of interest earned on the effective rate of 12 percent and the effective balance in the notes receivable account.

d. How much greater or less would the reported income of United Brands have been in both the year of sale and year of collection of the first principal and interest payment had the company not imputed the additional 8 percent interest?

20. *Just as it is commonly asserted that there is no such thing as a "free lunch," there is also no such a thing as "free money."*

The Davis County Land Development Co. sells real estate on terms of 10 percent down, the balance to be paid in annual installments over a three-year period. Customers are not specifically charged interest on their outstanding balances.

During 1982 the company sold several lots at a stated price of $8,000 each. The original cost to the company of each of the lots was $400. The interest rate on similar "loans" would be at a rate of 10 percent per year.

a. How much *income* do you think the company should recognize at time of sale (upon collection of the 10 percent down payment) assuming recognition of all *sales* (but not *interest*) revenue at time of down payment? Prepare a journal entry to record the transaction.

b. How much income should be recognized at the time of each of the three installment payments? What would be the balances in notes receivable and the related discount account immediately following each payment?

21. *Should a franchisor recognize revenue at the time it signs a sales contract or should it wait until it has performed substantially all of the terms of the contract?*

The Peter Pan Cheese Co., after successfully operating a single retail cheese store for several years, decided in 1982 to expand its operations. It offered to sell Peter Pan franchises, in several cities, for $40,000. For that amount an individual businessman acquired the right to sell under the name "Peter Pan" and to purchase from the franchisor several products bearing the company name.

The franchisee was required to pay $10,000 upon the opening of its outlet and could pay the balance over the next 10 years. It was to be charged interest at a rate of 8 percent per year on the balance outstanding.

The company estimated that the cost of initial services it would be required to provide the franchisee prior to the opening of his outlet would be $30,000. The company, in accord with recommendations of the franchise industry audit guide, elected to recognize revenue from the sale of the franchise at the *commencement of an outlet's operations.*

In 1982 the company signed sales contracts with 10 franchisees. Of these, 6 began operations during the year. The company incurred $180,000 in costs in connection with the outlets actually opened and $100,000 in connection with those expected to open in the following year.

In addition, the company had cash sales of merchandise to the outlets of $120,000; the cost of merchandise sold was $80,000.

The company collected $10,000 from each of six franchisees at the time their outlets began operations. It also collected a total of $6,000 in interest. The company estimated that 6 percent of the original balance of the notes would prove to be uncollectible.

a. Prepare an income statement for 1982 to reflect franchise operations. (Be sure to match expenses with revenues.)

b. Prepare a balance sheet as of year end. To simplify your presentation, do not include in notes receivable that portion of the notes associated with revenue that has not yet been realized. Assume that the company began the year with $200,000 in cash and owners' equity. All costs were paid in cash.

22. *An increase in the current ratio may not necessarily be indicative of an improved financial position.*

The president of a company, in requesting a renewal of an outstanding loan, wrote to an officer of a bank: "In spite of a decline in sales and earnings, we were able to strengthen our working capital position." He went on to cite the increase in the current ratio as evidence of the improvement.

The balance sheet of the company reported the following current assets and liabilities:

	December 31, 1983	December 31, 1982
Cash	$ 60,000	$120,000
Accounts receivable	270,000	190,000
Inventories	420,000	300,000
Total current assets	$750,000	$610,000
Accounts payable	$370,000	$330,000
Notes payable	140,000	140,000
Total current liabilities	$510,000	$470,000

The income statement (in summary form) revealed the following:

	1983	1982
Sales	$1,400,000	$1,560,000
Cost of goods sold	$ 840,000	$ 936,000
Other expenses	240,000	260,000
Total expenses	$1,080,000	$1,196,000
Net income	$ 320,000	$ 364,000

a. Determine the current ratio for both years.
b. (1) Determine the quick ratio.
   (2) Calculate number of days' sales in accounts receivable.
c. Provide a possible explanation for the increase in accounts receivable and inventories that would undermine the contention of the president that the firm's working capital position has improved. Has the current position of the company really improved?

23. *The manner in which a ratio is computed must depend on the purpose to which it is put; conclusions from ratios must be drawn with care.*

The following data (in millions of dollars) were taken from the 1979 annual report of the Hoover Company, the manufacturer of vacuum cleaners:

	1979	1978
Sales	$754.3	$691.8
Notes and accounts receivable less allowances for bad debts (in millions) of $2.4 in 1979 and $2.0 in 1978	143.6	143.7

a. On the basis of accounts receivable turnover, in which year did the firm employ its receivables more effectively? (Compute receivables turnover *gross*—that is, without reduction for allowances—and use year-end rather than average salaries).
b. Suppose that the firm sells on terms 2/10, n/30. What concern would be raised by a calculation of number of days' sales in accounts receivable?

Inasmuch, however, as the data combine notes receivable and accounts receivable, why *might* your concern be unwarranted?

c. A question is often raised as to whether ratios involving accounts receivable, such as the current ratio and the quick ratio, should incorporate accounts receivable gross or net of allowances for bad debts. Why might your response be different if you were providing an answer to a banker who is interested primarily in the ability of the firm to collect on its outstanding receivables and repay its debts than if you were responding to a manager who is concerned with minimizing the amount of funds tied up in "unproductive" assets?

SOLUTIONS TO EXERCISE FOR REVIEW AND SELF-TESTING

1. The fair market value of the equipment may be obtained by evaluating the value *today* of the note. Per table 2, the present value of $1 to be received one year hence, discounted at a rate of 12 percent is $0.8929. The present value of the note, therefore, is $1,040 × 0.8929—$928.62. The fair market value of the equipment, therefore would also be $928.62.

2. Notes receivable $1,040.00
    Notes receivable,
      discount $111.38
    Sales revenue   928.62
To record sale of equipment.

3. Cash $1,040.00
Notes receivable,
  discount   111.38
    Notes receivable $1,040.00
    Interest revenue   111.38
To record collection of the note and to recognize interest revenue for one year.

4. Sales-uncollectibles $7,000
    Notes receivable, allowance
      for uncollectibles $7,000
To record estimate of bad debts.

5. Notes receivable, allowance
  for uncollectibles $2,500
    Notes receivable $2,500
To write off specific notes that are uncollectible.

INVENTORIES 8 AND COST of Goods Sold

The term *inventory* refers both to goods that are awaiting sale and to those that are in the various stages of production. It includes the merchandise of a trading concern as well as the finished goods, the work in process, and the raw materials of a manufacturer. In addition, the term embraces goods that will be consumed indirectly as the enterprise manufactures its product or provides its service. Thus, stores of stationery, cleaning supplies, and lubricants would also be categorized as inventories. Proper accounting for inventories is critical not only because they often comprise a substantial portion of a firm's assets but also because they relate directly to what is frequently the firm's major expense—the cost of goods sold. The beginning inventory balance plus purchases minus the ending inventory balance equals the cost of goods sold. This chapter will be directed to several key accounting issues pertaining to inventory, some of which are currently at the center of active controversy. Among the questions to be raised are

What are the objectives of inventory measurement and valuation?

What costs should be included in inventory?

How should inventory quantities be determined?

What assumptions regarding the flow of costs are most appropriate in particular circumstances?

What accounting recognition should be given to changes in the market prices of inventories?

The discussion of inventories will be in the context of generally accepted accounting principles—how inventories are accounted for in practice. But consideration will also be given, in a concluding section, to alternatives that have been proposed but which are not presently viewed as acceptable.

EXHIBIT 8-1

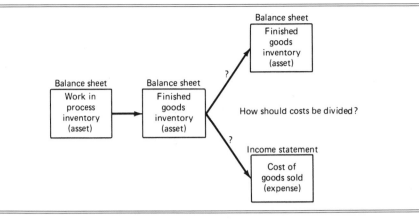

OBJECTIVES

The overriding objective of conventional inventory accounting is to match the costs of acquiring or producing goods with the revenues that they generate and thereby enable both managers and investors to evaluate organizational performance. In a typical operating cycle of a firm, the costs of goods which are either manufactured or purchased are included in inventory and reported as an asset. Even though the goods may have been paid for, their costs are not considered to be expenses; rather they are *stored* on the balance sheet until the goods are sold and the costs can be associated with specific revenues. In the course of a year, a portion of the goods remains on hand; a portion is sold to outsiders. A portion of the costs, therefore, must be assigned to the goods that remain on hand and the rest to the goods that have been sold. That portion of the costs that is assigned to the goods on hand will continue to be carried on the balance sheet, while that assigned to the goods that have been sold will be charged to an expense account, cost of goods sold, and reported on the income statement. The question facing the firm is,

How much of the total costs should be assigned to the goods on hand and how much to the goods that have been sold? Diagramatically the issue can be depicted as shown in Exhibit 8-1.

Insofar as a greater value is placed on the goods in inventory, a lesser amount will be charged as an expense. Insofar as a greater amount is charged as a current expense, then smaller amounts will remain on the balance sheet to be charged as expenses in future years.

COSTS INCLUDED IN INVENTORY

Inventories are conventionally stated at historical cost—that of acquisition or production. Cost, as applied to inventories, "means in principle the sum of the applicable expenditures and charges directly or indirectly incurred in bringing an article to its existing condition and location."* If goods are purchased from outsiders, then cost would include not only the invoice price but also

---

* *Accounting Research Bulletin No. 43.* Committee on Accounting Procedure, American Institute of Certified Public Accountants, 1961.

costs of packaging and transportation. Trade, cash, or other special discounts or allowances would ordinarily be deducted from the stated price.

As a general rule, all costs that can reasonably be associated with the manufacture or acquisition, with the storage, or with the preparation for sale of goods should be included as part of the cost of such goods. In determining whether a particular item of cost should be added to the reported value of inventory, the impact of the decision on both the income statement and the balance sheet should be taken into account. If costs are added to the reported value of goods on hand, they will be charged as expenses (as part of cost of goods sold) in the period in which the merchandise is actually sold. By contrast, if the costs are not assigned to particular items of inventory, then they will be charged as expenses in the periods in which they are incurred, regardless of when the merchandise is sold.

Example

A company purchased 100 units of product at $20 per unit. It was permitted a trade discount (one granted to all customers in a particular category) of 5 percent but had to pay shipping costs of $300. Cost per unit would be computed as follows:

Base price (100 units @ $20)		$2,000
Less trade discount (5%)	100	$1,900
Plus shipping costs		300
Total cost of 100 units		$2,200
Number of units		÷ 100 units
Cost per unit		$ 22

If goods are produced by the company itself, the problem of cost determination is considerably more complex. Cost would include charges for labor and materials that can be directly associated with the product as well as those for *overhead* such as rent, maintenance, and utilities that may be common to several products produced in the same plant. To determine the cost of a particular product, a company will have to allocate such common charges among the various products. In addition, however, the firm has to decide whether certain costs should be considered *product* costs and thereby added to the carrying value of the goods produced, or *period* costs and thereby charged off as an expense as incurred. The implications of classifying an outlay as a product rather than a period cost were discussed earlier in Chapter 4 in connection with the discussion of the manufacturing cycle and will be dealt with at length in Part 2 of this text.

ACCOUNTING FOR QUANTITIES ON HAND

Periodic versus Perpetual Bases

In Chapter 4 it was pointed out that inventories may be maintained on a perpetual or a periodic basis. A perpetual basis implies that accounting recognition is given to the diminution of inventories each time a sale is made, supplies are consumed, or raw materials are added to production. When goods are removed from inventory upon a sale, for example, the following journal entry would be made:

Cost of goods sold	xxxx	
Inventory		xxxx

The periodic method, on the other hand, requires that recognition be given to the reduction in inventory resulting from the sale or use of goods only periodically, perhaps once a year. As goods are added to inventory, the inventory account is debited with their cost.* As goods are removed however, no entry is made. Throughout the year, therefore, the inventory *account* misstates the cost of the goods actually on hand. At the end of the period, a *physical* count of goods is taken, the goods are valued on the basis of acquisition cost, and the inventory account is adjusted to reflect the resultant dollar amount. If, for example, at year end an inventory account reflects a balance of $10,000 but a physical count reveals inventory on hand of only $500, the following entry would be appropriate (assuming that the difference between the two amounts reflects merchandise sold and not damaged or pilfered):

Cost of goods sold	$9,500	
Inventory		$9,500

To adjust the year-end inventory account to reflect goods actually on hand.

Although this text is not primarily directed toward the record-keeping procedures of enterprises, the two alternative methods of accounting for inventories are explained here because they *may* have an impact on the reported value of inventories at year end. The circumstances in which a difference may occur will be identified in the following discussion of the flows of costs.

FLOWS OF COSTS

The critical issue of inventory accounting, that of flows of costs, arises because the acquisition or production costs of goods do not remain constant. As a consequence, it is

---

* Many firms, as they acquire inventory, debit an account entitled "purchases" rather than the inventory account itself. At year end, they transfer the balance in the purchases account to the inventory account by debiting "inventory" and crediting "purchases."

sometimes necessary to make assumptions as to which goods have been sold and which remain on hand—those with the higher costs or those with the lower. (Recall the example in the first chapter of the text pertaining to the cost of a liquid solvent.) In some situations, identification of specific costs with specific goods presents no problem. The goods have sufficiently different characteristics so that they can readily be tagged with specific costs. The costs to retailers of automobiles, appliances, or rare pieces of jewelry, for example, can easily be associated with specific units. Not so, however, with *fungible* (interchangeable) goods such as grains or liquids, purchases of which made at different times are mixed together, or with most small items, such as canned goods or items of clothing for which it is inconvenient to account for each unit independently. Moreover, for reasons to be indicated shortly, accountants sometimes find it desirable to make assumptions regarding the flow of *costs* which are in obvious conflict with available information regarding the flow of *goods*.

SPECIFIC INDENTIFICATION

The specific identification inventory method requires the enterprise to keep track of the cost of each individual item bought and sold. Ordinarily, a firm would either code the cost directly on the item itself or otherwise tag each item with a control number and maintain a separate record of costs.

Refer, for example, to the data provided in Exhibit 8-2, which indicates quantities of an item purchased and sold on various dates. Also indicated are the opening balance, the prices at which the various acquisitions were made, and the total cost of each acquisition. Assume that of the 200 items that were sold on 4/20, 100 units were taken from the lot that was on hand on 1/1 and 100 were taken from that purchased on 3/2. Of the 300 items sold on 11/8, 100 were taken from the lot on hand on 1/1 and 200 from that purchased on 5/25. The cost of goods sold would be computed as follows:

Sale of 4/20

From lot of 1/1	100 @ $5	$ 500
From lot of 3/2	100 @ $6	600
	200	$1,100

Sale of 11/8

From lot of 1/1	100 @ $5	$ 500
From lot of 5/25	200 @ $8	1,600
	300	$2,100
Cost of goods sold	500	$3,200

Total merchandise costs to be accounted for during the year (initial balance plus purchases) are $6,700. If the cost of goods sold is $3,200, then the balance of the total costs must pertain to the goods still on hand at year end—$6,700 minus $3,200 = $3,500. This amount can be verified by the following tabulation of ending inventory:

From lot of 1/1	100 @ $5	$ 500
From lot of 5/25	200 @ $8	1,600
From lot of 9/18	200 @ $7	1,400
Ending inventory	500	$3,500

The specific identification method is most appropriate for enterprises, such as automobile and appliance dealers, that sell relatively few items of large unit cost. It becomes burdensome to firms that sell large quantities of low-cost items. The specific identification method is rational in that it assures that the amounts charged as expenses are the actual costs of the specific goods sold. But at the same time, especially if the goods sold are similar to one another, it permits management the opportunity to manipulate income. If, in the above example, management wanted to report a higher income, it could simply have made certain that the units sold were taken from a lot of lower cost (e.g., the goods sold on 11/8 were taken from the $7 lot of 9/18 rather than from the $8 lot of 5/25).

FIRST IN, FIRST OUT

In most well-managed businesses, an attempt is made to sell goods in the order in which they have been acquired. This practice minimizes losses from spoilage and deterioration. In the absence of the ability or the willingness to expend the required time and effort to identify the cost of specific units sold, the assumption that goods acquired first are sold

EXHIBIT 8-2

Purchases and Sales of a Particular Item

	Purchases				
Date	No. of Units	Unit Cost	Total Cost	No. of Units Sold	No. of Units on Hand
1/1 (bal. on hand)	300	$5	$1,500		300
3/2	100	6	600		400
4/20				200	200
5/25	400	8	3,200		600
9/18	200	7	1,400		800
11/8				300	500
Total	1,000		$6,700	500	

first is likely to provide a reasonable approximation of the actual flow of goods. Under the first-in, first-out approach, commonly abbreviated FIFO, the flow of *costs* (that which is of primary concern to the accountant) is presumed to be the same as the usual flow of goods. The FIFO method can readily be demonstrated using the data presented in Exhibit 8-2.

To compute the cost of goods sold, the items sold on 4/20 would be assumed to have come from the lot that was purchased first—that on hand on 1/1. The items sold on 11/8 would be assumed to have come from the balance of the 1/1 lot and the lots of 3/2 and 5/25. Cost of goods sold, therefore, would be $2,900:

Sale of 4/20

From lot of 1/1	200 @ $5	$1,000

Sale of 11/8

From lot of 1/1	100 @ $5	$ 500
From lot of 3/2	100 @ $6	600
From lot of 5/25	100 @ $8	800
	300	$1,900
Cost of goods sold	500	$2,900

If 500 units were sold at a cost of $2,900, then still to be accounted for are the remaining 500 units, at a cost of $6,700 minus $2,900—$3,800. These items—the ones still on hand—would be assumed to be those that were purchased most recently:

From lot of 5/25	300 @ $8	$2,400
From lot of 9/18	200 @ $7	1,400
Ending inventory	500	$3,800

FIFO—An Evaluation

Proponents of the FIFO method point out that not only is the underlying assumption that goods purchased first are sold first in accord with conventional management practice but that the method eliminates the opportunities for income manipulation that are possible if costs are identified with specific units. Regardless of which items are actually sold, for accounting purposes it will be assumed that those purchased first have been sold first. Moreover, FIFO provides a balance sheet value that comprises those items purchased last. In most instances the most recent acquisitions are more indicative of current replacement costs than are those purchased earlier. Insofar as current values are of interest to investors and other readers of financial statements, then FIFO provides a more useful balance sheet valuation than do any of the other methods to be discussed. [But as pointed out previously, the balance sheet, in the context of currently accepted accounting principles, should be viewed as a compendium of *residuals* (unexpired costs) as opposed to current market values.]

WEIGHTED AVERAGE

The weighted average inventory method is based on the assumption that all costs can be aggregated and that the cost to be assigned to any particular unit should be the weighted average of the costs of the units held during the accounting period. The weighted average method assumes no particular flow of goods. The cost of any unit sold is simply the average of those available for sale—an average that is weighted by the number of units acquired at each particular price.

In the discussion of both the specific identification and FIFO methods no distinction was made between the methods as they would be applied by firms that maintain perpetual inventory records and those which update their records only periodically after taking a physical count of goods on hand. It would make no difference in either cost of goods sold or ending inventory whether the firm followed perpetual or periodic procedures. In applying the weighted average method, however, the results would not be the same. The weighted average cost of goods on hand at the end of the year may differ from those calculated at various times throughout the year. Hence the costs assigned to the various quantities sold would also differ.

To apply the weighted average method on a *periodic* basis, the firm would assign a cost to all goods—both those that were sold and those in inventory at year end—that represents the weighted average of the cost of *all* goods available for sale during the period. The cost of the goods on hand at the beginning of the year as well as those purchased during the year would be considered in the calculation of the average. The weighted average, based on the information in Exhibit 8-2, would be calculated as follows:

Balance 1/1	300 @ $5	$1,500
Lot of 3/2	100 @ $6	600
Lot of 5/25	400 @ $8	3,200
Lot of 9/18	200 @ $7	1,400
	1,000	$6,700

The average cost of goods available for sale would be $6,700/1,000 = $6.70.

Inasmuch as 500 units were sold during the period, the cost of goods sold would be 500 times $6.70—$3,350. Since, by coincidence, 500 units remain unsold at year end, the closing inventory would also be 500 times $6.70—$3,350.

Weighted Average—An Evaluation

The weighted average method can be set forth as representing the physical flow of goods when all goods available for sale are mixed together with one another—as would be the case with liquids or other fungible goods. When applied on a periodic basis, however, such justification becomes tenuous. If goods are purchased subsequent to the last sale of the year, then the cost of those goods will enter into the average cost of the goods sold during the year, even though such goods could not possibly have been sold during the year. Suppose that in the example presented, the firm on 12/1, well after the last sale of the year, acquired 1,000 units at $20 per unit. The 1,000 units at $20 per unit would be included in the computation of the average cost of the units sold, even though it is obvious that none of them were actually sold. The weighted average method, as applied on a periodic basis, owes its popularity to its convenience; if it may result in the inclusion in the cost of goods sold the costs applicable to merchandise purchased after the final sale of the year has been made, it is decidedly lacking in theoretical support.

If the weighted average method were to be applied on a perpetual basis (see Exhibit 8-3), then a new weighted (or *moving*) average of the cost of goods available for sale would have to be computed after each purchase at a different price. Such average cost would be assigned to both the goods sold and those that remain in inventory. For example, the average cost of goods available for sale, after the purchase of 3/2, would be calculated as follows:

Cost of goods available for sale on 4/20		
Balance 1/1	300 @ $5	$1,500
Lot of 3/2	100 @ $6	600
	400	$2,100

Average cost of goods available for sale would be $2,100/400 = $5.25.

The cost assigned to the 200 units sold on 4/20 would be 200 times $5.25—$1,050. That assigned to the 200 units that remain in inventory after the sale of 4/20 would also be $1,050.

EXHIBIT 8-3

Perpetual Inventory Record
Weighted (Moving) Average Method

	Purchases			Sales			Balance		
Date	Units	Unit Cost	Total Cost	Units	Unit Cost	Total Cost	Units	Unit Cost	Total Cost
1/1							300	$5.00	$1,500.00
3/2	100	$6.00	$ 600				400	5.25	2,100.00
4/20				200	$5.25	$1,050.00	200	5.25	1,050.00
5/25	400	8.00	3,200				600	7.0833	4,250.00
9/18	200	7.00	1,400				800	7.0625	5,650.00
11/8				300	7.0625	2,118.75	500	7.0625	3,531.25

The average cost of goods available for the next sale, that of 11/8, would be based on the average cost of goods on hand immediately following the last sale (i.e., 200 units at $5.25 per unit) plus that of the subsequent acquisitions. Thus:

Cost of goods available for sale on 11/8
Balance 4/20	200 @ $5.25	$1,050
Lot of 5/25	400 @ $8.00	3,200
Lot of 9/18	200 @ $7.00	1,400
	800	$5,650

Average cost of goods available for sale would be $5,650/800 = $7.0625.

The cost assigned to the 300 units sold on 11/8 would be 300 times $7.0625—$2,118.75—and that to the 500 units remaining on hand at year end would be 500 times $7.0625—$3,531.25 (or $5,650 minus the $2,118.75 assigned to the goods sold). The total cost of goods sold for the year would be the sum of the costs assigned to each of the two lots sold:

Total cost of goods sold during the year
Goods sold on 4/20	$1,050.00
Goods sold on 11/8	2,118.75
Total	$3,168.75

This compares to $3,350 calculated using the periodic procedures.

LAST IN, FIRST OUT

In recent years the last-in, first-out method has been the focus of accounting controversy pertaining to inventory valuation. As its name implies, the last-in, first-out method (LIFO) assigns to goods sold the costs of those goods that have been purchased last. It is based on the assumption that, irrespective of the actual physical flow of goods, the goods sold are those that have been acquired last and the goods that remain on hand are those that have been acquired first. No pretense is made that the flow of costs even approximates the usual flow of goods.

As with the weighted average method, there will be significant differences in the cost of goods sold, as well as in the ending inventory, if a firm follows periodic as opposed to perpetual inventory procedures. If the firm determines ending inventory and cost of goods sold based on a *periodic* (i.e., annual) inventory count, then the cost of goods sold will be the cost of products that were purchased *closest to the year end*. If the firm

EXHIBIT 8-4

Summary of Cost of Goods Sold and Ending Inventory

	Cost of Goods Sold	Ending Inventory	Total Costs Accounted For
First in, first out (FIFO)[a]	$2,900.00	$3,800.00	$6,700
Weighted average			
Periodic	3,350.00	3,350.00	6,700
Perpetual	3,168.75	3,531.25	6,700
Last in, first out (LIFO)			
Periodic	3,800.00	2,900.00	6,700

[a] Cost of goods sold and inventory would be the same regardless of whether inventory records were maintained on a periodic or a perpetual basis.

maintains *perpetual* records, then the cost of the goods sold will be considered to be the cost of units that were purchased closest to each individual sale. Only LIFO assuming periodic procedures will be illustrated here inasmuch as firms seldom use LIFO in association with perpetual systems.*

As indicated in Exhibit 8-2, the firm sold 500 units during the year. The cost to be assigned to those 500 units will be that of the 500 units purchased most recently, i.e., those purchased on 9/18 and 5/25:

Cost of goods sold

From lot of 9/18	200 @ $7	$1,400
From lot of 5/25	300 @ $8	2,400
Cost of goods sold	500	$3,800

Since there was a total of 1,000 items available for sale at a total cost of $6,700, the costs that would be assigned to the ending inventory would be $6,700 minus the $3,800 assigned to the goods sold—$2,900. Ending inventory would be composed of the 500 items, including those that were on hand at the beginning of the year, that were purchased

* For guidance on applying LIFO on a perpetual basis, see problem 2 at the conclusion of this chapter.

first:

Ending inventory

From lot of 1/1	300 @ $5	$1,500
From lot of 3/2	100 @ $6	600
From lot of 5/25	100 @ $8	800
Ending inventory	500	$2,900

Exhibit 8-4 summarizes the costs of goods sold and the ending inventories under the FIFO, weighted average, and LIFO methods.

THE RATIONALE FOR LIFO

Very few firms sell or use first the goods that they have acquired last. In some situations, a company might indeed store certain commodities in a pile and remove goods as needed from the top of the heap—that portion of total goods which presumably has been added last. Such would be the case in firms maintaining stores of coal or sand. But the use of LIFO is not confined to situations where the physical flow of goods follows a last-in, first-out pattern. It is applied even when there is no question but that the goods acquired first are sold first. The justification for the use of LIFO must be found in reasons other than that it is representative of the physical flow of goods.

Matching Current Costs with Current Revenues

The objective of inventory accounting, it was previously indicated, is to *match* the costs of acquiring or producing goods with the revenues that they generate. The more specific objective of the LIFO method is to match the *current costs* of acquiring or producing the goods with the current revenues from sales. Under LIFO the cost of goods sold is considered to be that of the goods most recently acquired.

Eliminating "Inventory" Profits

Proponents of LIFO point out that a business must maintain a minimum supply of goods on hand. This basic stock of goods is as essential to the firm's continued operations as are its fixed assets, such as machinery and equipment. Under generally accepted accounting principles, accounting recognition is seldom given to increases in the market value of fixed assets. Why, then, should accounting recognition be accorded increases in the market price of inventories? Suppose, for example, that upon its formation a business determines that it must have 100 units of product on hand. It purchases the 100 units at a price of $1,000 each. In the course of the first year of operations, it sells the units for $1,200 each. At the end of the year it replenishes its stock by purchasing another 100 units—this time, however, at a cost of $1,200 each. If inventory and cost of goods sold were to be determined on a FIFO basis, then ending inventory would be valued at $1,200 per unit; the cost of goods sold would be $1,000 per unit. The firm would

report a profit of $200 per unit—a total of $20,000. Is the firm really $20,000 better off than it was at the beginning of the period?

Since the firm deemed it necessary to maintain an inventory of 100 units, it would be unable to distribute to owners any funds from the business without contracting operations. It would be required to use the entire $20,000 gain to replace the goods that it had sold. The $20,000, according to proponents of LIFO, is not a "true" profit; rather it represents an *inventory* profit. The inventory profit is indicative of nothing more than the difference between the initial cost of acquiring a minimum stock of goods on hand and the current cost of doing so.

Under LIFO, ending inventory would be reported at $1,000 per unit and cost of goods sold at $1,200. Since the items were sold at a price of $1,200 per unit, the firm would report zero profit for the year. Inventory would be valued on the balance sheet at the amount initially invested in the 100 units. The firm would not appear to be $20,000 "better off" when, as the advocates of LIFO point out, it is in the identical position at the end of the year that it was at the beginning.

Reducing Distortions in Income Attributable to Inflation

LIFO represents an attempt to reduce distortions in the income statement attributable to inflation. In a period of stable prices, both inventory and cost of goods sold would be identical under FIFO and LIFO. In a period of rising prices, compared with FIFO, LIFO would ordinarily result in a lower reported value for inventory (since goods are being valued at the earliest prices paid) and correspondingly a lower reported income (since the cost of goods sold is being determined on the basis of the most recent purchases—those at the higher prices).

EXHIBIT 8-5

Five-Year Comparison between FIFO and LIFO

Table 1: FIFO

	Cost of Goods Purchased	FIFO Cost of Goods Sold		FIFO Ending Inventory	
	Per Unit	Per Unit	Total (1,000 units)	Per Unit	Total (1,000 units)
1978				$100.00	$100,000
1979	$110.00	$100.00	$100,000	110.00	110,000
1980	121.00	110.00	110,000	121.00	121,000
1981	133.10	121.00	121,000	133.10	133,100
1982	146.41	133.10	133,100	146.41	146,410
1983	161.05	146.41	146,410	161.05	161,050
Total			$610,510		

Table 2: LIFO

	Cost of Goods Purchased	LIFO Cost of Goods Sold		LIFO Ending Inventory	
	Per Unit	Per Unit	Total (1,000 units)	Per Unit	Total (1,000 units)
1978				$100.00	$100,000
1979	$110.00	$110.00	$110,000	100.00	100,000
1980	121.00	121.00	121,000	100.00	100,000
1981	133.10	133.10	133,100	100.00	100,000
1982	146.41	146.41	146,410	100.00	100,000
1983	161.05	161.05	161,050	100.00	100,000
Total			$671,560		

Table 3: Differences between FIFO and LIFO
(Table 1 Minus Table 2)

	Cost of Goods Sold		Ending Inventory	
	Per Unit	Total (1,000 units)	Per Unit	Total (1,000 units)
1979	$10.00	$10,000	$10.00	$10,000
1980	11.00	11,000	21.00	21,000
1981	12.10	12,100	33.10	33,100
1982	13.31	13,310	46.41	46,410
1983	14.64	14,640	61.05	61,050
Total	$61.05	$61,050		

Exhibit 8-5 compares reported cost of goods sold and year-end inventory for a five-year period. It is based on the assumption that at the start of 1979 a firm had on hand 1,000 units at $100 each. During each of the next five years the firm sold 1,000 units and purchased 1,000 units. The cost of the units purchased increased at a compounded rate of 10 percent per year.

As indicated in Exhibit 8-5, the difference each year in cost of goods sold is equal to the difference between the cost of goods purchased in the previous year and the cost of those purchased in the current year. Under FIFO goods sold in 1979 are assumed to be purchased in 1978; under LIFO goods sold in 1979 are assumed to be purchased in 1979. Proponents of LIFO argue that because FIFO matches current revenues with the cost of goods acquired in a previous period, it consistently understates the "true" cost of goods sold and as a result overstates income.

The difference in ending inventory is considerably more striking. Under FIFO goods on hand at the end of 1983 are assumed to have been purchased in 1983; under LIFO they are assumed to be purchased in 1978 (each year's sales were assumed to have been taken from the current year's purchases; the stock on hand at the start of 1979 is assumed to have never been depleted). The difference in ending inventory at the end of 1983 ($61,050) is the equivalent of the cumulative difference in cost of goods sold for the five-year period ($671,560 versus $610,510).

LIFO—SOME RESERVATIONS

The effects of LIFO on both the balance sheet and the income statement are, in the view of some managers and accountants, unaccept-able. LIFO results in a reported inventory that is continually out of date. If the firm never dips into its base stock (for example, in Exhibit 8-5, the inventory was never reduced below 1,000 units), then the reported inventory would be reflective of prices that existed at the time LIFO was first adopted, decades earlier perhaps. The balance sheet, as continually emphasized in this text, is not purported to be representative of current values. Nevertheless, many accountants feel uncomfortable when values that are hopelessly out of date are assigned.

More serious, however, is the impact of LIFO on reported income when the firm is required to dip into its base stock. If the firm is required to sell goods that are valued on the balance sheet at decades-old prices, then the cost of goods sold will be based on the same ancient prices. Refer back to Exhibit 8-5. Suppose that in 1983 the firm was unable to purchase its required 1,000 units. Instead, it sold its goods on hand and thereby reduced its end-of-year inventory to zero. The cost of goods sold would be $100 per unit—the price of the goods on hand when the company first adopted LIFO in 1979. This at a time when the current replacement cost of the goods is $146.41 per unit. If the cost of goods sold is misleadingly low, then reported income would, of course, be correspondingly high. Whatever its advantages when the firm is able to meet current sales out of current purchases, LIFO produces results that are absurd when it becomes necessary to reduce inventory below a level that is historically normal. Many accountants who are opposed to LIFO recognize the need to account for rapid increases in the replacement costs of inventories. They believe, however, that it should be done directly, by adjusting both cost of goods sold and goods on hand to reflect current values. Current value accounting as it applies to inventories will be discussed later in this chapter.

LIFO—ITS RECENT POPULARITY

From the mid-1970s on, several hundred major U.S. firms shifted from either a FIFO or a moving average to a LIFO inventory valuation method. The shifts were motivated almost entirely by the opportunities to reduce the federal income tax burden.

Since 1938, the Internal Revenue Code has recognized the acceptability of LIFO. In periods of rapid inflation, such as those experienced in many industrial nations in the 1970s and early 1980s, LIFO, by basing the cost of goods sold on the most recent purchases, reduces taxable income. The difference in taxable income between that determined on a FIFO or average cost as opposed to a LIFO basis may not be trivial. Du Pont, for example, estimated that its 1974 shift from average cost to LIFO reduced income by over $250 million and reduced its earnings per share by $3.02 (from $11.22 to $8.20). Other major corporations effected similar reductions in earnings and hence in taxes. Estimates of the overall loss in tax revenues to the federal government range up to $22 billion per year.

As a rule, when there are alternative accounting methods that are generally accepted, businesses are not required to use the same method in reporting to the Internal Revenue Service as they do in reporting to their stockholders. With respect to the method of determining inventories, however, the tax code makes an exception. If a company adheres to one method in reporting to the general public, it *must* use the same method in reporting to the IRS. As a consequence of this ruling, firms that wish to take advantage of the tax-savings opportunities provided by LIFO are required to switch to LIFO for general reporting purposes.

Quite apart from the tax advantages of LIFO, some financial analysts consider earnings of LIFO-based companies to be of higher "quality" than those of FIFO or average cost firms. What they mean is that were it not for the "inflated" value of their inventories, the earnings of the non-LIFO firms may have been considerably lower and growth trends somewhat more flat.

LIFO—CAN A FIRM AFFORD NOT TO ADOPT IT?

A large number of accountants and financial specialists assert that in periods of inflation the use of any inventory method other than LIFO cannot be justified. LIFO serves to reduce taxes and, thereby, to increase the amount of cash available for other corporate purposes. Yet not all firms have shifted to LIFO. There are several reasons for their reluctance.

Impact Not Significant

LIFO will not result in a significant tax saving for all firms. To the extent that a firm maintains a relatively small stock of goods on hand relative to sales (that is, inventory *turnover* is rapid), the difference between LIFO and FIFO or average cost earnings is likely to be small. In the grocery industry, for example, goods are sold within days of their arrival in a store. As a consequence, inventory, as a percentage of total cost of goods sold, is sufficiently small so that a change in method of valuing inventory will have only a minor impact on overall income. Moreover, although the United States has experienced an increase in the general level of prices, the prices of some items have remained stable, or have even declined. For firms which deal in such items, such as computers and other electronic devices, a change would increase taxable income. In addition, because of special features of the tax laws, many firms are able to report *taxable* losses—and thus have no tax obligations—for many years at a time even if under generally accepted accounting principles they are profitable.

Will Decrease *Reported* Earnings

LIFO, by decreasing the amount of cash that must be paid to taxing authorities, increases the true economic well-being of a firm. At the same time, however, it decreases the earnings that will be reported on the financial statements.

Many firms are reluctant to take any actions that will reduce reported earnings. They are afraid that a reduction in reported earnings will decrease the appeal of their securities to investors and thereby depress the prices at which they are traded. This would impair the ability of the firm to raise additional capital. There is, however, a substantial body of academic research to suggest that their fears are unfounded. Investors as a group are able to distinguish between substantive economic developments that affect a firm and mere accounting changes. They do not reduce the value they place on a firm's securities only because a change in accounting method has reduced the earnings that the firm reports.

Some managers may also be concerned that a reduction in reported earnings owing to a switch to LIFO would, in fact, have a negative *substantive* economic impact on the well-being of themselves as well as their firms. Such would be the case when the compensation of the managers is tied, by way of profit sharing or bonus arrangements, to reported earnings. It would also be true when con-

tractual arrangements with lenders or other parties specify that in order to be eligible for continued funding or other benefits the firm must maintain its reported earnings above a certain level.

Might Increase Taxes at a Time When the Firm Could Least Afford It

Some firms may also be concerned about the consequences of having to reduce their stock below normal levels. The reduction might be the result of a strike or economic downturn. It would cause a substantial increase in both reported and taxable income and a corresponding increase in taxes. The tax "savings" of several previous years might be offset entirely by an inordinately large tax expense in a single year. Since the firm might then have to replace the goods sold at the prices prevailing at the time, it might not have sufficient cash on hand both to replenish its inventory and to meet its tax obligations.

LOWER OF COST OR MARKET RULE

Regardless of which of the previously described inventory methods a firm adopts, the application of generally accepted accounting principles requires a departure from cost whenever the utility of the goods on hand has diminished since the date of acquisition. Loss of utility might be the result of physical damage or deterioration, obsolescence, or a general decline in the level of prices. Loss of utility should be given accounting recognition by stating the inventories at *cost or market, whichever is lower*. As used in the expression cost or market, *market* refers to the amount that would have to be paid to *replace* the goods by purchase or reproduction. This lower of cost or market rule is grounded in the concept of *conservatism*, which holds that firms should advance recognition of losses but delay recognition of gains.

Suppose that a jewelry retailer purchases a lot of 100 digital watches for $100 each, with the intention of selling them at a price of $125. Prior to sale, however, as a result of manufacturing efficiencies, the wholesale price of the watches drops to $80 and the corresponding retail price to $105. Application of the lower of cost or market rule would require that the stated value of the watches on hand be reduced from original cost of $100 to the current market (replacement) price of $80. The following journal entry would be appropriate to record the decline in price:

Loss on inventory
  (expense) $2,000
      Inventory (asset) $2,000

To record the loss attributable to the decline in the replacement cost of 100 digital watches from $100 to $80.

The lower of cost or market rule may be applied to inventories on an individual (item-by-item) or a group basis. If applied on an individual basis, then the cost of each item in stock is compared with its current replacement cost. If the replacement cost of an item is lower than its original cost, then the item is written down to its replacement cost. If applied on a group basis, then the original cost of the inventory pool (which may be either the entire inventory or a collection of similar items) is compared with its market value, and a reduction in book value is required only if total market value is less than total initial cost. The group basis is likely to result in a considerably higher inventory valuation than the individual basis since it permits the increases in the market prices of some items to offset the decreases in others. The two bases were illustrated in Chapter 6 as part of a discussion regarding the values to be assigned to portfolios of marketable securities.

The lower of cost or market rule has been adopted by the rule-making bodies of the profession, but it has been the subject of widespread attack by accounting theoreticians. Critics assert that the rule sacrifices consistency for conservatism. The rule introduces a measure of inconsistency into financial reports, since it gives recognition to decreases in market values but not to increases. Moreover, they contend that the rule requires the recognition of losses where none have really occurred. In the previous example, the firm purchased watches for $100 and will sell them for $105. Although it will not earn the full $25 profit that was expected, it will nevertheless realize a gain (excluding all other operating costs) of $5 per unit. If the lower of cost or market rule is adhered to, the accounts will reflect a loss of $20 per unit in the period of the write-down and a gain of $25 in the period of sale.* Critics contend that, as a consequence, earnings of both periods are distorted. In fact, they assert, the company earned a profit of $5 at the time of sale, not a loss of $20 in one period and a gain of $25 in the next.

PROPOSED ALTERNATIVE: USE OF CURRENT VALUES

Many accounting theoreticians have proposed that inventories be stated at their *current* values. In this way, they suggest,

---

* Authoritative pronouncements provide that inventory should never be reduced to a level that will lead to recognition of an unusually high profit in a subsequent period. Thus, if in the example the firm estimated that it would be able to sell the watches at retail for $115 rather than $105, it should reduce inventory to no less than $90. If it reduced inventory below $90, then when it sells a watch, its profit in the period of sale would be greater than its "normal" profit of $25 per unit.

many of the deficiencies of each of the alternative assumptions regarding flow of costs, as well as the inconsistencies of the lower of cost or market rule, can be overcome. Their suggestions are worth attention, not so much because they are likely to be accepted in the foreseeable future—although there is unquestionably a trend in the direction of current value accounting—but rather because they provide an insight into the components of gains or losses attributable to the sale of goods included in inventory.

Assume that on September 1, 1983, a merchant purchases 30 cans of tennis balls at $2.00 per can. In the remainder of 1980 he sells 20 cans at $3.00 per can. On December 31, 1983, the wholesale price of tennis balls is increased to $2.50 per can. As a consequence, the merchant raises the retail price to $3.50 per can.

In 1984 he sells the 10 cans that remain from 1983. According to the rules of conventional practice, he will record a gain of $1.50 per can (Sales price of $3.50 minus cost of $2.00.) The $1.50 is composed of two types of gains—a *holding* gain of $.50 and a *trading* gain of $1.00.

The trading gain arises out of the normal business activities of the firm. It represents a return to the merchant for providing the usual services of a retailer—providing customers with the desired quantity of goods at a convenient time and place. The holding gain, on the other hand, can be attributed to the increase in price between the times the merchant purchased and sold the goods. The magnitude of the holding gain depends on the quantity of goods held in inventory and the size of the price increase. Most merchants are required to maintain a stock of goods adequate to service the needs of their customers—that is, to make certain that they have a sufficient number of goods on hand to minimize the risk of outages and to provide customers with an ample choice of styles, sizes, and colors. Some merchants, however, intentionally maintain an inventory greater than that necessary to meet their operating needs. Hoping to take advantage of increases in price, they employ inventory as a means of speculation. Speculative holding gains (and of course losses) are especially common in those industries which deal in commodities—e.g., grains, cocoa, and metals—that are subject to frequent and substantial fluctuations in prices.

Were inventories to be stated at their current values, it would be relatively easy to distinguish—and report separately—the holding gains from the trading gains. And more significantly, the holding gains could be identified with the accounting period in which the increase in prices actually took place, rather than delayed until the period of sale. In the example at hand, the holding gain actually occurred in 1983, the year in which the price increase was announced. Management control and evaluation of performance would be facilitated because the elements of profit that are within the control of specific managers could be set forth. Gains or losses arising from changes in prices could be taken into account in appraising the record of a manager only when they are relevant to his or her accomplishments.

The following journal entry would be appropriate to recognize the holding gain of $.50 per can of tennis balls that took place during the year 1983:

Inventory	$5.00	
Holding gains on		
inventory (revenue)		$5.00

To record the holding gain on 10 cans of tennis balls that remained on hand at year-end.

When the 10 cans were sold in the following year, the cost of goods sold would be charged, and inventories credited, with their adjusted carrying value of $2.50 per can:

Cost of goods sold $25.00
     Inventory $25.00
To record the cost of goods sold.

Comparative income statements which give recognition to the sale in 1983 of 20 cans of tennis balls at $3.00 per can and the sale in 1984 of 10 cans at $3.50 per can would appear as follows:

	1983	1984
Sales	$60.00	$35.00
Holding gains	5.00	—
Total revenues	$65.00	$35.00
Cost of goods sold:		
20 cans @ $2.00	40.00	
10 cans @ $2.50		25.00
Income	$25.00	$10.00

Regardless of whether inventory was adjusted to reflect the holding gains or whether conventional procedures were followed, the total gain on the sale of the 30 cans of tennis balls would be $35. Conventional income statements, in which the holding gains were not recognized, would appear as follows:

	1983	1984
Sales	$60.00	$35.00
Cost of goods sold		
20 cans @ $2.00	40.00	
10 cans @ $2.00		20.00
Income	$20.00	$15.00

The effect of increasing the carrying value of the 10 cans in inventory and of concurrently recognizing a holding gain of $.50 per can would be to shift $5 of income from 1984, the year in which the cans were sold, to 1983, the year in which the price increase took place.

In the discussion to this point *current value* has been used to mean replacement cost, an *input* value. As indicated in an earlier chapter, however, current value can be viewed as an *output* value as well as an input value. Thus, some theoreticians suggest that inventories be stated at a current *output* value, such as the amount for which they could currently be sold or at net realizable value (the amount for which they are *likely* to be sold in the future, less any costs of bringing the goods to a salable condition.)

Regardless of which particular current value is employed, the suggestion that inventories be valued at some current value should not be viewed as particularly radical. Recall the discussion in Chapter 5 pertaining to recognition of revenue. It was pointed out then that when, in unusual circumstances, revenue is recognized in the course of production (as in long-term construction contracts) or upon completion of production (as in the mining of precious metals), inventory is in effect stated at a current value.

Since 1979 the Financial Accounting Standards Board has required that firms larger than a specified size provide in their annual reports supplementary data on the replacement value of inventories. The pronouncement of the Board (Financial Accounting Statement No. 33) does not prescribe that complete replacement cost statements be prepared, but it does mandate that firms indicate what the cost of goods sold and ending inventories would have been if calculated on the basis of current, as opposed to historical, values.

INVENTORY TURNOVER

The effectiveness with which a firm uses its inventory to support sales can be measured by way of an activity ratio, *inventory turnover*. Inventory turnover is the number of times the annual cost of sales exceeds average inventory. It is computed by dividing cost of goods sold by average inventory:

$$\text{Inventory turnover} = \frac{\text{Cost of goods sold}}{\text{Average inventory}}$$

The greater the number of times per year that inventory *turns over*, the more efficiently the inventory is being used. The smaller the inventory in relation to cost of goods sold, the greater the sales activity that the inventory is able to sustain.

Because inventory is more closely related to cost of goods sold than it is to sales, cost of goods sold rather than sales serves as the numerator. This is in contrast to the accounts receivable turnover ratio (discussed in Chapter 7) and the fixed asset turnover ratio (to be discussed in Chapter 9). As with the accounts receivable turnover ratio, the denominator should be based ideally on a 12-month average (as opposed to a beginning- and end-of-year average) in order to avoid distortions resulting from seasonal fluctuations.

Per its statements included in Chapter 7 Fruehauf Corp. reported cost of goods sold in 1980 of $1,688,619,307. Average inventory was $306,462,032. Inventory turnover was, therefore, 5.5.

$$\text{Inventory turnover} = \frac{\$1,688,619,307}{\$306,462,032} = 5.5 \text{ times}$$

It should be obvious that when a firm uses LIFO to account for its inventory, the usefulness of the inventory turnover ratio as a technique of management control or investment analysis is severely limited. If the inventory is being reported at values representing prices of a distant past, then a comparison of LIFO inventory with cost of goods sold (based on current prices) is of little or no significance.

SUMMARY

In this chapter we have dealt primarily with accounting issues pertaining to inventory within the traditional historical cost framework. Because of the overriding importance of inventories to most manufacturing and retail companies, selection of accounting alternatives may have a critical impact on both reported assets and earnings.

The primary objective of conventional accounting is to match the costs of acquiring or producing goods with the revenues that they generate. To realize such objective it is necessary to make assumptions as to the flow of costs—whether the cost of goods acquired first, or last, for example, should be associated with the revenues of a particular period. Strong arguments can be advanced in favor of or against each of the assumptions, and choice of assumption may have a significant effect on reported cost of goods sold as well as ending inventories.

Regardless of assumption, however, inventories should be restated at the lower of cost or market to reflect declines in their replacement cost. Although some accountants have suggested that accounting recognition be given to increases in market prices as well as to decreases, current practice favors conservatism over consistency, and gains from holding inventories are considered to be realized only at the time they are sold.

EXERCISE FOR REVIEW AND SELF-STUDY

The inventory records of the Simon Corp. indicate the following with respect to a particular item:

	Purchases				
Date	No. of Units	Unit Cost	Total Cost	No. of Units Sold	No. of Units on Hand
1/01/83[a]	400	$20	$8,000		400
2/24/83	200	21	4,200		600
6/16/83				300	300
9/23/83	100	22	2,200		400
11/15/83				300	100
12/28/83	100	23	2,300		200

[a] Beginning balance.

1. Determine the total number of units as well as the total costs to be accounted for during the year.

2. The firm maintains its records on a *periodic* basis. Determine year-end inventory and cost of goods sold assuming each of the following cost flows:
   a. First in, first out
   b. Weighted average
   c. Last in, first out

3. Suppose that the firm values its inventory on the FIFO basis. On December 31, the price per unit of the item falls to $21 and the anticipated selling price falls by $2. At what amount, in accord with the lower of cost or market rule, should year-end inventory be stated? What would be the effect of the write-down on earnings of 1983? What would be the effect on earnings of 1984 when the goods are sold?

4. Assume alternatively that the firm were to report inventory at current replacement cost (a practice *not* in accord with "generally accepted accounting principles") and that the price at year end remained at $23 per unit. At what amount should year-end inventory be stated? How much "holding gain" should be recognized? What would be the effect on cost of goods sold in 1984 of recognizing the holding gain in 1983, assuming that the goods are sold in 1984?

5. Determine inventory turnover. Assume the firm uses the FIFO inventory method. For convenience, consider average inventory to be one-half the sum of beginning-and end-of-year values.

QUESTIONS FOR REVIEW AND DISCUSSION

1. "Since it is the objective of asset accounting to assign fair values to goods owned by a firm, LIFO is an inappropriate means of accounting for inventories. LIFO may result in values that are far out of date." Do you agree? Comment.

2. "Firms make assumptions regarding the flows of goods only because it is costly and inconvenient to keep records of specific items actually sold. The specific identification method is theoretically superior to any of the other methods and eliminates the possibilities of income manipulation associated with those methods." Do you agree? Comment.

3. Very few businesses sell or use first the goods that have been received most recently. How, then, can the widespread use of LIFO be explained? Provide an example of a situation in which a company does in fact sell or use first the goods acquired last.

4. National Steel Corp. and Great Supermarkets, Inc., each has annual sales of approximately $10 million and earnings of $300,000. National Steel maintains an inventory equal in value to about 5 percent of cost of goods sold, and Great Supermarkets, about .5 percent. In other words, the inventory of National Steel *turns over* approximately 20 times per year and that of Great Supermarkets about 200 times a year. For which of the two firms would a shift from FIFO to LIFO have the greater impact on earnings? Explain.

5. It is sometimes asserted that LIFO provides a more meaningful income statement, albeit not necessarily a more meaningful balance sheet. Why does LIFO provide a more meaningful income statement? Does it always? Provide an example of a situation in which it may seriously distort income.

6. What is meant by the term market, as it is used in the expression "cost or market, whichever is lower." The lower of cost or market rule is often cited as an example of the possible conflict between conservatism and consistency. Why? Over a period of several years, is the lower of cost or market rule likely to decrease the overall income of a firm? Explain.

7. Suppose that inventories were to be stated on the balance sheet at current replacement values (which may exceed costs). What would be the impact on earnings of the year in which an increase in replacement cost was first recognized? What would be the impact on earnings of the year in which the goods were sold?

8. Conventional accounting practices require that inventories be stated at historical cost. How could a financial analyst obtain information on the replacement value of a firm's inventory?

9. Why does the use of LIFO limit the utility of the inventory turnover ratio.

10. A firm acquires a substantial quantity of inventory on December 31, subsequent to the last sale of the year. The price paid is considerably greater than that of previous purchases.

Why might use of the weighted average method, applied on a periodic basis, produce a cost of goods sold that many accountants would claim is overstated?

PROBLEMS

1. Choice of bookkeeping procedure may affect earnings.

As of January 1, 1983, a firm had 700 units of product on hand. The stated value was $1,400. During the year the firm had two sales—the first on January 17 of 600 units, and the second on November 11 of 700 units. On March 8 the firm received a shipment of 1,600 units at a cost of $4,800. Assume that the purchases were for cash.

Prepare those journal entries which would affect inventory assuming that the firm uses
a. Periodic inventory procedures:
   (1) FIFO
   (2) Weighted average
b. Perpetual inventory procedures:
   (1) FIFO
   (2) Weighted average
c. Compare the total cost of goods sold and the ending inventory under each of the alternatives.

2. This exercise serves to illustrate the three fundamental inventory valuation methods, each applied on both periodic and perpetual bases.

During 1983 the Whitman Co. engaged in the following purchases and sales of an item:

	Purchases		
	No. Units	Cost per Unit	Sales (No. Units)
Jan. 1 (Beginning bal.)	400	$5.00	
Feb. 11			150
May 6	200	5.10	
Sept. 8			220
Sept. 30	300	5.20	
Oct. 17			310
Nov. 26	100	5.25	
Dec. 16			50
	1,000		730

Determine December 31 inventory and cost of goods sold for 1983 assuming first that the company maintains inventory on a periodic basis and then on a perpetual basis. Assume also each of the following flows of costs: FIFO; weighted average; LIFO.

LIFO, applied on a perpetual basis, is not specifically illustrated in the text. The procedures are not difficult, however. Compute the cost of goods sold upon each sale. The goods sold would be assumed to be those which were acquired most recently up to the date of sale. For example, the 220 units sold on September 8 would be considered to be the 200 units acquired on May 6 plus 20 from the balance on hand as of January 1.

3. The specific indentification method, even if clerically feasible, may not be theoretically perferable.

As of December 1, 1983, Big Sam Appliance Co. has 300 refrigerators in stock. All are identical; all are priced to sell at $900. Each is tagged with a card indicating in code its cost to Big Sam. Of the 300 refrigerators on hand, 100 were acquired on June 15, at a cost of $800 each, 100 on November 1 at a cost of $650, and 100 on December 1, at a cost of $700 per unit. Big Sam estimates that, in the month of December, 200 refrigerators will be sold.

a. Determine cost of goods sold on a FIFO basis, assuming that 200 refrigerators were in fact sold.
b. Suppose that Big Sam uses the specific identification method and wishes to maximize reported earnings for the year. How can it accomplish its objective by discreet selection of the units to be sold?
c. Suppose that Big Sam uses the specific identification method and, to minimize taxes, wishes to minimize reported earnings. How can it accomplish its objective?

4. Is the impact of LIFO upon earnings the same in periods of falling prices as in periods of rising prices?

The Simmons Co. began operations on January 1, 1980. In 1980 the company produced 85,000 units at a cost of $12 per unit and sold 89,000 units. In each of the next three years the company produced 80,000 units and sold 80,000 units. Costs of production were $14, $16, and $18, respectively, in each of the years.

a. Compute both cost of goods sold and year-end inventory for each of the four years using first FIFO and then LIFO.
b. Do the same as in part a, assuming this time that production costs were $12, $10, $8, and $6 in each of the four years. (Omit consideration of the lower of cost or market rule.)
c. What generalizations can be made regarding the impact of LIFO as compared with FIFO on cost of goods sold and inventories in periods of rising prices versus periods of falling prices?

5. In the "long run," choice among accounting principles seldom makes a difference.

The Pittsfield Co. existed in business for a period of four years. During that period, purchases and sales were as follows:

	Purchases		Sales	
	Units	Unit Cost	Units	Sales Price
1980	12,000	$10	8,000	$15
1981	14,000	11	15,000	16
1982	9,000	12	9,000	17
1983	10,000	11	13,000	17

a. Determine income for each of the four years assuming first that the company uses FIFO and then that it uses LIFO.
b. Determine total income for the four-year period. Over the life of the business, does it matter which method of inventory is used?

6. Earnings based on LIFO are said to be of higher quality than those based on FIFO.

In December 1982, L. Minton established a door-to-door sales company. He invested $10,000 and purchased 2,000 units of inventory at $5 per unit—the minimum number of units required to sustain his business. He made his purchase at a propitious time, for the next day, before he had a chance to make a single sale, the price per unit of his inventory increased to $6.

During 1983 Minton purchased an additional 10,000 units at $6 per unit and sold 10,000 units at $7 per unit. He withdrew from the business for his personal use *all* cash except that necessary to assure that his inventory was maintained at its minimum level of 2,000 units.

a. Prepare journal entries to reflect the above transactions. First assume that Minton maintained his inventories on a FIFO basis; then assume that he maintained his inventories on a LIFO basis, and indicate any entries that would be different. Prepare income statements and balance sheets comparing results under the two methods.

b. How much cash was Minton able to withdraw during 1983? Compare his cash withdrawals with income as determined by both the FIFO and the LIFO methods. What do you suppose that some financial observers mean when they say that in periods of inflation LIFO results in earnings that are of "higher quality"?

7. *An invasion of the LIFO base may seriously distort earnings.*

As of January 1, 1980, the Byron Co. had 50,000 units of product on hand. Each unit had cost $.80 to produce. During each of the next three years the company produced 100,000 units and sold the same number. In the fourth year, as the result of a strike,

The company maintains its inventory on a periodic LIFO basis.

a. Determine the net income *after taxes* for each of the five years. Assume a tax rate of 40 percent of income.

b. Determine the *cash flow* for each of the five years. That is, determine total cash receipts less total cash disbursements. Assume that all sales were for cash and that all production costs and taxes were paid in cash.

c. In the view of a manager or a financial analyst, of what significance is the income of the firm for 1983?

d. Compare the total cash flow for 1983 and 1984 with that of the prior two-year period. Why is it lower?

8. *The lower of cost or market rule does not reduce the total profits to be realized on the sale of inventories; it only transfers them from one year to the next.*

The Roscoe Corp. started in business on January 1, 1980. Its purchases and sales, as well as the

	Purchases		Sales		Unit Replacement Cost at Year End
	Units	Unit Cost	Units	Unit Price	
1980	12,000	$20	10,000	$30	$15
1981	12,000	15	10,000	25	10
1982	6,000	10	10,000	20	5

the company was able to produce only 50,000 units, though it was able to maintain sales at 100,000. In the fifth year the company, in order to replenish its inventory, produced 150,000 units and continued to sell 100,000 units. Unit production costs and sales prices are indicated in the table.

	Units Produced		Units Sold	
	No. Units	Unit Cost	No. Units	Unit Price
1980	100,000	$1.00	100,000	$1.40
1981	100,000	1.20	100,000	1.60
1982	100,000	1.40	100,000	1.80
1983	50,000	1.60	100,000	2.00
1984	150,000	1.80	100,000	2.20

replacement cost of goods on hand at year end for its first three years of operations, are indicated in the table above. The company stated its inventory on a FIFO basis and applied the lower of cost or market rule.

a. Determine income for each of the three years.

b. Comment on the effect of the lower of cost or market rule on earnings over an extended period of time.

9. *The lower of cost or market rule provides that declines in the value of inventory be given prompt recognition.*

Indicated in the table following is the December 31, 1983, inventory of the Albany Company, along with current replacement costs and expected selling prices:

Items	Units	Unit Cost	Replacement Cost	Expected Selling Price
A	6,000	$10	$12	$18
B	4,000	8	6	9
C	12,000	6	4	6
D	2,000	4	2	6

It is the policy of the company to sell at 50 percent above cost, but sometimes market conditions force (or enable) the company to sell at a lower (or higher) price.

Apply the lower of cost or market rule to determine the value at which December 31, 1983, inventory should be stated. Apply the rule first on an item-by-item basis and then on a group basis. (In assigning a value to item D, be sure to refer to the footnote in the text that indicates that inventories should never be reduced to a level that will lead to recognition of an unusually high profit in a subsequent period.)

10. Problems 10 and 11 illustrate the advantages—and disadvantages—of a shift from FIFO to LIFO.

The 1976 annual report of E. I. du Pont de Nemours & Company contained the following footnote (figures are stated in millions):

If inventory values were shown at estimated replacement or current cost rather than at LIFO values, inventories would have been $489.9 and $410.6 higher than reported at December 31, 1976 and December 31, 1975, respectively.

a. In periods of rising prices, which valuation method, FIFO or LIFO, results in inventory values which most closely approximate current market prices?

b. Assume that replacement costs are approximately equal to inventory as computed on a FIFO basis. Ignoring the impact of income taxes, how much more, or less, as of December 31, 1975 and 1976, would retained earnings have been had the company remained on FIFO?

c. Considering the effect of the change in valuation method on retained earnings of 1975 and 1976,

how much more or less would earnings before taxes have been in 1976 if no change had taken place?

d. Based on your response to part c and assuming a tax rate of 40 percent, how much more or less would the tax obligation of the firm have been in 1976?

e. Comment on why, in a period of rising prices, a firm would deliberately select a method of accounting that would adversely affect reported earnings.

11. The same annual report of E. I. du Pont de Nemours & Company contained the following footnote pertaining to inventories (figures are stated in millions):

During 1975, inventory quantities were reduced from the abnormally high year-end 1974 level. This reduction resulted in a liquidation of LIFO inventory quantities carried at lower costs prevailing in prior years as compared with 1975 costs, the effect of which increased 1975 net income by approximately $38.9 or $.81 per share.

a. Explain in your own words why a liquidation of inventory served to increase net income.

b. If the liquidation served to increase the reported after-tax income by $38.9 million, by how much greater or less was the value of the goods sold based on current (1975) costs than on the historical costs at which they were actually carried on the books. Assume a tax rate of 40 percent.

c. It is clear that in 1975 the use of LIFO seriously distorted the firm's reported income. In fact, management felt compelled to include in its financial statements the previously cited footnote to warn readers of the aberrant earnings.

Why did not the company shift to FIFO for 1975 and then shift back to LIFO in subsequent years when earnings would not be distorted by inventory liquidations?

12. A CPA firm points out that there are no generally accepted standards of "preferability."

In 1977, the Susquehanna Corporation, a firm whose securities are traded on the American Stock Exchange, changed from the FIFO to the LIFO method of accounting for inventories. The change, according to a footnote to the financial statements, was made "to better match the most recent inventory acquisition costs against current sales, thereby minimizing the effects of inflation on earnings."

In a letter to the firm's board of directors, the company's auditors, Price Waterhouse & Co., wrote the following:

Note 2 to the consolidated financial statements of The Susquehanna Corporation, included in the Company's Annual Report to its stockholders for the year ended December 31, 1977 and incorporated by reference in the Company's Annual Report on Form 10-K for the year then ended, describes a change from the first-in, first-out method of accounting for inventories to the last-in, first-out method. We concurred with this change in our report dated February 10, 1978 on the consolidated financial statements referred to above. *It should be understood that preferability of one acceptable method of inventory accounting over another has not been addressed in any authoritative accounting literature and in arriving at our opinion expressed below, we have relied on management's business planning and judgment.* Based upon our discussions with management and the stated reasons for the change, we believe that such change represents, in your circumstances adoption of a preferable accounting principle in conformity with Accounting Principles Board Opinion No. 20.

a. What makes one accounting method perferable to another?

b. If a method of accounting, such as LIFO, is considered preferable to another method, such as FIFO, by both a company and its auditors, how can the use of the alternative method by a company in the same industry, whose financial statements might be examined by the same firm of auditors, be justified?

13. By shifting to FIFO from LIFO, a company may increase reported earnings but incur a substantial economic cost.

In November 1970, the president of an automobile manufacturer became concerned that actual earnings for 1970 would fall short of predicted earnings. In discussions with the corporate controller, he suggested that one way to boost earnings would be to shift from the last-in, first-out method of reporting inventories, which the company was presently using, to the first-in, first-out method.

Upon investigation, the controller found that anticipated inventories at year end would be approximately $100 million if stated on a LIFO basis. If valued on the basis of the cost of the most recent purchases (FIFO), they would be approximately $180 million.

a. What would be the effect on cost of goods sold if inventories for the year 1970 were stated on a FIFO rather than a LIFO basis? Explain.

b. What would be the impact on income tax obligations? Assume a combined federal and state tax rate of 50 percent. (In practice the Internal Revenue Service is likely to allow the company to pay the additional taxes attributable to the shift over a 20-year period.)

c. Comment on any advantages and disadvantages to the company of making the shift.

14. The LIFO method affords an opportunity for income manipulation.

As of January 1, 1983, the Elliot Corp. had 10,000 units of product on hand. Each had a carrying value of $20. In November of that year the president estimated that sales for the year would total 80,000 units. To date, the company had produced 70,000 units, at a cost of $25 per unit. If additional units were to be produced in the remainder of the year, they would cost $26 per unit. The company determines inventory on a periodic LIFO basis.

Determine cost of goods sold if

1. The president ordered that no additional units be produced during the year.
2. The president ordered that 10,000 additional units be produced.
3. The president ordered that 40,000 additional units be produced.

15. *Historical cost accounting may not properly reflect propitious acquisitions of inventory.*

The president of Carolina Textiles, Inc., was disappointed to learn from his controller that preliminary data indicated that his firm had suffered a loss of $25,000 in 1982. The president was surprised by the report of the controller since the price of print cloth, the product in which the company trades, had increased substantially during the year.

Determine income for 1982 assuming that inventories were stated at replacement cost in *both* 1981 and 1982.

16. *The conventional income statement can readily be modified to give effect to changes in inventory replacement costs.*

The F. C. Miller Co. trades in scrap metal. The company purchases the scrap from small dealers and sells it in bulk to the major steel manufacturers. As a matter of policy, the company sells the scrap to the manufacturers for $5 per ton more than the current price it pays the individual dealers. The price of scrap steel is volatile. The following table indicates several price changes that occurred in 1982 and the transactions engaged in by the F. C. Miller Co. in the periods between the price changes:

Period	Price Paid to Dealers	No. of Tons Purchased	No. of Tons Sold	Price per Ton
1/1	$ 82	5,000[a]		
1/2–3/11	85	16,000	18,000	$ 90
3/12–6/4	87	25,000	22,000	92
6/5–9/26	93	5,000	9,000	98
9/27–12/30	104	17,000	13,000	109
12/31	106	-0-	-0-	
		68,000	62,000	

[a] Opening inventory.

As of January 1, 1982, the company had on hand 400,000 yards of print cloth, for which it had paid $.25 per yard. The replacement cost of the cloth as of that date was $.27 per yard. As of December 31, 1982 the company had in inventory 600,000 yards of cloth for which it had paid $.30 per yard. If it were to replace the cloth on December 31, it would have to pay $.45 per yard.

The president believed that creditors would be misled by financial reports on which inventories were valued, and income determined, strictly on the basis of historical cost. He requested that the controller prepare supplementary reports in which inventories were valued at net realizable value and *holding gains* were specifically recognized in the computation of income.

During the year F. C. Miller incurred operating costs of $325,000.

a. Prepare a conventional income statement in which gains or losses are recognized only upon actual sale of goods. Use the FIFO method of inventory valuation.
b. Prepare an income statement in which gains or losses are recognized upon increases in wholesale prices. Cost of goods sold should be based on replacement costs applicable at the time the goods are sold. Be sure to indicate holding gains actually realized as well as those still unrealized. A holding gain actually realized represents the difference between replacement cost on the date the goods are sold and the amount paid to acquire them. An unrealized holding gain

represents the difference in the replacement cost at year-end of goods which have not yet been sold and the amount paid to acquire them.

17. A recent Supreme Court decision restricted the application of the lower of cost or market rule as it applies to federal income taxes. Henceforth, a firm will be able to write down its inventory to net realizable value only when it actually intends to make sales at the prices used to determine net realizable value. This ruling may have a significant impact on decisions made by managers in certain industries. Publishers, for example, assert that it will now be advantageous for them to sell their books as soon as possible, even if only at greatly reduced prices, rather than to retain them in inventory for sale at later dates at standard prices. There would be no financial incentive for them to carry in stock works of academic and literary merit that are "slow-moving" because of their limited market appeal.

Art Books, Inc., printed at a cost of $20 per copy, 20,000 copies of a scholarly art text. In 1983, the year of publication, it sold 10,000 copies at a price of $25 per copy. It estimates, however, that sales in the future will be limited to a relatively few collectors and scholars. It predicts that it will be able to sell, at $25 per copy, 1,000 copies per year for 10 years.

The prevailing income tax rate is 40 percent.

a. In your view, is the inventory still worth $20 per copy? What, for example, is the *maximum* amount a buyer would pay for the entire stock of 10,000 books if the decision criterion is present value of expected cash receipts? Assume a discount rate of 15 percent. In other words, what is the present value of the cash receipts (ignoring taxes) to be received from sales over the period of 10 years?

b. Suppose that Art Books, Inc., has a choice. It could retain the books in inventory and sell them over the period of 10 years. It would be permitted no immediate tax deduction to reflect the loss of the inventory value suggested by your response to part a. Over the 10-year period, it would, of course, be taxed on profits from the sale of the books (revenue less cost of goods sold) as they are earned.

Alternatively, the firm could sell its entire stock of books to a cut-rate bookstore for $10 per copy.

The tax loss on the sale (revenue less cost of goods sold) could be used to offset other corporate income. As a consequence, the firm would realize a cash saving equal in amount to 40 percent (the tax rate) of the loss. In an analysis of this course of action, the cash saving could be considered to be a cash receipt.

1. What is the present value, after taxes, of the cash to be received from the sale of books at the standard price of $25 over the period of 10 years? Assume a discount rate of 15 percent. The cash receipts for each year are equal to the *revenues* to be received less the taxes to be paid. Cost of goods sold, although an expense, does not require an outlay of cash inasmuch as the books to be sold have already been produced.

2. What is the present value, after taxes, of the total amount to be received from the immediate sale of the books to the cut-rate bookstore? Inasmuch as the cash will be received immediately, no discounting is necessary. Be sure to include the tax saving as a cash receipt.

3. Which course of action is likely to be chosen by management? To simplify the illustration, no mention has been made of the costs of holding the inventory, such as storage and insurance, and of selling and distributing the books. What impact would these costs have on the course of action decided upon? Comment on why the decision of the court would encourage firms to destroy, or sell as salvage, slow-selling works rather than to retain them.

18. An increase in reported earnings may not necessarily be reflected in the market price of a firm's common stock.

The president of a publicly held corporation was considering switching from the FIFO to the LIFO method of accounting for inventory. The shift would enable him to reduce his annual income tax payments. The president was reluctant to authorize the shift, however, because it would result in an immediate decline in reported earnings. Such a decline, he thought, might adversely affect the market price of the company's stock and thereby antagonize the shareholders.

As of January 1, 1983, the company had 1,000 (000s omitted) units of products on hand. They were carried on the books at $20 per unit, and because the company had recently reduced its inventory to zero, they would be valued at $20 regardless of whether the company remained on FIFO or switched to LIFO.

As of January 1, 1983, the president made the following estimate of purchases and sales for the following three years (000s omitted from quantities):

1983	Purchase 1,000 units @ $22;
	sell 1,000 units @ $30
1984	Purchase 1,000 units @ $24;
	sell 1,000 units @ $32
1985	Purchase 1,000 units @ $26;
	sell 1,000 units @ $34

a. Determine annual earnings after taxes for each of the three years assuming first that the company maintains its inventory on a FIFO basis and second that it shifts to LIFO. The effective rate of taxes is 40 percent. For convenience, disregard all costs other than cost of goods sold and taxes.

b. Determine the annual cash flows after taxes for each of the three years under both FIFO and LIFO. Compare them with annual earnings. Cash flows should represent sales minus purchases and taxes.

c. Assume that the market price of the firm's stock is based on anticipated corporate cash flows. The total market value of all shares outstanding is equal, at any time, to the present value of expected cash flows for a number of years into the future (in this case assume three years). In calculating the present value of expected cash flows use a discount rate of 8 percent. Determine the total market value of all shares outstanding assuming first that the company remains on FIFO and second that it shifts to LIFO. (For convenience assume that all cash flows occur at year end.)

d. Suppose that the company has 100,000 shares of stock outstanding. Determine the expected market price per share under both FIFO and LIFO.

e. If the capital markets are "efficient" (if they recognize or are able to distinguish between economic earnings and reported accounting earnings), are the reservations of the president justified?

SOLUTIONS TO EXERCISE FOR REVIEW AND SELF-TESTING

1. The total number of units to be accounted for is the sum of beginning balance and the purchases throughout the year—800 units. Similarly, the total cost to be accounted for is $16,700.

2. a. *FIFO*

Ending inventory

From purchase of				
12/28	100 @ $23	$2,300		
From purchase of				
9/23	100 @ 22	2,200	$ 4,500	

Cost of goods sold

From balance of 1/1	400 @ $20	$8,000		
From purchase of				
2/24	200 @ 21	4,200	12,200	
Total	800		$16,700	

b. *Weighted Average:* Average cost = $16,700/800 units = $20.875

Ending inventory	200 @ $20.875	$ 4,175
Cost of goods sold	600 @ $20.875	12,525
Total	800	$16,700

c. *LIFO*

Ending inventory

From balance of 1/1	200 @ $20	$ 4,000

Cost of goods sold

From purchase of			
12/28	100 @ $23	$2,300	
From purchase of			
9/23	100 @ 22	2,200	
From purchase of			
2/24	200 @ 21	4,200	
From balance of 1/1	200 @ 20	4,000	12,700
Total	800		$16,700

3. The 200 units on hand would have to be written down to $21 per unit—$4,200. The write-down from $4,500 would cause earnings to decrease by $300. Inasmuch as the carrying value of the inventory would be reduced, then cost of goods sold, when the goods are actually sold, would be reduced by $300 and earnings thereby increased by that amount.

4. The entire inventory must be stated at $23 per unit. The 100 units that would otherwise be reported at $22 per unit would have to be increased in value by $1 per unit—a total of $100. Thus, a holding gain of $100 would be recognized. The effect of writing up the inventory by $100 in 1983 would be to increase reported cost of goods sold and reduce reported income in 1984 by the same amount.

5. Beginning inventory is given as $8,000. Ending inventory is calculated in part 2a as $4,500. Cost of goods sold is computed in part 2a as $12,200.

$$\text{Average inventory} = \frac{\$8,000 + \$4,500}{2} = \$6,250$$

$$\text{Inventory turnover} = \frac{\text{Cost of goods sold}}{\text{Average inventory}}$$

$$= \frac{\$12,200}{\$6,250}$$

$$= 1.95 \text{ times}$$

LONG-LIVED ASSETS AND THE ALLOCATION of THEIR COSTS 9

This chapter will be directed to long-lived (often referred to as *fixed*) assets of the firm—assets that cannot be expected to be consumed within a single operating cycle of the business. Long-lived assets include plant assets (such as land, buildings, and equipment) as well as natural resources (such as minerals) and intangible assets (such as copyrights). Long-lived assets can be thought of as "bundles of services" which the firm will consume over time. Although they may be purchased and paid for in a single year, they will be used to generate revenues over a number of years.

From the perspective of managers the most significant questions relating to fixed assets are if and when they should be acquired and retired. These issues will be addressed in Part 2 of this text. This chapter will be concerned with the manner in which they should be accounted for and reported upon.

Because a long-lived asset provides services for a span of time longer than one year, its cost must be charged off as an expense over more than one accounting period. The cost of the asset must be matched with the benefits to be provided—with the revenues to be generated. The process of allocating the cost of an asset over several accounting periods is referred to as *depreciation* if the asset is plant and equipment; *depletion*, if natural resources; and *amortization*, if intangible.

The basic journal entry to record the acquisition of a long-lived asset, equipment, is (assume the asset to be equipment which cost $10,000)

Equipment	$10,000	
Cash (or notes payable)		$10,000
To record the purchase of equipment.		

The basic entry to record the periodic allocation of the cost of the asset over its useful life (assume a life of 10 years) is

Depreciation (expense)	$1,000	
Equipment, accumulated depreciation		$1,000
To record periodic depreciation expense.		

Fixed assets are reported on the balance sheet at original cost less accumulated depreciation.

The account for accumulated depreciation or amortization (often referred to as *allowance* for depreciation or amortization) is a contra account and is always reported directly beneath the particular group of assets to which it pertains. Use of the contra account enables the firm to provide information that is more complete than if the balance in the asset account were reduced directly. Thus, after one year, the equipment might be shown on the balance sheet as

Equipment	$10,000	
Less: Accumulated depreciation	1,000	$9,000

ISSUES OF VALUATION

The limitations of the historical cost approach to asset valuation—that which is taken in practice today—are particularly pronounced with respect to fixed assets. Fixed assets commonly constitute a major portion of total assets of a firm, and because they are replaced relatively infrequently, differences between the value based on initial cost and that based on current measures may be substantial. Financial statements in which long-lived assets are reported at historical costs are deficient in that they provide no information as to either the market value of the assets—the price at which they could be sold or which would have to be paid to replace them—or the value of the services to be provided to the particular user.

Market Values

Insofar as the financial reports fail to account for changes in market values, *both* the balance sheet and the income statement

may be of limited utility to managers as well as investors. The balance sheet fails to provide information on the total amount of resources available to management for which it should be held accountable. It serves inadequately, therefore, as a basis on which to determine the return generated by the assets. Corporate performance can be meaningfully measured only in terms of current values—not historical values. Current values provide an indication of the alternative uses to which the assets could be put—the amount for which they could be sold and the proceeds invested in other ventures.

The income statement fails to provide information on the periodic increases in the value of assets (and thus of corporate net worth) over time. If income is to be a measure of how much "better off" a firm is from one period to the next, then changes in the amount for which assets could be bought or sold may be as important in determining income as actual exchange transactions. Decisions as to whether to hold or to sell fixed assets may be critical to the long-run welfare of the company. Since historical cost-based income statements omit consideration of *holding* gains or losses until such time as the assets are sold or retired, they fail to account for an important dimension of corporate performance.

At the same time, the historical cost-based income statement provides no information with respect to the market value of the services consumed as an asset is used. Depreciation expense represents the cost of a portion of an asset's service potential. If the annual depreciation charge is determined on the basis of outdated historical costs, then in a period in which market values exceed historical costs the charge will understate the market value of the services consumed. A reader of the financial report may be led to infer that the firm is being operated with greater efficiency (less cost) than is in fact the case.

Similarly, a naive manager may improperly conclude that one plant is more cost effective than another. In fact, its lower costs may be the consequence of lower depreciation charges, which are attributable to the use of older and less costly assets. If, however, the current market values of the assets were the same, then the value of resources consumed would also be the same, despite the differences in the accounting numbers assigned to them.

Value to Users

Measures of value based on historical costs fail to take into account not only the amounts for which assets could be bought or sold but also the benefits to be provided to the particular users.

The value of an asset to its user is that of the services that it will provide—the revenues that it will generate or the cost savings that it will effect. It is a future-oriented measure of earnings potential.

The revenues to be generated or savings to be effected by a long-lived asset will be realized over a period greater than one year. Revenues or savings realized in the future, however, are of considerably less value than those to be realized at the present. The dollar values of services to be provided in the future must be discounted to take into account the time value of money.

Assume, for example, that a firm owns a building which it rents to outsiders. All operating expenses are paid by the tenants. The building has a remaining useful life of five years. The firm receives annual rental payments of $20,000. If the firm requires a rate of return of 8 percent on all assets, then (ignoring taxes) the value of the asset to the firm is the present value of a cash flow of $20,000 for five years. Per Table 4 in the Appendix, which indicates the present value of an annuity, present value of the rent payments (five periods, 8 percent) would be

$$\$20,000 \times 3.9927 = \$79,854$$

This amount, in that it indicates expected future returns, is likely to be more useful to users of financial statements than a value based on historical cost.

Historical cost-based income statements also fail to reveal the economic cost to the firm of the portion of the asset consumed during an accounting period. The economic sacrifice sustained by the firm is the loss of earnings potential. Such loss can be measured by the difference between the value of remaining asset services at the beginning of a period and that at the end. In the example of the building, the present value of the services of a building with a five-year useful life was determined to be $79,854. After another year, however, the asset could be expected to generate only four rental payments of $20,000. The present value of four payments of $20,000 discounted at 8 percent is, per Table 4,

$$\$20,000 \times 3.3121 = \$66,242$$

The economic loss, with respect to the building, sustained by the firm between the end of the fourth and the fifth years was therefore

$$\$79,854 - \$66,242 = \$13,612$$

Depreciation as conventionally determined is based on the cost to acquire an asset; it is past-oriented. It gives no explicit consideration to the loss of earnings potential sustained during the year.

Replacement Cost as An Alternative

One frequently proposed alternative to reporting assets on a historical basis is to state them at *current replacement cost.*

Current replacement cost is the cost of purchasing a similar asset (adjusted for age as well as technological factors) at the prevailing market price.

The use of current replacement costs would assure that the financial statements reflect at least an approximation of the costs that would have to be incurred if the asset were to be purchased in the current market. It would provide, in most instances, a reasonable estimate of the amount for which the asset could be sold. It would furnish the means to give recognition in the income statement to *holding gains* attributable to increases in market prices.

Current replacement costs do *not*, however, necessarily provide an indication of the value of the asset to the particular user. The value of an asset to a company that might use it with unusual efficiency might far exceed the price at which it is being traded in currently established markets. Nevertheless, the price that independent purchasers are willing to pay would, in general, be a reasonable approximation of the present value of the services to be provided by the asset. For most companies, replacement cost is likely to be a better indicator of value-in-use than historical cost. In fact, it is seldom feasible to measure directly the service potential of an asset. Most assets, unlike the building used in the previous example, cannot be identified with specific cash flows. They provide services only when used in conjunction with other assets. Equipment used in a manufacturing process, for instance, has value only when used along with the plant building and the land on which the plant sits. Replacement cost is, therefore, as good an approximation of value-in-use as a firm could ordinarily expect to obtain.

As indicated in the following example, recognition of increases in replacement cost could readily be effected in the accounts.

Example

The Jay Co. owns a building which originally cost $180,000 when purchased 10 years ago. It has an estimated useful life of 40 years and no salvage value. It is currently reflected on the balance sheet as follows:

Building	$180,000
Less: Accumulated depreciation	
($\frac{10}{40}$ of $180,000)	45,000
	$135,000

During each of the 10 years depreciation was recorded with the conventional journal entry

Depreciation	$4,500	
Accumulated depreciation		$4,500

To record annual depreciation expense.

Replacement cost had remained constant for the first 10 years of asset life.

At the end of the tenth year, however, it was noted that, owing to increases in construction costs, the replacement cost of the building had increased by $20,000.

The following entry would effect recognition of the increase in replacement cost:

Building	$20,000	
Accumulated depreciation		$ 5,000
Gain from appreciation		15,000

To record the increase in replacement cost.

The necessity for crediting accumulated depreciation for $5,000 may be unclear. It makes sense, however, considering that the useful life of the building has not changed. Thus, 25 percent of the building must still be considered as having been depreciated, regardless of the value placed on the building. The new value of the building is $200,000; hence 25 percent (10 years worth—

$50,000) of replacement cost must be reflected in the accumulated depreciation account.

In each of the following 30 years depreciation would be recorded in the standard manner, except that the charge each year would be $\frac{1}{40}$ of $200,000:

| Depreciation | $5,000 | |
| Accumulated depreciation | | $5,000 |

To record depreciation expense.

A primary objection to the use of replacement costs is the difficulty of obtaining a reasonable measure of such costs. Many assets are unique so that there do not exist readily available market prices.

How, for example, would you determine the current replacement cost of a tract of land? In some cases it may be possible to derive a value based on a recent offer to purchase the tract. In others, a reasonable value could be obtained by determining the amount for which similar tracts in the same neighborhood have recently been sold or by using price indices that reflect a general increase in commercial real estate value. Consider the problem, however, of estimating the value of land on which Ford Motor Company's River Rouge plant is located. The tract of land comprises several square miles, and the industrial influence of the plant is felt for many miles around the plant. Whatever value (or lack of it) the surrounding land has is attributable to the activities of Ford. It would be impossible to determine the value of the land either by looking at other recent offers (the plant is of such enormous value that it is reasonably certain that there have been few serious offers) or by looking at the sales prices of surrounding land (the Ford land determines the value of the surrounding land, not the other way around). Current replacement costs may be relevant for many decisions; they may not, however, be objectively determinable.

ADVANTAGES OF HISTORICAL COSTS

The disadvantages of historical costs are obvious. The advantages, however, should not be understated. Historical costs are objective; the amount paid for an asset can readily be verified. Moreover, financial statements in which assets are stated at acquisition costs (less accumulated depreciation, as appropriate) are transaction based. Assets are initially recorded at the amounts for which they were acquired. The cost of an asset is allocated among the periods in which the service of the asset is provided. The total amount charged as an expense (depreciation) is exactly equal to the actual net cost (cost less salvage value, if any) incurred by the firm. Subjective judgments are held to a minimum; the financial statements present a historical record based on actual arm's-length exchanges.

It is undeniably true that financial statements based on historical costs do not provide *all* information necessary to make adequate investment or management decisions. It is questionable whether financial statements prepared on any single basis could do that. The use of historical costs, however, by no means precludes the supplementary disclosure of current market values.

The Financial Accounting Standards Board has taken a position with respect to the value of long-term assets similar to that adopted with regard to inventories. It has recognized the importance of information on current values and the limitations of historical costs. It has prescribed, therefore, that publicly held corporations larger than a specified size reveal in their annual reports (as a supplement to the basic financial statements) the *replacement* costs of their long-lived assets. The firms must report not only the current value (net of depreciation) of property, plant, and equipment, but also what the depreciation expense would have been had it been based on replacement, rather than historical, costs. A more complete discussion of the requirements of FASB Statement No. 33, which sets forth the disclosure rules, will be presented in Chapter 15.

ISSUES OF OWNERSHIP

Generally, of course, a firm owns the fixed assets that it uses. But it is not essential that a firm have formal legal title to the assets in order to record them in its own accounts. Assets are defined by accountants in economic rather than legal terms. Assets, as viewed by the accountant, are the economic resources of the firm; the contractual right to use property may be as much of an economic resource as a certificate of title. The distinction between economic and legal resources is especially important in light of current financial practice. With increasing frequency the rights and obligations of ownership are being contractually assigned to parties other than those which hold legal title.

In a common installment purchase, for example, the seller often retains formal title to the property until the buyer has made final payment of his outstanding obligations. The asset should be accounted for on the books of the purchaser as soon as it first acquires rights to its use. In a more complex financial arrangement, a financial institution might hold title to assets for a major portion of their useful lives. The financial institution leases the property to the party that will use it. The terms of the lease arrangement may be such that the annual rental payments approximate what they would have been had the user bought the property outright and borrowed the purchase price from the financial institu-

tion. Moreover, the lease contract may specify that the lessee (the user of the property) has to bear all risks and obligations of ownership; that is, it must pay all maintenance and insurance costs and make all required tax payments. Under such an arrangement the user of the property is in substance its owner; the property should, therefore, be accounted for as an asset on the books of the user.

Leasing is common in many industries; the railroad industry is an example of but one. Many freight cars bear notations indicating that they are the property of well-known banks or leasing companies. The financial institutions obviously are not in the railroad business. Rather, they have loaned the railroad the cost of the cars and are retaining legal ownership until the railroad has repaid its loan. The loan may, however, take the form of a lease arrangement whereby the railroad rents the car from the financial institution. After such time as the railroad has made payments equal to the cost of the car (plus interest) the railroad would have the right to purchase the car for a nominal sum, perhaps $1. The railroad is, of course, the constructive owner of the car. The car should be recorded on the books of the railroad, not the bank.

Lease arrangements will be discussed in greater detail in Chapter 10 in connection with long-term liabilities. The point to be emphasized at this time is that the question of whether or not property should be accounted for as an asset must be answered independently of strict legal interpretations or the peculiarities of financing arrangements.

COST OF PLANT ASSETS

As a general rule, plant assets are shown on the balance sheet at original cost, with the accumulated depreciation to date shown in a contra account. Normally, plant assets are said to be valued at "cost less accumulated depreciation." The cost of an asset may not simply be its stated purchase price. It would include all costs that are necessary to bring it to a usable condition. Cost would include, in addition to actual purchase price, costs of freight, installation, taxes, and title fees, among others. The costs that are included as a part of the fixed asset are said to be *capitalized*. They were incurred to benefit several periods, not just one; they should be charged as expenses over the useful life of the asset rather than in the year in which they are incurred.

The catalog or advertised price of an asset may not always be the relevant purchase price. Oftentimes the stated price of an asset is nothing more than the starting point of the bargaining process. Frequently, dealers give trade discounts (not to be confused with trade-in allowances) to customers of a certain category and cash discounts for prompt payment. Such discounts must be deducted from the originally stated price, since the purchase price must be determined on the basis of value actually surrendered by the buyer and received by the seller—that is, the *current cash equivalent*.

Example

Assume that a firm purchases a machine for $10,000 under terms 2/10, n/30 (the company will receive a 2 percent discount if it pays within 10 days, but, in any event, must pay within 30 days). Transportation costs are $300, and the wages of the two workers who install the machine amount to $150. In addition, while the machine is being installed, three employees who worked in the vicinity of the new machine are idled for several hours, since power to other machines has to be disconnected. The wages paid to the workers while they are idle are $90. The cost of the new machine would be computed as follows:

Purchase price:	$10,000	
Less 2% discount	200	$ 9,800
Freight-in		300
Installation costs		150
Payment for idle time		90
		$10,340

It may appear illogical to add the wages of the idle employees to the cost of the machine. But could the machine have been installed without such loss of time? Was the cost necessary to bring the asset to a performing state? If the answer is yes, then such costs have been incurred to benefit future periods, rather than the current period, and should rightfully be capitalized as part of the asset and should be allocated (i.e., depreciated) over the useful life of the new machine. If the answer is no, then the wages of the employees should be charged in full as an expense in the period of installation.

Purchases of Land

The same general principle applies to purchases of land. If a company purchases a parcel of land on which it intends to erect a new building, then all costs necessary to make the land ready for its intended use should be capitalized as part of the land. Thus, should a firm purchase a plot of land on which stands an old building that must first be torn down before a new building can be constructed, then the demolition costs should be added to the purchase price of land; they will serve to benefit future accounting periods.

Example

A company purchases a plot of land for $100,000, with the intention of constructing a plant. Before construction can begin, however, an old building on the land must be removed. Demolition costs amount to $10,000, but the firm is able to sell scrap from the old building for $3,000. Title and legal fees incurred in connection with the purchase total $1,000. At what value should the land be recorded?

Purchase price		$100,000
Add: Demolition		
costs	$10,000	
Less: Sale of scrap	3,000	7,000
Title and legal fees		1,000
Net cost of land		$108,000

Land is somewhat different from other fixed assets in that it does not ordinarily lose either service potential or value with the passage of time. Indeed, most often it *appreciates* in value. Thus the cost of the land should not be depreciated or allocated over time as long as there is no evidence of a decline in its service potential or value. If the land does not decline in value and the firm can, at any time, sell the land for the amount that it originally paid, then there is no real cost to the firm and, thus, no expense need be charged. Land, therefore, is not ordinarily considered a *depreciable* asset.

THE DISTINCTION BETWEEN MAINTENANCE OR REPAIRS AND BETTERMENTS

A frequent question that faces firms is whether to treat certain costs associated with fixed assets, especially buildings and equipment, as repair (or maintenance) costs or as betterments. The distinction between the two is often unclear, but the accounting implications are significant. In general, repair or maintenance costs are incurred to keep assets in good operating condition. They are recurring costs and do not add to the productivity of the asset or extend its originally estimated useful life. Betterments, on the other hand, enhance an asset's service potential (e.g., extend its useful life or increase its productivity) from what was anticipated when it was first purchased.

Maintenance and repair costs are usually charged off as expenses as they are incurred. Betterments, on the other hand, are added to the original cost of the fixed asset and depreciated over its remaining useful life.

Example

In January 1982, the Z Company expended $500 to air-condition the cab of one of its trucks. At the same time, it spent $75 to replace a worn-out clutch. The journal entry to record the repair/betterment combination would be

Trucks (fixed asset)	$500	
Truck, repairs (expense)	75	
Cash		$575

To record repairs and betterments.

If the remaining useful life of the truck were five years, then during each of the five years, depreciation expense on the truck would be $100 (one-fifth of the air-conditioning costs) greater than what it was previously.

The "gray" area of maintenance costs involves those costs that recur every few years. Many firms have a policy of repainting their plants every, say, five years. Most of these firms, for the sake of clerical convenience, would record the cost of the paint job (assuming it was done by outside contractors) with the following journal entry:

Maintenance expense	xxxx	
Cash		xxxx

In effect, such firms are obtaining the benefit of the expenditure over a period of five years but charging the cost to one year. It would be considerably more sound to capitalize the cost of the paint job—to record it as a separate asset—and allocate the cost to each of the five years to be benefited by the expenditure.*

DEPRECIATION

Depreciation is the process of allocating (in a systematic and rational manner) the cost of a tangible asset, less *salvage* (also called *residual*) value, if any, over the estimated useful life of the asset. Allocation of cost is necessary if costs are to be matched with the revenues that they help to generate. By salvage value is meant the amount that can be recovered when the asset is either sold, traded in for a new asset, or scrapped. If an asset that originally cost $5,000 could be sold after 10 years (the longest the company expects to use the asset) for $500, then the total amount that must be depreciated, or allocated over useful life of the asset, is $5,000 less $500—$4,500.

Depreciation is a process of *allocation*, not *valuation*. The original cost of an asset less the accumulated depreciation (the amount of depreciation taken on an asset up to a given time) is often referred to as the *book* value of

* Refer to problem 8 for illustrations of unconventional practices in this area.

an asset. Accountants do not purport that the book value of an asset represents the value of the asset in the open market. The potential for conflict between the two values can be demonstrated in a simple example involving an automobile.

A company purchases an automobile for $13,000 with the intention of using it for five years. It estimates that the trade-in value of the auto after that time will be $1,000. The amount of depreciation to be charged each year can be calculated to be $2,400:

$$\frac{\text{Original cost} - \text{Salvage value}}{\text{Useful life}} = \frac{\$13,000 - \$1,000}{5}$$

$$= \$2,400$$

Indicated in Exhibit 9-1 is a comparison of book values and market values at the end of each of the five years of estimated useful life. The market value represents a "typical" pattern of the decline in value of an automobile.

Merely because the amounts in the last two columns are not the same it cannot be said that the decision to depreciate the asset at the rate of $2,400 per year was in error. It is *not* the objective of depreciation accounting to indicate what the asset could be sold for at the end of any given year.

It is often said that another objective of the depreciation process is to provide funds with which to replace assets when they must be sold or retired. Nothing can be further

EXHIBIT 9-1   Comparison of Book and Market Values for a Typical Automobile

End of Year	Original Cost	Depreciation Taken to Date	Cost Less Accumulated Depreciation ("Book" Value)	Estimated Market Value
1	$13,000	$ 2,400	$10,600	$9,200
2	13,000	4,800	8,200	6,200
3	13,000	7,200	5,800	3,800
4	13,000	9,600	3,400	2,200
5	13,000	12,000	1,000	1,000

from correct. The absurdity of such a proposition is evident by examining the basic journal entry for depreciation:

Depreciation   xxxx
   Accumulated
      depreciation   xxxx

Cash is neither debited nor credited; it is neither received from outsiders nor moved from one bank account into another. It is not possible for an accountant to assure that a firm will have sufficient cash on hand to purchase a new asset when an old one is retired merely by making an end-of-month or end-of-year adjusting entry.

Only in the most indirect sense can it be said that depreciation accounting provides funds for the future replacement of assets. Depreciation, like other expenses, is deducted from revenues in order to calculate annual income. To the extent that it reduces income, it also reduces income taxes. Insofar as it reduces income taxes, it enables the firm to save for asset replacement more cash than it would if it had not recorded depreciation. In the same vein, the reduction in income attributable to depreciation expense may discourage some firms from declaring cash dividends of the amount they might have if income were greater. In both cases, the relationship between depreciation and an asset replacement fund is far too removed to permit one to say that depreciation *provides* funds to replace assets.

ACCELERATED DEPRECIATION METHODS

Up until this point, whenever depreciation has been discussed, the annual depreciation charge has been calculated by dividing the total amount to be depreciated (cost less salvage value, if any) by the number of years that the asset was expected to be in use. The depreciation charges were thereby equal during each year of the asset's life. Such procedure of calculating depreciation is known as the *straight-line* method. There are, however, other means of allocating the cost of an asset to the various periods during which it will be used that result in unequal annual charges. Two of the most popular of these methods are known as the *sum-of-the-years' digits* method and the *double-declining balance* method. Both of these methods result in depreciation charges which decline over the life of the asset. That is, depreciation expenses are greater in the beginning years of the asset's life than they are at the end. Both are referred to as *accelerated* methods of depreciation.

Sum-of-the-Years' Digits Method

Under the *sum-of-the-years' digits* method a fraction of the asset's net depreciable cost is charged off each year. The denominator of the fraction remains constant over the life of the asset. It is determined by taking a sum of numbers starting with 1 and continuing to the estimated life of the asset. Thus, if the life of the asset is three years, the denominator would be $1 + 2 + 3 = 6$. If it were five years, it would be $1 + 2 + 3 + 4 + 5 = 15$. A shortcut technique eliminates the need to count on fingers. The life of the asset (n) may be multiplied by the life of the asset plus 1 ($n + 1$) and the product divided by 2, e.g., the denominator to be used for an asset with five years of useful life would be

$$\frac{n(n + 1)}{2} = \frac{5(6)}{2} = 15$$

The numerator of the fraction would vary over the life of the asset. Each year it would be equal to the number of years remaining in the asset's life. Thus, in the first year of the life of a five-year asset, $\frac{5}{15}$ of the asset's cost (less salvage value) would be depreciated. In the second year, when the asset has a remaining life of only four years, $\frac{4}{15}$ would be depreciated. In subsequent years $\frac{3}{15}$, $\frac{2}{15}$, and $\frac{1}{15}$ respectively would be charged to depreciation expense.

Example

A firm purchases an auto for $13,000. It estimates that the auto has a useful life of five years, after which it can be sold for $1,000. The net amount to be depreciated is $12,000 (original cost less estimated salvage value). Depreciation charges using the sum-of-the-years' digits method would be as follows:

Year	Net Depreciable Amount	Depreciation Fraction	Depreciation Charge
1	$12,000	$\frac{5}{15}$	$ 4,000
2	12,000	$\frac{4}{15}$	3,200
3	12,000	$\frac{3}{15}$	2,400
4	12,000	$\frac{2}{15}$	1,600
5	12,000	$\frac{1}{15}$	800
		$\frac{15}{15}$	$12,000

Double-Declining Balance Method

The *double-declining balance* method consists of applying to the current book value of the asset (cost less accumulated depreciation

to date) a percentage rate equal to twice the straight-line depreciation rate. In the earlier example of straight-line depreciation in which the asset had a useful life of five years, one-fifth or 20 percent of the net depreciable cost was charged off each year. Hence, the depreciation rate could be said to have been 20 percent. The appropriate rate for the double-declining balance method would therefore be twice that, or 40 percent. Unlike the straight-line or sum-of-the-years' digits methods, *the declining balance procedure requires that the rate be applied initially to the original cost of the asset—not original cost less salvage value.*

Example

Again, the asset to be considered cost $13,000, has a useful life of five years and an estimated salvage value of $1,000. Depreciation charges using the double-declining balance method would be based on a rate of 40 percent (twice the straight-line rate of 20 percent). The calculations are shown in Exhibit 9-2.

The double-declining balance method does not automatically assure that an asset will be depreciated exactly down to its salvage value. At the end of the fifth year, the book value of the asset would be $1,011—$11 more than

EXHIBIT 9-2   Double-Declining Balance Depreciation

Year	Cost Less Accumulated Depreciation (Book Value)	Depreciation Rate (%)	Depreciation Charge	Remaining Book Value
1	$13,000	40	$5,200	$7,800
2	7,800	40	3,120	4,680
3	4,680	40	1,872	2,808
4	2,808	40	1,123	1,685
5	1,685	40	674	1,011

the estimated salvage value of $1,000. To the extent that the firm continues to hold on to the asset beyond its originally estimated five-year life, then the additional $11 depreciation would be taken in the sixth year. An asset, however, should never be depreciated below its estimated salvage value. In the example, if the estimated salvage value were $1,200 instead of $1,000, the maximum amount of depreciation that could be charged in the fifth (and final) year of asset life would be $485 ($1,685 minus $1,200).

Remember, in applying the double-declining balance method the first-year depreciation charge must be based on the original cost of the asset—not original cost less estimated salvage value. Salvage value should be disregarded in computing first-year depreciation.

An additional observation pertaining to the two accelerated depreciation methods may be appropriate. Such methods, particularly the double-declining balance method, have grown increasingly popular in recent years. Some accountants aver that accelerated depreciation methods are preferable to the straight-line method since they tend to result in book values that more closely approximate market values. The values of many assets— autos, for example—decline by greater amounts in the early years of their lives than in later years. Such an assertion is specious, however, in that under conventional accounting there is no pretext that the book value of an asset should approximate its market value. Assets are not, by contrast, restated to reflect *increases* in market value. Others maintain that assets often provide greater services to the firm in their early years than they do in their later years. The productivity of many assets decreases with time as they operate less efficiently, require more maintenance, and are out of service for greater periods of time. Such a position is somewhat more convincing; in practice, however, accelerated depreciation methods are generally applied without consideration of the probable service patterns of particular assets. Moreover, the specific procedures were not developed on the basis of studies of asset productivity. They have received wide acceptance primarily because they provide an expedient and easily applied means for attaining a decreasing annual charge.

The popularity of the declining charge methods is most directly traceable to current tax laws. The Internal Revenue code permits taxpayers to use such procedures in calculating taxable income. Since the methods result in greater deductible expenses in the early years of an asset's life, they result in more immediate tax savings. Although the total that the code allows a taxpayer to deduct over time is the same (cost less a salvage value) regardless of the depreciation method used, a dollar saved today is worth considerably more than one to be saved in the future.

In contrast to the provisions with respect to inventories, the tax laws do not require that a firm use the same method of depreciation to calculate its tax obligation as it does for purposes of general reporting. Since the double-declining balance method allows for earlier write-offs than do other methods, there can be little or no justification for *not* using it to calculate taxable income. Only in the most unusual of circumstances would it be in the interest of a firm to use anything but the most accelerated method.

RETIREMENT OF FIXED ASSETS

Upon the retirement of an asset, either by sale or by abandonment, the asset *as well as the related accumulated depreciation* must be removed from the books. If the asset is sold for the amount and at the time originally estimated, then the retirement entry is especially simple.

Example

Return once again to the auto which originally cost $13,000 and had an estimated salvage value after five years of $1,000. At the end of five years the fixed asset account would have a debit balance of $13,000 (regardless of the choice of depreciation method), and the accumulated depreciation account a credit balance of $12,000 (slightly less if the double-declining balance method were used). If the asset is, in fact, sold for $1,000 then the appropriate journal entry would be

Cash	$ 1,000	
Accumulated		
depreciation, autos	$12,000	
Fixed assets,		
autos		$13,000

To record the sale of the asset.

If at any time during its life, the asset is either sold or abandoned for an amount greater or less than its book value then a gain or loss on retirement would have to be recognized.

Example

The firm has charged depreciation on the auto using straight-line depreciation. At the end of three years, after $7,200 of depreciation had been charged, the firm sold the auto for $4,000. The book value of the asset at time of sale would have been $5,800—$13,000 less $7,200. Hence, the firm has suffered a loss of $1,800.

Cash	$4,000	
Accumulated		
depreciation, autos	7,200	
Loss on disposal	1,800	
Fixed assets, autos		$13,000

To record the sale of the asset.

Bear in mind that if an asset is sold anytime before the close of the year, depreciation for the portion of the year which the asset was actually held must first be recorded before any gain or loss can be computed.

The nature of gains or losses on retirement merits comment. Such gains or losses arise only because a company was unable to have perfect foresight when it acquired the asset as to the time of retirement and the selling price. If it had such foresight, it would have determined its depreciation schedule accordingly and hence there would be no gain or loss upon retirement.

In the previous example, the $1,800 loss on retirement indicates that insufficient depreciation in the amount of $600 per year for the three years that the asset was held had been charged. If the firm had known that it would sell the asset (which cost $13,000) for $4,000 after using it for three years, then it would have allocated $3,000 of asset cost ($13,000 cost less $4,000 salvage value, divided by 3) to each of the three years—instead of the $2,400 per year actually allocated.

Meticulous accounting might therefore dictate that, rather than recognizing a loss on retirement in the year of sale, the company should correct the earnings of the prior years for the insufficient depreciation charges. Such a correction would have the effect of reducing retained earnings without burdening reported income in the year of retirement. In practice, such an approach is virtually never taken inasmuch as it would require an excessive number of prior period adjustments and thereby complicate the process of financial reporting.

TRADE-INS

A special problem is presented when a firm *trades in* an old asset for a new one. A firm surrenders an old car, plus cash, for a later model. The most logical way of handling a trade-in is to view it as two separate transactions. In the first, the old asset is sold—not for cash but instead for a *trade-in allowance*. In the second, the new asset is purchased—for cash plus the trade-in allowance. The critical step in implementing such a procedure lies in determining the price for which the old asset was sold. In many instances, the amount that the dealer says he is offering as a trade-in allowance bears no relationship to the actual fair market value of the old asset. In the auto industry, for example, it is common practice for new car dealers to offer unusually high trade-in allowances on the used vehicles of prospective new car purchasers. If the purchaser accepts the high trade-in allowance, he may be unable to avail himself of discounts that are generally granted to purchasers who come without used cars. He may, in effect, have to pay full, or nearly full, *sticker* price for the new car, something he would not ordinarily have to do if he came to the dealer without an old car to trade.

If a meaningful gain or loss on retirement is to be computed it is essential, therefore, that the company determine as accurately as possible the actual fair market value of the asset given up. This can usually be done by consulting industry publications, such as the car dealers' "blue" book of used car prices, or by obtaining data on transactions involving similar assets.

Example

The auto, which originally cost $13,000 (estimated life of five years, $1,000 salvage) is traded in for a new car after three years. The dealer grants a trade-in allowance of $7,000, but, according to a book of used car prices, the car is worth no more than $5,200. The sticker price of the new car is $16,800 but, in fact, an astute buyer would not normally pay more than $15,000. In addition to giving up its old car, the company pays cash of $9,800.

The book value of the old car, assuming straight-line depreciation, would at time of trade-in be

Original cost	$13,000
Accumulated depreciation (three years' times $2,400)	7,200
Book value	$ 5,800

Loss on the sale of the old car would therefore be $5,800 less $5,200 (fair market value of the old car)—$600.

The "sale" of the old car could properly be recorded as follows:

(a)

Loss on retirement	$ 600	
Accumulated depreciation, autos	7,200	
Trade-in allowance (a temporary account)	5,200	
Fixed assets, autos		$13,000

To record the "sale" of the asset.

The entry to record the purchase of the new auto would be

(b)

Fixed assets, autos	$15,000	
Cash		$9,800
Trade-in allowance		5,200

To record the purchase of the new asset.

Clearly, the two entries could be combined (and the trade-in allowance account eliminated).

This method of accounting for trade-ins allows the new asset to be recorded at its fair market value, which is equal to the cash price that an independent buyer would have to pay. At the same time, it permits the gain or loss on retirement of the old asset to be based upon its fair market value. It thereby gives recognition to the economic substance of the transaction, regardless of what amounts are arbitrarily assigned to the trade-in allowance and the price of the new asset.

The transaction just illustrated resulted in a reported loss on retirement. If, however, application of the accounting procedure described would have resulted in a *gain* rather than a loss, then the Accounting Principles Board (in Opinion No. 29) prescribes the use of a slightly different method. Under the APB method no gain on retirement would be recognized. The new asset would be recorded at an amount equal to the sum of:

1. The book value (cost less accumulated depreciation) of the old asset and
2. any additional cash paid.

For example, if a firm were to exchange an old auto having a book value of $8,000 (cost $10,000, accumulated depreciation $2,000) plus cash of $1,000 for a new auto that has a fair market value of $12,000, the following entry would be in order:

Accumulated depreciation (old auto)	$2,000	
Automobile (new)	9,000	
Automobile (old)		$10,000
Cash		1,000

To record trade-in of automobiles.

The entry gives no recognition to either the fair market value of the new asset or the obvious economic difference at the time of the trade between the fair market value and the book value of the old asset. The new balance in the automobile account would be depreciated over the useful life of the new auto.

The APB method serves to prevent a firm from recognizing a gain—and increasing reported earnings—merely by exchanging one asset for another of similar type and value. The APB method is based on the underlying assumption that such an exchange is not of sufficient economic substance to justify an increase in the reported value of a firm's assets.

The contrast between the two methods serves to highlight the fact that many current accounting issues can be attributable to the practice of reporting assets on the basis of historical cost rather than market value. If the reported value of an asset were periodically increased to reflect changes in market conditions, then at the time of retirement or trade there would be little need to recognize a gain or a loss. The reported value of the asset would be nearly identical to the amount for which it could be sold or traded.

DETERMINATION OF USEFUL LIFE

To this point in the text, no attention has been directed toward problems of determining useful lives. Assumptions regarding length of service potential have been haphazardly asserted. In practice, regrettably, whereas considerable attention is directed to selection of depreciation methods, estimates of useful life are often made capriciously. In many cases, however, overall income of the company may be as sensitive to variations in estimates of useful life as to method of depreciation.

The number of years that a firm will keep an asset is not a matter of determining only when the asset will deteriorate beyond the point at which repairs are economically feasible. Physical obsolescence is but one determinant of useful life. The service potential of an asset is to a large extent a function of technological factors. A technological breakthrough may enable a company to produce its product at considerably less cost than previously; hence the firm may decide to replace an old machine with a new one. Or, a technological development in either the same or a related industry may reduce or eliminate the demand for the firm's product—and thereby make many of its production facilities obsolete. The difficulties of making meaningful estimates of useful life cannot be overestimated, and, unfortunately, there are no easy-to-follow techniques available to either accountants or managers.

The importance of correct estimates cannot be overstated, especially in companies in which depreciable assets constitute a major portion of total assets. To the extent that the estimate of useful life is greater than what is proper, annual depreciation charges will be lower and, as a consequence, income greater. Because estimates of useful life must necessarily be based on "subjective judgment," a competent financial analyst should carefully scrutinize the number of years over which a firm depreciates its major assets.

Recently, for example, the depreciation practices of several companies in the computer leasing industry came under question. One company, for example, had been depreciating IBM 360 computers, its major asset, over a 10-year period. When a new series of computers was introduced, it became unlikely that the company could continue to profitably rent out to its customers its old-model data processing machines. Its auditors qualified their opinion that the annual report of the firm presented fairly its financial position because of reservations as to the company's ability to recover the remaining undepreciated costs on its computer leasing equipment.

The depreciation practices of major airlines further highlight the subjective nature of estimates of useful life. Whereas one airline may depreciate its 727 jets over a 10-year period, another may allocate the cost over a 12-year period. The estimates are not necessarily inconsistent with one another. One may *plan* to use its planes for a shorter period of time than does the other. But since the airline industry is competitive, the seemingly conflicting policies at the very least raise questions as to the reliability of the estimates and the credibility of the financial statements.

PLANT AND EQUIPMENT TURNOVER

The efficiency with which plant and equipment is utilized may be measured by the *plant and equipment turnover* ratio, determined by comparing sales to average book value (cost less accumulated depreciation) of plant and equipment:

$$\text{Plant and equipment turnover} = \frac{\text{Sales}}{\text{Average plant and equipment}}$$

Fruehauf Corporation in 1980 had average plant and equipment of \$454,970,608; sales for the year were \$1,878,746,434.

$$\text{Plant and equipment turnover} = \frac{\$1,878,746,434}{\$454,970,608}$$

$$= 4.1 \text{ times}$$

The greater the turnover ratio, the more effectively plant and equipment are being employed. In years when sales are down and physical facilities are not being used to capacity, the ratio would tend to decline. In years when sales are up and the plant is being used to the fullest extent possible, the ratio would tend to increase.

Although plant and equipment are conventionally stated in the ratio at book values, there is no reason why market values could not be used instead. Indeed, if management is concerned with comparing asset utilization among plants of different ages, then market values may provide a more appropriate measure of the resources over which plant executives have stewardship.

NATURAL RESOURCES AND DEPLETION

Natural resources, or *wasting assets*, as they are often referred to, are accounted for in a manner similar to plant and equipment. They are recorded initially at acquisition cost, and the value at which they are reported subsequently is reduced as their service potential declines.

Units of Output Basis

The process of allocating the cost of natural resources over the periods in which they provide benefits is known as *depletion*. The service potential of natural resources can ordinarily be measured more meaningfully in terms of quantity of production (e.g., tons or barrels) than number of years. Hence, depletion is generally charged on a *units of output* basis. As with other types of long-lived assets, the initial cost of a natural resource may be reported on the balance sheet for as long as it is in service. The accumulated depletion may be indicated in a contra account. In practice, however, a contra account is not always used; often the balance in the natural resource account itself is reduced directly by the amount of the accumulated depletion.

Example

A firm purchases mining properties for $2 million cash. It estimates that the properties will yield 400,000 usable tons of ore. During the first year of production, the firm mines 5,000 tons.

The following entry would be appropriate to record the purchase of the properties:

Mineral deposits $2,000,000
   Cash $2,000,000
To record the purchase of the ore deposit.

Since the deposit will yield an estimated 400,000 tons of usable ore, cost assignable to each ton is

$$\frac{\$2,000,000}{400,000 \text{ tons}} = \$5 \text{ per ton}$$

Depletion cost of the first year would be

5,000 (tons mined) × $5 per ton = $25,000

The entry to record the depletion would be

Depletion (expense) $25,000
   Mineral deposits, accumulated
    depletion $25,000
To record first-year depletion.

After the first year, the mineral deposits would be reported on the balance sheet as

Mineral deposits	$2,000,000
Less: Accumulated depletion	25,000
	$1,975,000

Depletion is a cost of production, to be added along with other production costs (labor, depreciation of equipment, supplies) to the carrying value of the minerals inventory. It will be charged as an expense (cost of minerals sold) in the accounting period in which the inventory is sold and the revenue from the sale is recognized.

Depreciation of Location-Specific Equipment

Often, a mining or drilling company will have to purchase or build equipment or structures that can be used only in connection with the recovery of a specific deposit. If such structures or equipment will be used for as long as the property continues to be exploited (and only so long), then depreciation charges should logically be determined using the same units of output basis as used to compute depletion.

Suppose, for example, that mining equipment cost $80,000 and can be used exclusively at a site with estimated ore content of 400,000 tons. Depreciation would be charged at a rate of $.20 per ton mined ($80,000 divided by 400,000 tons) regardless of useful life in terms of years. If, in the first year of operation 50,000 tons were mined, the depreciation charge would be $10,000 (50,000 tons @ $.20 per ton). Depreciation, if based on output, is more likely in such circumstances to assure that the cost of equipment or structures is matched with the revenues realized from the sale of the minerals than if based on useful life in terms of time.

INTANGIBLE ASSETS

Intangible assets are those assets characterized by the rights, privileges, and benefits of possession rather than by physical existence. Often, the service potential of intangible assets is uncertain and exceedingly difficult to measure. As a consequence, intangible assets frequently are the subject of controversy. Examples of intangible assets are patents, copyrights, research and development costs, organizational costs, and goodwill. In this section we shall deal specifically with only a few selected intangible assets with the aim of highlighting some key accounting issues. A discussion of goodwill, one of the more controversial intangible assets, will be deferred until the chapter pertaining to ownership interests among corporations, since goodwill conventionally arises only out of the acquisition of one company by another.

Intangibles are considered to be assets either because they represent rights to future benefits or because the expenditures that were made to acquire or develop them will serve to benefit a number of accounting periods in the future. Hence, the costs must be allocated to the periods in which the benefits will be realized.

Intangible assets are recorded initially at their acquisition or development cost. The cost is then amortized over (allocated to) the periods in which the benefits will accrue. The general accounting approach to intangibles may be illustrated with respect to copyrights.

Copyrights

A copyright is an exclusive right, granted by law, to publish, sell, reproduce, or otherwise control a literary, musical, or artistic work. As of January 1, 1978, in the United States, copyrights on most new works are granted for the life of the creator plus 50 years. The cost to secure a copyright from the federal government is minimal; however, the cost to purchase one from its holder on a work that has proven successful—on a best-selling novel or musical recording, for instance—may be substantial.

If a firm were to purchase a copyright, it would record it initially as it would any other asset. Assuming a cost of $20,000, for example, an appropriate journal entry might be

Copyright	$20,000	
Cash		$20,000

To record the purchase of the copyright.

If the remaining useful life were determined to be 10 years, then the following entry would be appropriate each year to record amortization:

Amortization of copyrights	$2,000	
Copyrights, accumulated amortization		$2,000

To record amortization of copyright.

Accounting practices with respect to copyrights focus attention on a question that is raised with respect to many types of intangibles—that of the number of years over which cost should be amortized. Although the legal life of a copyright may be firmly established, the copyright may be of significant economic value for a considerably shorter period of time. Actual useful life may depend on a multitude of factors such as public taste, critical acclaim, or future success of the author, none of which can readily be assessed. As with other long-lived assets, carrying value of the asset as well as amortization charges (the periodic decline in value) must be based, in large measure, on subjective judgments of corporate management and accountants.

Costs of Drilling Unsuccessful Oil Wells

Accounting practices in the oil and gas industry raise other important issues with respect to intangible assets. What is the nature of the costs to be included as part of the asset; how directly must a cost be associated with a future benefit before it should properly be capitalized? How broadly should an asset be defined? Despite highly sophisticated geological survey techniques, it is usually necessary for oil and gas companies, in their search for new reserves, to drill unsuccessfully in several locations before actually striking oil or gas. Obviously the cost of drilling the productive wells should be capitalized and amortized over the years during which oil or gas will be withdrawn from the ground. But what about the costs of drilling the *dry holes?* Should they be written off as incurred, or should they also be capitalized and amortized over the period in which oil is withdrawn from the successful wells? Should they be considered losses (corporate errors, in a sense) as opposed to expenditures that are statistically necessary

to discover the productive locations? Directly, the dry holes will produce no benefits to the company; indirectly they represent an inevitable cost of finding the productive wells.

If the asset is defined narrowly as a single hole, then there would be little justification for capitalizing it. It clearly has no future service potential. But if the asset is defined more broadly as an entire oil field, then the dry hole can be interpreted as an element of cost required to bring the field to a serviceable state.

In past years, some companies capitalized costs associated with unsuccessful prospects (dry hole costs), while others did not. Those that did were known as *full-cost* companies, inasmuch as the costs of the proven mineral reserves included the costs of drilling the unsuccessful as well as the successful wells. Those that did not were referred to as *successful-efforts* firms, because only the costs of drilling successful wells were added to the costs of the oil and gas properties; outlays associated with unsuccessful drilling efforts were charged to expenses as soon as it was concluded that the efforts at a particular location were a failure.

In 1977, the Financial Accounting Standards Board, in Statement No. 19, prescribed that all firms must use *only* the *successful-efforts* method. The decision of the FASB was a source of consternation on the part of those firms that had been using the full-cost method and the federal agencies concerned with administering the antitrust statutes. The full-cost method had been used by many small exploration firms. The switch to the successful-efforts method resulted, at least in the short run, in reductions in their reported earnings because the costs of unsuccessful wells were written off in the year of failure rather than over a number of succeeding years. It was thought that the reduction in reported earnings would make the firms less attractive to investors and lenders and, thereby, less able to acquire the capital necessary to compete with the giants of the industry, many of which were already using the successful-efforts method. The FASB and its defenders, however, asserted that fears of reduced competition were groundless because the change would affect only *reported* earnings. In terms of economic wealth—the present value of actual oil and gas reserves—the firms would be neither better nor worse off merely because they made use of one accounting method rather than another.

The Securities and Exchange Commission failed to support the directive of the FASB that mandated the use of the successful-efforts method. It took the position that both the successful-efforts and the full-cost methods were deficient because they failed to provide adequate information on the economic worth of the oil and gas reserves that had been discovered. The SEC proposed that a third method, referred to as *reserve recognition accounting*, be developed. The new method required that proved reserves be reported at an amount indicative of the present value of the cash flows that they were likely to generate. It required firms not only to estimate the quantities of oil and gas in their fields, but also to make assumptions as to the prices at which they would be sold and the costs of lifting them from the ground.

Owing in large measure to the difficulties of making the necessary estimates, reserve recognition accounting never gained the support of firms in the oil industry and eventually the SEC abandoned efforts to impose it upon them. In light of the initial opposition to successful efforts accounting on the part of the SEC, the FASB suspended the key provisions of Statement No. 19. As of 1982, firms can use either the full-cost or the successful-efforts method and the controversy over the accounting for oil and gas operations continues.

Research and Development Costs

Accounting procedures with respect to research and development costs are illustrative of an additional issue common to intangible assets—to what extent must theoretical concepts of intangible assets be tempered by "practical" considerations? Research and development costs are, by nature, incurred in order to benefit future accounting periods. Expenditures for research and development are made with the expectation that they will lead to new or improved products or processes that will in turn increase revenues or decrease expenses. The matching concept suggests that research and development costs be capitalized as intangible assets and amortized over the periods in which the additional revenues are generated or cost savings effected.

In practice, however, it has proven exceedingly difficult to match specific expenditures for research and development with specific products or processes. Some expenditures are for *basic* research; they are not intended to produce direct benefits. Others produce no benefits at all or result in benefits which could not have been foreseen at the time they were incurred.

The FASB in Statement No. 2 (1974) prescribed that expenditures for most types of research and development costs must be charged to expense in the year incurred rather than capitalized as intangible assets. The board was motivated by the great variety of practice among corporations as to the nature of costs that were capitalized and the number of periods over which they were amortized. Given almost unlimited flexibility in accounting for research and development, some firms capitalized costs that were unlikely to provide future benefits; others *wrote off* large amounts of previously capitalized costs in carefully selected periods so as to avoid burdening other accounting periods with amortization charges.

As a consequence of the board's actions, uniformity of accounting practice among companies has been enhanced. But research and development costs must now be charged as an expense as if they were to benefit but a single accounting period. And the period in which they are to be charged off—that in which they are incurred—is that which is, in fact, least likely to benefit from the expenditures, since research and development costs are almost always future-, rather than present-oriented.

The approach of the board is inconsistent with the notion that costs should be matched to the revenues with which they are associated. It substitutes a precise accounting rule for the professional judgment of managers and accountants. It can hardly be viewed as an ideal solution to the accounting problems related to intangibles. But the board's approach does represent an attempt to ensure greater consistency among firms and to eliminate reporting malfeasance on the part of at least a few corporations.

SUMMARY

Long-lived assets provide services over a number of accounting periods. Their cost, therefore, must be allocated over all of the periods benefited.

Long-lived assets are conventionally reported on the balance sheet at their original cost, less the amount assumed to have expired to date. The amount at which they are reported may, however, bear little relationship either to what it would cost to replace them or to their value to their specific users (the present value of the revenues that they will generate or the cost savings that they will effect).

The process of allocating the cost of a long-lived asset to the accounting periods which will benefit from its services is referred to as depreciation, depletion, or amortization. There are several basic methods of cost allocation. Among them are the straight-line method and the various *accelerated* methods.

Regardless of how a long-lived asset is accounted for—the method of allocation selected, the useful life estimated, or the means of recognizing changes in market value chosen—its impact on reported income over its useful life will be the same. The total cost of an asset—the amount to be charged as an expense—will be the price paid for the asset less the amount for which it can be sold at time of retirement. The manner in which an asset is accounted for may, however, have a significant effect on the earnings of each individual period in which it is used. As a consequence, the issues associated with long-lived assets are of critical concern to the accounting profession, to corporations and to investors.

EXERCISE FOR REVIEW AND SELF-TESTING

Airline Freight acquires a new cargo plane. The company pays $3,000,000 cash and gives to the seller marketable securities with a fair market value of $500,000. The company incurs additional costs of $6,000 to have the plane delivered to its home airfield and $94,000 to have it fitted with special equipment. The firm plans to keep the plane for 10 years; it estimates that it will be able to sell the cargo plane at the end of 10 years for $900,000.

1. At what amount should the plane be initially recorded?

2. What is the total dollar amount to be allocated as depreciation expense over the period during which the plane will be in service?

3. What should be the charge for depreciation for each of the 10 years of useful life if the firm were to use the straight-line method?

4. What should be the charge for depreciation for each of the first three years of useful life if the firm were to use the double-declining balance method?

5. Suppose that the firm used the double-declining balance method and that at the end of the sixth year of useful life the book value of the plane were $943,718—that is, depreciation of $2,656,282 had been charged to date. How much depreciation should the firm charge in the seventh year of service? How much in the eighth? Be sure your answers are consistent with your response to part 2.

6. Suppose that after the third year of using the plane the company elected to trade in the old plane for a new one. The company paid $7,000,000 cash for the new plane and surrendered the old cargo plane. Immediately prior to the trade, the firm had received offers from parties who were willing to buy the plane outright. All were willing to pay approximately $1,500,000 cash. At the time of the trade, the old plane had a book value of $1,843,200 (initial cost less accumulated depreciation of $1,756,800) based on use of the double-declining balance method. How much gain or loss should the firm report on the transaction? At what amount should it record the new plane?

QUESTIONS FOR REVIEW AND DISCUSSION

1. "Because fixed assets are stated on the *balance sheet* at values that are based on historical costs, the *income statement* is of limited value in evaluating corporate performance." Do you agree? Explain.

2. What is the value of an asset to a particular user? Why is it seldom feasible to measure the value of a fixed asset to a particular user?

3. It is generally agreed that market values of fixed assets are more relevant than historical values for most decisions that must be made by both investors and managers. Why, then, do accountants persist in reporting historical values?

4. A stockholder recently charged that the financial statements of a corporation in which he owned shares were false and misleading in that included among fixed assets was computer equipment which the company leased from a financial institution but did not actually own. Assuming the assertion to be correct—that leased equipment was included among assets—how might the company respond to charges that the statements were false and misleading?

5. A company recently purchased for $350,000 a parcel of land and a building with the intention of razing the building and using the land as a parking lot for employees. The land had an appraised value of $300,000, and the building, $50,000. The company incurred costs of $10,000 to remove the building. The firm recorded the parking lot on its books at $360,000. Can such value be justified?

6. A company purchased a parcel of land for $100,000, but was permitted by the seller to delay payment for one year with no additional interest charges. The prime lending rate at the time was 12 percent per year. Do you think that the company should record the land at $100,000 or at a greater or lesser amount? Explain.

7. The term *reserve* for depreciation is sometimes used instead of *accumulated* depreciation. Some managers point out that it is essential that firms, through the process of depreciation, make periodic additions to such reserve in order to make certain that they have the wherewithal to replace assets when they must be retired. Explain why (or why not) depreciation assures that a firm will have sufficient resources to acquire new assets as old ones wear out.

8. "Accelerated methods of depreciation are generally preferable to the straight-line method because most assets decline in market value more rapidly in the early years of their useful life than in later years." Do you agree?

9. A company incurred $1 million in advertising costs in 1982 for radio and television ads broadcast during the year. It elected to *capitalize*

such costs as an intangible asset and charge them off as expenses over a five-year period. Such practice is *not* in accord with generally accepted accounting principles. What arguments might the firm make, however, in defense of the practice? Why do you suppose that such practice is not generally accepted?

10. As an executive of a firm with two manufacturing plants, you are required to evaluate the effectiveness with which the managers of the plants utilize the resources within their control. One criterion by which you judge is plant and equipment turnover. The two plants are of substantially different ages. In computing turnover, why might you find it advantageous to state plant and equipment (including land) at market rather than book values.

PROBLEMS

1. Depreciation, regardless of the method used, is a means of allocating the cost of an asset over its productive life.

The Valentine Construction Corp. purchased a crane for $150,000. The company planned to keep it for approximately five years, after which time it believed it could sell the crane for $30,000.
a. Determine depreciation under each of the following methods for the first four years that the crane is in service:
   1. Straight-line
   2. Sum-of-the-years' digits
   3. Double-declining balance
b. At the start of the fifth year the company sold the crane for $60,000. Determine the gain under each of the three depreciation methods.
c. Determine for each of the methods the net impact on earnings (total depreciation charges less gain) of using the crane for the four-year period.

2. The useful life of one asset may depend upon that of another.

The James Co. purchases a small plant for $250,000. The plant has an estimated useful life of 25 years with no salvage value. Included in the plant is a boiler to provide heat and hot water. At the time of purchase the company is aware that the re-

maining useful life of the boiler is 15 years. The firm estimates the value of the boiler to be $25,000.
a. Record the purchase of the plant.
b. Record depreciation during the first year.
c. At the end of 15 years the boiler requires replacement, and the firm purchases a new boiler for $40,000. The useful life of the new boiler is also estimated to be 15 years.
   1. Record the replacement of the old boiler with the new.
   2. Record depreciation during the sixteenth year.
   3. Over how many years did you decide to depreciate the new boiler? What assumptions did you make?

3. The method of depreciation selected should provide the best possible match of costs to revenues.

The Strip Mining Co. decides to remove coal from a deposit on property it already owns. The company purchases for cash mining equipment at a cost of $850,000 and constructs a building on the site at a cost of $90,000. The equipment has a useful life of 10 years, an estimated salvage value of $50,000 and can readily be moved to other mining locations. The building has a potential useful life of 12 years but would have to be abandoned when the company ceases operations at the site.

The mine contains approximately 1 million tons of coal, and the company plans to remove it over a four-year period according to the following schedule:

Year 1	400,000 tons
2	250,000 tons
3	250,000 tons
4	100,000 tons

The property will be abandoned at the end of the fourth year.
a. Record the purchase of the equipment and the construction of the building.
b. Compute depreciation charges for the first year on both the building and equipment. Justify in one or two sentences your choice of depreciation method(s) and lives.

4. Trade-in transactions must be accounted for in a manner that reflects economic substance rather than form.

In January 1980 the Jarvis Co. purchased a copy machine for $6,000. The machine had an estimated useful life of eight years and an estimated salvage value of $500. The firm used the double-declining balance method to record depreciation.

In December 1982 the company decided to trade in the machine for a newer model. The new model had a *list* price of $12,000, but it is common in the industry for purchasers to be given a 15 to 20 percent trade discount off of list price. The manufacturer offered the company a trade-in allowance of $4,000 on its old machine. The company accepted the offer since it was considerably above the several offers of approximately $2,000 that the firm had received from other parties interested in purchasing the machine. The company paid $8,000 in addition to giving up the old machine.

Record the trade-in of the old machine and the purchase of the new. Assume that depreciation had already been recorded for 1982.

5. *Costs incurred at the end of an asset's useful life may be associated with revenues of previous accounting periods.*

National Auto Company agrees to participate as a major exhibitor at the North American Trade Fair. The company constructs and furnishes its exhibit hall at a cost of $8 million. The fair will last for three years, after which National Auto will be required to remove its building from the fair grounds. National estimates that removal costs will be approximately $100,000 but that the building materials and the exhibits can be sold for $300,000.

a. Record the exhibit hall on the books of National Auto. Assume all payments were made in cash.
b. Calculate first-year depreciation using the straight-line method.
c. Record the removal of the exhibit hall at the completion of the fair. Assume that removal costs were as estimated.
d. Suppose instead that removal costs would be approximately $700,000 and that the building materials and exhibits could be sold for $300,000. Prepare journal entries to record the exhibit hall, to account for the hall during the three-year period, and to remove it from the books after the three-year period. Over how many periods

should the removal costs (net of the amount to be salvaged) be charged as an expense?

6. *Changes in estimated useful life and residual value can have a material effect upon reported earnings.*

The 1976 financial report of American Airlines, Inc., contains the following note:

During 1975, American, in addition to expanding its Boeing 727 fleet, commenced various life improvement programs on its existing Boeing 727 aircraft. In recognition of the continued use and improvement of these aircraft, effective January 1, 1975, American extended the estimated useful lives of these aircraft from 12 to 16 years and reduced estimated residual values from 15% to 10% of cost.

Suppose that within the next several years American Airlines expects to acquire new Boeing 727 aircraft at a cost $1 billion. The firm uses the straight-line method of depreciation. By how much would the change described cause annual depreciation charges on the new aircraft to decrease?

7. *Periodic maintenance costs that benefit more than one accounting period may be accounted for in at least two different ways.*

Treetop Airlines conducts maintenance overhauls on all aircraft engines every three years. The cost of each overhaul is approximately $12,000. The company owns 24 engines. In 1980 the company overhauled 10 engines, in 1981, 8 engines, and, in 1982, 6 engines.

a. How much expense should the company report in 1982 in connection with engine overhauls?
b. A financial report of Braniff Airlines indicates that "expenditures for maintenance overhauls of aircraft engines and airframes are charged to expense as incurred." Is the policy of Braniff consistent with your response in (a)? If it is, can you think of, and justify, an alternative policy that might be as acceptable or even preferable? If it is not, then defend your response.
c. Suppose instead that it was the company practice to overhaul 8 engines each year. Would it matter, as far as reported expense is concerned, which accounting procedure the company used?

8. *Firms in some industries must adapt generally accepted accounting principles to their special needs.*

The two statements that follow were drawn from footnotes to the financial reports of U.S. corporations. Each indicates that the company records a particular financial event in a nonconventional manner. For each statement compare the described practice with the conventional practice and indicate whether (and under what circumstances) the described practice would result in higher or lower reported earnings and balance sheet values than the conventional practice.

1. *Chessie System, Inc., December 31, 1976.* "As prescribed by the Interstate Commerce Commission, certain items of road property (principally rails and ties) are not depreciated but are accounted for under an alternative generally accepted accounting method whereby replacements are charged to expense and only additions and betterments are capitalized."

2. *Yellow Freight System, Inc., December 31, 1976.* "The cost of tires, including those purchased with new equipment, is amortized over the estimated tire lives. The unamortized balance of the cost is included in prepayments."

9. *Depreciation and depletion costs, like those of labor and materials, may be considered production, rather than period, costs if they can be associated directly with the minerals recovered.*

Wildcat Minerals, Inc., was incorporated in 1983 for the specific purpose of mining a tract of land. The company acquired the tract at a cost of $6.2 million. It estimated that the tract contained 700,000 tons of ore and that after the property was completely mined (in approximately four years) it could be sold as farm land for $600,000.

The company built various buildings and structures at a cost of $1.4 million. Such improvements have a useful life of 15 years but have utility only when used at the specific mining site; they cannot be moved economically to other locations. In addition, the company purchased other equipment at a cost of $400,000. Such equipment has a useful life of five years and an estimated salvage value of $50,000.

In 1983 the company incurred labor and other production costs of $357,000 and selling and administrative costs of $224,000. It paid taxes of $105,000.

The company mined 100,000 tons and sold 80,000 tons of ore. The selling price per ton was $19.

The company elected to charge depreciation on a unit of output basis.

a. Determine total depreciation and depletion costs for 1983.

b. Determine the cost per ton of ore sold.

c. Determine net income.

d. Determine the ending inventory.

10. *Alternative accounting practices in the oil industry may result in substantial differences in reported earnings.*

Panhandle, Inc., in 1983 drilled three exploratory oil wells at a cost of $300,000 each. Of the three, only one proved successful. The company estimates that the property on which the successful well is located will provide a cash inflow of $600,000 per year, after taking into account recovery costs, royalties, and other cash outlays for each of the next 10 years, including 1983.

a. Determine earnings for 1983 assuming that the firm uses
   1. The "full-cost" method.
   2. The "successful efforts" method.

b. Assume that the firm uses the successful efforts method. It does not own the property on which it discovered oil; instead it pays a per barrel royalty to its owner.
   1. At what value should the oil reserves (including the capitalized drilling costs) be reported on the balance sheet as of the end of 1983?
   2. Do you think that such value fully and fairly reflects the value of the asset? What supplementary disclosures would you recommend?

11. *It is often unclear as to whether certain types of costs are necessary to bring an asset to a serviceable condition.*

On January 2, National General Corporation purchased for $10,000 an *option* on a tract of land in which it hoped to construct a plant. The option gave the company the right to purchase the land itself within a given time period and for a fixed price—in this case within 10 months and for $2 million. If the company decided to exercise its option, it would pay the seller an additional $2 million and receive title to the land. If it decided not to purchase the land, then it would allow the option to lapse and would be unable to recover the $10,000. The option arrangement allows the company additional time to decide whether to make the purchase and at the same time compensates the seller for giving the company the exclusive right to purchase the property.

a. On July 2, National General decided to purchase the tract of land for $2 million. Prepare journal entries to record both the purchase of the option and the subsequent purchase of the land. Should the cost of the option be added to the cost of the land?

b. Suppose instead that on January 2, National General purchased three options—each for $10,000—on three tracts of land. The company expected to purchase and build on only one of the three tracts; however, it wanted to locate its new plant by the side of a proposed highway, and the exact route of the highway had not yet been announced. The company purchased the three options in order to assure itself that the plant could be built adjacent to the road, regardless of which of three routes under consideration was selected for the highway. On July 2, the company exercised its option on one of the three tracts and purchased the land for $2 million. It allowed the other two options to lapse. Prepare journal entries to record the purchase of the three options, the purchase of the land, and the expiration of two of the options. Consider carefully whether the cost of all three options should be included as part of the cost of the land. Present arguments both for and against including the expired options as part of the cost of the land.

12. *Tax laws, as they affect depreciation, may encourage firms to sell assets long before the expiration of their useful lives.*

Commuter Airlines, Inc., was established in 1983. The firm issued common stock for $12 million and used the funds to purchase six small passenger jets at a total cost of $12 million. The firm plans to use the planes for 10 years, after which it believes they can be sold for a total of $2 million.

a. Compute depreciation for the first three years under each of the following methods:
1. Straight-line
2. Sum-of-the-years' digits
3. Double-declining balance

b. Assume that income before depreciation and taxes during each of the first three years is $3 million. Compute income taxes for those years if the tax rate is 40 percent. Which method results in the least tax burden in the early years of asset life?

c. Suppose that at the end of the second year the planes are sold for $10 million. The remaining useful life of the assets is eight years. If the new owner elected to charge depreciation for tax purposes using the double-declining balance method, what would be the first-year deduction for depreciation? Compare such deduction to that which would be permitted Commuter Airlines if it used the double-declining balance method. Why might it be said that the asset is "worth" more to the new owner than to the previous one?

13. *The impact on earnings of both alternative depreciation practices and errors may depend upon a firm's trend of growth.*

Collins Manufacturing Corporation, established in 1960, uses 18 lathes, each of which costs $10,000 and has a useful life of three years (with no salvage value). Each year the company retires 6 machines and replaces them with 6 others.

a. Compute total depreciation charges on the 18 lathes for the three-year period 1978, 1979, and 1980 using
1. The straight-line method.
2. The sum-of-the-years' digits method.

b. Suppose the company used an incorrect useful life in calculating depreciation charges. Even though it replaced the machines after a three-year period, it charged depreciation over a two-year period. It made no adjustment in the accounts for the "error"; it simply charged zero depreciation in the machines' third year. Compute depreciation using the straight-line method for the same three-year period.

c. In 1981 the company undertook an expansion program. In each of the next three years (1981,

1982, and 1983) the company purchased 7 machines and retired 6. Thus, in 1981, 1982, and 1983 the firm had in operation 19, 20, and 21 machines, respectively. Compute depreciation charges for the three-year period using

1. The straight-line method.
2. The sum-of-the-years' digits method.

d. Assume again that the firm used an incorrect useful life and depreciated the machines over a two-year period instead of three. Compute depreciation charges for the three-year period using the straight-line method.

e. What conclusions can you draw regarding the impact of choice of depreciation method and estimate of useful life on the income of a firm that is expanding its asset base as opposed to one that is maintaining it at a constant level?

14. *Complete journal entries can be reconstructed from limited amounts of data; annual reports sometimes contain misleading assertions.*

The following information relating to plant, warehouse, and terminal elevator equipment was taken from the 10-K report of General Mills, Inc., for the fiscal year ended May 29, 1977 (in thousands):

Equipment:

Balance at beginning of period	$346,838
Additions and miscellaneous adjustments	70,305
Balance at end of period	384,406

Equipment, accumulated depreciation:

Balance at beginning of period	173,964
Depreciation expense and miscellaneous adjustments	32,267
Balance at end of period	186,668

a. Based on the data provided, plus any other amounts that it may be necessary to derive from the data provided, prepare a journal entry that summarizes the retirement of equipment during the period. Assume that the equipment was sold for $10,000.

b. In a discussion of replacement cost information the report contains the following comment: "While inflation's annual impact on replacement of existing productive capacity is minimal because of the long time span over which replace-

ments occur, its long-run result is that accumulated depreciation is insufficient to replace fully depreciated productive capacity."

1. Prepare a journal entry that summarizes depreciation expense for the period.
2. Is it the purpose of depreciation accounting to provide for the replacement of equipment? In what way, if any, does the entry you proposed enable the company to accumulate funds for replacement?

15. *Revaluation of assets to reflect changes in market values would affect not only their recorded values, but also the allocation of earnings among the years that the assets were in service.*

The Rhinegold Chemical Co. constructed a new plant at a cost of $20 million. The plant had an estimated useful life of 20 years, with no salvage value. After the plant had been used for 4 years, its replacement cost had increased to $24 million. The company decided to recognize in its accounts the increase in the fair market value of the asset. (Such practice is not, of course, in accord with currently acceptable accounting principles.)

a. Prepare the journal entry to record depreciation for each of the first four years.

b. Prepare an entry to record the revaluation of the plant.

c. Prepare an entry to record depreciation in the fifth year, the first year subsequent to the revaluation.

d. At the *start* of the eighth year the company accepted an offer to sell the plant for $19 million. Prepare an entry to record the sale.

e. Suppose the company had not readjusted its accounts after the fourth year to recognize the increase in market value. How much gain would it have recognized upon sale of the plant? Compare total depreciation expense and total gains recognized if the company recognized the increase in market value with those that would have resulted if it adhered to conventional practice and did not recognize the increase.

16. *Conventional practices of depreciation do not adequately satisfy the information requirements of municipalities.*

In January 1982 the village of Rahavia acquired a new sanitation truck at a cost of $50,000. The useful life of the truck is estimated to be five years, with no salvage value anticipated. Officials of the village have budgeted $350,000 in additional expenditures for 1982. All such expenditures require the direct outlay of cash.

State law requires that the village operate on a "balanced budget"; taxes and other revenues must be sufficiently large to cover expenses.

1. Assume that the village elects to record depreciation on the new truck on a straight-line basis.
   a. What would be total reported expenses for 1982? What would be total required revenues?
   b. What would be total required *cash* outlays for 1982? Would the revenues as determined in part a be sufficient to cover required cash outlays?
   c. Comment on why traditional depreciation practices may be inappropriate for the types of decisions made by municipal budget officers.
2. In fact, generally accepted accounting principles as they apply to municipalities do not require that depreciation be charged on certain types of assets. Instead, the full cost of such assets is charged as an expense at the time that they are paid for and the full amount of any sums received when an asset is retired or sold is recognized as revenue. Suppose that at the end of 1983 the village of Rahavia sold its truck for $30,000. Other expenditures were again $350,000.
   a. Determine total reported expenses and the required amount of revenues, in addition to that from the sale of the truck, for both 1982 and 1983.
   b. A new mayor assumed office in 1983. He asserted that, inasmuch as both reported expenditures and required additional reve-

nues were lower in 1983 than in 1982, the village had been operated more efficiently in 1983 than in 1982. Do you agree? Comment on the usefulness in evaluating managerial performance of financial statements based on the special accounting principles applicable to municipalities.
3. Comment on the limitations of a single set of accounting practices in achieving a multiplicity of accounting objectives.

17. Ownership arrangements that are very different in form may be very similar in economic substance.

Deception, Inc., currently has a loan outstanding from the Gibraltar Insurance Co. that requires that Deception, Inc., maintain a *debt/equity ratio* no greater than 1 : 1. That is, the balance in all liability accounts can be no greater than that in the capital stock and retained earnings accounts. As of December 31, 1983, Deception, Inc., had total liabilities of $3 million and total capital stock and retained earnings of $3,150,000.

The vice-president of production of Deception, Inc., has proposed that the company purchase new equipment that would cost $257,710. The equipment would have a three-year useful life and no salvage value and during its life would result in substantial cost savings to the company. Aware that the company is short of cash, the vice-president arranged with the manufacturer of the equipment to give a three-year note for the purchase price. Interest would be at the rate of 8 percent on the unpaid balance. Payments would be made at the end of each of the three years as follows:

	Remaining Balance	Payment of Interest at 8%	Payment of Principal	Total Payment
1	$257,710	$20,617	$ 79,383	$100,000
2	178,327	14,266	85,734	100,000
3	92,593	7,407	92,593	100,000
			$257,710	

Annual rent would be $100,000 but Deception, Inc., would have to pay all maintenance and insurance costs. At the expiration of the lease, Deception, Inc., would have an option to purchase the machine for $1.

a. Prepare all journal entries that would be required on the books of Deception, Inc., if it agreed to *purchase* the machine and issued the note for $257,710. The company records depreciation on a straight-line basis.

b. Prepare all journal entries that would be required if the firm agreed to lease the machine.

c. What are the total charges associated with the acquisition of the machine under each of the two alternatives?

d. Comment on the difference, if any, in the *substance* of the two transactions. Viewing the transactions from the point of view of Gibraltar Insurance Co., how would you propose that the firm record the transaction if it decided to *lease* the equipment?

18. *Although not discussed in the text, increasing charge (as opposed to decreasing or accelerated charge) methods may also be used to calculate periodic depreciation charges.*

Machine Rentals, Inc., is considering purchasing a new computer that it will be able to rent to a customer for $10,000 per year starting January 1, 1982. The machine has a useful life of four years and no salvage value. The company expects a rate of return of 6 percent on all its assets.

a. What is the maximum amount the firm would be willing to pay for the machine? That is, what is the present value, discounted at a rate of 6 percent, of anticipated future cash receipts?

b. What is the present value of anticipated cash receipts at the end of each of the four years?

c. Suppose that the firm were able to purchase the machine for the amount computed in a. It elects to charge depreciation on the basis of what the

machine is worth to the company (the present value of anticipated cash receipts) at the end of a year as compared to what it was worth at the

beginning. How much depreciation should it charge during each of the four years? Determine total depreciation charges for the four-year period.

d. Comment on the trend of charges by this method of depreciation as compared to other methods. This method is not widely used in practice, but is regarded with favor by many theoreticians. How can it be justified?

SOLUTIONS TO EXERCISE FOR REVIEW AND SELF-TESTING

1. The amount at which the plane should be recorded must include the fair market value of all consideration (cash and property) paid to bring the asset to a usable condition. In this case, all amounts indicated ($3,000,000 cash payment plus $500,000 in marketable securities plus $6,000 delivery charges plus $94,000 furnishing costs) must be "capitalized" as part of the asset—a total of $3,600,000.

2. The total cost of using the plane for 10 years—the amount to be allocated—is the initial amount recorded ($3,600,000) less the anticipated residual value ($900,000)—$2,700,000.

3. If the straight-line method were used, annual depreciation charges would be $2,700,000 divided by 10, or $270,000 per year.

4. The straight-line rate of depreciation is 10 percent; twice that is 20 percent. This rate would be applied each year to the current book value (cost less accumulated depreciation) *without* regard to residual value (except as suggested in part 5 of this exercise). Thus,

Year	Book Value, Start of Year	Depreciation Rate (%)	Depreciation Charge	Book Value, End of Year
1	$3,600,000	20	$720,000	$2,880,000
2	2,880,000	20	576,000	2,304,000
3	2,304,000	20	460,800	1,843,200

5. Depreciation must never be charged so as to reduce the remaining book value below expected salvage value—in this case $900,000. In the

seventh year of service, therefore, the firm would charge only $43,718 of depreciation ($943,718 less $900,000); in the eighth year, zero.

6. In economic substance the firm sold an asset with a book value of $1,843,200 for $1,500,000—the apparent fair market value of the old plane. Hence, it should report a loss of $343,200. The new plane snould be recorded at an amount representative of the fair market value of the consideration paid—$7,000,000 cash plus $1,500,000, the fair market value of the plane surrendered—a total of $8,500,000.

Liabilities 10
and Related Expenses

In the preceding four chapters we addressed questions of valuing assets and of reporting the related revenues and expenses. This chapter will be directed to the equally important and controversial issues of valuing liabilities and of measuring their impact upon earnings of the firm.

This chapter is of concern to managers and investors for a number of reasons. Liabilities are, of course, as significant to the financial health of an enterprise as are assets; they are the claims upon the assets. The means by which liabilities are accounted for can have a substantial effect on reported income. Moreover, an understanding of liabilities is essential to an appreciation of the alternative sources from which firms can finance the acquisition of assets. This chapter will deal at length with bonds, but the principles of valuing and accounting for bonds are applicable to a wide range of financing arrangements. It is the principles, rather than the specifics, of bonds that are important because new instruments of debt are continually being evolved. Indeed, the high rates of interest, inflation, and taxes of the last decade have stimulated the development of borrowing plans that are as complex as they are creative. Also discussed in this chapter are issues of accounting for income tax liabilities. In light of the magnitude of tax obligations, the manner in which they are reflected in financial reports must be taken into account in all major managerial decisions.

BONDS

Corporations, as well as governmental units and nonprofit organizations, borrow funds to finance *long-term* projects, such as plant and equipment and major public works projects. Conventionally, borrowers provide the lender with bonds or notes as evidence of their obligations to repay the funds and to make periodic interest payments. A bond is a more formal certificate of indebtedness than a note. Characteristically bonds are evidence of long-term indebtedness (five years or more), while notes may be issued in connection with short- or long-term borrowings.

Corporate bonds are most commonly issued in denominations of $1,000. The *par* or *face* value of a bond indicates the *principal* amount due at the *maturity* or due date of the bond. Bonds ordinarily carry a stated annual rate of interest, expressed as a percentage of the principal. Most bond *indentures* (agreements which set forth the legal provisions of the bonds) require that interest be paid semiannually. Thus, a corporation which has issued $1,000-denomination bonds that specify an annual rate of interest of 12 percent would pay the holder of a single bond $60 on each of two interest dates six months apart.

Most corporate bonds are *bearer* bonds. Each bond typically contains a series of coupons which may be clipped and redeemed at six-month intervals for the interest due. Bearer bonds are distinguished from *registered* bonds in that on the latter interest is paid not to the bearer of the coupon but only to a specific party whose name is registered with the borrower.

Corporate bonds may be secured (collateralized) by property, such as a plant or land. Or they may be unsecured, with the lender relying primarily upon the good faith and financial integrity of the borrower for repayment. Secured bonds may be categorized by the type of legal instrument used to provide the lien on the property that is pledged—e.g., mortgage bonds and equipment trust bonds. Unsecured bonds are commonly called *debentures*.

Virtually all corporate bonds indicate a specific maturity date. However, many corporate issues provide for the early retirement of the debt at the option of the *borrower* (the corporation). Such a *call provision* ordinarily requires the company to pay the lender (the bond holder) a *call premium*, an amount in addition to the par value of the bond, as a penalty for depriving the lender of his "right" to interest payments for the original term of the loan.

Bonds are generally freely negotiable— they can be bought and sold in the open market subsequent to original issue. An active market for corporate bonds is maintained by both the New York and American Stock Exchanges. A lender who no longer wishes to have his funds tied up in a loan to the issuer of a bond can sell his bond to an investor who is seeking the type of return provided by that type of bond. The price at which the bond is sold need not be that for which the bond was initially issued. Rather, it would be determined in large measure by interest rates prevalent at time of sale.

THE NATURE OF BONDS

Bonds provide for interest payments of a fixed amount. Ordinarily, the more financially sound the lender, the lower will be the rate of interest. Yet interest rates for securities *within* the same category of risk are determined by the forces of supply and demand—the amount of funds being sought by borrowers, the amount being made available by lenders. Rates of interest that prevail throughout the country fluctuate from day to day and even from hour to hour. Although corporations conventionally set the coupon rate of interest—the amount that will be paid to the lender each interest period—and print it in the bond indentures several weeks prior to the date on which they are to be issued, the actual interest rate is determined at time of sale. The actual interest rate, often referred to as the *yield rate*, is established, not by changing the coupon rate, but rather by adjusting the price at which the bond is sold. Suppose, for example, that a $1,000 bond has a coupon rate of 8 percent—that is, the holder of the bond will be entitled to two payments of $40 each year. At the time of sale, however, the prevailing interest rate for that type of bond is $8\frac{1}{4}$ percent. Would a purchaser be willing to pay $1,000 for such a bond? Obviously not. He could lend his money to another similar company and receive $82.50 per year rather than $80. Therefore, he would be willing to pay something less than $1,000 for the bond. How much less will be considered in the next section. Similarly if the prevailing interest rate were lower than 8 percent—$7\frac{1}{2}$ percent, for example—a rational buyer would be willing to pay more than $1,000 for the bond. If he were to purchase the bonds of similar companies, he would receive only $75 per year in interest. He would be willing to pay something above $1,000 in order to receive a return of $80 per year. If a purchaser pays less than the face amount for a bond, then the difference between the face amount and what he actually pays is referred to as a bond *discount*. If he pays more than the face amount, then the additional payment is referred to as a *premium*.

A rational purchaser would undertake a similar analysis in deciding how much to pay for a bond that had been issued several years earlier, one to be purchased not from the issuing company directly but rather from the current holder of the bond. To the extent that prevailing interest rates are greater than the coupon rate of the bond, he would be willing to pay *less* than the face value of the bond, for he could receive the prevailing rate by purchasing a different bond on which the coupon rate is equal to the prevailing rate. To the extent that prevailing rates are less than the coupon rate, he would be willing to pay more, since the semiannual interest payments would be greater than what he could obtain elsewhere.

DETERMINATION OF DISCOUNT OR PREMIUM*

Determination of the amount that a rational purchaser would pay for a bond requires an understanding of the promises inherent in the bond agreement. A somewhat simplified and exaggerated example can be used to illustrate a logical approach to calculating the amount to be paid for a particular bond.

Suppose that on a particular day a corporation seeks bids on two bond issues. Bond A bears a coupon rate of 12 percent and bond B a coupon rate of 10 percent. Both bonds will mature in two years. Both pay interest semiannually. The prevailing annual rate of interest is 12 percent.

Both bonds contain a promise to pay the purchaser $1,000 upon maturity after two years—four semiannual periods hence. The present value of a single cash payment four semiannual periods away given an interest rate of 6 percent is, per Table 2 in the Appendix, $1,000 × .7921—$792.10. The 6 percent rate is one-half the annual rate of 12 percent; it reflects the semi-annual rather than the annual payment of interest. The 12 percent rate is the *prevailing* rate for bonds of that type, not necessarily the coupon rate on either of the two bonds in question. It is the rate that is relevant to the prospective purchaser since it is that which he could receive if he were to turn to alternative investment possibilities of comparable risk.

Bond A also promises four semiannual payments of $60. The present value of four semiannual payments, discounted at 6

* The reader is strongly urged to review the material on compound interest and present value contained in Chapter 6.

percent per period (one-half the *prevailing* annual rate), is, per Table 4, $60 × 3.4651—$207.90. The total present value of the two promises—the promise to pay principal of $1,000 plus the promise to make semiannual interest payments—discounted at the prevailing rate of 6 percent per semiannual period is $1,000 ($792.10 plus $207.90). The rational buyer would be willing to pay $1,000—in this instance, the face value—for the bond.

Bond B, on the other hand, promises four semiannual payments of only $50, since the coupon rate is 10 percent per year. The present value of four semiannual payments of $50, discounted at 6 percent is, again per

Table 4, $50 × 3.4651—$173.25. The rate of 6 percent is one-half the *prevailing* rate of 12 percent. The *prevailing rate is the one that must be used to evaluate an investment opportunity*, since it (rather than the coupon rate) is indicative of the return that the investor can expect to receive. The present value of the two promises combined is, therefore, $792.10 plus $173.25—$965.35. A rational purchaser would be willing to pay only $965.35 for the bond with a face value of $1,000 and a coupon rate of 10 percent. The discount of $34.65 would assure him a *yield* of 12 percent per year, even though the coupon rate is only 10 percent per year. The analysis can be summarized as follows:

	12 Bond A (12% Coupon)	10 Bond B (10% Coupon)
Present value of $1,000 to be received at the end of 4 periods, discounted at prevailing rate of 6% ($1,000 × .7921 per Table 2)	$ 792.10	$792.10
Present value of $60 to be received at the end of each of 4 periods, discounted at prevailing rate of 6% ($60 × 3.4651 per Table 4)	207.90	
Present value of $50 to be received at the end of each of 4 periods, discounted at prevailing rate of 6% ($50 × 3.4651 per Table 4)		173.25
Present value of bond	$1,000.00	$965.35

EXHIBIT 10-1

Bond A
12% Coupon; 12% Yield

Present value	1/1/82		6/30/82	12/31/82	6/30/83	12/31/83
$ 56.60		.9434	$60			
53.40		.8900		$60		
50.38		.8396			$60	
47.52		.7921				$60
792.10		.7921				$1,000
$1,000.00						

EXHIBIT 10-1 (continued)

Bond B
10% Coupon; 12% Yield

Present value	1/1/82		6/30/82	12/31/82	6/30/83	12/31/83
$ 47.17		.9434	$50			
44.50		.8900		$50		
41.98		.8396			$50	
39.60		.7921				$50
792.10		.7921				$1,000
$965.35						

Diagrammatically, the two bonds can be depicted as in Exhibit 10-1. Both bonds are evaluated at a rate of 6 percent per period—the prevailing yield on comparable securities. It is assumed that the bonds were sold on January 1, 1982. All discount factors are per Table 2. Bond A would sell at face value because its coupon rate is identical to the yield rate. Anytime there is a difference between the coupon and the yield rates, the bonds would be sold at an amount other than face value.

Alternative View

The discount of $34.65 on Bond B can be viewed from a slightly different perspective. If a purchaser can obtain a yield of 12 percent per year elsewhere, then from a $1,000 bond he expects interest payments of $60 every six months. In fact, Bond B will pay him only $50 per six months. He is "losing" $10 per period. The present value of $10 lost for four periods, discounted at a rate of 6 percent per period (one-half the prevailing yield of 12 percent), is, per Table 4, $10 × $3.4651—$34.65.

Computation of the bond premium or discount can be facilitated by asking four simple questions:

1. How much interest per period (based on the *coupon rate*) is a purchaser of the bond actually going to receive?
2. How much interest (based on the prevailing *yield* of comparable securities) would he expect to receive?
3. What is the difference between the two amounts?
4. What is the present value, discounted at the prevailing *yield rate*, of such difference?

The present value of the difference between the amounts a purchaser would expect to receive and what he will actually receive represents either premium or discount.

RECORDING THE SALE OF BONDS

The sale of Bond B for a price of $965.35 could be recorded by the following journal entry:

Cash (asset)	$965.35	
Discount on bonds (contra account to bonds payable)	34.65	
Bonds payable (liability)		$1,000

To record issuance of the bond.

If financial statements were to be prepared immediately after the sale, the liability would be reported as follows:

Bonds payable	$1,000.00	
Less: Discount	34.65	$965.35

As a consequence the *net* liability to be reported would be only $965.35 not the $1,000 face value of the bond.

NATURE OF PREMIUM OR DISCOUNT

The net liability of the company at the time of sale is only $965.35. That is the amount of cash actually received. It may be argued that the company will have to repay $1,000, the face value of the bond, and that that amount, therefore, is the liability to be reported. The company will, of course, have to pay $1,000 at time of maturity. But if it only borrowed $965.35, then the "extra" $34.65 must represent interest, in addition to the semiannual coupon payments, to be paid to the lender. The additional $34.65 has the effect of increasing the rate of interest paid by the company from 10 percent to 12 percent. Interest is not ordinarily reported as a liability and recorded as an expense until the borrower has had use of the funds for an appropriate period of time. Just as the liability for each of the periodic coupon payments of $50 will not be recorded until the interest has been earned, neither should the liability for the additional interest of $34.65 to be paid upon maturity of the bond. Instead, it should be added to the liability account over the remaining life of the bond issue—as the firm has use of the funds borrowed.* Similarly,

---

* It could, of course, be argued that the company has a legal liability for the full $1,000. Should the company go bankrupt, however, soon after the sale of the bonds, it would be highly unusual for a bankruptcy court to award the full $1,000 to a bondholder who recently had loaned the company only $965.35.

if the bonds were sold at a premium, at a price of $1,020, for example, then the amount borrowed by the company is the amount actually received, $1,020. The company will, of course, have to repay only $1,000. The $20 represents a reduction, over the life of the issue, of the firm's borrowing costs and should be accounted for as such.

RECORDING THE PAYMENT OF INTEREST

As a consequence of the price adjustments attributable to the premium or discount at which the bonds were sold, the effective rate of interest to be paid by the company is that established not by the coupon rate but rather by the *yield rate* (*the effective rate at time of issue*). *The reported interest expense should be based on such yield rate.*

In the previous example, the company borrowed $965.35 at an effective interest rate of 12 percent (6 percent per interest period). Each interest date, however, it must pay the bondholder only $50. On the first interest date, its effective interest expense is 6 percent of $965.35—$57.92, an amount that is $7.92 greater than the actual payment of $50 to be made to the bondholder. The $7.92 represents the first interest period's share of the $34.65 in additional interest to be paid upon the maturity of the loan. It is, therefore, the amount of the discount that must be amortized and charged as additional interest expense in the first period. The following journal entry would reflect this interpretation of the bond discount:

Interest expense	$57.92	
Cash		$50.00
Discount on bonds		7.92

To record payment of interest.

As a result of this entry, the unamortized portion of the bond discount has been reduced from $34.65 to $26.73. The bond would be reported in the liability section of the balance sheet as follows:

Bonds payable	$1,000.00	
Less: Discount	26.73	$973.27

The effective liability of the company has increased from $965.35 to $973.27 because the company now owes not only the original amount borrowed ($965.35) but also a portion of the interest which the bondholder has earned during the first interest period. The additional interest now owed is equal to the effective interest for the period ($57.92) less the amount actually paid ($50.00).

At the end of the second interest period, the interest expense would again be based on the effective interest or yield rate that prevailed at the time the bond was issued. But now the effective liability is not $965.35 as at the end of the first period but rather $973.27, an amount reflective of the amortization of a portion of the original discount. Hence, the effective interest expense is 6 percent of $973.27—$58.40. As in the first period, the actual payment to the bondholder would be only $50.00. The difference between the two represents the portion of interest earned by the bondholder but not yet paid to him—the amount that must be subtracted from the bond discount and thereby added to the effective liability. The following journal entry would be required on the second interest date:

Interest expense	$58.40	
Cash		$50.00
Discount on bonds		8.40

To record payment of interest.

As a result of this entry, the unamortized portion of the bond discount has been reduced from $26.73 to $18.33. After the second payment of interest the bond would be reported as follows:

Bonds payable	$1,000.00	
Less: Discount	18.33	$981.67

A history of the bond is summarized in Exhibit 10-2.

The effective liability, as of any date, can be determined by following the same procedures used to calculate the initial selling price of the bond. For example, as of 12/31/82 there are two interest payments of $50 remaining. The present value of such payments discounted at the effective interest or yield rate of 6 percent per period is, per Table 4, $50 × 1.8334—$91.67. The present value of the $1,000 to be received at maturity is, per Table 2, $1,000 × .8900—$890.00. The present value of the two sets of payments combined is $91.67 plus $890.00—$981.67.

The following example deals with a bond to be sold at a premium rather than a discount.

Example

A company wishes to sell 10-year debentures that bear a coupon rate of 10 percent. At the time of sale, bonds of comparable risk are being sold to yield 8 percent.

1. For how much will the company be able to sell each $1,000 bond?

The present value at the effective yield rate of 4 percent per half-year period (8 percent per year) of a single payment of $1,000, 20 periods hence, is, per Table 2, $1,000 × .4564—$456.40.

The present value of a stream of 20 payments of $50 each (based on the coupon rate discounted at 4 percent per period) is, per Table 4, $50 × 13.5903—$679.52. The sum of the two present values is $1,135.92, the amount for which the company will be able to sell the bond.

EXHIBIT 10-2

$1,000 Bond Issued on January 1, 1982; Matures on December 31, 1983;
10 Percent Coupon; Sold to Yield 12 Percent
(6 Percent per Semiannual Period)

Date	Interest (6% of Effective Liability)	Coupon Payment	Discount	Effective Liability
1/1/82	—	—	$34.65	$ 965.35
6/30/82	$57.92	$(50.00)	(7.92)	7.92
			26.73	973.27
12/31/82	58.40	(50.00)	(8.40)	8.40
			18.33	981.67
6/30/83	58.90	(50.00)	(8.90)	8.90
			9.43	990.57
12/31/83	59.43	(50.00)	(9.43)	9.43
			$ 0.00	$1,000.00

Present value of $1,000 to be received after 20 periods discounted at prevailing rate of 4% per period ($1,000 × .4564 per Table 2) $ 456.40

Present value of $50 to be received at the end of each of 20 periods, discounted at prevailing rate of 4% per period ($50 × 13.5903 per Table 4)   679.52

Present value of bond $1,135.92

Alternatively the same result could have been obtained by focusing on the premium. The company is offering the purchaser 20 payments of $50 each. The purchaser, based on the prevailing interest rate of 8 percent, would be willing to accept 20 payments of $40 each. The present value of the series of the $10 "bonuses" is, per Table 4, $10 × 13.5903—$135.90. The latter figure represents the bond premium; hence the sale price would be the face value of $1,000 plus a premium of $135.90—the same (with allow-ance for rounding discrepancies) $1,135.92 as computed earlier.

2. Prepare a journal entry to record the sale of one bond.

Cash	$1,135.92	
Bonds payable		$1,000.00
Premium on		
bonds payable		135.92

To record sale of the bond.

3. How would the bonds be reported on the balance sheet immediately after sale?

Bonds payable	$1,000.00	
Premium	135.92	$1,135.92

4. Prepare a journal entry to record the first interest payment. The total amount borrowed by the company was $1,135.92. The effective rate of interest, the yield rate, was 8 percent. The effective semiannual interest would therefore be 4 percent times the outstanding balance of $1,135.92—$45.43. The amount of interest actually to be paid at

the time of the first payment is, based on the coupon rate, $50.

Interest expense	$45.43	
Premium on bonds payable	4.57	
Cash		$50.00

To record payment of interest.

5. How would the bonds be reported immediately after the first payment of interest?

Bonds payable	$1,000.00	
Premium	131.35	$1,131.35

6. Prepare a journal entry to record the second interest payment. The effective liability just prior to the second payment of interest is $1,131.35. Effective interest charges, based on the yield rate at the time of sale, are $1,131.35 × .04—$45.25.

Interest expense	$45.25	
Premium on bonds payable	4.75	
Cash		$50.00

To record payment of interest.

The net liability will now be $1,131.35 less that portion ($4.75) of the premium just amortized—$1,126.60.

7. For how much could the bondholder sell the bond immediately after the second payment of interest, assuming that the prevailing interest rate is still 8 percent?

Present value of $1,000, 18 periods away, discounted at 4% per period (per Table 2), $1,000 × .4936	$ 493.60
Present value of 18 coupon payments of $50 each (per Table 4), $50 × 12.6593	632.97
Price at which the bond could be sold	$1,126.57

This amount is the same amount that would be reported on the books of the issuing company as calculated for part 6 of this example (save for a minor rounding discrepancy). It is the same only because the prevailing interest rate is the same as it was at the time when the bond was first issued—8 percent.

END-OF-YEAR ACCRUALS

If a bond interest date does not occur exactly at year end, it is necessary to accrue interest for the expense incurred from the time of either the issue date or the last payment date to the year end. Suppose, for example, that a 12 percent, 20-year coupon bond was sold on December 1, 1982 for $866.68—a price that would result in a yield of 14 percent. Interest is payable each year on May 31 and November 30. Interest expense for the first full six-month period would be 7 percent of $866.68—$60.67. That portion of the discount amortized would be the difference between the interest expense of $60.67 and the actual coupon payment of $60.00—$.67. The accrual entry on December 31, 1982, would reflect one-sixth of these amounts:

Interest expense ($\frac{1}{6}$ of $60.67)	$10.11	
Discount on bonds payable		$ .11
Accrued interest payable		10.00

To record accrual of interest.

The entry on May 31, 1983, when the first payment was made would be reflective of the remaining five-sixths (note that consistent with conventional practice the interest expense on May 31 is *not* based on the effective liability at December 31—after the *partial* amortization of the discount—but rather on the liability as of December 1):

Interest expense ($\frac{5}{6}$ of 60.67)	$50.56
Accrued interest payable	10.00
Discount on bonds payable ($\frac{5}{6}$ of $.67$)	$ .56
Cash	60.00

To record payment of interest.

STRAIGHT-LINE AMORTIZATION

Some firms, instead of determining interest charges and amortization of discount or premium as described in the preceding paragraphs, have in the past amortized the premium or discount on a straight-line basis. Total interest charges for the month are calculated by adding to the cash coupon payment (or subtracting from, in the case of a premium) the portion of the discount (or premium) amortized. The amount of the discount or premium amortized each period is determined simply by dividing the initial discount or premium by the total number of periods for which the bond will be outstanding. As a consequence, effective interest charges remain constant over the life of the issue. In the illustration used earlier, a 10 percent coupon bond was issued at a price of $965.35—a discount of $34.65. Since the bond would be outstanding for four periods, one-fourth of $34.65—$8.66—would be amortized each period. Total interest costs each period would be $58.66—the portion of the discount amortized plus the $50 coupon payment. The straight-line method is convenient; it eliminates the need to recompute interest each period. But it is deficient in that it results in a constantly changing *rate* of interest when interest expense is compared to effective liability (face value plus or minus discount or premium). Since, in the example, the effective liability would increase by $8.66

each period, the effective interest rates over the life of the bond (interest expense ÷ effective liability) would be as follows:

$$\frac{58.66}{965.35} = 6.08\%; \quad \frac{58.66}{974.01} = 6.02\%;$$

$$\frac{58.66}{982.67} = 5.97\%; \quad \frac{58.66}{991.33} = 5.92\%$$

The effective rate of interest tends to increase over time when a bond is sold at a premium. Because of such distortions, the Accounting Principles Board, in Opinion No. 21, "Interest on Receivables and Payables," specifically prohibited firms from using the straight-line method for their reports to the public.

REDEMPTION OF BONDS

When a firm redeems its bonds outstanding upon their maturity, no special accounting problems are presented. Once the interest expense of the final period is recorded, the discount or premium should have been amortized to zero. Thus, for a single bond, the following entry would be appropriate:

Bonds payable	$1,000.00
Cash	$1,000.00

To record redemption of the bond.

If, however, the firm decides to redeem the bonds before they mature, then the accounting questions are more complex.

Assume that a company 20 years ago had issued 30-year, 7 percent coupon bonds at a price of $1,025.50 to yield 6.8 percent. With 10 years remaining until maturity, the firm decides to redeem the bonds since it no longer needs the funds that it borrowed. According to the bond indenture agreement, the company has the right to call the issue any time after 15 years of issuing date at a price of $102. (Bond prices are frequently quoted in terms of $100 even though they are conventionally sold in denominations of $1,000. Thus the company would have to pay $1,020 to redeem a single bond.) The bond was originally issued at a price of $1,025.50; if the company had amortized the premium correctly, the net value of the bond after 20 years (10 years remaining) per the corporate books would be $1,014.34. If the company exercised its option to redeem the bond for $1,020.00, the following entry would be appropriate:

Bonds payable	$1,000.00	
Premium on bonds payable	14.34	
Redemption costs (call premium)	5.66	
Cash		$1,020.00

To record redemption of the bond.

The redemption costs represent a penalty payment that management has elected to make to the bondholders in return for depriving them of the return which their investment in the bonds was providing them.

A corporation may also realize a gain by redeeming its bonds prior to maturity. This is especially true if the company does not officially *call* its outstanding issue but instead purchases its bonds in the open market. The company would pay the current bondholders the prevailing price for the security. By purchasing the bonds outstanding the company would eliminate its liability to outsiders, and it would recognize as a gain the difference between the book value of the bonds and the purchase price.

Bond Prices Are Subject to Wide Fluctuations

Bond prices, as pointed out earlier, are determined by the relationship between the coupon rate and the prevailing return that an investor is able to obtain elsewhere. It is commonly believed that bonds are a relatively riskless investment—that bond prices remain reasonably stable. Nothing could be further from the truth. If, for example, prevailing interest rates increase from 12 percent to 14 percent, then the market price on a bond which bears a coupon rate of 12 percent and has 30 years remaining until maturity could be expected to decline from $100.00 to $85.96—almost a 14 percent change. If a company had initially issued such a 12 percent coupon bond at a price to yield 12.2 percent, then after 10 years (with 20 years—40 periods—until maturity) the bond would be recorded on its books at a net value of $98.51 (a discount of $1.49 per hundred dollars). The purchase (i.e., the redemption) of a single $1,000 bond at a price of $86.67 (which reflects a market rate of interest of 14 percent) would be recorded as follows:

Bonds payable	$1,000.00	
Cash		$866.70
Discount on bonds payable		14.90
Gain on redemption		118.40

To record redemption of the bond.

INTERPRETING GAINS AND LOSSES ON REDEMPTIONS

Gains or losses on the redemption of bonds must necessarily be interpreted with care by both managers and outside financial analysts. Such gains or losses are recognized and reported on the income statement in the year in which the redemption takes place. As a result, corporate management could readily time its redemptions in such a manner as to provide a source of discretionary income whenever it is believed that a boost in reported earnings would be helpful. Assume, for example, that in 1965 a firm issued (at par)

$10 million in 5 percent coupon bonds payable in 45 years. In 1980, 15 years later, the prevailing rate of interest for similar securities was 7 percent. A 5 percent bond with 30 years remaining until maturity would be traded in the open market for approximately $75. The company could purchase the entire issue for $7.5 million and thereby realize a $2.5 million gain. Insofar as management believes that interest rates in the 1980s will continue to remain substantially above the level of the earlier period, then management is free to select the year in which it redeems the bonds and thereby reports the gain.

Viewed from another perspective, a gain or loss on redemption of bonds may be seen as being very similar to a gain or loss on the sale of long-term assets. If a company is blessed with perfect foresight and is able to predict exactly when and for how much it will redeem its bonds, it would calculate its periodic charges or credits for the amortization of the bond discount or premium in a manner that would assure that the net book value of the bonds at time of redemption is exactly equal to the redemption price. Thus, there would be no gain or loss on redemption. If a company does not have perfect foresight, then, upon redeeming its bonds, it must make adjustment for its failure to amortize correctly the discount or premium in the years that the bond was outstanding. Just as the gain or loss on the retirement of long-lived assets may be interpreted as a correction of depreciation expense, the gain or loss on redemption of bonds may be considered to be a correction of the amortization of the bond discount or premium and, thus, as an adjustment to the interest charges of previous periods.

The gain on redemption that will be reported on the financial statements does not accrue to the corporation without a price. If the corporation must reborrow the funds used to redeem the outstanding issue, it will have to do so at the prevailing rates of interest—rates that are higher than those which it had been paying in the past. The new rates will, of course, be reflected on income statements of the future as greater interest expenses.

TIMES INTEREST EARNED

Insight into the ablity of a company to satisfy its fixed obligations to creditors may be obtained by comparing earnings with interest charges. Although the times interest earned ratio may be expressed in a variety of ways, the simplest form indicates the relationship between interest and income *before* deducting both interest and income taxes. The objective of the ratio is to indicate the margin of safety afforded bondholders and noteholders. If earnings only barely cover interest charges, then the creditors' promised interest payments are in jeopardy. If, however, earnings are several times greater than interest charges, then in the absence of a business reversal their return is reasonably assured.

Since the objective of the ratio is to indicate the earnings available for the payment of interest, it is important that the interest charges themselves be added back to net income. Moreover, since interest payments are a deductible expense in the determination of taxable income, income taxes should also be added back. In a sense, the payment of interest takes precedence over the payment of federal, state, and local income taxes. Required income tax payments are calculated after deducting payments to creditors. If the firm, after payment of interest, has zero income or a net loss, then the tax liability is also zero.

Fruehauf Corp. in 1980 reported net income after taxes of $32,213,012. (See statements in Chapter 7.) It incurred $81,872,552 in interest charges and $21,100,000 in income taxes. It covered its interest payments, therefore, 1.65 times:

Times interest earned

$$= \frac{\text{Net income} + \text{Interest} + \text{Income Taxes}}{\text{Interest}}$$

$$= \frac{\$32,213,012 + \$81,872,552 + \$21,100,000}{\$81,872,552}$$

$$= \frac{\$135,185,534}{\$81,872,552} = 1.65$$

LEASES

A financial arrangement that is of special concern to managers and accountants is *leasing*. In a strict sense a lease involves the right to use land, buildings, equipment, or other property for a specified period of time in return for rent or other compensation. In practice, however, many lease arrangements are the equivalent of installment purchases or other forms of borrowing arrangements.

Acquisition by Purchase

Suppose that a construction firm is in need of earth-moving equipment. The cost of the equipment is $100,000; the estimated useful life is 10 years. Since the company does not have sufficient cash on hand to purchase the equipment, it secures a loan for its full cost. The terms of the loan specify that principal and interest are to be paid in 10 annual installments of equal amount. The amount of each payment is to be determined on the basis of an annual interest rate of 12 percent. If $100,000 is viewed as the present value of an annuity for 10 periods, discounted at a rate of 12 percent, then the annual payment required to amortize the loan can be deter-

mined (per Table 4 of the Appendix) as follows:

$$\$100,000 = 5.6502x$$
$$x = \$17,698$$

Upon purchasing the equipment and borrowing the necessary funds, the company would make the following journal entries:

Cash	$100,000	
Note payable		$100,000

To record the loan of $100,000.

Equipment	$100,000	
Cash		$100,000

To record the purchase of earth-moving equipment.

Each year the company would make the required payment on the note and would record depreciation on the equipment. The division of the payment between principal and interest would, of course, vary from year to year. As the balance of the loan declines, a smaller portion of the payment would be for interest and a larger portion for reduction of the principal. The interest expense for the first year would be 12 percent of the $100,000 balance of the note—$12,000. The remainder of the total payment of $17,698 would be a repayment of the principal. The entry for the payment of the first year would be:

Interest expense	$12,000	
Note payable	5,698	
Cash		$17,698

To record the first payment of the note.

The entry for depreciation (assuming the straight-line method is being used) would be

Depreciation expense	$10,000	
Allowance for depreciation		$10,000

To record depreciation for one year.

Acquisition by Lease—Different from a Purchase Only in Form

Suppose instead, however, that the transaction took a slightly different form. The manufacturer of the earth-moving equipment, upon arrangement with the construction company, sold the equipment to a financial institution, such as a bank or an insurance company. The financial institution thereupon leased the equipment to the construction company. The agreement specified that the term of the lease was to be for 10 years, after which time the construction company would have the option to purchase the equipment for $1. Annual rental charges would be $17,698, and the construction company (the lessee) would have to pay all insurance, maintenance costs, and license fees on the equipment. In economic substance all parties are in the identical position in which they would have been had the company purchased the equipment outright and borrowed the required funds from the financial institution. Annual cash payments by the construction company are the same $17,698. Compare, however, the manner in which the lease, as opposed to the borrow/purchase, transaction might be accounted for. At the time the lease agreement was signed no entry would be required. Each year upon payment of the "rent" the following journal entry would be made:

Rent expense	$17,698	
Cash		$17,698

To record payment of rent for one year.

Depreciation, of course, would not be taken on the equipment, since the equipment itself would never be recorded on the books of the lessee (the construction company).

The fundamental accounting distinction between the transaction as a purchase/borrow arrangement and as a lease is that when con-sidered as a lease the company records on its books neither the asset nor the accompanying liability. From the standpoint of the company, the omission of the liability may represent an important advantage of the lease transaction. Potential creditors and investors may view with disfavor excessive amounts of debt appearing on a balance sheet. Moreover, some loan agreements specify the maximum amount of debt that a company is permitted to incur. The leasing arrangement would be a convenient means of circumventing such restrictions. In effect it would permit the company to arrange for "off the balance sheet" financing of its equipment acquisitions.

Accounting for Financing Leases

There would be little justification for permitting two transactions, the purchase/borrow arrangement and the lease, which are in economic substance identical, to be accounted for differently. The construction company, as a lessee, has the same rights and obligations as it would if it were the legal owner of the equipment. The company bears all risks and has acquired all rights of ownership. Should the equipment last for longer than the estimated 10 years, the company has the option to purchase it for a negligible amount. Should it suffer a major breakdown, the construction company has the obligation to repair it. Moreover, the company has both a legal and a moral obligation to make the specified payments over the life of the lease. The firm that holds title to the equipment, the financial institution, is the owner in name only.

The Accounting Principles Board determined, and the Financial Accounting Standards Board affirmed, that leases which are clearly in substance purchases of property (*financing leases*) should be recorded as such. The acquisition of the construction equipment would be recorded as a purchase. The transaction would be accounted for as the purchase illustrated previously except that appropriately descriptive account titles would be used for both the asset and the liability:

Equipment held
  under lease (asset) $100,000
      Present value
        of lease
        obligations
        (liability) $100,000

To record acquisition of earth-moving equipment under a lease arrangement.

The asset, "equipment held under lease," would be amortized over the useful life of the equipment;* the liability, "present value of lease obligations," would be accounted for as if it were an ordinary interest-bearing note:

Amortization of
  equipment held
  under lease (expense) $10,000
      Equipment held under
        lease, allowance for
        amortization $10,000

To record first-year amortization (straight-line method, useful life of 10 years).

Interest expense (12% of
  $100,000) $12,000
Present value of lease
  obligations   5,698
      Cash $17,698

To record the first lease payment.

Many lease agreements indicate only the amount of annual payments; they do not reveal either the actual purchase price (i.e., the fair market value) of the property trans-

---

* This asset could be amortized over the life of the lease if ownership of the property is not likely to be transferred to the lessee.

ferred or the interest rate used to determine the required amounts of the annual payments. Insofar as the lease agreement is silent on these points, the accountant must look to other borrowing arrangements into which the firm has entered to identify an appropriate rate at which to discount the periodic payments.

Accounting for Operating Leases

Not all lease arrangements are the equivalent of purchases. Businesses enter into rental agreements for a variety of reasons: they need property for only a short period of time; they do not wish to accept the risks of ownership; they do not have the cash necessary to make a purchase and are unable or unwilling to incur additional debt; they want the service and maintenance that might be provided by the lessor.

Traditionally, *operating* leases, those which cover merely the right to use property for a limited time in exchange for periodic rental payments, have been accorded no balance sheet recognition. No entry is made at the time the lease is executed; entries to record the rent expense are made periodically. Many accountants argue, however, that *all* lease agreements (assuming that they are not cancellable) create property rights as well as obligations that deserve to be reported on the balance sheet. A lessee has most of the rights of an owner, with the exception of the right to dispose of the property at its discretion. At the same time, it has the obligation to make rental payments as they come due. The present value of the rights obtained in a lease agreement, according to many accountants, should be *capitalized* and recorded as an asset; the corresponding present value of the obligation should be recorded as a liability. The asset should be amortized (depreciated) over the life of the lease. The stated value of the obligation should be reduced as the periodic rental payments are made. Each rental payment would be considered in part a payment of *principal*, the initial liability being equal to the present value of the property rights, and in part a payment of interest on the unpaid balance of the original obligation.

There are, however, serious obstacles to *capitalizing* (recording as an asset) the value of the property rights inherent in *all* noncancellable lease commitments. It is exceedingly difficult to measure the value of such property rights. Many leases, for example, provide not only for the right to *use* the property but also for services on the part of the lessor. The lessor of an office building, for example, may provide heat, electricity, and janitorial and security services. Consistent with other accounting principles, the rights to receive those types of services are not capitalized as assets—no more than accounting recognition is given to an employment contract at the time it is signed. The task of allocating the lease payments between the right to use the property and the other services provided is likely to be inordinately difficult. Moreover, determination of an appropriate rate at which to discount the lease payments to arrive at their present value is also likely to present difficulties. Whereas in transactions involving purchase-type leases the effective interest rate is often a subject for negotiation, in those pertaining to *operating* (nonpurchase) leases the question of interest may not even be specifically considered.

Distinguishing Criteria

In 1977 in Statement No. 13, the FASB set forth criteria for distinguishing between financing leases and operating leases. According to the board, leases should be considered financing leases and thus capitalized, if the present value of required lease payments is approximately equal to the fair market value of the lease property, if the term of the lease is 75 percent or more of the leased property's estimated useful life, if the lessee has the right either during or at the expiration of the lease agreement to purchase the property from the lessor at an amount less than what the property is actually worth, or if ownership is transferred to the lessee by the end of the lease term. If the agreement does not satisfy any one of these criteria, it should be considered an operating lease and not capitalized. Disclosure of the terms of the lease should be made in a footnote to the financial statements.

The economics of lease financing should be understood by managers, accountants, investors, and lenders. Lease financing may provide a firm with an opportunity to conserve working capital, to avoid some of the risks of ownership, and to take advantage of favorable provisions of the tax regulations. It should not, however, be permitted to result in financial statements which obscure its underlying nature and which imply substantive differences from purchase arrangements where none, in fact, exist.

ACCOUNTING FOR INCOME TAXES

For many companies, taxes based on income represent their single largest recurring expenditure. The combined federal, state, and local income tax rate is sometimes over 50 percent of earnings. Income taxes must obviously be a major factor to be accounted for in any business decision. The proper determination of tax liability is also a critical element of financial reporting.

Permanent as Distinguished from Timing Differences

As a general rule, corporate earnings on which income taxes are based are determined in the same manner as for general financial reporting. There are, however, a number of exceptions. The exceptions fall into two broad categories: permanent differences and timing differences. A permanent difference is one in which, because of special legislative consideration, particular revenues or expenses are omitted from computation of taxable income. Interest on municipal bonds, for example, is not taxable by the federal government and hence, in calculating the income on which the federal income tax is based, it would be omitted from the revenues. Similarly, under certain circumstances charitable contributions, officers' salaries, and life insurance premiums may be corporate expenses which are not deductible in the determination of taxable income and would therefore be excluded from expenses.

A timing difference, on the other hand, is one in which an item is reflected in income for tax purposes in one period but in income for general reporting purposes in another. For example, a dance studio may sell to a customer a series of dance lessons. The customer pays for the lessons in advance. As illustrated previously in the text, for purposes of general reporting the company would properly record the revenue in the periods in which the lessons were actually taken. In the computation of taxable income, however, the revenue would be taken into account in the period in which the cash was collected. An oil company, in searching for new oil, incurs costs of drilling dry holes. Such costs for general reporting purposes may be considered unavoidable costs of discovering the actual location of the oil and thereby capitalized and written off over the period during which the oil is removed from the producing wells. For tax purposes, however, the costs may be considered expenses in the year in which actually incurred.

Taxes Must Be Reported with Related Revenue or Expense

Because of the magnitude of the tax rate, financial statements can easily be distorted if the tax expenditure or deduction associated with a particular revenue or expense is reported in a period other than that in which the revenue or expense is recorded. Consider the following (exaggerated) example.

The income of a company before consideration of depreciation and income taxes is $1,000 in both year 1 and year 2. Equipment had been purchased at the beginning of year 1 for $1,000 and has an estimated useful life of only two years and no salvage value. For purposes of financial reporting the company computes depreciation using the straight-line method. Hence, depreciation is $500 per year. The Federal government, however, permits the use of accelerated depreciation for computation of taxable income. The company elects to compute depreciation for tax purposes using the double-declining balance method, because it would result in the postponement (though by no means the reduction) of taxes. Since, in the absence of a salvage value, the double-declining balance method results in a depreciation charge in the first year of twice that determined by the straight-line method, depreciation in year 1 would be $1,000. In year 2, the asset would have been fully depreciated; hence zero depreciation would be charged. (Note that in this particular case depreciation in year 2 is zero. As a general rule, however, the number of years over which an asset is depreciated is the same regardless of depreciation method used.) Assume that the tax rate is 40 percent.

As illustrated in Exhibit 10-3, reported income of the company, before income taxes, is $500 in both year 1 and year 2. *Taxable* income, however, is zero in year 1 and $1,000 in year 2. Therefore, required tax payments are zero in year 1 and $400 in year 2.

If the company were to report a tax expense of $0 in year 1 and $400 in year 2, then income after taxes in year 1 and year 2 would be $500 and $100, respectively:

	Year 1	Year 2
Income before taxes (from Exhibit 10-3)	$500	$500
Tax expense (from Exhibit 10-3)	-0-	400
Income after taxes	$500	$100

Many managers and accountants would aver, however, that such computation of income after taxes is misleading. They would question whether the company really earned $400 more in year 1 than in year 2. They would assert that to the extent that an investor relies upon earnings of the past as a guide to earnings of the future, he would be seriously misled by the year 1 report of income. They would contend that income before taxes was the same in both year 1 and year 2 and that since income taxes are based on income, the reported tax expense should be the same in each of the two years. At the end of the first year the company had an effective liability (though certainly not a legal one) for taxes of $200 (40 percent of $500). The Federal government, through special provisions of tax laws, allowed the company to *postpone* the payment of the taxes until the following year. The following journal

EXHIBIT 10-3

Reported Income as Compared to Taxable Income

Asset cost: $1,000
Useful life: 2 years
Tax rate: 40%
Methods of depreciation: Straight-line for general reporting purposes, double-declining balance for tax purposes.

Income Before Taxes—General Reporting Purposes

	Year 1	Year 2
Income before depreciation and taxes	$1,000	$1,000
Depreciation	500	500
Income before taxes	$ 500	$ 500

Required Tax Payment

	Year 1	Year 2
Income before depreciation and taxes	$1,000	$1,000
Depreciation	1,000	-0-
Taxable income	$-0-	$1,000
Tax rate	40%	40%
Required tax payment	$-0-	$ 400

entries, they contend, would give effect to the economic substance of the taxes on income:

Year 1

Tax expense (40% of $500)	$200	
Taxes deferred until future years (liability)		$200

To record tax expense.

Year 2

Tax expense (40% of $500)	$200	
Taxes deferred until future years	200	
Taxes payable in current year		$400

To record tax expense.

As the taxes are actually paid, the usual

recognition would be given to the payment:

Taxes payable in current year $400
  Cash $400

To record tax payment.

The procedure by which the reported tax expense is based on reported *income*, as opposed to the actual legal liability (the taxes indicated as due per the tax return), is often referred to as *interperiod tax allocation*. The Accounting Principles Board in Opinion No. 11, "Accounting for Income Taxes," specifically prescribed that interperiod tax allocation be an integral part of the determination of the income tax expense.

Reported Tax Expense Based on Reported Pretax Income

In essence, tax allocation requires that the reported income tax expense be based on pretax accounting income. The reported tax liability is divided into two parts: (1) the portion that is currently payable and (2) that which can be deferred until future periods.

The portion that is currently payable is based on the liability per the tax return (that is, on *taxable* income). The deferred portion is ordinarily the difference between the reported tax expense and the portion of the liability that is currently payable. In years in which the firm is able to postpone taxes, the deferred portion of the liability is ordinarily credited (that is, the deferred liability is increased); in years in which the firm must "repay" the taxes that had been postponed, the deferred liability is debited (and thereby decreased). The following example illustrates a timing difference in which revenue is included in years subsequent to those in which it is included in accounting (reported) income.

Example

The Ann Arbor Bridge Co. received in 1982 a $40 million contract to construct a bridge across the Huron River. The company estimates that construction costs will total $36 million and that the bridge will be built over a two-year period.

The company estimates that construction and collection of cash will adhere to the following timetable:

	Percent Completed in Year	Percent Cash Collected in Year
1982	20	—
1983	80	25
1984	—	75

The company decides to report in its financial statements earnings from the contract on a percentage of completion basis but elects to report the earnings on its income

EXHIBIT 10-4

		Required Tax Payments (Installment Basis)		
		1982	1983	1984
Revenue		$ -0-	$10,000,000 (25%)	$30,000,000 (75%)
Expenses applicable to revenues (36/40ths of revenues)		-0-	9,000,000 (25%)	27,000,000 (75%)
Taxable income		$ -0-	$ 1,000,000	$ 3,000,000
Tax rate		40%	40%	40%
Tax		$ -0-	$ 400,000	$ 1,200,000

EXHIBIT 10-4 (continued)

Income Statement for Purposes of Financial Reporting
(Percentage-of-Completion Basis)

	1982	1983	1984
Revenue	$8,000,000 (20%)	$32,000,000 (80%)	$ -0-
Expenses applicable to revenues (36/40ths of revenues)	7,200,000 (20%)	28,800,000 (80%)	-0-
Income before taxes	$ 800,000	$ 3,200,000	$ -0-
Tax expense (40%)	320,000	1,280,000	-0-
Net income	$ 480,000	$ 1,920,000	$ -0-

tax return on an installment basis (i.e., as cash is collected).

The tax rate is 40 percent. The required tax payments and income statement is shown in Exhibit 10-4.

In the income statement, the tax expense is based on the reported income before taxes, irrespective of the required tax payment. *The tax expense follows the income.*

The following journal entries would effect the appropriate *allocation* of taxes. It is assumed for convenience that the required tax payment (the current portion of the liability) is made entirely in the year to which it is applicable, although in practice a part of the payment is likely to be delayed until the following year.

Year 1982

Tax expense $320,000
 Taxes deferred until
  future years $320,000
To record tax expense. (No tax payment need be made in 1982; tax expense represents 40 percent of reported income before taxes of $800,000.)

Year 1983

Tax expense $1,280,000
 Taxes payable in
  current year $400,000
 Taxes deferred until
  future years 880,000

To record tax expense. (Required tax payment is $400,000; tax expense represents 40 percent of reported income before taxes of $3,200,000.)

Taxes payable in
 current year $400,000
  Cash $400,000
To record payment of taxes.

Year 1984

Taxes deferred until
 future years $1,200,000
  Cash $1,200,000
To record payment of taxes. (Required tax payment is $1,200,000; reported income is zero so no tax expense need be charged.)

The liability, "taxes deferred until future years" would be reported on the balance sheet among the current or noncurrent liabilities, depending on when it is likely to be liquidated. The balance in the account will increase in those years in which the tax expense exceeds the required tax payments and decrease in those years in which required tax payments exceed the tax expense.

Taxes deferred until future years

		(1982)	320,000
		(1983)	880,000
(1984)	1,200,000		

Controversy Continues

The issue of whether or not taxes should, in fact, be allocated among accounting periods, as presently required, has been the subject of considerable debate among accountants. Tax allocation is rooted in the matching concept; it is designed to give effect to a cause and effect relationship between income and tax expense. It is intended to prevent businesses from reporting a relatively high income in one period only to have to report a correspondingly low income in a future period when taxes that have been postponed from the earlier years must be paid.

Many accountants contend, however, that income taxes are sufficiently different from other types of costs that application of the matching principle may be inappropriate. Income taxes, they assert, are not functionally related to revenues or even to pretax reported income. They are related instead to *taxable* income. The accountants believe, therefore, that requirements that the taxes be matched to reported income are of questionable validity.

They also point out that tax allocation can result in financial statements in which liabilities are materially overstated in that deferred tax obligations may never, in fact, have to be paid. For most companies, the deferred tax liability is attributable primarily to the use of accelerated depreciation methods for tax purposes but straight-line depreciation for general financial reporting. Insofar as a company continually replaces its assets, each year it would be able to postpone a portion of its taxes. As the taxes associated with assets purchased earlier must be paid, taxes associated with the more recent acquisitions may be postponed. The deferred tax liability will continuously *roll over*, and in a sense be postponed indefinitely. If, on the other hand, the firm is expanding, then the deferred tax liability will increase year by year. The continuous buildup of such liabilities has been of concern to many financial analysts. They contend that, in reality, it is often unlikely that the reported deferred tax obligation will have to be liquidated in the foreseeable future. Therefore, they assert, the tax allocation process results in financial reports in which liabilities are substantially overstated.*

INVESTMENT TAX CREDIT

In the early 1960s, in an effort to stimulate corporate investment in plant and equipment, Congress provided for a tax credit of up to 7 percent of the cost of new facilities. Since then the credit has periodically been revoked and reinstituted; in 1975, the maximum credit was increased to 10 percent. From the time it was introduced, however, the proper means of accounting for the credit has been a major source of controversy.

A tax credit must be distinguished from a tax deduction. A tax deduction reduces the income on which tax is computed. A tax credit, by contrast, directly reduces the tax itself. The investment tax credit provides that up to 10 percent (1982 rates) of the cost of eligible plant and equipment can be used to offset a firm's required tax payment. If, for example, a firm purchased $500,000 of eligible plant and equipment, then it could

---

* The counter to the argument that the deferred tax liability will continuously roll over and thus be postponed indefinitely is that accounts payable also continuously roll over. As long as a firm continues to function at its present level or to expand, then its liability for accounts payable, like that for deferred taxes, is unlikely to ever be liquidated. Few, if any, accountants would argue that accounts payable should not be reported on the balance sheet.

reduce its current tax liability by $50,000. In addition, it could take *deductions* for depreciation on the full $500,000 (less any salvage value) over the useful life of the equipment.

The accounting question evoked by the investment tax credit is whether such credit should reduce the *reported* tax expense only in the year the equipment is purchased (and the year in which the credit is granted) or whether it should be spread over the useful life of the equipment. On the one hand, it has been argued that the credit represents a permanent reduction of tax (as opposed to the temporary reductions discussed in the preceding section) and that the benefits from such reduction should be reported to investors in the year in which they are granted. On the other hand, it has been asserted that the tax credit has the effect of reducing the net cost of the asset. The cost of an asset is charged to expense (through the process of depreciation) over its useful life. The tax credit should be accounted for in a way that would reduce the costs that would otherwise have to be charged as expenses over the useful life of the equipment.

The accounting method by which the credit reduces *reported* tax expense in the year in which it is granted is known as the *flow-through* method (because the credit "flows" directly into income) and the method by which it reduces expenses over the life of the property is referred to as the *deferral*, or *amortization*, method.

Deferral (Amortization) Method

Suppose that a firm has a tax obligation of $1,000,000 prior to consideration of an investment tax credit of $50,000. Useful life of the property acquired is ten years. If it were to use the deferral method, then in the year it acquired the property the firm would make the following two entries relating to income taxes:

(a)

Tax expense	$1,000,000	
Investment tax credit		$ 50,000
Cash (or taxes currently		
payable)		950,000

To record tax expense.

(b)

Investment tax credit	$5,000	
Tax expense		$5,000

To record the amortization of the investment tax credit (based on an estimated useful life of the property of 10 years).

The net effect of the two entries is to reflect a reported tax expense of only $995,000. During each of the remaining nine years of the asset's useful life, the reported tax expense would be reduced by $5,000 [by way of an amortization entry like (b)], and the remaining balance in the "investment tax credit" account would also be reduced by the same amount.* The "investment tax credit" account would, of course, always have a credit balance. It could be reported on the balance sheet either as a deferred revenue (similar to revenues received but not yet earned) or as an account contra to the property with which it is associated.

Flow-Through Method

If the firm were to use the flow-through method then reported tax expense would be equal to the required tax payment—$950,000. *Reported* tax expense would be $45,000 less in the year the property is acquired than if the deferral method were used. In each of the subsequent nine years, however, it would be $5,000 greater. The actual tax payments that

---

* Alternatively, the credit could be reflected each year as a reduction of depreciation expense rather than tax expense.

the firm is required to make would be unaffected by choice of method.

At one time, the Accounting Principles Board specified that the allowable investment credit should be reflected in income over the productive life of the acquired property (the deferral method) and not only in the year in which it is placed in service. Subsequently, however, while reaffirming its preference for the deferral method, it permitted firms to use either of the two methods.

Misplaced Concern over *Reported* Earnings

In 1971 Congress passed into law a provision that prohibited any professional accounting body (it was aimed at the Accounting Principles Board and the Securities and Exchange Commission) from requiring that firms use the deferral method exclusively. The provision was intended to ensure that the credit had maximum impact on earnings in the year a firm purchased the eligible property.

The Congressional action was significant for at least two reasons. First, it demonstrated that Congress has, and may sometimes be willing to exercise, the authority to establish accounting principles. Second, it emphasized the importance that some groups place on *reported* earnings of corporations. The legislation was apparently passed in response to pressure from both industry groups and the U.S. Treasury Department. They believed that the credit would provide a stimulus to the economy that was both more pronounced and more immediate if it could be reflected in full in corporate earnings in the year in which it was granted. Whether or not they are correct is questionable. Financial statements do not establish the financial health of an enterprise; they only report upon it. The tax credit serves to reduce taxes (and thereby reduce cash out-

flow) in the year in which the eligible property is purchased—regardless of the manner in which it is accounted for. The economic well-being of the corporation is, in substance, unchanged by the manner in which accountants elect—or are required—to describe it.

PENSIONS

Pensions represent periodic payments to retired or disabled employees owing to their years of employment. Although there is a great variety of pension plans, most require that a company make fixed monthly payments to an employee from the time of his retirement to the date of either his death or that of his surviving spouse.

At one time pensions were viewed as discretionary payments made by a company to its loyal and dedicated employees. Today they are contractual obligations of a company and are incorporated into almost all collective bargaining agreements.

The accounting issues pertaining to pension plans arise from the fact that payments to an employee do not have to be made until he retires, yet the cost to the company clearly arises from the service that he provides during his period of employment. Most companies make periodic payments into a pension fund in order to assure the availability of cash as required. The amount that a company must provide in current periods, in order to meet the future pensions of employees who are presently active, is *actuarially* determined. (An actuary is a statistician who computes insurance risks and premiums.) It is dependent on estimates of life expectancy, employee turnover (since only a portion of present employees is likely to remain with a company sufficiently long to be eligible for pension benefits), and the rate of return that the company will earn on investments purchased with the cash that has been contributed to the pension fund. The specific method that a firm uses to determine the amount of its required payments to the pension fund is referred to as its *actuarial cost method*.

The importance of proper accounting for pensions was vividly demonstrated in the mid-1970s when it became widely known that the financial states of several major U.S. cities were substantially worse than indicated by their financial reports. These cities did not adhere to generally accepted accounting principles and failed to disclose pension obligations of hundreds of millions of dollars to both current and previous employees.

Accrual Basis

Pension costs must be accounted for on an accrual basis. Regardless of when a company actually *funds* (makes the required payments to the pension fund) its pension plan, the company receives the benefit of an employee's services in the years in which he has actually worked. Pension costs, like direct wage payments, must be charged as expenses in the periods in which the employees provide their services.

The *pension fund* itself is ordinarily a separate legal and accounting entity. Its assets consist entirely of cash, securities, and other income-earning investments. Its liabilities are composed primarily of the *estimated* claims of the employees—the actuarial value of their vested (contractually required) benefits. Neither the assets nor the liabilities of the pension fund are reported on the balance sheet of the corporation.

Expense Represents *Required* Payments

The amount that the corporation reports as its pension expense represents its *required* payments to the pension fund as determined

by the actuarial cost method that it elects to use. The difference between the required payment and the amount that it actually pays into the fund is recorded as a liability (accrued pension expense) if the required payment exceeds the actual payment. The difference is recorded as an asset (prepaid pension expense) if the actual payment exceeds the required payment. Assume, for example, that the required payment to the pension fund, as determined by an appropriate actuarial cost method, is $500,000. In fact, however, the company contributes only $400,000. The following journal entries would be required:

(a)

Pension expense	$500,000	
Accrued pension costs (liability)		$500,000

To record pension expense.

(b)

Accrued pension cost (liability)	$400,000	
Cash		$400,000

To record contributions to the pension fund.

The pension liability, as reported on the balance sheet, is increased each year by the recorded pension expense; it is decreased by payments to the pension fund.

Prior Service Costs

The problem of accounting for pension costs is further complicated by the fact that when a firm first adopts a pension plan or makes significant improvements to its plan it is likely to incur an immediate obligation to make payments to the pension funds. That is because additional benefits will probably have to be made available to all employees presently on the payroll—including those who are near retirement age. The new benefits can be attributed to the employees' *prior service* to the company, but the company will not yet have funded such benefits.

It would generally cause a company serious economic hardship if it had to fund all *prior service costs* (those based on service in past years) in the year in which the plan or changes to the plan are adopted. Similarly, it would seriously distort income if the costs of such prior services were charged to income in a single year. As a consequence, firms are permitted to amortize (spread) such costs over a 40-year period. The amount of the liability for such past service costs must, however, be reported in footnotes to the financial statements.

Because there are several actuarial cost methods by which a firm can elect to determine its required payments to the pension fund, reported pension expenses of firms with similar pension obligations may not be readily comparable. The essential point to bear in mind, however, in reviewing financial reports is that the reported pension expense represents actuarially *required* payments to a pension fund (*not actual* payments to pensioners or even to the pension fund) and that the reported balance sheet liability represents the cumulative difference between such required payments and the actual payments (not the actual liability to the pensioners).

SUMMARY

In this chapter we have reviewed the means by which several types of liabilities—bonds, as well as those relating to leases, taxes, and pensions—are accounted for. Each of the liabilities is directly related to an expense—interest expense, income tax expense, and pension expense. A central theme of the chapter has been that the amount at which the liability is stated on the balance sheet has a direct impact upon the amount of expense reported on the income statement. As emphasized in each of the chapters pertaining to assets, all questions of balance sheet valuations must necessarily be considered within a context of income determination.

EXERCISE FOR REVIEW AND SELF-TESTING

On January 1, 1983, a company issued bonds. The bonds had an established coupon rate of 14 percent, but they were issued at a price that provided bondholders a return of only 12 percent. The bonds were to mature in 20 years.

1. For each $1,000 bond, how much interest will the company be required to pay each six months?

2. For each $1,000 bond held, how much interest would a bondholder expect to receive semiannually based on the prevailing yields of comparable securities?

3. What is the difference between the two amounts?

4. What is the present value of such a difference based on the effective yield rate (compounded semiannually) and the number of periods until maturity?

5. What is the amount of premium or discount at which the bond will be issued? What is the issue price of each $1,000 bond?

6. What is the amount of interest, based on the effective yield rate, that the company should record as an expense when, on June 30, 1983, it is required to make the first interest payment?

7. What is the actual amount of required payment?

8. What is the difference between the two amounts? By how much should the recorded value of the bond premium be reduced?

9. What is the effective liability of the company, per bond, on July 1, 1983?

10. What is the amount of interest expense that the company should record on December 31, 1983, when it is required to make its second payment of interest?

QUESTIONS FOR REVIEW AND DISCUSSION

1. A friend recently purchased $10,000 of American Telephone & Telegraph Company bonds. The company is considered as financially sound as any major U.S. corporation. The bonds are scheduled to mature in 30 years, but your friend intends to sell them within 2 or 3 years in order to provide funds for her child's education. She wants a "safe" investment. She decided not to purchase the common stock of the same company because she viewed it as too risky. Do you think she made a wise decision? Would she have been better off buying AT & T bonds that matured in only 3 years? Explain.

2. The account "discount on bonds payable" ordinarily has a debit balance. It has sometimes been argued that bond discount, like most other accounts which have debit balances, should be reported as an asset rather than as *contra* (as an adjustment) to a long-term liability. Considering the nature of bond discounts, do you agree?

3. For many years there has been controversy over the accounting for gains and losses which may arise when a company repurchases or redeems its own bonds at a price different from the value at which they are recorded on its books. Why have some financial observers charged that major corporations have engaged in repurchases or redemptions in order to give an artificial boost to earnings? How is this possible?

4. Why are some lease arrangements accounted for as if they were installment purchases? Why do some accountants believe that almost all long-term noncancellable lease agreements should be *capitalized* (i.e., assets and corresponding liabilities recorded) on the balance sheet? Why might a company believe that it is able to present a more favorable balance sheet by leasing, rather than purchasing, plant or equipment?

5. Why might a company report a tax expense on its income statement that is greater or less than the required tax payment as indicated on its income tax return?

6. Why do some financial experts contend that interperiod tax allocation results in an overstatement of liabilities, in that amounts which may never have to be paid are included among reported obligations?

7. Distinguish between a tax *deduction* and a tax *credit*.

8. What is the impact on both income and assets of accounting for the investment tax credit by the flow-through as opposed to the amortization method?

9. What does reported pension expense represent? What does the liability for accrued pension costs represent?

10. On the books of which accounting entity would a firm's actual liability to its employees for pension benefits be reported?

11. What is meant by "prior service costs?" How are they accounted for?

PROBLEMS

1. The amount for which a bond is issued, as well as subsequent charges to income, is dependent upon the prevailing yield rate at the time of issue.

On January 2, 1982, the Green Company issued 12 percent coupon bonds at a price which provided purchasers a yield of 10 percent. The bonds paid interest on June 30 and December 31 and were scheduled to mature at December 31, 1983.
a. Record the sale of a single $1,000 bond.
b. Determine interest expense for each of the four periods and record the first payment of interest.
c. Record the redemption of the bond (including final interest payment).

2. The prices at which outstanding bonds can be resold fluctuate with changes in the prevailing rates of interest.

On May 1, 1980, the Baltimore Co. issued at par (i.e., at a price of $100) $10 million in 8 percent, 20-year coupon bonds. Interest is payable semi-annually.

a. Within two years, prevailing interest rates had increased to 10 percent. At what price could a bondholder sell a single $1,000 bond in the open market?

b. By the fourth year, prevailing interest rates had increased to 12 percent. At what price could a bondholder now sell a single $1,000 bond?

c. What impact would the increase in prevailing interest rates have upon the reported interest expense of the Baltimore Co.?

d. "In comparison with common stocks, bonds provide a relatively risk-free investment." Do you agree?

3. Call provisions may establish a ceiling on the prices at which outstanding bonds are traded.

The Universal Drilling Co. issued, in 1965, $100,000 of 6 percent, 30-year bonds. The bond indenture agreement provided that the company could redeem the bonds any time after 1975 at a price of $102.

In 1980, with 15 years remaining until maturity, the company decided to retire the bonds. Since the prevailing interest rate was 8 percent, the company elected to repurchase the bonds in the open market at the prevailing price.

a. Determine the price that the company would have to pay for the bonds.

b. Assume instead that the prevailing annual interest rate in 1980 was 4 percent. Determine the price that the company would have to pay for the bonds. Be sure to consider the maximum price at which the bonds are likely to trade in light of the call provision.

4. Bonds may also be issued between interest dates, and, although not specifically discussed in the text, the accounting problems associated with such issues are not overly complex.

The city of Highland Hills on January 31, 1982, issues 6 percent coupon bonds to mature in 20 years. The bonds are sold, at par, to yield 6 percent. The bonds require the payment of interest on June 30 and December 31.

a. What will be the required interest payment on June 30, 1982, on a single $1,000-denomination bond? (All coupons, including the first, require the payment of the same amount of interest.)

b. Since the bondholder on June 30 would have held the bond for only five months, how much interest would he have earned (i.e., would he actually "deserve" to receive)?

c. Suppose the bondholder agreed to *advance* the company the amount of that portion of the first interest payment that he did not actually earn. How much would he advance the company?

d. Prepare a journal entry to record the issue of one bond, assuming that the company received the principal plus the unearned portion of the first interest payment.

e. Prepare a journal entry to record the first interest payment. The interest expense should represent the cost of borrowing funds only for the period during which the company had the use of such funds.

5. Principles of accounting for financial reporting may not be appropriate for managerial decision making.

In January 1955, the Bowman Co. issued $100,000 of 6 percent, 30-year coupon bonds. The indenture agreement stipulates that the company has the right to *call* (redeem) the bonds at a price of $103 any time after the bonds have been outstanding for 10 years. In 1980 the bonds were stated on the company's books at a value of $98,300; there was a reported discount of $1,700.

In January 1980, when 5 years remained until maturity, the company controller debated whether or not he should refund the entire bond issue—that is, whether he should redeem the bonds and reborrow the entire cost of redemption. The controller determined that he could acquire the entire $103,000 necessary to call the outstanding issue by issuing, at par, bonds that paid interest at an annual rate of 5 percent and matured in 5 years.

The company uses a discount rate of 8 percent to evaluate all financial opportunities.

a. Prepare a journal entry that would be required to record the redemption of the bonds.

b. In view of the fact that the company would have to report a loss on the redemption of the bonds, the controller decided against redeeming the bonds. Do you agree with his decision? [*Hint:* Identify all cash receipts and disbursements that would result in the next 5 years (10 semiannual periods) under both of the alternatives. Determine their present value *to the company*.]

6. *The straight-line method of bond amortization distorts the cost of borrowing.*

In the past, companies, wishing to avoid the complexities of the *effective interest* means of accounting for bond premium or discount, used the *straight-line* amortization method.

Suppose a company issues 12 percent coupon bonds at a price which would provide a return to the bondholders of 10 percent. The bonds will mature in 20 years.

a. Prepare a journal entry to record the issue of a single $1,000 bond.
b. Prepare journal entries to record both the *first* and the *last* payments of interest. Assume first that the company uses the effective interest method and second the straight-line method. Be sure to determine the *effective* liability outstanding at the *start* of each of the periods.
c. Determine the effective rate of interest recorded as an expense under each of the two methods for both the first and the last payments. That is, express the recorded interest expense as a percentage of the reported effective liability (bond payable plus unamortized premium).

7. *By redeeming its debt at a "bargain" price, a firm is able to realize a substantial gain.*

The 1976 financial statements of Chessie System, Inc., contained the following note:

During 1975 [the company] purchased $11.6 million principal amount of its $4\frac{1}{2}\%$ convertible debentures due 2010 at a price of $550 each under a tender offer. The resulting net gain was $2.6 million after related deferred Federal income taxes of $2.4 million.

a. Chessie System, Inc., was a financially sound company. Why do you suspect that it was able to redeem its outstanding debt at a "bargain" price?
b. The note makes reference to *deferred* federal income taxes. What does the use of the term *deferred* suggest about the provisions of the tax laws pertaining to gains on the redemption of bonds?

c. Suppose that the company was unable to pay off its debt without reducing the scale of its operations. It therefore had to reborrow the amount that it paid to the holders of the $4\frac{1}{2}$ percent debentures. How do you think the rate of interest on the new debt would compare with that on the old (much higher, much lower, etc.)? Will the company really be better off as a consequence of having "refunded" (paid off and reborrowed) its debt? What is the real nature of the gain of $5 million (before taxes)? When did the gain really occur—at the time of refunding or in the several previous accounting periods?

8. *An important issue facing banks and other financial institutions is whether they should give immediate accounting recognition to unfavorable modifications in the terms of debt arrangements.*

In January 1980 a bank acquired $1 million of the bonds of Gotham City. The bonds paid interest at a rate of 10 percent and were sold to yield 10 percent (that is, they were sold "at par"). The bonds were to mature in five years.

Shortly after the bank made its investment in the bonds, Gotham City faced a fiscal crisis. After a series of complex legal maneuvers, it was able to "restructure" its debt. The city was permitted to extend the maturity of the debt from five years to ten years and to reduce the rate of interest paid from 10 percent to 6 percent. The amount of principal owed (the face value of the bonds) was to remain unchanged.

a. What is the value to the bank of its Gotham City bonds immediately following the restructure? That is, what is the present value, discounted at the prevailing yield rate of 10 percent per year (5 percent per period), of the anticipated payment of $1 million in principal and the anticipated 20 semiannual payments of $30,000 in interest?
b. Do you think that the bank should "write down" the carrying value of the bonds from $1 million to the amount determined in Part a and thereby recognize an immediate loss? If it did, what would be the impact on earnings of the current year and future years as compared to that if it did not? Would total earnings, over the remaining life of the issue, be affected by a decision

to recognize an immediate loss? (*Note:* The question of how to account for "restructured debt," although not specifically dealt with in the text, was an important issue in the mid-1970s as a consequence of fiscal crises that faced New York City as well as a large number of firms in the real estate industry. The FASB, in Statement No. 15, ruled that in situations similar to the one described in this problem no write-down would be required. However, in cases where total anticipated receipts of both principal and interest, without regard to their *present* value, are less than the carrying value of the debt, an immediate loss would have to be recognized.)

9. Bonds can provide substantial returns to their holders—even if they pay zero interest.

The *Wall Street Journal* recently reported that PepsiCo, Inc., plans "to take out a 'loan' on which it won't have to pay any interest for 30 years."

According to the *Wall Street Journal*, the company would issue bonds that won't pay annual interest. Instead the bonds, known as "zero coupon" securities, would be sold at a "deep discount" from face value and then redeemed at the full amount upon maturity. The difference between the two would be the investors' return.

The *Wall Street Journal* indicated that PepsiCo would issue $25 million of the new securities. Initially, each bond with a face value of $1,000 would be priced at $270.

a. Suppose that a 30-year bond was priced to sell for $270. What would be the effective percentage yield (within 1 percent) to the purchaser. (In order to be able to make use of the tables in the appendix, assume that interest is compounded annually rather than semiannually.)

b. What would be the primary advantage to the borrower in issuing zero coupon bonds?

c. Suppose, as in Part a, that a bond was issued for $270. What journal entry would you propose that the firm make to record:
   1. Issuance of the bond?
   2. First-year interest expense?
   3. Second-year interest expense?

10. Principles of liability valuation are essential to assessing the assets of thrifts (saving and loan

associations) as well as financial institutions in general.

A letter to the *Wall Street Journal* stated: "'Threat to Thrifts' [a previous article] skirts the real, present financial plight of not only thrifts but of banking institutions in general. So-called 'net worth' is only an illusion, a distortion of reality resulting from the treatment of 8% mortgage loans with 15 years amortization as being worth the principal balance due on them rather than the market value, in today's 15% mortgage market, of less than 70% of the unpaid balance. (The Penn Central also had an impressive net worth prior to its bankruptcy.)" The author went on to suggest that a more meaningful measure of the assets (i.e., the mortgage loans outstanding) of a thrift institution would be their current market values.

Suppose that a thrift institution issued a 30-year mortgage loan of $100,000 at an annual rate of interest of 8 percent. Annual payments on the loan were $8,883. (Although mortgage notes often require monthly payments, assume for convenience in this problem that only one payment per year is required.) Each yearly payment would contain an element of interest (8 percent of the remaining loan balance) and an element of principal.

a. What would be the "book value" (i.e., the remaining principal balance) of the loan after 15 years?

b. What would be the most likely market value of the loan assuming that prevailing interest rates on mortgage loans had increased to 15 percent?

c. Is the letter writer correct in asserting that market value is likely to be less than 70 percent of the book value (unpaid principal balance)?

11. The distinction, in economic substance, between an installment purchase and a financial lease may be trivial.

The indenture agreement associated with the outstanding bonds of the Eastern Machine Co. stipulates the maximum amount of debt that the company can incur. The company wishes to expand its plant and purchase new equipment, but the company has insufficient funds to purchase the equipment outright. Since the company is prohibited by the existing bond indentures from borrowing the needed funds, the controller of the company has suggested that the firm arrange for the manufacturer of the equipment to sell the equipment to a lending institution. The lending institution would, in turn, lease the machine to the company. The lending institution would provide no maintenance or related services, and the company would have responsibility for insuring the equipment. Upon the expiration of the lease, the company would have the option of purchasing the equipment. If the company were to acquire the equipment outright, its cost would be $500,000. If it were to borrow the funds, it would be required to pay interest at the rate of 8 percent per year. The financial institution has agreed to a noncancellable lease with a term of 15 years, a term corresponding to the useful life of the equipment.

a. If the company decides to lease the equipment, what would be the most probable annual rental payments?

b. How do you suspect the controller intends to account for the acquisition of the equipment? What journal entries do you think he would propose at the time the equipment is acquired? At the time the first payment of rent is made?

c. Do the proposals of the controller in your opinion reflect the substance of the transaction? Are they in accord with provisions of the Financial Accounting Standards Board? What alternative journal entries would you propose?

12. *Recent pronouncements of the FASB are intended to prevent firms from avoiding balance sheet disclosure of financial obligations by leasing rather than purchasing long-lived assets.*

The managers of Business Services, Inc., are debating whether to buy or to rent a computer. A computer manufacturer has offered the company the opportunity to lease a machine for $100,000 per year over a period of 15 years. Alternatively, the company could purchase the machine outright and could borrow the purchase price from an insurance company at an annual rate of 10 percent. The note to the insurance company would be repaid in 15 equal installments, each installment representing both a repayment of principal and a payment of interest on the unpaid balance.

Costs of operating the equipment would be the same under either alternative; the salvage value after 15 years would be negligible.

Currently the company has total assets of $5 million, total liabilities of $2 million, and total owners' equity of $3 million.

a. What is the maximum that the company should be willing to pay to purchase the machine?

b. Suppose that the company paid such maximum amount. Compare total expenses that would be reported during the first year if the company purchased the machine as opposed to leasing it assuming that it accounts for the transaction as an operating lease (although under current FASB pronouncements the lease would satisfy the criteria of a financing lease). The company uses the straight-line method of depreciation.

c. Determine the ratio of total debt to total owners' equity under each of the alternatives immediately upon acquisition of the asset (prior to giving effect to first-year expenses).

13. *The perceptive financial analyst would adjust for differences between companies relating to the means of financing and accounting for long-term assets and obligations.*

As a financial analyst, you are reviewing annual reports for the year 1982 of two chains of discount department stores. The reports indicate that one of the two companies owns all of its stores; the other leases them. A footnote to the financial statements of the firm that leases contained the following information:

The company operates principally in leased premises. The basic terms of the leases generally range from 10 to 20 years. The leases meet the criteria of noncapitalized leases (operating leases) as defined by the Financial Accounting Standards Board and accordingly have not been included among long-term liabilities. Total minimum rental commitments are as follows (in thousands):

1983–1987	$30,000 per year
1988–1997	$25,000 per year
1998–2002	$10,000 per year

An additional note in the financial statements indicates that the company's cost of borrowing is 12 percent.

What adjustments to the assets and liabilities of the firm that leases its stores would make its financial reports comparable with those of the firm that owns the stores?

14. *Under deferred tax accounting, reported tax expense may differ from the required tax payment.*

A company acquires an asset at a cost of $30,000. The asset has an estimated useful life of three years and an estimated residual value of $6,000. The company computes depreciation on the straight-line basis for purposes of financial reporting but uses the sum-of-the-years' digits method in reporting to taxing authorities. In each of the three years that the company uses the asset, it expects to have earnings, before taking into account depreciation and taxes, of $20,000. The applicable tax rate is 40 percent.

Complete the following table:

	Year 1	Year 2	Year 3
Depreciation			
Reporting purposes			
Tax purposes			
Income before taxes			
Reporting purposes			
Tax purposes			
Taxes			
Reported expense			
Required payment			
Deferred tax account			
Amount to be added or subtracted during year			
Balance at end of year			

15. *Reported tax expense may be substantially greater than the required tax payment.*

In 1982 the ELS Company had income, before depreciation on assets purchased in that year and before taxes, of $20 million. During the year it purchased equipment for $4 million. The equipment has a useful life of eight years and no salvage value. All of the equipment purchased is eligible for the 10 percent investment tax credit.

The company charges depreciation on a straight-line basis for financial reporting purposes but uses the double-declining balance method for tax purposes. It accounts for the investment credit by the deferral method. The tax rate is 40 percent.

a. Compute the actual amount of taxes for 1982 that the company will be required to pay.
b. Determine reported tax expense and net income (i.e., income after taxes).

16. *By the time an asset is fully depreciated, the balance in the deferred tax account related to that asset should be reduced to zero.*

The Frost Co. purchased equipment in 1980 at a cost of $100,000. The equipment had an estimated useful life of 4 years with zero salvage value. The company elected to use straight-line depreciation for general reporting purposes but decided to take advantage of the provisions of the tax code which permit the use of accelerated (double-declining balance) depreciation to determine taxable income.

In each of the four years from 1980 through 1983 the company had earnings, before taking into account both depreciation on the equipment and taxes, of $50,000. The tax rate is 40 percent.

a. Determine taxable income and taxes for each of the four years. Assume that the asset is depreciated to zero in the fourth year.
b. Determine reported tax expense and net income for each of the four years, assuming that tax expense is based on reported, rather than taxable, income.
c. Prepare journal entries necessary to give effect to the allocation of taxes for each of the four years. Assume that all taxes are paid in the year in which they are incurred. Determine, and keep track of, the year-end balances in the deferred taxes account.

17. *As long as a company continues to expand, the balance in its deferred tax liability account will continue to increase.*

A company made purchases of fixed assets as follows:

1977	$ 60,000
1978	90,000
1979	120,000
1980	120,000
1981	0
1982	0

The company uses straight-line depreciation for accounting purposes but sum-of-the-years' digits depreciation for tax purposes. The useful life of all fixed assets purchased is three years; the assets have a zero salvage value. The income tax rate is 40 percent.

a. Determine, for each of the six years, total depreciation that would be reported on the financial statements and that which would be deductible for tax purposes. Indicate the difference each year.

b. Determine the taxes that would be *saved* (postponed) or would have to be *repaid* during each of the six years.

c. Determine the amount that would be reported as a deferred tax liability each year.

d. Suppose that the firm continued to increase its purchases of fixed assets after the third year. What would be the effect on the deferred tax liability? Why do you suppose some managers and accountants are opposed to *interperiod* tax allocation?

18. *A liability for taxes that will have to be paid in the future should be established whenever a company is permitted to recognize revenue for financial reporting purposes in one period and for tax purposes in a later period.*

The Arizona Land Co. was organized on January 1, 1982. The corporation issued 1,000 shares of common stock for $100,000 cash. The company elected to recognize revenue on the installment basis (i.e., upon collection of cash) for income tax purposes but at time of sale for general accounting and reporting purposes.

In 1982 the company purchased for cash a parcel of land for $60,000. In the same year it sold the land for $100,000; the buyer made a down payment of $50,000 and paid the balance in 1983.

In 1983 the company purchased for cash another parcel of land for $180,000 and sold it for $200,000. The buyer paid the entire amount in cash at time of sale.

The effective tax rate is 40 percent. The company pays all taxes in the year to which they are applicable. The company allocates taxes as appropriate.

Prepare a statement of income and a balance sheet for the years 1982 and 1983.

19. *The deferral method of accounting for the investment tax credit requires that the credit be taken into income over the life of the related asset.*

A firm acquires an asset at a cost of $32,000. The asset has an estimated useful life of eight years and qualifies for an investment tax credit of 10 percent. The firm estimates that in each of the next eight years it will have a tax obligation, prior to giving consideration to the investment tax credit, of $20,000.

Complete the following table assuming that the firm uses the deferral method to account for the tax credit:

	Year 1	Years 2 through 8 (per year)
Required tax payment		
Tax expense to be reported on income statement		
Net amount to be added to (subtracted from) deferred investment tax credit account on balance sheet		

20. *In comparing firms, differences in the methods used to report the investment tax credit must be taken into account.*

In analyzing the financial statements of two firms in the same industry, an investor noticed that one firm accounted for the investment tax credit by the flow-through method and the other by the amortization method.

The firm that accounted for the credit by the flow-through method had taxable earnings in 1982 of $100,000. In 1982 it acquired assets, which were eligible for the tax credit of 10 percent, of $300,000. The useful life of the equipment is 15 years. It has no salvage value. The applicable tax rate is 40 percent.

a. To make the two firms comparable, what adjustments to both the income statement and balance sheet of the flow-through firm would you suggest for 1982?

b. What adjustment would you suggest for the remaining 14 years over which the assets will be depreciated?

21. *The full cost of increasing employee pension benefits attributable to prior service with the firm does not necessarily have to be reflected in the income statement or balance sheet in the year of the change.*

The 1976 financial statements of the Colgate-Palmolive Company reported:

> Effective January 1, 1977, the Board of Directors, subject to stockholders' approval, amended the Colgate plan to increase the benefits. These amendments will create an additional unfunded prior service cost of $57,000,000. The effect on pension expense of the increased benefits, amortization of the increased prior service cost, and revision of the actuarial assumptions will be an increase of approximately $1,400,000 per year.

a. What is the effect of the change, as of January 1, 1977 (to the extent revealed or implied by the note), on
   1. Recorded expenses?
   2. Recorded liabilities?
   3. Cash disbursements?
b. Over how many years would you estimate Colgate is amortizing the prior service costs? (Assume the entire $1,400,000 relates to prior service costs.)
c. What would be the long-term effect of the change, during 1977 and subsequent years, on
   1. Reported expenses?
   2. Required cash payments?

22. *Pension costs should be charged as expenses when the firm receives the benefits of employee services, not when the firm makes cash payments to either the employees themselves or to a pension fund.*

A corporation reported on its income statement pension expense of $17 million. Its balance sheet indicated accrued pension costs (liability) of $6 million. A footnote to its financial statements revealed that the company's actual contribution to the pension fund was $14.5 million and that the actuarially computed liability for *unfunded* prior service costs was $36 million.

a. Prepare a journal entry to summarize the pension expense and the cash contribution to the pension fund for the year.
b. Distinguish between the liability for accrued pension cost as reported in the balance sheet and that for the unfunded prior service costs as reported in the footnotes.
c. From the information provided, is it possible to determine the present actuarial value of the firm's overall pension liability to its past and current employees? On the books of which accounting entity would such liability be recorded?

SOLUTIONS TO EXERCISE FOR REVIEW AND SELF-TESTING

1. 7% ($\frac{1}{2}$ of 14%) of $1,000—$70 interest payable each six months.

2. 6% ($\frac{1}{2}$ of 12%) of $1,000—$60 interest expected each six months.

3. $10 difference.

4. The present value of an annuity of $10 for 40 semiannual periods at a discount rate of 6% is, based on Table 4.

$$\$10 \times 15.0463 = \$150.46$$

5. Each bond will be issued at a premium of $150.46 and at a total price of $1,150.46.

6. 6% of $1,150.46—$69.03.

7. $70 (see Part 1).

8. $70.00 − $69.03 = $.97 amortization of bond premium.

9. $1,150.46 − $.97 = $1,149.49 effective bond liability on July 1, 1983.

10. 6% of 1,149.49—$68.97 interest expense.

TRANSACTIONS 11 between a Firm and Its Owners

This chapter is the first of two chapters that will be directed primarily to transactions between a firm and its owners. In this chapter we shall compare partnerships with corporations, consider the problems associated with the formation of a new enterprise, and identify the characteristics of preferred stock and common stock. In addition, we shall digress from our main concern with the accounting issues associated with commercial enterprises to explore some of the unique reporting problems of municipalities and other nonprofit organizations.

An underlying assumption of this chapter, indeed as with all of the other chapters, is that managers and investors must be aware not only of the economic substance of a transaction, but also the extent to which the economic substance is reflected by conventional accounting practices.

PROPRIETORSHIPS AND PARTNERSHIPS

There are three major types of business enterprises: the individual proprietorship, the partnership, and the corporation. The proprietorship is a business firm owned by a single party. The partnership is one owned by two or more parties. The corporation is a separate, legal entity which operates under a grant of authority from a state or other governmental body and is owned by one or more stockholders.

The proprietorship is far and away the most common type of business enterprise in the United States. Indeed, proprietorships comprise almost 70 percent of all business concerns, whereas partnerships account for about 17 percent of enterprises and corporations only 13 percent. Corporations, however, generate approximately 75 percent of the national income.

No Limits on Size

Corporations are often thought of as large enterprises whereas proprietorships and partnerships as small. While it is true that most proprietorships and partnerships are small businesses, *most* corporations are also relatively small, often family-owned firms. The corporation is associated with bigness because most large businesses—those that account for the major part of industrial output—are corporations. Nevertheless, many large enterprises are organized as partnerships. Service organizations such as brokerage firms and CPA firms are commonly organized as partnerships even though they generate hundreds of millions of dollars in annual revenues.

Unlimited Owner Liability

Proprietorships and partnerships are, in a legal sense, extensions of their owners. One or more parties simply establish a business. They purchase or rent whatever equipment or space is needed, acquire supplies or inventory, and obtain any local operating licenses that might be required. No formal charter or state certificates are required. If the business is to be operated as a partnership, it is generally wise to have an attorney draw up a partnership agreement which specifies the rights and obligations of each partner—how profits will be distributed, who will perform what services, how much each partner must contribute initially, what rights of survivorship will accrue to each partner's estate, what limitations there will be upon sale of a partner's interest in the business. But such a document is for the protection of the individual partners; it is not ordinarily required by law.

Significantly, a proprietor, as well as each partner of a partnership, is usually personally responsible for all obligations of his business. If the enterprise suffers losses, the owners are jointly and severally responsible for all debts incurred. A partner will generally be held liable not only for his share of the debts but, should his partners be unable to meet their share of the claims against the business, for those of his partners as well. As a consequence, few investors are willing to purchase an equity interest in a partnership as they might purchase one in a corporation. In the event the partnership is liquidated and fellow partners are unable to meet their share of obligations, the personal assets of the investors might be subject to the claims of creditors. Their risk of loss is unlimited, extending beyond their original investment.

There are no limits on the number of partners who might compose a partnership. Because of the extended liability to which each partner is subject, most partnerships are small—two or three members. However, many partnerships are considerably larger. Some CPA firms which are organized as partnerships have well over 1,000 partners.

Taxes Levied on Individual Owners, Not on Business Entity

Neither proprietorships nor partnerships are subject to federal or state taxes on income. Instead, the tax is assessed on the individual owners. If the organization is a partnership, then each partner is taxed on his share of partnership earnings. The rate of tax is determined by the tax bracket in which the individual partner falls after taking into account his earnings from nonpartnership sources. Each partner is taxed on his share of the entire earnings of the partnership, not just on his withdrawals from the business. Thus, especially if the partnership requires capital for expansion, a partner may be taxed on earnings that are retained in the business, and are not readily available for his discretionary use, as well as on funds actually taken from the business.

CORPORATIONS

A Legal "Person"

A corporation, by contrast, is a legal entity separate and distinct from its owners. It is a legal "person" created by the state. A corporation is owned by its stockholders, but its stockholders are not compelled to take an active role in its management. In many corporations there is a distinct separation of ownership and operating control, with managers typically holding only a small fraction of total shares outstanding. A corporation has an indefinite life. It continues in existence regardless of the personal fortunes of its owners. Its owners are commonly free to transfer or sell their shares of stock to anyone they wish.

Corporations, unlike proprietorships or partnerships, are creatures of the state. A corporation has the right to own property in its own name, and it can sue or be sued. Upon its formation, it must be chartered by the state. Although at one time charters were granted only upon special acts of the legislature, today they are routinely issued upon submission of certificates of incorporation and supplementary application forms, and payment of necessary fees. The certificate of incorporation specifies the name of the proposed corporation, its purposes (most certificates of incorporation are drawn so as to allow the company to engage in an unlimited range of business activities), the number of shares authorized to be issued, and the number of directors.

Once the charter has been issued the corporation has to adopt formal bylaws, which govern a number of critical areas of operation. They would cover such matters as the issuance and transfer of stock and the conduct of meetings of directors and stockholders.

Limited Liability

The single most significant distinction between corporations and proprietorships or partnerships is that the liability of stockholders of a corporation is limited to the amount of their initial investment in the company, whereas that of the owners of proprietorships or partnerships is unlimited. With few exceptions, the maximum loss that a stockholder can sustain on purchase of an interest in a corporation is the amount of his initial investment. Should the corporation fail, creditors can avail themselves of only the assets of the corporation; they cannot seek redress against the personal assets of the individual stockholders. Only in rare circumstances—the involvement of corporate stockholders in fraud, for example—is it possible for creditors or others who may have judgments against the corporation to "pierce the corporate veil" and bring a successful legal action against the individual stockholders. Because it is able to protect investors against unlimited loss, the corporation is a vehicle that is well suited to raise large amounts of capital. Large numbers of persons may be willing to purchase an ownership interest in a company knowing that they can share in the gains of the company to an unlimited extent but that their losses will be limited by the amount of their direct contributions. They need not be overly concerned with the day-to-day operations of their business, since neither the managers nor their fellow owners can so mismanage the business as to put any of their personal assets in jeopardy.

Corporations, like other legal persons, are subject to both federal and state income taxes. Earnings of a corporation are taxed regardless of whether or not they are distributed to its owners, albeit at rates different from those of individuals. The individual owners of the corporation, unlike those of a partnership, are not taxed on their shares of the earnings that are retained in the business; they are, however, taxed on the earnings as they are distributed to them in the form of dividends. Earnings of a corporation are taxed twice— once when earned by the corporation and again when they are distributed to the stockholders.

CORPORATIONS VERSUS PARTNERSHIPS: DISTINCTIONS IN PERSPECTIVE

It is easy to place too much emphasis on the distinctions between partnerships and corporations. For some businesses, especially smaller enterprises, the differences may be more of form than of substance. For a small business the corporate form of organization is unlikely to facilitate acquisition of required capital any more than would the partnership form. Most small enterprises have difficulty obtaining equity capital, not so much because potential investors are concerned about subjecting all of their personal assets to possible loss, but rather because they are unwilling to risk any funds on the venture. Small businesses are inherently hazardous, and the corporate form of organization does not measurably enhance prospects for success.

Corporate Form May Inhibit Capital Formation

Equally significant, the limited liability feature of the corporate form of organization may actually deter potential suppliers of capital. To a bank or other lending institution, the limitation on owners' liability is an obstacle rather than an inducement to making a loan. The bank, after all, wants assurance that in the event of default it can have access to all the assets of owners, not merely those devoted to the business. As a consequence, many lenders circumvent the limitations on stockholder liability by requiring that the stockholders personally co-sign any notes issued by the corporation.

Limitations on Partners Liability

The distinction between the corporate and partnership form of organization has been diminished further in recent years by legislation in some states which provides for the limitation on the liability of certain partners in selected circumstances. As long as there exists one *general* partner whose liability is unlimited, the liability of other partners, particularly those who take no part in the day-to-day management of the enterprise, may be limited.

Ease of Stock Transferability May Be Illusory

The advantage of a corporation over a partnership in that shares of ownership are readily transferable may also be more illusory than real. Although the shares of major corporations can be sold without difficulty, those of companies that are *closely held* by a small number of stockholders could probably not be sold any more easily than could a similar interest in a partnership. Indeed, agreements among stockholders of smaller companies sometimes provide that all sales of shares to outsiders must meet with the approval of existing owners.

Tax Distinctions Have Been Reduced

The tax distinctions between partnerships and corporations have also been diminished greatly by statute. The current federal tax code provides that if certain criteria are met small corporations may elect to be taxed as partnerships. As a consequence, small corporations can avoid the burden of "double" taxation; only stockholders and not the corporation will be taxed on corporate earnings.

DISTINCTIVE FEATURES OF PARTNERSHIP ACCOUNTING

There are relatively few differences between accounting for a proprietorship or partnership and a corporation. What differences there are relate primarily to the owners' equity accounts and are more of form than of substance. For accounting purposes the proprietorship may be viewed as a special case of a partnership—a "partnership" with only a single partner.

The owners' equity section of a partnership general ledger usually consists of one capital account for each partner. Each capital account is credited (increased) by the amount of a partner's contributions to the firm and by his share of partnership profits. It is debited (decreased) by a partner's withdrawals from the firm and by his share of partnership losses.

Example

Lee and Grant decide to form a partnership. Lee contributes $200,000 cash, and Grant contributes a building, which has been appraised at $150,000 but on which there is a mortgage of $50,000. The building had been carried on Grant's personal books at

a value of $75,000. The partnership agrees to assume the liability for the mortgage. The following entry would be required to establish the partnership:

(a)

Cash	$200,000	
Building	150,000	
Mortgage note payable		$ 50,000
Capital, Lee		200,000
Capital, Grant		100,000

To record formation of the partnership.

Property contributed is valued at its *fair market value*, regardless of the value at which it might have been carried on the books of the individual partners prior to being assigned to the partnership.

The partners agree to share profits and losses in the same ratio as their initial capital contributions, 2 to 1. During the first year of operations the partnership had revenues of $240,000 and expenses of $180,000—income of $60,000. The following *closing entry* would be required, assuming that revenues and expenses were properly recorded throughout the year.

(b)

Revenues (various accounts)	$240,000	
Expenses (various accounts)		$180,000
Capital, Lee		40,000
Capital, Grant		20,000

To close the revenue and expense accounts.

During the course of the year Lee withdrew $20,000 in cash, and Grant, $40,000. In addition, each partner was paid $25,000 in salaries, included in expenses above. At the time of withdrawal the appropriate entry would be:

(c)

Withdrawals, Lee	$20,000	
Withdrawals, Grant	40,000	
Cash		$60,000

To record withdrawals.

The "withdrawals" account is the equivalent of the "dividends" account maintained by corporations. At year end it would be *closed* to partners' capital:

(d)

Capital, Lee	$20,000	
Capital, Grant	40,000	
Withdrawals, Lee		$20,000
Withdrawals, Grant		40,000

To close withdrawals accounts.

It is critical that a partnership agreement set forth any amounts that the individual partners are to receive in salaries apart from the shares of earnings to which they are entitled. Payments of salaries to partners may be accounted for just as they would be if they were ordinary expenses. They have no direct impact on the withdrawals account or the individual capital accounts.

Lee, capital

(d)	20,000	**(a)**	200,000	
		(b)	40,000	
			220,000	

Grant, capital

(d)	40,000	**(a)**	100,000	
		(b)	20,000	
			80,000	

At the conclusion of the year, Lee would have a capital balance of $220,000, and Grant, $80,000. The capital balances would no longer be in the original ratio of 2 to 1.

Whether or not a partner should be permitted to draw his capital account below a specified level is a question that must be addressed in the partnership agreement. Some partnership agreements provide for the payment of interest to any partner who maintains an *excess* capital balance in relation to those of his partners.

CORPORATE CAPITAL ACCOUNTS

In contrast to the owners' equity section of a partnership balance sheet, in which the capital balances of the partners are reported, that of a corporation would indicate the par values of different classes of stock, the amount received by the corporation in excess of such par values, and the earnings retained in the business. Exhibit 11-1 illustrates the stockholders' equity section of Armstrong World Industries, Inc.

There are two major categories of capital stock: common stock and preferred stock. Common stock is the "usual" type of stock; when only one class of stock is issued, it is almost certain to be common stock. Preferred stock, when issued, ordinarily has certain preferences as to dividend payments and rights in liquidation.

As indicated in Exhibit 11-1, the balance sheet includes, often parenthetically, information on the numbers of shares of each class of stock authorized, issued, and outstanding. The number of shares *authorized* is the maximum number of shares, per its corporate charter, that the company is permitted to issue; the number of shares *issued* is the amount that has actually been put into circulation; the number of shares *outstanding* indicates those currently in circulation. It represents the number of shares issued less those that have been repurchased by the company. Shares held by the company, often

EXHIBIT 11-1

Armstrong World Industries, Inc.
Stockholders' Equity
(dollar amounts in thousands)

	December 31 1981	1980
Preferred stock, $3.75 cumulative, no par value. Authorized 161,821 shares; issued 161,522 shares (at redemption price of $102.75 per share)	$ 16,596	$ 16,596
Voting preferred stock. Authorized 1,500,000 shares	—	—
Common stock, $1.00 par value per share. Authorized 60,000,000 shares; issued 25,939,455 shares	25,939	25,939
Capital surplus	44,660	47,066
Retained earnings	543,457	524,146
	630,652	613,747
Less treasury stock, at cost:		
Preferred stock, $3.75 cumulative—43,373 shares	3,986	3,986
Common stock: 1981—1,501,352 shares; 1980—1,192,748 shares	25,143	22,702
	29,129	26,688
Total stockholders' equity	601,523	587,059

referred to as *treasury* shares, are considered to be issued but not outstanding.

COMMON STOCK: CHARACTERISTICS AND RIGHTS OF SHAREHOLDERS

Common stock is characterized by rights to income and of control. Common stockholders receive distributions of the assets of the corporation if and when dividends are declared by its board of directors. Common stockholders, however, have a *residual* interest in their company. Upon dissolution of the corporation, they have the right to share in the remaining assets of the company after all claimants, including preferred stockholders, have been satisfied.

Common stockholders ordinarily possess rights to vote. They can elect members of the board of directors and can vote on such matters of corporate policy as are specifically reserved in corporate bylaws for decision by the stockholders-at-large. Corporate voting is conducted on the basis of one *share* (not one shareholder), one vote.

PREFERRED STOCK: CHARACTERISTICS AND RIGHTS OF SHAREHOLDERS

Preferred stock is a hybrid between common stock and bonds: It combines some of the benefits—and limitations—of both. Preferred stock ordinarily stipulates that a fixed or minimum dividend will accrue to the holder each year. The dividend may be stated as a dollar amount (e.g., $3 per share) or as percentage of the par value (e.g., 5 percent). In this regard, preferred stock is similar to bonds. However, the obligation to pay such dividends is not quite as binding on the corporation as it would be if the company had issued bonds. Most commonly, the company would not be in immediate default if it failed to make a single dividend payment. Instead, the company would be prohibited from making any dividend payments to common stockholders until it satisfied its current and, in most instances, accumulated obligations to the preferred stockholders. Similarly, in the event of liquidation, the preferred stockholders would have preference over the common stockholders. Before any distributions could be made to the common stockholders, the preferred stockholders would have to have been returned both their initial investment as well as any accumulated dividends.

The specific features of preferred stock vary from issue to issue. Generally, preferred stockholders do not have voting rights, except when the company has failed to pay preferred stock dividends for a specified number of periods. Some issues, called *participating* issues, entitle the preferred stockholders to share in income in excess of the stipulated dividend. For example, an issue may carry a minimum dividend of $3 per share. It may provide that once the preferred stockholders have received their minimum dividend—and usually once the common shareholders have received a dividend of a stated amount—any additional funds available for distribution will be divided, in a specified proportion, between the two groups of stockholders.

Unlike bonds, preferred stock does not mature on a particular date. Usually, however, the corporation has the option to *call*

(redeem) the stock at a stipulated price after a number of years have elapsed. Many issues (approximately 40 percent in recent years) provide that preferred shares can be *converted*, at the option of the holder, into shares of common stock. The specific conversion ratio—how many shares of common stock may be exchanged for each share of preferred stock—is ordinarily established at the time the preferred stock is issued.

Dividends Not Deductable

From the standpoint of the issuing corporation, preferred stock has one critical disadvantage over bonds or other pure debt securities. The dividends on preferred stock (like those on common stock) are not deductible from corporate income for tax purposes, whereas interest payments are. The effective cost of the capital acquired through the issue of preferred stock is therefore magnified substantially. Suppose, for example, that a company wishes to raise $1 million in capital. It could issue bonds which could be sold to yield 6 percent or preferred stock which would bear a dividend rate of 8 percent. Preferred stock, especially if it is not convertible into common stock, often provides the holder with a higher return since interest payments take precedence over dividend payments. The interest payments would require an outlay of $60,000 per year, and the dividend payments, $80,000. If, however, the income tax rate were 46 percent, then the *effective* outlay would be $80,000/(1 − .46)— $148,148. That is, the company would have to earn $148,148 in order to meet its preferred stock dividend payments of $80,000:

Income before taxes	$148,148
Tax at 46%	68,148
Income available for payment of dividends	$ 80,000

By contrast, the company would have to earn only $60,000 to meet its required interest payments of $60,000. Since the interest payments are fully deductible, if the corporation earned $60,000 and paid interest of $60,000, it would have no taxable income and hence no tax liability. The full $60,000 of earnings could be used to meet the interest payments:

Income before taxes	$60,000
Taxes	0
Income available for payment of interest	$60,000

FORMATION OF A CORPORATION—ISSUANCE OF COMMON STOCK

The mechanics of forming a corporation are straightforward; the central accounting problems relate to the values to be placed upon the assets or services contributed by its organizers.

A corporation is ordinarily formed by one or more individuals known as promoters. The *promoters* organize the corporation, apply for a charter, and establish the bylaws under which the corporation will initially operate. Commonly, the promoters contribute cash, other assets, or services to the company in exchange for all or a portion of the capital stock to be issued. If additional equity (ownership) financing is required, then the promoters arrange for shares of the stock to be sold either to the general public or to specific parties known to the promoters. The promoters are in a fiduciary relationship—one of highest trust—to the corporation. They are under obligation to make certain that they themselves do not benefit at the expense of those who will subsequently purchase shares of corporate stock—that they receive an interest proportionate to the value of the assets or services which they have contributed.

Par Value

Corporate stock traditionally bears an indication of *par value* per share. Par value is the nominal value of the stock, a value that has been arbitrarily assigned. Common stock can be sold for an amount above or below par value. If sold above, it is said to have been sold at a *premium*, and if below, at a *discount*. Originally par value was intended to protect creditors. It was to provide them assurance that stockholders had contributed assets worth at least as much as the par value of the shares. If they had not—that is, if they had purchased the stock at a discount—then in the event of corporate dissolution they could be held responsible for the difference between what they paid for the stock and its par value, despite the usual limitations on stockholder liability.

Par value did not prove to be an effective means of protecting creditors because a new corporation could assign to its shares a par value far below the price at which it expected the shares to be sold. Many states have substituted a concept of *stated* or *legal* capital for par value. Commonly, stated or legal capital is either an amount established by the company (similar to par value) or that for which the stock was actually issued. Typically, stated or legal capital establishes a floor on the payment of dividends; the corporation is prohibited from paying dividends that will reduce its owners' equity below its stated or legal capital.

Assets Stated Initially at Fair Market Values

When a corporation issues common stock for cash or other assets, either to the original promoters or anytime subsequent to its formation, a simple journal entry is in order. Asset accounts are debited and owners' equity accounts are credited for the *fair market* value of the property received by the corporation. The credit to the capital account is divided into two parts—the par (or stated) value of the stock issued and the amount in excess of par (or stated) value. Suppose, for example, a corporation issues 10,000 shares of $2.50 par value stock at $80 per share. The appropriate entry would be

Cash	$800,000	
Common stock, par value		$ 25,000
Contributed capital in excess of par value, common stock		775,000

To record the issue of common stock.

The two credited accounts combined indicate the capital contributed by common stockholders. Some accountants believe that the significance of par value is sufficiently small so that the interests of clear and concise financial reporting would be better served if the two accounts were consolidated on the balance sheet into a single account, "capital contributed by common stockholders."

ISSUANCE OF ADDITIONAL SHARES

Should a firm issue additional shares of stock subsequent to its formation, similar entries would be in order. The resultant increase in owners' equity would be reflected first in the "common stock, par value" account, and then, to the extent of amounts received above par, in the account, "contributed capital in excess of par value."

The price at which additional shares of stock may be issued would be dependent on the market value as opposed to the book value of the company's existing shares outstanding.

Example

A firm has reported assets of $100,000, liabilities of $50,000, and owners' equity of $50,000. Owners' equity is composed of the following accounts:

Common stock, $1 par value, 10,000 shares issued and outstanding	$10,000
Contributed capital in excess of par value	25,000
Retained earnings	15,000
Total owners' equity	$50,000

The book value per share is $50,000 divided by 10,000 shares—$5 per share.

The company wishes to raise $100,000 in capital. The market price of the company's stock is $20 per share. (Large discrepancies between book value and market value are not uncommon. Book value is based on historical costs; market value is based on investor expectations as to future earnings.) Assuming that the market price is unaffected by the impending issue of the new stock (a major financial event which may itself affect investor expectations of future earnings), the company could acquire the $100,000 in needed capital by issuing an additional 5,000 shares at $20 per share.

The journal entry to record the issue would be

Cash	$100,000	
Common stock, par value		$ 5,000
Contributed capital in excess of par value		95,000

To record the issue of additional stocks.

Owners' equity would now be made up as follows:

Common stock, $1 par value, 15,000 shares issued and outstanding $ 15,000
Contributed capital in excess of par value 120,000
Retained earnings 15,000
$150,000

Book value per share would now be $10 ($150,000 divided by 15,000 shares), compared to $5 prior to the sale of the additional shares.

The increase in book value can be attributed to the willingness of the new investors to pay $20 per share for stock that had a book value of only $5 per share. The new investors contributed $100,000 in return for a one-third interest (5,000 shares out of 15,000 shares) in a company that will have *reported* net assets of $150,000. In effect, existing shareholders received a "bonus" reflecting the market's assessment of the company.

ISSUANCE OF PREFERRED STOCK

The mechanics of recording the issuance of preferred stock are almost identical to those of recording common stock. However, the characteristics of any amounts received in excess of or below par value are, in essence, more similar to the premium or discount associated with bonds than with common stock.

The amount that an investor will pay for a corporation's common stock is dependent on his expectation of the firm's earnings in the future. He will share in the *residual* income of the company—that which remains after the claims against earnings of bondholders and preferred stockholders are satis-

fied. The price that he is willing to pay for a share of common stock will rise and fall with his assessment of the company's earning potential.

The owner of preferred stock, however, is less concerned with anticipated profits of the company. His dollar share in the income of the company is contractually fixed. He will receive only the dollar amount of the dividend specified on his shares. As long as the company has sufficient earnings to meet its required dividend payments, he will be unaffected by swings in income.

The primary concern of the purchaser of preferred stock is the yield that he will obtain from one company as opposed to another with similar risk characteristics. Suppose, for example, the preferred stock of a company has a par value of $100 per share and a dividend rate of $6 per year. If similar securities are being sold to yield 7 percent per year, then a rational purchaser would be willing to invest in the shares only if he could purchase them at a discount sufficiently great to assure a return equivalent to the rate prevailing in the market. If similar securities are being sold to yield only 5 percent, then he would be willing to pay a premium of such magnitude as to reduce his return to that which he could obtain elsewhere. Preferred stock has many of the characteristics of bonds. The price at which a share of preferred stock is traded is determined in a manner similar to that of bonds.

Example

The ABC Co. wishes to issue 10,000 shares of $100 par value preferred stock which will pay dividends of $10 per year. On the day of issue the prevailing yield on similar types of securities is 9 percent.

For how much is each share likely to be sold?

Let x = the amount for which each share will be sold

$$.09x = \$10$$

$$x = \frac{\$10}{.09}$$

$$x = \$111.11$$

If a share of stock which pays dividends of $10 per year is to be sold to yield 9 percent, then it would be sold at a price equal to $111.11. Since, unlike bonds, there is no maturity date, the return can be assumed to be a perpetuity (one for an infinitely long duration); hence, there is no need to refer to present value tables to determine the selling price. Similarly, there is no need to amortize the premium ($11.11 per share in this case), which is commonly classified on the balance sheet as "Contributed capital in excess of par."

TRANSACTIONS IN A CORPORATION'S OWN SHARES

Companies may purchase their own outstanding shares of stock for a number of reasons. They may wish to reissue the shares to executives or other employees in connection with stock option or related compensation plans. They may desire to *invest* temporarily in their own shares, just as they might invest in shares of other corporations. Or they may want to reduce the scale of their operations—to return to stockholders a share of the capital they had contributed. Stock which is acquired and retained by the issuing corporation is known as *treasury stock*. Treasury shares may not be voted, do not receive dividends, and carry none of the usual rights of ownership.

The manner in which treasury stock is accounted for has a direct impact on a firm's reported capital structure. There are two primary methods of accounting for treasury stock. One method is referred to as the *cost* method and the other as the *par value* method. Under the cost method treasury shares are accounted for in a separate account. Under the par value method treasury shares are treated as stock to be permanently retired.

Cost Method

In general, if a corporation expects to reissue the shares acquired it should account for them by way of the *cost method*. Under the cost method the treasury shares are reported in a separate account, which is shown on the balance sheet *contra* to the other equity accounts. Thus:

Common stock, $1 par value, 10,000 shares issued, 100 shares held in treasury	$ 10,000
Contributed capital in excess of par value	20,000
Retained earnings	70,000
	$100,000
Less: Shares held in treasury (at cost)	1,500
Total owners' equity	$ 98,500

The amount recorded in the treasury stock account represents, as suggested by the name of the method, the *cost* of the shares acquired. The cost would be dictated by market conditions at the time of acquisition.

Some firms report treasury stock among the current assets, along with other marketable securities. The justification is that the shares can be sold and thereby converted to cash in the same manner as could other temporary investments. The overwhelming body of professional opinion rejects this contention, maintaining instead that a firm cannot "own itself." Shares reacquired by the company serve to reduce the claims of the owners (the owners' equity) against the firm's net assets; they are not themselves assets.

Should the company sell the shares, the treasury stock account is reduced by the amount at which the shares are recorded. If the selling price is different than the amount recorded in the treasury stock account, then any difference is added to or subtracted from the account, "Contributed capital in excess of par." The firm should *not* recognize a gain or loss in transactions in its own securities and the sale of treasury stock, unlike the sale of marketable securities, should not result in revenues or expenses to be included in the computation of net income.

Par Value Method

If a corporation does *not* expect to reissue the shares acquired, then it should account for them by way of the *par value method*. Under the par value method, the shares are, in essence, retired. First, both the common stock, par value, and the contributed capital in excess of par accounts are reduced by amounts reflective of the percentage of shares being retired. Then, retained earnings is adjusted by the difference between the price paid to acquire the shares and the amounts charged to the par value and the contributed capital accounts.

DEBT TO EQUITY RATIO

Financing ratios, one of which is the debt to equity ratio, compare claims of creditors with the equity of stockholders.

The debt to equity ratio relates capital provided by creditors with that supplied by owners. Debt includes all outstanding liabilities, both current and noncurrent. Equity includes balances in all owners' equity accounts—common and preferred stock, capital provided in excess of par, and retained earnings.

Total debt of the Fruehauf Corporation (see Chapter 7), composed of current liabilities, long-term debt, other liabilities, and deferred income taxes, is $995,876,096. Total stockholders' equity is $529,110,725. The debt to equity ratio as of December 31, 1980, therefore, is 1.9 to 1.

$$\text{Debt to equity ratio} = \frac{\text{Total debt}}{\text{Total equity}}$$
$$= \frac{\$995,876,096}{\$529,110,725} = 1.9$$

The debt to equity ratio is of particular concern to creditors. The claims of creditors against the assets of a firm have priority over those of the stockholders. The higher the debt to equity ratio, the greater the amount of the *priority* claims against the assets, and in the event the firm is unable to meet all its outstanding obligations, the less likely that any individual claim will be liquidated in full. Moreover, a high debt to equity ratio suggests the obligation to make high periodic interest payments. As a consequence, there is an increased risk that corporate earnings will be insufficient to cover all required principal and interest payments.

The debt to equity ratio is also of interest to managers and the stockholders they represent. Stockholders can expect no return on their investment, either periodically in the form of dividends or upon liquidation, until all senior claims of creditors have been satisfied. The lower the debt to equity ratio, the less the risk of loss assumed by stockholders. But in contrast to the possible preference of stockholders to be assured a return on their investment, there may be a conflicting desire to make use of *leverage*—the ability to take advantage of other people's money to enhance the return on their invested capital. Insofar as the debt to equity ratio is high as a consequence of reliance upon debt, then any earnings on the borrowed capital above the required interest payments would increase the return to stockholders. Leverage, however, works both ways. If the firm was unable to earn on its borrowed capital an amount sufficient to cover the cost of such capital, then the return on stockholders' equity would be comparably reduced.

ACCOUNTING FOR NONPROFIT ORGANIZATIONS

The accounting problems of municipalities and other nonprofit organizations have, until recently, received relatively little public attention. The fiscal crisis of New York City, which resulted in part because the financial reports of the city failed to warn of impending insolvency, represented a turning point with respect to active interest in, and concern for, nonprofit accounting on the part of the accounting establishment. Today, government accounting is one of the most controversial and rapidly expanding areas of the profession. Nonprofit organizations contribute a sizable proportion of the gross national product and are major recipients of private investment capital. In terms of dollar volume of new offerings, the market for municipal securities is only slightly smaller than that for corporate securities, and in recent years the number of individual offerings by municipalities has been over five times the number of primary corporate issues that have been registered with the SEC.

The accounting practices of nonprofit organizations are of concern to managers for at least two reasons. First, as the percentage of gross national product attributable to the nonprofit sector increases, so also does the probability that a manager will assume either a paid or voluntary position with such organizations. Second, corporations are usually major taxpayers in the communities in which they are located as well as important contributors to educational, health, and community organizations. It is in the interest of the corporations, and thus their managers, that the organizations are administered efficiently and effectively.

Accounting practices of nonprofit organizations are basically the same as those of commercial enterprises, but there are several noteworthy differences. In the discussion to follow attention will be directed to the accounting practices of municipalities; those of other nonprofit organizations are similar but not always the same in all respects.

The Accounting Entity

In commercial accounting, a single set of accounts is maintained for each corporation. In municipal accounting, by contrast, several sets of accounts are usually employed for a single government entity. Each set of accounts is known as a *fund*. The term *fund* as used here bears little relationship to the term as defined earlier with reference to commercial accounting (i.e., cash or working capital). A fund is used to account for certain related activities of a government enterprise. Conventionally, one fund is maintained for general operations of government, another for revenues that are restricted for special purposes, a third for capital projects under construction, a fourth for assets accumulated to repay outstanding loans, and a fifth for business-like enterprises, such as hospitals or utilities, that the municipality may control.

The accounts of each fund, like those of a commercial enterprise, are self-balancing and may be summarized by the fundamental accounting equation:

$$\text{Assets} - \text{Liabilities} = \text{Owners' equity}$$

The individual asset and liability accounts are comparable in nature and terminology to those described throughout this text. The owners' equity account like that of commercial organization represents a residual interest in the enterprise—what would remain if all assets were to be sold at amounts equal to their book values and all liabilities were to be liquidated. In nonprofit accounting, the residual interest is referred to *not* as owners' capital or capital stock, but rather as *fund balance*. Except for the name, however, it has most of the accounting characteristics of owners' equity.

The various funds are seldom combined. The financial statements of municipalities consist of several independent balance sheets and statements of revenues and expenditures.

The use of several accounting entities to account for a single economic entity can be explained by the need to maintain strict separation and control over assets that are *legally* earmarked for specific purposes. Should, for example, a municipality use funds that were acquired by issuing long-term utility bonds to finance day-to-day operations, then the responsible government officials may be in violation of applicable city or state statutes and bond covenants and subject to legal sanctions.

The Modified Accrual Basis

Municipalities and other nonprofit organizations generally recognize revenues and expenditures on the accrual basis, just as do commercial enterprises. There are, however, several important exceptions. The most prominent of these regards fixed assets.

Municipalities and other nonprofit organizations do not generally give formal accounting recognition in the individual funds to fixed assets or to the debt used to acquire them. If an asset is acquired for cash, then an expenditure account is charged at the time of purchase. If it is financed by long-term bonds, then the expenditure account is charged as payments are made to liquidate the debt. Neither the asset nor the debt is recorded on the balance sheets of the various funds. Instead, they are listed separately in special "groups of accounts" that are, in effect, nothing more than supplementary "memo" ledgers. Since as the expenses associated with the acquisition of assets are recorded when the cash payments are made, there is no need to reflect the cost a second time by way of charges to depreciation.

The accounting practices with respect to fixed assets can be traced directly to the relationship between tax revenues and expenditures. Tax rates are established so that a municipality can meet its expenditures. The municipality must gear its tax collections to cash payments, not to expenses as they might be determined using an accrual basis of accounting. The financial statements, therefore, report expenditures for fixed assets when cash disbursements are made, rather than, as in commercial accounting, as the services provided by the assets are consumed.

Most of the other modifications to the accrual basis further reflect the preferences of municipal managers and bondholders for information on cash receipts and disbursements rather than on inflows and outflows of resources. Revenues, for example, are generally recognized when they are both measurable and *available to meet current expenditures*.

Financial Statements

The financial statements of nonprofit organizations are comparable to those of commercial establishments. For each fund, a balance sheet, which indicates the assets, liabilities, and fund balance as of a particular point in time, is prepared. Inasmuch as nonprofit organizations do not attempt to "earn" income, no income statement is prepared. Instead, a statement that indicates revenues and expenditures is presented. Commonly, the statement would compare actual amounts with budgeted amounts. Such comparison reflects the greater importance attached to budgets in nonprofit organizations. In nonprofit organizations, the budget is not merely a set of managerial guidelines; it is a document that is formally adopted by the governing authorities. It sets forth the manner in which the resources of the organization are to be allocated, and it specifies the contributions that will be required from its members (e.g., citizens). In addition, the financial report of a nonprofit organization will generally include for each fund a statement of cash receipts and disbursements and a statement of changes in fund balance. The latter is comparable in many respects to the statement of changes in retained earnings that is required of commercial entities.

Each of these distinctive features of nonprofit accounting has come under attack. Within the next several years there are likely to be substantial changes in the manner in which nonprofit organizations are accounted for; many of these changes are likely to diminish the differences between nonprofit and commercial accounting procedures.

SUMMARY

In this chapter we have focused on the equity accounts of proprietorships, partnerships, and corporations. Although there are important legal and organizational differences among proprietorships, partnerships, and corporations, the accounting distinctions are relatively minor, affecting primarily the accounts comprising the owners' equity section of the balance sheet. We also in this chapter detoured from the main commercial road traveled in this text to consider the unique features of the accounting systems and financial reports of nonprofit organizations.

A corporation's transactions involving its own shares are seldom reported on its statement of income. Yet they can have a profound impact on its earning per share as well as on the value of outstanding shares.

In the 1960s, for example, many companies took advantage of relatively high stock market prices to issue additional shares. Since the price that the new investors were willing to pay was substantially above the *book* value of the new shares, the added premium served to increase the book value of the existing shares. Inasmuch as the cost of the capital acquired was low in relation to the return that could be generated by the additional capital, sale of the new shares served to increase overall earnings per share. Numerous firms that were previously privately owned *went public* in order to benefit from the ease of obtaining capital through the sale of common stock.

In the 1970s and early 1980s, when stock market prices were depressed, a number of companies engaged in the reverse process; they reacquired shares that they had issued previously. If the market price of the shares acquired was less than their intrinsic value, then the proportionate value of the remaining shares increased. Since relatively little capital had to be surrendered to reacquire the shares, the overall earnings capacity of the firms may have declined only slightly. But since earnings now had to be divided among a significantly smaller number of shares, earnings per share may have increased substantially.

The perceptive investor and financial analyst examines carefully the transactions between a company and its owners and the manner in which they are accounted for. They can have a critical effect on a stockholder's interest in past and future corporate earnings.

The skilled manager as well as the perceptive investor must be aware of the opportunities and pitfalls inherent in corporate dealings between a company and its owners and must be cognizant of how they will be reflected in the financial reports.

EXERCISE FOR REVIEW AND SELF-TESTING

Scopus, Inc., decides to reorganize its corporate structure. To facilitate additional financing, it is going to incorporate one of its divisions. The company will transfer to the new corporation plant and equipment that is presently recorded on its books at a cost of $8,900,000 less accumulated depreciation of $4,500,000 and patents that were developed by the company itself and have not been accorded formal accounting recognition. The fair market value of the plant and equipment is $8,200,000; that of the patents, $2,000,000.

1. The new company issues 100,000 shares of common stock, par value $50. Initially, all the shares will be held by the parent company.
    a. What value should the new company assign to the plant and equipment? To the patents?
    b. What value should the new company assign to "Common stock, par value"? To "Common stock, capital in excess of par"?
    c. Prepare a journal entry to record the issuance of the common stock.

2. The new company also issues 10,000 shares of preferred stock. The preferred stock is assigned a par value of $100 and pays dividends at a rate of 9 percent per year. At the time the stock is issued comparable securities are being sold to yield 8.5 percent.
    a. What is the dollar amount per share that the firm will pay in dividends?
    b. How much is an investor likely to pay for a share of stock that pays a dividend of such amount if he expects a return of 8.5 percent?
    c. Prepare a journal entry to record the issuance of the preferred stock, assuming that the stock is issued for cash at the price determined in Part b.

3. After a year, the new company acquires 1,000 of its outstanding shares of common stock for the

purpose of reissuing them to employees as part of a stock option plan. The company acquires the shares for cash at a price of $180 per share.
    a. Do you think that the acquisition of the treasury stock should be accounted for by the cost or the par value method?
    b. Based on your answer to Part a, prepare a journal entry to record the acquisition of the stock.

4. Shortly after reissuing the shares described in Part 3 the company reacquires an additional 20,000 shares of common stock with the intention of retiring them. The company purchases the shares for $160 each. At the time of purchase the company has a balance in its retained earnings account of $2,000,000.
    a. Do you think that the acquisition should be accounted for by the cost or par value method?
    b. By what percentage would the number of shares outstanding be reduced?
    c. By what percentage and by what amount should the balance in the account "Common stock, par value" be reduced?
    d. By what percentage and by what amount should the balance in the account "Common stock, capital in excess of par" be reduced?
    e. By what amount—the difference between total amount paid and the sum of the reductions in the other capital accounts—should the balance in "Retained earnings" be reduced?
    f. Prepare a journal entry to record the retirement of the shares.

QUESTIONS FOR REVIEW AND DISCUSSION

1. The risks of being a *silent* (one who takes no active role in management) partner of a business organized as a partnership are far greater than that of being a silent stockholder of a firm organized as a corporation. Do you agree? Explain.

2. It is often pointed out that the limitations on liability afforded stockholders of a corporation make it easier for a corporation as opposed to a

partnership to raise capital. Cite an example of a situation where the limitations on liability may, in fact, make it more difficult for a corporation to acquire needed funds.

3. A corporation, it is said, is a legal "person." Why is a corporation, but not a partnership or a proprietorship, so described?

4. Why is *preferred* stock preferred? What preferences are attached to it?

5. A friend wants to purchase "safe" securities for a period of two to three years. He wants assurance that the original amount of his investment will remain intact. Assume that you are satisfied that the company in which he is considering investing is sound—that it is highly unlikely that it will be unable to pay required preferred stock dividends or interest. Would you necessarily suggest to him that the preferred stock of the company is a safer investment than the common stock? What factors are most likely to influence the market price of the preferred stock, assuming that it is not convertible into common stock?

6. What are the critical accounting problems involved in the formation of a corporation? What warnings would you give to someone who is about to purchase the common stock of a newly organized corporation?

7. The financial statements of RCA Corporation contained the following footnote:

At December 31, 1980, 52,967 shares of treasury stock, included in Other Assets [a noncurrent asset] at cost to RCA of $1.3 million, were available to cover undistributed awards payable in RCA common stock.

What objections might many accountants have to classifying treasury stock as a noncurrent *asset*?

8. How does use of the term "funds" in nonprofit accounting differ from that in commercial accounting?

9. By accounting for long-lived assets on what is essentially a cash basis, governmental units are able to readily match tax collections to required cash outlays. What is an important disadvantage of accounting for long-lived assets on a cash basis?

PROBLEMS

1. The method of financing used by a "closely held" corporation must take into account the distinctions in the tax code between dividends and interest.

William Elton is the sole stockholder of the Elton Co. Mr. Elton intends to contribute $1 million of his personal funds to the corporation in order to finance expansion of a plant. He expects that the added capacity of the plant will enable the company to earn $300,000 per year additional income, before federal and state taxes. Mr. Elton has asked your advice as to whether he should have the corporation issue common stock or bonds in return for the $1 million. Mr. Elton intends to withdraw $100,000 of the additional earnings each year, either in the form of interest on bonds or dividends on the common stock. The corporation pays taxes at a rate of 48 percent. Mr. Elton personally is in a 60 percent tax bracket. Mr. Elton would be required to pay taxes on all returns from the corporation, regardless of whether in the form of interest or dividends.

What advice would you give to Mr. Elton?

2. The tax consequences of incorporating a closely held business depend to a great extent upon the owner's plans to withdraw funds.

John Albert operated his business as a sole proprietorship for several years. His attorney had advised him that in order to limit his liability he ought to incorporate his firm. He has asked you for an evaluation of the tax consequences.

The firm has annual earnings, before taxes, of $250,000. The effective corporate income tax rate would be approximately 40 percent. Since he has several additional sources of income, Mr. Albert is in the 70 percent personal income tax bracket (for federal and state taxes combined).

Were Mr. Albert to incorporate his business, he would be the sole stockholder.

a. Determine the total tax obligation on income attributable to the business assuming first that the business remains a sole proprietorship and alternatively that it is incorporated. Consider the total tax impact on both Mr. Albert and his firm—both corporate and personal taxes. Assume that Mr. Albert intends to withdraw $50,000 per year from the business (either in the form of proprietor withdrawals or corporate dividends) and retain the remainder of earnings in the business.

b. Again determine total tax obligations. Assume this time, however, that Mr. Albert intends to withdraw $150,000 per year from the business.

c. Can you generalize from your analysis?

3. *Accounting principles applicable to partnerships are essentially the same as those applicable to corporations.*

Simmons and Ross decided to form a partnership to engage in the sale of real estate. Simmons contributed land that had an appraised value of $400,000; Ross contributed cash of $100,000. The land was subject to a liability of $100,000, which the partnership agreed to assume. The land had been recorded on the personal books of Simmons at a value of $200,000. The partners agreed that profits and losses would be shared in proportion to the initial contributions of the owners. In addition, however, Ross would be paid a management fee of $10,000 per year.

During its first year of operations the partnership purchased additional land for $800,000, paying $150,000 cash and giving a note for the balance. It sold for $300,000 land that it had acquired for $200,000. The buyers paid cash of $90,000 and agreed to assume liabilities of $210,000 that the partnership had incurred when it had acquired the land.

During the first year the partnership borrowed $80,000 from Simmons. It agreed to pay Simmons interest at the rate of 6 percent per year. As of year end the loan had been outstanding for six months, but the partnership had neither paid nor accrued any interest.

The firm incurred additional interest expenses, paid in cash, of $40,000. At year end, Ross withdrew $30,000 cash from the partnership and, in addition, was paid his management fee; Simmons withdrew nothing. (Assume that all other operating expenses are negligible.)

a. Prepare all necessary journal entries to record the formation of the partnership and to summarize all transactions in which it engaged during its first year of operations. Prepare also any required adjusting and closing entries.

b. Prepare a balance sheet as of year end.

4. *Distributions to partners upon liquidation of a partnership must be based upon the balances, after appropriate adjustments, in the partners' capital accounts.*

After 10 years, Freeman Brothers Men's Shop is going out of business. Freeman Brothers is operated as a partnership. Just prior to liquidation, its balance sheet reflected the following:

Cash	$ 20,000
Merchandise inventory	80,000
Total assets	$100,000
Current liabilities	$ 5,000
Capital, J. Freeman	45,000
Capital, L. Freeman	50,000
Total liabilities and owners' equity	$100,000

The two Freeman brothers share profits and losses equally.

The firm holds a "going-out-of-business" sale and sells its entire merchandise inventory for $100,000. It pays its creditors and distributes the remaining cash between the two partners.

a. Prepare the required journal entries to record the sale of the merchandise and payment of the liabilities. (Prepare any closing entries that might be required with respect to any revenues and expenses associated with the sale of the merchandise.)

b. Determine the balances in the partners' capital accounts immediately prior to the final distribution of cash between the partners. How do you explain the fact that although the partners share profits and losses equally, their capital balances are not also equal?

c. How much cash should be distributed to each of the partners? Prepare a journal entry to record the final distribution to the partners.

5. *Partners' capital accounts are basically the same as owners' equity accounts of corporations.*

On the following page is an excerpt from the annual report of Price Waterhouse & Co., one of the "Big Eight" CPA firms.

a. To what corporate account would "Partners' capital" be comparable?

b. To what corporate account would "undistributed income" be comparable?

Worldwide Statement of Changes in Partners' Capital and Undistributed Income,
Years Ended June 30, 1980 and 1979
(thousands of dollars)

	1980	1979
Partners' capital		
Balance, beginning of year	$ 65,900	$ 53,500
Additional capital provided	10,700	17,900
Repayment of paid-in capital	(3,500)	(5,500)
Balance, end of year	$ 73,100	$ 65,900
Undistributed income		
Balance, beginning of year	$129,200	$119,300
Payments to retired partners	(1,300)	(3,300)
Net income of active partners	186,100	154,800
Distributions to active partners	(164,800)	(141,600)
Balance, end of year	$149,200	$129,200

c. What were the net assets of Price Waterhouse as of December 31, 1980?

d. Price Waterhouse has 1,487 partners worldwide. What were the average earnings per active partner in 1980? What was the average amount of payments (presumably in cash) to each of the active partners?

6. *The initial values assigned to the assets of a newly established corporation must be indicative of their fair market values.*

You have recently been offered the opportunity to purchase 1,000 shares of the common stock of Computer Service Corporation at a price of $15 per share (a price well below its book value). The company has just been formed; it has not yet commenced operations. It was organized by three computer systems analysts, who are presently the only stockholders. The company intends to lease office space and computers; it will provide automated bookkeeping services to small businesses.

A balance sheet provided you by the company reveals the following:

Cash	$100,000
Inventories and supplies	20,000
Goodwill	150,000
Total assets	$270,000

Common stock, par value $1 (20,000 shares authorized, 10,000 shares issued and outstanding)	$ 10,000
Common stock, contributed capital in excess of par	260,000
Total equities	$270,000

A footnote to the financial statements indicates that the $150,000 of goodwill represents the accumulated expertise of the founders of the corporation. All three promoters have had extensive experience with a leading computer manufacturer and have held management positions with other computer service companies. The goodwill was authorized by the firm's board of directors.

a. What reservations might you have about purchasing the stock of the company?

b. Assume instead that you were an independent certified public accountant called upon to audit the company shortly after its formation. What adjusting journal entry might you propose?

7. *The amount for which shares of common stock were issued can be derived from information provided upon their retirement.*

The financial report of Warner Communications, Inc., contains the following note:

During the year, 9,000,000 Common treasury shares, $1 par value, having an aggregate cost of $157,798,000 were retired resulting in charges of $9,000,000 to capital stock, 36,440,000 to paid in capital and $112,358,000 to retained earnings.

a. How much did the company pay to acquire each share?
b. What was the initial issuance price per share?
c. Prepare a journal entry to record the retirement of the shares assuming that just prior to their retirement they were recorded at acquisition cost in a treasury stock account.

8. *The price at which preferred stock, like bonds, is issued is reflective of the relationship between prevailing yields and the promises inherent in the security.*

The Thoreau Electric Co. has decided to issue 100,000 shares of preferred stock that will pay an annual dividend of $6 per share. The preferred stock will have a stated value of $100 per share. At the date of issue, similar grades of preferred stock are being sold to provide a return to investors of 7 percent.

a. At what price is the issue of Thoreau likely to be sold?
b. Prepare a journal entry to record the sale of the preferred stock.
c. Prepare an entry to record the payment of the first annual cash dividend.
d. Suppose instead that the preferred stock will have a stated value of $1 per share. Prepare an entry to record the sale of the stock.

9. *Preferred stock dividends are usually "cumulative."*

The *Wall Street Journal* of March 12, 1981, reported that "Cenco Inc., which has missed all but one of its preferred dividend payments since June 1976, said it now plans to pay the accumulated dividends." According to the *Journal*, "the dividends, totaling about $933,000 at $1.40 a share, will be payable April 27 to stockholders of record February 28." Cenco, the *Journal* indicated, "said the payment is subject to the condition that it won't violate the company's debenture agreements, which call for Cenco to have about $31.4 million in retained earnings before it can pay its preferred dividends." That requirement is the reason that Cenco was unable to pay its preferred dividends in the past.

Cenco's financial problems are attributable to a $25 million phony profit scheme that involved inflating both inventories and earnings. Several executives were convicted of conspiracy and fraud.

a. What is meant by the term "accumulated dividends"?
b. How many shares of preferred stock does the company have outstanding?
c. What entries, if any, does the *Wall Street Journal* report suggest that the firm made in those years that it failed to pay its dividends? Explain.

10. *Prices at which securities are issued and acquired can be derived from changes in the balances of owners' equity accounts.*

The stockholders' equity section of the balance sheet of the Intercontinental Corp. reveals the following:

	1980	1979
Common stock, $10 par value	$ 1,200,000	$ 1,000,000
Preferred stock, $100 par value, 8%	500,000	450,000
Contributed capital in excess of par		
Common stock	11,500,000	8,900,000
Preferred stock	8,000	—
Retained earnings	18,143,000	20,220,000
Less: Common stock held in treasury		
(1,300 shares in 1980, 1,000 shares in 1979)	(173,000)	(130,000)
	$31,178,000	$30,440,000

No treasury stock was retired or reissued during 1980.
a. How many shares of common stock did the company issue in 1980? What was the issue price per share?
b. How many shares of preferred stock did the company issue in 1980? What was the issue price per share?
c. What would you estimate to be the prevailing yield rate for comparable types of securities at the time the preferred stock was issued? That is, what was the yield rate used to determine the issue price of the preferred stock?
d. What was the price paid for the 300 shares of common stock acquired by the company in 1980?

11. *The price at which common stock of a newly formed corporation is issued should be reflective of the fair market value of the corporate assets.*

Filmore and Francis are partners in a firm that operates a chain of drug-stores. They decide to incorporate their business and sell shares in the enterprise to the general public. Filmore has a 60 percent interest in the partnership and Francis a 40 percent interest.

The net assets (assets less liabilities) of the partnership are recorded on the books of the partnership at $8 million. However, after considerable study and consultation with independent appraisers, the partners decide that the fair market value of their business is $12 million. Indeed, just prior to their decision to incorporate they received an offer to sell their entire business to an independent party for that amount.

The partners intend to issue 200,000 shares of common stock. They plan to keep 60 percent of such shares for themselves and sell the rest to the public. Each share of stock will have a par value of $20.
a. At what price should the shares be sold to the public?
b. Prepare any journal entries required to record the formation of the new corporation.

12. *The conversion of preferred stock to common stock requires an adjustment only to owners' equity accounts.*

The annual report of Chromalloy American Corporation, a firm listed on the New York Stock Exchange, contains the following note:

Preferred Stock—The Company's preferred stock is issuable in series and is entitled to one vote per share. The outstanding $5 Cumulative Convertible Preferred Stock is convertible at the rate of 3.888 shares of common for each share of preferred stock.

The stockholders' equity section of the balance sheet indicates the following:

Preferred stock—authorized 1,825,000 shares, par value $1 per share:	
$5 cumulative convertible preferred stock; outstanding 561,164 shares	$ 561,164
Common stock—authorized 20,000,000 shares, par value $1 per share; issued 10,748,462 shares	10,748,462
Other capital ascribed to shares	42,930,965
	$ 54,240,591
Retained earnings	122,696,044
	$176,936,635

Suppose that all 561,164 shares of preferred stock were converted (exchanged) into common stock. The company receives no cash in the exchange; it realizes no gain or loss; the transaction has no impact upon retained earnings.

Prepare a journal entry to record the exchange. Be sure that as the result of your entry the balance in the common stock, par value account is reflective of the new number of shares outstanding.

13. *A shift from partnership to corporate status is an event of sufficient economic and legal significance to justify revaluing the assets and liabilities of an enterprise.*

Bryan and Moore are partners in a retail stereo business. After several successful years of operation as a partnership, the two decide to incorporate their business as Stereo, Inc. Bryan and Moore share profits and losses in the ratio of 3:1. Prior to the liquidation of the partnership and its subsequent incorporation, the balance sheet of the partnership indicated the following:

Assets		
Cash		$ 12,000
Accounts receivable		26,000
Inventory		83,000
Furniture and fixtures	$ 75,000	
Less: Allowance for depreciation	22,000	53,000
Land		18,000
Building	$102,000	
Less: Allowance for depreciation	60,000	42,000
Total assets		$234,000

Liabilities and owners' equity		
Accounts payable		$ 29,000
Notes payable		80,000
Capital, Bryan		93,750
Capital, Moore		31,250
Total liabilities and owners' equity		$234,000

Prior to transferring the assets to the corporation, the partners decided to adjust the books of the partnership to reflect current market values.

The building had a current market value of $85,000; the land, $26,000; and the furniture and fixtures, $30,000.

The firm had not previously provided for uncollectible accounts. However, it was estimated that $4,000 of the accounts would be uncollectible. It was also determined that $8,000 of inventory was obsolete. The new corporation was to assume the liabilities of the partnership except as noted below.

The new corporation was authorized to issue 100,000 shares of $10 par value common stock. Common stock was to be issued at par value, with the number of shares proportionate to the fair market value of one's contribution.

Shares were also issued to the following parties in addition to the partners:

To an attorney for providing services pertaining to the organization of the corporation. The fair market value of the services was $8,000.

To the party holding the note payable. He agreed to accept common stock in full payment of his $80,000 note.

To a venture capital financial institution. It agreed to invest $50,000 cash in the new corporation.

a. Prepare journal entries to revalue the partnership, to transfer the assets to the new corporation in exchange for common stock, and to distribute the shares of the common stock to the partners.

b. Prepare journal entries to organize the new corporation.

c. Indicate the number of shares each investor would receive.

14. Transactions involving a firm's own stock are often based upon the price at which the shares are being traded in the open market.

The Frost Co. was organized on June 1, 1982. According to the terms of its charter, the firm was authorized to issue capital stock as follows:

Common stock: $2 par value, 100,000 shares.

Preferred stock: $100 par value, 5 percent dividend rate, 10,000 shares.

During the first year of operations the following transactions, which affected capital accounts, took place:

1. The corporation issued for cash 50,000 shares of common stock at a price of $30 per share.
2. The corporation issued for cash 10,000 shares of preferred stock at $90 per share.
3. The company purchased a building, giving the seller 10,000 shares of common stock. At the time of the purchase, the common stock of the company was being traded in the open market at $25 per share.
4. The firm's advertising agency agreed to accept 3,000 shares of common stock, rather than cash, in payment for services performed. At the time of payment the market price of the stock was $28 per share.
5. The firm agreed to purchase the stock of a dissident shareholder. The firm purchased 3,000 shares at a price of $30 per share.
6. The company subsequently sold the shares to another stockholder at a price of $31 per share.

Prepare journal entries to record the above transactions.

15. The value of a business, which is about to be acquired by another firm, can be established in a number of different ways.

Alliance Department Stores, Inc., has agreed to purchase McKay Bros. Discount Store. McKay

Bros. is operated as a partnership. The owners' equity accounts on the books of the partnership indicate that each of the two partners has a recorded capital balance of $100,000. An independent appraiser has determined that the value of the individual assets of the company (there are no significant liabilities) is $250,000. The partners, however, have had several offers to sell the entire business for $300,000.

Alliance Department Stores, Inc., has offered to purchase the store for shares of its own common stock. The number of shares to be issued is currently being negotiated between the two parties. Alliance currently has 50,000 shares of common stock outstanding. The par value of each share is $2. The company has $300,000 in capital in excess of par and $600,000 in retained earnings. The current market price for shares of Alliance is $25 per share.

Six possible ways of determining the number of shares to be issued to the McKay Bros. partners are under consideration. The value of a share to be issued by Alliance can be based on either its *book* or its *market* value. The value of the interest to be purchased by Alliance can be based on the book value of McKay Bros.' assets, the appraised value of its assets, or its market value as a going concern.

a. Determine the number of shares to be issued by Alliance under each of the six combinations:

Value of Alliance shares based on (1) book value *or* (2) market value, *and*

Value of McKay Bros. based on (1) book value, (2) appraised value, *or* (3) market value.

b. How do you account for the differences among book value, appraised value, and market value?

c. On which basis do you recommend the number of shares should be determined?

16. *Prevailing tax laws are a key factor in a corporation's decision as to whether it should issue bonds or preferred stock.*

A firm wishes to construct a new plant. The estimated cost of the plant is $5 million. The firm is undecided as to whether to raise the required capital by issuing bonds or preferred stock. The current prevailing yield on bonds of similar grade is 7 percent, and that on preferred stock is 9 percent.

What would be the minimum earnings, before taxes, that the firm would have to realize, under both alternatives, if it were to break even on the proposed project? The current tax rate is 40 percent.

17. *In choosing among alternative instruments of financing, a firm must take into account its expectations as to future earnings.*

A corporation has decided to construct an addition to its plant. The cost of the addition is $5 million; it is expected to increase earnings by $900,000 per year before taking into account income taxes.

The firm is considering three means of acquiring the needed $5 million capital:

1. Sell bonds. Current yield rates are 8 percent per year.
2. Issue preferred stock. Current yield rates are 12 percent per year.
3. Issue common stock. The firm currently has 600,000 shares outstanding. It estimates that additional shares could be sold at a price of $10 per share. The company has not paid any dividends on common stock in recent years and does not plan to do so in the foreseeable future. The current tax rate is 48 percent.

a. Prepare a table that has one column for each of the three options and the following headings:
   1. Anticipated additional earnings (before taxes)
   2. Required interest or dividend payments
   3. Additional "earnings" less direct cost of capital (1 − 2)
   4. Income taxes
   5. Net additional earnings (3 − 4)
   6. Shares of common stock outstanding
   7. Additional earnings per share of common stock (5 ÷ 6)

Which alternative do you think the company ought to select if impact on earnings per share of common stock is to be the most important criterion?

b. Suppose that anticipated earnings from the new addition were $1.5 million per year. Which alternative do you think the firm ought to select? (You need not recompute earnings per share; simply use judgment.)

c. Suppose that estimated additional earnings were $900,000 per year but that the market price of the firm's common stock was $20 per share. Which alternative should now be favored?

18. A corporation can increase the equity of existing (and remaining) stockholders by judiciously issuing and retiring shares of its own common stock.

In 1978 Mary Bells, Inc., reported earnings of $6 million. Its owners' equity at the end of that year was $30 million. The firm had 1 million shares of common stock issued and outstanding.

At the start of 1979 the company decided to expand its operations. To raise an additional $15 million in capital, it elected to issue additional common stock. It was able to issue the stock at a price of $100 per share. The additional capital enabled the firm to increase earnings by $3 million per year after taxes to $9 million.

a. Determine the *book* value per share and earnings per share both before and after the issue of the additional common stock.

b. In 1982 the market price of the firm's common stock had fallen to $50 per share. The firm decided to reacquire, at market price, $7.5 million of common stock. To avoid having to reduce its scale of operations the firm decided to issue long-term bonds for $7.5 million. The bonds could be sold at a price such that the effective interest cost to the company, after taxes, would be 5 percent. Determine the book value per share and earnings per share after the reacquisition of the shares and the issue of the bonds. Assume that in the intervening years, including 1982, all earnings had been distributed to stockholders in the form of dividends and that income, in 1982, before taking into account interest on the new bonds, was the same as that in 1979—$9 million.

SOLUTIONS TO EXERCISE FOR REVIEW AND SELF-TESTING

1. a. The assets should be recorded at their fair market values. Hence, plant and equipment, $8,200,000; patents, $2,000,000.

b. Common stock, par value: 100,000 shares × $50 per share = $5,000,000.

Common stock, capital in excess of par: $10,200,000 − $5,000,000 = $5,200,000.

c. Plant and
equipment $8,200,000
Patents   2,000,000
   Common stock,
      par value $5,000,000
   Common stock,
      capital in
      excess of par   5,200,000
To record issuance of common stock.

2. a. The firm will pay $9 per share in dividends.

b. $9 ÷ 0.85 = $105.88, which equals the market value per share of preferred stock.

c. Cash $1,058,800
   Preferred stock,
      par value $1,000,000
   Preferred stock,
      capital in
      excess of par   58,800
To record issuance of preferred stock.

3. a. Inasmuch as the company intends to reissue the shares in the near future they should be accounted for by the cost method.

b. Treasury stock $180,000
      Cash $180,000
To record acquisition of 1,000 shares of common stock.

4. a. Inasmuch as the company intends to retire the shares, they should be accounted for by the par value method.

b. 20%.

c. 20%; 20% of $5,000,000 = $1,000,000.

d. 20%; 20% of $5,200,000 = $1,040,000.

e. 20,000 shares × $160 per share minus $2,040,000 = $1,160,000.

f. Common stock,
      par value $1,000,000
   Common stock,
      capital in excess
      of par   1,040,000
   Retained earnings   1,160,000
      Cash $3,200,000
To record retirement of 20,000 shares of common stock.

Special Problems 12
of Measuring
and Reporting Dividends
and Earnings

This chapter, as did the previous one, will focus on transactions between a corporation and its owners. Specifically, it will consider the means of measuring and reporting distributions of earnings—dividends in cash, "in kind," and in stock. It will also deal with the unique problem of accounting for employee salaries when the compensation is in the form of options to acquire common stock, and it will examine the question of when an impairment of asset value should be considered a loss. It will conclude with a discussion of two controversial issues with respect to reports of earnings—those relating to calculation of earnings per share and those relating to the determination of earnings for an *interim* period.

The issues dealt with are of immediate concern to investors inasmuch as they affect directly both the magnitude and the proportion of their claims to corporate assets. They are of equal importance to managers because managers are the agents (representatives) of investors and their performance is likely to be evaluated on how competently and equitably they represent their interests. Moreover, the corporations that managers administer may themselves be investors, owning shares in other companies.

RETAINED EARNINGS AND CASH DIVIDENDS

Retained earnings represent the total accumulated earnings of a corporation less amounts distributed to stockholders as dividends and any amounts transferred to other capital accounts.

Dividends are distributions of *assets* (or shares of common stock) which serve to reduce retained earnings. They are *declared* by a formal resolution of a firm's board of directors. The announcement of a dividend would indicate the amount per share to be distributed, the *date of record* (that on which the stock records will be closed and ownership of the outstanding shares determined), and the *date of payment*. A typical announcement might read as follows: "The board of directors of the XYZ Corporation, at its regular meeting of December 9, 1982, declared a quarterly dividend of $2 per share payable on January 24, 1983, to stockholders of record on January 3, 1983."

Basic Entries

The entry to record the declaration of a dividend is straightforward. On the date of declaration, when the liability for payment is first established, the entry (in this case to record a dividend of $2 per share on 100,000 shares outstanding) would be

Common stock
dividends $200,000
    Dividends payable $200,000

To record declaration of the cash dividend on common stock.

At year end "common stock dividends" would be *closed* to retained earnings. When payment is subsequently made it would be recorded as follows:

Dividends payable $200,000
    Cash $200,000

To record payment of the dividend.

Ability to Pay Dividends Requires Availability of Cash or Other Assets

Although conventional (nonstock) dividends are *charged* to retained earnings, they are *paid* in cash or other tangible assets. It does not follow that merely because a company has a balance in retained earnings it has the wherewithal to make dividend payments. Retained earnings are a part of owners' equity. Owners' equity corresponds to the excess of assets over liabilities. It cannot be associated with specific assets to which stockholders have claim.

The nature of retained earnings is a common source of misunderstanding—a misunderstanding that can be attributed in large measure to the widespread use, until recently, of the term *earned surplus* in place of retained earnings. *Surplus* implies something extra— an amount over and above what is needed. Retained earnings may not, in fact, represent *surplus*. Rather, a balance in retained earnings may be indicative of earnings that have been reinvested in the corporation. By not distributing its earned assets to stockholders, the corporation may have internally financed expansion. The retained earnings, therefore, may not denote the availability of cash or other assets that can readily be distributed to stockholders; instead the company may have used its available resources to acquire land, buildings, and equipment. The owners' equity section of General Motors Corporation balance sheet (1980), for example, comprises the following accounts (in millions):

Preferred stock	$ 283.6
Common stock	496.7
Capital in excess of par	1,297.2
Retained earnings	15,737.1
	$17,814.6

Retained earnings account for 88 percent of owners' capital. It is obvious that distribution of assets represented by the entire $15.7 billion in retained earnings would force the company to retrench its operations back to the scale of its "horseless carriage" days.

Decisions as to when and how much of a dividend to declare are ordinarily made with primary reference to the corporation's current cash position and anticipated cash flow. The company must determine whether the available and projected cash is sufficient to meet its other operating requirements—the need to meet payrolls, maintain inventories, replace worn-out equipment, etc. In addition, however, the corporation must consider also the interests of shareholders. To the extent that assets are not distributed to stockholders, the stockholders are being forced to increase their investment in the corporation. Whether they wish to increase their investment will ordinarily depend in large measure on the return they could obtain from competing investment opportunities. If the funds to be retained in the corporation are likely to provide a return greater than stockholders could obtain elsewhere, then stockholders are often willing to permit the company to retain all or a portion of its assets. In fact, many corporations, particularly *growth* companies, omit payment of dividends for years at a time. Stockholders of such companies are willing to forgo immediate cash returns for long-term corporate expansion and enhancement of their investment.

The payment of dividends is sometimes constrained by statutory restrictions. The corporation laws of some states prescribe that dividends cannot be paid "out of capital"; they can be paid only "out of earnings." That is, the payment of dividends cannot serve to reduce the stockholders' equity of the company beneath the amount contributed by the stockholders. The motivating force behind such restrictions is protection of creditors. The state laws are designed to make certain that assets that should properly be used to liquidate outstanding debt are not, by way of dividends, returned to stockholders, who, because of their limited liability, are not otherwise responsible for the obligations of the corporation.

DIVIDENDS IN KIND

Although dividends are conventionally paid in cash, it is not uncommon for a company to distribute other types of assets. A company, for example, may own a substantial number of shares in another corporation and wish to distribute those shares in lieu of a cash dividend. Suppose, for example, the Gamma Co. owns 100,000 shares of XYZ Corporation stock. It declares and pays a *dividend in kind* (as such dividends in property are known) of 4 shares of XYZ stock for each of its own 25,000 shares outstanding. If the stock of the XYZ Corporation had been recorded on the books of the Gamma Co. at $5 per share but had a fair market value of $8 per share, then the following two entries would be in order:

XYZ Corp stock	$300,000	
Gain on investment		$300,000

To write up XYZ Corp. stock to reflect market value.

Common stock dividends	$800,000	
XYZ Corp. stock		$800,000

To record declaration and payment of dividend in kind.

As a consequence of the dividend, the corporation is able to realize a holding gain in the amount of the difference between book value and market value of the property distributed.

Many accountants assert, however, that a corporation should *not* be permitted to realize gains or losses as the result of discretionary, non-arm's-length transactions with stockholders. If it were, they contend, it could readily manipulate earnings by distributing to shareholders assets that it could not otherwise sell to outsiders at the value assigned to them. Other accountants point out, however, that the recipients of the assets would unquestionably record, and would be taxed upon, the property at fair market value. Moreover, they observe, a corporation should not have to incur the transaction costs of selling its assets to outsiders to realize a gain, when it could readily transfer them directly to its shareholders, who could sell them for as much cash as they would otherwise receive. By definition of the term "market value," they aver, assets distributed to the stockholders could alternatively have been sold to outsiders at the market values assigned to them. The Accounting Principles Board, in Opinion No. 29, held that dividends in kind should generally be accounted for at fair market values and appropriate gains or losses recognized.

Distributions of the stock of other companies (dividends in kind) should not be confused with *stock dividends*, which will be discussed in a following section.

STOCK SPLITS

Corporations will sometimes *split* their stock. That is, they will issue additional shares for each share outstanding. A firm might, for example, split its stock three for one, meaning that, for each one share presently held, a shareholder will receive an additional two.

Stock splits are ordinarily intended to reduce the market price per share, to obtain a wider distribution of ownership, and to improve the marketability of the outstanding shares. The common stock of a corporation might be trading at $300 per share. The board of directors determines that at such a high price the stock is less attractive to investors than it would be at a lower price. Many investors like to acquire stock in round lots of 100 shares since brokerage commissions are relatively higher when fewer shares are purchased. The board might, therefore, vote a three for one stock split. Each shareholder will end up with three times as many shares as previously, but the market price per share could be expected to fall to nearly one-third its previous price. Neither the corporation nor the individual stockholder

would be intrinsically better or worse off as a result of the split.

Commonly, the corporation would reduce the par value of the common stock to reflect the split and would so notify shareholders. If the stock previously had a par value of $1, it would subsequently have a new par value of $.33\frac{1}{3}$. As a consequence, no accounting entries are required to effect the split. Common stock, par value, will in total remain unchanged. So, too, will capital contributed in excess of par and retained earnings.

STOCK DIVIDENDS

Motivation

A special form of stock split is known as a *stock dividend*. As with a stock split, a stock dividend results in the issuance of additional shares. Ordinarily the ratio of new shares to outstanding shares is decidedly lower for a stock dividend than for a stock split. Seldom would the number of new shares to be issued exceed 20 percent of previously outstanding shares; generally it is less than 5 percent. More significantly, the motivation underlying a stock dividend is considerably different from that of a stock split. A corporation would issue a stock dividend not to improve the marketability of its shares but rather to provide its shareholders with tangible evidence of an increase in their ownership interest. A company may view a stock dividend as a substitute for a dividend in cash or other property. Lacking the available cash, it will distribute to each shareholder, on a *pro rata* basis, additional shares of its own stock. Sometimes, for example, a company that has consistently paid cash dividends will be caught in a *cash squeeze*. Rather than omitting the dividend entirely, the company will distribute additional shares of stock instead of cash. A stock dividend may also provide a means for a company to *capitalize* a portion of accumulated earnings. The company will transfer a portion of accumulated earnings from the retained earnings account (which is sometimes viewed as a temporary capital account) to common stock, par value and capital received in excess of par accounts (which are considered to be of a more permanent nature). Such a transfer provides formal evidence that a portion of accumulated earnings has been invested in the business and is no longer available for the payment of dividends.

In Essence a Stock Split

A stock dividend, like a stock split, has no effect on the intrinsic worth of the corporation. It leaves the shareholders neither better nor worse off than previously. A stock dividend has no effect on corporate assets and liabilities. As a consequence of the dividend, additional shares of common stock are outstanding. But since the net worth of the corporation remains the same, each share of common stock represents a proportionately smaller interest in the corporation.

Suppose, for example, that a corporation, prior to declaration of a stock dividend, had net assets of $100,000 and 1,000 shares of common stock outstanding. A stockholder who owned 100 shares would have held a 10 percent interest in a company with a book value of $100,000. If the corporation declared a 3 percent stock dividend, then the stockholder would receive 3 additional shares. He would now own 103 shares out of a total of 1,030 shares—still a 10 percent interest in a company with a book value of $100,000. Insofar as the market price for the stock is determined in a rational manner, then the market price per share could be expected to be reduced proportionately.

The underlying nature of a stock dividend has been well expressed by the U.S. Supreme Court. In a case in which the court was called upon to rule whether stock dividends constituted income subject to tax under the provisions of the Sixteenth Amendment, Justice Pitney affirmed a judgment in a previous case in which it was stated

> A stock dividend really takes nothing from the property of the corporation, and adds nothing to the interest of the shareholders. Its property is not diminished, and their interests are not increased. . . . The proportional interest of each shareholder remains the same. The only change is in the evidence which represents that interest, the new shares and the original shares together representing the same proportional interest that the original shares represented before the issue of the new ones.[*]

Accounting Practices Inconsistent with Economic Interpretation

Although stock dividends are, in essence, a form of stock split, the rule-making authorities of the accounting profession have determined that they should be accounted for differently. According to a pronouncement of a committee on accounting procedures, a predecessor of the Accounting Principles Board, when a corporation issues less than 20 percent additional shares as a dividend, it should transfer from retained earnings to "permanent" capital an amount equal to the *fair value* of the shares issued.[†] Assume, as before, a company which previously had 1,000 shares of stock outstanding declared a 3 percent stock dividend. Assume additionally that each share had a par value of $10 and that the market price at the time of

---

[*] Eisner *v.* Macomber (252 U.S. 189, 40 S. Ct. 189).

[†] American Institute of Certified Public Accountants, *Accounting Research Bulletin No. 43.* (New York, 1961), Chap. 7.

the declaration was $150 per share. The fair value of the 30 shares to be issued and the accumulated earnings to be capitalized would be 30 times $150—$4,500. Conventionally, because of the relatively small number of additional shares to be issued, a company would *not* reduce the par value of its shares. Instead, it would transfer from retained earnings to "common stock, par value" an amount reflective of the par value of the new shares to be issued—in this example $300—and to "common stock, contributed capital in excess of par" the remaining amount—in this example $4,200.

The following entry would give effect to the stock dividend:

Retained earnings	$4,500	
Common stock, par value		$ 300
Common stock, contributed		
capital in excess of par		4,200

To record the issue of a stock dividend.

Rationale behind Generally Accepted Practice

The rationale behind the *capitalization* of retained earnings rests largely with the interpretation placed upon stock dividends by the recipients. The professional committee which issued the official pronouncement with respect to stock dividends took note of the fact that a stock dividend does not, in fact, give rise to any change whatsoever in either the corporation's assets or its respective shareholders' proportionate interests. However, it said, "it cannot fail to be recognized that, merely as a consequence of the expressed purpose of the transaction and its characterization as a *dividend* in related notices to shareholders and the public at large, many recipients of stock dividends look upon them as distributions of corporate earnings and usually in an amount equivalent to the fair value of the additional shares received."

Moreover, the committee pointed out, in many instances the number of shares issued is sufficiently small in relation to shares previously outstanding so that the market price of the stock does not perceptibly decline. Hence, the overall market value of a stockholder's interest may, in fact, increase by the amount of the market value of the new shares. Because both recipients and the investing public *think* that the dividend shares are of value, the committee implied, the corporation should account for them as if they were of value. It should transfer a portion of accumulated earnings from "temporary" to "permanent" capital accounts so as to indicate that such portion of earnings is no longer available for the payment of dividends. Whatever merit the rationale of the committee might have had when it was first set forth has unquestionably been reduced by the increased sophistication of investors. Today, only the most naive of investors see the new shares *per se* as having value—although they do, of course, recognize that the earnings that they represent have served to enhance the value of their investment.

WHEN IS A LOSS A LOSS?

Inherent in almost all accounting issues is the question, "When is a company better off than it was previously?" Implicit in this question is its corollary, "When is a company worse off," or, to phrase it somewhat differently, "When should a loss be recognized as a loss?"

Suppose, for example, that a U.S. company that has interests abroad has been threatened with the expropriation of one of its foreign manufacturing facilities. Unquestionably, the mere threat of the expropriation leaves the firm worse off than it was previously. No doubt, the market price of the firm's outstanding common stock would fall in reaction to such a threat. But should the mere possibility of expropriation be a cause for the firm to write off its foreign assets and charge income with a "loss from expropriation"?

Consider also a company that has been accused by federal authorities of having engaged in price-fixing activities. As a consequence, its customers announce their intention to sue for recovery of damages. At what point should the firm recognize an impairment of its value: when the suit is actually filed; when an initial judgment against the firm is rendered; or when all available appeals have been exhausted?

Contingencies

The question of when to recognize such *contingencies* (losses that are uncertain as to both occurrence and amount) is particularly troublesome. On the one hand, the convention of conservatism dictates that prompt recognition be given to losses. But, on the other, financial statements must be objective. The probability of many types of losses does not suddenly go from remote to certainty. It increases gradually over a period of time. Firms cannot be permitted unlimited discretion in selecting the period in which to recognize losses. If they were, then reported income would be nothing more than an arbitrary determination of corporate management.

The difficulty of establishing guidelines as to when a loss should be recognized arises in large measure because the type of losses which firms incur form a continuum from "reasonably certain and estimable" to "remotely possible and not estimable." On the one end of the continuum are losses such as those arising from warranty obligations and uncollectible accounts. As indicated previously, such losses are conventionally recognized at the time of the related sale of merchandise. They are statistically certain to occur, and the amount of the loss is subject to reasonable estimation, even though the particular account that will have to be written off or the party to whom payment might have to be made is unknown at the time of sale. On the other end of the continuum are losses from fires and natural disasters, which, although sure to occur at some time, are in fact random happenings.

Loss Must Be Probable and Estimatable

The Financial Accounting Standards Board, in Statement No. 5, "Accounting for Contingencies," has prescribed that a loss may be charged to income only when

(1) information available prior to issuance of the financial statements indicates that it is probable that an asset had been impaired or a liability had been incurred at the date of the financial statements, *and*

(2) the amount of loss can be reasonably estimated.

These guidelines are, of course, vague, but the complete statement of the board provides a number of examples as to when various types of losses should be recognized. The statement directs that, even if a loss contingency does not satisfy the criteria for formal recording within the accounts, it must nevertheless be *disclosed* in a footnote to the financial statements. The disclosure must indicate the nature of the contingency and give, if possible, an estimate of, or range of, the possible loss.

EMPLOYEE STOCK OPTIONS

In recent years, stock options have become an increasingly popular means of compensating executives and other employees. They present intriguing accounting issues because of the uncertainty that attaches to the value of the compensation.

Stock options take many forms, but typically they permit an employee to purchase shares of his company's stock at a fixed price at some date in the future. Although the employee will have to pay for his shares, the price he will have to pay remains constant regardless of fluctuations in market value. Should the market value of the shares increase above the set price (the *exercise* price), he could acquire the shares at a considerable savings over what he would otherwise have to pay. Should the market price fall below the exercise price, then he need not exercise his option and could allow it to lapse.

Issues of Measuring Compensation Expense and Determining Share Values

The difficult accounting issues with respect to employee stock options relate to the measurement of the compensation paid and the value of the shares of stock to be issued. If the employee had to exercise the option immediately upon receipt, then the problems of valuation would be reasonably straightforward. The approximate value of the option would be the number of shares that could be purchased times the difference between the current market price of the stock and the exercise price of the option. If, for example, an option permitted an employee to purchase 100 shares of stock at $40 per share at a time when the stock was being traded at $45 per share, then the employee could "save" $5 per share. The value of the option would be

$$100(\$45 - \$40) = \$500$$

Most stock option plans stipulate that an option can be exercised only after a specified period of time has elapsed and only if the employee has remained with the company during that period. Indeed, one of the primary objectives of stock option plans is to reduce employee turnover. As a consequence, at the time the option is granted, neither the number of shares to be issued nor the total amount to be received from an employee as payment for his shares is known.

Moreover, once an option plan has been adopted, the exercise price—the price that the employees will have to pay for their shares—is adjusted only periodically. Because of fluctuations in the market price of the firm's shares, the exercise price may sometimes be *greater* than the market price. For example, the option may allow employees the right to purchase shares of stock at a price of $40 even though the current market price is only $35. If the value of the option is to be based on the excess of the exercise price over the market price, then the option would appear to have a negative value.

The option, however, clearly has a positive value regardless of the relationship between exercise and market prices. The recipient has the *right* to purchase the shares at $40 per share. If in the period during which he is eligible to exercise the option the market price increases to more than $40, he can purchase the shares at a *discount* price. If the price remains below $40 per share, he need not exercise the option; he has lost nothing.

Compensation Expense Must Be Matched with Employee Service

Despite these problems of measurement, the Accounting Principles Board has ruled that stock options should be recorded as compensation expense in the periods in which an employee performed the services for which the option was granted. The injunction of the board is intended to ensure that the cost of employee services is matched with the benefits (revenues) that they serve to generate. The value of the option should be determined as of the date that the option is granted.

The board prescribed that the value of each option be measured by the difference between the exercise price and the market price so long as the market price exceeds the exercise price. But, if, as in the situation just described, the exercise price is greater than the market price, then the option and the related compensation should be assumed to have a zero value. The board recognized that there is, in fact, value to options that are granted when the exercise price is greater than the market price. However, it considered the practical difficulties of determining such value to be insurmountable.

Example

On February 28, 1982, a firm grants an executive the option to purchase 1,000 shares of $1 par value common stock at a price of $8 per share. The option can be exercised during a five-year period beginning January 1, 1986, providing the executive is still employed by the firm. The market price of the stock on February 28, 1982, is $10 per share.

The compensation and the option would be assigned a value of 1,000 times $2 ($10 minus $8)—$2,000—and would be recorded on the date granted as follows:

Executive compensation (expense)	$2,000	
Capital received, stock options		$2,000

To record the issue of the employee stock options.

The account "Capital received, stock options" would be reported among the other owners' equity accounts. It would represent capital contributed by employees in the form of services rather than cash or other property. When the option is actually exercised, the issue of the 1,000 shares would be recorded as follows:

Capital received, stock options	$2,000	
Cash	8,000	
Common stock, par value		$1,000
Common stock, contributed capital in excess of par		9,000

To record the issue of 1,000 shares of common stock.

If, alternatively, the employees elected not to exercise the options and they lapsed, then no entry would be required (although "Capital received, stock options" could be reclassified to an account with a title indicative of the lapsed status of the options).

On March 31, 1982, the firm grants the executive an identical option. The market price of the stock has now fallen to $7 per share, however. Since the exercise price is greater than the market price, the option, for accounting purposes, is deemed to have a zero value; no journal entry is required to record the grant of the option.

When the option is actually exercised, the issue of the 1,000 shares would be recorded with the following entry:

Cash	$8,000	
Common stock, par value		$1,000
Common stock, contributed capital in excess of par		7,000

To record issue of 1,000 shares of common stock.

Note that the recorded value of the capital received is directly dependent on the market price of the common stock on the *date the options are granted* rather than the date on which the options are exercised and the shares issued.

EXTRAORDINARY ITEMS

Extraordinary items are those that are *unusual in nature and infrequent in occurrence*. In Opinion Nos. 9 and 15, the Accounting Principles Board directed that extraordinary items be segregated from other revenues and expenses and reported separately on the income statement. The board recommended that they be included as part of the income statement as follows:

Income before extraordinary items	$xxxx
Extraordinary items (less applicable taxes of $___) (Explanatory note:_____)	xxxx
Net income	$xxxx

As indicated by the suggested presentation, the taxes associated with the extraordinary items should be presented along with those items. The taxes applicable to the extraordinary items should, therefore, be excluded from the tax expense reported in the main body of the income statement.

To help assure uniformity of practice, the board established rigorous criteria as to what constitutes an extraordinary item. To qualify as extraordinary, an item (as set forth in Opinion No. 30) must be unusual in nature in that "the underlying event or transactions should possess a high degree of abnormality and be of a type clearly unrelated to or only incidentally related to the ordinary and typical activities of the entity." It should be characterized by infrequency of occurrence in that it should be "of a type not reasonably expected to recur in the foreseeable future." Examples of events or transactions that would ordinarily be categorized as extraordinary items are losses resulting from major casualties such as earthquakes, expropriations of property by foreign governments, or governmental prohibitions against the sale or use of products which the company had previously manufactured. Examples of events or transactions that would not be categorized as extraordinary items and should thereby be reported along with ordinary expenses are write-offs of receivables, losses on the sale of a plant, and losses from foreign currency revaluations.

EARNINGS PER SHARE

If there is any one single measure of corporate performance that is of primary concern to common stockholders and potential investors, it is unquestionably earnings per share (EPS). In its simplest form, calculation of earnings per share is straightforward:

$$\frac{\text{Net earnings} - \text{Preferred stock dividends}}{\text{Number of shares of common stock outstanding}}$$

Net earnings should be those after taxes. Preferred stock dividends must be deducted from earnings whenever the ratio is being computed for the benefit of common stockholders, since preferred dividends serve to reduce the equity of common stockholders.

Must Be Based on Average Number of Shares Outstanding

The number of shares outstanding should be based on the average number of shares outstanding during the year. Such average should be weighted by the number of months the shares may have been outstanding. The average number of shares outstanding, rather than simply the number outstanding at year end, must be used in the denominator to take into account the fact that the corporation may have had the use of the capital associated with any additional shares issued during the year only for a part of the year. The company's opportunity to generate earnings on the additional capital would have been limited by the number of months it had the use of such capital.

Example

A firm had earnings after taxes of $800,000. It paid preferred stock dividends of $200,000. It had 200,000 shares of common stock outstanding since January 1. On October 1, it issued an additional 100,000 shares of common stock.

Earnings available to common stockholders would be $600,000 (earnings after taxes less preferred dividends paid).

The average number of shares outstanding would be

200,000 shares × 9 months	1,800,000
300,000 shares × 3 months	900,000
	2,700,000
Divided by 12 months	÷ 12
	225,000 shares

Earnings per share of common stock would be

$$\frac{\$600,000}{225,000} = \$2.67$$

Must Account for Potential Dilution

As a consequence of the complex capital structures of many firms, the straightforward computation of earnings per share may be misleading. Although the average number of shares actually outstanding during a year is, by year end, a historical fact, many firms have commitments to issue additional shares in the future. If earnings per share are to have predictive value—if they are to be useful in forecasting future earnings—then the number of shares reasonably expected to be issued in the future must also be taken into account. Otherwise, earnings per share may take a precipitous drop in the period in which the additional shares are issued.

The obligation to issue the additional shares of common stock stems largely from commitments contained in other securities that may be outstanding: stock rights, warrants, and options as well as bonds and preferred stock that might be converted into common stock.

Stock rights, often called *preemptive* rights, represent commitments on the part of a company to issue, at an established price, a specified number of shares of common stock. A company would typically grant stock rights to existing shareholders whenever it intends to issue new shares of stock. The rights give the existing stockholders first opportunity to acquire the new shares and thereby to preserve their proportionate interests in the company.

Warrants, like rights, are promises on the part of a company to issue a stated number of shares at a set price. Warrants, however, are usually issued by companies in connection with the sale of bonds to make the bonds more attractive to prospective purchasers.

When a firm has a complex capital structure—one that includes such securities that could potentially result in the *dilution* of earnings per share—the calculation of earnings per share becomes both subjective and complicated: subjective because it must necessarily be based on a number of estimates and assumptions, and complicated because the issue of the additional shares will affect not only the number of shares outstanding but overall corporate earnings as well. The Accounting Principles Board, in Opinion No. 15, has set forth specific guidelines on the computation of earnings per share. An overview of its provisions will serve to indicate some of the difficulties of determining earnings per share when the capital structure is complex.

Opinion No. 15 requires that a firm with a complex capital structure present two types of earnings per share data on the face of its income statement. The first would indicate *primary earnings per share* and the second *fully diluted earnings per share.* The calculation of *both* of the earnings per share figures would take into account the impact of additional shares of common stock that might be issued. They differ, however, in that in the primary earnings per share calculation, the denominator (shares outstanding) of the EPS fraction is based on common stock presently outstanding as well as those other types of securities that are considered to be, in substance, *common stock equivalents.* In the computation of fully diluted earnings per share, the denominator includes all shares of common stock presently outstanding plus *all* (with a few exceptions) shares which the firm might have to issue in the future.

Number of Shares Must Be Adjusted for Common Stock Equivalents

Securities that are in substance *common stock equivalents* are those which are not, in form, common stock but which contain provisions which enable their holders to convert the securities into common stock. They are securities that derive their value from that of the common stock in that they can readily be converted into common stock. The holders of such securities can expect to participate in the appreciation of the value of the common stock and share in the earnings of the corporation. An option to purchase shares of common stock, for example, would ordinarily be considered to be a common stock equivalent as long as the exercise price is less than the prevailing market price of the common stock. As the common stock appreciates in value, so also will the option, since it can be converted into common stock.

Preferred stock that is convertible to common stock may or may not be a common stock equivalent. An issue of convertible preferred stock that provides its holders with a return approximately equal to that which they could obtain by purchasing similar securities without the conversion privilege would *not* be considered a common stock equivalent. It has a value in its own right; holders receive periodic dividend payments sufficient to provide them with a return comparable to that which they could obtain elsewhere. An issue of convertible preferred stock that provides its holders with a yield significantly less than they could obtain elsewhere *would*, however, be considered a common stock equivalent. Holders can be presumed to have purchased such securities in order to be able to convert their shares into common stock. The security derives its value primarily from the common stock into which it could be converted. Suppose, for example, that the prevailing rate of return that an investor could expect to receive is 12 percent. If an issue of convertible preferred stock is sold at a price to yield 12 percent, then it would *not* be considered a common stock equivalent; it does not derive its value primarily from the common stock. The potential number of shares of common stock to which it could be converted would not be taken into account in determining primary earnings per share. If, however, the stock is sold at a price to yield only 4 percent, then it would be considered to be a common stock equivalent, and the number of shares to which it could be converted would be included in the calculation of primary earnings per share. The convertible preferred stock that is not considered to be a common stock equivalent would, however, be taken into account in the calculation of fully diluted earnings per share. Opinion No. 15 sets forth, in detail, rules to be adhered to in determining whether a particular security is a common stock equivalent and whether the number of shares of common stock into which it could be converted should thereby be included in the computation of primary earnings per share. In general, a security would be considered a common stock equivalent if its yield *at the* *time it was issued* was less than two-thirds of interest rates (the average Aa corporate bond yield*) prevailing at the time.

Earnings Must Be Adjusted for Interest and Preferred Dividends Saved, as Well as Income from Additional Capital to Be Received

If, in computing earnings per share, both primary and fully diluted, it is assumed that certain securities will be converted into common stock and thereby increase the number of common shares outstanding, it is also necessary to give consideration to the impact of such conversion on the *earnings* of the company that are available to common stockholders. To the extent, for example, that it is assumed that outstanding bonds or preferred stock will be converted to common stock, the firm will no longer have to pay interest or dividends on such securities. The amounts saved will serve to increase the earnings in which the common stockholders have an equity interest. In determining the numerator (earnings) of the EPS fraction, the interest or dividends on preferred stock or bonds which are assumed to be converted into common stock must be added to the actual earnings for the year.

Outstanding stock warrants or options permit the holder to *purchase* (for cash) shares of common stock. If, in computing number of shares outstanding, it is assumed that warrants and options will be exercised and additional shares of common stock issued, it is also necessary to take into account the cash that will be received in exchange for the additional shares. Few firms will permit such cash to remain idle in a checking account.

Instead, they will invest it in income-producing projects. To the extent that the shares to be issued are added to the number of shares outstanding, it is necessary also to add the potential increase in corporate earnings to actual earnings for the year.

The Accounting Principles Board recognized the practical difficulties of estimating the additional income that would be derived from the cash received from the exercise of warrants and options. To avoid the confusion and diversity of practice that might result if each firm made arbitrary assumptions regarding income to be earned, the board directed that a firm presume that, instead of investing the proceeds from the exercise of the warrants and options in income-producing projects, the firm use the proceeds *to purchase and retire* shares of its own common stock; that is, to reduce the scale of its operations. The number of shares to be purchased and retired would be based on the present market price of the stock. If, for example, a company had 10,000 warrants outstanding, each of which could be used to acquire one share of common stock at a price of $54 per share, it would be assumed that the firm would receive $540,000 in cash. If the current market price of the common stock were $60 per share, then it would be assumed also that the $540,000 would be used to purchase and retire 9,000 shares of common stock. The effect of the method required by the board would be that 1,000 shares (10,000 shares issued less 9,000 assumed to be retired) would be added to the outstanding common shares but that no change in earnings would be assumed.

The board recognized that few firms would, in fact, use the proceeds from the exercise of warrants or options to retire common stock outstanding. It viewed the assumption as a practical means of taking into account the use of the funds received in exchange for the additional shares of common stock.

* The designation Aa refers to a rating of bond quality assigned by *Moody's* or *Standard & Poor's*, the leading bond rating services. Aa bonds are considered by both services to be high quality obligations of firms having a strong capacity to pay interest and repay principal.

Example

The capital structure of a firm included the following throughout all of 1983.

Common stock: 200,000 shares issued and outstanding.

Preferred stock, Class A: 50,000 shares issued and outstanding. Each share is convertible into *one* share of common stock. Each share pays a dividend of $2. The stock was initially sold to yield shareholders a return of 3 percent—a yield *substantially* below (less than two-thirds) the bond yields of 6 percent that prevailed at the time.

Preferred stock, Class B: 100,000 shares issued and outstanding. Each share is convertible into one share of common stock. Each share pays a dividend of $6. The stock was initially sold to yield shareholders a return of 7 percent—a yield approximately *equal* to the rate that prevailed at the time.

Executive stock options outstanding: Options to purchase 9,000 shares at a price of $40 per share are outstanding.

The current market price of common stock is $60 per share.

The firm had net earnings of $3 million. Out of this amount, $100,000 was paid in dividends to holders of preferred stock, Class A and $600,000 was paid in dividends to holders of preferred stock, Class B. Earnings available to common stockholders were, therefore, $2.3 million.

Preferred stock, Class B would *not* be considered a common stock equivalent, since it has value in its own right—its yield at time of initial issue was greater than two-thirds of prevailing bond yields.

Preferred stock, Class A would be considered a common stock equivalent, since it apparently would derive its value directly from the common stock—its yield at time of initial issue was less than two-thirds of prevailing bond yields.

The computation of earnings per share, both primary and fully diluted is shown in Exhibit 12-1.

EXHIBIT 12-1   Earnings per Share

Primary Earnings per Share		
Number of shares outstanding		
Common stock		200,000 shares
Common stock equivalents:		
Preferred stock, Class A		50,000
Options	9,000 shares	
Less: Shares of common stock assumed to be purchased and retired with proceeds of $360,000 ($40 × 9,000); $360,000 ÷ $60 (market price)	6,000	3,000
Shares outstanding for primary EPS calculation		253,000 shares
Earnings		
Earnings available to common stockholders (per information provided)		$2,300,000
Add: Dividends on preferred stock, Class A, considered to be a common stock equivalent		100,000
Income for primary EPS calculation		$2,400,000

$$\text{Primary EPS} = \frac{\$2,400,000}{253,000 \text{ shares}} = \$9.49$$

EXHIBIT 12-1 (continued)

Fully Diluted Earnings per Share

Number of shares outstanding	
Per primary EPS calculation	253,000 shares
Preferred stock, Class B (not a common stock equivalent	
but nevertheless convertible into common stock)	100,000
Shares outstanding for fully diluted	
EPS calculation	353,000 shares
Earnings	
Income for primary EPS calculation	$2,400,000
Add: Dividends on preferred stock, Class B assumed	
in calculation of number of shares outstanding to	
be converted into common stock	600,000
Income for fully diluted EPS calculation	$3,000,000

$$\text{Fully diluted EPS} = \frac{\$3,000,000}{353,000 \text{ shares}} = \$8.50$$

INTERIM FINANCIAL REPORTS

Publicly traded corporations are required, and many other firms elect, to issue interim financial reports. Interim financial reports are those that cover less than a full year; commonly they cover a quarter- or half-year period. The interim reports of most companies are not nearly so detailed as their annual reports; usually they indicate only a few key indicators of performance such as sales or net income and earnings per share.

The accounting principles to be followed in calculating income for a period of a quarter or half year are the same as those followed for a full year. Nevertheless, meaningful determination of income for short periods presents inherent difficulties. In an earlier chapter it was pointed out that over the life of an enterprise determination of income is relatively simple. Most accounting problems arise because of the need for financial information on a periodic basis. Revenues and expenses must be assigned to specific accounting periods long before the full consequences of a transaction are known with certainty. Prepaid and deferred costs must be *stored* in asset and liability accounts pending allocation to earnings of particular years. To the extent that interim periods are shorter than annual periods, the related problems of income determination and asset valuation are correspondingly greater. It becomes considerably more difficult to associate revenues with productive effort and to match costs with revenues.

Revenues and Expenses May Be Based on Annual Measures

The problems of preparing interim financial reports are compounded by the fact that whereas a period of one year will often correspond to a firm's natural business cycle, periods shorter than a year may be characterized by seasonal fluctuations in both revenues and expenses. Indeed, some revenues and expenses are determined on an annual basis; they cannot readily be calculated for a period less than a year until results for the entire year are known. As a consequence, meaningful interim reports cannot be prepared for any one period without consideration of anticipated financial activities in subsequent periods.

A corporate compensation plan may require a firm to pay year-end bonuses to employees based on annual measures of performance, such as corporate earnings or a salesperson's gross sales. The amount of the bonus cannot be determined, and will not be paid, until the end of the fourth quarter. Yet the bonus unquestionably represents compensation for services rendered throughout the year, not just the final quarter.

Some firms permit customers quantity discounts based on cumulative purchases during the year. The discounts may not take effect until the customer has reached a specified level of purchases—a level not likely to be attained until the third or fourth quarter of the year. Prices—and revenues—will appear to be higher in the earlier quarters than the later ones. Unless an adjustment to revenues is made to take into account the discounts to be granted in the future, the interim reports will overstate earnings.

In the same vein, firms may traditionally incur certain major costs in a particular season. Major repairs, for example, may be undertaken during a firm's "slow" season, but they benefit the entire year. Property taxes may be paid at the year end, but they represent an operating cost for the entire year. Unless these expenditures are taken into account and spread over the entire year, the interim reports for each individual period may be misleading.

Each Interim Period Should Be Viewed as Part of an Entire Year

An opinion of the Accounting Principles Board (Opinion No. 28) deals specifically with issues of interim reports. It emphasizes that each interim period should be viewed as an integral part of an annual period and that, as appropriate, adjustments should be made to expenses and revenues to take into account benefits received or costs incurred in other periods.

Although the opinion helped provide for greater uniformity of practice among firms, it did not (and, of course, could not) eliminate the underlying weaknesses of interim reports. Interim reports necessarily are based on an even greater number of subjective assumptions, estimates, and allocations than are annual reports. They provide financial information for a relatively short period of time; especially if a business is seasonal, they cannot be relied upon as predictors of earnings for the remaining periods of the year. If carefully prepared, they can serve as a useful means of comparing performance in one quarter with that in a corresponding quarter of a prior year, though usually not among quarters of the same year. Interim reports unquestionably provide information that is of value to investors and other users of financial reports—but only if the users are aware of their inherent limitations.

SUMMARY

In this chapter we have dealt with distributions of earnings, stock options, losses and contingencies, earnings per share, and interim reports. Although we discussed several diverse accounting problems, the general approach to resolving them must, in essence, be the same as that to the issues discussed in previous chapters. Accountants must discern the substance, as well as the form, of a transaction, they must measure and assign values to the goods, services, or securities exchanged and must make a judgment as to the appropriate accounting period in which to give recognition to the impairment or enhancement of company resources.

A corporation had earnings after taxes and preferred dividends of $500,000. It had, for the entire year, 100,000 shares of common stock outstanding.

The company also had outstanding 10,000 shares of preferred stock. The shares were issued at par ($100) and provide the holders with a return of 4 percent. Each share is convertible into one share of common stock. At the time the shares were issued, the prevailing rate of interest, as measured by Aa corporate bond yields, was 10 percent.

The firm's capital structure also includes 2,000 convertible bonds, each of which is convertible into 15 shares of common stock—a total of 30,000 shares of common stock. Each bond pays interest at a rate of 8 percent per year. The bonds were issued at a time when the Aa corporate bond yield was also 8 percent. Total annual interest costs are $160,000, but after-tax interest costs are only 52 percent (one minus the tax rate of 48 percent) of that amount—$83,200.

1. Which of the two issues of convertible securities would be considered a *common stock equivalent?* Why?

2. In determining *primary* earnings per share, how many shares of common stock should be considered outstanding? Such amount would include the actual number of shares of common stock plus the number of shares of common stock into which the common stock equivalent could be converted.

3. If the common stock equivalent were converted into common stock, by how much would interest or preferred dividends be reduced? What would be total earnings available to common stockholders?

4. Based on the calculations in (2) and (3), what would be *primary* earnings per share?

5. How many additional shares of common stock would the company be required to issue if the convertible security that is not considered a common stock equivalent were converted? How many shares of common stock should be con-

sidered outstanding in determining *fully diluted* earnings per share?

6. If the bonds were converted into common stock, by how much more would interest (after taking into account tax costs) be reduced? What would now be total earnings available to common stockholders?

7. Based on the calculations in (5) and (6), what would be *fully diluted* earnings per share?

QUESTIONS FOR REVIEW AND DISCUSSION

1. The *Wall Street Journal* reported that Gulf & Western Industries, Inc., declared a 100% stock dividend, said it intends to raise its quarterly dividend by the equivalent of 2.5 cents a current share and predicted record earnings for the coming fiscal year. Explain the significance of each of the three elements of the announcement. Which of the three is of most significance to the welfare of the stockholders? Which is of the least?

2. Dividends are sometimes said to be "paid out of retained earnings." Yet for many corporations, especially those that have been in existence for, and have expanded over, a period of several years, the balance in retained earnings is of little consequence in the decision as to the amount of dividends that can be declared. Why?

3. A firm owns 10,000 shares of stock in another corporation. It wishes to distribute the stock to its shareholders as a dividend in kind. The stock was purchased by the company as a temporary investment at a price of $4 per share. It has a present market value of $10 per share. If the company were to distribute the shares to its stockholders, how much gain on the transaction should the company report? Some accountants oppose recognizing gains or losses on distributions to stockholders. Why?

4. The following excerpt of a conversation was overheard in a crowded elevator in a Wall Street office building: "I just heard that IBM is going to split its stock two for one. The

announcement will be made later this week so you'd better purchase a few hundred shares before everyone else hears about it and the price skyrockets." Assuming that the tip is reliable, is there any reason for the price of IBM to "skyrocket"?

5. Why is it important that accounting recognition be given to executive stock options in the period that they are first issued? Why would it not be preferable to wait until the period in which the options are exercised—and the company actually receives cash and issues the additional shares—to record the option transactions?

6. In calculating earnings per share, why is it necessary to make assumptions as to what a firm will do with any cash received when options are exercised? Why not simply add the potential number of shares to be issued to the number of shares currently outstanding?

7. What is the distinction between primary earnings per share and fully diluted earnings per share? Are primary earnings per share necessarily based on the average of the actual number of shares outstanding during the year?

8. A firm incurred unusual losses on two of its six plants in 1982. Each plant had a book value, prior to the loss, of $100 million. One plant was destroyed by flood. Insurance covered only $60 million of the loss. The other plant was sold for $60 million. Should either of the losses be considered *extraordinary*? Explain.

9. Under what circumstances would income taxes for the current year be reported as an extraordinary item? Why?

10. "The deficiencies and limitations of financial statements are magnified many times when such reports are prepared on a quarterly rather than annual basis." Do you agree? Explain.

PROBLEMS

1. *Are stockholders really better off if they receive a cash, rather than a stock, dividend?*

As of January 1, 1983, the owners' equity section of Arrow Industries contained the following

balances:

Common stock, ($2 par value, 12,500,000 shares issued and outstanding)	$ 25,000,000
Capital in excess of par value	230,000,000
Retained earnings	300,000,000
	$555,000,000

In 1983 the company had earnings of $20,000,000.

In 1982 the company had declared cash dividends of $1.50 per share. In 1983, however, the board of directors wished to use all available cash to expand facilities. It decided instead to issue a stock dividend "equivalent in value" (based on market prices) to the cash dividend.

The market price of the firm's common stock on December 31, 1983, was $60 per share.

a. How many additional shares of common stock should the company issue?

b. Prepare a journal entry to record the distribution of the additional shares.

c. Comment on whether the stockholders are as well off having received the stock as the cash dividend.

2. *You be the judge. Does a stock dividend represent income to the recipient?*

The case before the court presents the question whether, by virtue of the Sixteenth Amendment, Congress has the power to tax, as income of the stockholder, a *stock dividend* made lawfully and in good faith against earnings accumulated by the corporation since March 1, 1913.

The facts, as outlined, are as follows:

On January 1, 1916, the Standard Oil Company of California declared a *stock dividend;* the company issued additional shares to its stockholders and transferred a portion of its retained earnings to permanent capital (common stock and capital received in excess of par).

Plaintiff, a shareholder of Standard Oil Company of Cailfornia, received her pro rata number of additional shares. She was called on to pay, and did pay under protest, a tax imposed on the shares. The amount of the supposed income was her proportionate share of the retained earnings transferred to the other capital accounts.

Plaintiff has brought action against the Collector of Taxes to recover the tax. In her complaint she contends that the stock dividend was not income within the meaning of the Sixteenth Amendment.

Put yourself in the position of a judge hearing the case. Outline an opinion in which you decide whether the shareholder can recover the tax paid. The only issue you need to consider is whether a stock dividend constitutes income. Make certain that in your outline you summarize the arguments most likely to be made by *both* plaintiff (shareholder) and defendant (tax collector).

3. The economic as well as the accounting impacts of three types of dividends of "equal value" may be somewhat different.

The balance sheet of Cannon Industries reports the following amounts:

Cash		$ 2,000,000
Marketable securities		4,000,000
Other assets		14,000,000
Total assets		$20,000,000
Liabilities		$ 7,000,000
Common stock ($1 par value, 500,000 shares issued and outstanding)	$ 500,000	
Common stock, capital in excess of par	3,500,000	
Retained earnings	9,000,000	13,000,000
Total liabilities and owners' equity		$20,000,000

Marketable securities include 300,000 shares of Consolidated Industries, which were purchased at a cost of $6 per share.

In past years the company has paid annual dividends of $4 per share. This year the company is considering two other alternatives to a cash dividend which it hopes will have "equal value" to shareholders:

1. A dividend in kind of shares of Consolidated Industries. The market value of the shares is $8 per share. The company would distribute to stockholders one share of Consolidated for each two shares of Cannon owned—a total of 250,000 shares.
2. A stock dividend. The market value of Cannon Industries' stock is $80 per share. The company would distribute one additional share for each 20 shares presently owned—a total of 25,000 shares.
   a. Prepare journal entries that would be required if the company were to issue (1) the dividend in kind, (2) the stock dividend, (3) the cash dividend of $4 per share.
   b. Comment on any problems the company might face in issuing the cash dividend.

4. Although a stock dividend is comparable in economic substance to a stock split, it is not accounted for in the same manner.

The owners' equity section of the Cortland Co. includes the following balances as of June 30, 1982.

Common stock (80,000 shares par value $20, issued and outstanding)	$ 1,600,000
Common stock, capital in excess of par	9,200,000
Retained earnings	30,000,000
	$40,800,000

As of June 30 the market price of the firm's stock was $700 per share. On that date the firm issued to its stockholders an additional 16,000 shares.

a. Record the issuance of the additional shares if the transaction were to be accounted for as (1) a six-for-five stock split, (2) a stock dividend.
b. At what price would you anticipate the common stock would be traded subsequent to the issuance of the new shares?
c. Comment on how the individual stockholders should account for the additional shares received in their own books and records. How much income should they report for federal tax purposes?

5. The distinction between a stock split and a stock dividend may be a source of confusion.

Barron's contained the following two news items, back-to-back in the same article:

McQuay-Perfex, Inc., declared a 50% stock dividend and raised its quarterly cash dividend to 24 cents a share from 20 cents.

Stanley Works directors declared a three-for-two stock split and boosted the cash dividend on presplit shares to 40.5 cents from 36.0 cents.

a. Assume that the stockholders' equity of both firms comprised the following:

Common stock, par value $3	
(100,000 shares outstanding)	$ 300,000
Additional paid-in capital	800,000
Retained earnings	2,000,000
	$3,100,000

Prepare the journal entry, if any, that each of the firms would make to record the stock "dividend" or stock split.

b. Comment on why accountants, businessmen, as well as journalists are sometimes accused of using needlessly confusing jargon.

6. A firm accounts for dividends in kind in apparent violation of generally accepted accounting principles.

The 1976 annual report of American Express Company explains that the company had recently declared a dividend in kind. It distributed to its shareholders approximately 1,955,000 shares of the common stock of Donaldson, Lufkin & Jenrette, Inc. (DLJ), that it had held as an investment. The shares of DLJ had been carried on the books of American Express at $26,773,000 ($13.70 per share). The market value of the shares on the date of the declaration of the dividend was only $6,352,000 ($3.25 per share).

a. Prepare any journal entries that the company should make in connection with the dividend in kind. Remember that generally accepted accounting principles require that property distributed to shareholders be valued at market value and the difference between that value and carrying value should be reflected as a gain or loss.

b. The annual report of American Express also notes: "In management's opinion, the difference between the carrying value and market value of the DLJ investment . . . did not represent a permanent impairment in value (in which case a charge to income to the extent of the impairment would have been required under generally accepted accounting principles). Accordingly, the entire carrying value of the DLJ investment . . . was charged to retained earnings."

Prepare the entry most likely made by the company.

c. What reservations might you have regarding the manner in which American Express accounted for the dividend in kind?

7. Restrictions on the payment of dividends that are based on balances in retained earnings may be inappropriate for some companies.

The Mineral Wells Mining Co. was organized for the sole purpose of extracting ore from a deposit that the company intended to purchase. It is anticipated that after the property is mined, the company will be dissolved.

The company issued 10,000 shares of common stock ($1 par value) at a price of $110 per share. It purchased the properties for $1 million cash.

During its first year of operations the company extracted 25 percent of the available ore. It had sales revenue of $400,000 and operating expenses and taxes of $100,000, *excluding* depletion. All revenues were received, and all operating expenses were paid, in cash.

The company estimates that it requires an operating cash balance of $100,000.

a. Prepare an income statement and a balance sheet which would reflect the results of operations for the first year.

b. Based entirely on the cash requirements of the firm, what is the maximum cash dividend it can afford to pay?

c. Prepare a journal entry to record payment of such "dividend." (Debit owners' equity accounts directly rather than "dividends.")

d. The statutes of many states prohibit companies from paying dividends in amounts greater than the existing balance in retained earnings. The purpose of the restriction is to assure that distributions of corporate assets are not made to stockholders at the expense of creditors. Do you think that such restrictions should apply to companies organized to extract minerals from specific properties? What would be the impact, over time, of such restrictions on the assets of the companies?

8. *Employee stock options represent a cost of compensating employees. They should be recorded as an expense in the accounting period during which the employees perform the related services.*

The Warwick Co. has adopted a stock option plan which entitles selected executives to purchase shares of its common stock at $40 per share, the price at which the stock was being traded in the open market on the date the plan was adopted.

The plan provides that the options may be exercised one year after being received provided that the executive is still employed by the company. The options lapse, however, $2\frac{1}{2}$ years after they have been issued.

Each option entitles the executive to purchase one share of common stock, which has a par value of $5.

The following transactions or events with respect to the option plan took place over a period of years:

12/31/80: The company issued 1,000 options to its executives. Market price of the stock on that date was $52.

12/31/81: The company issued an additional 2,000 options. Market price of the stock was $35.

7/1/82: Executives exercised 800 of the options issued in 1980. Market price of the common stock was $42.

3/6/83: Executives exercised 1,000 of the options issued in 1981. Market price of the common stock was $48.

6/30/83: The remaining 200 of the options issued in 1980 lapsed. Market price of the common stock was $47.

Prepare journal entries, as required, to record the above transactions and events.

9. *Owing to outstanding stock appreciation rights, an increase in the market price of a firm's shares caused a decrease in reported earnings.*

In a recent column, the *Wall Street Journal* called Texas International, an Oklahoma City-based exploration company, one of the year's "hottest trading stocks." In 1980 and the first

quarter of 1981 the price of the stock increased more than four-fold. It traded as high as $46\frac{7}{8}$, which, as the *Wall Street Journal* indicated, is "not bad" for a company that had 1980 earnings of only 76 cents a share.

But the *Wall Street Journal* pointed to a dark cloud in front of the silver lining. Both the chairman and the president of the company hold "stock appreciation rights." These rights entitle the officers to *cash payments* based on the increase in the market value of the company's shares. For each right held, the officers will receive the difference between the per share selling price as of specified dates and a stated exercise price ($4\frac{3}{8}$).

Every fiscal quarter, according to the *Wall Street Journal*, the company must charge an expense account with an amount reflective of the stock's rise and the corresponding increase in the firm's obligation to the officers. In the first quarter of 1981 the firm had to charge about $5.2 million to earnings—earnings which, after the charge, were less than $3 million.

a. Distinguish between the stock appreciation rights described in this problem and the employee stock options described in the chapter.

b. Why must Texas International charge an expense each period to reflect the increase in the market price of the shares? Why can't the company record the full amount of compensation expense at the time the rights are granted, as it would if it had granted stock options?

c. Is the company really as badly off economically as implied by the substantial charges against income? Suppose that first quarter 1981 earnings, prior to charges relating to stock appreciation rights, were $8.2 million. The firm's obligation to holders of stock appreciation rights increased during the quarter by $5.2 million. The firm had outstanding 9.5 million shares of common stock.

   1. The firm decides to acquire the $5.2 million in cash needed to satisfy the rights obligations by issuing new shares of common stock. Assume that the market price per share is $50. How many new shares would the firm have to issue?

   2. What would be earnings per share, assuming no charge to earnings for stock appreciation

rights, based on 9.5 million shares of common stock outstanding?

3. What would be earnings per share, assuming no charge to earnings for stock appreciation rights, based on the number of shares outstanding after the additional shares had been issued?

10. This problem provides a review of several types of transactions that affect owners' equity.

As of January 1, 1982, the owners' equity section of the Green Mountain Co. contained the following balances:

Common stock, $4 par value (100,000 shares issued and outstanding)	$ 400,000
Common stock, capital received in excess of par	600,000
Retained earnings	800,000
	$1,800,000

During 1982 the following events took place:

1. On January 7, the company issued to executives options to purchase 2,000 shares of common stock at a price of $25 per share. The market price of the common stock on that date was $28 per share.

2. On February 1, the company purchased 2,000 shares of its own stock in the open market at a price of $20 per share. The firm intended to use the stock to satisfy obligations on outstanding options.

3. On February 10, the company declared a cash dividend of $.50 per share. The dividend was paid on February 23.

4. On March 7, executives exercised options to purchase 2,000 shares. The market price of the common stock on that day was $26 per share.

5. On May 10, in lieu of its usual quarterly cash dividend, the company declared and paid a dividend in kind. The company distributed to shareholders 5,000 shares of Pacific General Co. common stock that had been held as an investment. The prevailing market price for the shares was $10 per share; they had been purchased previously, and recorded on the books of Green Mountain Co., at a price of $2 per share.

6. On August 10, the company declared and paid a stock dividend equal in value (based on the current market price of the shares issued) to the $.50 per share of its traditional quarterly dividend. The market price of the shares on that date was $25.

7. On December 17, the company declared a stock split. For each old share owned, stockholders would be given *two* new shares.

8. On December 28, the company issued to executives the options to purchase 4,000 shares at a price of $12.50 per share. The market price of the common stock on that date was $10 per share.

Prepare journal entries to record the above events. (Debit any dividends directly to the owners' equity accounts affected rather than to "dividends.")

11. End-of-year changes in number of shares outstanding will have but little effect upon earnings per share.

In November 1983, the controller of a firm estimated that net earnings for the year ending December 31 would be approximately $500,000, an amount considerably less than the $600,000 for the previous year. Aware that the newspapers commonly focus on earnings per share, the controller devised a scheme to boost EPS. On December 1, the firm would acquire in the open market 20,000 shares of its own common stock. It would immediately retire those shares. The acquisition and retirement would serve to reduce the denominator of the EPS ratio and thereby boost EPS. Throughout 1982 and the first eleven months of 1983 the firm had 100,000 shares of common stock outstanding.

a. Determine EPS for 1982 and 1983, based on 100,000 shares outstanding.

b. Determine EPS for 1983 as the controller apparently expects it will be computed.

c. Will the scheme of the controller be successful? Determine EPS for 1983 in accord with generally accepted accounting principles.

12. An understanding of the principles underlying the computation of earnings per share helps in interpreting information contained in a firm's annual report.

The following information pertaining to earnings per share appeared in an annual report of the Monsanto Company. Income and the number of shares used in the computation of earnings per common and common equivalent share were determined as shown.

Earnings per Common Share

	Primary	Fully Diluted
Income (millions of dollars)		
Net income	$ 366.3	$ 366.3
Preferred dividends	(2.2)	
Interest (less tax) on:		
Loan stock of Monsanto Limited	0.3	0.3
Debentures of Monsanto International Finance Company		0.5
	$ 364.4	$ 367.1
Number of Shares (thousands of shares)		
Weighted average shares:		
Outstanding	35,835	35,835
Incremental shares for outstanding stock options	161	167
Shares issuable upon conversion:		
Loan stock of Monsanto Limited	276	276
Debentures of Monsanto International Finance Company		269
$2.75 preferred stock		983
	36,272	37,530

a. Is the firm's $2.75 preferred stock a common stock equivalent? How can you tell?
b. Why were preferred dividends of $2.2 million deducted from the computation of primary earnings but not fully diluted earnings?
c. Are the debentures (bonds) of Monsanto International Finance Company (a consolidated subsidiary) common stock equivalents? How can you tell?
d. Why is the term "incremental" used in describing the shares to be issued in connection with outstanding stock options?

13. The procedure for determining earnings per share, although complex, is designed to make certain that potential dilution is taken into account.

In 1982 the Sutton Company had earnings after taxes and before dividends of $300,000. The company has 100,000 shares of common stock issued and outstanding. The corporate income tax rate may be assumed to be 40 percent.

In addition, the company has outstanding $500,000 of bonds that are convertible into common stock. Each $1,000 of bonds may be converted into 40 shares of common stock. The bonds were sold to yield 4 percent. When they were issued, corporate Aa bond yields were 8 percent.

The company also has outstanding 3,000 shares of $100 par value convertible preferred stock. Each share of preferred stock may be exchanged for five shares of common stock. The preferred stock carries a dividend rate of $10 per share. The stock was issued at par (no discount or premium) at a time when the prevailing Aa corporate bond yields were 7 percent.

a. Determine primary earnings per share.
b. Determine fully diluted earnings per share.

14. In computing earnings per share a firm must make an assumption as to what it does with cash received when outstanding stock options are exercised.

Riggs Corporation had earnings after taxes in 1983 of $800,000. The company had 200,000 shares of common stock outstanding. The current market price of the common stock is $25 per share.

In 1979 the company adopted a stock option plan. Outstanding as of year-end 1983 are 5,000 options which enable the holder to purchase one share each at $20 per share and 10,000 options which may be exercised for one share each at $10 per share.

The company has 10,000 shares of 8 percent convertible preferred stock outstanding. Par value of the stock is $100; each share is convertible into *three* shares of common stock. The year-end 1983 market price of the preferred stock is $105. The preferred stock was issued at a time when the prevailing Aa corporate bond yields were 6 percent.

a. Determine primary earnings per share.
b. Determine fully diluted earnings per share.

15. *The question of how best to report upon pending litigation and final settlement of claims resulting from such litigation has always been a troublesome one to accountants.*

Assume the following facts:

In 1978 a major manufacturer of electrical equipment is charged by a group of customers with engaging in pricing practices that are in violation of antitrust statutes. The alleged illegal activities took place in the years 1975 to 1977. The customers file suit in federal court; they seek treble damages totaling $36 million. Attorneys for the defendant confidentially advise their client to "be prepared for a final judgment between $10 million and $20 million."

In 1981, after a lengthy trial, the company is found liable to the plaintiffs for $20 million in damages. The company announces its intention to appeal.

In 1982 an appeals court reverses the decision of the lower court and orders a new trial.

In 1983 the company agrees to an out-of-court settlement with the plaintiffs. The firm will pay damages of $6 million.

In 1984 the company pays the agreed-upon amounts to the plaintiffs.

How, in your judgment (irrespective of any official pronouncements on the subject), do you think the company ought to account for the litigation? Indicate any specific journal entry that you think the company should make during or at the end of each of the years in question. Consider the possibility of making supplementary disclosures in footnotes to the financial statements. Bear in mind that the financial statements will be public documents, available to the plaintiffs and their attorneys.

16. *When is a gain a gain?*

The following is an excerpt from a *Wall Street Journal* report of March 25, 1980:

Peabody International Corp. said net income of 71 cents a share reported for the fiscal fourth quarter included 30 cents a share of what it expects to recover from litigation against two subcontractors. That's about 44% of the earnings.

The company, in its first quarter report to shareholders, also disclosed that the Securities and Exchange Commission is investigating the inclusion in earnings of the hoped-for court awards.

As reported earlier this year, Peabody is seeking damages exceeding $2,566,000 against Dynamech Systems Inc. and more than $1,288,000 against Inseco Inc., two subcontractors Peabody terminated on a contract in Craig, Colo. Peabody filed suits against them in federal court in Denver, which are still pending.

Based on the 10.5 million Peabody shares outstanding, the expected awards totaled more than $3 million of Peabody's earnings of $6.9 million for the fiscal fourth quarter, ending Sept. 30.

a. Based on the limited information provided in the article, what do you think is the basis of the Securities and Exchange Commission investigation? In what other way might the litigation have been accounted for and reported?

b. How do you think Dynamech Systems, Inc., and Inseco Inc., accounted for and reported the suit?

17. *Getting out of diapers can be costly.*

The *Wall Street Journal* of February 12, 1981, reported that "Johnson & Johnson has thrown in the diaper. The big medical care and consumer health products concern said it will soon stop selling its disposable diaper in the U.S., thereby conceding the $1.8 billion U.S. market to Procter & Gamble Co. and Kimberly-Clark Corp."

The *Wall Street Journal* indicated that "Johnson & Johnson said the action will result in an estimated charge of $14 million to $16 million against first quarter earnings."

Industry sources, according to the *Journal*, considered a competitive product, Luvs, superior to the Johnson & Johnson brand because "Luvs contours more closely to a baby's bottom and contains elastic around the legs, which Johnson's doesn't provide."

a. Why should "throwing in the diaper" result in a charge against earnings? What journal entry would the firm most likely make? What types of assets would most likely be written-off?

b. Based on the criteria outlined in the chapter, do you think the loss should be classified as ordinary or extraordinary?

18. *Seasonal businesses have special problems of interim reporting.*

Lakeview, Inc., operates a summer resort. The resort is open for guests during the summer months only. All of its revenue is earned during the summer months. In the first quarter (January 1 through March 31) of its fiscal year the company had zero revenues but made cash disbursements as follows:

Property taxes for the period January 1 to December 31	$ 60,000
Administrative salaries for the first quarter	30,000
Advertising	12,000
Repair and maintenance (annual overhaul of boats and docks)	7,000
Total disbursements	$109,000

a. For each disbursement consider whether, for purposes of interim reporting, (1) it should be charged as an expense as incurred, (2) it should be allocated evenly to each of the four quarters, or (3) it should be allocated on some other basis. (Use your judgment; the answer cannot be found in the text.)

b. Comment on the special difficulties faced by seasonal businesses in preparing interim reports. (In practice, policies with regard to the allocation of costs such as those indicated in this problem vary from firm to firm. There are no specific professional guidelines that deal with seasonal industries.)

19. *First period "interim" earnings must be adjusted to take into account events of subsequent periods.*

For the first three months in 1982, the Warwick Company, according to its president, had earnings before taxes of $140,000, determined as follows:

Sales		$420,000
Cost of goods sold	$200,000	
Other expenses	80,000	280,000
Income before taxes		$140,000

The following additional information has come to your attention:

1. The company gives quantity discounts to its customers based on total purchases for the year. No quantity discounts have been allowed to date. The firm estimates that total sales for the year, at *gross* sales price, will be $2 million. After taking into account quantity discounts, $200,000 of the sales will be at 95 percent of gross sales price (a discount of $10,000) and $400,000 will be at 90 percent of gross sales price (a discount of $40,000). Average selling prices for the year are thus somewhat lower than those implied by sales revenue of the first quarter.

2. The company uses the LIFO inventory method and determines year-end inventory and the annual cost of goods sold on the basis of a periodic inventory count, which is taken on December 31 of each year. The cost of goods sold for the quarter ending March 31 was calculated as follows:

Goods on hand 1/1:		
30,000 units @ $5	$150,000	
Production, 1st quarter:		
10,000 units @ $10	100,000	$250,000
Estimated goods on hand 3/31:		
10,000 units @ $5		50,000
Cost of goods sold, 30,000 units		$200,000

The company estimates that it will complete the year with an inventory of 30,000 units. As a consequence, the ending inventory will be stated at $5 per unit: The firm will not have to "dip" into its LIFO stock. The cost of goods sold for the entire year will be based on current production costs of $10 per unit.

3. The company overhauls its plant once a year in July at a cost of $20,000. The cost of the overhaul has not been taken into account in computing first-quarter expenses.

4. Each December the company gives its salaried employees a bonus equal to approximately 10 percent of their annual salaries. First-quarter salaries (included in other expenses), without

taking into account the bonus, amounted to $75,000.

5. Assume that the current federal income tax rate is 22 percent of the first $25,000 of taxable income and 48 percent on all earnings above that amount. The company estimates that taxable income for the entire year will be $80,000. Thus, its average effective rate for the year will be different than that based on first quarter earnings alone.

Determine earnings after taxes for the first quarter of 1982 as you believe they should be reported to the general public.

SOLUTIONS TO EXERCISE FOR REVIEW AND SELF-TESTING

1. A convertible security is considered a common stock equivalent if it derives its value from the common stock. The pragmatic test is whether its yield at the time it was issued was less than two-thirds of the Aa corporate bond rate. The preferred stock was issued to yield 4 percent at a time when the Aa rate was 10 percent. It would, therefore, be considered a common stock equivalent. The convertible bonds were issued to yield 8 percent at a time when the prevailing rate was also 8 percent. It would not, therefore, be considered a common stock equivalent.

2. 100,000 shares of common stock + 10,000 shares that would be issued if the preferred stock were converted = 110,000 shares.

3. Preferred dividends would be reduced by $40,000. Total earnings available to common stockholders would be $540,000.

4. Primary earnings per share = $540,000/110,000 shares = $4.91.

5. An additional 30,000 shares would be issued; 140,000 shares would now be outstanding.

6. Interest would be reduced by $83,200, after taking into account income taxes. Total earnings available to common stockholders would be $540,000 + $83,200 = $623,200.

7. Fully diluted earnings per share = $623,200/ 140,000 shares = $4.45.

INTERCORPORATE 13 INVESTMENTS AND EARNINGS

In this chapter we shall consider issues of accounting for and reporting intercorporate investments. Because they are sometimes of major magnitude, intercorporate investments are a source of continuing controversy. The means by which an investment in another company is recorded initially and updated subsequently are likely to be of considerable consequence for the valuation of assets and the determination of income.

It is, therefore, of utmost importance that both managers and investors understand how intercorporate activity will be reported. The impact on the financial statements of intercorporate events will affect policies not only of companies that own or may in the future own other firms, but also of those that are already owned by or may be an acquisition target of another.

MOTIVATION FOR, AND MEANS OF, OWNERSHIP

A corporation may acquire an equity interest (ownership of common or preferred stock) in another company for a number of reasons. A company may have cash that is temporarily idle. It may use this cash to purchase a relatively small number of the shares of another company in order to obtain a short-term return—as an alternative, perhaps, to purchasing short-term government notes or certificates of deposits. Such securities are categorized on the books of the acquiring corporation as "marketable securities"; the accounting for current marketable securities was discussed in Chapter 6. On the other hand, a company may purchase the stock of another corporation as a long-term investment. It may do so because it believes that the securities will provide a long-term return equivalent to, or greater than, that which could be obtained by internal use of available funds. Or, it may seek to obtain a sufficient number of shares to exercise a measure of influence and control over the other corporation in order to gain entry into new markets or new industries, to develop sources of raw materials, or to integrate its own operations with those of the other company. This chapter pertains to long-term investments.

A company may acquire the stock of another company by purchasing it for cash or other assets. Or, especially if it intends to get possession of all, or almost all, of the outstanding shares, it may exchange shares of its own common stock for those of the company it seeks to acquire. Moreover, a firm may obtain shares of another company simply by itself organizing such a company and retaining all, or a portion, of the shares issued. Many companies, to satisfy various legal requirements, to obtain certain tax advantages, or to enhance organizational efficiency, divide their operations into several subsidiary corporations, in each of which the *parent* corporation will hold controlling interest. Each subsidiary corporation may represent nothing more than a manufacturing or sales division or even a branch office. To take an extreme example, a well-known commercial loan company maintains separate corporations not only for each of its numerous branch offices but for each major type of loan made within a branch office. The parent corporation owns 100 percent of the common stock of all of the individual corporations.

LEVEL OF INFLUENCE

The critical determinant of the means by which intercorporate investments are accounted for is the degree of influence that the investor corporation exerts over the acquired company. To the extent that the investor corporation exerts relatively minor

influence, the investment would generally be accounted for by the *cost* method; to the extent that it exerts substantial influence, it would be accounted for by the *equity* method. (Both of these methods will be defined and evaluated shortly.) Insofar as the investor company is able to *control* the other company (control ordinarily being defined as ownership of over 50 percent of the voting stock), the investment is commonly reported by means of *consolidated financial statements.* Consolidated financial statements report the financial positions and earnings of two or more corporations as if they were a single entity. The three methods of accounting for corporate investments—the cost, the equity, and the consolidated statement method— are not, it should be emphasized, categorically consistent. *Since each corporation is a separate legal entity, a separate set of accounting records must, by law, be maintained for it. On the books of the investor corporation the shares of the other company must be accounted for by* either *the cost or the equity method. If, however, the investor company has control over another corporation, then, for purposes of reporting, the individual financial statements of the two companies can be combined into a single, consolidated, set of statements.* The relationships and distinction among the methods will be brought out in the next several sections.

Criteria for Presumption of Significant Influence

Where an investor corporation is unable to maintain significant influence over the company in which it owns an interest because of the small proportion of its holdings, then it should account for its investment by the cost method. Evidence of an ability to influence significantly the key financial and operating policies over an investee company may be manifest by several factors: percentage of shares owned, representation on the corporate board of directors, membership on key policy-making committees, interchange of managerial personnel, material purchases or sales between the two companies, and exchanges of technological information. Even though a company may not own a majority of a corporation's outstanding shares, it may nevertheless exercise a predominant impact on that company's policies. The Accounting Principles Board recognized that degree of influence cannot be readily measured. In order to make practice more uniform, however, it prescribed (in Opinion No. 18, 1971) that an investment of 20 percent or more should lead to a presumption that the investor has the ability to exercise significant influence over the investee. It directed, therefore, that investments of less than 20 percent of voting stock should be accounted for by the cost method. Those of 20 percent or more should generally be accounted for by the equity method. But if an investor company can demonstrate that even though it owns 20 percent or more of a firm's stock it, in fact, has little or no influence over the investee's operating and financial policies, then it should use the cost rather than the equity method.

COST METHOD

Under the cost method, a company records its investment in the stock of another company at cost—the amount paid to acquire the stock. It recognizes revenue from its investment only to the extent that the investee company actually declares dividends. In the absence of unusual declines in market values, the investment would be maintained on the books of the investor at original cost. The carrying value of the investment would be unaffected by changes either in the market value of shares owned or in the net worth of the company that they represent.*

Example

On January 2, 1982, the Adams Company purchases 10,000 of 100,000 (10 percent) shares of the outstanding common stock of the Cain Company. It pays $30 per share. The following entry would be required on the books of the *investor* company, the Adams Company:

Investment in Cain
  Company $300,000
    Cash $300,000
To record the purchase of 10,000 shares of Cain Company common stock.

On December 31, 1982, the Cain Company announces that earnings for the year were $500,000 ($5 per share of common stock).

No entry is required to record the announcement of the annual earnings. The Adams Company recognizes revenue from its investment only upon the actual declaration of dividends by the company whose shares it owns.

On the same date, December 31, 1982, the Cain Company declares dividends of $2 per share, payable on January 20, 1983.

Dividends receivable $20,000
  Revenue from investment
    in Cain Company $20,000
To record dividends to be received from the Cain Company.

* Financial Accounting Standards Board Statement No. 12, "Accounting for Certain Marketable Securities" (1976), provides that investments in other corporations which are accounted for by the cost method should be reported and valued in a manner similar to marketable securities in general. They should be valued at cost unless the market value of the entire portfolio of securities is less than its cost. In such event, the entire portfolio should be written down to, and reported at, market value.

The cost method of maintaining investments is that illustrated in previous chapters in connection with marketable securities and recognition of dividend revenue. Dividends are recognized as revenue when they are declared, not when they are received.

EQUITY METHOD

Under the equity method, a company records its investment in another company at cost (the same as under the cost method), but it periodically adjusts the carrying value of its investment to take into account its share of the investee's earnings subsequent to the date it acquired the stock. It recognizes its share of increases or decreases in the net worth of the investee as soon as they are known to it. If net worth increases as a result of investee corporate earnings, then the investor company recognizes promptly, on its own books, revenue in the amount of its proportionate share of such earnings; it does not wait until such earnings are distributed in the form of dividends. Since earnings of the investee company serve to increase the equity of the investor company in the investee company, the investor company will concurrently increase the carrying value of its investment by its share of total revenue recognized.

If net worth of the investee corporation decreases, then the investor will also recognize such decreases. Net worth will decrease as a consequence of operating losses. But it will also decrease whenever dividends are declared (a liability for the payment of a dividend is established; retained earnings are decreased). Hence, as the investee company declares a dividend, the investor company recognizes the dividend receivable and at the same time adjusts the carrying value of its investment to reflect the decline in the net worth of the investee. An example may help to clarify the accounting procedures.

Example

Assume the same facts as in the previous example, except that this time, on January 2, 1983, the Adams Company purchases 20,000 of 100,000 (20 percent) shares of the common stock outstanding of the Cain Company. Again, it pays $30 per share. This time, however, since Adams has acquired 20 percent of the shares outstanding, it may be presumed that it exerts substantial influence over the Cain Company; hence, it is appropriate to account for the investment by the equity method.

(a)

Investment in Cain		
Company	$600,000	
Cash		$600,000

To record the purchase of 20,000 shares of Cain Company common stock for $30 per share.

This entry is identical in form to that illustrated previously in connection with the cost method.

On December 31, the Cain Company announces that earnings for the year were $500,000 ($5 per share of common stock).

(b)

Investment in Cain		
Company	$100,000	
Revenue from investment		
in Cain Company		$100,000

To record the proportionate share of the 1982 income reported by the Cain Company.

The net worth of the Cain Company increased by $500,000 as a consequence of 1983 earnings. The Adams Company must recognize 20 percent of that amount as its own revenue. Since the Adams Company receives no cash or other assets as a direct result of the Cain Company having realized the income, its share of the earnings would be reflected by an increase in the carrying value of its investment.

When the Cain Company declares a dividend of $2 per share, the Adams Company would establish a receivable account for the dividends but would recognize a corresponding *decrease* in the carrying value of its investment.

(c)

Dividends receivable $40,000
     Investment in Cain
       Company $40,000
To record dividends to be received from the Cain Company.

Upon learning that the Cain Company had declared a dividend, the Adams Company would *not*, under the equity method,

would be reduced by the amount of the dividend received because, as a result of cash distributions to its shareholders, the Cain Company has reduced both its assets and its retained earnings. The share of the Adams Company in such retained earnings has thereby been proportionately reduced.

As indicated in the accompanying T accounts, the net effect of the last two entries (**b** and **c**) has been to increase the assets of the Adams Company by $100,000 (investment in Cain Company, $60,000; dividends receivable, $40,000). Correspondingly, the Adams Company recognized $100,000 in revenue from its investment in the Cain Company. The $100,000 represents, of course, 20 percent of the reported earnings of the Cain Company.

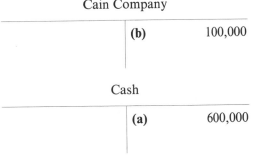

Investment in Cain Company			
(a)	600,000	(c)	40,000
(b)	100,000		

Revenue from investment in Cain Company		
	(b)	100,000

Dividends receivable	
(c)	40,000

Cash		
	(a)	600,000

The investment account of a corporation is increased (debited) when the net assets of the company that it owns increase as a consequence of periodic earnings.

The investment account is decreased (credited) when the net assets of the company that it owns decrease as a consequence of dividend declarations.

recognize revenue. Revenue representing the earnings of the Cain Company had been recognized at the time it was first reported. To recognize it again when it is distributed to shareholders in the form of dividends would be to count it twice. The carrying value of the investment in the Cain Company

COST AND EQUITY METHODS COMPARED

The justification for the cost and the equity methods and the distinctions between them can readily be appreciated when the two methods are viewed within the context of issues of revenue recognition. A company owns stock in another company. If the investee company is profitable, the investor company is obviously better off than if the investee company is not. Since, in the long run, earnings of a company represent revenue to its owners, earnings of the investee company signify revenue to the investor company. The question facing the accountant of the investor company relates to the point in time at which such revenue should be recognized.

Under the cost method the investor company recognizes as revenue its share of investee corporation earnings only as the investee corporation actually declares dividends—that is, as it announces its intention to distribute to shareholders the assets corresponding to the earnings available for distribution. The cost method is thereby more conservative than the equity method. Under this method revenue is recognized by the investor company only as cash (assuming that the dividend is to be paid in cash) is about to be received. The cost method makes sense when an investor company has but little influence on the dividend or other operating policies of the company in which it owns shares, for although the investee company may be profitable, it need not necessarily declare dividends, and the investor company cannot require it to do so. It may be many years, therefore, before earnings of the investee company are translated into liquid assets of the investor company.

Cost Method Permits
Income Manipulation

Under the equity method, the investor company recognizes as revenue its share of investee company earnings as soon as such earnings are reported, regardless of when such earnings are likely to be distributed to shareholders in the form of dividends. The equity method is appropriate when the investor company does have significant impact on the dividend policy of the investee firm. The rationale for the equity method can easily be understood if the consequences of *not* using the method are considered. If the investor had sufficient influence on the investee so that it could control if and when the investee could declare dividends, then it could readily control its own earnings. If the investor firm otherwise had an unprofitable year, it could direct that the investee firm increase its dividend payout. Its share of the dividends would be reflected immediately in higher reported revenues. If the investor firm otherwise had an unusually profitable year and did not "need" additional revenues in order to report satisfactory earnings, it could request that the investee firm delay payment of dividends until future periods. In Chapter 5 it was pointed out that revenue should be recognized only when it can be objectively measured and when eventual collection of cash can reasonably be assured. When a firm is able to exert substantial influence (characterized by the Accounting Principles Board as ownership of 20 percent or more of voting stock) over the company in which it maintains an interest, then the two criteria are reasonably satisfied at the time the investee company reports its earnings. The equity method is thereby considered more appropriate. When the firm is unable to exert such influence, then the criteria are not reasonably satisfied until the investee company declares its intention to distribute cash or other assets. Hence, the cost method is more appropriate.

CONSOLIDATED REPORTS

When a company is able to control, as opposed to merely influence, the financial and operating policies of another company, then the interests of investors as well as other users of financial statements are usually most meaningfully served by the preparation of consolidated financial statements. Consolidated financial statements report the financial position and results of operations of two or more corporations, each a separate legal entity, as if together they were a single economic entity. They are designed to give effect to the economic substance as opposed to the legal form of the corporate relationship. They combine the assets, liabilities, equities, revenues, and expenses of the two or more companies into a single balance sheet and income statement.

Consolidated statements are a means of *reporting*. The preparation of consolidated financial statements does not preclude the preparation of individual financial statements for specific purposes. Indeed, each member of a group of corporations whose financial statements may be combined into a single consolidated set of statements must maintain separate accounting records. An investor corporation must, therefore, account for its ownership in other companies by either the cost or the equity method—although, as will be seen shortly, choice of method becomes immaterial since both the investment accounts and the revenue from investment accounts are eliminated in the process of consolidation.

The usual condition for consolidated statements is voting control of one company by another—that is, ownership of more than 50 percent of the voting stock. There are, however, exceptions to this rule. Consolidated statements would not generally result in the most meaningful presentation and are, therefore, not required when the two or more companies are not, in fact, a single economic entity (if, for example, voting control is likely to be only temporary). Similarly, if a subsidiary company is in a specialized industry,

one in which unique accounting practices are adhered to, the presentation of individual reports might be more useful to investors than a consolidated report.

As a general rule, if an investor company owns less than 20 percent of the voting stock of another company, it would *account* for its investment on the cost basis; if it owns 20 percent or more, then it would *account* for its investment on an equity basis; if it owns over 50 percent, it would *report* to stockholders on a consolidated basis, unless because of special circumstances consolidation is deemed inappropriate.

A company that has control (over 50 percent ownership) of another company is referred to as a *parent;* the controlled company is known as a *subsidiary.*

PRINCIPLES OF CONSOLIDATION— BALANCE SHEET

In simplest form consolidated statements represent the sum of the balances in accounts of the individual companies which are to form the consolidated entity. However, as will be demonstrated in the discussion and examples to follow, certain eliminations and adjustments are required if double counting is to be avoided.

The objective of consolidated statements is to depict the financial position and results of operations of two or more companies as if they were a single economic entity. It is necessary, therefore, to adjust for the effect of certain intercompany transactions on both the income statement and the statement of position. Consider the following: If a parent company sells for $100 merchandise to a subsidiary company, which in turn sells it to outsiders for $120, then the sum of the sales of the two companies would be $220. But if the two companies were viewed as a single entity, then the sale from the parent to the subsidiary would be accounted for as an internal transfer rather than a sale. Total sales—those to outsiders—would be only $120. Elimination of the sale from parent to subsidiary is thereby required. Similarly, the cost of the goods sold by the parent to the subsidiary would have to be eliminated, and if the subsidiary is still indebted to the parent for the goods which it purchased, so also would the account receivable (on the books of the parent) and the account payable (on the books of the subsidiary).

The examples to follow will center first upon the effects of consolidation on the balance sheet and then on the income statement.

Inter-Company Investments and Debts

Assume that Parent company purchases 100 percent of the common stock outstanding of Subsidiary company. Immediately after acquisition, the trial balances of the two individual companies appear in condensed form, as follows:

	Parent	Subsidiary
Cash	$ 20,000	$10,000
Account receivable (from subsidiary)	10,000	
Investment in subsidiary	40,000	
Other assets	80,000	40,000
	$150,000	$50,000
Account payable (to parent)		$10,000
Common stock	$ 30,000	10,000
Retained earnings	120,000	30,000
	$150,000	$50,000

Since the balances indicated are those immediately following acquisition, it is clear that the parent company must have paid $40,000 to acquire the subsidiary—the amount indicated in its investment in sub-

sidiary account. If the two companies are to be combined, there is no need for an investment in subsidiary account; from a consolidated standpoint, a company cannot have an investment in itself. At the same time, if the two sets of statements are to be combined, it would be inappropriate to report $40,000 owners' equity (common stock, $10,000, plus retained earnings, $30,000) of the subsidiary, since it is the parent company which is the sole owner of the subsidiary and which has such equity in the subsidiary. To effect a consolidation, it would be necessary to eliminate *both* the investment in the subsidiary *and* the equity of the owners. For convenience, the eliminations can be expressed in journal entry form:

(a)

Common stock (of subsidiary)	$10,000	
Retained earnings (of subsidiary)	30,000	
Investment in subsidiary (by parent)		$40,000

To eliminate the investment in subsidiary and corresponding subsidiary owners' equity accounts.

The trial balance indicates that the subsidiary company owes the parent company $10,000. From the standpoint of the combined enterprise, both accounts receivable and payable would be overstated if assets and liabilities were simply added together; a company cannot have a payable to or a receivable from itself. The payable and receivable must be eliminated:

(b)

Account payable (to parent)	$10,000	
Account receivable (from subsidiary)		$10,000

To eliminate intercompany payable and receivable.

EXHIBIT 13-1   Eliminating Inter-Company Investments and Debts

	Original Statements		Adjustments		Combined Statements
	Parent	Subsidiary	Debit	Credit	
Cash	$ 20,000	$10,000			$ 30,000
Account receivable (from subsidiary)	10,000			(b) $10,000	
Investment in subsidiary	40,000			(a) 40,000	
Other assets	80,000	40,000			120,000
	$150,000	$50,000			$150,000
Account payable (to parent)		$10,000	(b) $10,000		
Common stock	$ 30,000	10,000	(a) 10,000		$ 30,000
Retained earnings	120,000	30,000	(a) 30,000		120,000
	$150,000	$50,000	$50,000	$50,000	$150,000

The two adjustments would be made to the books of neither *the parent nor the subsidiary. They are nothing more than* worksheet *eliminations to effect a combination of the two individual sets of statements.* Thus, the consolidated balance sheet would appear as indicated in the far right-hand column in Exhibit 13-1.

Interests of Minorities

A firm does not always acquire 100 percent of the outstanding common stock of another firm. *Minority stockholders* may also own an equity interest in an investee firm. Assume facts similar to those in the previous example, but this time suppose that the parent company purchased only 80 percent of the common stock of the subsidiary. The parent company paid $32,000 for its interest, an amount exactly equal to 80 percent of the *book value* of the subsidiary, as represented by common stock of $10,000 and retained earnings of $30,000.

The parent company's investment in subsidiary of $32,000 must be eliminated against $32,000 of the $40,000 owners' equity of the subsidiary:

Common stock (of subsidiary)	$ 8,000
Retained earnings (of subsidiary)	24,000
Investment in subsidiary (by parent)	$32,000

To eliminate investment in subsidiary and corresponding amounts in subsidiary's owners' equity accounts.

But that leaves $8,000 remaining in the owners' equity accounts of the subsidiary. This amount represents the equity of the minority shareholders—those who hold the remaining 20 percent interest in the firm. Consolidated financial statements are prepared from the perspective of the *majority* stockholders, those of the parent company. From the standpoint of a majority stockholder, it would be both confusing and misleading to report on the balance sheet common stock and retained earnings in two companies—those of the parent and those of the subsidiary. Hence, the minority interest in each of the owners' equity accounts (the amounts that remain after the majority interest has been eliminated) are reclassified into a single account, "minority interest in subsidiary":

Common stock (of subsidiary)	$2,000	
Retained earnings (of subsidiary)	6,000	
Minority interest in subsidiary		$8,000

To reclassify the equity of minority shareholders in the subsidiary.

The minority interest in subsidiary account represents the equity of the minority shareholders in the consolidated corporation. It is, in a sense, the portion of the residual interest in the subsidiary that may be assigned to the minority rather than the majority stockholders. Common practice is to report minority interest in subsidiaries on a single line between long-term liabilities and owners' equity. The amounts reported in the owners' equity section of the consolidated balance sheet represent only the equity of the parent company stockholders.

Acquisition Price in Excess of Investment Book Value

In the discussion so far, the price paid by the parent to acquire its investment in the subsidiary was exactly equal to its proportionate share of the *book value* (which is equal to the *owners' equity*) of the subsidiary. If, as is common, the parent company acquires its interest at an amount greater than the book value of the assets acquired, then such excess must be accounted for and reported in a manner indicative of its nature.

Assume now that Parent Co. paid $45,000 to acquire a 100 percent interest in Subsidiary Co. but that the net assets of Subsidiary Co. as recorded on its own books are only $40,000. As in the previous examples, if the financial positions of the two individual companies are to be shown as if they were a single economic entity, then both the investment of the parent and its corresponding owners' equity as recorded on the books of the subsidiary must be eliminated. This time, however, although the investment would be recorded on the books of the parent at $45,000, the corresponding equity is recorded on the books of the subsidiary at only $40,000.

The portion of the investment ($40,000) that represents its value as recorded on the books of the subsidiary can be eliminated against the corresponding owners' equity with an entry identical to that made in a previous example. That leaves $5,000 (the excess of $45,000 paid over the corresponding book value of $40,000) of the investment still to be accounted for.

specific tangible or intangible assets

This excess of cost over book value is often a source of confusion and misunderstanding. There are at least two reasons a firm may pay for an interest in a subsidiary an amount in excess of the book value of such interest. First, the book value of individual assets (and hence the recorded owners' equity) is based on historical cost—the amount initially paid to acquire the assets, less amortization and depreciation. Book value, as frequently emphasized throughout this text, is not necessarily indicative of fair market value. Thus, the price paid by the company to acquire its shares of stock in the subsidiary may be indicative of the fair market value of the individual assets represented by such shares. If such is the case, then the excess of cost over book value should be assigned to the particular assets acquired. Consistent with the historical cost basis of accounting, assets should be valued at purchase price. The mere fact that the parent company may not have purchased the assets directly, but instead acquired the common stock of the company that has title to the assets, does not change the substance of the transaction. Nor should it change the manner in which the assets are to be accounted for. Sometimes, in fact, as is the case with intangible assets, the assets acquired may not even be recorded on the books of the subsidiary. In accord with generally accepted accounting principles, patents, copyrights, or trademarks when developed internally (as opposed to purchased from outsiders) are not given accounting recognition. When such assets are obtained in connection with the purchase of a subsidiary, they should be stated at their fair market values and an appropriate share of the excess of the cost over the book value assigned to them. The following additional adjustment would be required insofar as the excess of cost over book value is to be allocated to specific assets:

Specific assets (land, buildings, equipment, patents, etc.)	$5,000	
Investment in subsidiary		$5,000

To allocate the excess cost of investment over book value to specific assets.

Subsequent to the acquisition, the consolidated enterprise should base its charges for depreciation and amortization on the amounts at which the assets are recorded on the consolidated balance sheet. Depreciation and amortization charges, as a consequence, may be greater on the consolidated income statement than the sum of the separate depreciation charges on the financial statements of the two individual companies. The acquired subsidiary, on its own financial statements, will maintain its assets and continue to base depreciation and amortization at the initial values of the assets.

goodwill

Second, a firm may pay to acquire another company an amount in excess of recorded book value because the company possesses certain intangible assets that cannot be specifically identified. Such assets may arise because of favorable customer attitudes toward the company, unusual talents of corporate managers, advantageous business locations, or special monopolistic or political privileges. Or they may arise because the individually identifiable assets when used together are worth considerably more than the sum of the fair market values of the assets employed independently. Whatever may be the attributes of such assets, however, they enable the firm to earn amounts in excess of "normal" returns. Such assets—that is, the amount in excess of book value that cannot be specifically allocated to other assets—may be classified as *goodwill*:

Goodwill	$5,000	
Investment in subsidiary		$5,000

To allocate the excess of cost over book value of investment to goodwill.

Goodwill, in a sense, is a residual. It represents that portion of the cost of acquiring a subsidiary that cannot be assigned directly to any specific assets. Goodwill is one asset that arises *only* out of business combinations. Although firms may over a number of years develop the attributes that comprise goodwill, they may not, under conventional accounting principles, give recognition to them. Goodwill may be recorded only when one firm purchases another and the excess of cost over book value cannot be specifically assigned to other assets.

As a consequence of the very nature of goodwill—it is a residual asset—its useful life is not readily determinable. Nevertheless, the Accounting Principles Board has prescribed that firms should make their best efforts to estimate the useful lives of all intangible assets, including goodwill, and that such assets should be amortized over their useful lives.* In no event, however, should the amortization period exceed 40 years. To the extent, therefore, that a consolidated entity records goodwill, it must each year reduce the balance in the goodwill account (a credit to goodwill) and increase expenditures by a like amount (debit to amortization of goodwill) by no less than one-fortieth of the initial amount recorded. Both the goodwill itself and the charge for amortization would appear only on the consolidated statements, not on those of either the parent or the subsidiary by itself.

PRINCIPLES OF CONSOLIDATION— INCOME STATEMENT

In essence, the consolidated income statement, like the consolidated balance sheet, presents the sum of the balances in the accounts of the component corporations. However, as with the balance sheet, numerous adjustments and eliminations may be necessary to give effect to transactions among the individual companies.

The consolidated income statement provides an indication of the change in enterprise welfare between two points in time as if the various components of the enterprise were a single economic entity. Principles of revenue and expense recognition must be applied as if the individual companies whose statements are to be consolidated were, in fact, combined into a single company. As a consequence, revenues and expenses, if they are to be recognized, must be the result only of arm's-length transactions with parties *outside* of the *consolidated* entity.

Intercompany transactions take many forms; the specific eliminations and adjustments that might be required must be determined in light of the particular nature of the transactions. Some typical intercompany transactions may be used to provide an insight into the general approach to consolidations.

Assume the following statements of income of Parent Co. and Subsidiary Co.

	Parent Co.	Subsidiary Co.
Sales	$400,000	$300,000
Gain on sale (to subsidiary) of fixed assets	6,000	
Interest revenue (from subsidiary)	7,000	
Total revenues	$413,000	$300,000
Cost of goods sold	$240,000	$210,000
Interest expense (to parent)		7,000
Other expenses	80,000	53,000
Total expenses	$320,000	$270,000
Income	$ 93,000	$ 30,000

Parent Company owns 80 percent of Subsidiary Company.

Interest

The individual components of a company may enter into arrangements which result in revenues to one company and expenses to

* American Institute of Certified Public Accountants, "Intangible Assets," Opinion No. 17 of the Accounting Principles Board (New York, 1970).

another but involve no transactions with outsiders. Suppose, for example, that a parent company makes a loan to its subsidiary. Interest on the loan would be recognized as a revenue to the parent and as an expense to the subsidiary. From the standpoint of the consolidated entity, the "loan" is nothing more than an intracompany transfer of funds from one "division" to another. Just as any intercompany payable and receivable outstanding at year end would be eliminated from the consolidated balance sheet, so too must the interest revenue and expenses be eliminated from the income statement. If $7,000 of the interest revenue and expense reported on the individual statements were intercompany interest, then the following elimination would be required:

(a)

Interest revenue	$7,000	
Interest expense		$7,000

To eliminate intercompany interest.

Sales and Cost of Goods Sold

From the standpoint of a consolidated enterprise, a sale of merchandise by one member of a consolidated group to another is not an event worthy of revenue recognition. A sale takes place only when merchandise is sold to a party outside of the consolidated enterprise. Intercompany sales should, of course, be given accounting recognition on the books of the individual companies; they must, however, be eliminated when reporting on the operations of the companies as a consolidated economic entity.

Assume, for example, that included in the revenues of the parent are $100,000 in sales to the subsidiary. The goods sold to the subsidiary were manufactured by the parent at a cost of $80,000. The subsidiary company in turn sold the goods to outsiders at a price of $120,000. The transactions would be reflected in the books of the two companies as follows:

	Parent	Subsidiary
Sales revenue	$100,000	$120,000
Cost of goods sold	80,000	100,000

From the standpoint of the consolidated firm, sales to outsiders were $120,000 and the cost of goods sold only $80,000. It is necessary to eliminate $100,000 in both sales revenue (the sale by the parent to the subsidiary) and cost of goods sold (the cost of the goods sold by the subsidiary to outsiders):

(b)

Sales revenue	$100,000	
Cost of goods sold		$100,000

To eliminate intercompany sales.

The required adjustments for intercompany sales become considerably more complex when, at year end, one member of the corporate group has not yet sold to outsiders its entire stock of goods purchased from another member. It then becomes necessary to reduce the value of inventory in the amount of any profit recognized on its sale from one company to another. Inventory must be stated at its cost to the consolidated entity, rather than at the intercompany selling price.

Sales of Fixed Assets

Fixed assets must be reported on the consolidated statements on the basis of their initial cost to the consolidated enterprise. If a fixed asset has been sold by one member of the consolidated group to another, then the amount at which the asset is carried on the books of an individual company may be greater or less than that based on original cost.

Assume, for example, that the $6,000 in the account of the parent company, "gain on sale of fixed assets" represents in its entirety the gain on the sale of land to the subsidiary. The land was sold to the subsidiary at a price of $45,000; it had originally cost the parent $39,000. After the sale, the land would be recorded on the books of the subsidiary at its purchase price of $45,000—an amount $6,000 greater than that paid for it by the two companies viewed as a single, consolidated entity.

To report the consolidated results of operations and financial positions of the two companies, it is necessary to eliminate the effects of transactions that would be considered nothing more than internal transfers if the two companies were viewed as a single economic entity. Thus:

(c)

Gain on sale of fixed assets (by parent)	$6,000	
Land (of subsidiary)		$6,000

To adjust for gain on intercompany sale of land.

This adjustment, as is the case with many consolidation adjustments, would affect both the income statement and the balance sheet.

The intercompany sale of land will have to be accounted for in the preparation of consolidated statements in years subsequent to that in which the sale took place—in fact, for as long as the asset remains on the books of the subsidiary. The land will continue to be "overvalued" by the amount of the gain recognized by the parent. Since, on the books of the parent, the gain will have been *closed* at year end to retained earnings, retained earnings will be permanently overstated.

The complexities of adjusting for the sale of fixed assets are substantially compounded when the assets transferred are subject to depreciation. From the standpoint of the consolidated enterprise, depreciation charges must be determined on the basis of the original cost of the asset to the first member of the consolidated group that acquired it. On the

books of the company on which the asset is presently recorded, however, it would be maintained on the basis of the price paid to the seller company, a member of the consolidated entity. If, for example, the fixed asset sold were equipment rather than land, then the subsidiary would properly depreciate, on its own books, an asset that had cost $45,000. If the useful life were 10 years and zero salvage value were assumed, annual depreciation charges would be $4,500. For purposes of consolidated reporting, however, the asset initially cost only $39,000, the original acquisition cost of the parent (seller) corporation. Hence annual depreciation charges would be only $3,900. Adjustment would be required to reduce annual depreciation charges by $600. But, in addition, adjustments would also be required in each year after the first to "correct" for the cumulative effect on "accumulated depreciation" attributable to the previous "overstatements" of depreciation charges.

Amortization of Goodwill

As was indicated in the discussion relating to the interpretation of the excess of investment cost over book value, *goodwill* is an asset that arises exclusively out of the process of consolidation. Goodwill is recorded only on a consolidated balance sheet, not on those of the component companies of a consolidated group. When, in accordance with authoritative professional pronouncements, the goodwill is amortized, then the amortization expense is reported only on the consolidated income statement, not on those of the individual companies.

Assume that Parent Co. paid $200,000 for an 80 percent interest in Subsidiary Co. and that the book value of Subsidiary Co. was $225,000. The book value of the 80 percent interest was, therefore, $180,000. The excess of cost over book value—assumed in this case to represent goodwill—was, at time of acquisition, $20,000.

If the goodwill is to be amortized over 40 years, the maximum amortization period permitted by current professional pronouncements, then the following consolidation adjustment would be in order:

(d)

Amortization of goodwill (expense)	$500	
Goodwill (asset)		$500

To amortize goodwill.

Minority Interests in Earnings of Subsidiary

Consolidated statements, as already emphasized, are prepared from the perspective of the stockholders of the parent corporation. The parent corporation, however, is entitled to only a portion of the earnings of its sub-sidiary. The minority stockholders of the subsidiary are then entitled to remaining earnings. Conventionally, therefore, the portion of subsidiary earnings that can be ascribed to the minority stockholders is deducted from total consolidated income to arrive at net consolidated income.

The earnings of Subsidiary Co. as indicated in its income statement were $30,000.

Inasmuch as Parent Co. owns only 80 percent of the outstanding shares of Subsidiary Co., the minority share of subsidiary earnings would be 20 percent of $30,000—$6,000.

By summing the amounts reported in the income statements of the individual companies, taking into account the consolidating adjustments, and giving recognition to the minority interest in the earnings of the subsidiary, a consolidated statement of income can be prepared. A worksheet is shown in Exhibit 13-2.

EXHIBIT 13-2   Income Statement Adjustments

Parent Co.
Consolidated Statement of Income

	Individual Statements		Adjustments That Affect Income Statement Dr. (Cr.)	Consolidated Statement of Income
	Parent Co.	Subsidiary Co.		
Sales	$400,000	$300,000	$100,000 **(b)**	$600,000
Gain on sale of fixed assets	6,000		6,000 **(c)***	
Interest revenue	7,000		7,000 **(a)**	
Total revenues	$413,000	$300,000	$113,000	$600,000
Cost of goods sold	$240,000	$210,000	($100,000) **(b)**	$350,000
Interest expense		7,000	(7,000) **(a)**	
Other expenses	80,000	53,000		133,000
Amortization of goodwill			500 **(d)**	500
Total expenses	$320,000	$270,000	($106,500)	$483,500
Total income	$ 93,000	$ 30,000	$ 6,500	$116,500
Less: Minority interest in earnings of subsidiary				6,000
Consolidated income				$110,500

* Corresponding credit would be to Land, which would be reported on the balance sheet.

A company may, of course, purchase for cash all, or a portion, of the outstanding stock of another corporation. But quite often interests in other companies are obtained in exchange

reported profits even in the absence of any substantive improvements in the operations of either the parent or the subsidiary company. Consider the following additional information pertaining to the acquisition of Beta by Alpha:

Selected Financial Data Immediately Prior to Acquisition

	Alpha	Beta
Number of shares outstanding	100,000 shares	500,000 shares
Net assets	$1,000,000	$5,000,000
Capital stock ($1 par value)	$ 100,000	$ 500,000
Retained earnings	$ 900,000	$4,500,000
Book value per share	$ 10	$ 10
Latest annual income	$ 200,000	$ 500,000
Latest earnings per share	$ 2	$ 1
Market price of common stock	$ 100 per share	$ 10 per share

for the common stock of the acquiring corporation. If the investment is accounted for as a purchase (an alternative means will be discussed shortly), no special accounting problems are presented. Suppose, for example, Alpha Company acquired 500,000 shares of Beta Company at a price of $10 per share. In exchange for the shares, Alpha Company issued to Beta Company stockholders 50,000 shares of its own common stock, each share having a market value of $100. The common stock has a par value of $1 per share. The following journal entry would be in order:

Investment in
Beta Co. $5,000,000
   Common stock, par
    value $ 50,000
   Common stock, capital
    in excess of par   4,950,000
To record purchase of Beta Co. by Alpha Co.

An acquisition for stock, rather than cash, may have a striking impact on the reported earnings of the parent company. Indeed, acquisitions may result in instant increases in

Alpha Company is the smaller of the two companies in terms of assets and total earnings. Yet investors obviously consider its prospects for future earnings to be more promising than those of Beta. The price/earnings ratio (market price of common stock to earnings per share) of Alpha is 50 to 1 and that of Beta is only 10 to 1. Suppose that the exchange of stock were to be based on the market prices of the shares of the two companies. The 500,000 shares of Beta Company have a total market value of $5 million (500,000 shares at $10 per share). Since each share of Alpha has a market value of $100, the number of shares that Alpha would be required to issue would be $5 million divided by $100—50,000.

If Alpha Company were to issue 50,000 additional shares to the owners of Beta Company, then it would have outstanding a total of 150,000 shares. Consolidated earnings, assuming no substantive improvement in the operations of either firm, would be the sum of the earnings of the two individual companies—$700,000 ($200,000 plus

$500,000). No amortization of excess of cost over book value is required since the total market price of Beta Company stock is exactly equal to its book value. Earnings per share of Alpha Company, reported on a consolidated basis, would now be $4.66 ($700,000 divided by 150,000 shares)—an increase of 133 percent over previously reported earnings of $2 per share.

The ramifications of this simplified example are critical to an understanding of the merger movement of the 1960s and 1970s. In that period numerous firms acquired subsidiaries. Frequently, the acquired companies were in industries totally unrelated to those of the parents. Usually the acquisitions were made for common stock rather than cash, and often, as in the example, a whale of a firm was swallowed up by a minnow.

The acquisition in the example, as is common in practice, was facilitated by the substantial difference in the price/earnings (P/E) ratios of the two firms. The P/E ratio of Alpha was considerably higher than that of Beta. Stock market prices are likely to be influenced by the trend in earnings over a number of years. The relatively high P/E ratio of Alpha might be explained, at least in part, by a trend of rapidly increasing earnings. The acquisition of Beta would likely help sustain that trend or even accentuate it. The P/E ratio of Alpha may thereby remain high or even increase, thus making it even easier for the firm to acquire additional firms in the future. And future acquisitions may further add to reported earnings per share. To a considerable degree, the recent merger movement was supported by the circle of acquisition, increase in earnings, increase in market price of stock, additional acquisitions, etc.

It must be pointed out, however, that the increase in earnings is seldom as dramatic as in the example. To the extent that the acquiring corporation pays to stockholders of the company to be acquired a price in excess of the firm's book value, then the excess might (exceptions will be discussed below) have to be amortized over a number of years. The charge for amortization would serve to reduce earnings.

POOLING OF INTERESTS

Rationale

In the discussions of business combinations to this point it has been assumed that one company acquires another. The combinations have been accounted for as purchase-type transactions—one company purchases, either for cash or common stock, the outstanding common stock of another. In those instances where a business combination is effected by an exchange of common stock—where one company, be it a new or existing company, acquires substantially all of the voting stock of another in return for its own common stock—the transaction may be accounted for as an alternative type of business combination—a pooling of interests. The financial consequences of accounting for a business combination as a pooling of interests rather than a purchase may be profound; reported earnings as well as values assigned to assets may be significantly different.

Underlying the pooling of interests method of accounting for business combinations is the rationale that two firms join together to operate as a single economic enterprise. Neither of the two purchases the other, and the owners of both of the component companies are granted a proportionate interest in the combined enterprise. The combination represents a marriage of equals, or if not exactly of equals, then at least a marriage where one party does not clearly dominate the other.

No Increase in Asset Values

The key feature of the pooling of interests method is that each of the component companies retains its former basis of accounting. That is, the assets and liabilities of neither company are revalued at the time of combination. The recorded assets and liabilities of both companies are carried forward to the consolidated enterprise at their previously recorded amounts. So also are their retained earnings. *No accounting recognition is given to goodwill, nor are other assets written up to their fair market values.* Retention of the former basis of accounting is justified on the grounds that there has been no sale of the assets of one firm to another; there has

firm to reflect an excess of purchase price over book value. No goodwill need be recorded. Therefore, the firm does not have to charge either depreciation or amortization on the amounts by which the fair market values of either of the two firms exceed their book values. An example can be used to illustrate the pooling of interests approach and to highlight the differences between the pooling of interests and the purchase methods of accounting for business combinations.

Example

Indicated in the table following is selected information about two firms, Delta Corp. and Echo Corp., prior to their merger:

Balance Sheet

	Delta Corp.	Echo Corp.
Miscellaneous assets	$1,500,000	$6,000,000
Miscellaneous liabilities	$ 500,000	$1,000,000
Common stock, par value $1	100,000	500,000
Contributed capital in excess of par	300,000	700,000
Retained earnings	600,000	3,800,000
	$1,500,000	$6,000,000
Number of shares outstanding	100,000	500,000
Net income, in year prior to merger	$ 200,000	$ 500,000
Earnings per share	$ 2	$ 1
Recent market price per share	$ 100	$ 20

merely been a fusion of two companies into one.

The pooling of interests method has great appeal to firms effecting business combinations in that in most circumstances it permits the consolidated enterprise to report higher earnings than if the combination were accounted for as a purchase. The pooling of interests method may result in higher reported earnings because it does not require the consolidated enterprise to increase the carrying values of the assets of the acquired

Delta and Echo agree to combine their operations. Delta Corp. will issue to the current stockholders of Echo Corp. new shares of its own common stock in exchange for their existing shares in Echo Corp. The number of shares to be issued by Delta will be based on the relative market prices of the shares just prior to the negotiations leading to the merger. Since the shares outstanding of Echo Corp. have a current market value of $10 million (500,000 shares at $20 per share), Delta Corp. will have to issue 100,000 shares

($10 million divided by $100, the market price of Delta Corp. stock).

Under the pooling of interests method, the accounting entries are a bit tricky. The consolidated balance sheet, however, would reflect the sum of the assets and liabilities of each of the two companies. The common stock, par value account would indicate the par value of the shares outstanding (those of the "parent" company). The balance in the retained earnings account would represent the sum of the previous balances of the two individual companies. The balance in the contributed capital in excess of par account would, in essence, be a "plug"—whatever amount is required to assure that assets less liabilities are equal to owners' equity.

Consolidated Balance Sheet

Miscellaneous assets	$7,500,000
Miscellaneous liabilities	$1,500,000
Common stock, par value $1	
(200,000 shares outstanding)	200,000
Contributed capital in excess of par	1,400,000
Retained earnings	4,400,000
Total liabilities and owners' equity	$7,500,000

The assets and liabilities are stated on the same basis as on the books of the component companies. In contrast to the purchase method no adjustment has been made to asset values—either by revaluation of specific assets or by the addition of goodwill—to reflect the difference between the market value of the common stock issued by Delta Corp. ($10 million) and the value at which the assets were recorded on the books of the Echo Corp. ($5 million).

If there were no substantive increase in the earnings of the two firms as a consequence of the merger, then earnings after the merger would be the sum of the earnings of the two individual firms—$200,000 contributed by Delta, $500,000 contributed by Echo, a total of $700,000. The earnings per share, based on 200,000 shares of Delta Corp. stock outstanding, would be $3.50. The earnings per share of Delta Corp., the firm whose stock remains outstanding, would thereby have increased as a result of the merger by $1.50 from what they were rior to the merger—an increase that can be attributed entirely to the *instant earnings* effect described earlier.

By contrast, if the combination had been accounted for as a purchase, then the combined entity would either have reported goodwill of $5 million or increased the carrying value of specific assets by that amount. If the $5 million in additional assets or in goodwill were depreciated or amortized over a period of, say, 20 years, then earnings would be $250,000 per year lower than under the pooling method. If earnings of the two individual firms after the merger were the same as those prior to the merger, then consolidated earnings, if the combination were accounted for as a purchase, would be only $450,000. By contrast, they would be $700,000 if the combination were accounted for as a pooling. Hence, earnings per share would be only $450,000 divided by 200,000 shares—$2.25.

Abuses and Reforms

The term *pooling of interests* was at one time used to describe a type of business combination rather than an accounting method. Two corporations of similar size joined together to carry out their operations. The owners of the two firms obtained, and retained, an interest in the new firm proportionate to their respective contributions, and the new company was managed jointly by the previous managers of the two firms. A pooling of interests was viewed as a merger of two great rivers as contrasted with a purchase which was seen as a stream feeding into a river. The merger of the New York Central Railroad and the Pennsylvania Railroad into the Penn-Central Corp. was a classic example of a pooling of interests.

In the late 1950s and early 1960s the traditional criteria for a pooling of interests began to erode. Business combinations that were not in spirit poolings of interests were accounted for as if they were. First, the relative size test was abandoned. Combinations of giant firms, often conglomerates, with small firms were treated as poolings of interests. Then, the criteria of continuity of ownership and management were disregarded. One of the two firms involved in the combination may have paid sizable amounts of cash, rather than common stock, for a portion of the common stock of the other firm. Thus, the owners of one of the firms were, to the extent that they received cash payments, *bought out* by those of the other. Eventually, even those combinations in which it was clear that one company had acquired (purchased) another were accounted for as poolings. *Poolings of interests* and *purchases* came to be recognized as *accounting* alternatives from which managements could select, rather than as types of business combinations.

Today, as set forth in Opinion No. 16, "Business Combinations," issued by the Accounting Principles Board in 1970, a business combination may be accounted for as a pooling of interests only if a number of specific conditions are satisfied. Primary among the criteria for a pooling of interests is that the merger must be effected almost entirely by an exchange of common stock. Purchases of stock for cash (except in minor amounts) are prohibited and one company must acquire substantially all (at least 90 percent) of the common stock of the other firm. Moreover, stockholders who receive the newly issued shares must either retain them or sell them to outsiders; they cannot redeem them for cash to the issuing corporation.

Opinion No. 16 does not require adherence to the spirit of the traditional pooling of interests in the sense that the two combining companies must be of similar size. One company is permitted to be dominant over another. But Opinion No. 16 does restrict the freedom of firms to choose whether a combination should be accounted for as a purchase or as a pooling of interests. If it satisfies certain criteria, it *must* be accounted for as a pooling of interests; if it does not, it *must* be accounted for as a purchase.

Despite the issuance of Opinion No. 16, the issue of business combinations remains controversial. The critical issue on which attention is focused relates to the values that should be assigned to the assets of the combining companies—and most particularly those of a company acquired by another. The values assigned to the assets have, of course, a direct bearing on depreciation and amortization charges and, hence, on reported earnings. In a pooling, the assets of each company are stated at their previous bases; in a purchase, assets are restated to reflect the consideration paid for them.

SUMMARY

Intercorporate ownership may take a variety of forms. The objective of accounting is to give effect to the economic substance of the relationship between the parties involved.

As a general rule, the manner in which the interest of one company in another is accounted for is determined by the degree of control that it is able to exercise. If an investor company is unable to exert substantial influence over the company whose shares it owns, it would account for its interest on the *cost basis*. If it is able to exercise substantial influence, it would account for its interest on the *equity basis*.

When a corporation has control over another, then the information needs of the stockholders of the controlling company are usually best served by combining the financial positions and results of operations of the merging firms into a single set of *consolidated* financial statements. If the business combination were effected entirely by an exchange of common stock, then the consolidated statements would ordinarily be prepared on a pooling of interests basis. If, on the other hand, one company acquired for cash or other assets the outstanding stock of another, the combination would be accounted for as a purchase.

EXERCISE FOR REVIEW AND SELF-TESTING

Parent Co. acquired 90 percent of the outstanding common stock of Subsidiary Co. On January 1, 1983, immediately following the acquisition, the balance sheets of the two firms revealed the following:

	Parent Co.	Subsidiary Co.
Investment in Subsidiary Co.	$320,000	—
Other assets	500,000	$300,000
Capital contributed by stockholders	200,000	120,000
Retained earnings	620,000	180,000

Subsidiary Co. reported earnings for the year ending December 31, 1983, of $30,000 and declared dividends of $10,000. Parent Co. reported earnings, *excluding* any revenues attributable to Subsidiary Co., of $100,000.

1. Parent Co. maintains its investment in Subsidiary Co. on the equity basis.

a. What would be the amount that it should report in 1983 as earnings from subsidiary?

b. At what amount should it value "Investment in Subsidiary Co." on December 31, 1983, after the declaration of the dividend?

2. If the financial statements of Parent Co. and Subsidiary Co. were to be consolidated, what amount should be reported on the balance sheet as excess of cost over book value (goodwill) prior to amortizing such excess in 1983?

3. What would be the amount of Subsidiary Co.'s 1983 earnings that could be ascribed to minority stockholders?

4. If the excess of cost over book value were to be amortized over a period of 40 years, by how much would the combined earnings of the two companies be reduced when the income statements of the two firms were consolidated?

5. What would be the consolidated income of the two companies, assuming that the earnings of the subsidiary company owing to minority stockholders was considered as an expense?

6. Suppose alternatively that Parent Co. acquired 100 percent of the stock of Subsidiary Co. in exchange for shares of its own common stock. At time of acquisition, the common stock issued by Parent Co. had a fair market value of $400,000 and the book value of Subsidiary Co. was $300,000. What would now be the consolidated income of the two companies for 1983 assuming that the merger satisfied the conditions of the pooling of interests accounting method?

QUESTIONS FOR REVIEW AND DISCUSSION

1. Under what circumstances should a firm account for an investment in another company by the cost method? By the equity method? When should it prepare consolidated financial statements?

2. Why is the cost method considered inappropriate for investments in which the investor company can exert significant influence over the operating policies of the investee?

3. Why, under the equity method, does a firm

reduce its balance in its investment account upon declaration of a dividend by the investee?

4. When under the equity method does an investor recognize revenue attributable to the earnings of the company in which it maintains an investment? When under the cost method? When is revenue recognized if consolidated statements are prepared?

5. Why do consolidations relate only to corporate *reports* rather than to the underlying corporate books and records? On which set of books, those of the parent or the subsidiary, those of both, or those of neither, are consolidation adjustments made?

6. From the standpoint of which group of stockholders—those of the parent, those of the subsidiary, or those of both—are consolidated statements prepared?

7. Under what conditions may a company improve its earnings per share simply by acquiring controlling interest in another company?

8. What is *goodwill?* When is it recorded? From what does it arise? Suppose a firm acquires an interest in a subsidiary for an amount in excess of its book value. What difference might it make on consolidated net income if such excess were classified as goodwill rather than assigned to specific assets?

9. What is the underlying rationale of a pooling of interests? What critical differences arise in terms of asset valuation and income determination if a combination is accounted for as a pooling rather than as a purchase?

10. What four accounts—two income statement accounts and two balance sheet accounts—appear only on consolidated financial statements, never on those of individual companies?

PROBLEMS

1. *The equity method provides for more timely recognition of subsidiary earnings and losses than does the cost method.*

On January 2, 1982, the Colorado Co. purchased for $60 per share (cash) 2,000 of the 10,000 outstanding shares of the Denver Corp.

On July 5, 1982, the Denver Corp. reported earnings of $40,000 for the first six months of the year.

On July 15, the board of directors of the Denver Corp. declared and paid a $1 per share cash dividend.

On December 31, the Denver Corp. reported a loss of $15,000 for the second six months of the year.

a. Prepare journal entries to account for the investment of the Colorado Corp. in the Denver Corp. using first the *cost* method and then the *equity* method.

b. Compare total revenues of the Colorado Co. attributable to its investment under the two alternative methods. Compare the year-end carrying values of the investment.

2. *The earnings of a subsidiary can be derived from information on the carrying value of the investment and dividends declared.*

On January 1, 1978, the Eagleton Co. purchased for $80,000 a 40 percent interest (4,000 of 10,000 shares) in the common stock of Alexander, Inc.

On December 31, 1980, the Eagleton Co. sold 1,000 of the shares at a price of $25 per share. It recorded a gain of $2,000 on the sale.

On December 31, 1982, the remaining shares were reported on the books of Eagleton at a value of $78,000.

During the five-year period from 1978 through 1982, Alexander, Inc., paid annual dividends of $1.50 per share.

a. Determine the earnings of *Alexander, Inc.,* during the period January 1, 1978, to December 31, 1980.

b. Determine the earnings of Alexander, Inc., during the period January 1, 1981, to December 31, 1982.

3. *The equity method prevents an investor company from regulating its own earnings by manipulating the dividend practices of the investee firm.*

The Maine Co. owned 40 percent (10,000,000 shares) of the voting stock of the Bangor Corp. and controlled a majority of seats on the latter's board of directors. Toward the end of 1982, it was estimated by the controllers of the two firms that Maine Co. would have earnings for the year of approximately $10,000,000 (exclusive of earnings attributable to Bangor Corp.) and that Bangor Corp. would have earnings of approximately $50,000,000.

The president of Maine Co. was disappointed that his firm would earn only $10,000,000 plus its share of Bangor Corp. earnings. Prior to 1982, Maine Co. had increased its earnings by 10 percent each year; consistent with that trend, Maine Co. would have to report total earnings in 1982 of $45,000,000.

a. In accord with APB guidelines, Maine Co. accounts for its interest in Bangor Corp. on the equity basis. If Bangor Corp. were to declare its usual dividend of $.50 per share, what would be the total reported income of Maine Co.?

b. The president of Maine Co. suggested to his controller that Bangor Corp. be directed to declare a special dividend of $3 per share in addition to the $.50 per share. What impact would the additional dividend have on earnings of Maine Co.?

c. Suppose that Maine Co. accounted for its investment in Bangor Corp. on the cost basis. What would be the total reported earnings of Maine Co. if the latter declared its regular dividend of $.50 per share? What impact would the additional dividend specified in Part b have on earnings of Maine Co.?

d. Comment on why the equity rather than the cost method is considered appropriate for firms which can exert substantial influence over companies in which they have an interest.

4. A firm is ordered to pay its earnings from a subsidiary to the U.S. Treasury.

The following is an excerpt from a news report in the *Wall Street Journal* of December 1, 1980:

A Federal Trade Commission hearing officer ruled in Washington that Beatrice Foods Co. must divest itself of Tropicana Products, Inc., and pay its Tropicana profits to the U.S. Treasury.

The decision by an FTC administrative law judge, James P. Timony, was based on a finding that Beatrice's 1978 purchase of Tropicana, valued at about $490 million, violated federal antitrust law.

If upheld, the ruling would represent a unique financial penalty in the field of antitrust enforcement, FTC officials believe. Antitrust specialists suspect that many companies involved in takeovers are willing to risk government challenge because of the profits to be earned from the acquired company while the challenge is pending. However, the FTC didn't allege, nor did Mr. Timony find, that Beatrice had such a motive in acquiring Tropicana.

Although Beatrice doesn't break out Tropicana's earnings in its financial statements, industry specialists estimate that Tropicana contributed about $57 million to the income of Beatrice in 1979.

a. By which method, cost or equity, is it likely that Beatrice accounted for its interest in Tropicana?

b. Suppose that since being acquired by Beatrice, Tropicana declared either no dividends or dividends in an amount less than annual earnings. Would recorded *earnings* from subsidiary be a reasonable measure of the economic value of the benefits that Beatrice received from Tropicana during the period of ownership? What might be a better measure?

c. It is really possible for a firm to "pay its *profits* to the U.S. Treasury"? Comment.

5. Consolidating adjustments may have varying effects on consolidated earnings.

The consolidated income of two companies is the sum of their individual earnings after certain adjustments have been made. For each of the transactions listed, indicate with brief explanation whether the required adjustments would increase, decrease, or have no effect upon consolidated income, as determined simply by summing the earnings of the two individual companies. Assume that company A owns 100 percent of the outstanding shares of common stock of company B.

1. Company B acquired $100,000 of bonds issued by company A. Company A paid company B interest of $8,000.

2. Company B sold $100,000 of the merchandise to company A. The goods had cost company B $80,000 to produce. By year end company A had resold all of the goods to outsiders.

3. Company A sold $50,000 of merchandise to company B. The goods had cost company A

$30,000 to produce. At year end all the goods remained in the inventory of company B.

4. Company B owned 5,000 shares of the preferred stock of company A. Company A paid dividends of $3 per share on the preferred stock.

5. Company A sold Company B land for $25,000. The land had cost company A $40,000.

6. Two years earlier, Company A sold Company B equipment for $10,000. The equipment had cost company A $6,000. The equipment had an estimated useful life of 10 years and zero salvage value. Company B has been charging depreciation based on its cost of $10,000—$1,000 per year.

6. Consolidated income represents the sum of the earnings of the individual firms plus or minus any revenues or expenses that would not have been recognized had the individual firms been divisions of a single entity.

Chicago Corp. owns 100 percent of the outstanding stock of the Woodlawn Co. In 1982 Chicago Corp. had earnings of $200,000 (exclusive of its share of Woodlawn Co. earnings) and Woodlawn Co. had earnings of $80,000. Given the additional information that follows, determine consolidated earnings for the year:

1. Chicago Corp. sold merchandise to Woodlawn Co. at a price of $60,000. The cost of the merchandise was $48,000. Woodlawn Co. has not yet resold any of the merchandise.

2. Chicago made a loan of $100,000 to Woodlawn. During the year, Woodlawn Co. paid interest on the loan of $6,000.

3. Chicago Corp. purchased from Woodlawn equipment for $25,000. The equipment has a remaining useful life of 10 years and no anticipated salvage value. The equipment had a net value on the books of Woodlawn of $15,000 (cost of $30,000 less accumulated depreciation of $15,000). Woodlawn had been depreciating the equipment over a period of 20 years ($1,500 per year). Chicago Corp. charged a full year's depreciation (based, of course, on its cost).

4. Woodlawn Co. leased office space from Chicago Corp. In 1982 Woodlawn made rent payments of $500 per month—a total of $6,000 during the year.

5. Chicago Corp. paid for its interest in Woodlawn an amount that was $60,000 in excess of Woodlawn Co.'s book value. The $60,000 was allocated entirely to goodwill and is being amortized over a period of 20 years.

7. The sale of equipment by one member of a consolidated group of firms to another may result in complex adjustments to a number of accounts for as many years as the equipment is used.

The Wayside Co. purchased manufacturing equipment from its subsidiary, The Gardner Co. The Wayside Co. paid $40,000. The equipment had been recorded on the books of the Gardner Co. at a cost of $50,000 less accumulated depreciation of $25,000. The Gardner Co. had been depreciating the asset over a period of 10 years. The Wayside Company will depreciate the asset over its remaining useful life of 5 years.

a. At what amount should the Wayside Co. record the asset on its own books? How much depreciation should it charge each year?

b. At what amount should Wayside Co. report the asset on its consolidated balance sheet? How much depreciation should it report?

c. Suppose that depreciation charges on the equipment enter into the computation of cost of goods sold. Explain the nature of any adjustments to cost of goods sold that might have to be made when a consolidated income statement is prepared. Suppose that not all goods manufactured in the course of a year are actually sold. Explain the nature of any adjustments to year-end inventory that might have to be made.

8. Intercompany sales may require the adjustment of inventory as well as sales and cost of goods sold.

Retail Co. serves as the marketing division of Manufacturing Co. It purchases all the goods that it sells to outsiders from Manufacturing Co. Manufacturing Co., which sells only to Retail Co., does so at prices that exceed costs by 66 2/3 percent.

The following data were taken from the year-end trial balances of the two firms:

	Manufacturing Co.	Retail Co.
Sales revenue	$200,000	$216,000
Cost of goods sold	120,000	180,000
Ending inventory	—	20,000

Neither company had inventory on hand at the beginning of the year. The financial statements of the two firms are to be consolidated.

a. What is the total amount that should be reported as sales (i.e., sales to outsiders)?

b. What was the cost (to the consolidated entity) of the goods sold?

c. What is the amount at which the ending inventory should be reported (i.e., what was its cost to the consolidated entity)?

d. Prepare a journal entry to eliminate intercompany sales and cost of goods sold and to eliminate any "unearned" profit from the ending inventory. Such entry should serve to reduce the combined trial balances of the two firms to the amounts computed in Parts a, b, and c.

9. *The financial statements of three or more companies can be consolidated using the same principles that are applicable to consolidation of two firms.*

Condensed balance sheets of three companies, A, B, and C, appear as follows:

	A	B	C
Miscellaneous assets	$500,000	$140,000	$80,000
Investment in B (80 percent)	190,000		
Investment in C (60 percent)		60,000	
	$690,000	$200,000	$80,000
Common stock	$ 50,000	$ 5,000	$10,000
Retained earnings	640,000	195,000	70,000
Total owners' equity	$690,000	$200,000	$80,000

Company *A* just acquired its interest in Company *B*; Company *B* just acquired its interest in Company *C*.

a. Make any necessary adjustments to eliminate, for purposes of consolidation, the investment of B in C, to recognize goodwill, and to reclassify the interest of the minority stockholders.

b. Make any necessary adjustments to eliminate the investment of A in B, to recognize goodwill and to reclassify the interest of the minority stockholders.

c. Combine the remaining balances into a consolidated balance sheet.

10. *This exercise can serve as a review of the various types of adjustments that are generally*

required to effect a consolidation of financial statements.

Indicated on the next page are the preclosing trial balances of X Co. and its subsidiary Y Co. as of December 31, 1982.

The following information suggests adjustments to the accounts of the two firms that must be made before they can be summed:

1. X Co. owns 60 percent of the common stock of Y Co. It acquired its interest in Y Co. on January 1, 1982. The difference between what it paid for its interest ($29,000) and the book value of such interest ($24,000) can be attributed entirely to the fact that land owned by Y Co. was worth more than its recorded value. (Be sure to eliminate the entire investment in Y Co. against land as well as X Co.'s interest in the three owners' equity accounts of Y Co. Also, reclassify the equity of Y Co.'s minority stockholders as "Minority interest in subsidiary.")

2. In 1982 X Co. made $20,000 of sales to Y Co. None of the goods purchased by Y Co. remains in its inventory. Hence, from a consolidated perspective, sales and cost of goods sold are overstated by $20,000

3. Y Co. still owes X Co. $6,000 for the merchandise purchased.

4. In the course of the year X Co. made loans to Y Co. X Co. charged Y Co. $2,000 of interest on the loans. Although there was no outstanding balance on the principal of the loans at year end, Y Co. was still indebted to X Co. for $1,000 of interest. Both companies have properly accrued the interest revenue or expense.

5. During the year X Co. sold to Y Co. some land. Selling price was $6,000. The land had originally

	X Co.		Y Co.	
	Dr.	Cr.	Dr.	Cr.
Cash	$ 20,200		$ 3,000	
Accounts and notes receivable	50,000		16,000	
Interest receivable	4,000		3,000	
Inventory	25,000		10,000	
Fixed assets	185,000		30,000	
Investment in Y Co.	29,000			
Accounts and notes payable		$ 44,000		$ 17,000
Interest payable		2,000		1,000
Common stock		10,000		10,000
Capital contributed in excess of par		50,000		20,000
Retained earnings		181,200		10,000
Sales		100,000		40,000
Interest and other revenues		12,000		2,000
Cost of goods sold and related expenses	80,000		32,000	
Interest expense	6,000		6,000	
	$399,200	$399,200	$100,000	$100,000

cost X Co. $3,000. X Co. included the gain on the sale of land in "Interest and other revenues."

6. In preparing a consolidated balance sheet from the adjusted trial balance, it is important to remember that the balance in X Co. "Retained earnings" does not reflect earnings for 1982. Correspondingly the balance in "Minority interest in subsidiary" (an account established by your journal entries) does not include the interests of the minority stockholders in the earnings of the subsidiary in 1982. It will be necessary, therefore, to add to the balance sheet account, Minority interest in subsidiary, the minority share of 1982 earnings and to add to retained earnings net consolidated income of 1982.

a. Make all adjustments necessary to effect consolidated financial statements.

b. Prepare a consolidated income statement and balance sheet. Be sure to include minority share of subsidiary earnings as a deduction from consolidated income. You will probably find it useful to prepare a worksheet in which you establish columns for original balances, adjustments, and consolidated balances.

11. If management were not required to amortize goodwill, it could avoid "income statement responsibility" for amounts paid to acquire assets.

Shortly after the Accounting Principles Board imposed the requirement that goodwill be amortized over a period of not longer than 40 years, International Telephone & Telegraph Corporation (ITT) indicated in a footnote to its financial statements that it disagreed with the position of the board because, it asserted, the value of goodwill does not necessarily diminish over time.

a. If an asset, such as goodwill or land, does not diminish in value over time, do you think that it should be amortized?

b. Suppose that a company, such as ITT, wishes to acquire a plant that manufactures solar energy cells. Solar Energy, Inc., offers to sell the company such a plant, its only asset, for $1 million. The remaining useful life of the plant is 40 years. Its value on the books of Solar Energy, Inc., is $100,000.

Alternatively, the *owners* of Solar Energy, Inc., offer to sell their *stock* (not the plant) to ITT for $1 million.

1. Assume that ITT acquires the *plant* for $1 million. How much depreciation would it charge each year?

2. Assume instead that ITT acquires the *stock* for $1 million. Based on the "judgment" of management it allocates the entire excess of

cost of its investment in Solar Energy, Inc., over its book value of $100,000 to goodwill. If the company were not required to amortize goodwill, how much depreciation would it charge each year? If, instead, it were required to amortize goodwill over a period of 40 years, what would be the combined charge for depreciation and amortization?

3. Why do you suppose the APB decided as it did that goodwill must be amortized?

12. A merger or acquisition, particularly if accounted for as a pooling, may provide "instant earnings" to the firm whose shares remain outstanding.

The following information pertains to the Cambridge Co. and the Leeds Co. as of December 31, 1982.

	Cambridge Co.	Leeds Co.
Number of shares of common stock outstanding	1,000,000	500,000
Net assets	$15,000,000	$5,000,000
Latest annual income	$ 2,000,000	$1,000,000
Recent market price of common stock (per share)	$40	$20
Earnings per share	$ 2	$ 2

The Cambridge Co. and the Leeds Co. have agreed to a business combination. Cambridge Co. will acquire 100 percent of the common stock of Leeds Co. at the recent market price of $20 per share.

a. Suppose that Cambridge Co. were to purchase all 500,000 shares of Leeds Co. for $20 per share in cash. Cambridge Co. would borrow the required funds at an interest rate (after taxes) of 5 percent per year. The combination would be accounted for as a purchase, and the excess of cost over book value would be amortized over a period of 20 years. Determine anticipated earnings per share of Cambridge Co. after the acquisition, assuming no substantive changes in the earnings of either company.

b. Suppose alternatively that Cambridge Co. were to acquire all 500,000 shares in an exchange of stock. The number of shares to be issued would be based on relative market values, and the

combination would be accounted for as a pooling of interests. Determine the anticipated earnings per share of Cambridge Co.

13. Alternative means of effecting a merger may have differing impacts upon reported assets and equities.

Indicated as follows are condensed balance sheets of the MNO Co. and PQR Co.

	MNO Co.	PQR Co.
Assets	$5,000,000	$2,000,000
Common stock, par value $10	$1,000,000	$ 500,000
Contributed capital in excess of par	1,500,000	650,000
Retained earnings	2,500,000	850,000
Total owners' equity	$5,000,000	$2,000,000

Prepare balance sheets of the MNO Co. (consolidated as appropriate) to reflect the acquisition of the PQR Co. by the MNO Co. under each of the following conditions:

1. The MNO Co. purchases the *assets* of the PQR Co. at a price of $2.5 million cash. To raise the necessary cash, MNO Co. issues 50,000 shares of common stock at $50 per share.
2. The MNO Co. purchases 100 percent of the outstanding stock of the PQR Co. at a total price of $2.5 million cash. To raise the necessary cash, MNO Co. issues 50,000 shares of common at $50 per share.
3. The MNO Co. issues 50,000 shares of its own common stock in exchange for 100 percent of the outstanding shares of the PQR Co. The market price of the MNO Co. stock at the time of the exchange is $50 per share. The transaction is to be accounted for as a pooling of interests.

14. Alternative means of accounting for excess of cost over book value can have substantially different effects on reported earnings.

In 1983, the National Products Company acquired, for $200,000 in common stock, 100 percent control of State Industries, Inc. At the time of the acquisition the net assets (assets less liabilities) of State Industries were recorded on its books at a value of $120,000. In 1984, National Products had

earnings of $90,000, exclusive of earnings of State Industries, Inc. State Industries, Inc., had earnings of $20,000. There were no material intercompany transactions during the year. Determine the consolidated earnings of National Products Company and its subsidiary under the following alternative assumptions:
1. The combination is accounted for as a purchase, and the excess of acquisition cost over book value is allocated to various fixed assets that have an average remaining useful life of 10 years.
2. The combination is accounted for as a purchase, and the excess of acquisition cost over book value is allocated entirely to "goodwill." The goodwill is to be amortized over the maximum period allowed by Accounting Principles Board guidelines—40 years.
3. The business combination is accounted for as a pooling of interests. (A firm cannot in practice choose whether to account for a merger as either a purchase or a pooling. If, and only if, an acquisition satisfies the criteria for a pooling can it be accounted for as such. Otherwise, it must be accounted for as a purchase.)

15. *The equity method of accounting for an investment will have an effect on parent company earnings comparable to that of a full-scale consolidation.*

The preclosing trial balances of the Mann Co. and the Rudolph Co. as of December 31, 1982, are as follows:

	Mann Co.	Rudolph Co.
Cash	$100,000	$20,000
Investment in Rudolph Co.	54,000	
Other assets	76,000	75,000
Common stock	10,000	10,000
Retained earnings	190,000	80,000
Sales	140,000	60,000
Cost of goods sold	95,000	50,000
Other expenses	15,000	5,000

The Mann Co. owns 60 percent of the outstanding stock of the Rudolph Co. It acquired its investment in January 1982 for $54,000 at a time when the net worth of Rudolph Co. was $90,000. Mann maintains its investment in Rudolph on the equity basis.

Mann Co. has not yet taken into account its share of Rudolph Co.'s 1982 earnings.
a. Prepare a 1982 income statement and balance sheet for Mann Co. assuming that it is deemed *inappropriate* to consolidate its accounts with those of Rudolph.
b. Prepare a *consolidated* income statement and balance sheet. Be sure that the last line of the income excludes the minority share of Rudolph Co. earnings.
c. Compare net worth and income under the two procedures. Why is the equity basis of accounting for business combinations sometimes referred to as a *one-line consolidation?*

16. *The "value" of shares received by stockholders of a firm being acquired may be less than what is readily apparent.*

Octopus Corp., a conglomerate, decided to acquire controlling interest in Meek Co.

The common stock of Octopus Corp. had been trading at $20 per share and that of Meek Co. at $60 per share. Octopus had 1 million shares outstanding, and Meek had 300,000 shares outstanding.

The management of Meek Co. was opposed to the takeover. To circumvent the opposition of management, Octopus offered to purchase all outstanding shares of Meek Co. stock at a price of $80 per share—a price that was $20 greater than the market price prior to the announcement of its offer. Octopus would not, however, pay cash for the stock. Instead it would issue to Meek stockholders common stock of Octopus Corp. with a market value of $80 for each share that it received. Hence, it would issue four shares of Octopus stock for each share of Meek Co. stock received.

In the year prior to the offer, Octopus Corp. had earnings of $500,000; Meek had earnings of $1 million. At the time of the offer, Meek Co. had a book value (net worth) of $15 million.
a. Determine the earnings per share of Octopus Corp. in the year prior to the acquisition.
b. Determine the earnings per share of Octopus in the year immediately following the acquisition. Assume that Octopus will prepare consolidated financial statements and that the operating earnings of the two individual companies will remain unchanged. Any excess of cost over book value will be assigned to goodwill and amortized

over a period of 40 years. Assume also that only 80 percent of the outstanding shares of Meek were tendered (sold) to Octopus. The remainder are being retained by minority shareholders.

c. Suppose an investor owned 1,000 shares of Meek. How much better off is he in terms of market value of his holdings after he sold his shares to Octopus than before?

d. How much better (or worse) off is he with respect to earnings that can be ascribed to his shares?

SOLUTIONS TO EXERCISE FOR REVIEW AND SELF-TESTING

1. a. Parent Co. would report as earnings from subsidiary in 1983 90 percent of Subsidiary Co. income of $30,000—$27,000.

b. It would value "Investment in Subsidiary" at $338,000. Such amount is the original investment of $320,000 plus $27,000, its share of subsidiary earnings, less $9,000 of dividends received (or recognized as receivable) from the subsidiary.

2. Parent Co. paid $320,000 for a 90 percent interest in a firm with a book value of $300,000. The excess of cost over 90 percent of total book value ($270,000) is $50,000.

3. Subsidiary Co. had earnings of $30,000. The minority share would be 10 percent of earnings—$3,000.

4. Inasmuch as excess of cost over book value is $50,000, consolidated earnings would be reduced by one-fortieth of that amount—$1,250.

5. Consolidated earnings would be the combined earnings of the two firms, $130,000, less the minority interest in earnings of $3,000 and less amortization of the excess of cost over book value of $1,250—$125,750.

6. If an acquisition is accounted for as a pooling, then the investment in subsidiary is recorded on the books of the parent at the book value of its equity in the subsidiary—in this case, $300,000. No goodwill is recognized; none need be amortized. Consolidated earnings would simply be, therefore, the sum of the earnings of the two individual companies—$130,000.

STATEMENT 14
of Changes in
Financial Position

The statement of changes in financial position is the third of the three primary financial statements. Equal to the income statement and the balance sheet by way of official pronouncement, although not tradition, the statement of changes in financial position became a required element of financial reporting in 1971. In Opinion No. 19 the Accounting Principles Board prescribed that it must be presented as a basic statement for each period in which an income statement is shown. The statement of changes in financial position reports on the sources from which working capital was derived and the uses to which it was put. An example is presented in Exhibit 14-1.

The sources and uses of working capital are of critical concern to investors as well as managers. Working capital is composed of cash and other liquid assets such as marketable securities, accounts receivable, and inventories—those that could be transformed into cash within a relatively short period of time—less accounts payable and other liabilities that would be expected to consume cash within the same short period of time. As a general rule, cash is what is needed by a business to satisfy its obligations as they come due, to meet day-to-day operating expenses, and to make distributions of assets to stockholders eager for a return on their investment.

Investors are interested in flows of cash because the returns that they receive from their investment will ordinarily be in the form of cash. Dividends are paid in cash, and the market value of a business at any particular time reflects investor predications as to the amount of dividends that will be paid in the future.

Managers pay attention to flows of cash in order to be sure that the firm has the wherewithal to satisfy its obligations and to meet the dividend expectation of investors. Moreover, the economic consequences of virtually all decisions that managers are called upon to make can generally best be evaluated in terms of cash receipts and disbursements rather than increases or decreases in reported profits.

EXHIBIT 14-1

Consolidated Statements of Changes in Financial Position
Alberto-Culver Company and Subsidiaries
Years Ended September 30, 1980 and 1979

	1980	1979
Sources of working capital		
Provided from operations		
Earnings before extraordinary gain	$10,435,786	3,671,195
Add charges (deduct income) not affecting working capital		
Depreciation	2,560,435	2,242,769
Amortization of trade names and goodwill	549,152	795,193
Deferred income taxes	104,000	292,000
Disposals of property, plant and equipment	4,117	(165,939)
Sale of foreign trademarks	(8,893,422)	—
Other	(215,200)	3,699
Total provided from operations	4,544,868	6,838,917
Extraordinary gain		
Proceeds from settlement of litigation, net of related expenses and income taxes	—	2,128,576
Deferred litigation costs not affecting working capital	—	1,202,424
Proceeds from sale of trademarks, net of related costs	9,409,828	—
Dividend received from Japanese Joint Venture	726,468	—
Increase in long-term debt	509,783	1,154,036
Sales and retirements of property, plant and equipment	124,217	923,944
Proceeds from exercise of stock options	38,930	—
Change in other assets	124,470	51,800
	15,478,564	12,299,697
Applications of working capital		
Capital expenditures	2,593,316	3,224,788
Reduction in long-term debt	808,532	1,030,978
Net noncurrent assets of acquired company	4,704,901	—
Cash dividends	1,436,343	1,504,132
Stock purchased for treasury	2,427,403	956,631
Additions to trade names and goodwill	945,435	699,182
Other	—	75,983
	12,915,930	7,491,694
Increase in working capital	$ 2,562,634	4,808,003
Increase (decrease) in components of working capital		
Cash and short-term investments	$ (569,037)	586,197
Receivables	6,050,233	2,760,953
Inventories	8,117,933	9,181,303
Prepaid expenses	312,790	144,604
	13,911,919	12,673,057
Notes payable and current maturities of long-term debt	704,599	2,111,854
Accounts payable and accrued expenses	8,892,028	6,032,738
Income taxes	1,752,658	(279,538)
	11,349,285	7,865,054
Increase in working capital	$ 2,562,634	4,808,003

In fact, a central theme of Part 2 of this text, which is directed to "managerial" accounting, is that it is cash, not income, on which managers should focus their analyses of alternative courses of action.

The statement of changes in financial position presents a summary of all significant transactions that involve the receipt or disbursement of working capital. Included in the statement are transactions pertaining to the financing and investing activities of the firm, such as the sale of new securities, the purchase of fixed assets and the payment and repayment of debt—transactions of the type that are excluded from the income statement because they generate neither revenues nor expenses. The statement of changes in financial position is intended to provide an additional resource on which investors, managers, and other users of financial reports can rely to examine the history of company activities and to make predications about cash flows of the future.

MORE OBJECTIVE THAN
INCOME STATEMENT

The statement of changes in financial position is generally seen as being more objective than the statement of income. The statement of income is necessarily tainted by estimates, allocations, and choices among accounting principles and methods. By contrast, the report on inflows and outflows of working capital is relatively free of independent judgments.*

* "Relatively" rather than "absolutely" free of independent judgments mainly because the value of accounts receivable is affected by estimates of bad debts and choice of principles of revenue recognition; the value of inventory is affected by choice of valuation method (FIFO, LIFO, etc.)

USUALLY DEPICTS FLOWS
OF WORKING CAPITAL
RATHER THAN CASH

The statement of changes in financial position is often referred to as a *statement of sources and applications of funds*. "Funds" has alternative meanings, and in practice there is considerable variation in the nature of the statements. On the one hand, "funds" is sometimes interpreted to mean *cash;* as a consequence, the statement of changes in financial position is a summary of cash receipts and cash disbursements. More commonly, "funds" is interpreted to mean *working capital*—current assets less current liabilities—and the statement of changes in financial position is a summary of the means by which the enterprise accumulated working capital and the uses to which it was applied.[†] In this chapter we shall be concerned primarily with the statement of changes in financial position based on the working capital concept of funds; a section of the chapter will, however, be directed to the statement based on the cash concept of funds.

In light of the importance of cash, it may seem odd that it is the working capital, rather than the cash, concept of funds that is most widely accepted. But it is the statement of changes in financial position based on the broader concept of funds that is likely to serve as the more reliable basis on which to predict cash flows of the future. Current assets generally can be either readily transformed into cash or may obviate the need for future disbursement of cash. Current liabilities usually require the near-term payment of cash. For example, the total sales of a

[†] In nonprofit accounting "fund" is used to signify an independent accounting entity with a self-balancing set of accounts.

company during a period—sales for cash as well as on credit—are likely to be a better indicator of the ability of a firm to generate cash than merely the total cash collections from sales. Credit sales would immediately serve to increase working capital but not cash. In the normal course of business, however, the accounts receivable generated by the credit sales would shortly be converted into cash.

CHANGES IN WORKING CAPITAL

Working capital represents the current assets of a firm (commonly cash, marketable securities, accounts receivable, and inventories) less the current liabilities (wages and salaries payable, accounts payable, and short-term notes payable).

By the very nature of the accounting equation and the double-entry bookkeeping process, changes in working capital must be associated with changes in nonworking capital accounts—noncurrent assets, noncurrent liabilities, and owners' equity. A change in one working capital account that is offset by a corresponding change in another working capital account will have no effect on net working capital.

The basic accounting equation indicates that current assets (CA) plus other assets (OA) are equal to current liabilities (CL) plus other liabilities (OL) plus owners' equity (OE); that is,

$$\$CA + \$OA = \$CL + \$OL + \$OE$$

By rearranging the terms in the equation, it can be seen that working capital (current assets minus current liabilities) must equal other liabilities plus owners' equity minus other assets:

$$\underbrace{\$CA - \$CL}_{\text{Working capital}} = \overbrace{\$OL + \$OE - \$OA}^{\text{All other accounts}}$$

Changes in working capital can be identified with changes in other liabilities, owners' equity, or other assets. *Increases* in working capital can be explained by *increases* in noncurrent liabilities or owners' equity (such as those attributable to the issuance of bonds or stock) and by *decreases* in noncurrent assets (such as those attributable to the sale of long-lived assets). *Decreases* in working capital can be explained by *decreases* in noncurrent liabilities or owners' equity (such as those attributable to the repayment of debt or the declaration of dividends) or *increases* in noncurrent assets (such as those attributable to the purchase of long-lived assets). Changes in working capital may also, of course, be associated with profits and losses—in effect, increases and decreases in owners' equity (retained earnings). To summarize:

Sources of Working Capital (Events Associated with Increases in Working Capital)	Uses of Working Capital (Events Associated with Decreases in Working Capital)
Increases in noncurrent liabilities	Decreases in noncurrent liabilities
Increases in owners' equity (including those attributable to periodic income)	Decreases in owners' equity (including those attributable to periodic losses and declarations of dividends)
Decreases in noncurrent assets	Increases in noncurrent assets

THE STATEMENT OF CHANGES IN FINANCIAL POSITION: A REPORT ON LONG-TERM FINANCIAL AND INVESTMENT ACTIVITY

Changes in working capital are necessarily associated with changes in noncurrent assets, noncurrent liabilities, and owners' equity. Thus the statement of changes in financial position can also be seen as a report that focuses on the long-term financing and investing activities of a firm. It indicates how much the firm spent on the acquisition of plant, equipment, or other long-term assets and how it obtained the financial wherewithal to do so.

In a broad sense, there are only three types of transactions in which a firm can engage:

1. Those in which the components of working capital are affected but the net amount of working capital remains unaffected.
2. Those in which the net amount of working capital is changed but so also are one or more of nonworking capital accounts (noncurrent assets or liabilities or owners' equity).
3. Those in which no working capital account is affected; only noncurrent asset, noncurrent liability or owners' equity accounts are increased or decreased.

Report on Transactions Involving Changes in Working Capital

The statement of changes in working capital does not indicate the transactions in which net working capital remains unchanged (type 1). It focuses primarily on the second type of transactions in which working capital and, correspondingly, long-term assets, long-term liabilities, or owners' equity change. In addition, however, it reports upon the third type of transactions—those that involve changes in only noncurrent asset, noncurrent liability, or owners' equity accounts. This type of transaction has no effect upon working capital. But it may have an important impact upon the firm's productive capacity as well as the structure of its debt and equity.

Report on Selected Transactions that Do Not Involve Working Capital

Suppose, for example, that a firm acquires a new plant in exchange for long-term notes. No cash is paid, nor is any other component of working capital involved in the transaction. If the statement of changes in financial position were to report only those transactions which directly affect working capital, then the acquisition of the plant would be omitted from the statement. Moreover, since the acquisition would have no effect on revenues or expenses (except insofar as depreciation is charged) in the year of exchange, it could not properly be reported on the income statement.

Because of the long-term significance of such transactions, the Accounting Principles Board directed that they be specifically reported upon in the body of the financial statements. It prescribed that they should be reported "as if" they were made for cash. That is, the issuance of the long-term notes should be reported as a source of funds and the acquisition of the plant as a use of funds. In other words, such transactions should be reported as offsetting sources and uses of funds. Commonly, a note beside the reported amounts would indicate the nature of the transaction.

Other examples of transactions that do not directly affect working capital but which should be reported as if they did are those involving exchanges of one noncurrent asset for another, acquisition of assets in exchange for common or preferred stock, exchanges of one class of stock for another (e.g., common stock for preferred), or redemption of long-term debt in exchange for common or preferred stock.

CHANGES IN COMPONENTS OF WORKING CAPITAL

The statement of changes in financial position comprises two related tables. One indicates the change between two points in time in the balances in the accounts that constitute working capital. The other indicates the reason for the change in working capital— that is, the changes in those other accounts (noncurrent assets and liabilities and owners' equity) that provide an explanation for the change in working capital.

The table that indicates the change in the components of working capital is easily understood and can be prepared in a straightforward, mechanical manner.

Current assets and liabilities (per the balance sheet) at the beginning of the year are compared to those at the end of the year and the differences computed. The net change in current liabilities is then subtracted from the net change in current assets. The table on the next page, for example, indicates the change in working capital of the Kingston Corp. during 1983.

Working capital increased during the year by $24,000—an increase that would have to be accounted for in the second table.

Importance of Makeup of Working Capital

The importance of changes in the components of working capital should not be overlooked. In the Kingston Corp., for exam-

ple, net working capital increased. The increase, however, is primarily attributable to a build-up of accounts receivable and inventories and would, in fact, have been much greater had it not been for a substantial increase in current notes payable. The build-up in receivables, payables, and inventories, if not associated with an increase in sales, could be a sign of financial deterioration rather than strength. The customers of the firm may not be paying their bills on time, the firm may be unable to sell the goods that it has produced, and it may have had to resort to short-term borrowing to meet its obligations.

EXPLANATION OF CHANGES IN WORKING CAPITAL

The table that explains the changes in working capital is typically divided into two parts. The first indicates the sources (i.e., the inflows) of working capital; the second the uses (i.e., the outflows). The most common sources of working capital are income, borrowings, sale of long-lived assets and issuance of new stock. The most common uses are purchases of long-lived assets and repayment of debt.

The accountant who prepares the table of explanation must be a detective. He must gather, from a number of sources, bits and pieces of information which together account for the entire change in working capital. His primary sources are the income statement and the balance sheet, but sometimes he must delve further into the underlying accounts.

In light of the fact that changes in working capital can be explained in terms of changes in other balance sheet accounts, the preparer's basic approach is to reconcile the beginning balance with the ending balance in each noncurrent asset, noncurrent liability,

Kingston Corp.
Changes in Working Capital (000s omitted)

	December 31, 1983	December 31, 1982	Increase (Decrease)
Current assets			
Cash	$ 41	$ 28	$ 13
Accounts receivable (net of allowance for uncollectibles)	231	180	51
Note receivable	11	—	11
Inventories	275	219	56
Prepaid expenses	8	6	2
Total current assets	$566	$433	$133
Current liabilities			
Accounts payable	$114	$110	$ 4
Wages and salaries payable	42	39	3
Notes payable	196	83	113
Interest payable	5	2	3
Dividends payable	5	5	0
Taxes payable	14	28	(14)
Total current liabilities	$376	$267	$109
Working capital	$190	$166	$ 24

and owners' equity account. He attempts to reconstruct the transactions or events that resulted in an increase or a decrease in the account and to determine which of those transactions or events created a source of working capital.

EARNINGS AS A SOURCE OF WORKING CAPITAL

Retained earnings are conventionally increased as a consequence of periodic income; they are decreased by the declaration of dividends. Operations, *as represented by income*, are a source of working capital, and dividends, a use.

Income is a primary measure of an increase in working capital in that *most* components of income—that is, most revenues and expenses—involve either cash receipts or disbursements, or short-term promises of cash receipts or disbursements. Suppose, for example, that income of a merchandising company was $20,000, determined as follows:

Sales revenue		$100,000
Less: Cost of goods		
sold	$40,000	
Salaries	25,000	
Taxes	8,000	
Other expenses	7,000	80,000
Income		$ 20,000

Adjustments Required

Insofar as sales revenue resulted in an increase in cash or accounts receivable and that the expenses resulted in a decrease in cash or inventories, or an increase in a short-term payable (all being components of working capital), then operations (income) were a *source of funds* in the amount of $20,000. However, if income is to be considered a source of funds, *it must be adjusted to take into account any revenues or expenses that were not associated with increases or decreases in working capital.*

Depreciation

Suppose that of the $7,000 in other expenses, $3,000 represented depreciation on store and office equipment. The likely journal entry to record the depreciation expense was:

Depreciation expense $3,000
    Store and office
      equipment,
      accumulated
      depreciation $3,000
To record depreciation.

The depreciation did not require an outlay of cash or other current assets in the current year. Neither did it result in an increase in current liabilities. "Store and office equipment—accumulated depreciation" is a contra account to a noncurrent asset; no components of working capital were affected by the charge for depreciation.

Under the assumption that $3,000 of the other expenses represented depreciation charges, sales revenue resulted in an increase in working capital of $100,000, but expenses resulted in a decrease of working capital of only $77,000. Operations, therefore, served to increase working capital by $23,000. $3,000 of expenses were of the type that did not require an outlay of cash or other components of working capital. Therefore, $3,000 must be added to reported net income to derive the total increase in working capital attributable to operations.

It is common for firms to report depreciation as a source of funds. Thus (assuming no other sources of funds):

Sources of working capital:

Net income	$20,000
Depreciation	3,000
	$23,000

Such reporting practice has no doubt contributed to a great deal of misunderstanding with respect to depreciation. Depreciation is *not* a source of funds. Depreciation provides no cash to an enterprise. It neither increases nor decreases current assets or current liabilities. Depreciation is nothing more than an expense that does not require a current outlay of cash. It is a means of allocating to a current year a cost that had been incurred in a previous year. It is a source of funds only in the sense that if reported income is to be considered a source of funds, then reported income must be adjusted (increased) by the amount of depreciation included among reported expenditures. A statement of changes in financial position is likely to be more meaningful to investors if depreciation, when included among the sources of working capital, is specifically described as an adjustment to net income, required because it is an expense that does not result in a current year reduction of working capital.

Amortization and Depletion

In addition to depreciation there are other components of income that do not result in either an increase or decrease in working capital. They, too, must be either added to or subtracted from net income if operations are to be considered a source of funds.

Most similar to depreciation are charges for amortization or depletion of noncurrent assets. The amortization of patents, copyrights, franchises, or goodwill or the depletion of mineral deposits requires a charge to income that results in the reduction of a long-term asset rather than an outlay of working capital. Insofar as income is categorized as a source of funds, those expenditures that did not result in a reduction of working capital must be added back to net income.

Amortization of a bond discount is another type of expense that does not result in a reduction of working capital. When a bond discount (a contra account to a liability—hence an account that has a debit balance) is amortized, the net balance of long-term liabilities is reduced. No cash, other assets, or liabilities are exchanged. The amount of the amortization expense must be *added* to net income; it is a charge that does not require the use of funds.

Correspondingly, amortization of a bond premium must be *subtracted* from income. A bond premium has a credit balance and is reported as an addition to bonds payable. The amortization of a bond premium serves to *reduce* interest expense. Recall, for example, that if a $1,000 bond is sold at a premium, then the effective interest rate must be less than the coupon rate. If, for example, a 20-year, 12 percent, $1,000 bond were sold to yield 10 percent (at a price of $1,171.60), then the following entry might be made to record the first semiannual interest payment:

Bond premium	$ 1.40	
Interest expense	58.60	
Cash		$60.00

To record payment of interest.

The enterprise would record an interest expense of $58.60, but a cash payment of $60.00 would be made to the bondholder. The amortization of the premium serves to understate reported expenses as a use of funds and thereby to overstate reported income as

a source of funds. In this example, as is typical, the amortization was not recorded in a separate account (e.g., amortization of bond premium, a credit) but was instead reflected as a reduction of interest expense. The amortization of the bond premium ($1.40) must be subtracted from reported income if reported income is to be shown as a source of funds.

Gains and Losses

Gains or losses on the sale of fixed assets are additional types of revenues and expenses for which income must be adjusted. Consider, for example, the sale of a parcel of land. The land had cost $5,000 and had been carried on the books at that value. It was sold for $7,000. The following entry would have been made to record the sale:

Cash	$7,000	
Land		$5,000
Gain on sale of land		2,000

To record the sale of land.

The sale of the land would provide the firm with $7,000 in working capital. Included among the sources of funds would be a separate item, "sale of land—$7,000." But included in reported income would be the $2,000 gain on the sale of land. If income, including the gain of $2,000, were shown as a source of funds and so also was the $7,000 received in exchange for the land, then sources of funds would be overstated by $2,000; the gain would have been counted twice. If reported income is to be presented as a source of funds, any recognized gains on sale of noncurrent assets must be backed-out. Similarly, any losses must be added to income. Such losses, although they reduced reported income, did not reduce working capital.

Deferred Income Taxes

A further adjustment to income is required to take into account the difference between reported tax expense and taxes that are actually payable. In Chapter 10, it was pointed out that the reported income tax expense is conventionally determined as a percentage of reported earnings. Yet special features of the tax laws—those which permit the use of *accelerated* methods of depreciation, for example—often provide for long-term postponement of taxes. A typical journal entry to record an annual tax liability might appear as follows:

Tax expense	$100,000	
Taxes payable in		
current year		$80,000
Taxes deferred		
until future		
years		20,000

To record tax expense.

That portion of the tax which is payable in the current year increases current liabilities and hence decreases working capital; it is a use of funds. But that portion which is deferred until future years increases a long-term liability; it has no effect on working capital. Insofar as reported income has been reduced by reported tax expense ($100,000), net income as a source of funds is understated by the portion of taxes deferred until future years ($20,000), for only the portion of the tax that is payable in the current year ($80,000) resulted in a reduction of working capital. The deferred portion of income taxes must therefore be added back to net income.

Other Changes in Retained Earnings

Retained earnings are characteristically increased by earnings and decreased both by losses and by dividends. Dividends paid in cash are a use of working capital and should be reported as such. Stock dividends, like cash dividends, result in a decrease in retained earnings. But stock dividends do not result in a reduction of working capital. Stock dividends result in an increase in common stock and contributed capital in excess of par. They should not, therefore, be classified as a use of funds.

CAPITAL STOCK AND RELATED ACCOUNTS

Changes in capital stock accounts usually result from either the issuance of additional shares or the redemption of existing shares. Suppose, for example, that a firm's common stock and the related contributed capital in excess of par accounts contained the following balances at the beginning and at the end of 1983:

	December 31, 1983	December 31, 1982
Common stock (par value $1)	$120,000	$100,000
Contributed capital in excess of par	524,000	480,000
	$644,000	$580,000

Changes Should Be Reported Even If They Did Not Involve Working Capital

Assume that the combined increase of $64,000 was attributable to the issuance of 20,000 shares of common stock. Insofar as the shares were issued in exchange for cash or other current assets, they represent a *source* of funds and should so be reported.

If, however, the shares were issued to acquire noncurrent assets (to acquire a new corporation, for example) or in exchange for outstanding bonds or preferred stock, then the addition to the capital accounts would *not* represent a source of funds. Nevertheless, because the transaction would have had an important effect upon the firm's long-term financial structure, it would be reported "as if" it involved working capital. The issue of the new securities would be reported as a source of working capital; the acquisition of the assets or retirement of the debt would be reported as a use.

Changes in the balance in preferred stock and related accounts are also likely to be attributable to the issue or redemption of shares in exchange for cash. The analyst must therefore account for all changes in such balances and verify whether in fact they resulted in increases or decreases in working capital.

NONCURRENT ASSETS

The amount paid to acquire a long-lived asset is a use of funds; the amount for which a long-lived asset is sold is a source of funds.

Activity in fixed asset accounts is reflected on the statement of changes in financial position in several ways: purchases are uses of working capital; sales are sources of working capital; gains and losses, as well as depreciation, are adjustments to earnings. The following example illustrates how typical changes in fixed asset accounts are reported on the statement of changes in financial position.

Assume that the reported balances in an equipment account and the related accumulated depreciation account at the end of years 1983 and 1982 appear as follows:

	December 31, 1983	December 31, 1982
Equipment	$310,000	$290,000
Accumulated depreciation	75,000	90,000
	$235,000	$200,000

The underlying accounts reveal:

Amount (in cash) for which equipment was sold	$ 3,000
Original cost of equipment sold	60,000
Accumulated depreciation on equipment sold	56,000
Loss on sale of equipment	1,000
Annual depreciation charge on all equipment	41,000
Purchase of new equipment	80,000

The activity in the fixed asset accounts was associated with several changes in working capital:

1. Equipment was acquired at a cost of $80,000. Purchase of equipment usually requires the *use* of cash or other components of working capital.

2. Equipment was sold for $3,000. The cash received served to increase working capital. The sale of equipment can be considered a *source* of working capital.

3. The equipment that was sold for $3,000 had a book value of $4,000 (initial cost of $60,000 less accumulated depreciation of $56,000). If the price at which equipment is sold is reported as a source of working capital, then the related gain or loss cannot also be reflected in income, if income is to be considered a source of funds. The recorded loss on the sale of equipment ($1,000) must be added back to income.

4. Periodic charges for depreciation are a type of expense that does not require the use of funds. If income is considered a source of funds, then depreciation charges, in this example $41,000, must also be added back to income.

In summary, the activity would be reflected as follows:

Sources of working capital			
Adjustments to income (expenses not associated with an outflow of working capital)			
Add: Annual depreciation charges		$41,000	
Loss on sale of equipment		1,000	$42,000
Sale of equipment			3,000
Total sources associated with equipment			$45,000
Uses of working capital			
Purchase of new equipment			$80,000
Net *use* of working capital associated with activity in equipment accounts			$35,000

NONCURRENT DEBT

The issuance of long-term bonds is a source of funds and the retirement a use. When bonds are issued at a premium or a discount the amount to be reported as a source of funds is the actual amount received—that is, the face value of the bonds plus the premium or minus the discount. When bonds are retired the amount to be reported as a use is the actual amount paid to retire the bonds, irrespective of their book value (face value plus unamortized premium or less unamortized discount). Gains or losses on the retirement of bonds can be accounted for identically to gains or losses on the sale of fixed assets; they should be considered as adjustments to income not involving an inflow or outflow of working capital.

PREPARATION OF FUNDS STATEMENT—AN EXAMPLE

An example of the derivation of a statement of changes in financial position from an income statement and a balance sheet may help to clarify the relationships between changes in working capital and changes in other accounts. The example is based on the income statement, balance sheet, and other information of the Taconic Corp., presented in Exhibit 14-2.

Although there are many approaches that may be taken in preparing a statement of changes in financial position, the one illustrated here will be that of first determining the change in working capital to be accounted for and then reconstructing, in summary form, the journal entries that most likely affected each of the *nonworking capital* accounts. The reconstructed entries will be slightly different from the original entries, however.

First, whenever one side of the original entry involved a working capital account, the debit or credit in the reconstructed entry will not be to that working capital account. Instead, it will be to either "Sources of working capital" or "Uses of working capital." A brief explanation as to why working capital was received or disbursed will be provided in parentheses.

Second, whenever one side of the original entry involved a revenue or expense that did not result in either an inflow or an outflow of working capital (and must thereby be added to or subtracted from income) the debit or credit in the reconstructed entry will not be to that revenue or expense. Instead, inasmuch as income represents a source of funds, it will be to "Sources of working capital." A few words indicating that the entry represents an adjustment to income and the reason for the adjustment will be placed in parentheses.

The reconstructed entries will be posted to a worksheet. The worksheet will have four columns: one for beginning balances, two

EXHIBIT 14-2

		1983	1982
Taconic Corp.			
Comparative Statement of Position			
December 31, 1983 and 1982			
Assets			
Current assets			
Cash		$ 40,000	$ 30,000
Accounts receivable		76,000	80,000
Inventories		60,000	62,000
Other current assets		160,000	50,000
Total current assets		$336,000	$222,000
Other assets			
Buildings and equipment		$403,000	$328,000
Less: Accumulated depreciation		90,000	72,000
		313,000	256,000
Land		40,000	40,000
Investment in subsidiary		6,000	
Miscellaneous assets		27,000	27,000
Total other assets		$386,000	$323,000
Total assets		$722,000	$545,000
Liabilities and owners' equity			
Current liabilities			
Accounts payable		$ 50,000	$ 48,000
Other current liabilities		12,000	8,000
Total current liabilities		$ 62,000	$ 56,000
Other liabilities			
Income taxes deferred until future years		$ 69,000	$ 62,000
Bonds payable		378,000	261,000
Premium on bonds payable		3,000	
Total bonds payable		$381,000	$261,000
Total other liabilities		$450,000	$323,000
Owners' equity			
Common stock ($1 par value)		$ 13,000	$ 12,000
Contributed capital in excess of par		127,000	122,000
Retained earnings		70,000	32,000
Total owners' equity		$210,000	$166,000
Total liabilities and owners' equity		$722,000	$545,000

EXHIBIT 14-2 (continued)

Taconic Corp.
Statement of Income
Year Ended December 31, 1983

Sales	$1,045,000	
Other revenues	26,000	$1,071,000
Cost of goods sold (excluding depreciation)	$895,000	
Depreciation	51,000	
Interest	11,000	
Taxes	30,000	
Other expenses	24,000	1,011,000
Net income		$ 60,000

Other information (from journal entries or specific accounts):

1. The company declared dividends of $22,000.
2. It acquired buildings and equipment at a cost of $112,000.
3. It sold assets for $10,000. The assets had originally cost $37,000. At time of sale depreciation of $33,000 had been accumulated. The gain on sale of $6,000 is included in "Other revenues."
4. The subsidiary was acquired in exchange for 1,000 shares of common stock. The stock was valued at $6 per share.
5. The company paid $23,000 in taxes. The difference between that amount and tax expense of $30,000 was credited to "Income taxes deferred until future years."
6. The company issued for $120,000 bonds having a face value of $117,000.

for the reconstructed entries, and one for ending balances. The top portion of the worksheet will contain one line representing working capital and other lines for each of the nonworking capital balance sheet accounts. The lower portion of the worksheet will contain accounts descriptive of the reasons for the changes in working capital—the

EXHIBIT 14-3

Taconic Corp.
Change in Working Capital

	December 31, 1983	December 31, 1982	Increase (Decrease)
Current assets			
Cash	$ 40,000	$ 30,000	$ 10,000
Accounts receivable	76,000	80,000	(4,000)
Inventories	60,000	62,000	(2,000)
Other current assets	160,000	50,000	110,000
Total current assets	$336,000	$222,000	$114,000
Current liabilities			
Accounts payable	$ 50,000	$ 48,000	$ 2,000
Other current liabilities	12,000	8,000	4,000
Total current liabilities	$ 62,000	$ 56,000	$ 6,000
Working capital	$274,000	$166,000	$108,000

part of the reconstructed journal entries that do not involve debits or credits to the nonworking capital accounts.

The mechanics of preparing the worksheet are reflective of the relationship between working capital and nonworking capital accounts. Changes in working capital must be associated with increases or decreases in nonworking capital accounts. The worksheet is a means of assuring that all changes in nonworking capital accounts have been analyzed and that their impact upon working capital has been described.

During 1983, the working capital (current assets less current liabilities) of the Taconic Corp. increased by $108,000. The changes in the component accounts are indicated in Exhibit 14-3.

The $108,000 increase in working capital may be accounted for by reconstructing the entries, in summary form, that affected each of the nonworking capital balance sheet accounts.

Retained Earnings

Retained earnings increased by $38,000 in 1983. This increase can be accounted for by income of $60,000 less dividends of $22,000 (per other information). Income (subject to adjustments for noncash revenues and expenses) represents a source of funds and dividends a use of funds:

(a)

Sources of working
  capital (net income) $60,000
    Retained earnings $60,000
To record net income.*

---

* Unfortunately, this very first entry represents a minor exception to the general policies to be followed in reconstructing the original entries. Throughout the year as revenue was earned, a working capital account was debited and a revenue account was credited. As expenses were incurred, a working capital account was credited and an expense account was debited. At year end, the revenues and expenses were closed to retained earnings.

(b)

Retained earnings $22,000
  Uses of working
    capital (declaration
    of dividends) $22,000
To record declaration of dividends.

Buildings and Equipment

The next nonworking capital balance sheet account for which it is relatively easy to account for the change during the year is "Buildings and equipment." "Buildings and equipment" increased by $75,000. As indicated in other information, new equipment was acquired at a cost of $112,000, and equipment that had an initial cost of $37,000 was retired during the year. These two transactions account for the entire increase of $75,000.

The entry to record the acquisition of equipment can be reconstructed as follows:

(c)

Buildings and
  equipment $112,000
  Uses of working
    capital
    (purchase of
    buildings and
    equipment) $112,000
To record the purchase of buildings and equipment.

The equipment was sold at a price of $10,000. At the time of sale it had a book value of only $4,000 (initial cost of $37,000 less accumulated depreciation of $33,000). The company realized a gain of $6,000 on the sale. The amount for which the equipment was sold is, of course, a source of funds. Because the $10,000 is reported as a source of funds, the gain on sale must be subtracted from income if double counting is to be

---

In the entry given the credit to retained earnings represents, therefore, the net amount closed to retained earnings—the difference between revenues and expenses.

avoided. Thus, in the following reconstructed entry, the gain is recorded as a reduction of (credit to) sources of working capital:

(d)

Sources of working capital (selling price of the equipment)	$10,000	
Accumulated depreciation	33,000	
Buildings and equipment		$37,000
Sources of working capital (adjustment to income owing to gain on sale of equipment)		6,000

To record the sale of equipment.

Accumulated Depreciation

Accumulated depreciation, per the comparative balance sheets, increased by $18,000. The balance in the account was reduced by $33,000 as the result of the sale of equipment (see entry **d**). Depreciation charges for the year, per the income statement, were $51,000. The difference between the two amounts is equal to the net $18,000 change to be accounted for.

Depreciation charges are a nonfund expense; they must be added back to income if income is to be considered a source of working capital. Thus,

(e)

| Sources of working capital (adjustment to income owing to depreciation charges, a nonfund expense) | $51,000 | |
| Accumulated depreciation | | $51,000 |

To record depreciation.

Investment in Subsidiary; Capital Accounts

Taconic Corp. acquired its investment in the subsidiary, $6,000, in exchange for 1,000 shares of $1 par value common stock (per the comparative balance sheets and other information). As a consequence of the transaction, the balance in the common stock account must have increased by $1,000 and that in the contributed capital in excess of par account by $5,000. In fact, the increases of $1,000 and $5,000, respectively, account for the entire changes in the two accounts during the year.

The acquisition of the interest in the subsidiary in exchange for common stock neither increased nor decreased the working capital of the company. Nevertheless, the issue of common stock in exchange for noncurrent assets is included in that category of transactions that are considered sufficiently significant that they should be reported in the statement of changes in financial position *as if* they resulted in offsetting sources and uses of funds. Thus,

(f)

Sources of working capital (issuance of common stock)	$6,000	
Common stock		$1,000
Capital contributed in excess of par		5,000

To record the issue of 1,000 shares of stock.

(g)

| Investment in subsidiary | $6,000 | |
| Uses of working capital (acquisition of subsidiary) | | $6,000 |

To record the acquisition of the subsidiary.

Deferred Income Taxes

Of the $30,000 in taxes reported on the income statement, only $23,000 was actually paid. Hence only $23,000 served to reduce working capital. The remaining $7,000 did not require an outlay of funds; along with other expenses that did not require an outlay of funds, it must be added back to reported income.

(h)

| Sources of working capital (adjustment to income owing to taxes that were deferred and thereby did not require an outlay of working capital) | $7,000 | |
| Income taxes deferred until future years | | $7,000 |

To record deferred portion of tax expense.

(There is no need to record the portion of the tax expense that is not deferred inasmuch as it was included in the determination of reported earnings and does not require adjustment.)

Bonds Payable and Bond Premium

Per the supplementary information, and consistent with the changes in the appropriate balance sheet accounts, bonds with a face value of $117,000 were issued for $120,000—at a premium, therefore, of $3,000. The issuance of the bonds increased working capital by $120,000.

(i)

Sources of working capital (issuance of bonds)	$120,000	
Bonds payable		$117,000
Premium on bonds payable		3,000

To record the issuance of bonds.

Completing the Statement

When all the entries have been posted to the worksheet (Exhibit 14-4), the changes in all of the nonworking capital accounts will have been accounted for, and the $108,000 increase in working capital will have been explained.

Exhibit 14-5 summarizes the various sources and uses of working capital.

STATEMENT OF CHANGES IN FINANCIAL POSITION ON A CASH FLOW BASIS

Accounting Principles Board Opinion No. 19, which requires that a statement of changes in financial position be included in a firm's annual report along with the income statement and the balance sheet, allows a company to prepare the statement on a cash rather than a working capital basis. A statement which indicates the sources and uses of cash may be of more utility to some investors than one dealing with working capital in that it provides direct information on the one resource, cash, that is likely to be of greatest interest. As pointed out previously, however, a statement which focuses on cash may, ironically, be of less value in predicting future flows of cash than one which focuses on working capital. Some of the elements of working capital other than cash may be interchangeable with cash and can readily either be exchanged for cash at the discretion of management or will be converted into cash in the ordinary course of business operations within a short period of time.

Change in Cash Equals Changes in All Other Accounts

The statement of changes in financial position on the basis of working capital is grounded on the fact that a net change in working capital can be explained by changes in all nonworking capital accounts. Similarly, the statement of changes in financial position on the basis of cash finds its roots

EXHIBIT 14-4

Taconic Corp.
Worksheet for Preparation of Statement of
Changes in Financial Position
(Working Capital Basis)

	Beginning Balance (12/31/82) Debit (Credit)	Reconstructed Journal Entries		Ending Balance (12/31/83) Debit (Credit)
		Debits	Credits	
Working capital	$166,000	$108,000		$274,000
Noncurrent assets				
Buildings and equipment	328,000	(c) 112,000	(d) $ 37,000	403,000
Accumulated depreciation	(72,000)	(d) 33,000	(e) 51,000	(90,000)
Land	40,000			40,000
Investment in subsidiary		(g) 6,000		6,000
Miscellaneous assets	27,000			27,000
Total assets	$489,000			$660,000
Noncurrent liabilities and owners' equity				
Income taxes deferred until future years	$ (62,000)		(h) 7,000	$ (69,000)
Bonds payable	(261,000)		(i) 117,000	(378,000)
Premium on bonds payable			(i) 3,000	(3,000)
Common stock ($1 par value)	(12,000)		(f) 1,000	(13,000)
Contributed capital in excess of par	(122,000)		(f) 5,000	(127,000)
Retained earnings	(32,000)	(b) 22,000	(a) 60,000	(70,000)
Total noncurrent liabilities and owners' equity	$(489,000)			$(660,000)
Sources of working capital				
Income		(a) 60,000		
Adjustments to income:				
Depreciation		(e) 51,000		
Gain on sale of buildings and equipment			(d) 6,000	
Deferred income taxes		(h) 7,000		
Sale of equipment		(d) 10,000		
Issuance of common stock		(f) 6,000		
Issuance of bonds		(i) 120,000		
Uses of working capital				
Declaration of dividends			(b) 22,000	
Purchase of buildings and equipment			(c) 112,000	
Acquisition of subsidiary			(g) 6,000	
Net increase in working capital (per first line)			108,000	
		$535,000	$535,000	

EXHIBIT 14-5

Taconic Corp.
Statement of Changes in Financial Position
Year Ended December 31, 1983

Sources of working capital			
Net earnings		$ 60,000	
Adjustments to net earnings			
Add: Depreciation	$51,000		
Income taxes deferred until future years	7,000	$ 58,000	
Deduct: Gain on sale of equipment		(6,000)	$112,000
Sale of buildings and equipment		10,000	
Issue of bonds		120,000	
Issue of common stock[a]		6,000	136,000
Total sources of working capital			$248,000
Uses of working capital			
Dividends declared			$ 22,000
Purchase of buildings and equipment			112,000
Acquisition of interest in subsidiary[a]			6,000
Total uses of working capital			$140,000
Net increase in working capital (see Exhibit 14-3)			$108,000

[a] 1,000 shares of common stock (par value $1) were issued in exchange for an interest in a subsidiary. At the time of acquisition the fair market value of such interest was $6,000.

in a comparable relationship. Changes in cash must be associated with changes in non-cash accounts. The basic accounting equation indicates

Cash + All other assets
$$= \text{Liabilities} + \text{Owners' equity}$$

Therefore,

$$\text{Cash} = \text{Liabilities} + \text{Owners' equity} - \text{All other assets}$$

An increase in cash can be associated with an increase in a liability or equity account or a decrease in any other asset account. And a decrease in cash can be associated with a corresponding decrease in a liability or equity account or an increase in any other asset account.

The statement of changes in financial position based on cash is, therefore, not very different from that based on working capital. Indeed, the statement of changes in cash will ordinarily report all financial events that would be reported in the statement of changes in working capital. The major distinction between the two results from the fact that increases or decreases in cash may be attributable to increases or decreases in the other elements of working capital as well as in noncurrent assets, noncurrent liabilities, and owners' equity.

Cash, like working capital, is derived primarily from operations. But if net income is to be reported as a source of cash, several adjustments must be made—all of the adjustments that have to be made when the statement is prepared on the basis of working capital, plus a few others. The additional adjustments arise because revenues and expenses are conventionally reported on the accrual rather than on the cash basis of accounting. Whereas a sale generally results in a corresponding increase in working capital (i.e., accounts receivable), it does not necessarily result in an increase in cash. Similarly, the cost of goods sold can usually be associated with a decrease in working capital (i.e., inventory) but not necessarily in cash.

A simple example can highlight the distinctions between the statement of changes in financial position on a cash basis and on a working capital basis.

Example

The following information was taken from the books and records of a firm after its first year of operations.

Sales	$100,000
Cost of goods sold	65,000
Net income	35,000
Cash collections	95,000
Total goods purchased	80,000
Total goods for which payment was made	30,000

At year end its balance sheet showed

Cash	$65,000
Accounts receivable	5,000
Inventory	15,000
Total assets	$85,000
Accounts payable	$50,000
Owners' equity (retained earnings)	35,000
Total equities	$85,000

Working capital increased by $35,000 (assets, all current, of $85,000 less accounts payable of $50,000). The statement of changes in financial position based on working capital would attribute the entire increase to a single source, net income.

By contrast, cash increased by $65,000. The statement of changes in financial position on a cash basis would appear as follows:

Sources of cash	
Net income	$35,000
Increase in accounts payable	50,000
Total sources of cash	$85,000
Uses of cash	
Increase in accounts receivable	$ 5,000
Increase in inventory	15,000
Total uses of cash	$20,000
Net increase in cash	$65,000

The statement of changes in financial position on the cash basis, unlike that on the working capital basis, makes clear that

1. not all sales resulted in collections of cash. This is indicated by the $5,000 increase in accounts receivable.

2. not all the cost of the goods sold required the disbursement of cash. As revealed by the $15,000 increase in inventory, the firm acquired more goods than it sold, but, as shown by the $50,000 increase in accounts payable, it paid for only a portion of the acquired inventory.

SUMMARY

Investors, managers, and other users of financial statements have a vital interest in the uses to which a firm puts its cash and in the manner in which it is derived. In the short run, cash is what is needed by an enterprise to meet its day-to-day expenses and to satisfy its obligations as they come due. In the long run, investors, who likely acquired for cash an interest in the enterprise, expect to receive cash returns that exceed the amount of their initial sacrifice.

The statements of income and position fail to reveal directly the sources of a firm's cash and the uses to which it was applied. Both statements are prepared on the accrual basis of accounting. As a consequence, they provide little information on those transactions that involve exchanges among assets, liabilities, and equities but which do not affect the overall level of resources on hand.

The statement of changes in financial position is intended to supplement the income statement and the balance sheet by focusing directly upon changes in funds. Most commonly, the statement of changes in financial position indicates sources and uses of working capital rather than cash. Changes in working capital are seen as providing a better means of assessing future cash flows since working capital can readily be converted into cash.

The statement of changes in financial position is commonly prepared by accounting for all changes in nonworking capital accounts. Income (a change in retained earnings) is a primary source of funds. But reported income may include numerous nonfund revenues and expenses. Reported earnings, if they are to be considered sources of funds, must be adjusted for the nonfund elements such as depreciation and gain on disposal of fixed assets.

The statement of changes in financial position may be prepared on a cash as well as on a working capital basis. The underlying procedures are the same, but a few additional adjustments are required to take into account increases or decreases in cash attributable to changes in the other components of working capital.

EXERCISE FOR REVIEW AND SELF-TESTING

A firm's condensed balance sheets for the years ending December 31, 1983 and 1982 and statement of income for 1983 indicated the following:

	1983	1982
Balance Sheet		
Assets		
Working capital	$189,000	$140,000
Fixed assets	245,000	250,000
Accumulated depreciation	(36,000)	(30,000)
Total assets	$398,000	$360,000
Equities		
Deferred income taxes	$ 11,000	$ 4,000
Bonds payable	200,000	200,000
Discount on bonds payable	(4,000)	(5,000)
Contributed capital	15,000	15,000
Retained earnings	176,000	146,000
Total equities	$398,000	$360,000

Statement of Income		
Sales revenue	$274,000	
Gain on sale of fixed assets	2,000	$276,000
Cost of goods sold	$200,000	
Depreciation	10,000	
Interest	17,000	
Taxes	19,000	246,000
Net income		$ 30,000

1. By how much did working capital change during 1983? What must be the net change in the combined balances of all nonworking capital accounts?

2. Suppose that net income is to be considered a source of working capital. In which *nonworking* capital, balance sheet, account is income of $30,000 reflected?

3. Did net income really provide exactly $30,000 in working capital? How much working capital was required by depreciation expense? If, for example, depreciation did not affect working capital, then which nonworking capital account did it affect?

4. The accounts reveal that the firm actually paid $12,000 in taxes. Hence working capital was reduced by only $12,000, rather than by $19,000 as suggested by reported tax expense. In which balance sheet account is the difference of $7,000 reflected? How should income be adjusted to take into account the difference between taxes charged as an expense and taxes actually paid?

5. The accounts also indicate that the firm sold for $3,000 equipment that had originally cost $5,000. The firm had already charged $4,000 of depreciation on the equipment; its book value was only $1,000.
   a. If the sale of equipment is to be reported as a source of $3,000 in working capital, can the $2,000 gain on sale of fixed assets be properly included in income, inasmuch as income is also to be reported as a source of working capital? How should income be adjusted?
   b. In what two nonworking capital balance sheet accounts is the sale of fixed assets reflected?

6. Interest expense of $17,000 is reported on the statement of income. In light of the decrease in discount on bonds payable of $1,000, how much interest did the firm actually pay? What journal entry did it most likely make upon paying the interest? How should income be adjusted to take into account the portion of interest expense that did not require the outlay of working capital?

7. Have all the changes in nonworking capital accounts been fully accounted for? (Note that the accumulated depreciation account is affected by both the depreciation charges and the sale of equipment.)

8. Prepare a schedule in which you summarize the adjustments that must be made to income if it is to be considered a source of working capital, and indicate all other sources of working capital. Does the sum of all sources of working capital equal the increase in working capital as determined in question 1?

QUESTIONS FOR REVIEW AND DISCUSSION

1. A statement of changes in financial position, especially one based on the cash concept of funds, is sometimes said to be more "objective" than an income statement. Do you agree? Why?

2. Why are changes in the working capital balance of a firm, as well as reasons for such changes, of vital concern to managers, investors, creditors, and other users of financial statements?

3. In a recent collective bargaining session, management argued that even though reported earnings were at record highs, the company was nevertheless unable to afford even a small increase in wages. In another session involving different companies and unions, the union asserted that even though the company incurred a severe loss, the company could well afford to grant a substantial wage increase. What do you think the two positions have in common? What argument with respect to reported earnings is likely to be made in both sets of negotiations?

4. A magazine article contained the following comment with respect to a major U.S. corporation: "For the first time, the company's cash flow exceeded its income. The firm was basking in riches as depreciation write-offs poured a golden stream of cash into its treasury." In what way is such a statement misleading?

5. Why do most firms elect to define funds in terms of working capital rather than cash?

6. Why must reported earnings be adjusted before they can properly be included as a source of funds?

7. Why are some types of transactions (e.g., an

exchange of bonds for preferred stock) reported as sources and uses of funds even though they resulted in neither an increase nor a decrease in working capital? Provide examples of such transactions.

8. "The statement of changes in financial position is superfluous. A sophisticated analyst can derive from comparative balance sheets and the income statement all the information contained in the statement." Do you agree? Explain.

9. In what way does the statement of changes in financial position based on a cash concept of funds differ from that based on a working capital concept? In preparing the statement based on the cash concept, what additional accounts must be analyzed?

10. The president of Presidential Realty Corporation, a firm whose shares are traded on the American Stock Exchange, made the following comment in his letter to stockholders: "In our opinion, however, conventionally computed 'operating income' has never adequately measured the performance of real estate development and investment companies such as ours. We believe that the best measure of our performance is the 'Sum' of the operating income, the non-cash charges against such income (consisting of rental property depreciation, write-off of mortgage origination costs, and deferred federal income taxes), and the funds generated from net gains from capital transactions. It is this 'Sum' that is available for all corporate purposes, such as payment of mortgage debt, reinvestment in property replacements and new properties or enterprises, and distributions to shareholders."

The president of the company is, in essence, advocating a cash basis of reporting. Why, in light of his comments, has the accounting profession insisted that financial statements be prepared on the accrual basis and that noncash as well as cash charges be deducted from revenues in determining income? Do you believe that a better measure of performance is obtained if noncash expenses are added back to income? Can you think of any special

characteristics of the real estate industry that may have influenced the position of the president?

PROBLEMS

1. *Seemingly similar types of transactions may have very different effects on working capital.*

Indicate the impact each of the following transactions would have on the working capital position of a company. Specify whether it would increase (I), decrease (D), or have no effect on (NE) working capital.
1. Declaration of a $150,000 stock dividend.
2. Declaration of a $150,000 cash dividend.
3. Purchase of marketable securities for $12,000 cash.
4. Sale, for $15,000 cash, of marketable securities that had initially cost $12,000.
5. Declaration of $8,000 in dividends by a firm in which the company has a 5 percent interest.
6. Declaration of $8,000 in dividends by a firm in which the company has a 40 percent interest.
7. Write-off of an uncollectible account of $3,000 against the allowance provided.
8. Acquisition of another company in exchange for $1 million in long-term notes.
9. Acquisition, for $4,500 cash, of treasury stock.
10. Sale for $600 of merchandise that had cost $400.

2. *Transactions that affect working capital may not affect cash; those that affect cash may not affect working capital.*

The following describes several transactions in which the Ramara Corp. engaged in 1983.
1. Sold merchandise, on account, for $6,000. Cost of the goods sold was $5,000.
2. Collected $3,200 of the amount owed by customers.
3. Purchased additional inventory for $1,700 (on account).
4. Paid $1,500 of the amount owed to suppliers.
5. Purchased marketable securities for $700 cash.
6. Sold the marketable securities for $500 cash.
7. Recorded one month's interest on notes payable, $50.
8. Paid one month's interest on the notes payable, $50.

9. Recorded one month's rent due from tenant, $200.
10. Received payment of one month's rent from tenant.
   a. Indicate whether the transactions would increase (I), decrease (D), or have no effect on (NE) the working capital of the corporation.
   b. Indicate whether the transactions would increase (I), decrease (D), or have no effect on (NE) the cash balance of the corporation.

3. "Missing" information on sources and uses of funds may be deduced by analyzing the changes in nonworking capital accounts.

The following account balances appeared on the financial statements of the Rackham Corp.:

	1982	1981
Buildings and equipment	$475,000	$400,000
Accumulated depreciation	125,000	100,000
Depreciation	40,000	35,000
Gain on sale of equipment	12,000	57,000

During 1982 the Rackham Corp. purchased $134,000 in new equipment.
a. Compute the increase in funds attributable to the *sale* of equipment in 1982. (*Hint*: Analyze the changes in the buildings and equipment and related accumulated depreciation accounts, giving consideration to the types of events that cause their balances to increase or decrease.)
b. Indicate any adjustments to 1982 income that would be required if income were to be considered a source of funds.

4. Careful analysis of owners' equity accounts can provide information on sources and uses of funds.

The owners' equity section of the Driscoe Corp. balance sheet as of December 31, 1983 and 1982 contained the following balances:

	1983	1982
Common stock (par value $10)	$105,000	$100,000
Contributed capital in excess of par	43,000	40,000
Retained earnings	256,000	244,000

At the start of 1983 the company declared a cash dividend of $.50 per share and a stock dividend of $.20 per share (200 shares). Reported earnings of the firm included a loss of $20,000 attributable to a fire at a company plant, depreciation of $10,000, and a gain of $2,000 on the retirement of outstanding bonds.

The company issued for cash 300 shares of common stock in 1983.

Based on the above information, determine, as best you can, the increase in working capital associated with changes in the owners' equity accounts.

5. Statements of changes in financial position of actual companies often include one or more items of an unusual nature.

Examine the statement of changes in financial position of Alberto-Culver Company (Exhibit 14-1 in the chapter).
a. The company reported income tax expense in 1980 of $6,917,000. How much income tax was it most likely assessed in 1980? Explain the difference between the captions "Deferred income taxes" (under sources of working capital) and "Income taxes" (under increase or decrease in components of working capital).
b. Notes to the financial statements indicate that the company acquired the *net assets* of another company for $9.9 million in cash and promissory notes. Explain the application of working capital, "net noncurrent assets of acquired company" in the amount of only $4,704,901.
c. Why is sale of trademarks included twice in the statement—once as an adjustment to earnings not affecting working capital (under sources of working capital, $8,893,422); again as a source of working capital, $9,409,828? Explain the nature of the transaction.

6. Actual reporting practices may sometimes differ from those described in the text.

The 1980 statement of changes in financial position of Pan American World Airways, Inc., contains two items of note:
1. As a source of working capital the statement includes, "Book value of property, equipment and investments sold."
2. Also as a source of working capital the statement includes, "Conversion of debentures." As a use

of working capital, the report indicates, "Decrease in long-term debt due to conversion of debentures." Both items are of the same dollar amount.

a. How is the presentation of Pan American with respect to sale of fixed assets different from that described in the text? Are there any adjustments to income described in the text that would be unnecessary in the statement of Pan American?

b. How, if at all, does the conversion of debentures (bonds) into common stock affect working capital? Explain why the conversion is reported as it is.

7. *Reported changes in flow of funds as well as reported earnings can be "manipulated" by actions of management.*

The president of Trans-Dakota Airways is considering several means of improving financial performance in 1982.

a. Indicate the likely impact of each of the following suggestions on 1982 (1) reported earnings, (2) flow of funds (defined as working capital) and (3) flow of cash. Ignore any income tax implications.

1. Change from the LIFO to the FIFO method of accounting for inventories. (The prices of the goods purchased by the company have been consistently increasing.)

2. Recognize revenue from the sale of tickets at the time a ticket is sold rather than at the time a passenger completes his flight. In 1982 the number of tickets sold exceeded the number of flights taken.

3. Delay payments to certain suppliers until 1983.

4. Delay until 1983 required payments to the firm's pension fund.

5. Amortize (for reporting purposes) prior period service costs relating to pensions over a period of 20 years rather than 10 years, as is done currently.

b. Another suggestion was to depreciate the company's fleet of 727 jets over a period of 15 years—the number of years over which a competitor depreciates similar planes—rather than 10 years, as is currently done. The initial cost of the planes was $30 million. What would be the impact of the change on reported earnings and flow of working capital? Assume that the company pays income taxes at a rate of 40 percent and that the change would have to be made for tax as well as reporting purposes.

c. It is sometimes asserted that the statement of changes in financial position provides a more "objective" measure of financial performance than does the statement of income. Do you agree? Does it make a difference whether the statement of changes in financial position is based on working capital as opposed to cash? Comment.

8. *The reason for a change in working capital is more important than the magnitude.*

Crown Industries is contemplating acquiring Omega Co. Although Omega reported a loss in 1983, management of Crown is impressed with its increase in working capital.

Comparative balance sheets and income statements of Omega are as follows:

	1983	1982
Balance Sheet (millions)		
Assets		
Cash	$ 1	$ 2
Accounts receivable	12	6
Inventory	14	8
Long-lived assets	50	50
Accumulated depreciation and amortization	(17)	(10)
Total assets	$60	$56
Equities		
Accounts payable	$12	$10
Long-term debt	25	21
Owners' equity	23	25
Total equities	$60	$56

Income Statement (millions)		
Sales	$80	$70
Cost of goods sold (including depreciation and amortization)	62	50
Gross margin	$18	$20
Other expenses	20	18
Net income (loss)	($ 2)	$ 2

a. By how much did working capital increase during 1983?

b. What were the sources of the increase?

c. Comment on whether the increase in working capital is more likely indicative of financial strength or weakness.

   1. Compute and compare accounts receivable turnover for 1983 and 1982 (based on year-end accounts receivable balances).

   2. Compute and compare inventory turnover for 1983 and 1982 (based on year-end inventory balances).

   3. What is a possible reason for the increases in accounts receivable and inventory?

9. *For some decisions information on changes in working capital may be more relevant than that on income.*

The Badlands Mining Co. was organized to remove ore from a specific tract of land over a period of five years. In its second year of operations the company incurred a loss of $200,000, determined as follows:

Sales of ore		$2,000,000
Less: Depletion of ore	$1,000,000	
Depreciation on equipment	200,000	
Wages and salaries	400,000	
Other operating costs	600,000	2,200,000
Net loss		$ 200,000

In spite of the loss the president of the company recommended to the board of directors that it declare a dividend of $300,000. One member of the board declared the recommendation to be nonsense. "How can we justify declaring a dividend in a year when we 'took a financial beating'?"

a. How, in fact, might the board justify the declaration of a dividend?

b. Why would a statement of changes in financial position provide a better indication of the ability of the company to declare dividends than would a statement of income?

c. Suppose that the company had to acquire during the year $400,000 of equipment. Prepare a schedule which would support the position of the president that the company could "afford" to declare a dividend despite the required outlay for the equipment.

10. *In some industries changes in fund balances may provide a better measure of corporate performance than income.*

In January 1983 Real Estate Investors Corp. purchased an apartment building for $1 million. The company paid $100,000 in cash and gave a 10-year note for the balance. The company was required to pay only interest on the note for the first 5 years. In years 6 through 10 it was required to make principal payments of $180,000 per year.

In 1984 (the second year after the purchase of the property) the income statement of the company appeared as follows:

Revenues from rents		$200,000
Less: Depreciation	$90,000	
Interest	54,000	
Other expenses	60,000	204,000
Net loss		$ 4,000

Depreciation was based on the double-declining balance method with an estimated useful life of 20 years.

a. Determine net cash inflow during 1984.

b. Compute return on investment on a cash basis (cash inflow divided by company investment in the apartment building).

c. Comment on why some real estate experts believe that the statement of changes in financial position provides a better indication of corporate performance in the real estate industry than does the statement of income. Consider the fact that many properties are sold long before the end of their useful (depreciable) lives.

11. *After only one year of a firm's operations it is relatively easy to identify the sources of working capital and the uses to which it was put.*

The Earl Company began operations in 1982. Its income statement and balance sheet for its first year of operations are as follows:

Earl Company
Statement of Income
Year Ended December 31, 1982

Sales		$ 94,000
Less: Cost of goods sold	$48,000	
Depreciation	3,000	
Amortization of		
organization costs	2,000	
Taxes	7,000	
Interest[a]	1,000	
Other expenses	20,000	81,000
Net income		$ 13,000

[a] The reported interest expense of $1,000 represents, in its entirety, amortization of discount on note payable.

Balance Sheet
as of December 31, 1982

Assets		
Current assets		$ 37,000
Plant and equipment	$53,000	
Less: Accumulated		
depreciation	3,000	50,000
Land		20,000
Organization costs	$10,000	
Less: Accumulated		
amortization	2,000	8,000
Total assets		$115,000
Equities		
Current liabilities		$ 19,000
Income taxes deferred		
until future years		2,000
Note payable	$40,000	
Less: Discount	6,000	34,000
Common stock		50,000
Retained earnings		10,000
Total liabilities and		
stockholders' equity		$115,000

Reconstruct, as necessary, the transactions of the year and prepare a statement of changes in financial position. (*Hint:* Try to account for the change in each nonworking capital account. Make assumptions that are consistent with the information presented and with standard accounting practice. For example, inasmuch as income was $13,000, but the ending balance in "Retained earnings" is only $10,000, it may be assumed that dividends of $3,000 were declared.)

12. *It is possible to derive a statement of changes in financial position entirely from comparative balance sheets and a statement of income.*

Comparative income statements and balance sheets of the Hassel Corp. are as follows:

Hassel Corp.
Statement of Income
Years Ending December 31

	1982	1981
Sales	$160,000	$146,000
Gain on sale of land sold	8,000	
	$168,000	$146,000
Less: Cost of goods sold[a]	$118,000	$ 95,000
Other expenses	20,000	10,000
Income taxes	8,000	11,000
	$146,000	$116,000
Net income	$ 22,000	$ 30,000

[a] Included in cost of goods sold is depreciation expense of $10,000 in 1982 and $9,000 in 1981.

Balance Sheet
as of December 31

	1982	1981
Assets		
Current assets	$ 60,000	$ 47,000
Equipment	$150,000	$120,000
Less: Accumulated		
depreciation	(40,000)	(30,000)
	$110,000	$ 90,000
Land	35,000	50,000
Total assets	$205,000	$187,000

Balance Sheet
as of December 31 (*continued*)

	1982	1981
Equities		
Current liabilities	$ 20,000	$ 31,000
Income taxes deferred		
until future years	9,000	7,000
Notes payable	30,000	25,000
Common stock	100,000	100,000
Retained earnings	46,000	24,000
Total liabilities and		
owners' equity	$205,000	$187,000

a. Determine the net change in working capital.

b. Analyze each of the nonworking capital accounts. Determine the most likely reason for the change in each of the accounts and reconstruct the journal entries that affected each account. Identify the entries associated with sources or uses of working capital.

c. Prepare a statement of changes in financial position.

13. *Use of a worksheet facilitates preparation of the statement of changes in financial position.*

The table following gives the balance sheets of the Inman Corp. as of June 30, 1982 and 1981, and the income statement for 1982:

Inman Corp.
Balance Sheet
as of June 30, 1982 and 1981

	1982	1981
Assets		
Current		
Cash	$ 46,000	$ 13,000
Accounts receivable	65,000	12,000
Inventories	66,000	54,000
Total current assets	$ 177,000	$ 79,000
Noncurrent		
Property, plant, and equipment	$ 925,000	$1,090,000
Less: Accumulated depreciation	228,000	298,000
	$ 697,000	$ 792,000
Investment in subsidiary	230,000	219,000
Other assets	120,000	140,000
Total noncurrent assets	$1,047,000	$1,151,000
Total assets	$1,224,000	$1,230,000
Liabilities and shareholders' investment		
Current		
Accounts payable	$ 40,000	$ 35,000
Other payables	145,000	15,000
Total current liabilities	$ 185,000	$ 50,000
Noncurrent		
Notes payable	74,000	280,000
Shareholders' investment		
Common stock ($2 par value)	$ 20,000	$ 20,000
Contributed capital in excess of par	80,000	80,000
Retained earnings	865,000	800,000
Total shareholders' investment	$ 965,000	$ 900,000
Total liabilities and shareholders' investment	$1,224,000	$1,230,000

Statement of Income
Year Ending June 30, 1982

Sales	$555,000	
Proportionate share of subsidiary earnings	26,000	$581,000
Less: Cost of goods sold	326,000	
Interest	20,000	
Taxes	30,000	
Other expenses	140,000	516,000
Net income		$ 65,000

Other information:

1. Included in cost of goods sold and other expenses is a total of $90,000 in depreciation.
2. The company incurred an uninsured loss at its plant. Equipment that had a book value of $80,000 (original cost $240,000, accumulated depreciation $160,000) was destroyed. The loss is included among "Other expenses." No other "Property, plant and equipment" was sold or retired. The remaining change in the account balance ($75,000) can be attributed to the purchase of new equipment.

3. Other assets include patents of $40,000 in 1982 and $60,000 in 1981. Amortization expense of $20,000 is included in other expenses.
4. The company owns a 30 percent interest in another company. It accounts for its investment by the equity method. The sudsidiary paid cash dividends of $15,000 to Inman Corp. during 1982.
5. The entire decrease in the balance of "Notes payable" is the result of repayment of the liability.

Prepare, on a working capital basis, a statement of changes in financial position. You will probabily find it useful to reconstruct the journal entries that affected the nonworking capital accounts and to post them to a worksheet.

14. Preparation of a statement of changes in financial position requires the analysis of each nonworking capital account.

The consolidated balance sheets of the Sorrells Co. as of December 31, 1983 and 1982, are as follows. So also is the income statement for 1983.

Sorrells Co.
Consolidated Balance Sheet
as of December 31, 1983 and 1982

	1983	1982
Assets		
Current		
Cash	$ 88,000	$ 61,000
Accounts receivable	250,000	211,000
Inventory	269,000	245,000
Total current assets	$ 607,000	$ 517,000
Other assets		
Plant and equipment	$ 950,000	$ 958,000
Less: Accumulated depreciation	180,000	102,000
	$ 770,000	$ 856,000
Investment in unconsolidated subsidiary	50,000	-0-
Goodwill	65,000	74,000
Total other assets	$ 885,000	$ 930,000
Total assets	$1,492,000	$1,447,000

Sorrells Co.
Consolidated Balance Sheet
as of December 31, 1983 and 1982 (*continued*)

	1983	1982
Equities		
Current liabilities		
Accounts payable	$ 218,000	$ 179,000
Other current liabilities	63,000	176,000
Total current liabilities	$ 281,000	$ 355,000
Other liabilities		
Deferred income taxes	$ 24,000	$ 20,000
Bonds payable	$ 200,000	$ 200,000
Less: Unamortized discount	13,000	14,000
	$ 187,000	$ 186,000
Total other liabilities	$ 211,000	$ 206,000
Owners' equity		
Common stock ($1 par value)	$ 110,000	$ 100,000
Contributed capital in excess of par	340,000	300,000
Retained earnings	550,000	486,000
Total owners' equity	$1,000,000	$ 886,000
Total liabilities and owners' equity	$1,492,000	$1,447,000

Sorrells Co.
Statement of Income
Year Ended December 31, 1983

Sales		$883,000
Less: Expenses		
Cost of goods sold	$596,000	
Depreciation	87,000	
Amortization of goodwill	9,000	
Interest	13,000	
Other expenses	8,000	
Income taxes	76,000	789,000
Net income		$ 94,000

Using the statements as well as the other information provided below, prepare a statement of changes in financial position. Use the working capital concept of funds. Reconstruct journal entries as required and post them to a worksheet.

Be sure to review the statement of income for any reported expenses that may not have required the use of working capital.

Other information:

1. The company declared cash dividends of $30,000.
2. "Other expenses" includes a loss of $2,000 on equipment sold. The equipment had cost $17,000 and had a book value at time of sale of $8,000 (cost less accumulated depreciation of $9,000). It was sold for $6,000.
3. The firm also acquired new equipment. (By analyzing the plant and equipment account you should be able to determine the cost of the equipment purchased.)
4. The bonds payable carried a 6 percent coupon rate. They had been sold at a discount. (By examining the accounts related to the bonds payable you should be able to determine any required adjustments to net income—the difference between interest charged as an expense and interest actually paid.)
5. The company acquired a 15 percent interest in the unconsolidated subsidiary in exchange for 10,000 shares of common stock. There were no other changes in the common stock accounts during the year.

6. The company credits the difference between taxes reported on the income statement and those actually payable within one year to "deferred income taxes."

15. *Preparation of a statement of changes in financial position on a cash basis requires the analysis of all accounts other than cash.*

Comparative income statements and balance sheets for the Rushmore Sales Corp. for the years ended December 31, 1983 and 1982, are indicated as follows:

Rushmore Sales Corp.
Balance Sheet
as of December 31, 1983 and 1982

	1983	1982
Assets		
Cash	$ 40,000	$ 19,000
Accounts receivable	60,000	45,000
Inventories	20,000	28,000
Fixed assets (net of accumulated depreciation)	107,000	112,000
	$227,000	$204,000
Equities		
Accounts payable	$ 89,000	$ 85,000
Common stock	100,000	100,000
Retained earnings	38,000	19,000
Total equities	$227,000	$204,000

Income Statement
for Years Ending December 31, 1983 and 1982

Sales	$100,000	$ 85,000
Cost of goods sold	$ 70,000	$ 50,000
Depreciation	5,000	5,000
Other expenses	6,000	8,000
Total expenses	$ 81,000	$ 63,000
Net income	$ 19,000	$ 22,000

a. All sales were made on account. By analyzing "Accounts receivable," determine the amount of cash collected in 1983.

b. All "Other expenses" were paid directly in cash.

Indicate the amount of cash applied to the payment of "Other expenses."

c. Determine the amount of inventory purchased during 1983. Then, by analyzing "Accounts payable," determine the amount of cash payments made during the year in connection with purchases of inventory in 1983 and in prior years.

d. Indicate any other expenses not requiring an outlay of cash.

e. Prepare two statements of changes in financial position based on the cash concept of funds. In the first, indicate directly all sources and applications of cash (e.g., collections, purchases). In the second, start with net income as a source of cash and indicate any required adjustments (e.g., for changes in inventories, accounts receivable).

SOLUTIONS TO EXERCISE FOR REVIEW AND SELF-TESTING

1. Working capital increased by $49,000, an amount that must be equal to the net change in the nonworking capital balance sheet accounts.

2. The net income of $30,000 is reflected in an increase of the same amount in retained earnings.

3. Income did not provide $30,000 in working capital; some revenues and expenses involved neither an inflow nor an outflow of working capital. Depreciation did not require the use of working capital. It served to increase accumulated depreciation by $10,000.

4. The $7,000 difference is reflected in the deferred tax account. Inasmuch as only $12,000 in taxes was actually paid, $7,000 must be added to income if income is to be considered a source of working capital.

5. a. The $2,000 cannot be included in the determination of income if income is to be considered a source of funds. It must be deducted from income; otherwise it would be counted twice.

b. The sale of fixed assets is reflected in "Fixed assets" ($5,000) and its related contra account, "Accumulated depreciation" ($4,000).

6. The firm paid only $16,000, the difference of $1,000 being reflected by the reduction in the bond discount account. It probably recorded interest as follows:

Interest expense	$17,000	
Cash		$16,000
Discount on bonds payable		1,000

To record interest expense.

The amortization of the bond discount, $1,000, must be added to income, if income is to be considered a source of working capital.

7. All the changes in nonworking capital accounts would now have been accounted for.

8.

Net income		$30,000
Adjustments to net income		
Depreciation	$10,000	
Income taxes deferred	7,000	
Amortization of bond discount	1,000	
Gain on sale of land	(2,000)	16,000
Net income as a source of working capital		$46,000
Other source: Sale of fixed assets		3,000
Total sources of working capital		$49,000

The sum of all sources of working capital equals the change in working capital computed in Question 1.

15

Accounting for Increases in Prices and Values

Changes in prices and values are a factor that must be taken into account in making any business decision. In this chapter we shall deal with the need for, and means of, explicitly adjusting financial statements to take into account changes in the general level of prices as well as in the value of specific resources held by a firm.

HISTORICAL COSTS: ADJUSTING FOR CHANGES IN THE LEVEL OF PRICES

One of the implicit assumptions underlying traditional accounting is that the basic unit of measure (e.g., the U.S. dollar) is stable. To this point in the text, for example, it has been assumed that the U.S. dollar has remained unchanged in value over time—that a dollar was worth the same in 1982 as it was in 1967. It is for this reason that measurements (e.g., costs of assets) taken in 1967 could readily be added to those of 1982. In fact, of course, such an assumption is patently untenable. Between 1967 and 1982 the general level of prices in the United States approximately tripled. In a sense, therefore, the dollar of 1982 was worth about one-third that of 1967.

Inflation has been a major factor in the economy of the United States. Inflation works to the benefit of some parties and to the detriment of others. A firm, for example, that issued bonds in 1967 with the stipulation that they be redeemed in 1982 may have benefited from the increase in the general level of prices. The dollars that it borrowed in 1967 could purchase considerably more goods and services than those which it had to repay in 1982. By contrast, the parties which purchased the bonds in 1967 sacrificed far more purchasing power when they surrendered the cash to acquire the bonds than they received in return 15 years later.

Financial statements that do not take into account the changing value of the dollar are deficient in that they fail to provide a basis for assessing the impact of inflation upon the company being reported upon. They establish no basis on which to determine whether the firm has gained or lost from the increase in prices. Effective in 1980, large publicly-traded corporations have been required by FASB Statement No. 33 (1979) to provide in their annual reports two sets of supplementary financial disclosures. One takes into account changes in the general level of prices (*constant-dollar* data); the other gives recognition to changes in the replacement costs of the specific resources held by the firm (*current-cost* data).

Changes in Prices versus Changes in Values

Prices of goods and services increase (or decrease) for at least two reasons. First, there might be a change in either the demand for or the supply of a specific product. An increase in demand would cause the price to increase; a decrease in supply would also cause the price to increase. Second, as a consequence of inflationary forces in the economy, there might be a general increase in the prevailing level of prices. The dollar itself may decline in value. On average, taking into account *all* goods and services purchased by consumers as well as businesses, a dollar might buy less today than it did in a previous period. This section is directed exclusively to increases in prices resulting from a *general* increase in the level of prices. It does *not* deal with changes in the *value* of *specific* goods or services. Such changes will be discussed later in this chapter.

Suppose that in 1967, $1,000 could have served to acquire a *basket* of goods or services of a typical consumer. By the end of 1982

that same basket of goods had a cost of $3,000. Suppose further that the increase in prices (200 percent) was typical of the rise in prices throughout the economy. In terms of goods and services—the only terms in which a dollar has meaning—it can be said that 1.00 1967 dollar was the equivalent of 3.00 1982 dollars:

$$\$^{67}1.00 = \$^{82}3.00$$

If a company had purchased a parcel of land in 1967 for $1,000, then assuming no change in the inherent value of land—that is, assuming that there was no change either in the demand for such land or in the availability of similar parcels of land—one would expect that the parcel of land would be priced at $3,000 in 1982. Indeed, in terms of 1982 dollars, the price paid for such land was $3,000. The *historical cost* of the land can be expressed as either $\$^{67}1,000$ or $\$^{82}3,000$.

Many accountants and managers have come to recognize that it is inappropriate to add together, in the same financial statements, dollars of one year with dollars of another. Financial information, they point out, should be expressed in terms of the dollars prevailing at the time the statements are issued (e.g., 1982 statements should be based on 1982 dollars). Stated values of goods or services which were acquired with different monetary units (e.g., 1967 dollars) should be *translated* into the monetary unit in use as of the date of the financial statements (e.g., 1982). Thus, the land referred to in the previous paragraph should be reported on the balance sheet at $\$^{82}3,000$ as opposed to $\$^{67}1,000$.

It is essential that proposals to state all values in terms of current dollars be distinguished from those (to be discussed later in this chapter) which require that all assets be expressed in terms of current-*market* values. Proposals to express all values in terms of current *dollars* are firmly rooted in the historical cost basis of accounting. They require that assets be stated at historical cost expressed in terms of current purchasing power. They differ from proposals to take into account changes in market value in that, as under conventional reporting, changes in prices resulting from increases in supply or in demand will remain unrecognized until an asset is actually sold. Under proposals to recognize changes in market values, increases in market prices, regardless of cause, will be recognized as soon as they occur.

Suppose, for example, that the market value of the land purchased in 1967 for $1,000 was $3,500 in 1982. Under proposals to adjust for price level changes the land would be reported on the balance sheet at $3,000—its historical cost expressed in 1982 dollars. Were the company to sell the land in 1982, it would report a gain of $^{82}500—the difference between its historical cost of $^{82}3,000 and its selling price of $^{82}3,500. Had the market value decreased in 1982 to $^{82}2,200, then the company would report a loss of $^{82}800—the difference between the price paid of $^{82}3,000 and the selling price of $^{82}2,200.

Restatement Using Index Numbers

The key to restating financial statements so that they are expressed in common (constant) dollar terms is the translation of dollars of the past into dollars of the present. The U.S. Department of Labor maintains an in-dex, known as the Consumer Price Index (CPI), which expresses prices of various years as percentages of prices of a selected base year. The index is updated monthly. As of 1982, the base year was 1967. Hence the price level of 1967 is expressed as 100. The average price level which prevailed in 1980, for example, is expressed as 246.8, indicating that prices increased by 146.8 percent between 1967 and 1980.

To translate a value into current dollars, it is necessary to multiply the value, which is expressed in dollars of the past, by the ratio of the CPI (or any other similar index) for the current year to that of the past year.

Example

A company acquired a building in 1976 for $200,000. The building had a useful life of 20 years. At the end of 1982, it was carried on the books as follows:

Building	$200,000
Less: Accumulated depreciation	70,000
	$130,000

Assume that the CPI was 300 at the end of 1982. It was 170 at the time of acquisition in 1976. To translate the carrying value of the building to current dollars, it is necessary to multiply both the building and the accumulated depreciation by the ratio of 300 to 170:

Asset	Cost in Unadjusted Dollars	Conversion Factor	Cost in 1982 Dollars
Building	$200,000	300/170	$352,941
Accumulated depreciation	70,000	300/170	123,529
	$130,000		$229,412

The building would be reported on the 1982 balance sheet at the adjusted historical cost of $352,941 less accumulated depreciation of $123,529. Depreciation charges to be reported on the 1982 income statement would be one-twentieth of the adjusted historical cost of $352,941—$17,647 (or $10,000 unadjusted depreciation per year times 300/170).

Assume further that the company had prepaid insurance at yearend of $5,000. The insurance was acquired at midyear, at a time when the CPI had a value of 290. The value at year end was 300. Prepaid insurance would be converted by multiplying the $5,000 by the ratio of 300 to 290:

Asset	Cost in Unadjusted Dollars	Conversion Factor	Cost in Year-End 1982 Dollars
Prepaid insurance	$5,000	300/290	$5,172

Monetary versus Nonmonetary Items

Not all balance sheet items should properly be translated from original to current dollars. Many assets and liabilities are classified as monetary items. Monetary items are assets and liabilities which are contractually fixed or which are convertible into a fixed number of dollars regardless of changes in prices. Suppose, for example, that in 1967 a company deposited $1,000 in a non-interest-bearing bank account. The price index increased from 100 to 300 between the date of deposit and the end of 1982. But, if at the end of 1982 the company elected to withdraw its funds, it would still receive only $1,000. Over the years, the company clearly suffered a loss in purchasing power. But the bank is unlikely to indemnify the company for such loss and return to the company $3,000. Although the company in 1967 deposited $823,000, it holds a promise from the bank of only $821,000. It would be improper, therefore, to report the cash at a value greater than that stated on its face.

Other monetary items include accounts and notes receivable as well as most forms of debt. If a firm holds a note receivable, the amount that it will receive is contractually fixed. The company will receive no more or no less than the stated amount of the debt regardless of changes in the purchasing power of the dollar. Similarly, if the firm has obligations to make contractually fixed payments, its liability will be unchanged by fluctuations in the value of the dollar. In periods of inflation, creditors incur purchasing power losses as they are repaid with dollars worth less than those promised at the date of the contract. Debtors, on the other hand, reap purchasing power gains as they are able to repay their obligations in devalued dollars.

Nonmonetary items are defined as all assets and liabilities which are not contractually fixed in terms of a specific dollar amount and include all items which are not classified as monetary items. Among nonmonetary assets are common stocks held as marketable securities; inventories; most prepaid costs such as insurance, advertising, and rent; property, plant, and equipment; and goodwill. Among nonmonetary liabilities and equities are *deferred revenues* (e.g., obligations to perform services), common stock, contributed capital in excess of par, and retained earnings.

Adjusting the Balance Sheet

The unadjusted balance sheet of a company can readily be converted to one expressed entirely in current dollars by multiplying each of the *nonmonetary* items by an appropriate conversion factor. The conversion factor would represent the ratio of the current value of the price index to the value at the time each nonmonetary asset was acquired or each nonmonetary liability was incurred. No adjustment need be made for monetary assets or liabilities since the amount to be paid or received is contractually fixed.

Common stock is considered to be a nonmonetary item, one that must be adjusted, since it does not carry a promise to pay a fixed amount. Retained earnings is also a nonmonetary item. Retained earnings is a residual amount; it represents undistributed earnings of several accounting periods. It can be adjusted most readily by adding to or subtracting from the unadjusted amount the sum of the adjustments made to the other accounts.

Example

The December 31, 1982, balance sheet of the Inflation Co. appears as follows:

Inflation Co.
Balance Sheet at December 31, 1982

Assets		
Cash		$ 20,000
Accounts receivable		90,000
Inventory		80,000
Land		40,000
Plant and equipment	$180,000	
Less: Accumulated depreciation	72,000	108,000
Total assets		$338,000
Liabilities and owners' equity		
Accounts payable		$ 30,000
Rent received in advance		5,000
Bonds payable		50,000
Common stock		100,000
Retained earnings		153,000
Total liabilities and owners' equity		$338,000

The following information is also relevant:

The inventory was acquired in the fourth quarter of 1982. For computational purposes it may be assumed to have been acquired at year end. $10,000 of land was acquired at the end of 1968 and $30,000 at the end of 1970.

Plant and equipment was acquired at the end of 1978.

The rent paid in advance represents six months' rent on property owned by the company. The rent was received in the second quarter of 1982.

The common stock was issued at the end of 1968. Selected values of an appropriate price index may be assumed to have been:

1968		1982	
(year end)	71	(1st quarter)	170
1970		1982	
(year end)	75	(2nd quarter)	175
1978		1982	
(year end)	122	(3rd quarter)	179
1981		1982	
(year end)	167	(4th quarter)	183
		Average for 1982	= 177

The balance sheet can be adjusted as is shown at the top of page 442.

Special note should be taken of two accounts. The land is reported and adjusted in two parts to give recognition to acquisitions that were made in two separate years. Adjusted retained earnings of $108,000 represent unadjusted retained earnings of $153,000 plus the difference between unadjusted and adjusted amounts of assets less the differences between unadjusted and adjusted amounts of liabilities and common stock. More simply, it may be viewed as a "plug"—the adjusted assets less the sum of the adjusted liabilities and the adjusted common stock.

As a consequence of the adjustments, each *nonmonetary* item is expressed in terms of

Inflation Co.
Adjusted Balance Sheet at December 31, 1982

	Unadjusted Amounts	Conversion Factor	Adjusted Amounts (1982 dollars)
Assets			
Cash (monetary item)	$ 20,000	—	$ 20,000
Accounts receivable (monetary item)	90,000	—	90,000
Inventory (4th quarter 1982)	80,000	183/183	80,000
Land (1968)	10,000	183/71	25,775
Land (1970)	30,000	183/75	73,200
Plant and equipment (1978)	180,000	183/122	270,000
Accumulated depreciation (1978)	(72,000)	183/122	(108,000)
Total assets	$338,000		$450,975
Liabilities and owners' equity			
Accounts payable (monetary item)	$ 30,000	—	$ 30,000
Rent received in advance (2nd quarter, 1982)	5,000	183/175	5,229
Bonds payable (monetary item)	50,000	—	50,000
Common stock (1968)	100,000	183/71	257,746
Retained earnings	153,000	—	108,000
Total liabilities and owners' equity	$338,000		$450,975

its *historical* exchange value. Historical exchange value, however, is expressed in dollars of December 31, 1982, rather than dollars of a time past. Each *monetary* item, by contrast, is expressed at its contractually stated amount. The difference between that amount and the value that would have been reported had the item been adjusted represents a cummulative purchasing power gain or loss, a concept to be discussed in the section that follows.

Adjusting the Income Statement—Gains and Losses in Purchasing Power

One of the important measures to be derived by adjusting financial reports for changes in the overall level of prices is that of the net gain or loss from holding monetary items. Insofar as a company holds monetary assets, be they cash or receivables, during a period in which the level of prices is increasing, it suffers a monetary (purchasing power) loss. The dollars or the promises of dollars are worth less—they could be used to acquire fewer goods or services—at the end of the period than at the beginning.

Assume, for example, that at the start of 1982, when a price index was at 167, a company held cash and accounts receivable (monetary assets) of $100,000. During 1982 the level of prices increased by 9.6 percent and the price index, by year end, increased to 183. At year-end 1982 the company held the same cash and receivables; it engaged in no transactions during the year. As a consequence of holding the monetary assets, the company incurred a purchasing power loss of 9.6 percent. Had it held assets that could have been transformed into current, year-end 1982 dollars, then it would have been able to exchange such assets (assuming no change in substantive values) for $100,000 times 183/167—$109,581—and would have retained the same purchasing power that it had at the start of the year. Instead, however, it had at the end of 1982 only $100,000 in purchasing power, at a time when $109,581 was required to acquire the same goods and services that a year earlier cost only $100,000. In terms of current, year-end 1982 dollars, the company incurred a loss in purchasing power of $9,581. Price-level-adjusted statements would reflect such losses on the statement of income.

The overall gain or loss in purchasing power associated with a monetary item can readily be determined by subtracting the face amount of the item from the amount of current dollars that would be required to achieve the same degree of purchasing power as when the asset or liability was first acquired. The gain or loss within a particular period of time may be computed by subtracting the purchasing power of the item (expressed in current dollars) at the start of the period from that at the end of the period.

If a company acquires a monetary item in the middle of a year, then the purchasing power gain or loss with respect to that item must be measured from the date acquired to the end of the year. If during the year it disposed of a monetary item that it had on hand at the beginning of the year, then the gain or loss must be determined from the start of the year to the date of disposal. As a consequence, it is necessary to determine exactly (or otherwise make reasonable assumptions) as to when monetary items were acquired and disposed of.

Example

The illustration of the Inflation Co. will be continued. Assume that on January 1, 1982, the company held the following monetary items:

Assets		
Cash	$20,000	
Accounts receivable	32,000	$52,000
Liabilities		
Accounts payable	$30,000	
Bonds payable	50,000	80,000
Net monetary assets (liabilities)		($28,000)

Evenly throughout the year, the company made sales of $495,000. At the end of the second quarter of the year it collected rent on land leased to outsiders in the amount of $15,000. Of this, $10,000 represented revenue for 1982; $5,000 a prepayment for rent of 1983.

Evenly throughout the year the firm purchased $360,000 of merchandise and incurred various expenses (excluding depreciation) of $92,000. At year end, therefore, it had net monetary assets of $30,000:

Net monetary assets (liabilities), January 1, 1982		($ 28,000)
Add: Sales	$495,000	
Rent received	15,000	510,000
		$482,000
Less: Purchases	$360,000	
Various expenses (excluding depreciation)	92,000	452,000
Net monetary assets, December 31, 1982		$ 30,000

To determine the gain or loss on purchasing power, each of the monetary inflows and outflows will be translated into year-end 1982 dollars (index = 183) by multiplying the amount of the flow by the ratio of the index at year end to that existing at the time of the flow. In this illustration, all purchases and sales are assumed to have taken place evenly throughout the year. For convenience, they will be converted using the average value of the price index. The rent, however, was received in the second quarter. Thus, it will be converted using the second-quarter value. The difference in the ending balance of net monetary assets between that computed using the adjusted and that using the unadjusted data will constitute the gain or loss in purchasing power:

gain or loss in purchasing power attributable to holding monetary assets (that computed previously).

In adjusting the income statement, each revenue and expense must be related to the transaction from which it arose. The conversion factor must be based on the level of prices that existed at the time such transaction took place. Depreciation, for example, arises from the acquisition of fixed assets. Depreciation expense, therefore, must be adjusted by the ratio of the current value of the price index to the value of the price index at the time fixed assets were first acquired.

	Unadjusted Amounts	Conversion Factor	Adjusted Amounts (12/31/82 dollars)
Net monetary assets (liabilities), January 1, 1982	($ 28,000)	183/167	($ 30,683)
Add: Sales	495,000	183/177	511,780
Rent	15,000	183/175	15,686
	$482,000		$496,783
Less: Purchases	$360,000	183/177	$372,203
Various expenses	92,000	183/177	95,118
	$452,000		467,321
Net monetary assets, December 31, 1982	$ 30,000		$ 29,462
Less:			
Net monetary assets, December 31, 1982— unadjusted amounts			30,000
Difference—Loss (gain) in purchasing power			($ 538)

By being in debt for a portion of a year in which the price index rose from 167 to 183 the company realized a gain in purchasing power of $538.

Adjusting the Statement of Income—Other Accounts

The conventional statement of income can be translated into end-of-period dollars by adjusting each of the individual revenues and expenses and by adding or subtracting any

Similarly, cost of goods sold arises from the purchase of merchandise. Since a portion of goods sold during the current year may have been purchased in a previous year or at different times during the current year, the differences in dates of acquisition must be taken into account.

Example

The unadjusted income statement of the Inflation Co. for 1982 appears as follows:

Inflation Co.
Statement of Income
for the Year Ended December 31, 1982

Sales	$495,000	
Rent revenue	10,000	$505,000
Less: Cost of goods sold	$370,000	
Depreciation	18,000	
Various expenses	92,000	480,000
Net income		$ 25,000

As noted in the discussion of purchasing power gains and losses, sales took place evenly throughout the year. Hence, the average value (177) of the price index for 1982

These goods had been acquired at year-end 1981 when the price index was 167. As stated earlier, $360,000 of merchandise was acquired evenly throughout 1982, when the price index was, on average, 177. The ending inventory as of December 31, 1982, was $80,000. The ending inventory cannot be assumed to have been acquired evenly throughout the year. If the company maintains its inventory on a FIFO basis, it is more reasonable to assume that it was acquired during the fourth quarter of the year—when the price index was at 183. Cost of goods sold, expressed in terms of year-end 1982 dollars, can be determined as follows:

	Original Amounts	Conversion Factor	Adjusted Amounts (1982 dollars)
Inventory, January 1, 1982	$ 90,000	183/167	$ 98,623
Add: Purchases, 1982	360,000	183/177	372,203
Goods available for sale, 1982	$450,000		$470,826
Less: Inventory, December 31, 1982	80,000	183/183	80,000
Cost of goods sold, 1982	$370,000		$390,826

may be used to restate sales in terms of December 31, 1982, dollars. Thus,

$$495,000 \times 183/177 = 511,780$$

Also per the previous discussion, a rent payment of $15,000 was received in the second quarter of 1982. Of this amount $10,000 represented revenue for 1982 (the rest, prepaid rent). The price index when the payment was received in the second quarter was 175. Rent revenue could be restated in terms of end-of-year 1982 dollars as follows:

$$10,000 \times 183/175 = 10,457$$

Cost of goods sold arises out of purchases of inventory. Assume that the inventory on hand as of January 1, 1982, was $90,000.

Depreciation expense may be attributed to the acquisition of fixed assets. In the case at hand, plant and equipment was acquired at the end of 1978 when the price index was at 122. Depreciation ($18,000) may be adjusted as follows:

$$18,000 \times 183/122 = 27,000$$

Other expenses ($92,000), it will be assumed, arose out of transactions occurring evenly throughout 1982 and can be adjusted on the basis of the average value of the price index in 1982. Thus,

$$92,000 \times 183/177 = 95,119$$

The adjusted statement of income, taking into account the gain in purchasing power of $538, would appear as follows:

Inflation Co.
Adjusted Statement of Income
for the Year Ended December 31, 1982
(expressed in terms of current 1982 dollars)

	Original Amounts	Conversion Factors	Adjusted Amounts (1982 dollars)
Sales	$495,000	183/177	$511,780
Rent revenue	10,000	183/175	10,457
Gain on purchasing power	—	See computation	538
Total revenues	$505,000		$522,775
Cost of goods sold	$370,000	See computation	$390,826
Depreciation	18,000	183/122	27,000
Various expenses	92,000	183/177	95,119
Total expenses	$480,000		$512,945
Net income	$ 25,000		$ 9,830

Price-Level Adjustments: Why Bother?

Price-level adjustments unquestionably add a measure of complexity to financial reporting. Is the additional complexity worth the benefits to be obtained? The arguments in favor of price-level adjustments are persuasive.

First, price-level adjustments increase the internal consistency of financial statements. They assure that all revenues and expenses and all assets and liabilities that appear on the financial statements of a particular year are expressed in dollars of the same value, rather than in a mixture of dollars of varying values for a number of different periods.

And second, price-level-adjusted statements enable managers and stockholders of an enterprise to determine whether the "real" capital of the business has increased or decreased within an accounting period. The difference between adjusted and unadjusted earnings may be substantial. Studies have demonstrated that many firms which had been reporting healthy profits over a long period of time had, in fact, incurred losses when the impact of inflation was taken into account. Moreover, price-level-adjusted statements specifically set forth the gains or losses attributable to holding monetary items.

Factors that Determine Magnitude of Price-Level Adjustments

The primary determinants of the magnitude of the difference between constant-dollar earnings and conventional earnings are:

1. The rate of inflation
2. The average age of the firm's assets
3. The composition of its balance sheet in terms of monetary and nonmonetary items

rate of inflation

The greater the rate of inflation, the greater its impact on earnings. Indeed, interest in price-level adjustments has been influenced to a large extent by the prevailing rate of inflation. The roots of price-level accounting

EXHIBIT 15-1

Illustration of Impact of Inflation on Depreciation Expense

	Years since Acquisition of Assets		
	3	*6*	*9*
Historical cost of assets, unadjusted	$100,000	$100,000	$100,000
Accumulated depreciation, unadjusted	30,000	60,000	90,000
Depreciation expense, unadjusted	10,000	10,000	10,000
Historical cost of assets, adjusted[a]	133,100	177,156	235,795
Accumulated depreciation, adjusted[a]	39,930	106,294	212,215
Depreciation expense, adjusted[a]	13,310	17,716	23,580

[a] Unadjusted amount times $(1.10)^n$, where n = number of years since acquisition.

may be traced to Germany, which, in the years following World War I, experienced a period of exceedingly rapid cost-of-living escalation. Serious interest in price-level adjustments in the United States developed in the 1970s when the price level was increasing at rates in excess of 10 percent per year.

Suppose a firm had fixed assets that cost $100,000. They had a useful life of 10 years. If the rate of inflation were 10 percent per year, then the difference between adjusted and unadjusted depreciation charges can be seen in Exhibit 15-1.

The difference in annual depreciation charges by the ninth year of useful life is dramatic—adjusted depreciation charges are 235 percent of unadjusted charges.

rate of turnover

The slower the turnover of assets and liabilities, both monetary and nonmonetary, the greater will be the difference between adjusted and unadjusted financial statements. Insofar as assets and liabilities turn over rapidly, they are carried on the books at dollars that are either current or nearly current.

Constant-dollar statements will have significantly different effects on firms in differ-

ent industries. Compare, for example, a firm in the retail grocery business with that in the steel industry. The firm in the grocery business maintains relatively small amounts of fixed assets. Its primary asset, inventory, turns over daily or weekly. It offers no credit and hence has no accounts receivable. Insofar as its outstanding debt is also low, its assets and liabilities are all likely to be stated in current dollar terms; price-level accounting would have but a small impact on its financial reports. The firm in the steel business, by contrast, must maintain substantial amounts of plant and equipment, the useful lives of which are likely to be long. As a consequence, a major portion of its assets is likely to be stated in dollars of many years past, and its depreciation expense, if no adjustments are made, will be expressed in such earlier dollars. Were its statements to be recast in price-level-adjusted format, then reported fixed assets and depreciation charges would be substantially higher.

composition of balance sheet

Two general guidelines may be expressed with respect to the composition of the balance sheet and its impact on price-level-adjusted earnings. The greater the proportion of net monetary items, the greater will be the purchasing power gains or losses; the greater the proportion of fixed assets, the greater will be the difference in depreciation charges.

Companies which have high debt to equity ratios—and in particular those whose debt consists of long-term obligations—will generally report substantially *higher* earnings if price-level adjustments are taken into account. Suppose, for example, that a company had issued $1 million in bonds. If the rate of inflation were 10 percent, then each year, as the inflation rate is compounded, the company would realize a purchasing power gain of over $100,000.

The greater the proportion of fixed assets, the greater will be the increase in the carrying value of assets and, hence, the greater will be the increase in depreciation charges. The earnings of firms that are *capital intense* (i.e., that require large amounts of fixed assets) will likely be reduced substantially when their financial statements are adjusted to take into account the effects of inflation.

The financial reports of some firms—public utilities, for example—are likely to be significantly altered by price-level adjustments. Such companies must maintain large amounts of plant and equipment and conventionally finance such plant and equipment with large amounts of bonds. Hence, their earnings are likely to be decreased by additional charges for depreciation but increased by purchasing power gains on outstanding debt.

AN ALTERNATIVE APPROACH TO ACCOUNTING—CURRENT VALUES

Price-level accounting is nothing more than an extension of the traditional historical cost approach to accounting. Assets and liabilities are stated at values resulting from exchange transactions. Similarly, the determination of

income is firmly rooted in historical exchange transactions. The primary difference between price-level accounting and traditional accounting is that all accounting measurements are expressed in terms of common (i.e., current) dollars instead of a mix of current and previous dollars.

There are, however, other *models* of accounting that are not based primarily on historical exchange prices.

Current-Cost Model

One model of financial reporting in which firms are forced to venture outside of the relatively safe harbor of historical costs is based on *current* costs. Assets are stated on the balance sheet at their current costs; expenses are reported on the income statement at the current cost of the resources consumed. Current cost of property, plant, and equipment, as the term is defined by the FASB, is the amount that would have to be paid to *acquire the same service potential*. This could be the cost of either a new asset (less an allowance for depreciation, to take into account the portion of the asset already consumed) or of a used asset in the same condition and of the same age as the asset owned.

Under the current-cost model an increase in the current cost of an asset is given recognition in the period in which the increase takes place. In sharp contrast to the historical cost approach, there is no need to wait for an exchange transaction with outsiders (i.e., the asset is sold) before accounting for the gain. An asset is periodically *written-up* to reflect its current cost and correspondingly a holding gain is recorded.

One form of the current-cost model (there are any number of variations) explicitly takes into account changes in the purchasing power of the dollar as well as changes in value.

Monetary assets and liabilities are reported at their stated values, just as under traditional historical cost accounting and price-level accounting. All other items, such as marketable securities, inventories, deferred charges, property plant and equipment, intangibles, obligations under warranties, and deferred credits, are reported at their current values.

In the determination of income, revenues and some expenses are reported at end-of-period (i.e., price-level adjusted) dollars. Cost of goods sold and depreciation, however, are both derived from asset accounts, which would be reflected on the balance sheet at current costs. Cost of goods sold, therefore, is stated at the *current* cost of the merchandise sold. Depreciation is expressed as a proportion of the *current* cost of the assets that expired during the year.

The computation of income also includes gains or losses in purchasing power that result from holding monetary assets or being obligated for monetary liabilities. The gains or losses in purchasing power are calculated in the manner described previously in this chapter in the section dealing with price-level adjustments.

The gains or losses from holding nonmonetary assets (property, plant, and equipment, for example) represent only the changes in current cost that can be ascribed to changes in value. The changes attributable to changes in the level of prices are calculated and deducted from the total change in current cost.

A simple example can be used to illustrate the general approach to current-cost accounting.

Example

Postal Express, Inc., began operations on January 1, 1982, with $100,000 cash and corresponding owners' equity.

On January 1, 1982, it acquired delivery vehicles and other fixed assets for $80,000 cash. The assets had an estimated useful life of four years (no salvage value).

During 1982 the firm realized cash revenues from deliveries of $60,000 and incurred cash expenses (depreciation not included) of $20,000. Revenues and expenses were spread evenly throughout the year.

The replacement cost of the fixed assets increased during the year by 30 percent ($24,000) from $80,000 to $104,000.

The general level of prices increased during the year by 20 percent, as reflected in a consumer price index which went from 100 on January 1, 1982, to 120 on December 31, 1982. On average during the year it was 110.

Holding Gain on Fixed Assets

The current cost of fixed assets increased by $24,000 during the year. This represents the difference between the undepreciated balance in the fixed asset account at the *beginning of the year* expressed in beginning-of-year costs and that expressed in end-of-year costs. Thus:

December 31, 1982, replacement cost of undepreciated fixed assets on hand at beginning of year	$104,000
January 1, 1982, replacement cost of undepreciated fixed assets on hand at beginning of year	80,000
Holding gain	$ 24,000

Of the holding gain of $24,000, only $8,000 can be ascribed to changes in value. The other $16,000 is attributable to the 20 percent increase in the general level of prices. The part of the holding gain owing to changes in value is sometimes referred to as a *real* gain; that owing to changes in the general level of prices as a *fictional* gain:

Total increase in replacement cost
  (30% of $80,000) $24,000
Less: Increase in replacement cost
  due to increase in general level
  of prices (20% of 80,000);
  fictional gain   16,000
    Real holding gain on fixed
      assets (10% of $80,000) $ 8,000

Statement of Income

A current-cost statement of income can now be prepared by adjusting revenues and other expenses so that they are expressed in end-of-year dollars and by computing depreciation based on the current cost of the fixed assets.

Income Statement
for the Year Ended December 31, 1982

	Historical Cost	Conversion Factor	Current Cost
Delivery revenues	$60,000	120/110	$65,455
Less: Depreciation	(20,000)		(26,000)^a
Other expenses	(20,000)	120/110	(21,818)
Operating income	$20,000		$17,637
Loss on purchasing power			(7,637)
Gain from holding fixed assets (total gain of $24,000			
less price level gain of $16,000)			8,000
Net income	$20,000		$18,000

^{a} Current cost of $104,000 divided by useful life of 4 years.

Loss on Purchasing Power

The loss on purchasing power from holding monetary assets can be calculated exactly as illustrated in the section of the chapter pertaining to general price-level adjustments:

Balance Sheet

The current cost balance sheet would report monetary assets at stated values and fixed and other assets at current costs.

	Unadjusted Amounts	Conversion Factor	Adjusted Amounts (12/31/82 dollars)
Monetary assets (cash), January 1, 1982	$100,000	120/100	$120,000
Delivery revenues	60,000	120/110	65,455
Expenses (other than depreciation)	(20,000)	120/110	(21,818)
Purchase of fixed assets	(80,000)	120/100	(96,000)
Monetary assets (cash) December 31, 1982	$ 60,000		$ 67,637
Less: Monetary assets, December 31, 1982, unadjusted			60,000
Loss on purchasing power			$ 7,637

**Balance Sheet
as of December 31, 1982**

	Historical Cost	Current Cost
Assets		
Cash	$ 60,000	$ 60,000
Fixed assets	80,000	104,000
Less: Accumulated depreciation	(20,000)[a]	(26,000)[a]
Total assets	$120,000	$138,000
Equities		
Contributed capital	$100,000	$120,000[b]
Retained earnings	20,000[c]	18,000[c]
Total equities	$120,000	$138,000

[a] Depreciation for 1982.
[b] Unadjusted contributed capital of $100,000 times price-level conversion factor of 120/100.
[c] Income for 1982.

Pros and Cons
of the Current-Cost Model

The advantages and disadvantages of the current-cost model as compared with the historical-cost model have been debated extensively in the accounting literature. A few of the main points (each subject to challenge) can be summarized briefly:

*advantages of the current-
cost model*

1. It provides more relevant information for making predictions regarding future economic performance (and, more specifically, future cash flows) than does the historical cost model. First, it supplies data on earnings arising from both routine operations and changes in prices. Thus, it enables analysts to forecast future performance in light of their own estimates as to both changing operating conditions and expected increases in prices. Second, it provides a measure of the current value of the resources within the command of the organization. Cash flows of the future are more likely to be related to the current value of such resources than to a past value.

2. It provides more relevant information on which to evaluate the past performance of corporate managers. Corporate managers should be held accountable for earning an adequate return on the current value of the assets under their control. The cost of using the assets is more meaningfully determined on the basis of their current rather than their past economic value.

3. The current-cost model, if used by all corporations, would facilitate comparisons among firms. The resources held and consumed by each firm would be expressed in terms of their value today rather than as of the dates they were acquired, which vary from firm to firm.

*disadvantages of the current-
cost model*

1. The values assigned to assets may be highly subjective. In an era of rapid technological change, it is exceedingly difficult to determine the "replacement" value of an asset that, in fact, will not and cannot be replaced in the same form. Although there are ways to estimate the replacement costs of "service potential" (e.g., industry price indices and catalogs of used equipment prices), the range of managerial discretion may be sufficiently wide so as to detract from the credibility of the statements taken as a whole.

2. Current costs may not be relevant to investors and other groups of statement users if a firm has no intention of either selling or replacing its assets in the near future. The reported holding gains may never be realized,

and the amounts at which the assets are reported may never be received or paid by the company.

3. The current-cost model often increases substantially reported cost of goods sold and depreciation, but it usually has only a minor effect upon sales revenue. Many firms base their selling prices upon the actual (historical) costs of producing or purchasing their products. As such costs increase, the firms compensate by raising prices. Financial statements based upon replacement costs may give the false impression that earnings of the future may be lower than those of the present or past, when in fact they will not.

FASB STATEMENT NO. 33

FASB Statement No. 33 represents the most far-reaching departure to date on the part of a rule-making body from the relatively safe confines of the historical cost model. Statement No. 33, however, requires only supplementary reporting of a limited number of current-cost and price-level-adjusted measures. It does not prescribe that complete current-cost or price-level-adjusted statements be presented. The statement applies only to companies that have either inventories and property plant and equipment (before deducting depreciation) of more than $125 million or total assets of more than $1 billion.

Statement No. 33 requires that the following data be reported:

1. Income adjusted for the effects of general inflation (price-level changes).
2. Purchasing power gains or losses on monetary items.
3. Income adjusted for changes in current costs.
4. The current cost of inventory and property, plant, and equipment.

5. Holding gains on inventory and property, plant, and equipment.

The pronouncement is designed to hold to a minimum the adjustments required to convert from historical cost to current cost and constant dollar measures. Only inventory, property, plant, and equipment and the related cost of goods sold and depreciation expenses need be adjusted. In contrast to the presentation in this chapter, the price-level adjustments can be based on the *average* value of a price index during the year rather than the year-end value. Moreover, the purchasing power gain or loss from holding monetary items should not be included in the computation of income. It should be reported beneath net income.

The provisions of Statement No. 33 are viewed by the Board as well as the financial community as experimental. If the information that it requires be presented proves useful to investors, then the Board is certain to extend its application to additional income statement and balance sheet accounts and to specify in greater detail the manner in which price-level and current cost adjustments are to be made.

SUMMARY

Historical cost financial statements are deficient in two separate, albeit related, respects:

First, they are grounded on the assumption—clearly untenable in a period of high inflation—that the *value of the monetary unit* remains constant over time. They thereby fail to take into account changes in prices owing to changes in the general purchasing power of the dollar.

Second, they are based on the principle that recorded amounts of assets and liabilities, as well as revenues and expenses, should be the result of transactions with outsiders in which the entity has engaged. They thereby fail to take into account changes in prices owing to changes in the value of specific assets or liabilities.

Price-level-adjusted (constant-dollar) statements are an effort to remedy the first deficiency. Price-level-adjusted statements express all amounts—those reported on the income statement as well as the balance sheet—in terms of dollars of the current period. Price-level-adjusted statements do *not* represent a departure from the historical cost model of accounting. They express historical costs in terms of a present-day monetary unit.

Current-cost statements are intended to eliminate the second deficiency. Reported amounts reflect the cost to replace both the resources on hand and those consumed. Gains from holding assets or liabilities are recognized as they occur—not only in the period in which the assets or liabilities are sold or liquidated.

No manager or investor can afford to ignore changes in prices or values in evaluating results of the past or making predictions about the future. Changes in prices or values do not affect all companies uniformly. Price-level-adjusted and current-cost statements indicate their impact on the specific company being reported on.

EXERCISE FOR REVIEW AND SELF-TESTING

A firm was organized on January 1, 1982. On that date it issued common stock in exchange for $100,000 cash. The values of the price index during 1982 were as follows:

January 1, 1982	110
Average for 1982	120
December 31, 1982	130

Provide two answers to each of the questions. Assume first that the firm will prepare price-level-adjusted (constant-dollar) statements and then that it will prepare current-cost statements.

1. On January 1, 1982, the firm acquired equipment for $60,000 cash. The useful life of the equipment is 10 years; it has no anticipated salvage value. The firm records depreciation on a straight-line basis. By December 31, the replacement cost of the equipment had increased to $75,000.
   a. At what amount should the firm report the equipment on December 31, 1982, prior to adjusting for depreciation?
   b. How much depreciation expense should it record?
   c. What should be the reported net book value of the equipment?

2. Sales revenue, which was received evenly throughout the year, was $50,000. At what amount should the firm report sales revenue? (The same for both price-level and current-cost statements.)

3. Sundry expenses other than depreciation were incurred evenly throughout the year and amounted to $30,000. At what amount should the firm report the sundry expenses? (The same for both price-level and current-cost statements.)

4. At what amount should it report common stock? (The same for both price-level and current-cost statements.)

5. What was the amount of the loss in purchasing power that the firm incurred by holding various amounts of monetary assets (in this example, only cash) during the year? (The same for both price-level and current-cost statements.)

6. What was the gain from holding equipment during the year? Of this amount how much was attributable to inflation and how much was "real"? (This need be computed only for current-cost statements; only the real portion would be added to operating income.)

7. Prepare an income statement for 1982 and a balance sheet as of December 31, 1982, assuming that the firm uses each of *three* accounting models: historical cost, no price-level adjustments; historical cost, with price-level adjustments;

current cost. Be certain that the amount reported for retained earnings is equal to net income.

QUESTIONS FOR REVIEW AND DISCUSSION

1. It has been suggested that price-level adjustments are required because one of the underlying assumptions of traditional accounting is untenable. What assumption is this?

2. Increases in the prices of goods and services can be attributable to at least two fundamental economic forces. What are these forces? With which of the two do price-level adjustments attempt to deal?

3. "Price-level adjustments in no way undermine the historical transaction-based underpinning of financial accounting. Constant-dollar statements must be distinguished from those in which assets are recorded at current market values in that the former are firmly rooted in historical costs, while the latter are not." Do you agree? Explain.

4. "U.S. corporations should logically oppose price-level adjustments because in a period of inflation they result in lower reported earnings." Does such a statement make sense? Do price-level adjustments necessarily reduce reported earnings? Explain.

5. What is the difference between monetary and nonmonetary items? Why is it generally unnecessary to convert monetary items into current dollars?

6. What are purchasing power gains or losses? How are they computed?

7. What are the major determinants of the difference between price-level-adjusted earnings and conventional earnings?

8. What is meant by the *current cost* of an asset? Is it possible to derive a current cost of an asset even if the asset is no longer being produced in the same form?

9. What is a *holding gain* on nonmonetary assets? Distinguish between the *real* portion and the *fictional* portion.

10. What are the primary advantages and disadvantages of the current-cost model over the historical cost model?

PROBLEMS

1. *In adjusting for changes in price levels, monetary items must be distinguished from nonmonetary items.*

Indicate whether each of the following items should be considered a monetary (M) or a nonmonetary (N) item:
1. Cash on hand
2. Cash in bank
3. Marketable securities (e.g., common stocks)
4. Accounts and notes receivable
5. Inventories
6. Refundable deposits
7. Property, plant, and equipment
8. Accumulated depreciation
9. Goodwill
10. Patents, trademarks, licenses
11. Accounts and notes payable
12. Dividends payable
13. Bonds payable
14. Common stock, par value
15. Common stock, capital contributed in excess of par
16. Retained earnings

2. *Increases in prices must be distinguished from increases in value.*

In 1977 a certain grade of lumber sold for $115 per 1,000 board feet. In 1982 the same grade of lumber sold for $165 per 1,000 board feet. In 1977 the GNP Deflator, a widely used price index, was at 135; in 1982 it was at 188. By how much did the cost of lumber actually increase, after taking into account the decline in the overall value of the dollar? Express your answer in terms of 1982 dollars.

3. *Price-level adjustments affect not only the carrying value of fixed assets, but also related deprecia-*

tion charges and gains and losses from disposition of such assets.

As of December 31, 1982, a company reported a balance in its truck account of $106,000 and a balance of $62,800 in the related accumulated depreciation account. Supporting documentation reveals the following:

Year	Number of Trucks Acquired	Cost per Truck	Balance in Truck Account	Balance in Accumulated Depreciation Account
1979	3	$12,000	$ 36,000	$28,800
1980	2	15,000	30,000	18,000
1981	2	20,000	40,000	16,000
1982	0	—	—	—
			$106,000	$62,800

Depreciation is recorded on a straight-line basis. The useful life of a truck is assumed to be five years; salvage value is considered to be zero. Assume that all acquisitions are made at the start of the year.

For the years 1979 to 1982 a consumer price index was at the following levels:

January 1, 1979	148
January 1, 1980	159
January 1, 1981	178
January 1, 1982	184
December 31, 1982	188

a. Determine depreciation charges for 1982 on both a conventional and a price-level adjusted basis.

b. Suppose that on December 31, 1982, after 1982 depreciation had been recorded, one of the trucks acquired in 1979 was sold for $3,000. Determine the gain or loss to be recognized under both conventional and constant-dollar accounting.

4. "Earnings" from marketable securities may, in fact, be more than offset by losses in purchasing power.

As of the beginning of 1982 an investor had $200,000 in cash. On the first day of the year he purchased for $100,000 a certificate of deposit and for $50 per share, 2,000 shares of common stock (a nonmonetary asset) of a well-known company.

In the course of the year, the investor earned interest of $6,000 on the money placed in the certificate of deposit. He earned dividends of $3,000 on the common stock which he held. At year end, he sold the 2,000 shares of common stock at a price of $52 per share.

A general-purpose price index at the start of 1982 was at a level of 159. On average during the year it was at 170, and at year end it was at 178.

a. Determine income for the year on a conventional basis.

b. Determine the gain or loss in purchasing power for the year.

c. Determine the gain or loss, on a price-level-adjusted (constant-dollar) basis, from the sale of the common stock.

d. Determine price-level-adjusted earnings for the year, including the gains or losses in purchasing power and from the sale of common stock.

e. Reconcile, on a price-level-adjusted basis, the equity of the investor at the start of the year with that at the end. (Express beginning-of-year equity in terms of end-of-year dollars.)

5. A constant-dollar balance sheet requires that each nonmonetary asset and liability be adjusted by the ratio of the current price index to the price index at the time the asset or liability was acquired or incurred.

The balance sheet of the Daedalus Flying Service, as of December 31, 1982, appears as follows:

Daedalus Flying Service
Balance Sheet as of December 31, 1982

Assets
Cash		$ 5,000
Accounts receivable		6,000
Inventories		9,000
Planes and equipment	$320,000	
Less: Accumulated depreciation	80,000	240,000
Total assets		$260,000

Liabilities and owners' equity
Accounts payable	$ 7,000
Wages payable	2,000
Tickets sold for trips not yet taken	1,000
Notes payable	150,000
Common stock	40,000
Retained earnings	60,000
Total liabilities and owners' equity	$260,000

The inventory was acquired throughout 1982. On average during 1982 the GNP Deflator, a general-purpose price index, was 170.

The planes and equipment were acquired in 1978 at a time when the price index was at 135.

Accounts receivable, accounts payable, wages payable, and tickets sold for trips not yet taken arose from transactions that took place during the third and fourth quarters of 1982. The average GNP Deflator for those quarters was 175.

The notes payable were issued in connection with the purchase of the planes and equipment in 1978 when the price index was 135.

The common stock was issued in 1977 when the price index was at 128.

The price index as of December 31, 1982, was at 178.

Prepare an adjusted balance sheet expressed in terms of year-end 1982 dollars.

6. *Price-level adjustments have varying effects upon the earnings of firms in different industries.*

Two companies, firm A and firm B, are in different industries. Both, however, are of the same size and do the same volume of business. The 1983 income statements and balance sheets for the two firms are as follows:

Income Statements
for the Year Ending December 31, 1983

	Firm A	Firm B
Sales	$1,000,000	$1,000,000
Cost of goods sold (excluding depreciation)	$ 700,000	$ 850,000
Depreciation	200,000	50,000
	$ 900,000	$ 900,000
Net income	$ 100,000	$ 100,000

Balance Sheets as of December 31, 1983

	Firm A	Firm B
Inventory	$ 200,000	$ 800,000
Fixed assets	800,000	200,000
Total assets	$1,000,000	$1,000,000
Owners' equity	$1,000,000	$1,000,000

The fixed assets of both firms were acquired in 1979 at a time when the price index was at 144.

Ending inventory was acquired in the fourth quarter of 1983 at a time when the price index was at 178.

It may be assumed that sales and purchases of merchandise were made evenly throughout 1983. The average price index for 1983 was 170.

a. Prepare constant-dollar income statements for each of the two companies.

b. Comment on the reason for the differences in price-level-adjusted earnings.

7. *The constant-dollar income statement articulates (through retained earnings) with the constant-dollar balance sheet.*

University Book Store, Inc., comparative balance sheets for the years ending December 31, 1983 and 1982, and an income statement for 1983 are as follows:

University Book Store, Inc.
Balance Sheets as of December 31

	1983	1982
Assets		
Cash	$ 15,000	$ 10,000
Accounts receivable	36,000	40,000
Inventory	130,000	135,000
Plant and equipment	$125,000	$100,000
Less: Accumulated depreciation	(84,000)	(60,000)
Net plant and equipment	$ 41,000	$ 40,000
Total assets	$222,000	$225,000
Liabilities and owners' equity		
Accounts payable	$ 65,000	$ 50,000
Notes payable	70,000	100,000
Common stock	60,000	60,000
Retained earnings	27,000	15,000
Total liabilities and owners' equity	$222,000	$225,000

Income Statement
for the Year Ending December 31, 1983

Sales		$200,000
Cost of goods sold	$115,000	
Depreciation	24,000	
Taxes	8,000	
Other expenses	41,000	188,000
Net income		$ 12,000

Year	Average during Year	Value at Year End
1978	85	90
1979	97	104
1980	106	108
1981	112	115
1982	117	120
1983	125	130

Of the plant and equipment, $25,000 was acquired throughout 1983, the remainder was purchased uniformly throughout 1978. Depreciation charges include $4,000 applicable to the assets purchased in 1983. The company accounts for its inventory on a LIFO basis. The inventory on hand at year end may be assumed to have been acquired evenly throughout 1979. All sales, purchases of both inventory and fixed assets, and other expenses may also be assumed to have occurred evenly throughout 1983. Common stock was issued uniformly throughout 1978.

The value of the dollar is reflected in the following general-purpose price index.

a. Prepare a price-level-adjusted balance sheet for the year ended December 31, 1983, based on constant (i.e., year-end 1983) dollars. (*Note:* Retained earnings equal $50,890.)

b. Determine any purchasing power gains or losses for 1983. Be sure to take into account all changes in monetary items (i.e., those resulting from purchases of plant and equipment and of inventory as well as from revenues and expenses).

c. Prepare a price-level-adjusted statement of income for 1983. Be sure to take into account the fact that as a result of the reduction in inventory between year-end 1982 and 1983 a portion of the goods sold must be assumed to have been purchased in 1979.

d. Prepare a schedule reconciling, on a price-level-adjusted basis, retained earnings as of December 31, 1983, with those of December 31, 1982. Assume that historical-cost retained earnings of December 31, 1982 ($15,000), expressed in terms of year-end 1982 dollars would be $38,775.

8. *Use of LIFO may compensate, in part, for failure to adjust for changes in the value of the monetary unit.*

Two companies, the FIFO Co. and the LIFO Co., engage in operations in an identical manner. The former, however, maintains its inventory on a FIFO basis and the latter on a LIFO basis.

As of the start of 1983, each firm had 5,000 units of product on hand. The units of the LIFO Co. were assumed to have been acquired in 1974 and were carried on the books at a value of $170,000 ($34 per unit). Those of the FIFO Co. were assumed to have been acquired in 1982 and were carried on the books at a value of $250,000 ($50 per unit).

In 1983 each company purchased 24,000 units of product as follows:

1st quarter	6,000 units @ $51 =	$ 306,000
2nd quarter	6,000 units @ 52 =	312,000
3rd quarter	6,000 units @ 54 =	324,000
4th quarter	6,000 units @ 56 =	336,000
	24,000	$1,278,000

During the year each company sold 21,000 units; at year end each had 8,000 units remaining in inventory.

Relevant values of a general price index are as follows:

1974	111
1982	159
1983	
1st quarter	164
2nd quarter	167
3rd quarter	172
4th quarter	178

a. Determine cost of goods sold and year-end 1983 inventory for each of the two firms on a historical cost basis. Indicate the differences in amounts between the two firms.

b. Determine cost of goods sold and year-end 1983 inventory for each of the two firms on a price-level-adjusted basis. Indicate the differences in amounts between the two firms.

c. Comment on the use of LIFO as a substitute for price-level adjustments insofar as cost of goods sold is concerned.

9. *A decision as to how best to finance a capital investment may be altered by price-level adjustments to estimates of earnings.*

A company is planning to construct an addition to its plant. The addition would cost $4 million. The company has under consideration two means of financing the cost of construction. First, it could issue 10-year bonds at an annual interest rate of 10 percent. Second, it could sell an additional 30,000 shares of common stock. The company presently has 300,000 shares of common stock outstanding and in recent years had annual earnings, after taxes, of $2.1 million.

The plant is expected to provide an annual cash inflow of $900,000. Such amount has been determined without regard to financing costs or taxes. Moreover, in determining income, depreciation charges of $400,000 (based on a 10-year useful life, straight-line method) would also have to be deducted.

The applicable income tax rate may be assumed to be 40 percent.

a. Based on a criterion of increase in earnings (unadjusted) per share, do you think the company should finance the construction by issuing additional common stock or bonds?

b. The level of prices is expected to increase at a compound rate of 5 percent per year. The anticipated price level index for the 10-year period is indicated in the following table:

Year	Index	Year	Index
1	100	6	128
2	105	7	134
3	110	8	141
4	116	9	148
5	122	10	155

Determine constant-dollar earnings per share for year 5 under each of the two alternatives. Express the earnings in current dollars applicable to that year. Assume that the cash inflow as well as earnings will increase proportionately to the rate of inflation. Taking into account the increase in the price level, do you think the company should finance construction by issuing common stock or bonds? (*Note:* Be sure to take into account the purchasing power gain on the bonds between the end of year 4 and the end of year 5. And remember that taxes are levied on unadjusted rather than adjusted earnings.)

10. Price-level adjustments may alter return on investment.

A state public utilities commission establishes rates such that utilities within its jurisdiction are permitted to earn a return of 7 percent on total invested capital. A condensed balance sheet and an income statement of Atlantic Gas and Electric Co. for the year ending December 31, 1982, appear as follows:

divided by total assets. Thus, $676,200 divided by $9,660,000 equals 7 percent.

The funds represented by the long-term debt were borrowed in a period in which, on average, the general price index was at 110. The fixed assets were acquired when the price index was, on average, at the same level.

Revenues, operating expenses, taxes, and interest were incurred evenly throughout 1982. The average price index value for 1982 was 154.

The company paid dividends in 1982 of $400,000. They may be assumed to have been paid evenly throughout the year.

At the start of 1982, when the price index was at 148, the company had net monetary liabilities (monetary liabilities less monetary assets) of $5,116,200.

Supplies and inventory were acquired at year end. The price index at year end was 159.

Atlantic Gas and Electric Co.
Balance Sheet as of December 31, 1982

Assets		
Cash and accounts receivable		$1,500,000
Inventories and supplies		160,000
Plant and equipment	$11,000,000	
Less: Accumulated depreciation	3,000,000	8,000,000
Total assets		$9,660,000
Equities		
Current liabilities		$1,000,000
Long-term debt		5,000,000
Stockholders' equity		3,660,000
Total equities		$9,660,000

Statement of Income
for the Year Ending December 31, 1982

Revenues		$4,026,200
Operating expenses		
and taxes	$2,500,000	
Depreciation	500,000	
Interest	350,000	3,350,000
Net income		$ 676,200

Return on investment is defined as net income

a. Determine the actual rate of return for 1982 on a price-level-adjusted basis. Be sure to take into account any gains or losses in purchasing power.

b. Comment on why utility firms are particularly likely to favor the price-level-adjusted "model" of accounting.

11. Tax rates can increase, even without legislative action.

Irving Hirsch was generally pleased with the earnings of his office supplies business. Between 1976, when he began operations, and 1981, his withdrawals from the business increased from $25,000 to $45,000. "The improvement in earnings may not have been spectacular," commented Hirsch, "but at least it's outrunning the rate of inflation."

a. Taking into account the impact of inflation, by how much have the earnings of Hirsch increased? The value of a general-purpose price index in 1976 was, on average, 115; in 1981 it was 194. Express earnings of each year in terms of 1981 dollars.

b. Assume that the following is an excerpt from the federal individual income tax table:

Taxable Income (A)	Regular Tax on Amount in (A) (B)	Amount of Taxable Income in Excess of (A) But Not in Excess of (C) is Taxed at Rates Shown in (D)	
		(C)	(D)
$22,000	$ 5,990	$26,000	40%
26,000	7,590	32,000	45
32,000	10,290	38,000	50
38,000	13,290	44,000	55
44,000	16,590	50,000	60

Assume that Irving Hirsch is not married and had income from other sources in 1976 and 1981 which was just adequate to cover the miscellaneous deductions and exemptions allowed by the Federal Tax Code. Comment on whether his earnings after *taxes* kept pace with the rate of inflation.

c. It is often pointed out that Congress, by mere inaction, had been legislating increases in taxes. In light of the example above, what do you think is meant by such assertion?

12. In current-cost accounting, added depreciation charges may more than offset real holding gains.

Greenlawn, Inc., a lawn service company, began 1982 with $80,000 in working capital (all monetary items) and five trucks that had cost, in total, $600,000 but had a book value of $150,000 (after taking into account accumulated depreciation). The replacement cost of the service potential provided by the trucks (i.e., comparable used trucks) was $300,000.

During 1982 the firm realized sales revenues of $700,000 and incurred expenses, excluding depreciation, of $550,000. It charged $60,000 in depreciation. Sales and expenses were spread uniformly throughout the year.

During 1982 the replacement cost of trucks similar to those used by the company increased by 20 percent, to $360,000. The consumer price index was 130 on January 1, 140 on average throughout the year, and 150 on December 31. Current cost depreciation expense in *1981* was $120,000.

a. Prepare a current-cost income statement for 1982. Be sure to take into account the loss in purchasing power from holding monetary assets as well as the *real* portion of the holding gain on the trucks.

b. Prepare a current-cost balance sheet. Be sure that owners' equity at the beginning of year ($380,000 based on current costs) expressed in year-end dollars plus income is equal to owners' equity at the end of the year.

13. The separation of holding gains into realized and unrealized portions facilitates an understanding of the relationship between income statement and balance sheet accounts.

A firm began operations on January 1, 1983. On that date it had $1 million in cash and a corresponding amount of paid-in capital. At the start of the year the firm acquired fixed assets at a cost of $400,000. The assets have an estimated useful life of four years with no salvage value. Throughout the year the firm made purchases of inventory at a cost of $900,000. The historical cost income statement of the firm for its first year of operations indicates the following:

Income Statement
(Historical Costs)

Sales revenue		$1,200,000
Cost of goods sold	$700,000	
Depreciation	100,000	
Other expenses	100,000	900,000
Income		$ 300,000

By December 31, 1983, the replacement cost of the fixed assets acquired at the start of the year had increased by 15 percent, to $460,000. The replacement cost of inventory on hand at year end had increased by 5 percent, from $200,000 to $210,000. The replacement costs of the $700,000 in goods that were sold were, at times of sales, $735,000. All sales and purchases of goods and services were for cash. There was no general inflation during the year; hence all holding gains were "real."

Assume that the firm will prepare current-cost financial statements.

a. What was the total holding gain related to inventory and cost of sales during the year? Of this amount, how much was realized (reflected in cost of goods sold) and how much unrealized (reflected in ending inventory)?

b. What was the total holding gain related to fixed assets? Of this amount, how much was realized (reflected in depreciation) and how much unrealized (reflected in year-end fixed assets)?

c. Prepare a current-cost statement of income. Distinguish between realized and unrealized holding gains.

d. Prepare a current-cost balance sheet.

14. *Forest-product firms have special problems of determining current cost.*

The following is an excerpt from the supplementary inflation accounting information

Champion International Corporation

	As Reported in the Historical Dollar Statements	Adjusted for General Inflation	Adjusted for Changes in Specific Prices
Net sales	$3,753	$3,753	$3,753
Cost of products sold (excluding depreciation and cost of timber harvested)	2,985	3,032	3,011
Depreciation and cost of timber harvested	148	218	230
Selling, general and administrative expenses (excluding depreciation)	369	369	369
Interest and debt expense	58	58	58
Other (income) expense—net	(31)	(31)	(31)
	3,529	3,646	3,637
Income before income taxes	224	107	116
Income taxes	42	42	42
Income from continuing operations	$ 182	$ 65	$ 74
Gain from decline in purchasing power of net amounts owed		$ 127	$ 127
Increase in specific prices (current cost) of inventories, property, plant and equipment, and timber and timberlands held during the year			$ 446
Effect of increase in general price level (constant dollar)			478
Excess of increase in general price level over increase in specific prices			$ 32

contained in the 1980 annual report of Champion International Corporation, a producer of paper, building materials, and other forest-related products. (Amounts are in millions of dollars.)

a. Why are net sales as well as several other categories of revenues and expenses the same under each of the three models of accounting?

b. Did the cost of the products sold increase in *value* (as opposed to price) since the products were acquired? Explain.

c. Did the firm, on average, hold net monetary assets, or was it obligated for net monetary liabilities during the year? Explain.

d. Did the current-cost adjustments pertaining to inventories and property, plant, and equipment serve to increase or decrease income (after taking into account real holding gains) relative to historical cost income?

e. A substantial portion of the firm's assets are in standing timber (i.e., trees). How would you propose that the firm determine the current cost of its standing timber?

15. *The supplementary inflation data required by FASB Statement No. 33 can be presented in a variety of ways, not all of which are perfectly consistent with the discussion in this chapter. Regardless of how presented, though, the effects of inflation can have a major impact on financial measures of performance.*

The following table was part of the financial statements of International Telephone and Telegraph Corporation (ITT) for 1980:

a. Does income as reported under "Results for 1980" include holding or purchasing power gains or losses?

b. What is the significance of the "constant dollar adjustment" of $1,553?

c. Notes to the table (not shown) make it clear that the holding gain (current cost) of $948 includes real as well as fictional (owing to changes in the general level of prices) gains (or losses). Taking into account the holding gain and the related constant dollar adjustment reported under the constant dollar column, what was the *real* gain (or loss) from holding nonmonetary assets?

d. In light of the absence of a purchasing power gain under current costs, how does the current-cost model of ITT differ from that described in the chapter?

e. What percent of earnings (as computed in each of the three ways) has the company paid out in dividends in 1980? Consider earnings to be "total changes" after adding back dividends declared.

f. Calculate and compare return on stockholders' equity (earnings defined as in part e) under each of the three accounting models.

g. Calculate and compare fixed asset turnover (sales revenue divided by plant, property, and equipment) under each of the three accounting models.

h. In explaining its inflation adjustments the company comments: "It is significant that no tax effect has been ascribed to the hypothetical restatements." Why is it significant? In what ways could taxes be taken into account?

International Telephone and Telegraph Corporation
Summary of Effects of Inflation, Unaudited
(dollars in millions)

	Historic Cost (As Reported)	Constant Dollar	Current Cost
	Results for 1980		
Sales and revenues	$23,819	$23,819	$23,819
Cost of sales and services	13,820	14,171	13,901
Depreciation	520	706	914
Other costs and expenses	8,297	8,446	8,395
Minority equity in income	47	23	16
U.S. and foreign income taxes	331	331	331
Income	$ 804	$ 142	$ 262

International Telephone and Telegraph Corporation
Summary of Effects of Inflation, Unaudited (*continued*)
(*dollars in millions*)

	Historic Cost (As Reported)	Constant Dollar	Current Cost
	Reconciliation of Stockholders' Equity		
December 31, 1979			
Inventories	$ 3,647	$ 3,873	$ 3,709
Plant, property and equipment, net	5,084	8,082	8,635
Other assets (liabilities) less minority	(3,096)	(3,348)	(3,168)
Stockholders' equity	5,635	8,607	9,176
Changes during 1980			
Income	804	142	262
Gain on sale of Canadian timber facilities	90	90	90
Dividends declared	(359)	(359)	(359)
Other—including minority effects	104	110	66
Holding gains [on inventories and plant]	—	1,553	948
Constant dollar adjustment	—	(1,553)	—
Purchasing power gain	—	327	—
Total changes	639	310	1,007
December 31, 1980			
Inventories	3,599	3,474	3,697
Plant, property and equipment, net	5,215	7,905	9,105
Other assets (liabilities) less minority	(2,540)	(2,462)	(2,619)
Stockholders' equity	$ 6,274	$ 8,917	$10,183

SOLUTIONS TO EXERCISE FOR REVIEW AND SELF-TESTING

1.	Price-Level-Adjusted Statements	Current-Cost Statements
a. Equipment (gross)	$60,000 × 130/110 = $70,909	$75,000
b. Depreciation	$6,000 × 130/110 = $7,091 (or 1/10th of $70,909)	$7,500 (1/10th of $75,000)
c. Equipment (net)	$70,909 − $7,091 = $63,818	$75,000 − $7,500 = $67,500
2. Sales revenue	$50,000 × 130/120 = $54,167	
3. Sundry Expenses	$30,000 × 130/120 = $32,500	
4. Common stock	$100,000 × 130/110 = 118,182	

5. Loss on purchasing power

	Unadjusted Amounts	Conversion Factor	Adjusted Amounts (year-end dollars)
Cash balance, January 1	$100,000	130/110	$118,182
Add: Sales	50,000	130/120	54,167
Deduct: purchase of equipment	(60,000)	130/110	(70,909)
Sundry expenses	(30,000)	130/120	(32,500)
Cash balance, December 31	$ 60,000		$ 68,940
Less: Cash balance, December 31 (unadjusted)			$ 60,000
Loss on purchasing power			$ 8,940

6. Equipment holding gain

December 31, 1982, replacement cost of undepreciated equipment at beginning of year		$75,000
January 1, 1982, replacement cost of undepreciated equipment at beginning of year		60,000
Total holding gain		$15,000
Less: Gain attributable to inflation		
January 1, 1982, replacement cost of undepreciated equipment expressed in dollars of end of year ($60,000 × 130/110)	$70,909	
Less: January 1, 1982, replacement cost of undepreciated equipment expressed in dollars of beginning of year	60,000	10,909
Real portion of holding gain		$ 4,091

7.

Statement of Income
for the Year Ending December 31, 1982

	Historical Costs	Price-Level-Adjusted Costs	Current Costs
Sales	$50,000	$54,167	$54,167
Sundry expenses	$30,000	$32,500	$32,500
Depreciation	6,000	7,091	7,500
Total expenses	$36,000	$39,591	$40,000
Operating income	$14,000	$14,576	$14,167
Purchasing power loss		(8,940)	(8,940)
Real portion of equipment holding gain			4,091
Net income	$14,000	$ 5,636	$ 9,318

Balance Sheet
as of December 31, 1982

	Historical Costs	Price-Level-Adjusted Costs	Current Costs
Assets			
Cash	$ 60,000	$ 60,000	$ 60,000
Equipment (act of depreciation)	54,000	63,818	67,500
Total assets	$114,000	$123,818	$127,500
Equities			
Common stock	$100,000	$118,182	$118,182
Retained earnings	14,000	5,636	9,318
Total equities	$114,000	$123,818	$127,500

16

Financial Reporting and Analysis: An Overview

With Chapter 16 we conclude the first major division of the text, that which pertains to *financial* accounting. In the second division we direct attention to *managerial* accounting. The overriding purposes of this chapter are, first, to summarize and place in perspective the key ideas developed so far, and second, to provide a link between the two main sections of the text.

In the first part of this chapter we shall examine the objectives of financial reporting and show why accrual accounting is necessary to achieve these goals. Correspondingly, we shall consider some of the adverse consequences of accrual accounting. We shall be particularly concerned with the limitations of accrual accounting for decisions that managers are called upon to make. We shall also summarize the types of information that firms are required to report in notes supplementary to the three primary financial statements. In large measure the additional disclosures are intended to overcome the constraints of the primary statements.

In the second part of the chapter we shall discuss the relationship between financial reporting and financial analysis. We shall describe and evaluate in detail a ratio that has been cited previously—*return on investment*. Return on investment is considered the single most significant measure of financial performance, and as such it is focused upon by both managers and investors. Yet, as we shall demonstrate, efforts on the part of managers to maximize return on investment may not necessarily serve the interests of corporate owners.

OBJECTIVES OF FINANCIAL REPORTING

In 1978 the FASB published a statement of objectives of financial reporting by business enterprises. The objectives were intended to serve as the foundation on which a logical and orderly set of accounting standards could be constructed.

According to the Board, financial reports should be directed primarily to potential *investors* and *creditors*. They should provide information that is useful in making investment, credit, and similar decisions. By implication, financial reports should not be specifically directed to managers and parties internal to the organization. Managers and other internal parties, unlike investors and creditors, have the authority to prescribe the information they want and can obtain it from sources other than general-purpose financial reports.

The Board states that financial reports should provide information that will help users to assess the amounts, timing, and uncertainty of *future cash* that they will receive. Investors and creditors contribute cash to a business in the expectation of receiving more cash than they give up. Their cash returns will be in the form of dividends, interest payments, and proceeds from the sale, redemption, or maturity of securities and loans. Obviously, the prospects of investors and creditors receiving cash are dependent upon the ability of the enterprise itself to generate cash through its income-producing activities. Thus, financial reporting must facilitate predictions of enterprise cash flows.

In addition, financial reporting should help investors, creditors and others to assess an enterprise's financial performance during a period. It should serve as a basis for evaluating how well management has carried out its stewardship responsibilities to the owners of the business.

NEED FOR ACCRUAL ACCOUNTING

Although a key objective of financial reporting is to assist investors and creditors to predict the *cash* that an enterprise will generate, financial statements that reported merely changes in cash balances would inadequately satisfy that objective. The amount of cash to be generated in the future depends mainly on the economic resources available to the firm. The resources include the complete array of future economic benefits—tangible as well as intangible assets. Moreover, the performance of an organization over a specified period of time must be measured by the changes in those resources. *Accrual accounting*, unlike cash accounting, captures the changes in many more of a firm's resources. It gives recognition to transactions when they have their substantive economic impact rather than when cash is received or disbursed. Accrual accounting, for example, records an increase in level of resources when a firm makes a sale, regardless of whether the proceeds are received before or after the date of sale. It records a decline in resources when equipment is consumed over time, not when it is acquired and not necessarily when it is paid for. Accrual accounting is therefore generally seen as providing more useful information than cash accounting for both predicting cash flows and assessing the periodic performance of the firm and its managers.

CONSEQUENCES OF ACCRUAL ACCOUNTING

Complexity

Because accrual accounting reports upon changes in the full scope of a firm's resources and not just cash, it is necessarily more complex than cash accounting. Cash accounting involves little more than the identification, classification, and summarization of cash inflows and outflows—something that could be accomplished by an analysis of a firm's checkbook. Comparability of practices among firms could be achieved by merely establishing reasonable categories for classifying cash receipts and disbursements. There would be no issues of asset valuation; the only asset to be valued would be cash. There would be no questions of revenue or expense recognition; revenues or expenses would be concurrent with receipts or disbursements of cash.

Accrual accounting, by contrast, is concerned with *income*, not cash flows. The process of resource enhancement in a firm takes place over time and involves a series of related activities. In a manufacturing enterprise, for example, it includes the purchase of plant and equipment, the acquisition of raw materials, the manufacture and sale of the product, and the collection of cash. Accrual accounting requires a firm to determine (or make assumptions about) how much each particular activity contributes to increases in the firm's well-being—what the firm's resources are at any particular time and how much they have changed between two points in time.

If comparability of accounting reports is to be achieved, then guidelines of income measurement must be established. But the commercial activities in which firms of the modern era engage, are both diverse and complicated. Financial arrangements that are similar in substance may differ considerably in form. To date it has proven impossible to promulgate a set of simple accounting principles that captures the economic essence of all transactions in which firms engage.

As recently as twenty years ago, however, guidelines of accrual accounting were few in number and broad in scope. Individual firms had considerable freedom in reporting upon their activities. The resultant diversity of practice decreased the comparability of reports and allowed for some clear-cut instances of intentional deception. In the last two decades the rule-making authorities of the accounting profession have narrowed dramatically the range of reporting options available to firms. But as a consequence, the set of rules that firms must adhere to has become detailed and cumbersome. Greater comparability of reports has been achieved at the cost of great complexity.

The trade-off between comparability and complexity has proven especially difficult to avoid because *uniformity* of practice does not necessarily ensure comparability of financial reports. The value of a firm's resources—the extent to which they will generate cash in the future—depends upon circumstances that are unique to each firm. The benefits to be derived from a fixed asset in the control of one company may differ considerably from those from an identical asset in the control of another. Accounting rules which were to require identical useful lives and patterns of depreciation may make the financial reports of the two firms uniform, but certainly not comparable.

Opportunities to Influence Reported Earnings

Despite the strides in recent years toward greater uniformity of practice, individual firms still have opportunities to influence *reported* (as opposed to substantive economic) earnings. These opportunities exist because of the inherent characteristics of accrual accounting. Over time they may be reduced in number, but they will likely never be eliminated. It is essential that managers and investors be cognizant of them, not only so they can spot blatant attempts at income manipulation, but more importantly, so that they can compensate for differences in reporting policies among firms.

The section that follows summarizes the ways in which management can influence reported earnings. Although the emphasis is on *earnings*, it must be remembered that any actions that affect earnings must necessarily affect assets or liabilities and owners' equity.

There are three primary ways in which management can have an impact on reported earnings:

1. By choosing judiciously among acceptable accounting methods;
2. By making biased estimates;
3. By timing transactions so that changes in value which have occurred over time are given accounting recognition in the most opportune periods.

choosing among available accounting methods

In the preceding chapters a number of areas were discussed in which alternative accounting methods may be used. Among them are:

a. *Revenue recognition.* Although most businesses recognize revenue at time of sale, they may do so at other times as well. For example, revenue on a long-term project may be recognized as work is carried out (a percentage of completion basis), when the project is completed, or when cash is collected.

b. *Cost of goods sold.* Cost of goods sold and inventory values may be established by a number of methods, the most popular of which are first-in, first-out and last-in, first-out.

c. *Depreciation.* Firms may select among straight-line and various patterns of accelerated depreciation.

d. *Investment tax credit.* The investment tax credit may be used to reduce reported income tax expense in the year in which the eligible property is acquired or over its useful life.

e. *Matching of costs to revenues.* Costs should be charged as expenses in the periods in which the revenues that they serve to gen-

erate are recognized. Management, however, has considerable latitude in determining whether a cost should be considered a period cost to be charged as an expense as it is incurred, a product cost to be inventoried and charged as an expense as part of cost of goods sold, or a capitalizable cost to be amortized over several accounting periods.

f. *Cost of drilling unsuccessful oil wells.* Costs of drilling unsuccessful wells may be written-off as incurred (the successful efforts method) or capitalized as part of the cost of the successful wells (the full-cost method).

Some accountants and analysts characterize earnings in terms of their *quality*. The higher the quality of earnings, the more conservative are the accounting methods on which they are based. Conservative accounting methods are those which recognize revenues as late as possible and expenses as early as possible.

making estimates

Accrual accounting requires that numerous management estimates be incorporated into the financial reports. Among them are those of:

a. *Useful lives.* Management must determine the number of years over which to amortize the cost of fixed assets and intangibles, including goodwill.

b. *Losses on bad debts.* Management must estimate the percentage of sales or accounts receivable that will prove uncollectible, and credit such amount to an allowance for uncollectibles contra account.

c. *Warranties.* Because expenses must be matched with revenues, management must estimate repair and replacement costs that will be incurred subsequent to the period in which revenue is recognized and must establish appropriate allowances.

timing gains and losses

Gains or losses from changes in the value of assets or liabilities are ordinarily recognized when the assets or liabilities are sold or liquidated, not in the periods in which the changes take place. As a consequence, a firm which owns assets that have appreciated in value or owes liabilities that have depreciated in value has a "reserve" of earnings that it can draw upon at its discretion. It can engage in two types of transactions to realize the earnings in the reserve:

1. It can sell appreciated assets (such as marketable securities). The gain would be recognized entirely in period of sale, regardless of when the increase in value actually took place.
2. It can retire long-term bonds that have depreciated in value. Bonds would be traded at a price less than book value if interest rates have increased since the bonds were issued. The firm could purchase, and then retire, the bonds at an amount less than that at which they are recorded, and thereby recognize a gain in the period of retirement.

Both of these types of transactions may be economically insignificant because the assets surrendered by the firm (such as the marketable securities or the cash used to repay the debt) may be replaceable without loss of economic utility. The assets may be repurchased at the price for which they were sold; the cash may be reborrowed at a rate of interest reflective of the price at which the debt was retired.

Limitations for Managers

Financial statements, based on the principles of accrual accounting are designed for investors and creditors, not managers. Managers, as opposed to investors and creditors, are responsible for planning and controlling the activities of an enterprise. Seldom do they focus on predicting cash flows or evaluating the performance of the firm as a whole. Instead, they are concerned with the cash flows that could be generated by *specific* projects, activities, and assets; they are required to evaluate the performance of *individual* managers or corporate segments.

Managers need information that is tailor-made for the decisions at hand. Reports intended for investors and creditors are often inappropriate because they fail to isolate the changes in the resources that will be affected by the decision. Revenues and expenses as reported in the income statement, for example, are usually poor predictors of the cash consequences of any particular management action. They are "contaminated" by the estimates, allocations, and choices of accounting principles required by accrual accounting. Suppose that a manager must decide whether to increase production volume over what it had been. The expense, cost of goods sold, would provide little guidance as to the additional manufacturing costs that would be incurred. Cost of goods sold includes allocations of fixed costs (such as those for plant maintenance) which will be unchanged by the increase in volume. Moreover, it is influenced by estimates (such as that of the useful life of existing plant and equipment), and choice of inventory method (such as that between LIFO or FIFO), which will affect reported expense, but not actual manufacturing costs. Management would require a report that focuses directly upon the incremental cash flows attributable to the increase in production volume.

Similarly, when managers review the accomplishments of departments or divisions of the firm, they must focus attention exclusively on those elements of performance over which the unit has control. Earnings, as computed in accordance with accepted principles of accrual accounting, incorporate elements that are likely to be beyond the influence of the managers of a specific unit. Depreciation expense, for example, reflects decisions of the past. It is based on the amount paid to acquire an asset—an asset that may have been purchased in a period prior to that in which present managers took charge. Over time, of course, present managers can decide to dispose of old assets and buy new ones. But in the short run they are saddled with depreciation charges which they can do little or nothing to reduce.

Correspondingly, units may be credited with revenues or charged with expenses that are established "arbitrarily" at corporate headquarters. The revenues of a production unit may represent intra-company "sales" to a marketing division. The sales price (in actuality a *transfer* price since it represents the price at which goods are transferred from one unit of the firm to another) would be determined by the company itself. Its expenses may include allocations of common corporate costs (such as administrative and financing costs), also decided upon by company executives. Insofar as the unit lacks control over one or more key components of income, income cannot be used as a valid indicator of performance.

It would be incorrect to infer that financial reports based on accrual accounting are useless to managers and completely adequate for investors and creditors. Managers are themselves investors or creditors when they acquire securities of, or make loans to, other firms. And investors and creditors must make analyses similar to those of management when they decide whether to provide financial support for proposed corporate projects. On balance, however, accrual accounting is considered the preferred means of communicating financial information to investors and creditors. Reports that are specifically designed for the decisions at hand are required by managers.

REDUCING DEFICIENCIES THROUGH DISCLOSURE

The three basic financial statements are not a satisfactory means of conveying financial data to *all* investors and creditors. Users differ in their information requirements and preferences. The accounting and reporting practices which underlie the statements are the product of compromises and arbitrary decisions by rule-making authorities, the firm's managers, and its independent auditors. Moreover, the quantitative, tabular form of accounting statements can never fully capture all the events and circumstances that bear upon a firm's financial health. They must be supplemented by verbal reports and explanations.

In recent years there has been a sharp increase in the amount of information contained in notes which accompany the three basic statements. These notes form an integral part of the financial report and are intended, in large measure to reduce the inherent deficiencies of the statements themselves. The information contained in the supplementary notes varies from company to company. The following, however, are among the more significant types of disclosures and an indication of the deficiencies that they are intended to reduce:

1. *A summary of significant accounting policies.* The flexibility allowed firms in selecting accounting principles diminishes the objectivity and comparability of financial statements. The importance of the principles chosen is reduced, however, when the firm describes the principles used and provides the particulars of the transactions reported on. The user of the report is then able to adjust the statements to reflect his own preferred principles. The accounting policies a firm must describe in the supplementary notes are those over which a firm has discretion.

They include those relating to inventories and cost of goods sold, depreciation, income taxes, revenue recognition, retirement plans, and consolidations. Presently, firms are not generally required to provide sufficient details of the underlying transactions to permit accurate adjustments. But the information on accounting policies facilitates at least estimates of what the adjustments would be.

2. *Details of transactions.* The three primary statements may not reveal all important aspects of transactions in which a firm engages. For example, if a firm "defers" a portion of its income taxes, then the income statement would not indicate the amount of taxes actually paid. Similarly, if a firm capitalizes its lease obligations, then the reported lease (or interest) expense would differ from the actual cash paid. Typical of transactions about which additional information should be provided in supplementary notes are those involving income taxes, retirement plans, leases, research and development costs, and employee stock options.

3. *Breakdown of reported amounts.* The main body of each statement summarizes groups of accounts into single figures. But there is no optimum level of data aggregation. What is necessary detail to one user may be *information overload* to another. A firm can best satisfy differing preferences of users by indicating summary balances on the face of the statements and supporting amounts in supplementary notes. In this way, the firm is able to present the necessary data in a way that is both clear and complete. Among the accounts for which supporting detail is often provided are long-term debt, interest expense, fixed assets, and owners' equity.

4. *Outstanding commitments.* Generally accepted accounting principles do not require that all commitments be given accounting recognition. Yet some commitments may have a material impact on a firm's financial well-being and should thereby be disclosed. Examples are obligations for rent payments under noncancellable leases, promises to redeem preferred stock and pledges to issue stock under employee stock options.

5. *Contingent losses.* Contingent losses are potential losses. They would be transformed into actual losses only if certain unfavorable events were to occur. They frequently result from pending litigation, threats of expropriation, and guarantees of the indebtedness of others. Contingent losses are reported on the income statement only if the outcome of the related event can be predicted with a reasonable degree of certainty. But the consequences of an unfavorable event may overwhelm the information contained in the main body of the financial statements. If, for example, an unfavorable antitrust action were to cause the firm to be divided into several smaller units, then the asset values that it reports (based on the concept of the going concern) would have little meaning. Firms are required (by FASB Statement No. 5) to explain the nature of a contingency and to give an estimate of the possible range of loss.

6. *A five- or ten-year summary of operations.* The body of a financial statement generally covers the fiscal year just ended plus only one (and occasionally two) preceding periods. Evaluations of past performance, as well as prediction of future results, require analysis of trends over time. Consequently, many firms summarize the financial statements of five to ten years. Among the key figures they indicate are sales, net income, working capital and owners' equity.

7. *Information on lines of business and on classes of products.* Many firms are engaged in a number of different types of business endeavors. Some companies are *conglomerates;*

they are composed of divisions in a number of unrelated industries. Their consolidated financial statements combine the financial position and results of operations of all their activities, and provide no indication of the corporate resources devoted to any particular industry or to the profits derived from them. Yet financial analysis is meaningful only when it is possible to make comparisons among different firms in the same industry. If the financial statements fail to provide data by industry, such comparisons are impossible.

Firms traditionally have been reluctant to disclose financial information for individual lines of business. They cite the inherent difficulties of allocating common expenditures, such as headquarters costs, to the separate businesses and of classifying all products into lines of business. They have also feared that the additional data on product lines might aid their competitors. Nonetheless, both FASB and SEC pronouncements require that firms report revenues, income and assets for each major line of business.

8. *Management explanations and interpretations.* The numbers in the primary financial statements describe quantitatively a firm's results of operations and financial position. But they fail to explain and interpret them. Managers, however, can be expected to have insights into the firm's financial history and prospects that extend beyond the reported data. They can increase the usefulness of the reported information—and in fact are required to do so—by identifying transactions, events or circumstances that have a bearing on the firm's financial well-being but are not obvious from the statements themselves. Among the matters that management should address in notes to the financial statements are favorable and unfavorable trends, changes in product mix, acquisition and dis-

posal of major assets or lines of business, and unusual gains and losses.

9. *Information on the impact of changes in prices and value.* The primary financial statements are based on historical costs; for the most part they do not take into account changes in prices and values. Firms are required to provide supplementary information on the impact of inflation. The nature and extent of the mandated disclosures were discussed in Chapter 15.

FINANCIAL ANALYSIS, AN OVERVIEW

Financial reporting supplies information that assists investors, creditors, and other users in predicting cash flows of the future and assessing enterprise performance of the past. It does not, however, provide actual forecasts or evaluations. Investors, creditors, and other users must do their own forecasting and evaluating.

With respect to the role that financial reports can play in facilitating forecasts and evaluations, two contradictory messages must be conveyed. The first is that financial statements provide an abundance of information about the company whose financial affairs they describe. The financial statements of a company enable a manager or an analyst to gain an insight into its economic well-being with a clarity that cannot be matched by any other documents or sources of information. A measure of expertise, however, may be required to discern the true nature of the firm's financial situation. Financial statements may readily be compared to aerial photographs. An untrained observer may not only learn considerably less from an examination of the photographs than a skilled analyst, but the conclusions that he draws from them may be seriously misleading. A layman, for example, may see in a series of aerial photographs nothing more than a pastoral landscape of rolling hills and farms dotted with residential homes and barns. An expert, however, by carefully focusing on changes over time and relationships among the various structures, roadways, and power lines, may detect the presence of underground missile batteries. Similarly, a casual observer may see in a set of financial statements a seemingly stable, financially sound corporation. A skilled manager or analyst, however, by studying trends over time and relationships among accounts, may discern the existence of financial factors that point to fiscal turbulence.

The second message is that the importance of financial statements can easily be overemphasized. For any decisions in which the financial prospects of a company must be taken into account, an analysis of the data contained in the financial statements is unquestionably necessary. But it is hardly sufficient.

Financial statements do not explicitly provide information on a number of factors that are likely to have an effect on the future success of a company. Financial statements, for example, do not generally report upon scientific or technological breakthroughs that the company might have made. And they are generally silent about changes in the economic or social environment in which the firm operates. Changes in the real income or in the tastes of the consumers served by the firm could have a major impact on its profitability, but even a detailed examination of financial reports may not provide a hint of such changes.

Expertise in accounting must be accepted with humility. It enables one to prepare and interpret financial statements. But financial statements are only one source of information among many (albeit a critical source) that must be taken into account in deciding whether to invest in a corporation. For every millionaire whose investment success can be attributed to his keen ability to interpret financial statements, there is undoubtedly another who cannot distinguish a debit from a credit.

Financial analysis is founded upon ratios. Inasmuch as no accounting numbers, including net income, have meaning in and of themselves, ratios are necessary to extricate information of significance from financial reports. Ratios can be developed to describe quantitatively a firm's solvency and liquidity, its profitability and its effectiveness in employing all, or selected categories of, the resources within its control. The ratios discussed throughout this text are summarized in Exhibit 16-1.

RETURN ON INVESTMENT

Return on investment is the single most important measure of corporate profitability and efficiency. It encompasses all revenues and expenses as well as all assets and liabilities, and it is widely used as an evaluative criteria by managers as well as investors and creditors. Return on investment was discussed briefly in Chapter 2. In this section we shall expand upon its significance and indicate its limitations.

Return on investment may be computed in numerous ways. The differences among three of the more common ways point out the importance of adapting ratios to the particular objectives of the financial review which is being undertaken.

First, return on investment may be interpreted as a measure of the profitability of the enterprise without regard to the manner in which it has been financed. Income, before taking into account distributions to the

EXHIBIT 16-1 *Summary of Selected Ratios*

Name	Formula	Objective
I. Profitability and activity ratios		
A. Return on investment (all capital)	$$\frac{\text{Net income} + \text{Interest after taxes}}{\text{Average assets}}$$	To indicate effectiveness of business in employing *all* resources within its command
B. Return on investment (stockholders' equity)	$$\frac{\text{Net income}}{\text{Average stockholders' equity}}$$	To indicate effectiveness of business in employing capital provided by stockholders
C. Return on equity of common stockholders	$$\frac{\text{Net income} - \text{Preferred stock dividends}}{\text{Average equity of common stockholders}}$$	To indicate effectiveness of business in employing capital provided by common stockholders
D. Price/earnings ratio	$$\frac{\text{Market price per share}}{\text{Earnings per share}}$$	To measure return on market value of common stock
E. Inventory turnover	$$\frac{\text{Cost of goods sold}}{\text{Average inventory}}$$	To measure efficiency of employment of inventory
F. Accounts receivable turnover	$$\frac{\text{Sales}}{\text{Average accounts receivable}}$$	To measure efficiency of employment of accounts receivable
G. Number of days' sales in accounts receivable	$$\frac{\text{Accounts receivable}}{\text{Average sales per day}}$$	To determine the average number of days in which accounts receivable are outstanding
H. Plant and equipment turnover	$$\frac{\text{Sales}}{\text{Average plant and equipment}}$$	To measure efficiency in employing plant and equipment
II. Liquidity ratios		
A. Current ratio	$$\frac{\text{Current assets}}{\text{Current liabilities}}$$	To measure firm's ability to meet current obligations as they come due
B. Quick ratio	$$\frac{\text{Cash} + \text{Marketable securities} + \text{Accounts receivable}}{\text{Current liabilities}}$$	To measure, by a more severe test, the firm's ability to meet current obligations as they come due
III. Financing ratios		
A. Debt to equity ratio	$$\frac{\text{Total debt}}{\text{Total equity}}$$	To indicate proportion of capital provided by creditors rather than by owners
B. Times interest earned	$$\frac{\text{Net income} + \text{Interest} + \text{Income taxes}}{\text{Interest}}$$	To measure firm's ability to meet fixed interest charges

parties which supplied the capital—that is, interest or dividends—is related to total capital employed in the business. Total capital may be represented by either total assets (the left-hand side of the accounting equation) or total liabilities plus total owners' equity (the right-hand side).

Second, return on investment may be seen as a measure of the return to the stockholders, both common and preferred. Net income, after taking into account distributions to all parties other than the owners, is related to equity of the stockholders. Interest, a distribution to creditors, is considered an expense no different than other operating costs.

Third, return on investment may be taken as an indicator of the return to the *common* stockholders alone. Net income, less the distributions to preferred stockholders (i.e., preferred dividends) is related to the equity of the common stockholders (i.e., contributed capital plus retained earnings).

The first measure of profitability, return on investment (*all capital*), is of primary concern to managers of the firm since it reveals the success of the business in employing *all* the resources within its command. The latter two, return on investment (*stockholders' equity*) and return on *equity of common stockholders*, are of more immediate interest to stockholders in that they relate their share of income to the capital in which they have a residual interest.

The three measures will be illustrated with reference to Beatrice Foods Co., one of the world's largest food processors and distributors. Excerpts from its 1980 annual report are presented in Exhibit 16-2.

Return on Investment (All Capital)

During 1980 Beatrice Food Co. employed on *average* $3,827,234,000 in capital. This was determined by summing the *total assets*

EXHIBIT 16-2 Selected Data from Financial Statements of Beatrice Foods Co.
(in thousands of dollars)

	1980	1979
Total assets (or total liabilities and stockholders' equity)	$3,980,279	$3,674,189
Total liabilities (including minority interests in subsidiaries and deferred credits)	1,975,443	1,833,622
Stockholders' equity:		
Preferred stock (no par value)	261,043	264,814
Common stock (no par value)	179,349	178,202
Capital surplus	91,102	81,468
Retained earnings	1,473,342	1,316,083
Total equity of common stockholders	1,743,793	1,575,753
Total stockholders' equity	2,004,836	1,840,567
Interest expense	90,873	72,590
Income before taxes	575,640	513,360
Provision for income taxes	285,500	251,200
Net income after income taxes	290,140	262,160
Preferred stock dividends	17,179	7,153

at the end of 1979 and 1980 and dividing by two. It is preferable to base the computation on the average capital rather than that at a single date in order to avoid distortions that would result if capital had been acquired or returned to investors during the year. Since the firm would not have had use of such capital for an entire year, it should not be expected to have earned a return on it for a full year.

In 1980 Beatrice Foods had earnings *after taxes* of $290,140,000. Deducted from revenues in the calculation of net income was interest expense of $90,873,000. This amount had been paid to the parties which supplied debt capital. The interest must be added back to net income if total income available to suppliers of capital is to be related to total capital employed by the company.

Interest, however, is a tax-deductible expense. The cost to the company of the interest paid was not the amount charged as interest expense; it was the interest expense less the tax saving. Assume that Beatrice paid taxes (including state taxes) at an incremental rate of 49 percent. Its effective interest cost was $90,873,000 less 49 percent of $90,873,000—a net of $46,345,230.

Beatrice Foods in 1980 had a return on investment (all capital) of 8.8 percent:

Return on investment (all capital)

$$= \frac{\text{Net income} + \text{Interest after taxes}}{\text{Average assets}}$$

$$= \frac{\$290,140,000 + \$46,345,230}{\$3,827,234,000} = 8.8\%$$

Return on Investment (Stockholders' Equity)

The firm's entire net income (after interest and tax expenses) of $290,140,000 may be assigned to its owners, the common and preferred stockholders. The average equity of the stockholders during 1980 (calculated by averaging *total* stockholders' equity for years-end 1979 and 1980 was $1,922,701,500. Return on investment (stockholders' equity) was, therefore, 15.1 percent:

Return on investment (stockholders' equity)

$$= \frac{\text{Net income}}{\text{Average stockholders' equity}}$$

$$= \frac{\$290,140,000}{\$1,922,701,500} = 15.1\%$$

Return on Equity of Common Stockholders

Earnings applicable to common stockholders represent net income less dividends declared to preferred stockholders. The equity of common stockholders includes common stock at par value, capital received in excess of par, and retained earnings—that is, total stockholders' equity less preferred stock and applicable preferred premiums or discounts. Beatrice Foods declared preferred stock dividends in 1980 of $17,179,000. Average equity of common stockholders (based on the average of 1979 and 1980 amounts) was $1,659,773,000. The return to common stockholders was, therefore, 16.4 percent:

Return on equity of common stockholders

$$= \frac{\text{Net income} - \text{Preferred stock dividends}}{\text{Average equity of common stockholders}}$$

$$= \frac{\$290,140,000 - \$17,179,000}{\$1,659,773,000} = 16.4\%$$

Return on Investment as an Indicator of the Successful Use of Leverage

The extent to which common stockholders use capital supplied by lenders and preferred stockholders is known as *leverage*. It is to the advantage of common stockholders to acquire funds from outsiders whenever the firm is able to generate a dollar return from those funds that exceeds the interest and preferred stock dividends that they are required to pay on them. Interest and preferred stock dividends are fixed in amount; any earnings in excess of the required payments accrue entirely to the common stockholders.

The use of capital supplied by parties other than common stockholders is not, of course, without risk, and leverage can be employed to the detriment of common stockholders. If earnings on the funds received are less than the cost of those funds, then the deficit must be made up entirely from the returns to the common stockholders.

The success of a firm in employing leverage is indicated by a comparison of return on equity of common stockholders with return on investment (all capital). If the return on equity of common stockholders exceeds that of return on investment (all capital), then the firm has increased the return to common stockholders by earning a return on funds acquired from other parties that exceeds the required payments to them.

Suppose, for example, that a firm earned, after taxes, $1 million and its only capital was $10 million in common stockholders' equity. Its return on common stockholders' equity as well as return on investment (all capital) was, therefore, 10 percent. If it were able to borrow $2 million at an after-tax rate of 8 percent ($160,000) and earn $200,000 after taxes on the additional capital, then the stockholders would be $40,000 better off than they were without the loan. Income would increase to $1,040,000, but equity of common stockholders would remain the same. Return on common stockholders' equity would increase to 10.4 percent:

$$\frac{\text{Net income}}{\text{Average stockholders' equity}} = \frac{\$1,040,000}{\$10,000,000}$$
$$= 10.4\%$$

By contrast, return on investment (all capital) would remain at 10 percent as income before interest would increase by $200,000 to $1,200,000 and total capital (or assets) would increase by $2 million to $12 million:

$$\frac{\text{Net income} + \text{Interest after taxes}}{\text{Average assets}} = \frac{\$1,200,000}{\$12,000,000}$$
$$= 10\%$$

Since the return on equity of common stockholders of Beatrice Foods was 16.4 percent and the return on investment (all capital) was only 8.8 percent, the company made effective use of leverage.

The lower the rate of interest on amounts owed and the lower the rate of dividends on preferred stock, the greater the potential for effective leverage. Some types of liabilities, such as accounts payable and deferred taxes do not require the payment of interest. The acquisition of such "interest-free" capital automatically increases the return on common stockholders' equity relative to return on investment (all capital). If managers or investors wish to focus upon the extent to which *long-term* capital supplied by outsiders has been used to the benefit of common stockholders they can modify the return on investment (all capital) ratio. Instead of using in the denominator total assets (or its equivalent, total liabilities and stockholders' equity), they could deduct the "temporary" capital and use total assets less current liabilities (or its equivalent, total stockholders' equity plus long-term debt).

Deficiencies of Return on Investment as an Evaluative Criteria

Return on investment is a comprehensive measure of performance. But taken by itself, it is not an adequate measure, since it is based upon accrual accounting and thereby incorporates all of its limitations. What is more, it may not always reflect the interests of *existing* corporate owners.

incorporates limitations of accrual accounting

Return on investment, in that it relates earnings to resources is appropriate as an evaluative criteria only to the extent that the accounting measures of earnings and resources are appropriate. As indicated previously in this chapter, earnings—particularly over a short period of time—may not be a valid indicator of either management or enterprise accomplishments. Both reported earnings and resources may be subjective in that they are dependent upon arbitrary choices among accounting principles; they can readily be manipulated by nonsubstantive management actions; they may be influenced by unreliable or biased estimates; and they may be reflective of decisions that were made prior to the period under review. Moreover, because assets are generally stated at historical costs, the denominator of the ratio is likely to be an unsatisfactory indicator of the economic value of the resources which are committed to the enterprise.

may lead to dysfunctional management decisions

Management decisions taken with a view toward maximizing return on investment can lead to a reduction in the earnings per share of common stockholders. Actions taken to increase return on investment may therefore be counter to the interests of existing owners. By way of illustration, assume that a firm has the opportunity to acquire a parcel of land which it would lease to outsiders. It would finance the acquisition by issuing 50,000 shares of common stock. The following data

are relevant to the proposed acquisition:

Cost of land	$1,000,000
Expected rent revenue per year (after taxes)	120,000
Number of shares of common stock that the firm would issue to acquire necessary capital ($20 per share)	50,000

Other factors which affect return on investment and earnings per share are as follows:

Present assets	$10,000,000
Present liabilities	4,000,000
Present stockholders' equity	6,000,000
Expected income, prior to taking into account rent revenue from proposed acquisition	1,100,000
Interest (after taxes) on outstanding debt (10% of $4 million)	400,000
Present number of shares of common stock outstanding	1,000,000 shares

If the firm decided *not* to acquire the land, then return on investment (all capital) would be:

$$\frac{\text{Net income} + \text{interest}}{\text{Assets}} = \frac{\$1,100,000 + \$400,000}{\$10,000,000}$$

$$= 15\%$$

Return on investment (stockholders' equity) would be:

$$\frac{\text{Net income}}{\text{Stockholders' equity}} = \frac{\$1,100,000}{\$6,000,000} = 18.3\%$$

Earnings per share of common stock would be:

$$\frac{\text{Net income}}{\text{Number of shares outstanding}} = \frac{\$1,100,000}{1,000,000}$$

$$= \$1.10$$

If the firm elected to acquire the land and finance the purchase by issuing 50,000 shares of common stock at the assumed market price of $20 per share, then income would increase by $120,000 and stockholders' equity by $1,000,000. Return on investment (all capital), would decline:

$$\frac{\$1,100,000 + \$400,000 + \$120,000}{\$10,000,000 + 1,000,000} = \frac{\$1,620,000}{\$11,000,000}$$
$$= 14.7\%$$

So, too, would return on investment (stockholders' equity):

$$\frac{\$1,100,000 + \$120,000}{\$6,000,000 + \$1,000,000} = \frac{\$1,220,000}{\$7,000,000} = 17.4\%$$

Yet, earnings per share of common stock would *increase*:

$$\frac{\$1,100,000 + \$120,000}{1,000,000 + 50,000} = \frac{\$1,220,000}{1,050,000} = \$1.162$$

Were the firm to use return on investment, regardless of whether all capital or stockholders' equity, it would turn down the proposed land acquisition. But by doing so it would be passing up an opportunity to increase the dollar return to existing stockholders. The anomaly occurs because the percentage return on the additional investment of $1 million would be less than the *average* return that the firm was earning on previously invested capital. Nevertheless, the additional return of $120,000 would be greater than the cost of the additional capital. The cost of the additional capital would be $58,100—the dollars of earnings assigned to the newly issued shares (50,000 shares times income per share of $1.162). Thus, the existing shareholders would be better off by $61,900 ($120,000 minus $58,100?).

Residual Income as a Means of Avoiding Dysfunction Decisions

The danger that corporations will inadvertently maximize return on investment at the expense of returns to existing stock-

holders, is especially pronounced in divisionalized firms. Corporations commonly permit their divisions broad discretion in making investment decisions. The divisions receive capital from the corporation and are charged interest for it; they have no control over how the capital is obtained. Their performance is evaluated on the basis of return on investment. Therefore, there are decided risks that the divisions will reject any projects that do not increase their returns on investment, even if acceptance would work to the benefit of existing shareholders.

One means of avoiding this danger is to substitute *residual income* for return on investment as an evaluative criterion. Residual income is defined as *net income* (excluding any actual interest costs) *less an imputed cost of capital*. The imputed cost of capital would be determined by multiplying total assets by the minimum rate of return that top corporate managers or owners demand on invested capital.

Assume that in the previous illustration the company demands a minimum return of 11 percent on invested capital. If it did not acquire the land, the company would have $10 million in invested capital. It would be charged, therefore, $1.1 million in imputed capital costs (11 percent of $10 million). Its residual income would be $400,000, determined as follows:

Net income (given)	$1,100,000	
Add: Interest after taxes (given)	400,000	$1,500,000
Less: Imputed cost of capital (11% of $10,000,000)		1,100,000
Residual income		$ 400,000

Were the firm to acquire the land, then it would earn an additional $120,000 in revenue. It would be charged with an additional $110,000 in capital costs (11 percent of $1 million). Residual income would increase by $10,000. Aware that its performance is being evaluated on the basis of residual income, management would elect to acquire the land—a decision consistent with the interests of stockholders.

Measures of Performance that Supplement Return on Investments

In light of the limitations of return on investment—or any other individual income-based measure—it is generally necessary for firms to develop supplementary criteria of performance. These criteria can be tailored to the specific objectives of the firm. Among criteria that are widely used are *profit margin* (net income as a percent of revenues), *gross margin* (1 minus cost of goods sold as a percentage of revenues), share of market, innovations in product and manufacturing processes, productivity of labor, and rate of growth. Although these measures cannot be summed to provide an overall performance "score", and may be even more subjective than return on investment, taken together they may provide a fairly complete accounting of firm or divisional accomplishment.

Ratio Analysis as the Starting Point for Financial Analysis

Until recently (the 1960s), financial analysis was generally not carried beyond the calculation of ratios. Today, however, ratios serve as the starting point of financial analysis. The following are merely suggestive of the ways in which ratios are used:

Ratios are incorporated into statistical models that are intended to predict financial distress;

They are used in making forecasts of earnings and cash flows;

They are integral elements in investment models of asset valuation;

They are used in assessing the risk of individual securities and portfolios of securities;

They serve as the basis of comparing one firm with others in the same industry. Statistical tests have been developed to assess the significance of deviations from industry norms.

Financial statement analysis has become a specialized area within the disciplines of both accounting and finance. There is an abundant body of literature on the topic in textbooks, scholarly journals, and practice-oriented magazines.

SUMMARY

Financial reporting is directed primarily to investors and creditors. It should enable them to assess future cash receipts and to evaluate the fiscal performance of firms in which they have an actual or potential interest. Accrual accounting, in that it captures the periodic changes in the full range of a firm's resources, better serves the objectives of financial reporting than does cash accounting, a far simpler and more objective form of accounting. But accrual accounting requires the development of an elaborate set of principles and rules and affords firms considerable leeway to influence the earnings that they report. They can do so in selecting among acceptable principles, in making required estimates, and in timing planned transactions. Moreover, because reported amounts are based upon allocations, estimates, and choices among accounting principles, they tend to be inappropriate for many types of decisions required of managers. Managers usually need reports specially tailored to the decisions at hand—reports which focus upon cash flows associated with proposed projects and assets or upon activities under the control of specific organizational units.

Because of inherent constraints, the three primary statements can never fully report upon all events and circumstances relevant to a firm's fiscal well-being. They must be supplemented by notes which explain accounting policies and give details of balances and transactions, indicate commitments and contingencies, and interpret the numerical data.

Financial analysis begins with calculation of ratios. Return on investment is the most encompassing of the ratios discussed in this text. But it incorporates all of the weaknesses of the underlying accounting numbers. Although the performance of corporations and their divisions is often evaluated using return on investment as a criterion, efforts on the part of managers to maximize return on investments can run counter to the interests of stockholders.

EXERCISE FOR REVIEW AND SELF-TESTING

The following are the 1980 balance sheets and income statements of Eastern and Delta airlines. They have been recast from those included in their annual reports in order to make them comparable.

Balance Sheet, 1980
(in thousands)

	Eastern (December 31)	Delta (June 30)
Assets		
Current		
Cash	$ 18,830	$ 37,963
Short-term investments, at cost	264,358	101
Accounts receivable (net allowance for uncollectibles)	337,143	283,039
Materials and supplies	165,936	37,836
Prepaid expenses and other current assets	24,350	10,558
Total current assets	$ 810,617	$ 369,497
Noncurrent		
Property, plant, and equipment	$3,185,942	$2,761,601
Allowance for depreciation	(1,317,443)	(1,208,772)
	$1,868,499	$1,552,829
Advance payments for new equipment	95,678	90,952
Other assets	41,383	29,261
Total noncurrent assets	$2,005,560	$1,673,042
Total assets	$2,816,177	$2,042,539
Liabilities and owners' equity		
Current		
Accounts payable	$ 418,365	$ 237,349
Notes payable	84,656	—
Other	277,853	$ 313,215
Total current liabilities	$ 780,874	$ 550,564

	Eastern (December 31)	Delta (June 30)
Noncurrent		
Long-term debt (including obligations for leases)	$1,442,544	$ 147,901
Deferred tax credits and other liabilities	17,961	422,105
Total noncurrent liabilities	$1,460,505	$ 570,006
Preferred stock	$ 139,342	—
Common stock (par value and additional contributed capital)	$ 379,201	$ 139,730
Retained earnings	56,255	782,239
Equity of common stockholders	$ 435,456	921,969
Total liabilities and owners' equity	$2,816,177	$2,042,539

Income Statement, 1980
(in thousands)

	Eastern (December 31)	Delta (June 30)
Operating revenues	$3,452,542	$2,956,960
Operating expenses	3,450,685	2,864,323
Operating profit	$ 1,857	$ 92,637
Nonoperating revenues (expenses)		
Interest expense	($ 109,836)	($ 11,062)
Gain on disposal of aircraft	17,886	36,091
Other (net)	43,826	6,952
Total nonoperating revenues (expenses)	($ 48,124)	$ 31,981
Income before taxes and extraordinary item	($ 46,267)	$ 124,618
Provision for (reduction in) income taxes	(4,255)	31,460
Income before extraordinary item	($ 42,012)	$ 93,158
Extraordinary gain, net of taxes	24,654	—
Net income (loss)	($ 17,358)	$ 93,158

a. Which of the two firms had greater earnings, prior to taking into account the cost of capital, in relation to all the resources within its command? That is, which provided the greater return on investment (all capital)? Base your response to this and the following questions on year-end (rather than average) values, and on earnings *before* extraordinary items. Assume, in calcu-

lating interest after taxes, that each firm pays taxes at an incremental rate of 48 percent.

b. Which of the firms provided the greater return to common stockholders as measured by income available to them as a percentage of their equity? In 1980 Eastern paid preferred dividends of $4,035,000.

c. Which of the two firms was the more highly

leveraged as measured by the ratio of total debt to total stockholders' equity?

d. Which of the two firms made more effective use of leverage?

e. Which of the firms appeared to be better able to meet its fixed interest obligations; that is, which firm "covered" interest the greater number of times with earnings?

f. Which of the firms was more likely to be able to meet its current obligations as they came due as indicated exclusively by the current ratio?

QUESTIONS FOR REVIEW AND DISCUSSION

1. Per the objectives of the FASB, to which main groups of potential users should financial reports be directed? What two main functions should financial reports facilitate?

2. Why is accrual accounting more consistent with the objectives of financial reporting than is cash accounting?

3. Why is accrual accounting necessarily more complex than cash accounting?

4. What are three ways in which the management of a firm can exercise discretion over reported earnings?

5. Financial statements report the financial history of an organization. Managers as well as investors and creditors are concerned with what the organization has accomplished in the past. If accounting is to be objective, how can there be justification for presenting the history differently to investors and creditors than to managers?

6. What is meant by a *transfer price?* Why do transfer prices introduce additional elements of subjectivity into the determination of earnings of a corporate division?

7. Supplementary notes serve to reduce some of the deficiencies of the basic financial statements. Provide illustrations of several types of disclosures made in supplementary notes and indicate the deficiencies that they reduce.

8. The manner in which a ratio is determined should depend on the specific decision at hand.

Illustrate this statement by comparing return on investment using total investment with that computed using stockholders' equity.

9. What is meant by *residual income?* In what way does it overcome a deficiency of return on investment?

10. The *Wall Street Journal* of April 8, 1981, in a story about Federated Department Stores, Inc., reported that the newly appointed chief executive officer said that Federated will continue to keep an eye on the bottom line. He added, however, that the company is also making a concerted effort, particularly at the divisional level, to stress such other yardsticks as return on investment, share of market and gross profit margin. Why is the "bottom line" (net income), by itself, an inadequate indicator of corporate or divisional performance?

PROBLEMS

1. A forward-looking management should understand the impact of its actions upon widely used financial ratios.

What effect would each of the following transactions have on a firm's (1) current ratio, (2) quick ratio, (3) debt to equity ratio? Indicate whether each transaction would cause the ratio to increase (I) or decrease (D) or whether it would have no effect (NE). Assume that any transactions involving revenues or expenses have an immediate impact upon retained earnings. Assume that all ratios were initially *greater* than 1:1.

1. The firm sells goods on account. Assume that the firm maintains its inventory records on a perpetual basis and that the price at which the goods are sold is greater than their initial cost.

2. The firm collects the amount receivable from the customer to whom it made the sale.

3. The firm issues long-term bonds.

4. The firm issues preferred stock in exchange for cash.

5. The firm declares, but does not pay, a dividend on common stock.

6. The firm pays the previously declared dividend.

7. The company purchases merchandise inventory on account.

8. The company pays for the merchandise previously purchased.
9. The firm purchases equipment, giving the seller a three-year note for the entire amount payable.
10. The firm recognizes depreciation for the first year.

sume average investment to be the same as year-end investment.

b. Determine return on investment by "filling in" each of the boxes in the diagram and carrying out the required operations. "Other expenses" should be included net of interest revenue.

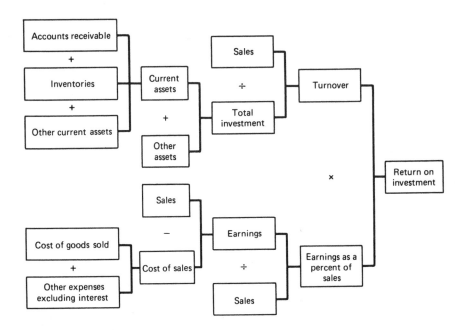

11. The company writes off an uncollectible account receivable against the allowance for uncollectibles.
12. The firm writes off inventory as obsolete.

2. The factors that affect return on investment may be depicted graphically.

Return on investment may be computed several ways. One way, often associated with the Du Pont Company, is illustrated in the accompanying diagram. The diagram is intended to direct the attention of management to the various elements that have an impact upon return on investment.

a. Refer to the 1980 financial statements of Adolph Coors Company as contained in problem 4. Determine return on investment (all capital) *before* income taxes (i.e., add to income before taxes the full amount of interest expense). As-

3. Financial ratios incorporate all of the deficiencies of the underlying accounting data.

A friend, who is president of Statistical Software, Inc., invited you to invest in his company. In explaining to you the advantages of such an investment, he pointed to the firm's profitability as evidenced by a high rate of return on stockholders' equity and the security of the investment as measured by *times interest earned*.

The firm develops and sells to industrial firms customized computer programs. The programs are intended to enable a firm to generate statistical information about its operations.

The president of Statistical Software, Inc., provided you with the company's 1983 financial statements. The statements of earnings and of changes in financial position (cash basis) are as follows:

Statistical Software, Inc.
Statement of Changes in Financial Position
Year Ended December 31, 1983

Sources of cash		
From operations		
Income	$120,000	
Add: Depreciation and amortization	60,000	
Subtract: Gain on sale of land	(160,000)	$ 20,000
Sale of land		220,000
Total sources of cash		$240,000
Uses of cash		
Increase in accounts receivable		$170,000
Increase in advertising and promotion costs expected to benefit future periods		30,000
Increase in program development costs applicable to software to be delivered in future		120,000
Total uses of cash		$320,000
Decrease in cash		$ (80,000
Cash balance beginning of year		410,000
Cash balance end of year		$330,000

Statistical Software, Inc.
Statement of Income
Year Ended December 31, 1983

Sales	$540,000	
Other revenues	260,000	$800,000
Cost of programs developed	$530,000	
Other expenses	90,000	
Interest	20,000	
Taxes	40,000	680,000
Net income		$120,000

The balance sheet reveals that average stockholders' equity during the year was $600,000.

a. Determine the rate of return on stockholders' equity and the times interest earned measure of coverage of fixed charges.

b. Review carefully the two statements presented. Recognizing that no investment decisions can be made on the basis of statements for a single year, what questions would you raise (or what reservations would you have) pertaining to the firm's *quality* of earnings?

4. *Price/earnings ratios do not necessarily reflect financial strength as measured by other financial ratios.*

The following are the 1980 income statements and balance sheets of Adolph Coors and Company and Pabst Brewing Company.

Statement of Income
(in thousands)

	Coors	Pabst
Sales	$887,897	$719,902
Cost of goods sold	$629,758	$607,526
Other operating expenses	160,549	90,953
	$790,307	$698,479
Operating income	$ 97,590	$ 21,423
Other expenses (revenue):		
Interest revenue	($ 16,514)	($ 3,471)
Interest expense	1,563	2,005
Miscellaneous	6,764	1,422
	($ 8,187)	($ 44)
Income before taxes	$105,777	$ 21,467
Income taxes	40,800	8,825
Net income	$ 64,977	$ 12,642
Earnings per share of common stock	$ 1.86	$ 1.55

Balance Sheet
(in thousands)

	Coors	Pabst
Assets		
Current assets		
Cash and short-term investments	$ 87,883	$ 37,346
Accounts receivable (net of allowances)	57,930	20,312
Inventories	149,504	78,421
Prepayments and other current assets	34,892	7,457
Total current assets	$330,209	$143,536
Property, plant, and equipment (net of depreciation)	556,419	276,740
Other assets	7,757	10,058
Total assets	$894,385	$430,334
Liabilities and owners' equity		
Current liabilities	$116,094	$ 89,323
Deferred income taxes	60,149	44,900
Other long-term debt	6,042	14,679
Equity of common stockholders, including retained earnings	712,100	281,432
Total liabilities and owners' equity	$894,385	$430,334

a. Compare the two companies with respect to the following, using year-end rather than average balance sheet values:
1. Return on investment (stockholders' equity)
2. Return on investment (all capital). Assume an incremental tax rate of 48 percent in calculating interest after taxes.
3. Gross margin
4. Debt to equity ratio
5. Inventory turnover

b. Based on your comparison, which firm do you think should command the relatively higher market price per share of common stock?

c. The average 1980 market price per share of Coors was $16.25; that of Pabst was $14.00.
1. Compute the price to earnings ratio for each of the firms.
2. Are the ratios consistent with your response to Part b? If not, explain.

5. *Differences in return on investment may be more apparent than real.*

Rent-a-Truck, Inc., was founded in January 1983. The company issued 300,000 shares of common stock at $10 per share.

The company acquired trucks at a cost of $3 million. The useful lives of the trucks were estimated to be five years, with zero salvage value.

During its first year of operations the revenues of the firm, less all expenses other than depreciation and income taxes, were $1.3 million.

The applicable income tax rate is 40 percent. The company *defers* its tax expense; that is, reported tax expense is based on *reported* income; it is not indicative of the required current tax payment.

a. Determine the first year's return on investment (stockholders' equity) under each of the following assumptions:
1. The firm uses straight-line depreciation for book purposes and straight-line depreciation for tax purposes.
2. The firm uses double-declining balance depreciation for book purposes and double-declining balance depreciation for tax purposes.
3. The firm uses straight-line depreciation for book purposes and double-declining balance depreciation for tax purposes.

Base your computation on year-end stockholders' equity as opposed to average stockholders' equity.

b. Comment on any substantive (i.e., "real" economic) differences in rate of return under each of the three methods.

6. *Use of return on investment as a criterion of*

corporate performance may lead to dysfunctional management decisions.

The president of Burnside, Inc., is faced with the decision as to whether to expand the corporation by acquiring a new plant. The cost of the new plant would be $500,000. The necessary capital could be acquired by issuing bonds which would provide a return to lenders of 12 percent per year. The new plant would increase corporate pretax earnings by $70,000 prior to taking into account required interest payments of $60,000.

Burnside, Inc., in recent years has had annual pretax income, after deducting $50,000 in interest payments, of $250,000. The firm, as of December 31, 1983, has outstanding debt of $500,000 and owners' equity of $1.5 million.

The financial vice-president favors acquisition of the new plant, arguing that corporate earnings would be increased by $10,000. The corporate controller opposes acquisition, maintaining that it would result in reduction of the firm's return on invested capital.

a. Determine return on investment (all capital) if (1) the plant is not acquired and (2) the plant is acquired. Assume that earnings on the old facilities will be the same in the future as they have in the past. Disregard income taxes (i.e., add back to income the full amount of interest costs). Base your computations on year-end as opposed to average values. Assume also that all earnings are distributed as dividends.

b. Calculate earnings per share under the two alternatives. The company has 10,000 shares of common stock outstanding.

c. Suppose instead that the company could acquire the necessary $500,000 in capital by issuing 2,000 shares of common stock. Compute return on investment (stockholders' equity) and earnings per share assuming first that the company did not expand and then that it did.

d. Do you think the company should acquire the plant? Explain.

e. Comment on the potential dangers of using return on investment as a criterion for making investment decisions.

f. What criterion might be preferable to return on investment?

7. *The advantages of debt as opposed to equity financing may be illusory.*

The Dement Corporation has $30 million in total assets. It has $10 million in current liabilities outstanding and $20 million in stockholders' equity. There are presently 100,000 shares of common stock outstanding. After-tax earnings over the past several years have averaged $2.1 million per year.

The company has decided to expand its operations by constructing a new plant. The new plant will cost $6 million, and it is estimated that it will increase earnings by $360,000 after taxes, not taking into account costs of financing.

The company has two options available to it to finance the plant. First it can issue additional shares of stock. The additional shares could be sold for $400 per share.

Alternatively, it can raise the required $6 million by issuing bonds. The bonds would be sold to yield purchasers 10 percent per year. The interest costs would be tax deductible to the company. The applicable tax rate is 48 percent.

a. Assume that the company will construct the new plant. For each of the alternatives determine anticipated (1) return on investment (all capital), (2) return on investment (stockholders' equity), and (3) earnings per share.

b. After reviewing the figures just computed, the president of the company stated, "It is obvious that we are better off financing expansion with debt rather than equity. In the future, let's finance all additions by issuing bonds rather than stock." Comment on the logic of the president.

8. *Insofar as financial statements fail to take into account current values, so also do the financial ratios.*

The financial statements of the Yorkville Bottling Co. revealed the following data for 1983:

Current assets	$ 420,000
Other assets (property, plant and equipment)	6,580,000
Current liabilities	670,000
Other liabilities	2,308,000
Sales	11,500,000
Interest expense, net of taxes	350,000
Net income	1,400,000

a. Determine the following relationships (based on year-end balances):
1. return on investment (all capital).
2. current ratio.

3. debt to equity.

4. plant and equipment turnover.

b. Investigation reveals that included in current assets are marketable securities that are recorded at a cost of $100,000. Their current market value is $350,000. Moreover, the company's plant is located on land that had originally cost $500,000. The land currently has a fair market value of $1 million. Recompute the above relationships to take into account the additional information. Which set of relationships do you think is more relevant to most decisions required of both managers and investors?

c. Comment on how the revised ratios may affect the analyst's view of both financial position and operating performance.

9. *Adjustments for changes in prices and values dramatically alter financial measures.*

The statement below was taken from an addendum to the financial statements of Delta Airlines (which are presented in the exercise for review and self-testing):

Compute the ratios or other measures indicated below for amounts:

1. expressed in historical costs;

Statement of Income Adjusted for Changing Prices (Unaudited)
For the year ended June 30, 1980

	As Reported in the Financial Statements (Historical Cost)	Adjusted for General Inflation (Fiscal 1980 Constant Dollar)	Adjusted for Change in Specific Prices (Current Cost)
	(In Thousands Except for Per Share Data)		
Operating revenues	$2,956,960	$2,956,960	$2,956,960
Depreciation and amortization expense	194,094	286,648	317,748
Operating expenses (excluding depreciation and amortization)	2,670,229	2,670,229	2,670,229
Gain on disposition of property	(36,444)	(34,146)	(39,835)
Other expense (income), net	4,463	4,463	4,463
Income taxes provided	54,433	54,433	54,433
Amortization of investment tax credits	(22,973)	(32,100)	(32,100)
Total expenses	2,863,802	2,949,527	2,974,938
Net income (loss)	$ 93,158	$ 7,433	$ (17,978)
Net income (loss) per share	$ 4.69	$ .37	$ (.90)
Gain from decline in purchasing power of net amounts owed		$ 62,948	$ 62,948
Effect on property and equipment of: Increase in specific prices (current cost)			$ 349,688
Increase in general price level (constant dollar)			298,813
Excess of increase in specific prices over the increase in the general price level			$ 50,875
Net assets (stockholders' equity) at June 30, 1980	$ 921,969	$1,872,077	$1,866,641

2. adjusted for general inflation;
3. adjusted for changes in specific prices (current costs).

In calculating ratios based upon general inflation data, net income as presented should be adjusted to include the gain in purchasing power; in calculating those based upon current cost data net income should be adjusted to include the gain in purchasing power as well as the "real" gain from changes in specific prices (that is, the total gain in specific prices less the portion of the gain attributable to the increase in the general price level).

The measures to be computed are:

a. Return on investment (stockholders' equity).
b. Earnings per share. There were 19,880,577 shares outstanding.
c. Price-earnings ratio.
d. Effective tax rate (income taxes as a percentage of income before taxes).
e. Dividend payout (dividends as a percentage of income). The firm paid dividends of $1.20 per share.

10. *A balance sheet and an income statement can be derived from selected financial ratios.*

The Ventnor Company had net earnings in 1983 of $50,000.

a. Its return on investment based on stockholders' equity as of year end was 10 percent. Determine year-end stockholders' equity.
b. The firm's debt to equity ratio was 0.4:1. Determine year-end debt.
c. Ventnor Company's return on investment (all capital) was 7.6571 percent based on year-end capital. It paid taxes at an incremental rate of 40 percent. Determine interest expense for the year.
d. Its *times interest earned* ratio was 13:1. Determine income taxes.
e. The company's net earnings as a percent of sales was 5 percent. Determine sales.
f. Its gross margin was 40 percent. Determine cost of goods sold.
g. Its inventory turned over 6 times. Determine inventory.
h. The firm's accounts receivable turned over 25 times. Determine accounts receivable.

i. Its fixed assets turned over 2 times. Determine fixed assets.
j. Its only remaining asset was cash. Determine year-end cash.
k. Its current ratio was 2:1. Determine current liabilities.
l. All expenses not yet determined may be classified as "sales and administration." Reconstruct, as best you can, the income statement of Ventnor company for 1983 and its balance sheet as of year-end 1983.

11. *Ratio analysis may assist an investor in predicting whether a firm will "turn around" or go bankrupt.*

The financial statements as of January 31, 1974 and 1975, of the M. R. Lee Co. are presented below and on page 492. The M. R. Lee Co. operates a chain of low-priced department stores located in 42 states. Most of its merchandise is priced under $10, but the stores also carry a line of major appliances.

a. Explain as best you can the reason for the decline in earnings in 1975.
b. Compare the liquidity of the company in 1975 with that of 1974.
c. Compare the debt to equity ratio of 1975 with that of 1974.
d. Comment on the firm's ability to meet fixed interest charges.

Consolidated Statement of Income
(000s omitted)

	Years ended	
	1/31/75	1/31/74
Net sales	$1,761,952	$1,845,802
Other revenues	10,700	15,617
Total revenues	$1,772,652	$1,861,419
Cost of goods sold	$1,303,267	$1,282,944
Selling and other expenses	726,420	546,202
Interest	37,771	18,082
Income tax expense (refund)	(117,466)	3,289
Total expenses	$1,949,992	$1,850,517
Net income (loss)	$ (177,340)	$ 10,902

M. R. Lee Co.
Consolidated Balance Sheet as of January 31
(000s omitted)

	1975	1974
Assets		
Current		
Cash and Equivalent	$ 79,642	$ 45,952
Accounts receivable (net)	431,191	540,802
Inventories	407,357	450,636
Other current assets	6,591	7,299
Total current assets	$ 924,781	$1,044,689
Noncurrent		
Property and equipment (net)	$ 101,932	$ 100,983
Investment in subsidiaries	49,764	44,251
Other assets	5,790	5,063
Total noncurrent assets	$ 157,486	$ 150,297
Total assets	$1,082,267	$1,194,986
Liabilities and stockholders' equity		
Current		
Accounts payable	$ 50,067	$ 58,192
Notes and other payables	600,995	453,096
Miscellaneous accruals	79,144	46,691
Taxes payable	19,700	103,078
Total current liabilities	$ 749,906	$ 661,057
Noncurrent		
Notes payable	$ 99,005	$ 100,000
Bonds payable	117,336	120,336
Other liabilities	2,183	18,845
Total noncurrent liabilities	$ 218,524	$ 239,181
Stockholders' equity		
Preferred stock	$ 7,465	$ 7,464
Common stock ($1.25 par value)	18,599	18,599
Capital in excess of par	83,914	85,909
Less: Stock held in treasury	(33,815)	(36,696)
Retained earnings	37,674	219,472
Total stockholders' equity	$ 113,837	$ 294,748
Total liabilities and stockholders' equity	$1,082,267	$1,194,986

e. Comment on the critical problems that the firm will face in the following year. Do you see any bright spots? Do you believe that the ability of the firm to survive is in question?

12. The following news item serves to highlight the deficiencies of accounting information as the basis of investor decisions.

"Depending on who's talking," the *Wall Street Journal* of February 2, 1981, began a news item, "the value of American Financial Corp.'s common stock is somewhere between $5 and $70 a share. Small wonder, then that some shareholders don't find the company's proposed offer of $28 very attractive."

The story went on to relate that Carl Lindner, chairman, president, and founder of American Financial, who, along with his family owns 45 percent of the firm's outstanding shares of common stock, is seeking to "take the company private" by acquiring the 55 percent of the stock held by parties other than the Lindner family.

Within days after Lindner offered to purchase the outstanding shares, minority stockholders filed suit charging that the price of $28 was unfair and inadequate. One suit, the *Journal* indicated, "charges that the offer doesn't take into account future profits of American Financial and that it is less than the company's value as a going concern." The latter assertion, according to the *Journal*, was backed by a financial analyst who estimated what American Financial would get for its assets if the firm were to be broken up and sold. Among the assets were insurance companies, convenience stores, savings and loan institutions, and investment positions in "a half-dozen or so companies." The analyst said "he based his estimates of the subsidiaries' values on the percentage amounts above or below book value that companies in their industries have fetched lately in the market." He valued American Financial's stock holdings at current market prices. Based on these estimates he valued the company at between $54 and $70 per share.

The *Journal* reported that American Financial "pooh-poohs the estimate of the analyst. In fact, the company says its book value of $23.53 a share is deceptively high. The company believes tangible book value of its assets is closer to $5 a share, in large part because the goodwill of its subsidiaries accounts for more than half of the common's book value."

a. Comment on why book values cannot serve as the basis for establishing a fair value of the company in light of the assertion of the firm's auditors that the "financial statements present fairly" its financial position.

b. How would you assess the reliability of the procedure used by the financial analyst to estimate the values of the firm's subsidiaries.

c. Evaluate the explanation of American Financial as to why the book value of $23.53 is deceptively high.

13. Are reported earnings a measure only of short-term, not long-term, well-being?

The *Wall Street Journal*, of April 14, 1981, described a proxy fight in which a group of dissident shareholders attempted to unseat the existing board of directors of American Bakeries Co. Although the firm is small, the effort to oust the directors raised an important issue, according to the *Journal*: "the extent to which managers of publicly held companies can dare to sacrifice short-term profits and dividends for long-term growth, as Japanese companies often do."

The dissident shareholders cited several measures of what they considered the firm's dismal performance: "a decline in net income to $2.1 million last year from $5.8 million in 1977; omission of the past two quarterly cash dividends; sluggish sales growth from 1976 to 1981; a decline in profitability to 0.39% of sales in 1980 from 1.38% in 1975."

According to the *Journal*, the chairman of American Bakeries "bristles at the suggestion that declining financial results of the past five years reflect management incompetence." He says the decline stemmed from "the biggest capital spending program—$84 million—in our history, over the five years that ended in 1980." He called that effort "absolutely crucial to this company's competitiveness and growth prospects."

There is no question, the *Journal* says, that "earnings performance over the past five years clearly was a casualty of the company's big capital-spending program. The American Bakeries executives' acknowledge that the company's annual depreciation expense rose nearly 40% during the period to more than $11 million in 1980 and that interest expense soared to $6.1 million last year from $2.1 million in 1976."

a. Reported earnings are supposed to be a measure of corporate well-being. Is it not a deficiency of financial reporting that if a firm takes measures, such as increasing capital spending, which are admittedly in its long-run interests, it may have to report lower earnings?

b. Comment on the dangers of using reported earnings alone to evaluate management performance.

c. Would the firm be saddled with the lower reported earnings if it adhered faithfully to the *principle of matching*? Explain. What changes in accounting practices would enable a firm to avoid having to report lower earnings in periods prior to those in which the benefits of a capital spending program were realized?

SOLUTIONS TO EXERCISE FOR REVIEW AND SELF-TESTING

a. Return on investment (all capital):

$$\frac{\text{Net income} + \text{Interest after taxes}}{\text{Assets}}$$

Interest after taxes = $(1 - \text{incremental tax rate})$ interest expense

1. Eastern:

$$\frac{(\$42,012) + (1. - .48)\$109,836}{\$2,816,177}$$

$$= \frac{\$15,103}{\$2,816,177} = 0.5\%$$

2. Delta:

$$\frac{\$93,158 + (1. - .48)\$11,062}{\$1,042,539}$$

$$= \frac{\$98,910}{\$2,042,539} = 4.8\%$$

Delta had the greater earnings relative to the resources within its command.

b. Return on investment (common stockholders' equity):

$$\frac{\text{Net income} - \text{Preferred stock dividends}}{\text{Equity of common stockholders}}$$

1. Eastern: no return, as income minus preferred stock dividends is negative.

2. Delta:

$$\frac{\$93,158 - \$0}{\$921,969} = 10.1\%$$

Delta provided the greater return to common stockholders.

c. $\qquad \text{Debt to equity ratio} = \dfrac{\text{Total debt}}{\text{Total equity}}$

1. Eastern:

$$\frac{\$780,874 + \$1,460,505}{\$139,342 + \$435,456}$$

$$= \frac{\$2,241,379}{\$574,798} = 3.9 \text{ to } 1$$

2. Delta:

$$\frac{\$550,564 + \$570,006}{\$921,969}$$

$$= \frac{\$1,120,570}{\$921,969} = 1.2 \text{ to } 1$$

Eastern was the more highly-leveraged, as it made greater use of debt capital relative to equity capital.

d. Delta used leverage more effectively. By using borrowed funds (including those recorded as accounts payable and deferred taxes which required no payments of interest), Delta increased the return to common stockholders. The return on the investment of common stockholders exceeded that to all suppliers of capital. Eastern, by contrast, was unsuccessful in its use of leverage. After taking into account interest payments, the return to common stockholders was less than that to all suppliers of capital.

e. Times interest earned

$$= \frac{\text{Net income} + \text{Interest} + \text{Income Taxes}}{\text{Interest}}$$

Eastern:

$$\frac{(\$42,012) + \$109,836 + (\$4,255)}{\$109,836}$$

$$= \frac{\$63,569}{\$109,836} = .58 \text{ times}$$

Delta:

$$\frac{\$93,158 + \$11,062 + 31,460}{11,062}$$

$$= \frac{\$135,680}{11,062} = 12.3 \text{ times}$$

Eastern failed to cover its interest costs. Delta covered them 12.3 times.

f. $\text{Current ratio} = \dfrac{\text{Current assets}}{\text{Current liabilities}}$

Eastern:

$$\frac{\$810,617}{\$780,874} = 1.04 \text{ to } 1$$

Delta:

$$\frac{\$369,497}{\$550,564} = .67 \text{ to } 1$$

Eastern had the higher current ratio, and based solely on this ratio, would appear to have been in the better position to repay its short-term obligations as they came due. But ratios cannot be examined in isolation of one another. The financial statements presented seem to indicate that overall Delta was, by far, the stronger of the two firms. It would be imprudent, however, to draw conclusions regarding the fiscal health of the companies from the ratios alone. Information of the type ordinarily included in footnotes and supplementary sections of the annual report as well as "nonfinancial" data such as market shares, route structures, and general economic conditions of areas served, must also be taken into account.

FOCUS ON COSTS 17

MANAGEMENT ACCOUNTING AS A KEY ELEMENT OF THE PROCESS OF PLANNING AND CONTROL

With this chapter we begin a new section of this text. To this point we have focused primarily on the role of accounting information as it relates to parties external to the organization. We have taken care, however, to point out transactions that may cause increases or decreases in earnings that are not reflective of corresponding changes in the economic well-being of the organization. In the remainder of the text we shall concentrate on accounting information as it can be used by managers in carrying out their primary functions: planning and controlling organizational activities.

Management (as opposed to *financial*) accounting is intended to provide managers with the information necessary to answer two broad and interrelated categories of questions. The first category is directed to *planning:* By what courses of action can the organization accomplish its mission most efficiently and effectively? This category is associated with management decisions relating to acquiring long-term assets, establishing prices, adding new products, and discontinuing operating segments. The second category pertains to *control:* How well is an individual or organization carrying out its mission, and what, if anything, should be done to improve unsatisfactory performance? This category relates to the procedures that management establishes to measure the deviations from plans, to affix responsibility for them, and to assure that they do not reoccur.

Because cost information is central to the management functions of planning and control, this chapter and the one that follows will be directed to the nature and behavior of costs and the means by which they can be assigned to organizational units as well as particular products and services. The following three chapters will be concerned with the contribution of accounting to management planning. They will stress the importance of establishing organizational objectives and will discuss and illustrate the role of the budget in operationalizing those objectives. Moreover, they will describe approaches to analyzing and selecting among courses of action that will affect the organization over both the short and long terms. A sixth chapter will point out techniques of routine control and highlight considerations to be taken into account in reporting to management the results of operations.

It is both convenient and common to distinguish between management activities that involve planning and those that involve control. In fact, however, the two functions are intertwined and, in practice, often inseparable. Similarly, it may be useful analytically and pedagogically to classify management activities as affecting either the long term or the short term. In reality, the time span affected by a management decision can seldom be known for sure and to a great extent the ultimate direction that an organization takes is the result of a series of seemingly short-term maneuvers. Management is an ongoing, continuous process in which executives take action in response to information about the results of past performance as well as anticipated conditions of the future. Management accounting is an inherent part of the management process. As such, it too is not as neatly divisible into topics of planning and control, or time frames of long and short terms, as is often implied.

BASIC THEMES

Underlying the remaining chapters will be several related themes.

1. *Information must be relevant to decisions at hand.* Accounting information is intended to facilitate management decisions. The ultimate criterion in determining the nature and form of accounting data is their utility. In presenting information to parties within the organization, accountants are unconstrained by pronouncements of outside regulatory authorities. Calculations and reports can be tailor-made for the individual managers who will use them.

2. *Decisions should focus on incremental receipts and disbursements.* For virtually all decisions that managers are called upon to make, only *incremental* receipts and disbursements should properly be taken into account. Incremental receipts and disbursements are those that will be affected by the outcome of the decision. They are distinguished from those that will remain the same regardless of course of action selected and need not therefore be given analytical consideration.

A corollary to this theme is that only future receipts and disbursements should be brought to bear on a decision. Past receipts and disbursements are relevant only to the extent that they serve as a guide to those of the future.

3. *Time value of money and uncertainty must be taken into account.* In evaluating cash flows, both the time value of money and the uncertainty surrounding the cash flows must be taken into account. A dollar to be paid or received sooner is worth more than one to be paid or received later. In assessing the financial impact of alternative courses of action, the analyst must "discount" all future inflows and outflows by a factor (such as the firm's "cost of capital") that equates dollars of the future with those of the present.*

---

* It is common, and perfectly reasonable, to ignore the time value of money when the time frame of a decision is sufficiently short so that the effect of discounting will be immaterial. With interest rates as high as they have been in the 1980s, the period of immateriality may be exceedingly short, however.

Similarly, a dollar to be paid or received with certainty is worth more than one to which there is risk attached. Anticipated cash flows must, therefore, be adjusted to take into account the degree of uncertainty with which they are associated.

4. *Only cash, not income, matters.* Insofar as it is the objective of management to maximize the economic well-being of an organization (with economic well-being defined in the conventional monetary terms that exclude consideration of environmental, psychological, and sociological factors), then only *cash*, not income, matters. Organizations are interested in returns of cash. It is cash, not income, that can be used to acquire goods or services or invested to earn additional returns. Whereas income may serve as an acceptable measure of organizational performance or may be the best available predictor of future cash flows, management must be concerned with when cash is actually received or paid. Income is calculated on an accrual basis and neither revenues nor expenses necessarily correspond to the receipt or disbursement of cash.

5. *Accountability should be confined to matters over which a party has control.* In evaluating the performance of managers or the units of the organizations for which they are responsible, accountability should be confined to those costs or revenues over which they have control. It is common, and for some types of reports appropriate, to allocate the costs incurred by one unit of an organization to those of other units to which it provides services. The costs, for example, of operating a maintenance department may be allocated to manufacturing units. Under some allocation schemes, the costs assigned to an individual manufacturing unit may depend not only on the amount of service that it requests from the maintenance department but also on the overall costs incurred by the maintenance department. The amount of such costs may be a function of both the efficiency of the maintenance department and the amount of service provided to all other manufacturing units—factors which are beyond the control of any individual manufacturing unit. In evaluating the performance of any individual manufacturing unit, costs which it can control must be distinguished from those which it cannot.

Each of these themes will be developed in several different contexts. An appreciation of them will tie together and facilitate an understanding of much of the material that follows.

BEHAVIOR OF COSTS

Of all the ways that costs can be classified, unquestionably the most significant, from the perspective of managers, is by degree of variability. Managers must be able to estimate the effect of their actions on costs to be incurred in the future.

Fixed costs are those which will remain the same regardless of changes in volume. *Variable costs* are those which change in direct proportion to changes in volume. In both definitions, "volume" refers to the output of the activity under consideration. In a manufacturing enterprise volume may be expressed in terms of physical units or dollar value of production. In service organizations or support units it could be expressed in units of service performed, such as customers called upon, patients or clients seen, documents processed, or miles driven. In sales departments it could be expressed as dollars of sales.

Fixed costs are *not* unchanging. Air conditioning and heating costs are almost always categorized as fixed costs, in spite of their volatility. They vary, however, with the weather, not with the output of the organization. Costs of repairs are usually classified as fixed, even though they may also vary considerably from period to period. The magnitude of repair costs most frequently depends on unpredictable breakdowns, which are random occurrences, rather than on number of units produced.

The levels of some costs that are categorized as fixed are within the discretion of management. Expenditures for advertising, research and development, and community relations can be freely altered by management. Such programmable or discretionary costs are considered fixed because they vary at the option of management, rather than in response to change in output.

Costs which are fixed overall are variable *per unit*. As volume increases and the costs are spread over a larger number of units, the cost per unit decreases. Correspondingly, costs which are variable overall are fixed per unit. As volume increases total costs increase, but per unit costs remain constant.

Fixed costs can be depicted graphically, as in Exhibit 17-1, which indicates the cost of rent incurred by a restaurant in relation to number of customers served. The horizontal line reveals that the rent in dollars (the vertical axis) remains constant regardless of output (the horizontal axis).

Variable costs can by shown graphically, as in Exhibit 17-2, which indicates the cost of food in a restaurant. The upward-sloping line signifies that food costs are directly proportional to number of customers served.

Costs which contain both a fixed and a variable element are referred to as *mixed* costs. Electricity costs, for example, sometimes contain a fixed element, a monthly service charge, plus a variable element, a charge for each kilowatt used. The broader the classification of costs, the more likely is a particular category of cost to have both fixed and variable elements. Shipping costs will have both fixed and variable components in relation to number of packages shipped. The salaries of mailroom personnel and the

EXHIBIT 17-1

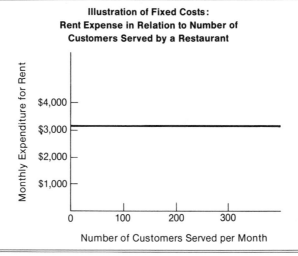

Illustration of Fixed Costs:
Rent Expense in Relation to Number of
Customers Served by a Restaurant

EXHIBIT 17-2

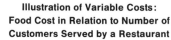

Illustration of Variable Costs:
Food Cost in Relation to Number of
Customers Served by a Restaurant

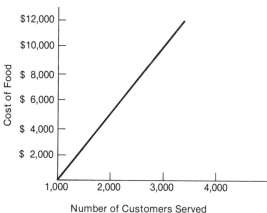

Number of Customers Served

depreciation on mailroom equipment will be primarily fixed. The cost of packaging materials will, however, likely be variable. Mixed costs present no conceptual problems. For analytical purposes they can be viewed as consisting of two independent elements of cost, one fixed, the other variable.

RELEVANT RANGE

In practice no costs are completely fixed. They are fixed only within a particular range of output. Among costs that are often thought of as fixed are rent, executive and supervisory salaries, and janitorial costs. Each of these costs will change if output expands or contracts to a point where the firm must make changes in its capacity. In the example of the restaurant, rent is fixed only as long as the firm can operate within the same amount of space. Should it require additional space, then rental costs would, of course, increase.

Fixed costs, therefore, are defined as being fixed within a *relevant* range. The *relevant* range is simply the range that is appropriate for the decision at hand.

No costs can be inherently categorized as being either fixed or variable. For a decision as to whether to serve an additional eight customers per day the cost of waiters may be fixed; no additional employees need be hired nor additional hours worked. For a decision as to whether to serve an additional 100 customers, the cost of waiters may be variable; experience may indicate that one additional waiter is required for each 10 customers. Within the range of 100 customers, the cost of waiters would, when shown graphically, appear in the form of a series of steps (Exhibit 17-3).

In fact, all costs, both fixed and variable, usually can most correctly be described by a step function. Exhibit 17-4 depicts rent costs over a range of 5,000 customers, with the assumption that the maximum capacity

EXHIBIT 17-3

Illustration of Stepped Costs:
Expenditures for Waiters in
Relation to Customers Served

EXHIBIT 17-4

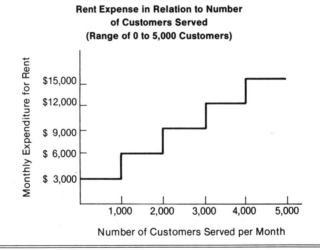

Alternative View of "Fixed Costs":
Rent Expense in Relation to Number
of Customers Served
(Range of 0 to 5,000 Customers)

of a single restaurant (or wing) is 1,000 customers. For each increment of 1,000 customers, additional space must be leased.

Exhibit 17-5 indicates food costs over a range of 24 customers. It is based on the assumption that acquisitions of food can be fine-tuned only to increments of four customers and that the additional food costs incurred to serve fewer than four customers are negligible.

The primary distinction, therefore, between fixed and variable costs, is in the size

EXHIBIT 17-5

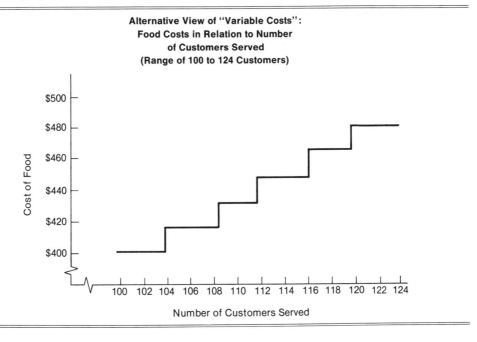

**Alternative View of "Variable Costs":
Food Costs in Relation to Number
of Customers Served
(Range of 100 to 124 Customers)**

of the step. If, within the range relevant for a particular decision, the costs are confined to a single step, then they are considered as fixed. If they increase by a sufficiently large number of steps that for the degree of accuracy required the steps can be decomposed into an upward sloping line, then they are classified as variable. If within the relevant range the costs are not confined to a single step and the steps are sufficiently large so that they cannot be considered as an upward-sloping line, then they must be described as being in a step function and, accordingly, cannot be represented or analyzed by simple linear equations.

AVERAGE COST

The most common expression of cost is average cost. Average cost represents total cost—

that is, fixed cost plus variable cost—divided by number of units of output or activity.

Although average cost may be a convenient summary of the components of unit cost, it has very little applicability to the decisions that managers are called on to make. Indeed, there are few, if any, decisions for which use of average cost is appropriate and for which a manager would not be better served by decomposing average cost into its fixed and variable elements.

Managerial decisions in which costs must be taken into account invariably require forecasts of costs that will be incurred in the future. As long as total number of units produced will be different from that of a previous period, average unit cost will also be different. Thus, it would be incorrect to estimate future costs simply by multiplying total number of units by average cost. In forecasting costs of the future, the manager must be cognizant of the stability of some elements of unit cost and of the variability of others. Use of average cost, unfortunately, is an unacceptable shortcut to relevant cost analysis. For almost all of the decisions to be discussed in the remainder of this text, a breakdown of costs into fixed and variable portions is required.

DIRECT VERSUS INDIRECT COSTS

Costs may be classified by degree of association with a product, activity, or department. Direct costs are those which are clearly traceable and easily identified with a product, activity, or department. Indirect costs are those which are not.

With regard to a product, for example, *direct materials* are those, such as component parts, which enter directly into the product and form an integral part of it. By contrast, *indirect materials*, such as cleaning supplies and machine lubricants, are those that cannot be readily associated with specific units of product. *Direct labor* is that which is applied and can be ascribed directly to the product. The services of machine operators and assemblers would ordinarily be categorized as direct labor. *Indirect labor* is that which has only an oblique connection to the product. The contribution of foremen, maintenance personnel, and supply clerks would usually be considered indirect labor. Other indirect costs with respect to a product include power, heating, rent, depreciation, and supervision.

The distinction between a direct and an indirect cost depends on the unit under consideration. Whereas the salary of the foreman of an assembly department may be an indirect cost of the products being assembled, it is a direct cost of the assembly department.

Indirect costs are commonly referred to as *overhead* costs.

DETERMINING THE BEHAVIOR OF COSTS

The importance of distinguishing between fixed and variable portions of cost cannot be overemphasized; neither unfortunately can the difficulties of establishing specific relationships between costs and volume.

Although certain types of costs are often considered to be either fixed or variable, there is considerable risk in making assumptions about costs without examining historical data and making adjustments for changes that may take place in the future. Direct labor, for example, by definition can be traced to units of product. Direct labor is a prime example of a cost that varies with volume of output, particularly when employees are paid on an hourly basis. But as the proportion of compensation paid as "fringe benefits" increases, direct labor becomes more of a fixed cost and less of a variable cost. If, for example, a company pays the medical insurance premiums of its employees, then the portion of compensation representing the insurance premiums may be fixed; changes in hours worked will have no effect on medical insurance cost. Similarly, in some industries, owing to Supplementary Unemployment Benefits (SUB) employees are guaranteed a specified percentage of their earnings, regardless of number of hours actually worked. Temporary reductions in the size of the work-force, therefore, will have only a minimal impact on labor costs.

In relating costs to volume, the variable selected to represent volume must depend on the decision at hand. If management needs to estimate production costs at various levels of output, then number of units produced may serve as an appropriate indicator of volume. In that case, total costs of production, including labor, materials, depreciation, and maintenance, may be compared to number of units produced. But if, on the other hand, management wishes to establish a pattern of maintenance costs for purposes of control, then machine hours may be a more useful indicator of volume. The amount of maintenance required is more likely to be influenced by the number of hours that machinery is in use than it is by the number of units produced.

There are several methods of determining relationships of costs to volume. The methods range widely in both accuracy and sophistication; selection of method must be based on comparison of the added cost of using a particular method to the value of the incremental accuracy to be obtained.

Each of the following methods, with the exception of the first, involves analysis of data of the past. They are appropriate for making decisions that will affect the future, therefore, only insofar as conditions of the future will be similar to those in the past.

NORMATIVE ANALYSIS

Normative analysis indicates the way costs *should* behave in relation to volume. Normative analysis of costs is often associated with, and carried out by, industrial engineers.

Normative analysis requires the study of each element that goes into producing the goods or providing the service. A team of industrial engineers, for example, might determine the number of units of raw materials and minutes of labor required to produce the desired output, assuming that production was carried out in a reasonably efficient manner. It would take into account the time and materials required to start up and shut down a process as well as the elements of production, such as maintenance and supervision, that do not vary directly with output. It would also make allowance for normal waste and errors. Working with budget analysts or accountants it would assign appropriate costs to the units of material or hours of labor. The result of its efforts would be a schedule of anticipated costs at various levels of output or a formula that expresses the relationships between costs and output.

Normative analysis is particularly suited for production processes that are repetitive and exhibit a close relationship between inputs and outputs. It is not very useful where the product or service must be customized or where a high percentage of costs is "indirect" and cannot readily be traced to output. It would be more suitable for determining cost relationships on an automobile assembly line than in an automobile repair shop.

Normative analysis rests on the assumption that the engineers or others making the analysis have taken into account all factors that affect the input–output relationships. People or processes seldom operate as they should, however; at the very least, therefore, normative relationships should be tested against actual experience before they are considered reliable.

SCATTER DIAGRAM

Historical data can be plotted on a graph. Relationships between cost and volume can be observed visually or a curve can be fitted by hand and eye without mathematical techniques.

Suppose that Rapid-Lube, a chain of auto service stations specializing in lubrication and oil changes, wishes to establish the relationship between labor costs and number of cars serviced. In one region, the data that follow were observed over a period of 12 months.

EXHIBIT 17-6

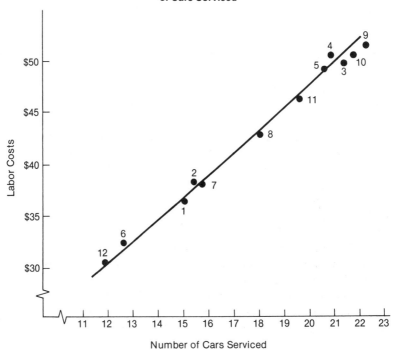

Illustration of Scatter Diagram:
Relationship of Labor Costs to Number
of Cars Serviced

Number of Cars Serviced

a Curve has been fitted visually.
Numbers refer to months of the year.

Operating Costs at Various Levels of Activity

Month	Number of Cars Serviced	Labor Costs
January	15,000	$37,200
February	15,400	38,200
March	21,600	49,500
April	21,300	50,000
May	20,700	48,000
June	12,600	32,500
July	15,800	38,100
August	18,000	43,500
September	22,200	51,300
October	21,600	50,150
November	19,200	46,200
December	12,000	30,700

Exhibit 17-6 indicates the data plotted on a scatter diagram. The curve that runs through the points reflects a clear relationship between volume and labor costs. At a volume of 14,000 cars serviced, the curve indicates that labor costs were approximately $35,000. At a volume of 19,000, costs were approximately $45,000. For each change of 5,000 cars served (19,000 − 14,000) labor costs increased by $10,000 ($45,000 − $35,000). It appears therefore that variable costs are approximately $2 ($10,000 ÷ 5,000 cars) per car serviced. Since total labor costs comprise a variable and a nonvariable element, once the variable element is known, the nonvariable can readily be deduced. At a volume of 14,000 cars serviced, the curve indicates that total costs would be approximately $35,000. Variable costs would be $28,000 (14,000 × $2). Hence, the nonvariable element would be $7,000 ($35,000 − $28,000). The relationship between costs and volume can be expressed in equation form as

$$Costs = \$7,000 + \$2 \text{ per car serviced}$$

HIGH–LOW METHOD

The high–low method establishes cost–volume relationships based on only two points—a high-volume point and a low-volume point. In the data presented the highest volume was in September; the lowest, in December. The following table indicates activity, costs, and changes:

Month	Volume	Cost
September	22,200	$51,300
December	12,000	30,700
Change	10,200	$20,600

Variable costs would be approximately $2.02, determined as follows:

$$\frac{\text{Change in costs}}{\text{Change in volume}} = \frac{\$20,600}{10,200} = \$2.0196$$

Remaining costs—those not explained by changes in volume—would be approximately $6,465:

Total costs at volume of 22,200	$51,300
Variable costs (22,200 × $2.0196)	44,835
Remaining costs	$ 6,465

In equation form,

$$\text{Total costs} = \$6,465 + \$2.0196X$$

where X is the number of cars serviced.

A danger of using the high–low method is that either the high or low points will be "outliers," atypical of normal cost relationships. It is useful, therefore, to use the high–low technique in conjunction with the scatter diagram approach. Should either the high or low point be inordinately far from the plotted line, then that point should be replaced by one that is closer to the line. In addition, results of the high–low method can be verified for reasonableness by carrying out the same analysis using selected other points, such as the second highest and the second lowest.

It must also be recognized that no conclusions regarding the behavior of costs can be inferred for levels of activity above the high point or below the low point. The constant in the cost equation—the amount that cannot be explained by the changes in level of activity—is often thought of as representing fixed costs. The costs would, however, represent true fixed costs only if the linear relationship established between the high and low points extended to zero volume. If the data include no points near the zero level of activity, there are no grounds for assuming that the relationship is constant. Sometimes, high–low analysis will indicate that fixed costs are negative. Negative fixed costs should be interpreted as indicating nothing more than if the line described by the equation were extended to zero activity it would cross the Y axis at a negative point.

LINEAR REGRESSION ANALYSIS

Linear regression is a mathematical means of relating changes in one variable with changes in one or more variables on which its value depends. For example, changes in costs may be associated with production volume. The variable whose value depends on the other variable is known as the dependent variable;

the one or more variables that have an influence on the dependent variable are referred to as independent variables. Linear regression analysis in which only one independent variable is taken into account is called *simple* regression; that in which more than one independent variable is examined is called *multiple* regression.

Simple linear regression establishes a mathematical expression of the relationships between dependent and independent variables by taking into account all available data points—not just two as does the high-low method. The resultant equation is of a line that best fits between the points as plotted on a scatter diagram—one that minimizes the distances between the points and the line. The "goodness of fit" can be measured and expressed as a coefficient of correlation (r) or coefficient of determination (r^2).

In simple linear regression, the relationship between dependent and independent variable is expressed as an equation of the form

$$Y = a + bX$$

where Y is the dependent variable, such as total costs

X is the independent variable, such as volume

a is the Y intercept, indicative, for example, of fixed costs

b is the regression coefficient, indicative of the slope of the line or the unit variable cost

The regression coefficient (b) representing the variable portion of cost can be determined by solving the following equation:

$$b = \frac{n \sum XY - \sum X \sum Y}{n \sum X^2 - (\sum X)^2}$$

where n is the number of observations. Then, using the results of that equation, the Y intercept (a) can be determined by solving

$$a = \frac{\sum Y}{n} - b\left(\frac{\sum X}{n}\right)$$

Exhibit 17-7 indicates the computation of the regression equation based on the data pertaining to the chain of auto service stations presented earlier.

The derivation of the formulas used to determine the regression equation as well as an adequate discussion of the uses and limitations of regression analysis is beyond the scope of this book. The example is provided merely to put readers on notice that there are available a variety of statistical techniques, many of which are exceedingly sophisticated and reliable, that can assist the manager in establishing historical relationships between costs and volume.

ECONOMISTS' VERSUS ACCOUNTANTS' VIEWS OF COSTS

The accountant views fixed costs as a straight horizontal line and variable costs as a straight upward-sloping line. He sees variable cost *per unit* as remaining constant. Total costs, being the simple sum of fixed and variable costs, is thereby also seen as a straight upward-sloping line. Average cost, by contrast, is seen by the accountant as a downward-sloping curve that is relatively steep at lower levels of activity but which flattens out at higher levels. Average cost decreases as volume increases because the fixed costs are spread over a larger number of units. The curve flattens out as volume increases because the dollar change in fixed costs per unit gets continually smaller as the number of units increases. If, for example, fixed costs are $1,000, then an increase in number of units produced from 10 to 20 would decrease fixed costs per unit from $100 to $50—a decrease of $50. By contrast, an increase in number of units from 20 to 30 would decrease

EXHIBIT 17-7

**Example of Regression Analysis:
Relationship between Labor Costs and Number
of Cars Serviced in a Chain of Auto Service Stations**

Month	X Number of Cars Serviced	Y Labor Costs	X² (000s omitted)	XY (000s omitted)
1. January	15,000	$ 37,200	225,000	558,000
2. February	15,400	38,200	237,160	588,280
3. March	21,600	49,500	466,560	1,069,200
4. April	21,300	50,000	453,690	1,065,000
5. May	20,700	48,000	428,490	993,600
6. June	12,600	32,500	158,760	409,500
7. July	15,800	38,100	249,640	601,980
8. August	18,000	43,500	324,000	783,000
9. September	22,200	51,300	492,840	1,138,860
10. October	21,600	50,150	466,560	1,083,240
11. November	19,200	46,200	368,640	887,040
12. December	12,000	30,700	144,000	368,400
	215,400	$515,350	4,015,340	9,546,100

$$b = \frac{n\sum XY - \sum X\sum Y}{n\sum X^2 - (\sum X)^2}$$

$$= \frac{12(9,546,100,000) - 215,400(515,350)}{12(4,015,340,000) - (215,400)^2} = 1.984873$$

$$a = \frac{\sum Y}{n} - b\left(\frac{\sum X}{n}\right)$$

$$= \frac{515,350}{12} - 1.984873\left(\frac{215,400}{12}\right) = 7,317$$

$$Y \text{ intercept } (a) = \$7,317$$

$$\text{Variable element of cost } (b) = \$1.985$$

In equation form, labor costs (Y) are related to number of cars serviced (X) as follows:

$$Y = \$7,317 + \$1.985X$$

The coefficient of determination (r^2) of this linear cost function (computation not shown) is .99. This means that 99 percent of the variance of labor costs around its mean can be explained by changes in volume. The remaining 1 percent is attributable either to other variables or to random variation.

fixed costs per unit from $50 to $33.33—a decrease of only $16.67.

The economist also views fixed cost as a straight horizontal line (at least in the short run). Unlike the accountant, however, he views variable costs as a curve that rises, first at a decreasing rate, then at a constant rate and finally at an increasing rate. Variable costs *per unit*, according to the economist, decrease at first, because a firm is able to take advantage of economies of scale both in the purchase of raw materials and in production processes. As the firm reaches its optimum capacity, the economies of scale are eliminated and variable costs per unit remain constant. Then, as the firm goes beyond optimum capacity, it faces increases in the price of raw materials and inefficiencies in production processes, and variable costs per unit increase. The economist's view of average cost is similar to that of the accountant, except that the curve turns upward (at the point that variable costs per unit begin to increase) rather than continuing downward. The two views of costs are contrasted in Exhibit 17-8.

The views of the economist and the accountant are not inconsistent with one another. The accountant provides information for decisions for which the relevant range is one in which variable costs per unit remain relatively constant and the total variable cost curve is linear. The relevant range for the economist is considerably broader and includes those ends of the curves which represent both decreasing and increasing variable costs per unit.

COST–VOLUME–PROFIT ANALYSIS

The basic relationship that total costs equal fixed cost plus variable costs, with variable costs being equal to variable cost per unit times number of units sold, can be used to facilitate a number of common types of management decisions.

Suppose that the Rapid-Lube Company referred to in the preceding section incurs monthly fixed costs of $24,000. This amount includes not only the fixed component of labor costs (the previous example dealt only with labor costs) but also rent, advertising, supervision, interest, and supplies. Total variable cost of changing oil and providing lubrication service, including materials and the variable portion of labor, is $14 per car. The standard charge for the service is $16 per car.

Total revenue earned by the company will be equal to selling price per unit ($16) times number of cars serviced.

Income will be equal to total revenue minus total costs—or

Income = (Selling price × Number of cars serviced)
— Fixed costs — (Unit variable costs
× Number of cars serviced)

Based on this relationship the types of questions that follow can readily be answered.

1. How many cars must be serviced each month in order for the company to "break-even" (earn profit of zero)?

Let X = the unknown, number of cars
that must be serviced

Desired income = (Selling price per unit)X
— Fixed costs
— (Unit variable costs)X

$$0 = \$16X - \$24,000 - \$14X$$

$$\$24,000 = 2X$$

$$X = 12,000 \text{ cars}$$

2. What number of cars must be serviced each month in order for the company to earn a profit of $20,000?

Let X = number of cars that must be
serviced

EXHIBIT 17-8

Accountants' versus Economists' Views of Costs

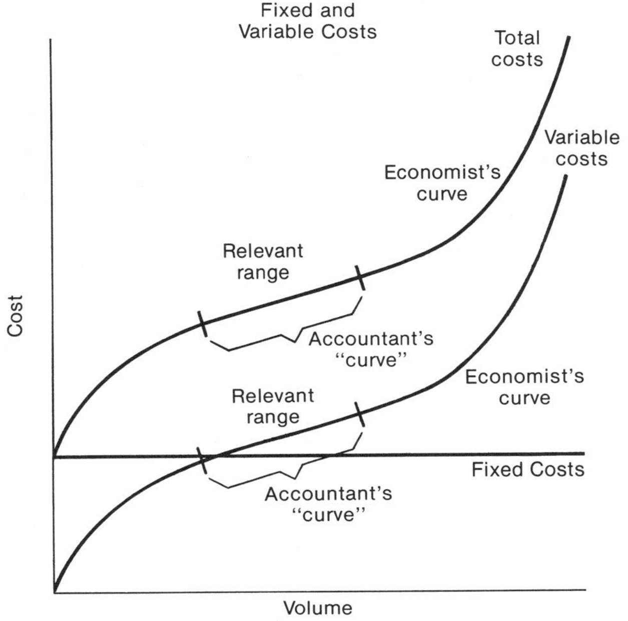

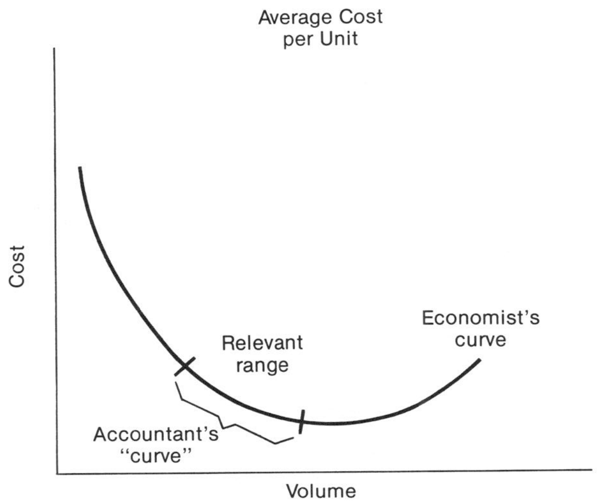

Fixed and Variable Costs

Total costs

Variable costs

Economist's curve

Economist's curve

Accountant's "curve"

Accountant's "curve"

Relevant range

Relevant range

Fixed Costs

Cost

Volume

Average Cost per Unit

Economist's curve

Relevant range

Accountant's "curve"

Cost

Volume

Desired income = $20,000

$$\$20,000 = \$16X - \$24,000 - \$14X$$

$$\$44,000 = 2X$$

$$X = 22,000 \text{ cars}$$

In solving each of the equations in the two illustrations, the variable cost per unit ($14) was subtracted from the revenue per unit ($16). The difference between the two represents the *contribution margin*. Contribution margin is defined as the excess of sales price over variable costs. Each unit of service *contributes* $2 toward covering overhead and realizing the profit objective. Also, in each of the illustrations, this contribution margin of $2 was divided into the sum of desired income and fixed costs in order to determine required volume of unit sales. Thus, to look at the relationship from a slightly different perspective:

Required output (in units)

$$= \frac{\text{Fixed costs} + \text{Desired income}}{\text{Contribution margin}}$$

The break-even point (i.e., zero desired income) may be determined as

$$\text{Break-even point} = \frac{\$24,000 + 0}{\$2} = 12,000 \text{ units}$$

The contribution margin is often expressed as a ratio or percentage rather than an absolute dollar amount. The ratio is calculated as follows:

Contribution margin ratio

$$= 1 - \frac{\text{Variable costs per unit}}{\text{Selling price per unit}}$$

In the example,

$$\text{Contribution margin ratio} = 1 - \frac{\$14}{\$16}$$

$$= 1 - .875 = .125$$

$$= 12.5\%$$

Unit variable costs are 87.5% of unit selling price. Therefore, the remaining 12.5% is a contribution toward fixed costs and desired income.

The contribution margin expressed in decimal or percentage form facilitates questions relating to the *dollar* volume of sales required to achieve a particular level of earnings.

3. What is the dollar volume of sales (i.e., revenues) necessary for the firm to break even?

Desired income at the break-even point is, as before, zero.

Variable costs ($14 per unit) are 87.5 percent of revenues ($16 per unit).

$$\begin{aligned} \text{Desired income} &= \text{Revenue} - \text{Fixed costs} \\ &\quad - \text{Variable costs} \end{aligned}$$

$$\begin{aligned} \$0 &= \text{Revenues} - \$24,000 \\ &\quad - \text{Variable costs} \end{aligned}$$

$$\begin{aligned} \$24,000 &= \text{Revenues} - \text{Variable costs} \\ &= \text{Revenues} - .875(\text{Revenues}) \\ &= .125(\text{Revenues}) \end{aligned}$$

$$\begin{aligned} \text{Revenues} &= \frac{\$24,000}{.125} \\ &= \$192,000 \end{aligned}$$

The required dollar volume of sales could have been computed by making direct use in the equation of the contribution margin. In the final step of the solution the sum of fixed costs and desired income ($24,000 + $0) was divided by the contribution margin (.125) to arrive at the required revenues. The equation could, therefore, be reformulated as:

$$\text{Required revenues} = \frac{\text{Fixed costs} + \text{Desired income}}{\text{Contribution margin}}$$

$$= \frac{\$24,000 + 0}{.125} = \$192,000$$

Because the selling price is $16 per unit, revenues of $192,000 is the equivalent of

EXHIBIT 17-9

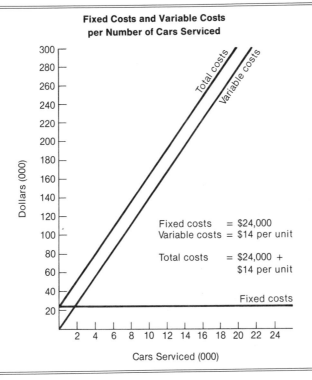

**Fixed Costs and Variable Costs
per Number of Cars Serviced**

Dollars (000)

Total costs

Variable costs

Fixed costs   = $24,000
Variable costs = $14 per unit

Total costs   = $24,000 +
                 $14 per unit

Fixed costs

Cars Serviced (000)

12,000 cars serviced; that is, $192,000 divided by $16.

The relationships between costs and revenues can be shown diagrammatically. Exhibit 17-9 indicates the fixed costs, variable costs, and total costs of servicing cars at various levels of volume. The line representing total costs indicates the sum of the fixed costs ($24,000) and the variable costs ($14 per unit of service); hence it is parallel to the line representing variable costs and each point is $24,000 greater than the point for corresponding volume on the variable cost line.

Exhibit 17-10 illustrates a *cost–volume–profit* chart. It indicates total cost (from Exhibit 16-9) and total revenue ($16 times number of units of service). In the shaded area total cost exceeds total revenue; hence the firm incurs a loss. The point of intersection (at 12,000 units; $192,000) is the break-even point. Beyond the point of intersection the firm earns profits, the amount of which at any particular volume of service will be the dollar difference between the two lines.

Exhibit 17-11, known as a *profit–volume* chart, focuses on profits rather than costs or revenues. The area below the horizontal axis represents a loss; that above, a profit. The income line indicates the profit at the various levels of volume. Each point along the income line represents the difference between the total cost and total revenue lines of Exhibit 17-10. The net income line crosses the horizontal axis (the zero income level) at the

EXHIBIT 17-10

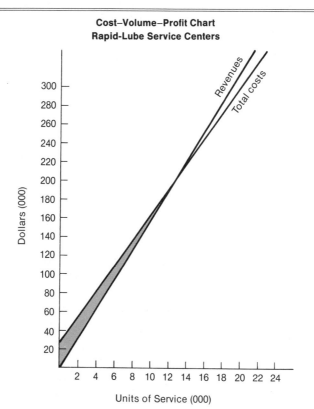

Cost–Volume–Profit Chart
Rapid-Lube Service Centers

EXHIBIT 17-11

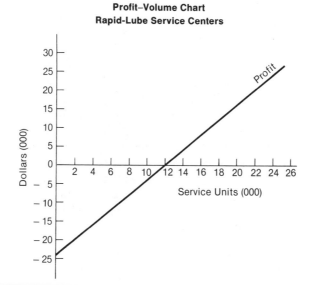

Profit–Volume Chart
Rapid-Lube Service Centers

break-even point. It meets the vertical axis (the zero volume level) at $24,000, an amount representing the fixed costs.

Charts of this type are perhaps of greater interest to managers of the 1980s than they were to those of earlier years. Increasingly, desktop computer terminals with visual display capability will be as common a tool for managers as electronic calculators. In conjunction with software that is widely available today, the computers permit a manager to vary assumptions regarding prices and costs and instantaneously obtain a graphic display of anticipated profits at various levels of volume.

Balancing of Costs

The same basic relationships between fixed costs and variable costs can be used to better understand other types of common issues facing managers. Balancing of costs between fixed and variable components is but one example. Suppose that Rapid-Lube has the opportunity to lease new equipment which would reduce variable labor costs by $.15 per car serviced. Equipment rental charges would be $2,100 per month. The effect of the acquisition would be to increase fixed costs from $24,000 to $26,100 and to decrease variable costs from $14.00 to $13.85 per car serviced. What volume of cars serviced per month would justify the added fixed costs?

The acquisition of the equipment would be justified as long as the volume of cars is sufficiently great so that the cost saving of $.15 per car is equal to or greater than the additional fixed costs of $2,100.

Let X = the required volume of cars

$.15X = \$2,100$

$X = 14,000 \text{ cars}$

Under the existing configuration of inputs without the new equipment, total costs at a level of 14,000 cars would be $220,000—fixed costs of $24,000 plus variable costs of 14,000 times $14. Under the proposed configuration total costs at a level of 14,000 would be the same $220,000—fixed costs of 26,100 plus variable costs of 14,000 times $13.85. At any volume greater than 14,000, total costs would be less under the proposed configuration.

Significance of the Break-Even Point and Opportunity Cost

Cost–volume–profit analysis is commonly referred to as "break-even" analysis, and discussions (such as those in this text) often focus on the "break-even" point. The break-even point unquestionably has "psychological" attraction. An activity that results in losses is considered far more of a failure than one that reports profits, no matter how meager. It is hard to see, however, why the break-even point, at least as traditionally calculated, has very much economic significance. A profit-oriented firm does not enter into ventures merely to "break even." Rather, it does so in order to provide returns to owners greater than can be obtained from other investment opportunities. A firm, for example, that earns a return of zero dollars on an investment of $1 million can hardly be considered to have "broken even" if, by purchasing risk-free Treasury notes it could have earned a return of $80,000. At the very least, the loss of the opportunity forgone is $80,000. The difference in return that results from employing resources to less than their optimum advantage is known as an *opportunity cost*. In considering proposals for the investment of resources the opportunity cost can readily be incorporated into cost–profit–value analysis either by including it as an additional expenditure (a cost of capital, for example) or by taking it into account in establishing "desired income."

Cost–Volume–Profit Analysis— Some Caveats

Cost–volume–profit analysis requires the separation of costs into fixed and variable elements. Whatever specific form the analysis takes, it is a useful—indeed essential— element of the planning process. Its limitations, however, cannot be overlooked.

First, cost–volume–profit analysis is based on static relationships. It assumes that the association between costs and volume will remain constant, at least within the relevant range. But cost–volume relationships are, in fact, seldom stable. Management is, or at least should be, continually searching for ways to reduce cost and increase output. Similarly, in a dynamic economy—and most certainly in an inflationary one—the prices of either inputs or outputs seldom remain the same for long. Moreover, changes in costs, technology, and prices are intertwined, rather than independent as implied by the simple cost–volume–profit relationships illustrated in this text and often assumed by managers. Although accountants are careful to distinguish between the short run and the long run, changes evolve over time; they cannot empirically be categorized into convenient time divisions.

Second, the linear relationships of cost–volume–profit analysis imply that firms can freely move up or down the cost and revenue curves without altering the shape or position of the curves. Such may not be the case. There may, for example, be substantial costs associated with reduction of volume. These may take the form of supplementary unemployment benefits, loss of favorable relationships with suppliers, and hiring and startup costs when volume is subsequently increased to previous levels. At the same time, in the absence of a perfectly competitive market, the firm may be unable to sustain a linear revenue curve. In order to increase sales volume the firm may have to reduce prices, either across the board or by way of quantity or other special discounts.

Third, the cost and revenue functions used in cost–volume–profit analysis are no better than the underlying accounting data. They may be affected by all of the choices among accounting methods, estimates, and allocations that have been discussed in the text to this point and will be discussed in the chapters that follow.

Fourth, cost–volume–profit relationships may lead to inferences as to causal associations that are unwarranted. Changes in volume may require increases in some types of costs. If, for example, a firm is to produce a greater number of units, then it may have no choice but to purchase a greater amount of raw materials. But other types of costs, although analytically associated with changes in volume, may in fact vary with volume only because management elects to allow them to. As a matter of tradition or implicit policy decisions, for example, management may budget research and development costs as a percentage of sales. It cannot be said that the increase in volume "caused" an increase in research and development costs. Still other types of costs may be the moving force behind the changes in volume, rather than the other way around. Advertising costs, for example, may drive, as opposed to be driven by, sales volume. Thus, if cost–volume–profit relationships are to be analytically useful, it is essential that dependent and independent variables be correctly categorized.

SUMMARY

Several themes underlie the practice of management accounting, one of which is that only future, not past costs, are relevant to virtually all decisions that managers are called upon to make. In estimating costs that will be incurred in the future, managers must be able to discriminate between those that are likely to change as a result of managerial action and those that will remain the same. This chapter has focused on the distinction between fixed costs and variable costs. It has highlighted the means of classifying costs by degree of variability and of analyzing the impact of changes in volume upon costs and profits. The fundamental cost–volume–profit relationships set forth in this chapter underlie many of the principles of managerial accounting and analysis that are adhered to in practice and will be discussed in the remaining sections of this text.

QUESTIONS FOR REVIEW AND DISCUSSION

An analysis of a firm's monthly costs reveals the following:

	Fixed Elements	Variable Elements (per unit)
Direct labor	$11,000	$1.80
Direct materials		5.90
Power	400	
Rental of plant and equipment	5,000	
Maintenance	2,000	.20
Other costs	1,600	.10
Total	$20,000	$8.00

Selling price per unit is $10.

1. How much does the sale of each unit contribute toward covering fixed costs?
2. How many units must the firm produce and sell to break even—that is, to assure that total contributions to fixed costs are exactly equal to fixed costs?
3. How many units would the firm have to produce and sell in order to cover all costs and earn a profit of $6,000?
4. What would be the profit of the firm if it were to produce and sell

a. 12,000 units?
b. 8,000 units?

5. Suppose that the firm was able to rent additional equipment, at a cost of $2,000 per month, which would reduce variable costs by $.20 per unit. How would this change affect:
a. The break-even point?
b. Profit, if the firm were to produce and sell 12,000 units?
c. Profit, if the firm were to produce and sell 8,000 units?

6. In general, what is the effect on the break-even point and the contribution margin (per unit contribution to fixed costs and earnings) of:
a. An increase in fixed costs?
b. An increase in selling price?
c. An increase in variable costs?

EXERCISE FOR REVIEW AND SELF-TESTING

1. Distinguish between "financial" and "management" accounting. With what types of questions is management accounting concerned?
2. What are four themes that underlie the practice and study of management accounting?
3. Fixed costs are fixed in amount. In the short run they are the same from month to month. Do you agree?
4. "There is no conceptual difference between fixed and variable costs. In fact, as is clearly evident when the two types of costs are displayed graphically, their behavior with respect to changes in volume is remarkably similar." Do you agree? Explain.
5. The most common expression of cost is "average" costs. For what types of decisions, if any, would a manager be better served by using average costs as opposed to fixed costs and variable costs?
6. Under what circumstances would normative analysis of costs—the type of analysis performed by industrial engineers—be most appropriate? Why must normative analysis usually be supplemented by other forms of analysis?

7. What is an important pitfall to be on guard against when performing a high–low analysis of costs?

8. What is the significance of the break-even point? Why do many accountants and financial analysts prefer the term "cost–volume–profit" analysis to "break-even" analysis?

9. What are three critical limitations of break-even analysis?

10. "Accountants and economists have totally different views of the behavior of costs. Any effort to reconcile the two is likely to be an exercise in frustration." Do you agree? Explain.

PROBLEMS

1. Changes in the fixed as opposed to the variable elements of earnings will have significantly different impacts on a profit–volume line.

Unsatisfied with its recent performance, the Deakin Co. is considering ways to reduce its operating losses. Presently, the firm faces a profit–volume relationship as indicated in the chart that follows. This chart is based on monthly fixed costs of $40,000, variable costs of $22 per unit, and a selling price of $30 per unit.

Prepare a profit–volume chart similar to the one illustrated. Include the line representing the present revenues and costs. Add additional lines to indicate the effect of each of the contemplated changes, considered independently:

a. The firm will decrease advertising costs by $10,000.

b. It will decrease variable manufacturing costs by $2 per unit.

c. It will increase selling price by $2 per unit.

d. It will decrease selling price by $2 per unit and reduce advertising costs by $10,000.

2. Some changes result in only a shift in the position of a cost or revenue curve; others, in a shift of slope.

A firm charges $140 per unit of its product. Fixed manufacturing costs are $200,000; variable costs are $100 per unit.

a. On a sheet of graph paper, plot two curves: one representing revenues in relation to sales volume; the other total cost in relation to sales volume. Determine the break-even point. Use algebraic procedures to verify your determination of the break-even point.

b. Suppose that the firm was able to increase sales price by 10 percent. Plot a new revenue curve and determine the revised break-even point. Verify algebraically.

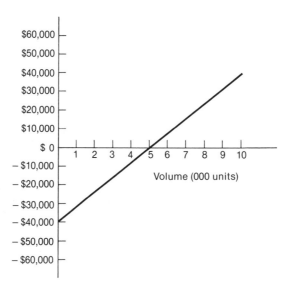

Volume (000 units)

c. Suppose alternatively that the firm was able to decrease fixed costs by 50 percent. Plot a new total cost curve and determine the revised break-even point. Verify algebraically.

d. Suppose instead that the firm was able to decrease variable costs by 70 percent. Plot a new total cost curve and determine the revised break-even point. Verify algebraically.

e. Which of the changes caused the curves to shift position yet retain the same slope? Which resulted in a shift in slope?

3. *In banks and related industries output may best be measured by amount of deposits or outstanding loans.*

First City Savings Association pays its depositors interest at the rate of 6 percent. It is able to make loans at the rate of 10 percent. Fixed costs of operating the bank are $600,000 per year.

a. Assume that the bank is able to lend 100 percent of its deposits.

  1. Prepare a cost–volume–profit chart in which you indicate, for various levels of deposits, fixed costs, variable costs, and revenues.

  2. What is the break-even point? At what level of deposits will the bank realize income of $200,000? Verify your answer with appropriate computations.

  3. Prepare a profit–volume chart in which you indicate income at various levels of deposits. Be certain that this graph is consistent with the cost–profit–volume chart; that is, at any particular level of deposits the difference between the revenue and total cost line per the first chart should be equal to the amount of profit per the second chart.

b. Assume that the bank is required by bank regulatory authorities to maintain reserves of 10 percent; that is, it is able to lend out only 90 percent of the amount on deposit. Repeat Part a under the revised assumption. You need not redraw the charts. Simply add an alternate revenue line.

4. *Cost–volume–profit analysis can take various related forms.*

Fairmont, Inc., incurs fixed costs of $270,000 and variable costs of $12 per unit. Selling price of its product is $20 per unit. The firm has established an annual earnings objective of $30,000.

a. Using the basic algebraic expression that includes price (P), fixed costs (F), variable costs (V), and desired income (I), determine the number of units (u) that Fairmont, Inc., would be required to manufacture and sell if it is to achieve its annual earnings objective. Calculate total sales revenue at that volume.

b. Determine the contribution margin (C) expressed in dollar terms. Formulate a mathematical expression of the number of units (u) that must be manufactured and sold in order to achieve a profit objective that incorporates the contribution margin in place of selling price and variable costs. Apply the expression to the case at hand.

c. Determine the contribution margin *ratio* (R)— a ratio which relates contribution margin to selling price. Formulate a mathematical expression of dollar sales volume for a firm to achieve a target income that incorporates such ratio in place of the contribution margin expressed in dollar terms. Apply the expression to Fairmont, Inc.

5. *Break-even analysis can be used to assist management in pinpointing changes that could have the greatest impact on earnings.*

Management has been dissatisfied with the performance of a division inasmuch as in the past month it was unable to do better than break even. A performance report for the month indicated the following:

Sales revenue (10,000 units @ $50)		$500,000
Costs		
Variable		
(10,000 units @ $20)	$200,000	
Fixed	300,000	500,000
Income		$ -0-

Management has established an earnings goal of $20,000 for the next month. It is contemplating several measures to increase revenue and or reduce costs.

a. Determine the number of units that the firm would be required to produce and sell in order to achieve the goal if the following changes (each to be considered separately) were made:
  1. Sales price were increased by 10 percent.

2. Fixed costs were decreased by 10 percent.
3. Variable costs were decreased by 10 percent.
4. Fixed costs and variable costs were decreased by 10 percent.
5. No changes were made in costs or prices.

b. Suppose instead that at a volume of 10,000 units total costs were, as as before, $500,000, but that fixed costs were $200,000 and variable costs were $300,000 ($30 per unit). How many units would have to be sold to increase earnings to $20,000?

6. *Cost–volume–profit analysis facilitates equipment balancing decisions.*

Flexi-Industries, Inc., was considering acquiring new manufacturing equipment which would enable it to substantially reduce direct labor costs. The equipment would cost $500,000 and would enable the firm to save $2 per unit in variable costs. The firm would have to borrow the amount required to purchase the equipment; as a result, interest costs would increase by $75,000. In addition, maintenance and miscellaneous costs would increase by $25,000.

In 1984, the firm produced and sold 100,000 units; sales price was $14 per unit. The actual income statement and year-end balance sheet, as well as *pro forma* statements indicating results as they would have been had the firm owned the new equipment, appear below.

Depreciation per unit was determined by dividing the *original cost* of plant equipment ($500,000 or $1,000,000) by useful life (five years) and by dividing

December 31, 1984

	Actual	Pro Forma
BALANCE SHEET		
Assets		
Plant and equipment (net of allowance for depreciation)	$400,000	$ 800,000
Other assets	250,000	250,000
Total assets	$650,000	$1,050,000
Equities		
Notes payable	—	$ 500,000
Stockholders' equity	$650,000	550,000
Total equities	$650,000	$1,050,000
Income Statement		
1984		
Sales revenue	$1,400,000	$1,400,000
Cost of goods sold	900,000	800,000
Gross margin	$ 500,000	$ 600,000
Administrative and other costs, including interest	400,000	500,000
Income before taxes	$ 100,000	$ 100,000
Cost of goods sold was determined as follows:		
Direct materials	$3.00	$3.00
Direct labor	5.00	3.00
Depreciation	1.00	2.00
	$9.00	$8.00
Number of units manufactured and sold	100,000 units	100,000 units
Cost of goods sold	$900,000	$800,000

the result ($100,000 or $200,000) by number of units manufactured and sold (100,000).

After reviewing the actual and *pro forma* financial statements the vice-president for manufacturing commented: "Inasmuch as overall profits would not be improved by the acquisition, it would be senseless for us to undertake it. After all, why trade a decrease in variable costs for an increase in fixed costs? Our low fixed costs have always been our strength relative to our competitors. They have enabled us to adjust quickly to changes in demand."

a. In the schedule of cost of goods sold, should depreciation be considered a fixed or a variable cost? Explain.

b. If you knew for certain that volume in coming years would be 150,000 units per year, would you recommend acquisition of the equipment? Assume that your objective was to maximize *reported* earnings. Support your answer with an appropriate schedule.

c. If you knew for certain that volume would be only 70,000 units, would your response be the same? Prepare a supporting schedule.

d. What is the break-even point if the equipment is not acquired?

e. What is the break-even point if the equipment is acquired?

f. Do you agree with the vice-president for manufacturing that a relatively small proportion of fixed costs assures flexibility with regard to changes in demand? Comment.

7. Contribution margin affects preferences for tax alternatives.

The annual revenues and expenditures of River View Hotel were as follows:

Revenues		$1,000,000
Expenditures		
Fixed	$300,000	
Variable	600,000	900,000
Income		$ 100,000

In order to finance the construction of a new convention center the city in which the hotel is located is considering several alternative types of taxes to be imposed on hotels. Under one alternative, hotels would pay a per room franchise fee to the city. The annual cost to River View would be $85,000.

Under the other alternative, the city would levy a 10 percent tax on all hotel revenues. The tax would be paid entirely by hotel customers. However, since River View is in competition with similar hotels in an adjoining town, management estimates that the tax would result in a 15 percent decline in annual sales.

a. Which of the alternatives would River View prefer? Determine the effect on income of each of the two proposals.

b. Assume that the city elected to impose the per room franchise fee. The hotel decides not to increase the prices charged to customers. Instead, it endeavors to make an effort to attract new business. By how much would revenues need to increase, assuming no increases in fixed costs other than the $85,000 franchise fee, in order for River View to maintain income at $100,000?

c. Assume instead that the city imposed the tax on revenues and that the hotel decided that in order to remain competitive it must now reduce the prices charged to customers by approximately 10 percent. What would be the amount of revenue required to maintain income at its previous level of $100,000?

d. Assume instead that the city decided to impose a 2 percent tax on net income (revenues less expenditures). By how much would revenues need to increase, assuming no increase in prices charged to customers, in order for the hotel to maintain income at $100,000?

8. Contribution margin affects profit potential of promotional strategy.

Two executives in related industries were discussing the merits of distributing free samples as a means of increasing sales. Both executives were from firms that sold their products to fashionable book and art shops. The first executive represented a publishing concern which produced and distributed expensive art books; the second represented a china firm which manufactured artistic plates, each of which was, in part, hand painted.

Coincidentally, the selling price and cost of the two products were the same. Based on estimated production and sales volume of 10,000 units the costs of the two products were as follows:

Art Books

Costs of design and production of plates	$300,000
Costs of printing, binding, materials, and distribution; 10,000 books at $10 per book	100,000
Total costs	$400,000

Artistic Plates

Costs of design and molds	$ 50,000
Costs of labor, materials, and distribution; 10,000 plates at $35 per plate	350,000
Total costs	$400,000

Thus, the average cost of both books and plates were $40 per unit. The selling price of each was $60 per unit.

Both executives agreed that a sample of a product, given free to a retail store, could be expected to generate sales of 10 units. The executive representing the publishing firm asserted that sampling represented an effective means of promoting sales and thereby increasing profits. The executive representing the china company was decidedly less enthusiastic about sampling, preferring to concentrate his firm's efforts on increasing the number of different plates available for sale.

a. Explain why each executive might view sampling as he does. Determine the impact on the earnings of each of the companies of distributing 100 free samples to the book and art stores with which they trade.

b. Indicate why it is to the relative advantage of the china company, as opposed to the publishing company, to introduce new products rather than concentrate on increasing sales of existing ones.

9. In determining the impact of changes in volume on earnings, cost "step functions" must be taken into account.

The Riverdale Transit Co. operates a commuter bus service between a suburban community and the downtown area of a major city.

The company presently operates 10 buses. Each bus has a practical capacity of 300 passengers (rides) per day. As the number of riders increases, the company can schedule more frequent service. However, each time the number of passengers increases by a multiple of 300, another bus must be added. The additional bus must be scheduled for the same number of daily trips as the others.

The company presently provides service for approximately 2,900 passengers per day. Inasmuch as the company does not operate on weekends or holidays it bases all monthly calculations on the assumption that there will be 22 days of service per month. Thus, the company currently provides 63,800 rides per month.

The company leases, rather than purchases, its buses. Operating costs for a recent month were as follows:

Monthly costs per bus	
Lease charges	$ 1,500
Wages of drivers	3,000
Fuel costs	1,800
Variable maintenance and miscellaneous costs	600
Total costs per bus	$ 6,900
Number of buses	× 10
Total direct costs of operating buses	$69,000
Administration, general, and fixed maintenance costs	25,000
Total monthly costs	$94,000

The fare for each ride is $2. Monthly revenues are $127,600.

a. In making plans for future months, the president of the firm estimates that ridership will increase by 3 percent. He has estimated that earnings before taxes will also increase by 3 percent. Do you agree? If not, determine the amount by which you believe earnings will change.

b. The controller of the firm, somewhat more knowledgeable about accounting than the president, has estimated that ridership will increase by 5 percent. He has determined that earnings will increase by the difference between additional revenue and additional variable costs. He has computed variable costs to be $69,000 divided by average monthly ridership of 63,800— that is $1.08 per rider. Do you agree with his computations? If not, determine the amount by which you believe earnings will change.

c. In light of your computations, do you believe

that the firm should make an effort to increase ridership by 5 percent or would it be better off by attempting to restrict ridership to its present level?

10. *Cost–volume–profit analysis is as applicable to nonprofit organizations as it is to private businesses.*

A nonprofit nursing home estimates that its variable costs per patient are $100 per week and fixed costs are $7,200 per week.

a. The home presently serves 80 patients. What is the least amount that it could charge each patient and still break even?

b. Suppose that the rate charged was $230 per week. What would be the minimum number of patients the home must serve in order to break even?

c. Assume, as in part b, that the rate is $230 per week. What is the number of patients that the home would be required to serve for it to realize a margin of $2,000 per week?

d. Assume that the home presently serves 80 patients. What is the rate per week that it should charge in order to realize a margin of 10 percent of patient revenues received?

e. In the current year the firm expects its revenues to exceed total expenses by $500 per week. It estimates that both fixed costs and variable costs will increase by 10 percent. Assuming that it will serve 80 patients per week, what rate should it charge next year if it is to continue to realize an excess of revenues over expenditures of $500 per week?

11. *Cost functions take a variety of forms, some of which appear to be inconsistent with the usual assumptions made by accountants.*

a. For each of the following descriptions of cost, draw a graph that indicates the relationship between dollar cost and an appropriate measure of level of activity (e.g., production, customers served, sales, etc.). The first one is done for you as an example and is shown below.

1. Employer contributions to a state unemployment compensation fund are 2.2 percent of each employee's wages, with a maximum contribution of $348. The size and composition of the work force remained constant during the year.

2. A commercial bank estimates that one teller is required for each 100 customers served per day.

3. Copying costs are $.08 per page for the first 100 copies, $.07 for the next 100, $.06 for the next 100, and $.05 for all copies thereafter.

4. Electric costs are $.031 for the first 10,000 kilowatt hours of electricity, $.032 for the next 10,000, $.033 for the next 10,000, and so on to a maximum charge of $.035 for each kilowatt hour over 50,000.

5. The salary of the company president is $100,000 per year.

6. Salary and bonus of the plant manager are $30,000 per year plus $.10 per unit for each unit of product over 100,000.

7. Rent on a retail gas station is $2,000 per month plus $.02 per gallon of gasoline sold over 10,000 gallons. Maximum rental payment in any one month is $4,000.

8. Depreciation on a factory building is calculated by the straight-line method.

9. Depreciation on factory equipment is calculated by the units-of-output method.

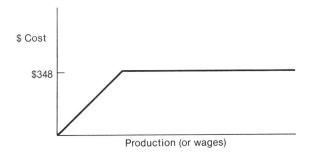

10. When acquiring raw materials, the company is allowed a discount of 2 percent once the total purchased during the year exceeds $100,000.

b. It is often convenient for the accountant to categorize costs as being either fixed or variable. He or she assumes that variable costs may be depicted as straight upward-sloping lines and fixed costs as horizontal lines. Yet many of the cost functions which you have just drawn do not conform to that pattern. Are the assumptions of the accountant unrealistic? How can you reconcile your graphs with the assumptions of the accountant?

12. Analytical relationships will be affected by the accounting methods used to establish the underlying data.

As a manager you wish to determine the relationship between selling expenses and dollar sales. From the records of your company you are able to abstract the following data for a period of 14 months:

Month	Sales	Selling Costs
December (1983)	$95,000	$5,600
January (1984)	85,000	5,700
February	74,000	5,100
March	63,000	4,400
April	90,000	3,800
May	92,000	5,400
June	67,000	5,500
July	69,000	4,000
August	88,000	4,100
September	86,000	5,300
October	79,000	5,200
November	83,000	4,700
December (1984)	62,000	5,000
January (1985)	80,000	3,700

a. Plot the data on a scatter diagram. Visually fit a curve to the points and if possible describe in equation form the relationships between sales and selling costs. Comment on the reliability of your equation; that is, how much of the variation in selling costs is explained by the equation?

b. You subsequently learn that the selling costs account is composed almost entirely of commissions of salesmen. Each month the account

is debited with the amount actually paid to the salesmen. The amount paid is based on sales of the previous month. (At year end, when annual financial reports are to be prepared, an adjustment is made so that commission expense is matched to the sales revenue of the proper period.) Prepare a second scatter diagram in which selling costs are matched to the sales of the previous month. Visually fit a curve to the data points and describe the relationship in equation form.

c. Suppose that you were called upon to study the behavior of electricity costs in relation to production. Why might you face a problem similar to that suggested by this example?

13. Relationships derived from correlations of one variable with another may be inappropriate for distinguishing the fixed from the variable elements of cost or for making predictions about costs to be incurred in the future.

During the five-year period between 1979 and 1983 a firm reported advertising costs and sales revenue as follows:

Year	Sales	Advertising Costs
1979	$5,000,000	$220,000
1980	4,800,000	208,000
1981	5,700,000	262,000
1982	6,400,000	304,000
1983	6,200,000	292,000

a. Using the high–low method, express in equation form advertising costs as a function of sales.

b. Based on the equation, determine the variable and the nonvariable elements of costs at a sales volume of (1) zero; (2) $50,000.

c. Explain the significance (or lack thereof) of the nonvariable portion of the costs at sales volume of zero and $50,000. Is it possible for fixed costs to be negative?

d. In preparing a budget for the firm you learn that the sales department estimates that sales volume in the following year will be $6,000,000. What is the amount that you would forecast for advertising costs?

e. Do you believe that the equation that you developed can really be used to make reliable predictions of advertising costs? Explain.

14. *This is a simple exercise in regression analysis which highlights the need for caution in drawing conclusions from it.*

A mail-order firm wishes to project the costs of packaging and shipping customer orders. It projects that sales for 1984 will be $870,000.

Sales and packaging and shipping costs for the previous five years were as follows:

Year	Sales	Packaging and Shipping Costs
1979	$700,000	$61,200
1980	890,000	67,000
1981	840,000	65,200
1982	970,000	69,100
1983	760,000	62,600

a. Following the form of the example in the text, prepare a table in which you determine the sums of x (sales), y (packaging and shipping costs), x^2 and xy. For computation convenience, divide each number by 1,000; e.g., $61.2 in place of $61,200.

b. Using the formulas in the example, determine (1) the y intercept and (2) the slope of the regression equation.

c. Based on the regression equation, estimate packaging and shipping costs for 1984.

d. Do you think that your equation could be used to predict packaging and shipping costs if sales were $3 million? Explain.

e. In this example your analysis is based on only five data points. How would the small number of observations affect the conclusions that you can draw from your analysis?

SOLUTIONS TO EXERCISE FOR REVIEW AND SELF-TESTING

1. Each unit contributes $2—the difference between selling price of $10 per unit and variable costs of $8 per unit.

2. Inasmuch as each unit contributes $2 toward covering fixed costs and there are $20,000 of fixed costs to be covered, the firm must produce and sell 10,000 units—$20,000 divided by $2.

3. In order to cover fixed costs of $20,000 and earn profits of $6,000, the firm must produce and sell 13,000 units—$26,000 divided by $2.

4. a. The production and sale of 12,000 units, each with a contribution margin of $2, would contribute $24,000 toward covering fixed costs of $20,000. Hence, profit would be $4,000.

b. The production and sale of 8,000 units would contribute only $16,000 toward covering fixed costs of $20,000. Hence, the firm would incur a loss of $4,000.

5. a. The change would cause fixed costs to increase to $22,000 and the contribution margin to increase to $2.20. Since both the fixed costs and the contribution margin increased in the same proportion—10 percent—the break-even point would remain the same: $22,000/$2.20 = 10,000 units.

b. The production and sale of 12,000 units, each with a contribution margin of $2.20, would contribute $26,400 toward covering fixed costs of $22,000. Hence, profit would be $4,400.

c. The production and sale of 8,000 units would contribute only $17,600 toward covering fixed costs of $22,000. Hence, the firm would incur a loss of $4,400.

6. a. An increase in fixed costs would cause the break-even point to increase, but would have no effect on per unit contribution to fixed costs and earnings (the contribution margin).

b. An increase in selling price would cause the break-even point to decrease and would increase the per unit contribution to fixed costs and earnings.

c. An increase in variable costs would cause the break-even point to increase and would decrease the per unit contribution to fixed costs and earnings.

ESTABLISHING THE COST 18
OF A PRODUCT

One of the key functions of an accounting system is to establish the cost of the products that an organization manufactures and sells or the services that it provides. Determination of cost is not, regrettably, merely a matter of mechanically recording outlays and dividing total outlays by number of units produced. Cost is affected by choices among accounting principles, methods of allocations, and means of making estimates. To be sure, issues of product costing are significant because the way in which cost is determined has an impact on earnings as reported to parties external to the organization. Equally important, however, managers must make decisions in which cost of product or service is a factor to be considered. It is critical, therefore, that they understand the elements of which it is composed and the principles by which it has been computed.

NATURE OF THE PROBLEM

Product cost consists of three primary elements: direct labor, direct materials, and overhead. Direct materials and direct labor can, by definition, be readily identified with specific units of product. Overhead (indirect) costs, however, are those which cannot directly be ascribed to particular units of product. Overhead costs include expenditures for rent, power, supervision, lubricants, supplies, and overtime premiums. They are as essential to the manufacturing process as direct labor and materials. They must, therefore, be included in the total product cost and procedures must be adopted to assign overhead costs to particular units of product.

This chapter will focus on principles of determining the cost of goods manufactured. Many of the concepts to be discussed are applicable also to services provided. As was pointed out earlier in the text, administration and selling, like manufacturing costs, are incurred to generate revenues. They should, therefore, be included in product cost and, in order to effect a proper matching of costs and revenues, charged as an expense in the period in which the goods are sold. However, in recognition of substantial difficulties of assigning them to particular units of product, and in respect to long-standing tradition, selling and nonfactory administrative costs are conventionally accounted for as *period* costs. They are *omitted* from the cost of the product and thereby *excluded* from inventory. Instead, they are charged as expenses in the periods in which they are incurred. Some accountants have urged that indirect factory costs that cannot readily be identified with specific units of product should also be charged to expense as incurred—a method of accounting known as *direct costing*, which will be considered later in this chapter. Generally accepted accounting principles require, however, that they be included in product cost and inventoried as assets until sold.

Most manufacturing firms are organized on a departmental basis. Some departments, known as *production* departments, engage directly in manufacturing operations. Assembly, molding, finishing, and painting departments are examples of production departments. Other departments, known as *service* departments, provide support services to the production departments. Among the functions carried out by service departments are personnel administration, warehousing and materials handling, telephone service, building maintenance, and equipment repair. Most departments, whether production or service, are also *cost centers*. A cost center is an organizational unit for which costs are accumulated. Some cost centers (or cost pools) are not operating departments. When certain costs, such as building occupancy costs, are common to a number of departments, they are assigned initially to a non-operating cost pool and then allocated to the user departments.

Allocation versus Absorption

The assignment of overhead costs to specific units of product is a two-stage process. First, since only production departments are directly associated with the manufactured products, costs that are accumulated in nonproduction cost centers must be assigned to the production departments. Second, the overhead costs from the nonproduction cost centers must be combined with the overhead costs of the production departments themselves and assigned to particular units of product.

The process of assigning overhead costs from the service departments and other nonproduction cost centers to the production departments is referred to as *allocation*. That of assigning overhead costs from the production departments to the particular units of product is known as either *absorption* or *application*.

Job Order versus Process Costing

In industries characterized by the production of customized units or batches of product, each of which requires different amounts of labor and materials, specific records must be maintained of the actual labor hours and materials used for each unit or batch. The method in which it is necessary to maintain cost records of the individual units or batches is known as *job order* costing. Job order costing, as the name implies, is used in those industries where each job is unique: construction, book publishing, shipbuilding, and furniture. In general, it is used by those firms that accept orders for products that require some degree of customization.

In industries characterized by continuous processing of identical goods, costs are accumulated by period in each production department. Cost per unit is calculated by dividing total costs by number of units produced during the period. This method of accumulating costs by department and then averaging them over the number of units produced in a period is known as *process costing*. Process costing is most closely identified with continuous processing industries, such as oil refining, chemicals, plastics, food processing, paper, and cement. It may also be used in service industries, such as banking and insurance, to account for the processing of checks, invoices, and similar documents.

Job order costing will be illustrated first; then process costing.

JOB ORDER COSTING

Direct Labor and Materials

Each job must be assigned three types of costs: direct labor, direct materials, and overhead. As each of the elements is assigned to a job an appropriate cost is added to the account, *work in process*. Work in process, however, is a control account, which may encompass more than one job. Costs applicable to each specific job are recorded in a subsidiary ledger composed of *job cost sheets*, one for each job in process. The ledger may be maintained manually or by computer.

Suppose that in a particular month Virginia Furniture Co. undertakes several jobs. Some are for chairs, some for tables and some for cabinets. The example that follows focuses on one of those jobs, number 101, for 100 custom-designed tables. As materials, which can be used for some or all jobs are purchased, ledger entries similar to

the following would be made:

(1)

Raw materials (or stores control, parts, etc.)	$800,000	
Accounts payable		$800,000

To record purchase of raw materials.

As materials are requistioned for job 101, the release of the goods from the storeroom would be recorded as:

(2)

Work in process	$60,000	
Raw materials (or stores control, parts, etc.)		$60,000

To record requisition of raw materials for job 101.

The cost of the materials would also be recorded on a job cost sheet. A job cost sheet is illustrated in Exhibit 18-1.

Direct labor costs may be accounted for in a variety of ways. Under most systems, however, entries such as the following two would be made:

(3)

Direct labor	$900,000	
Payroll (or wages payable)		$900,000

To record direct labor used on a number of jobs.

(4)

Work in process	$40,000	
Direct labor		$40,000

To assign direct labor to work in process, job 101.

Direct labor could be assigned directly to work in process, thereby bypassing the direct labor account. The direct labor account, however, is utilized in order to maintain a record of total direct labor costs. As with direct

EXHIBIT 18-1 *Job Order Cost Sheet*

Virginia Furniture Co.

Job Cost Sheet

Job. No. _101_   Date started _6/2_

Description _COLONIAL TABLES_   Date completed _6/30_

No. of units _100_

Direct Labor		Materials		Factory Overhead	
6/9	$ 8,200	6/9	$ 25,300	6/9	$ 5,125
6/16	7,680	6/11	10,615	6/16	4,800
6/23	12,912	6/19	12,650	6/23	8,070
6/30	11,208	6/24	8,945	6/30	7,005
		6/26	2,140		
		6/28	350		
Totals	$40,000		$60,000		$25,000

Total costs $ _125,000_   Per unit cost $ _1,250_

materials, the entry to the work in process control account would be accompanied by a corresponding notation on each job cost sheet.

Overhead

Overhead, by its very nature, cannot readily be traced to specific jobs. It cannot, therefore, be assigned directly. If product costs are to include overhead costs—which, in terms of magnitude may be as great as those of labor and materials—then they must be assigned indirectly.

The most common mechanism for assigning overhead costs to specific jobs is the *overhead charging rate,* commonly referred to as the *burden rate.* The overhead charging rate relates the overhead costs attributable to a production department to some measure of departmental volume, such as direct labor hours, direct machine hours, or direct labor dollars. If the measure of activity were to be direct labor hours, then the overhead charging rate for a productive department would be

$$\frac{\text{Total overhead}}{\text{Total direct labor hours}}$$

The amount of overhead charged to each job would be equal to the overhead charging rate times the number of direct labor hours worked on that job.

The overhead to be included in the numerator of the overhead charging rate fraction would include not only the costs traceable to the particular production department (e.g., costs of inspection, supervision, maintenance, and supplies) but also those *allocated* from other cost centers (e.g., costs of heat and light, materials handling, plant supervision, and plant maintenance).

predetermined charging rates

Overhead charging rates *could* be calculated so as to relate *actual* overhead costs to *actual* units of volume. Usually, however, overhead charging rates are *predetermined*, based on *estimates* of both costs and activity. There are at least two advantages to using *predetermined* overhead charging rates. First, predetermined overhead charging rates facilitate computation of unit cost prior to the end of an accounting period. Since some overhead costs (e.g., repair costs) are incurred only intermittently, the actual costs of a period may not be known at the time a job is completed and transferred to finished goods. Similarly, total volume into which costs must be divided may also be unknown. Second, predetermined overhead charging rates assure a constant per unit overhead charge throughout the period covered by the rate. This advantage stems from the fixed

nature of some overhead costs. Those costs, although not traceable directly to specific units of product, nevertheless vary with output. For example, costs of supplies, machine maintenance, and inspection may increase with increases in output. Other overhead costs, such as rent, taxes, heat, and light, are fixed; they bear no relation to volume. If the overhead charging rate were to be determined on the basis of actual volume, then per unit charges of fixed overhead costs would fluctuate in response to changes in volume. In periods of increased production, overhead cost per unit would decrease as the costs were spread over a larger number of units. In periods of decreased production, overhead cost per unit would increase. To avoid this type of fluctuation a firm can determine its overhead charging rate at the start of its fiscal year and continue to use it throughout the year unless actual experience indicates that its estimates were acutely in error.

Suppose that Virginia Furniture estimates that annual overhead costs, including those allocated from service departments and other nonproduction cost centers, to be incurred by the furniture production department will be $4,000,000. The firm forecasts that it will utilize 800,000 hours of direct labor. The overhead charging rate will thus be $5 per direct labor hour:

$$\frac{\text{Estimated overhead costs}}{\text{Estimated direct labor hours}} = \frac{\$4,000,000}{800,000} = \$5$$

If on job 101 the firm used 5,000 hours of direct labor, then the amount of overhead charged to that job would be 5,000 × $5 = $25,000.

Overhead costs are accumulated initially in accounts that provide management with information as to their nature and origin (e.g., maintenance, depreciation, supervision). They are then transferred to, and summarized in, a control account, "Factory overhead." From the factory overhead account, by means of the overhead charging rate, the overhead costs are added to work in process. Extension of the Virginia Furniture Co. example may serve to clarify the general approach to accumulation of overhead costs and their assignment to specific units.

Actual overhead costs in the furniture production department during the month of June were as follows:

Supervision	$ 60,000
Maintenance	50,000
Depreciation of equipment	20,000
Other overhead costs incurred by the department	90,000
Overhead costs allocated from other cost centers	110,000
Total overhead costs of the department	$330,000

Based on annual estimates the overhead charging rate has been established at $5 per direct labor hour. Since the production department applied 5,000 direct labor hours to job 101, the following type of journal entries would serve to assign overhead costs to work in process:

(5)

Supervision	$ 60,000	
Maintenance (various specific accounts)	50,000	
Depreciation	20,000	
Other costs	90,000	
Overhead costs allocated from other cost centers	110,000	
Payroll and accounts payable		$200,000
Accumulated depreciation		20,000
Accounts of other departments		110,000

To record actual costs incurred and those allocated from other cost centers.

(6)

Overhead control	$330,000	
Supervision		$ 60,000
Maintenance (various specific accounts)		50,000
Depreciation		20,000
Other costs		90,000
Overhead costs allocated from other cost centers		110,000

To summarize overhead costs in the overhead control account.

(7)

Work in process	$25,000	
Overhead control		$25,000

To assign overhead to work in process, job 101. (The amount assigned is determined by multiplying the 5,000 direct labor hours by the overhead charging rate of $5. As will be discussed in the section that follows, the total amount assigned to all jobs is not necessarily equal to the actual costs incurred.)

Upon completion of the job, its cost (including direct labor, direct materials, and overhead) would be transferred from work in process to finished goods:

(8)

Finished goods inventory	$125,000	
Work in process		$125,000

To record the completion of job 101 and its transfer to finished goods inventory.
(The amount transferred is equal to the sum of the direct materials, the direct labor, and the overhead assigned to job 101.)

Inasmuch as job 101 consists of 100 tables, cost per table would be $1,250 (that is, $125,000 divided by 100).

basis for the overhead charging rate

The basis for assigning overhead costs to product should be the variable that is most closely associated with the overhead costs.

In most organizations a significant portion of overhead costs are labor related. Hence, the overhead charging rate is labor based—on either direct labor hours or direct labor dollars. In unusual situations an overhead charging rate based on machine hours or materials usage may be justified. If, for example, most of the overhead costs were attributable to machine maintenance, then machine hours would be an appropriate basis for the overhead charging rate. If warehousing or materials handling costs constituted the bulk of overhead costs, then materials usage would be an appropriate basis.

Where overhead costs vary in response to different factors, it is desirable to separate overhead costs into two or more overhead pools and to use different bases to apply each cost pool. A pool of labor-oriented costs might be assigned on the basis of direct labor hours or dollars; a pool of maintenance costs might be assigned on the basis of the machine hours used. The advantages, in terms of more refined cost allocations, of numerous overhead pools must always, of course, be weighed against the resultant increases in clerical costs and inconveniences.

Exhibit 18-2, using the data for Virginia Furniture Co. and focusing on job 101, summarizes the flow of costs in a job order cost system.

over- or underabsorbed overhead

The overhead charging rate is based on estimates of annual overhead costs and direct labor hours or some other measure of activity. Should either of the estimates be in error—and in the absence of an uncommon degree of managerial prescience there is every likelihood that they will be—then either more or

EXHIBIT 18-2 Summary of Job Order Costing (with Focus on Job 101)

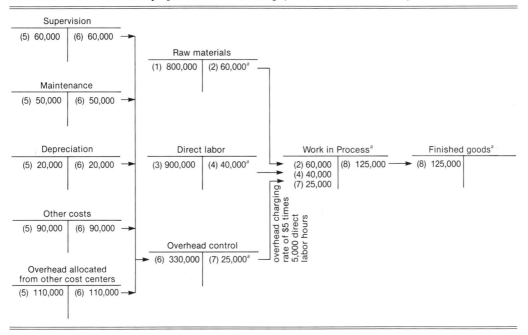

[a] Amounts shown are for job 101 only. Similar entries would be made for other jobs.

less than actual overhead costs will be assigned to products. Suppose, for example, that the actual overhead costs of the production department of Virginia Furniture Co. for the year were not $4,000,000 as estimated, but rather $4,300,000. Actual direct labor hours were not 800,000 as estimated but 820,000. Since the *predetermined* overhead charging rate was $5, only $4,100,000 ($5 × 820,000 direct labor hours) of overhead costs would have been assigned to the products produced during the year. At year end a balance of $200,000 would remain in the overhead control account:

Overhead control	
Actual	
costs $4,300,000	4,100,000

If the amount applied to products (transferred to work in process) is less than actual costs, then a *debit* balance would remain in the overhead control account and overhead would be *underabsorbed*. If the amount applied to the products is greater than actual costs, then a credit balance would remain in the overhead control account and overhead would be *overabsorbed*. The question of how to dispose of the balance in the overhead control account—the amount that is over- or underabsorbed—is a particularly interesting one because it casts light on the relationship between "managerial" and "financial" accounting. Discussion of the issue will be postponed until Chapter 22, which deals with standard costs, so that it may be discussed as part of the broader question of how to account for all variances owing to management estimates and standards that are not met. Suffice it to say for now that many firms transfer the entire balance to an expense account, such as cost of goods sold,

but that it is preferable to prorate it among cost of goods sold and ending inventory.

PROCESS COSTING

Process costing is appropriate for mass production industries in which each unit of product is nearly identical. Because each unit is almost the same, there is no need to accumulate costs by job or batch. The total costs incurred in a period of time can be divided by the number of units produced, after accounting for partially completed goods in beginning and ending inventory.

Work in process	
Amount absorbed $5 × 820,000 d.l.h.	4,100,000

Suppose, for example, a production department in a chemical plant has an output of 10,000 gallons of solvent in a particular month. Costs are incurred as follows:

Direct materials	$35,000
Direct labor	20,000
Overhead (including costs allocated from other cost centers)	10,000
Total costs	$65,000

Cost per gallon of output would be $6.50, determined by dividing total costs incurred by total output—$65,000 divided by 10,000 gallons.

Process costing becomes considerably more complex when there are beginning or ending inventories that have been only partially completed and when labor and material are not added either concurrently or uniformly throughout the production process. For example, materials may be added first at the beginning of the production cycle but not again until the end; labor may be added uniformly throughout. It may be possible, therefore, for a product to be in differing stages of completion with respect to the different factors of production.

In order to account for goods that are partially complete, it is necessary to express production in terms of *equivalent* units. Equivalent units are the number of completed units that are the equivalent of some number of partially completed units. Two units that are each one-half complete are the equivalent of one that is fully complete.

Suppose that costs were, as in the previous example, $65,000. Assume this time that the firm completed and transferred to finished goods only 9,000 gallons. There was no work in process at the start of the year, but at year end 1,000 gallons remained in work-in-process inventory. These 1,000 gallons were 100 percent complete with respect to materials, but only 60 percent complete with respect to labor. One thousand gallons that are 60 complete are the equivalent of 600 units that are fully complete. With regard to labor, therefore, production of the period was 9,600 units; with respect to materials production was 10,000 gallons.

	Materials	Labor
Units completed and transferred to finished goods inventory	9,000 gal	9,000 gal
Units in inventory at year end	600[a]	1,000[b]
Total units to be accounted for	9,600 gal	10,000 gal
Less: Beginning inventory	-0-	-0-
Production during period (equivalent units)	9,600 gal	10,000 gal

[a] 1,000 gallons 60 percent complete.
[b] 1,000 gallons 100 percent complete.

Costs per unit can be determined by dividing costs incurred *for each factor* during the period by equivalent production *for that factor.* In process costing overhead costs are assigned in essentially the same manner as in job order costing with the exception that overhead need not be assigned to specific jobs. Based on estimates of costs and activity (most commonly direct labor hours or direct labor dollars) an overhead charging rate is calculated. For each unit of activity used by a production department, a fixed dollar amount of overhead is added to product cost. In this example, assume that overhead is assigned on the basis of direct labor dollars. It is estimated that direct labor for the year will be $240,000 and that total overhead will be $120,000. Thus, for each $1.00 of direct labor charged to work in process, $.50 of overhead will be charged. For computational purposes direct labor and overhead costs can be grouped together; they will be referred to as *conversion* costs. Per unit costs can be determined as follows:

	Materials	Conversion Costs
Costs incurred during period	$35,000	$30,000[a]
Equivalent units of production	10,000 gal	9,600 gal
Cost per unit	$3.50	$3.125

[a] Direct labor	$20,000
Overhead ($20,000 × $.50)	10,000
	$30,000

Per unit cost of each completed unit would be the sum of the materials and the conversion costs—$6.625. The $65,000 total costs incurred during the month may be divided between work still in process and that transferred to finished goods as follows:

	Work in Process	Transferred to Finished Goods	Total
Materials ($3.50 per gal)	(1,000 gal) $3,500	(9,000 gal) $31,500	$35,000
Conversion costs ($3.125 per gal)	(600 gal) 1,875	(9,000 gal) 28,125	30,000
Total	$5,375	$59,625	$65,000

This illustration is limited to a single processing department. Some products may have to be processed in two or more departments. In such situations, the accounting entries should reflect a transfer first from one department to another rather than directly to finished goods inventory. The goods transferred into a department are from the perspective of that department, raw materials, and they should be accounted for as such (although they may be labeled "goods transferred from other departments"). They should be stated initially at the total cost (both materials and conversion costs) assigned in the previous department.

In-process inventories and transfers to other departments or to finished goods may be accounted for by any one of the basic inventory methods. The weighted-average method is the most widely used, with a modified version of FIFO a distant second.

In summary, the essential difference between job order costing and process costing is that in job order costing the focus is on the individual job, whereas in process costing it is on the production department. In a job order system, costs are accumulated initially by department but then they are assigned to particular jobs. Unit costs are determined by dividing costs assigned to a particular job by the number of units in that job. In a process costing system, unit cost is determined directly; costs incurred by a department are divided by the number of units produced, taking into account any adjustments for partially completed units in beginning or ending inventory.

ALLOCATION

In the discussion of job order costing, we dealt with the means of *absorbing* or *applying* overhead costs of a production department into the actual product. This section is concerned with the *allocation* of overhead costs from one department or cost center to others. *Allocation* is the process of assigning overhead costs from service departments or cost centers to production departments. *Absorption* is the process of applying overhead costs from production departments to products. The distinction between absorption and allocation is set forth graphically in Exhibit 18-3. It will be our objective not only to indicate widely used techniques of allocation, but more importantly, to comment upon their objectives and limitations. The discussion will center on the allocation of costs from service departments to production departments. It could readily be generalized to the allocation of any common costs (e.g., home office costs) to the various operating units of a corporation or other type of organization.

Overhead costs may be initially incurred by, or assigned to, nonproduction cost centers because they cannot be associated directly with specific production centers. Indirectly, or course, they have been incurred to benefit production departments and, ultimately, the product itself. But there are often

EXHIBIT 18-3   *Allocation and Absorption*

Allocation

Assignment of Overhead Costs from Service Departments
(or Cost Centers) to Production Departments

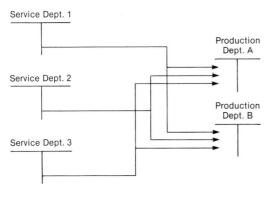

Absorption

Assignment of Overhead Costs from
Production Departments to Products

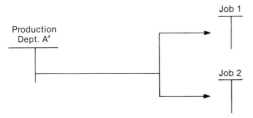

[a] Includes overhead costs of the department itself as
well as those allocated from service departments.

no clear-cut measures of benefits received.
Thus, there are also no self-evident bases
of allocation.

Objectives of Allocation

Allocation of costs may serve a number
of purposes. First, and most prominently,
allocation is a means of associating costs
with the revenues that they produce. The
matching principle requires that costs be
charged as expenses in the same accounting
period as the related revenues are realized.
This principle is applied when manufacturing
costs are held in inventory until point of sale
and then charged off as "costs of goods sold."
The matching principle implies that *all* manufacturing costs—indirect as well as direct—
be assigned to the product. If they are to be
assigned to products, then they must first be
assigned to the departments which produce
them.

Second, allocation may serve as a means
of motivating the employees of the production departments to assist in controlling overhead costs. If a department is charged for a
service on the basis of amount used, it is
likely that it will avail itself of the service
only when the benefits that it will receive
exceed their cost. But even if the department
is charged for a cost (such as air conditioning)
over which it may have no, or at best minimal
control, it may do its best to put pressure on
those departments which can influence the
magnitude of the cost. At the very least, cost
allocation serves to remind managers of the
various production departments that they
are receiving the benefits of a number of
activities and services being carried out on
their behalf.

Third, allocation may facilitate several
types of management determinations. Fore-
most among these are the selling prices of
the company's products. In a perfectly competitive market, a firm may be a price-taker;
it can sell only at the prevailing market price.
But in less than perfectly competitive markets, and particularly when a firm negotiates
contractual prices, product cost is an important element to be taken into account.

Nature of Overhead Costs

Two characteristics of overhead costs are
especially relevant to a determination as to

the most appropriate means of allocation. First, overhead costs may be classified as to degree of variability. Some overhead costs are fixed, having little or no relationship to level of activity. Examples are rent, depreciation of building and equipment, property taxes on plant, plant insurance, factory heat, air conditioning and light, most factory office costs, and many factory management costs (e.g., the salary of the plant manager). Others are, to some extent, variable. Indirect labor and supplies are typically influenced by volume. Machine maintenance and power costs are likely to be affected by machine usage, which in turn is affected by level of output. Fixed costs often provide basic operating capacity; they must be incurred for the firm to operate at even a minimum level of activity. Variable costs represent the portion of overhead costs that increases once the minimum level of activity has been exceeded.

Many types of overhead costs have both fixed and variable elements. A service department that repairs and maintains factory equipment must be sufficiently large to react to unforeseen equipment breakdowns. If the factory is to operate at all, the department must have the capability to provide assistance when called upon. But as volume increases, machines require greater amounts of maintenance and hence the costs incurred by service department increase.

The second characteristic of overhead costs that bears upon the appropriate means of allocation is that they may be classified by degree and source of control. Overhead costs may be controlled in two ways: by adjusting the quantity of service provided; by monitoring the efficiency by which it is provided.

The *quantity* of some overhead services is beyond the control of the firm, subject to minimal influence by the firm, or once established by company policy not subject to short-term fluctuations. In this category are heating and air conditioning, insurance, and building maintenance. The quantity of other services is subject to the control of the departments that benefit from them. Machine maintenance and repair service, for example, may be provided at the request of the various production departments. Purchasing services are rendered in response to requisitions of materials, supplies, or equipment. Personnel and payroll services are made available as new employees are added to the work force.

The *efficiency* with which services are provided is commonly under the control of the department that provides them. Given a specified or requested quantity of service, the costs of building maintenance, machine maintenance and repair, purchasing, and personnel services are dependent on the service departments rather than on production or beneficiary departments.

Guidelines for Overhead Allocations

There are two useful guidelines for the allocation of overhead costs. First, allocations should reflect benefits received. This can usually be accomplished by a two-step process: allocate fixed or capacity costs to the various departments in proportion to their long-range requirements for the service provided; allocate variable costs in proportion to actual usage.

Second, allocations should be made in such a way that the amount charged to a particular department does not vary from what is normal as a consequence of either (1) a change in quantity of service demanded by other departments or (2) a change in the efficiency with which the service is provided by the service department. Consistent with this guideline it is generally preferable to base allocations on *estimated* rather than *actual* overhead costs and to use different bases for allocating the fixed and variable components of the costs

Allocation of Fixed Costs

In allocating overhead costs, it is necessary to select a criterion by which to measure benefits received. For example, the benefits of building occupancy costs that are primarily fixed, such as rent, janitorial service, heat and air conditioning, and light, may be related to the number of square feet occupied. Suppose that monthly building occupancy costs in a plant are $12,000. There are three production departments: machining, assembling, and polishing. The number of square feet occupied by each of the departments and the resultant allocations based on square feet are as follows:

services received. Some bases for allocating variable costs (or the variable portion of costs that have both fixed and variable elements) are:

Type of Cost	Basis for Allocation
Power	Kilowatts consumed
Telephone (toll calls)	Actual billings
Machinery repairs (variable portion)	Number of machine hours
Purchasing Department services	Number of requisitions
Materials handling	Raw materials usage

If, for example, variable power costs are $.05 per kilowatt hour and a department uses 10,000 kilowatt hours in a period, then its

	Production Department			
	Machining	Assembling	Polishing	Total
Square feet	20,000	50,000	30,000	100,000
Percent of total	20%	50%	30%	100%
Share of cost ($12,000)	$2,400	$6,000	$3,600	$12,000

Some frequently used bases for allocating other overhead costs that are primarily fixed are:

Type of Cost	Basis for Allocation
Personnel	Number of employees, dollar amount of payroll
Warehousing	Number of square feet occupied
Machinery repairs (fixed portion)	Number of machines
Telephone service (basic charge)	Number of telephones

Allocation of Variable Costs

Where overhead costs are variable it is necessary to measure the actual quantity of

charge for power would be $500 (10,000 hours @ $.05).

Advantages of Dual Allocation Schemes Based on Estimated Costs

The desirability of dual allocations based on *estimated* rather than actual costs can be demonstrated by way of an illustration. A division of an insurance company has two main clerical departments. One is responsible for life insurance policies; the other, for pensions and annuities. Both rely on a central data processing service for computer support. The Life Insurance Department normally uses 240 hours per month of computer time; the Pensions and Annuities Department uses 160 hours. Monthly costs of operating the data processing center are:

Fixed costs	$24,000
Variable costs	$30 per computer hour

Total normal costs of operating the center are thus $36,000:

Fixed costs		$24,000
Variable costs (240 hours for the Life Insurance Department plus 160 hours for the Pensions and Annuities Department)		
400 hours @ $30		12,000
Total normal operating costs		$36,000

A dual allocation scheme based on estimated costs could assure that the allocation to each department is unaffected by fluctuations in volume or efficiency of other departments. The charge to each operating department for the fixed portion of the costs incurred by the service center would be that of providing the capacity to fulfill normal requirements. The allocation would be based on *estimated normal costs* of the service center and normal hours of service required by the operating departments. In the example at hand, normal fixed costs of the data processing center are $24,000. Inasmuch as the Life Insurance Department normally uses 60 percent (240 hours) of the services provided, its charge would be $14,400 (60 percent of $24,000). The Pensions and Annuities Department normally uses 40 percent (160 hours) of services provided; its charge would be $9,600 (40 percent of $24,000). The allocation of fixed costs would be constant from month to month, regardless of actual costs incurred by the service center or actual number of hours used by the operating departments.

The charge to each operating department for variable costs would be the normal incremental cost of providing an hour of service. In the example at hand, it would be $30 per computer hour. The *amount per hour* would remain constant regardless of the actual costs incurred by the service center.

Consider the amounts to be allocated to the two departments under three sets of circumstances.

1. Actual costs of the data processing center are normal ($36,000); computer hours used by each of the operating departments are also normal (Life Insurance Department, 240 hours; Pensions and Annuities Department, 160 hours).

In this case, since both actual costs and hours are as estimated, the costs allocated to each of the departments are in proportion to hours of service required and all costs are fully allocated.

2. Owing entirely to the inefficiency of the data processing center, its actual costs

	Life Insurance Department	Pensions and Annuities Department	Total
Allocation of fixed costs ($24,000)	$14,400	$ 9,600	$24,000
Allocation of variable costs ($12,000)	7,200[a]	4,800[b]	12,000
Total allocation	$21,600	$14,400	$36,000

[a] 240 hours @ $30.
[b] 160 hours @ $30.

are $38,000 instead of $36,000 as estimated. Computer hours used by each of the two operating departments are as expected. The allocation would be identical to that in situation 1. The amounts charged to both of the operating departments would be unaffected by the inefficiency of the service department. The amount ($2,000) representing the inefficiency of the service department would *not be allocated;* it would remain in the accounts of the service departments.*

3. Actual costs of the data processing department are less than normal ($34,800) owing entirely to decreased usage by the Life Insurance Department. The Life Insurance Department used 200 hours instead of 240 hours as anticipated. The Pensions and

mal, reflecting less than normal use of service. The reduction in its allocation is exactly equal to the amount saved by the data processing center: $1,200, which represents 40 hours at *variable* cost per hour of $30.

The dual allocation scheme results in charges to operating departments that reflect the benefits received. Each department is charged for the capacity that the service department makes available to it as well as for the actual services rendered. Once the capacity charge and the per-unit rate have been established, its share of costs is affected only by its demand for service. It is unaffected by the efficiency of the service department or the volume of service provided to other departments.

	Life Insurance Department	Pensions and Annuities Department	Total
Allocation of fixed costs ($24,000) based on normal hours and costs	$14,400	$ 9,600	$24,000
Allocation of variable costs ($14,800)—based on actual hours and standard cost per hour	6,000[a]	4,800[b]	10,800
Total allocation	$20,400	$14,400	$34,800

[a] 200 hours @ $30.
[b] 160 hours @ $30.

Annuities Department used 160 hours as expected.

The allocation to the Pensions and Annuities Department is the same as it would have been had total hours been normal; it is unaffected by changes in hours of service used by other departments. The allocation to the Life Insurance Department is less than nor-

* The unallocated balance could be analyzed and reported upon similarly to underabsorbed overhead: that is, prorated between cost of goods sold and ending inventory. The question of how to dispose of underabsorbed balances will be discussed in Chapter 22, which pertains to control.

Allocations Among Service Departments

In the discussion to this point, it has been assumed that costs of service centers could be allocated directly to production departments. Commonly, however, direct allocation would be inappropriate as service centers themselves render and receive services from other service centers. A maintenance department, for example, occupies space in a building and uses heat, air conditioning, and power. At the same time, it maintains and repairs the equipment that provides these services.

Many companies do, in fact, allocate costs directly from service centers to production departments and thereby ignore the services rendered among service departments. Alternatively, service department costs can be assigned using a step procedure. First, the costs of the department providing services to the greatest number of other service departments are allocated among all service departments and production departments. Then, the costs, including those which were just allocated to it, of the service department rendering services to the second greatest number of service departments are similarly allocated. The process continues until all service department costs are allocated. This step procedure takes into account services rendered by some service departments to others. But it is deficient in that it fails to give consideration to *reciprocal* relationships among service departments—those in which one service department both renders and receives services from another department. Insofar as the information requirements of a firm warrant such refinements, a firm can give recognition to reciprocal relationships by setting up and solving a series of linear equations in which the cost of each department is expressed as a proportional share of the costs of all other departments.

Limited Value of Allocations

One of the central themes underlying our discussion of management accounting is that in deciding among alternative courses of action, managers must distinguish between those costs that will change as the result of a particular action and those that will not. In using financial data that include costs that have been allocated from one department to another, there is substantial risk that costs that are fixed—and thus not subject to change—will be mistakenly classified as variable. This is because the costs may be variable from the perspective of a department, yet fixed from the standpoint of the firm at large. Consider a decision whether to abandon a particular production department. It may appear as if all costs of operating the department are, for purposes of this decision, variable. Included in the costs attributable to the department may be those, such as building occupancy costs, that have been allocated from other cost centers. Assume, for example, that the department's share of rent, heat, air conditioning, and light is $10,000. If the department is abandoned, the *department* would obviously "save" $10,000, but there may be no appreciable saving to the firm as a whole. The $10,000 in building occupancy costs would now have to be reallocated among the remaining departments in the plant.

Data that include allocations of cost must always be viewed as being tainted with arbitrariness. There is seldom a "correct" basis for allocations. Alternative allocation schemes may be equally logical yet yield dissimilar assignments of cost. Whereas allocations must be made for some purposes—e.g., product costs that are carried forward to external financial reports—they need not, and should not, be made for internally circulated reports unless they will indeed serve to facilitate the management decision for which the reports will be used.

Allocations for Advocacy

However limited may be their utility for many types of decisions made by managers, allocations are essential to a number of regulatory functions in our society in which outcomes are cost or income based. In the area of utility regulation, for example, rates are established at the level required to assure a fair return on investment. It is almost always necessary to determine the costs associated with providing service to a particular region, group of customers or class of service. Because many costs are common to two or more regions, groups, or classes, appropriate means of allocating the common costs must be devised. Similarly, in the field of taxation, levies may be based on the cost of products or on earnings within a particular jurisdiction. Again, costs must be allocated among products or jurisdictions.

Accounting data, presumably neutral and objective, are in fact the underlying cause of many disputes over taxes and regulated rates. Familiarity with the various means of allocating costs and knowledge of their limitations can serve as a potent weapon in the arsenal of those advocating a particular position. Consider several types of disputes in which allocations of costs are a central issue.

Established phone companies (e.g. the "Bell" companies) are facing increasing competition from upstart firms providing telephone services to commercial organizations, while at the same time they retain a near monopoly over residential services. It is to the advantage of the established companies to maintain relatively low rates for those services for which the competition is the greatest and to offset any lost revenues by increasing the rates on services for which competition is less intense. This can be accomplished by allocating a lesser proportion of common costs to business services and a greater proportion to residential services. At a number of rate hearings throughout the country representatives of consumer groups have asserted that the allocations of common costs to residential services are excessive, bearing no relation to the cost of providing these services; company representatives have countered by attempting to draw connections between costs assigned and services provided.

United Parcel Service is in direct competition with the U.S. Postal Service in the delivery of packages. It is in the interest of United Parcel Service that Postal Service rates for parcel post are set as high as possible. United Parcel Service consistently testifies before the Postal Rate Commision that the Postal Service improperly uses revenue from regular letters and other classes of business to subsidize its parcel mail. Central to its position is that the allocations of common costs to parcel service are improperly low.

A multinational corporation is taxed on earnings at higher rates in one country than in others. In an effort to reduce the reported earnings in the country with the high tax rates it allocates a disproportionately high share of common costs, such as home office costs, to that country. Tax officials of that country argue in favor of alternative allocation schemes that result in higher reported earnings.

A multidivision firm is engaged in collective bargaining with employees of one of its divisions. It asserts that it cannot yield to union demands because the division is "unprofitable." The extent to which they are "unprofitable," however, is a function of the amount of firm-wide costs charged to the particular division.

"DIRECT" COSTING

Generally accepted accounting principles require that product cost include all manufacturing overhead costs. The deficiencies, as well as the attendant opportunities for income manipulation, of this *full* or *absorption* costing "model", that assigns all overhead costs to units produced, can be appreciated by comparing it to *direct costing*. Direct costing is *not* an accepted alternative for general purpose reporting to the public. However, it is a means of presenting results of operations to internal management that provides substantially greater insight into cost behavior than does full costing.

Direct costing is a procedure whereby only *variable* costs are included in product cost. *All* fixed costs are classified as period costs and thereby carried directly to the income statement. Product cost under direct costing would include direct materials, direct labor, and the portion of overhead that is variable. As distinguished from full costing, it would exclude the portion of the overhead that is fixed. Fixed overhead, along with selling and administrative costs (costs which are also considered as period costs under full costing, regardless of whether fixed or variable) would be reported in the year incurred irrespective of when the products to which they relate are actually sold.

Direct costing remedies two primary deficiencies of full costing. First, it eliminates the need to allocate fixed overhead from one department to another and then to assign the overhead from the departments to the products. Such allocations and assignments, in that they are based on criteria that are within the choice of management, are necessarily arbitrary. Under direct costing, such allocations and assignments need not be made because all fixed costs are period costs and charged directly to earnings.

Second, direct costing eliminates fluctuations in product cost that are attributable to changes in volume. Under full costing, the cost assigned to each unit produced depends upon the number of units over which fixed costs can be spread. The greater the number of units produced, the less will be cost per unit.* As a consequence, management is able to reduce cost of goods sold, and thereby

* This is true even if overhead is assigned by means of a predetermined overhead burden rate because any under- or overabsorbed burden must be prorated among inventory and cost of goods sold.

increase reported earnings, in any single accounting period. It merely has to increase the volume of production. Even if sales decline, the decrease in cost per unit can cause income to increase. Under direct costing, by contrast, fixed costs do not enter into the determination of product cost; they are charged-off in full as they are incurred. Income, under direct costing, is driven entirely by sales. Assuming that selling prices, unit variable costs and total fixed costs remain constant, the only way to increase reported income is by increasing sales.

The example that follows compares income and ending inventory under full costing and direct costing. It covers a period of three years, one in which units produced equals units sold, one in which units produced exceeds units sold and one in which units produced are less than units sold.

Example

A firm manufactures a single product. Its books and records reveal:

Fixed manufacturing costs per year		$100,000
Variable manufacturing costs per unit		
Direct labor	$ 5	
Direct materials	4	
Variable overhead	3	
Total variable manufacturing costs per unit	$12	
Selling price per unit	$25	

Selling and administrative costs shall be ignored in this example as they are accounted for identically under both full and direct costing.

The Exhibit 18-4 indicates volume, costs, and inventory over the three-year period:

EXHIBIT 18.4

	Year		
	1	2	3
Sales volume (in units)	10,000	10,000	10,000
Production volume (in units)	10,000	18,000	2,000
Fixed costs (per above)	$100,000	$100,000	$100,000
Variable costs ($12 × production volume)	$120,000	$216,000	$ 24,000
Total costs (fixed costs + variable costs)	$220,000	$316,000	$124,000
Cost per unit produced under absorption costing (total costs ÷ production volume)	$22.00	$17.5556	$62.00
Ending inventory (in units)	-0-	8,000	-0-

Income and ending inventory under direct and absorption costing is shown in Exhibit 18.5

costing) also remains constant. When production exceeds sales, income is greater under absorption costing than under direct costing.

EXHIBIT 18.5

	Year		
	1	2	3
Direct Costing			
Income			
Sales @ $25	$250,000	$250,000	$250,000
Cost of goods sold (variable costs of $12 per unit)	120,000	120,000	120,000
Gross margin	$130,000	$130,000	$130,000
Fixed costs	100,000	100,000	100,000
Total income	$ 30,000	$ 30,000	$ 30,000
Ending inventory	$ -0-	$ 96,000[a]	$ -0-
Absorption Costing			
Income			
Sales @ $25	$250,000	$250,000	$250,000
Cost of goods sold	220,000[b]	175,556[c]	264,444[e]
Total income	$ 30,000	$ 74,444	$(14,444)
Ending inventory	$ -0-	$140,444[d]	$ -0-

[a] 8,000 units @ $12.
[b] 10,000 units @ $22.
[c] 10,000 units @ $17.5556.
[d] 8,000 units @ $17.5556.
[e] 8,000 units (from inventory) @ $17.5556 + 2,000 units @ $62.

Notice that because sales remain constant, income under direct costing (but not full

This is because under absorption costing a portion of the fixed costs is "stored" in inventory rather than charged in full against income. Correspondingly, when sales exceed production, income is less under absorption costing than under full costing because the fixed costs that were previously stored in inventory are now released and included in cost of goods sold. As with other circumstances in which there is a choice among accounting procedures, in the long run (in this case over any series of periods in which total sales are equal to total production) earnings will be the same under both direct and full costing.

A key advantage of direct costing from the perspective of managers is that it dovetails so naturally with cost–volume–profit analysis. Both contribution margin (sales less variable costs) and fixed costs are clearly set forth, and changes in earnings owing to changes in sales can readily be determined.

SUMMARY

One important function of an accounting system is to provide information on the cost of goods or services. Generally accepted accounting principles require that the cost of a unit of product—that to be matched with the revenue from sales—include not only those costs that can be directly associated with it, but also those that are common to other units of the same as well as different products.

If common costs are to be included in product cost then they must be assigned in a rational and systematic manner. There are, regrettably, no perfectly objective means by which to associate common costs with particular units of output. The product values which result from application of the procedures and techniques described in this chapter are no more objective than the bases of allocation which underlie them. Different companies, as well as different managers and accountants within the same company, could justifiably allocate similar costs by dissimilar means.

Reports that are used solely within a firm, as opposed to those intended for parties external to the organization, do not require that product costs include a share of common costs. Allocations need be made only when they serve to facilitate the decisions for which the reports will serve as information. Direct costing, as opposed to full or absorption costing, is a costing procedure whereby all fixed costs—those which are usually the least directly tied to units of output—are charged-off as period costs and thereby excluded from product cost.

Reports based on direct costing procedures are untainted by allocations of fixed costs and, at the same time, they set forth separately fixed costs and variable costs. They are, therefore, especially helpful to managers in conducting cost–volume–profit analysis.

EXERCISE FOR REVIEW AND SELF-TESTING

The Community Health Clinic must determine the cost of serving individual patients in order to obtain reimbursement from both private insurance companies and sponsoring government agencies. The clinic is divided into several patient-care departments, one of which is pediatrics. Direct costs of treating each pediatric patient are:

Physicians' salaries, per hour	$30
Nurses' salaries, per hour	10

Overhead costs of the *pediatrics* department for a *typical* month *excluding* allocations of costs of the clinic at large are:

Salaries of physicians and nurses applicable to activities other than patient care	$ 5,000
Depreciation of equipment	4,000
Supplies and medicines	3,000
Total	$12,000

In a typical month the payroll of physicians and nurses applicable to direct patient care in the pediatrics department is approximately $32,000.

All costs of the clinic that cannot be directly assigned to the patient-care departments are assigned initially to two cost pools; occupancy costs and administrative costs. The following information relates to the allocation of the costs in these pools:

	Occupancy Costs	Administrative Costs
Basis of allocation	Floor space	Fixed amount[a] + $1 per patient served
Cost incurred during month of June (same as estimated costs per month)	$5,000	$22,500[b]

[a] Based on proportion of estimated number of patients served per month.
[b] $15,000 in fixed costs + $7,500 in variable costs

	Pediatrices Department	All Other Patient-Care Departments
Amount of floor space	4,000 sq ft	16,000 sq ft
Number of patients served in June (same as estimated number of patients per month)	1,500	6,000
Allocation of fixed administrative costs ($15,000)	$3,000	$12,000

Overhead costs of the pediatric department (including allocations of occupancy and administrative costs) are assigned to individual "jobs" (i.e., patients) by way of a predetermined overhead charging rate. The overhead charging rate is applied on the basis of patient-care payroll dollars (i.e., salaries of physicians and nurses) and is determined by dividing estimated monthly overhead costs by estimated monthly patient care payroll dollars.

In the month of June, patient D. Short received 5 hours of physicians' services and 10 hours of nurses' services.

1. Allocation of at-large clinic costs to patient-care departments
   a. How much of the $5,000 in occupancy costs incurred in June should be allocated to the pediatrics department?
   b. How much of the $22,500 in administrative costs should be allocated to the pediatrics department?

2. Determination of overhead charging rate
   a. What would be the total estimated overhead costs of the pediatrics department, *including* its share of occupancy and administrative costs?
   b. What would be the predetermined overhead charging rate, based on $32,000 estimated patient-care payroll dollars?

3. Assignment of costs to a particular patient
   a. What would be the physicians' and nurses' costs assigned to D. Short?
   b. What would be the overhead costs assigned to D. Short?

4. Suppose that during the month of June, actual administrative costs of the clinic were $19,000 (instead of $22,500 as estimated) and actual patient-care payroll dollars were $35,000 (instead of $32,000 as estimated). How would these variances affect the dollar cost assigned to D. Short? Explain.

QUESTIONS FOR REVIEW AND DISCUSSION

1. What is overhead? Why can it not be applied to a product in the same manner as direct labor or direct materials?

2. Distinguish between *allocation* and *absorption* as the terms are commonly used in the literature of accounting.

3. What is the essential difference between job order and process costing? If a firm produces a

single product, all units identical to one another, which method would be most appropriate?

4. What is an *overhead charging rate?* What is the advantage of using a *predetermined* charging rate?

5. Under what circumstances would each of the following bases for an overhead charging rate be most appropriate:
a. Direct labor hours?
b. Direct labor dollars?
c. Machine hours used?

6. Suppose that a substantial portion of overhead costs was most directly associated with direct labor, but another equally substantial portion was most directly associated with direct materials. What would be the most appropriate basis for an overhead charging rate? Can the potential dilemma be resolved without conflict? At what price?

7. Many accountants aver that because of the arbitrary nature of the allocation process, little is accomplished by allocating service department costs to production departments. What purposes are, in fact, served by cost allocation?

8. What are the primary advantages of using a dual allocation scheme to distribute costs that have both a fixed and variable element?

9. In the "long-run" income as determined by direct or absorption costing will be the same. Under what circumstances will absorption cost income exceed direct cost income in a particular period? Under what circumstances will absorption cost income be less than direct cost income?

10. In a rate hearing before the utility commission of a northeastern state, representatives of a CPA firm engaged by the commission to undertake an independent study of costs testified that the cost to the electric company of providing electricity in that state was $.052 per kilowatt hour. The utility company serves a five-state area. The competence and integrity of the CPA firm is beyond dispute. Assuming that you are an attorney representing either the utility company seeking higher rates or a consumer group seeking lower rates, how could you impugn the cost figure provided by the CPA firm?

PROBLEMS

1. *Journal entries can serve to describe the flow of costs in a job order cost system.*

The data that follow relate to the manufacturing activities during May of Specialty Tools, Inc., and more specifically its finishing department. The firm uses a job order cost system to account for its production operations.
1. The finishing department incurred direct wage costs of $14,250. Of this amount $6,000 was applicable to job 168. Job 168 was started in May.
2. The department received from the assembly department partially completed goods that had an assigned cost of $12,760. Of this amount $9,000 was applicable to job 168.
3. The finishing department incurred the following overhead costs:

Indirect labor	$4,800
Supplies and materials (requisitioned from stores)	520
Depreciation	1,700
Total	$7,020

In addition, it was allocated $1,800 in overhead costs from other cost centers within the firm.
4. The finishing department completed job 168 and transferred it to finished goods inventory.

The finishing department assigned overhead to work in process and specific jobs by means of a predetermined charging rate based on direct labor dollars. At the start of the year it estimated that total overhead costs (including those allocated from other departments) would be $112,500 and that total direct labor dollars would be $187,500.

Prepare all journal entries suggested by the information provided as it applies to the finishing department.

2. *Unless a predetermined rate is used to apply overhead, product cost may be subject to wide fluctuations.*

Manfred Industries, Inc., manufactures two types of products, Product A and Product B. The firm estimates that in the current year overhead costs (all fixed) will be as follows:

Rent and other fixed occupancy costs	$ 300,000
Depreciation	180,000
Supervision	240,000
Indirect labor costs	540,000
Total overhead costs	$1,260,000

The firm also estimates that production of the two products will require a total of 360,000 direct labor hours.

The present wage rate per direct labor hour is $8. Each unit of Product A requires 20 hours ($160) of direct labor and $150 of direct materials. Overhead is applied on the basis of direct labor hours.

In a four-month period during the year, actual direct labor hours used in the manufacture of each of the two products were:

Direct Labor Hours

	June	July	August	September
Product A	20,000	20,000	10,000	20,000
Product B	10,000	10,000	10,000	15,000

In the same period actual overhead costs were as estimated, $105,000 per month ($1,260,000/12 months), with the exception of July, in which they were $150,000. Number of units of Product A manufactured was 1,000 per month, with the exception of August, in which only 500 were manufactured.

a. Assuming that the company applies overhead based on *actual* overhead costs and *actual* direct labor hours used, determine cost per unit of Product A during each of the four months.

b. Assuming alternatively that the company applies overhead by way of a *predetermined* overhead charging rate, based on *estimates* of overhead costs and direct labor hours to be used in the course of an entire year, determine cost per unit of Product A during each of the four months.

c. Unless a *predetermined* overhead charging rate is used to apply overhead to products, cost per unit of product is subject to wide fluctuations. Based on your responses to Parts a and b indicate three factors which, if different in magnitude than anticipated, would cause product cost to deviate from that which is expected.

3. *Alternative bases of overhead absorption may have substantially different impacts on the amount to be paid by a customer.*

A sporting goods manufacturer has agreed to produce 10,000 units of camping equipment for the Air Force at a price that will be determined, to a considerable degree, upon actual production costs.

The equipment to be sold to the Air Force is similar to that manufactured for sale through usual commercial channels, except that it is made of heavier and more durable materials. Comparative per unit labor and material costs of manufacturing the equipment are:

	For Commercial Use	For Military Use
Direct labor	$100	$100
Direct materials	600	900

The firm estimates that manufacturing overhead related to the equipment is approximately $4 million. It expects to produce a total of 20,000 units of the equipment—10,000 for the military and 10,000 for commercial sale.

a. In the past the company has used a predetermined overhead charging rate based on *direct material dollars* to apply overhead to the product. It intends to calculate costs of goods sold to the Air Force on the same basis. Determine per unit cost of equipment produced under the contract with the Air Force.

b. Air Force contract officers have argued that an overhead charging rate based on direct material dollars results in an allocation of costs that is unfair to the military. It asserts that the rate should be based instead on direct labor dollars. Determine the per unit cost of equipment sold to the Air Force based on the alternative charging rate.

c. How, in your opinion, should the difference be resolved? Under what circumstances can a rate based on materials as opposed to labor be justified?

4. *Some labor-related costs should be considered direct labor costs; others should be included in the pool of overhead costs.*

Precision Instruments, Inc., estimates that it will incur the following costs in the forthcoming year:

Direct labor	
(100,000 hours @ $19)	$1,900,000
Direct materials	2,500,000
Overtime premium	
(10,000 hours @ $9.50)	95,000
FICA (Social Security)	100,000
Pension contributions	114,000
Medical insurance	75,000
Vacation pay	130,000
Other overhead costs	800,000

The applicable FICA rate is 6.7 percent of wages to a maximum of $36,000 in wages.

Of the 100,000 hours of direct labor, 90,000 will be worked at the regular rate of $19; the remaining 10,000 at the overtime rate of $28.50. The overtime premium of $9.50 is charged to a separate overtime premium account. The firm's contribution to the employees' pension fund is, per union contract, a straight 6 percent of all direct labor costs (excluding overtime premiums). Medical insurance costs are approximately $1,400 per employee.

In the period December 27 to December 31, the firm began work on, and completed, job 56. The job ticket indicates the following charges:

Direct labor	400 hours
Direct materials	$16,700

Of the 400 hours worked on the job, 350 were paid at the overtime rate of $28.50, the remainder at the straight-time rate of $19. The overtime had been routinely planned. Job 56 was worked on during overtime hours only because it was scheduled for the end of the week when several employees had already worked the number of hours beyond which overtime pay is required. Inasmuch as all employees who worked on job 56 had already surpassed $36,000 in earnings, the firm was not required to make FICA payments on their behalf during December.

The firm bases its overhead charging rate on direct labor hours.

a. Determine an appropriate overhead charging rate based on estimated costs for the year. Should all labor-related costs except for direct labor be included in the overhead pool or should one or more be added to the direct labor rate? Explain.

b. Determine the cost, including overhead, of job 56.

c. In a sentence or two justify the way in which you accounted for both overtime premium and FICA.

5. *The key to process costing is the determination of equivalent units of production.*

Love Chemical has determined that the cost of producing Florex, under standard conditions, should be $4.90 per gallon.

Love uses a process costing system to account for chemical production.

Raw materials are added only at the start of the production process. There should be no waste or shrinkage of raw materials.

As of July 1, there was no work in process. During July the company put into production 600,000 gallons of materials at a cost of $2,400,000.

It used 25,000 hours of direct labor. Direct labor is charged at a rate of $14 per hour. Overhead is charged at a rate of $8 per direct labor hour.

During July the firm completed and shipped out 560,000 gallons of Florex. At month end, 40,000 gallons of Florex remained in work-in-process inventory. The Florex in process was 25 percent complete with respect to labor.

Did the company operate efficiently during July? How much greater or less were actual per gallon costs than standard costs?

6. *Partially completed beginning and ending inventories add a measure of complexity to process costing calculations.*

Note: This exercise goes beyond the discussion in the text. However, with the help of the "hints" provided, it should provide insight into process cost calculations when there are beginning and ending inventories.

Kalman Chemicals, Inc., uses a process cost system to account for the manufacture of Blue Dye 1.

As of June 1, 1984, the company had in process 4,000 gallons of dye. The dye was fully complete with respect to materials, but only one-fourth complete with regard to labor.

During the month of June, the company began work on, and added materials for, 60,000 gallons of dye. It completed and transferred to finished goods 58,000 gallons.

As of June 30, the company had in process 6,000 gallons of dye. The dye was fully complete with respect to materials and one-third complete with regard to labor.

Relevant cost data are as follows:

	Materials	Labor
Costs in beginning inventory	$ 8,000	$ 3,600
Costs added during month	110,000	168,000
Total costs to be accounted for	$118,000	$171,600

a. With regard to materials:
1. Determine the per gallon cost of materials added to production in June.
2. Determine the weighted-average cost per gallon of the dye transferred to finished goods and still in process at month end.

b. With regard to labor:
1. Determine the per gallon cost of labor added to production in June. *Hint:*
   (a) In addition to the gallons that were transferred to finished goods, what is the equivalent number of gallons in month-end work-in-process inventory that could be considered to have been produced during the month?
   (b) Of the goods that were transferred to finished goods, what is the equivalent number of gallons that were in beginning inventory and were thereby produced in a previous month?
2. Determine the weighted-average cost per gallon of the dye that was transferred to finished goods and still in process at month end. *Hint:*
   (a) What is the number of gallons that were transferred to finished goods?
   (b) What is the equivalent number of gallons that are in work-in-process inventory at month end?

c. Determine total (labor and materials) weighted-average cost per gallon of dye transferred to finished goods inventory.

7. *Under some allocation schemes the amounts charged to a unit will be affected by factors beyond its control.*

A municipal fire department is divided into two primary divisions: operations, which includes all firefighting activities, and support services, which includes fire prevention, education, maintenance, and training. In addition, there is a clerical pool which prepares routine reports for each of the two divisions.

Studies have indicated that the cost of operating the clerical pool is $3,500 per month plus $4 for each document prepared.

The operations division has estimated that it will require the preparation of an average of 270 documents per month in the forthcoming year. The support services division has estimated that it will require 360 documents per month.

The fire department is considering three schemes for allocating the costs of the clerical pool to the two primary divisions.

a. Each division will be charged with a pro rata share of *estimated* monthly costs based on an *estimate* of the number of reports that it will submit to the clerical pool. Thus, the charge to each department will be the same each month.

b. Each division will be charged with a pro rata share of *actual costs* of the clerical pool based on the *actual* number of reports submitted to the clerical pool by the two divisions.

c. Each division will be charged with a pro rata share of *estimated fixed* monthly costs (i.e., $3,500) of the clerical pool based on *estimated* number of reports and, in addition, with a variable charge based on *estimated* per report variable costs (i.e., $4) and *actual* number of reports submitted.

(a) Prepare a table in which you indicate the amount to be allocated to the operations division under each of the three allocation schemes and each of the following four sets of assumptions of actual numbers of reports and costs:

warehousing costs. With respect to factory office costs, some managers assert that they should be allocated on the basis of number of employees; others, on the basis of total payroll dollars. The mixer department has 30 percent of factory employees, but inasmuch as its employees are highly skilled,

	Number of Reports		
	Operations Division	Support Division	Costs Incurred by Clerical Pool
1. Number of reports and costs as estimated	270	360	$6,020[a]
2. Number of reports as estimated; clerical division inefficient	270	360	7,000
3. Operations division submits greater than estimated number of reports; clerical division efficient	300	360	6,140[b]
4. Support division submits fewer than estimated number of reports; clerical division efficient	270	330	5,900[c]

[a] $3,500 + 630($4).
[b] $3,500 + 660($4).
[c] $3,500 + 600($4).

(b) In light of your results, evaluate each of the three allocation schemes in terms of equity and desired motivational effects on the two divisions.

8. *In the view of many accountants and managers, allocations of service department costs are both arbitrary and unnecessary for most types of decisions.*

Appliance Industries, Inc., has a separate department devoted to the manufacture of heavy-duty kitchen mixers. The variable costs of producing mixers are:

Direct labor	$ 48
Direct materials	52
Variable overhead	50
Total variable costs	$150

Fixed overhead costs of the mixer department excluding the two allocated costs discussed below are $260,000.

Within the company there is disagreement as to the basis for allocating factory office costs and

it pays 40 percent of payroll dollars. Annual factory office costs are $400,000.

With regard to warehousing costs, some managers aver that the costs should be allocated on the basis of square footage occupied in the warehouse; others, on the basis of dollar value of goods stored. The mixer department occupies 20 percent of the square footage, but its goods account for 50 percent of the total dollar value. Annual warehouse costs are approximately $100,000.

The firm anticipates production volume of 10,000 units in the coming year.

a. Determine the total cost per mixer making four alternative assumptions as to the allocation of the office and warehouse costs (i.e., first office costs allocated one way and warehouse costs allocated each of the two ways, and then office costs allocated the other way and warehouse costs again allocated each of the two ways).

b. Suppose that the company was asked to enter into a contract with a retailer that required the sale of 2,000 mixers at a price of $191. The 2,000 units would be in addition to the 10,000 that the firm planned to produce. The company has the capacity to fulfill the contract and the production of the additional units would in no way affect the production volume or selling prices of mixers or other products that the firm manufactures. All fixed costs would similarly remain unchanged. Should the firm accept the contract assuming each of the four combinations of allocation bases? Explain.

c. Suppose that the firm faced a "purely" competitive market for the sale of its mixers. As a consequence, it had no influence over sales price. Its only decision would be as to the number of units to produce and sell. Do you think that bases of allocation should affect the firm's determination of how many units to produce and sell? Explain.

d. By what criterion should the firm select between alternative bases of allocation? What other information would you recommend that the decision maker try to obtain?

9. Can a department really incur a loss on a machine that is apparently profitable?

The manager of a clerical department would like to install a snack vending machine for the convenience of employees. He believes that it would serve to boost morale. The machine would be owned, stocked and maintained by a reputable vending service, which would pay the department a commission of $.04 for each item sold.

The machine, which measures 3 feet by 3 feet, would be placed in a corner which would otherwise be vacant. The manager estimates that approximately 5,000 items per year would be dispensed by the machine. Inasmuch as any "profits" would be contributed toward the annual company picnic the manager thought that the machine would serve the interests of the department. That is, until he discussed the idea with the company accountant.

The accountant pointed out that: (1) Occupancy costs are allocated to the various corporate departments at an annual rate of $12 per square foot. (2) The machine would inevitably require some attention on the part of the manager in the way of bookkeeping time and calls to the vending service when the machine was inoperable. He estimates that the manager would spend at least 10 hours per

year on matters pertaining to the machine. The salary of the manager is $40,000 per year; fringe benefits and related payroll costs amount to an additional $10,000 per year. The manager works an average of 2,000 hours per year.

a. Determine net income (or loss) as it would most probably be calculated by the accountant.

b. Based on financial considerations alone, do you think the department should install the machine?

10. Utility rates are severely affected by allocation basis.

Southwest Gas Co. serves a 12-county region in a southwestern state. Each municipality within that region has the authority to establish rates for the customers within its jurisdiction. The municipality of Burnt is presently holding hearings regarding the rates that it will charge. It has been generally agreed that the rates should be set so as to allow the company a return of 8 percent on assets. What is in dispute is the basis for allocating to Burnt both common costs and common assets. Burnt has no industry; virtually all of its customers are residential or small commercial establishments. As a consequence, the average consumption of gas per customer is substantially less than that for the entire 12-county region served by the company. Nearby municipalities are heavily industrialized and therefore have a number of customers who use many times more gas than the typical residential customer.

Southwest Gas Co. has provided the regulatory commission of Burnt with audited cost data. Costs and assets that are common to all customers within the 12-county area have been allocated to Burnt on the basis of its pro rata share of *number of customers*. Representatives of consumer groups assert, however, that the company's allocation of common costs and assets discriminates against the customers of Burnt. They aver that common assets and costs should be allocated on the basis of *share of gas used* rather than number of customers.

The regulator commission has been presented with the data that follow at the top of page 554. Amounts in parentheses indicate Burnt's percentages of totals. (MCF = thousand cubic feet.)

a. For each of the two alternative means of allocating common assets and costs, determine:

1. The total asset base of Burnt.

	Burnt	12-County Area Including Burnt
Number of customers	10,000 (5%)	200,000
Number of MCF consumed annually	960,000 (3.33%)	28,800,000
Value of assets that can be associated with specific jurisdictions	$3,000,000 (5%)	$60,000,000
Annual depreciation and other fixed costs that can be associated with specific jurisdictions	$600,000 (5%)	$12,000,000
Annual direct cost of gas ($1.50 per MCF)	$1,440,000 (3.33%)	$43,200,000
Value of assets that are common to all jurisdictions		$90,000,000
Annual fixed costs that are common to all jurisdictions		$48,000,000

2. The amount, based on the total asset base and the allowable earnings rate of 8 percent, that the company would be permitted to earn within Burnt.
3. The total costs that would be attributable to Burnt.
4. The total revenues that the company would be required to generate within Burnt.
5. The allowable rate per MCF.

b. Indicate briefly the primary arguments in favor of their positions that would be made by the representatives of both the company and the consumer groups.

11. *This problem illustrates the flow of costs from service departments to a particular job.*

The Ilan Co. has two service departments (Office and Materials Handling) and two production departments (A and B). At the start of 1984 it made the estimates shown below.

Overhead costs of the service departments are allocated as follows. First, the costs of the office are allocated to each of the other departments (including materials handling) on the basis of number of employees. Then, the costs (including those allocated from the office) of the materials handling department are allocated to the two

	Service Departments		Production Departments	
	Office	Materials Handling	A	B
Annual fixed costs (prior to allocations from other departments)	$80,000	$60,000	$200,000[a]	$18,000[a]
Variable costs	—	$40 per requisition received	$10 per d.l.h.[b]	$12 per d.l.h.[b]
Number of employees	5	10	22	18
Annual number of warehouse requisitions	—	—	500	300
Annual number of direct labor hours	—	—	25,000	20,000
Materials purchases (prior year)	—	—	$350,000	$450,000

[a] Fixed overhead traceable to the department.
[b] Variable overhead traceable to the department (d.l.h. = direct labor hour).

production departments. The fixed portion of the materials handling costs (including the share of office costs) are allocated on the basis of prior year purchases of materials. The variable portion is allocated on the basis of *actual* number of warehouse requisitions in a given month. Overhead costs of Department A are charged to specific jobs by means of a predetermined overhead charging rate. The rate is based on estimates of total annual overhead costs and direct labor hours.

a. Determine the overhead charging rate of Department A for 1984.
b. During February 1984 Department A was charged with 2,000 direct labor hours. It issued 40 warehouse requisitions. Actual fixed overhead costs traceable to the department (prior to allocations from the service departments) were $16,000. Department A's monthly share of the office department costs and the fixed portion of the materials handling costs is simply one-twelfth of its annual allocation (as calculated as part of the solution to item a).
   1. Determine the total overhead costs to be charged to the overhead account of Department A during February.
   2. Determine the amount of under- or over-absorbed overhead for the month.
c. During February Department A spent 150 direct labor hours on job 342. How much overhead should be charged to job 342?

12. Universities sometimes adopt overhead allocation schemes that appear especially arbitrary.

A large state university permits its component academic departments, bureaus and research institutes to enter into research contracts with outside organizations. Out of the negotiated price, the contracting unit must pay all direct costs pertaining to the project which it undertakes. In addition, however, it is charged by the university for "overhead." The charge is an amount equal to 60 percent of the direct wage and salary costs that will be incurred in fulfilling the contract.

The university maintains an office of "contract research," whose mission it is to assist the academic departments, bureaus and research institutes in obtaining and administering contracts. The cost of maintaining the office is approximately $200,000 per year. For the most part, however, the overhead for which the units undertaking contract research are charged represents costs that are incurred to carry out the traditional academic functions of the university—expenditures for buildings and grounds maintenance, libraries, laboratories, administration, athletic facilities, etc. Such costs are fixed; they are unaffected by any single contract research project.

Most contracts, particularly those with government agencies, are reimbursement-type agreements. A unit gets reimbursed for all costs, including overhead, that it incurs, but earns no "profit." Some contracts, however, are for a negotiated amount that provides for payments in excess of costs incurred. When such contracts are entered into, the unit performing the research is permitted to retain the excess of revenues over costs and use it to supplement university budget allocations. The primary motivation of conducting contract research is that it provides funding for projects that faculty and research associates want to conduct but which otherwise would have no financial support.

In recent years the contract value of sponsored research was $20 million.

Critically evaluate the policy of the university of imposing a charge for overhead.

a. What do you think are the primary purposes of the charge?
b. What effect do you think it has on the motivation of the various units to conduct research? On the ability of the units to obtain research contracts?
c. How do you think the 60 percent amount was arrived at?
d. What objections might be raised to the policy?
e. What are alternatives to the policy?

13. The costs of a corporate consulting department should be allocated in a manner that is equitable and that encourages efficient distribution of its services.

A multidivision corporation operates an internal consulting department. The department was organized for two primary reasons. First, it was recognized that many units within the organization were not operating at maximum efficiency and could thereby benefit from consulting services. Second, numerous units were continually spending large sums of money to obtain the services of outside management consulting firms. It was calculated, after extensive cost–benefit analysis, that the use of outside firms was sufficiently great that considerable savings could be effected by hiring consultants directly rather than paying their salaries (plus a premium) indirectly via a consulting firm.

The consulting department provides services in two ways. First, either on its own initiative or upon request of corporate management it surveys selected operations of the firm. It reports its finding to corporate management and, at the same time, advises division managers as to how their operations could be improved. Second, upon request of division managers, it undertakes specific consulting projects (e.g., assisting in instituting a computerized reporting system).

The budget for the consulting department has been established by corporate management at $1,500,000 per year. It is able to provide approximately 30,000 hours of consulting services.

On what basis do you think the costs of the consulting department should be allocated to the divisions that it serves? Be sure to take into account the objectives of the consulting department and the influence that any allocation scheme might have on the ability of the consulting department to fulfill its objectives.

14. *Direct costing facilitates cost–volume–profit analysis.*

A firm prepared the following income statement, which is based on *direct costing:*

Sales		$1,350,000
Variable costs		
Manufacturing	$750,000	
Selling	150,000	900,000
Contribution margin		$ 450,000
Fixed costs		
Manufacturing	$300,000	
General and		
administrative	170,000	470,000
Loss		$ 20,000

During the period the firm produced 20,000 units and sold 15,000 units.

a. How many units would the firm have to sell in order to earn a profit equal to 10 percent of sales revenue? Assume that production will equal sales.

b. Recast the income statement to one based on absorption costing.

c. Could the answer to part a have been derived solely from the absorption cost statements and the information on number of units sold and produced? Explain.

d. Determine end-of-period inventory that would be reported under both absorption costing and direct costing. Is the difference between the two amounts equal to that between the difference in reported earnings?

15. *Direct costing generally provides better guidance for management control.*

The president of a manufacturing concern has accused the vice-president for production of inefficiencies within his department. He has just received financial reports for February and they indicate a $5,000 deficit for the month as opposed to an anticipated $35,000 surplus. Since sales as well as general and administrative costs were as budgeted, he concluded that the fault must lie with the production department.

Upon investigation, the vice-president for production was provided the report shown on the top of the next page.

The financial statements that the president examined were prepared on a full-cost basis. Production for the month was less than budgeted because, owing to a severe snowstorm, the president had ordered the manufacturing plant closed for a few days.

a. Prepare a statement of income—as it was likely presented to the president—on a full-cost basis.

b. Recast the statement as it might have been prepared on a direct costing basis.

c. Was the production department inefficient during February? Explain. Which set of financial statements provides greater insight into the nature of the variance in costs from what was budgeted?

16. *Direct costing has obvious advantages over absorption costing; why then is it not "generally accepted" for purposes of external reporting?*

Electro-Games, Inc., began operations in 1981. In that year, it produced 1,000 electronic games, but its first shipments were not until the following year. Production, sales and year-end inventory

	Actual	Budgeted
Sales (5,000 units @ $150)	$750,000	$750,000
Production (in units)	4,000 units	5,000 units
Fixed manufacturing costs	$248,000	$250,000
Variable manufacturing costs	$272,000	$350,000
General and administrative costs	$115,000	$115,000
Beginning of month inventory (1,000 units, each of which included direct manufacturing costs of $70 and fixed manufacturing costs of $50)	$120,000	$120,000

(in units) for a four-year period were:

	Production	Sales	Year-End Inventory
1981	1,000	-0-	1,000
1982	1,000	1,000	1,000
1983	1,500	1,250	1,250
1984	250	1,500	-0-
Total for four years	3,750	3,750	

Production was curtailed for several months in 1984 owing to a labor dispute.

Fixed manufacturing costs during each of the four years were $100,000. Variable manufacturing costs were $300 per unit. Sales price per unit was $500.

a. Determine earnings and year-end inventory (in dollars) during each of the four years under:
   1. Direct costing
   2. Absorption costing
   Omit consideration of nonmanufacturing costs, as they will be accounted for the same under both methods. The firm maintains inventory on a FIFO basis.
b. Under which of the two methods is income most responsive to sales volume?
c. Suppose that a company attempts to artificially inflate reported earnings of a particular year by producing more units than it sells. Under which of the two costing methods would the scheme be effective? Explain.
d. In your opinion, which of the two methods results in the better match of costs with revenues? Explain, with reference to your calculation in Part a.

SOLUTIONS TO EXERCISE FOR REVIEW AND SELF-TESTING

1. a. The pediatrics department occupied 20 percent (4,000 of a total of 20,000 square feet) of the floor space of the clinic. It would be charged with 20 percent—$1,000 of the occupancy costs.
   b. The charge for administrative costs would be $3,000 plus $1 for each of the 1,500 patients typically served—a total of $4,500.

2. a. Total overhead costs of the pediatrics department

Overhead directly attributable to pediatrics department (given)		$12,000
Overhead allocated from other cost pools		
Occupancy costs	$1,000	
Administrative costs	4,500	5,500
Total overhead costs		$17,500

   b. The overhead charging rate would be

$$\frac{\text{Estimated overhead costs (per part a)}}{\text{Estimated patient-care payroll dollars}}$$

$$= \frac{\$17,500}{\$32,000} = \$.5469$$

3. a. Physicians' and nurses' costs assigned to D. Short

Physicians (5 hours @ $30)	$150
Nurses (10 hours @ $10)	100
Total direct patient-care costs	$250

b. Overhead costs assigned to D. Short

Total direct patient-care payroll dollars assigned to D. Short	$ 250
Overhead charging rate	× .5469
Overhead assigned to D. Short	$136.73

The total cost of services provided to D. Short would be $250 + $136.73 = $386.73.

4. A deviation of overhead costs or volume from those estimated would have no effect on the amount charged to any particular patient (or job) because the overhead absorbed is based on the predetermined rate. Indeed, the very purpose of using a predetermined rate is to avoid variations in "product" cost owing to fluctuations in either overhead costs or "production" volume.

Budgeting 19

This chapter is directed to budgeting. A budget is a quantified plan of organizational activities. Effective budgeting is a key to successful management, for the budget is the primary instrument of planning and control. The budget reflects virtually all management decisions having financial consequences. It serves as the benchmark by which the progress of the organization in achieving its objectives is measured. The term "budgeting" is sometimes used synonomously with *profit planning.**

Budgets can be executed for the organization in its entirety or for any of its component units. They may encompass all activities or only specific types of revenues or expenditures. A *master* budget is a comprehensive plan comprising a series of related schedules, each of which focuses on a particular function or phase of activities. A master budget will be illustrated later in this chapter. A *capital* budget is a program for the acquisition of long-term assets, including plant, buildings, equipment, and other companies. Capital budgeting will be discussed in Chapter 21. A *cash* budget indicates anticipated receipts and disbursements.

The time period covered by budgets, as well as the length of the segment into which they are divided, reflect management's planning horizon for the decisions at hand. Capital expenditure budgets, in that they indicate major acquisitions that have to be planned for years in advance, may extend for five years or more and may be segmented into periods as long as a year. Long-range cash budgets, which must

---

* In Chapter 17 we set forth as a theme of this section of the text, "only cash, not income, matters." In this chapter we refer to "profit planning" and suggest that maximization of profit is the primary objective of most commercial entities. The apparent contradiction is eliminated when it is recognized that as the length of the measurement period increases the difference between net cash inflow (excluding owner contributions and withdrawals) and net income approaches zero. Indeed, over the life of an enterprise net income is equal to the difference between the cash the owners withdrew from the business and that which they contributed.

be closely coordinated with capital expenditures, may cover correspondingly long periods. Short-term cash or production budgets, which by contrast are used to plan and control activities for which there are short lead times, may cover quarters or months and contain projections by weeks or even days.

Because a year is the typical operating cycle, master budgets usually cover a period of a year. Some firms make it a practice to revise their one-year budgets each month, dropping off the month just ended and adding the month one year out.

The budgeting process serves at least five primary functions:

First, it provides a means of developing and expressing organizational objectives.

Second, it facilitates the allocation of organizational resources.

Third, it allows the organization to formulate and communicate its plans for realizing its objectives. Concurrently, it promotes coordination of the activities in which it engages.

Fourth, it encourages increased productivity and other forms of behavior that are in the interests of the organization.

Fifth, it establishes the criteria by which the performance of individuals as well as organizational units will be judged.

The first four of these functions will be discussed in this chapter. The last will be dealt with in Chapter 22, pertaining to control.

THE BUDGET AS AN EXPRESSION OF OBJECTIVES

Although budgeting is often seen as little more than a perfunctory exercise in accounting intended to fulfill "paperwork" obligations, it provides an opportunity for an organization (or any of its subunits) to engage in periodic self-examination. In order to plan and allocate resources an organization and its managers must consider what it is they are planning for and what it is that should be accomplished by the resources that will be expended.

Limitations of Profit Maximization as an Objective

The explicit goal of most corporations or other profit-oriented enterprises is generally that of maximizing income—of ultimately returning to their owners more cash than they contributed. The objectives of both the subunits of an entity as well as the individual managers and employees may, however, be quite different from that ascribed by top management to the organization as a whole. It is a challenge to both managers and accountants to recognize potential differences—even conflicts—in goals and to design systems of budgeting and performance measurement that encourage the subunits and individual employees to act and make decisions that are consistent with the stated goal of profit maximization.

Profit maximization is not generally the objective of a subunit of a corporation because the subunit is unlikely to be a *profit center*. Its objective may be to maximize or minimize one or more elements of profit, but not profit per se. A *profit center* is a unit of an organization that has responsibility for both revenues and expenses and can be evaluated on the basis of profit earned. In practice, relatively few components of a corporation have complete responsibility for both revenue and expenses. Those that come closest are usually major divisions of conglomerates. But even seemingly autonomous divisions seldom have control over *all* expenses that enter into the determination of profit. It is unusual, for example, for divisions to have the authority to acquire long-term capital independently. Thus, they have but limited influence on the cost of capital (e.g., interest) or the quantity or quality of the fixed assets. As component units get smaller and more specialized (e.g., production centers, sales divisions, or service departments) the number of profit elements over which they have control is likely to be further reduced. A production department is generally concerned with output; it has substantial influence over manufacturing costs but little over selling prices or sales effort. A sales division can control selling prices and marketing programs, but may have little impact on production costs or product design.

It is convenient, yet simplistic, to assume that the purpose of every corporate subunit or activity is to "maximize profit." While it may be true that, from the organization as a whole, all activities should be intended to enhance long-term profitability, the impact of some activities on overall profitability is so indirect that profitability cannot adequately serve as an *operational* or workable objective. The objectives of accounting, legal, personnel, advertising, and stockholder relations departments are all, in some way, related to profit maximization. But the day-to-day—or even year-to-year—performance of none of these departments can meaningfully be evaluated in terms of contribution to profit. Characteristic of each of these departments is the need to express its objectives in terms of output that can be quantified and measured.

In this regard, the problems of management accounting in corporations are remarkably similar to those in not-for-profit organizations. Many nonprofit organizations never seriously consider what it is they are seeking to accomplish. To be sure, they may have goals that are as vague as they are noble, e.g., "to improve the quality of life" within a particular area of human endeavor. Such statements of purpose are not *operational*. They fail to imply standards of accomplishment. As a consequence, they cannot serve as a basis for comparing the benefits to be achieved by alternative courses of action or for measuring the extent to which they have been realized. Both types of organizations must decide where it is they want to go before they can determine the best route to take or periodically assess whether they have made progress in getting there.

LINK BETWEEN GOAL SETTING AND BUDGETING

Although it has been averred that a firm must establish its objectives before it can prepare a budget that reflects those goals, goal-setting and budgeting are, in fact, integrally linked. The wherewithal of a firm both to pursue and to achieve its objectives is dependent on the availability of resources and the competing demands on them. Suppose, for example, a successful brewer sets as an objective diversification into products and services other than beer (as Anheuser-Busch did in the late 1970s). It considers acquiring corporations in other industries, developing new products such as soft drinks and snack foods, and constructing "educational parks" which feature rides and amusements tied to a particular theme such as Sesame Street.

The transformation of the strategic goal, that of diversification, from a broad statement of aspirations to targets which the management of the firm can strive to accomplish, must be carried out within the constraints of the corporate budget. A long-term budget will indicate the sources and the amount of resources that can be directed toward the objective and will determine, to a great extent, the form that the diversification efforts will take. Whether or not, for example, the firm should, in fact, seek out new ventures depends very much on the return that existing products will generate in comparison to those which can be expected from the new lines of business, the amount of new investment that they will require and the funds that they make available for diversification. At the same time, of course, the corporate goals affect corporate plans as reflected in the budget. Budgeting and goal-setting are interactive processes; neither can be separated from the other. The budget must incorporate projections of revenues and expenditures. Insofar as the difference between the two is less than the firm's profit objective, then means must be developed to either increase revenues or reduce expenditures. As a consequence, the budget serves as an effective catalyst for creative thinking about new products, markets, production methods, administrative procedures, and financial policies.

THE BUDGET AS A MEANS OF ALLOCATING RESOURCES

In any organization there are competing demands upon limited resources. Factions of managers believe that funds should be directed to projects or activities in which they have a special interest. At the same time there are often automatic claims upon a sizable proportion of resources. To the extent that a firm establishes a sales target for a particular product, for example, the funds required to satisfy production demands must be provided. There are inevitably, however, some resources for which different divisions or departments must contend with one another. The ultimate allocation of funds is the consequence of pleadings by, and

negotiations among, responsible managers. The resultant budget, therefore, may be seen as very much of a political document.

The political nature of the budget, in an extreme form, can be appreciated by considering the budgetary process in a governmental organization, such as a municipality. In contrast to business organizations, which are to a considerable extent controlled by the forces of the "market," government organizations are regulated by their budgets. By way of the budgetary process municipality officials determine how much revenue the municipality will receive (e.g., they establish tax rates) and what will be its sources. They decide on the types and levels of services to be provided and the extent to which they will be funded. Whereas the revenues and expenditures incorporated in the budget of a business organization may only be estimates subject to the vicissitudes of the market, those settled on in the budget of a government organization can be backed by the authority of law. The revenue estimates see expression as enforceable tax levies; the expenditure estimates take the form of mandates from which little deviation may be permitted.

The similarity between business and government organizations with regard to budgeting should not be overlooked. Ultimately, of course, it is expected that each dollar expended by a business will provide a return. The budgetary process is designed to allocate resources to the activities from which the return per dollar will be the greatest. Insofar as the ultimate return associated with expenditures can be determined with reliability, the criteria for allocation in businesses are considerably more concrete and objective than those in nonbusiness organizations. There are, however, any number of projects undertaken or activities carried out by a business in which the association with profit is so tenuous as to limit the utility of the return criterion. Funds expended on new office complexes, institutional advertising, legal services, public relations, and executive perquisites are expected to operate to the ultimate benefit of the firm. The extent to which they will succeed, however, defies measurement or even estimate. Thus, the amounts allocated to these projects or activities owe more to the persuasiveness and stature of the parties who have a vested interest in them than to their ability to meet quantitative tests of financial return. The ultimate budget, therefore, like that of the government organization, is as much the product of internal political processes as of objective techniques of profit maximization.

THE BUDGET AS AN OPERATIONAL PLAN

The budgeting process enables the firm to set forth specifically how it intends to realize its objectives and to coordinate the various activities that it will be required to carry out. The process helps to assure that there will be goods on hand to satisfy projected sales, that there will be cash available to make required payments, that plant and equipment will be adequate to sustain the planned production, that the advertising and marketing strategies are consistent with anticipated sales, and that administrative and sales staffs are capable of supporting the forecasted sales and production.

FORMULATING THE REVENUE OBJECTIVE

In business organizations, the key target that must be established is sales revenue. To a great extent, once sales revenue is determined, the other variables that affect profit can be determined as a function of sales.

Developing targets, be they for revenues or expenditures requires concurrent consideration of what will be and what should be. Management must first forecast revenues or expenditures in the context of a given set of conditions and management policies. It must then determine if and how the firm can alter those conditions and policies so that the resultant revenues or costs will allow for the overriding profit objective to be met.

Sales forecasting is complex. Each of the broad categories of forecasting techniques that are indicated in the discussion that follows can be used independently; it is generally preferable, however, that they be used in conjunction with one another.

1. *Economic models.* Economic models are sets of equations representing selected segments of the economy. They are most useful in providing initial guidance as to future sales, especially in those industries which are affected by general economic conditions, such as automobiles, steel, and housing. In the automobile industry, for example, economic models have been used to forecast with considerable accuracy the total number of cars that will be sold in the United States. Inasmuch as there are but a small number of domestic producers and each firm's share of the total market is predictable, each company can estimate its own most likely sales volume. The use of economic models need not, however, be limited only to giant firms. Firms that supply parts or services to the automobile manufacturers usually find that their revenues are tied directly to automobile sales. As a consequence, the models are as relevant to them as they are to the automobile manufacturers. Only a relatively few firms are of sufficient size to justify a full-time staff of economists;

smaller firms can obtain the benefits of economic models by engaging the services of consulting economists.

2. *Statistical techniques.* Statistical procedures, such as regression and correlation analysis, can also be used to project sales. These techniques, which were discussed briefly in Chapter 17 with respect to behavior of costs, relate sales to the factors which cause them to vary. Some of these variables may be external to the company and beyond its control. Examples are economic factors, such as personal income, the level of unemployment and the level of consumer prices; the marketing efforts of competitors; and sales of products for which those of the company are either complements or substitutes. Other variables may be within the control of the company, such as advertising dollars and selling prices.

3. *"Ground-up" forecasts.* Sales forecasts based on either economic models or statistical techniques are commonly developed by staff departments associated with high levels of management. The more traditional and, in the view of many, still the more reliable means of projecting sales is by combining forecasts from field representatives. Individual sales persons who are the most familiar with their territories will indicate the sales volume that they believe they are capable of generating. Their estimates, modified by managerial judgments as to the extent to which salespersons are overly optimistic or cautious (perhaps out of reluctance to commit themselves to estimates to which they might later be held accountable), will be combined into district, regional, and eventually national forecasts. One advantage of this approach is that it benefits from the judgments of persons who, by being close to those who will make the purchasing decisions, have a sense of the market that may be lacking in those at corporate headquarters. Another is that it

involves in the budgetary process the parties that will be required to fulfill the forecasts that are included in the budget. Budgets are widely perceived as a means of pressuring employees to meet targets imposed by higher levels of management. This feeling can be alleviated, at least in part, by widespread and genuine contributions to the budget by those who will be required to carry it out.

FORMULATING EXPENDITURE TARGETS

Variable expenditures are, by definition, a function of volume. Hence, once revenue forecasts are made and translated into units of output, the procedures described in Chapter 17 in the section regarding cost behavior can be employed to project variable costs. The budget process, however, provides the opportunity to review the historic relationships between cost and volume to see if cost reductions are feasible. By contrast, many types of fixed costs are discretionary; management determines the level of service for which it is willing to pay. Maintenance, clerical, advertising, and supervisory costs are within this category. The budgetary process is a means by which management can consider explicitly the levels of service that are optimum and, at the same time, examine ways in which the costs of obtaining the required services can be held to a minimum.

EXAMPLE OF THE BUDGETARY PROCESS

The example that follows is meant to illustrate the general approach to planning sales, production, income, and cash receipts and disbursements. The schedules presented can properly take any number of forms and it should not be inferred that the forms shown are necessarily the most preferable. Each

EXHIBIT 19-1

Town Lake Industries
Expected Statement of Position
January 1, 1984

Assets		
Cash		$ 2,450,000
Accounts receivable		1,800,000
Inventory—raw materials for product 101:		
97,000 lb @ $1.10 = $106,700		
raw materials for product 202:		
101,000 lb @ $1.30 = $131,300		238,000
Inventory—finished goods of product 101:		
60,000 units @ $13 = $780,000		
finished goods of product 202:		
20,000 units @ $21 = $420,000		1,200,000
Plant and equipment	$10,000,000	
Less: Accumulated depreciation	4,000,000	6,000,000
Total assets		$11,688,000
Liabilities and owners' equity		
Accounts payable		$ 1,400,000
Owners' equity		
Common stock	$ 5,000,000	
Retained earnings	5,288,000	10,288,000
Total liabilities and owners' equity		$11,688,000

may be viewed as a summary of more detailed plans. Worthy of special note in the example is the extent to which it incorporates many of the principles of both financial and managerial accounting that have been discussed throughout this text. The budgeting process as illustrated begins with the balance sheet as it is expected to appear at the start of the period for which the plan is being formulated and concludes with one for the end of the period. The manner in which the two are linked together by the intermediate schedules is tribute to the simplicity, order and logic of the double-entry accounting model.

The time frame of the illustrated budget is one year—a typical period for a comprehensive budget. In practice, however, many of the schedules would be broken down by quarter or month. The detailed estimates are omitted from the illustration in order to focus on the relationships among the several schedules. For examples of more complete schedules the reader is referred to a comprehensive text on budgeting.*

Town Lake Industries manufactures two products, 101 and 202. Exhibit 19-1 is its balance sheet as management *expects* it to appear at the start of 1984.

THE SALES BUDGET

The sales budget indicated management's projection of sales. It requires estimates of

* See, for example, Glenn A. Welsch, *Budgeting: Profit Planning and Control* (Englewood Cliffs, N.J.: Prentice-Hall, Inc., 1976).

SCHEDULE I

Estimated Sales for 1984

	Unit Price	Total Units	Total Dollars
Product 101	$22.00	480,000	$10,560,000
Product 202	28.00	360,000	10,080,000
Total			$20,640,000

unit selling prices and number of units to be sold. It may reveal sales by regions or major categories of products. Schedule I represents a sales budget in summary form.

PRODUCTION BUDGET

Production plans are derived from the sales budget. The number of units that the firm will produce depends on expected sales, the number of units on hand at the start of the period, and the number of units that the firm considers necessary to have in stock at the end. Assume that management estimates its end-of-year required stock to be approximately one month's sales, i.e., 40,000 units of product 101 and 30,000 units of product 202. Schedule II.A indicates required production.

Once the number of units to be produced has been determined, then the cost of production can be calculated. The standard for

direct labor is as follows:

Product 101   .5 hour @ $16 — $ 8.00
Product 202   .8 hour @ $16 — $12.80

Schedule II.B reveals estimated outlays for direct labor.

The standard for raw materials is as follows:

Product 101   3 lb @ $1.10 = $3.30
Product 202   4 lb @ $1.30 = $5.20

Management estimates that ending inventory of raw materials should be approximately one month's supply—115,000 lb for product 101 and 123,000 lb for product 202. Schedule II.C summarizes raw material requirements.

Schedule II.D indicates predicted overhead costs (all assumed) and the resultant overhead charging rate.

Schedule II.D focuses on anticipated overhead costs at but a single level of activity. Whereas a schedule of this type may be useful

SCHEDULE II.A

Number of Units to be Produced

	Product 101	Product 202
Sales (per sales budget)	480,000	360,000
Add: Required ending inventory (per discussion)	40,000	30,000
Total requirements	520,000	390,000
Less: Beginning inventory (per January 1, 1984, balance sheet)	60,000	20,000
Number of units to be produced	460,000	370,000

SCHEDULE II.B

Direct Labor Cost

	Product 101	Product 202	Total
Units to be produced (per Schedule II.A)	460,000	370,000	
Hours per unit (per discussion)	× .5	× .8	
Required hours	230,000	296,000	526,000
Cost per hour	× $16.00	× $16.00	× $16.00
Direct labor cost	$3,680,000	$4,736,000	$8,416,000

SCHEDULE II.C

Raw Material Required to Be Used and Purchased

	Product 101		Product 202		
	Units	Dollars @ $1.10 per lb	Units	Dollars @ $1.30 per lb	Total Dollars
Units to be produced	460,000	—	370,000	—	—
Pounds per unit (per discussion)	× 3	—	× 4	—	—
Manufacturing requirements	1,380,000	$1,518,000	1,480,000	$1,924,000	$3,442,000
Add: Required ending inventory (per discussion)	115,000	126,500	123,000	159,900	286,400
Total requirements	1,495,000	$1,644,500	1,603,000	$2,083,900	$3,728,400
Less: Beginning inventory (per January 1, 1984, balance sheet)	97,000	106,700	101,000	131,300	238,000
Required purchases	1,398,000	$1,537,800	1,502,000	$1,952,600	$3,490,400

SCHEDULE II.D

Overhead Costs and Charging Rate

Supplies	$ 200,000
Indirect labor	1,500,000
Depreciation	1,100,000
Insurance and local taxes	150,000
Building occupancy costs	180,000
Other costs	26,000
Total overhead costs	$3,156,000
Number of direct labor hours (per Schedule II.B)	÷ 526,000
Overhead charging rate	$ 6.00

in planning overall expenditures and in calculating the overhead charging rate, it is of limited value in controlling expenditures and in evaluating deviations from plans. Unless actual volume is exactly equal to that budgeted, the schedule provides no insight into the amount that overhead costs "should be." To facilitate the control function, a *flexible* budget—one that distinguishes between fixed and variable overhead costs (to be described in Chapter 22)—is required.

Schedule II.E combines the direct labor, direct materials, and overhead costs to

SCHEDULE II.E

Unit Cost of Goods Manufactured

	Product 101	Product 202
Direct labor		
.5 hour @ $16	$ 8.00	
.8 hour @ $16		$12.80
Direct materials		
3 lb @ $1.10	3.30	
4 lb @ $1.30		5.20
Overhead ($6.00 per direct labor hour		
as indicated in Schedule II.D)		
.5 hour @ $6.00	3.00	
.8 hour @ $6.00		4.80
Unit cost of goods manufactured	$14.30	$22.80

arrive at the cost per unit of goods manufactured.

COST OF GOODS SOLD

Once manufacturing costs as well as beginning and ending inventory levels have been projected, then cost of goods sold can be calculated. Schedule III illustrates the computation of cost of goods sold, and indicates the value to be assigned to ending inventory on the end-of-year balance sheet.

SELLING AND ADMINISTRATIVE BUDGET

Schedule IV summarizes selling and administrative expenses. In a comprehensive sys-

SCHEDULE III

Cost of Goods Sold and Ending Inventory

	Product 101	Product 202	Total
Finished goods inventory,			
January 1, 1984 per balance sheet			
60,000 units @ $13	$ 780,000		
20,000 units @ $21		$ 420,000	$ 1,200,000
Add: Cost of goods manufactured			
460,000 @ $14.30	6,578,000		
370,000 @ $22.80		8,436,000	15,014,000
Goods available for sale	$7,358,000	$8,856,000	$16,214,000
Less: Finished goods inventory,			
December 31, 1984 (per discussion			
of production budget)			
40,000 @ $14.30	$ 572,000		
30,000 @ 22.80		$ 684,000	$ 1,256,000
Costs of goods sold	$6,786,000	$8,172,000	$14,958,000

SCHEDULE IV

Selling and Administrative Budget

Selling expenditures, including sales commissions	$1,300,000
Executive salaries	800,000
Clerical costs	950,000
Audit and legal costs	85,000
Other costs	670,000
Total selling and administrative costs	$3,805,000

tem of budgeting each of the expenditures indicated would be supported by subsidiary budgets.

PROJECTED INCOME

Given the projections of revenue and the major categories of expenses, a forecast of income before taxes, tax expense, and income after taxes is straightforward. Schedule V represents a *pro forma* statement of income for the year ending December 31, 1984. The tax rate is assumed to be 40 percent.

CASH BUDGET

A budget of cash receipts and disbursements permits management to evaluate the adequacy of its cash resources. It enables the firm to make arrangements to borrow any additional funds that might be necessary if it is to satisfy its obligations as they mature and to invest or distribute to shareholders any excess cash.

Schedule VI.A indicates projected cash receipts as well as the year-end balance in accounts receivable. It is premised on the assumption that 98 percent of the beginning-of-year balance in accounts receivable and 90 percent of the 1984 sales will be collected in cash during 1984. The remaining amounts will be carried forward in accounts receivable to 1985.

Schedule VI.B projects cash disbursements and the December 31, 1984, balance in accounts payable. The schedule is based on the assumption that the entire opening balance in accounts payable will be liquidated during the year. All manufacturing, selling, and administrative expenses are recorded as accounts payable prior to payment. Of these manufacturing, selling and administrative costs incurred during 1984, only 95 percent will be paid during the year; the remaining 5 percent will be reported as accounts payable at year end.

The schedule has been prepared on the additional assumption that the firm has projected its purchases of plant and equipment to be $2,000,000. This amount as well as the

SCHEDULE V

Pro Forma Statement of Income for the Year
Ending December 31, 1984

Sales revenue (per Schedule I)	$20,640,000
Less: Cost of goods sold (per Schedule III)	14,958,000
Gross margin	$ 5,682,000
Less: Selling and administrative expenses (per Schedule IV)	$ 3,805,000
Income before taxes	$ 1,877,000
Less: Income taxes @ 40%	750,800
Net income	$ 1,126,200

SCHEDULE VI.A

**Cash Receipts and December 31, 1984
Balance in Accounts Receivable**

Accounts receivable, January 1, 1984, (per January 1 balance sheet)		$ 1,800,000
Add: 1984 projected sales (per Schedule I)		20,640,000
Total available for collection		$22,440,000
Less: Projected cash receipts, 1984		
98% of January 1 balance in accounts receivable ($1,800,000)	$ 1,764,000	
90% of 1984 projected sales	18,576,000	$20,340,000
Accounts receivable, December 31, 1984		$ 2,100,000

SCHEDULE VI.B

**Cash Disbursements and Projected December 31, 1984
Balance in Accounts Payable**

Accounts payable, January 1, 1984, (per January 1 balance sheet)			$ 1,400,000
Add: Manufacturing, selling, and administrative obligations, 1984			
Purchases (per Schedule II.C)		$3,490,400	
Direct labor (per Schedule II.B)		8,416,000	
Overhead (per Schedule II.D)	$3,156,000		
Less: Depreciation	(1,100,000)	2,056,000	
Selling and administrative costs (per Schedule IV)		3,805,000	$17,767,400
Beginning balance and obligations credited to accounts payable			$19,167,400
Less: Projected December 31, 1984, balance in accounts payable (5% of $17,767,400 in obligations incurred during 1984)			(888,370)
Disbursements for manufacturing, selling, and administrative costs			$18,279,030
Add: Disbursement for acquisition of plant and equipment (per discussion)		$2,000,000	
Disbursement for income taxes (per Schedule V)		750,800	$ 2,750,800
Total projected cash disbursements			$21,029,830

obligation for taxes owing to 1984 earnings will be paid in full during the year.

Of special note in the schedule is that the disbursement for overhead costs excludes depreciation. Depreciation, of course, is a noncash expense.

Schedule VI.C summarizes expected activity in the cash account during 1984.

SCHEDULE VI.C

Projected Balance in Cash Account
December 31, 1984

Balance, January 1, 1984 (per January 1 balance sheet)	$ 2,450,000
Add: Cash receipts (per Schedule VI.A)	20,340,000
Sum of beginning balance and cash receipts	$22,790,000
Less: Cash disbursements (per Schedule VI.B)	(21,029,830)
Projected balance, December 31, 1984	$ 1,760,170

PROJECTED BALANCE SHEET

The schedules that have been prepared to this point indicate the year-end balances in several of the balance sheet accounts. The remaining balances can be obtained by analyzing the fixed asset and retained earnings accounts.

Schedule VII.A describes the activity in the fixed asset account. As indicated previously, the firm plans to acquire $2,000,000 in plant and equipment.

Schedule VII.B summarizes the activity in retained earnings. No dividends are expected to be declared during the year.

Schedule VII.C, a projected balance sheet for December 31, 1984, ties together each of the other schedules.

THE BUDGET AS A MOTIVATOR

By way of the budgeting process the organization establishes overall goals as well as specific targets for subunits. Managers are

SCHEDULE VII.A

Projected Balance in Plant and Equipment
Accounts, December 31, 1984

	Plant and Equipment	Accumulated Depreciation
Balance, January 1, 1984 (per January 1 balance sheet)	$10,000,000	$4,000,000
Expected purchases, 1984 (per discussion)	2,000,000	
Depreciation, 1984 (per Schedule II.D)		1,100,000
Projected balance, December 31, 1984	$12,000,000	$5,100,000

SCHEDULE VII.B

Projected Balance in Retained Earnings,
December 31, 1984

Balance, January 1, 1984 (per January 1 balance sheet)	$5,288,000
Income, 1984 (per Schedule V)	1,126,200
Projected balance, December 31, 1984	$6,414,200

Pro Forma Statement of Position, December 31, 1984

Assets		
Cash (Schedule VI.C)		$ 1,760,170
Accounts receivable (Schedule VI.A)		2,100,000
Inventory—raw materials (Schedule II.C)		286,400
Inventory—finished goods (Schedule III)		1,256,000
Plant and equipment (Schedule VII.A)	$12,000,000	
Less: Accumulated depreciation (Schedule VII.A)	5,100,000	6,900,000
Total assets		$12,302,570
Liabilities and owners' equity		
Accounts payable (Schedule VI.B)		$ 888,370
Owners' equity		
Common stock (January 1, 1984, balance sheet)	$ 5,000,000	
Retained earnings (Schedule VII.B)	6,414,200	11,414,200
Total liabilities and owners' equity		$12,302,570

made aware of what is expected of them and *may*, as a consequence, be motivated to achieve the budgeted results.

There is no doubt that budgets can have a powerful influence on the managers and employees whose performance is covered by them. But the nature and direction of that influence is an open question. The "behavioral" aspects of accounting—the effect of budgets as well as other forms of accounting information on decisions and performance—is an area about which there is little understanding. Researchers have demonstrated the significance of behavioral issues; they have yet to resolve them.*

The manner in which budgets are prepared and administered may color an individual's attitudes toward the organization as a whole. Evidence suggests that hostility toward budgets is associated with diminished job satisfaction, less commitment to the organization,

* See Michael Shiff and Aria Y. Lewin, *Behavioral Aspects of Accounting* (Englewood Cliffs, N.J.: Prentice-Hall, Inc., 1974) for an anthology of literature in this area.

and greater willingness to leave the firm. These negative attitudes are likely, in turn, to reduce productivity.

Owing to past experience with budgets, or popular misconceptions about them, employee feelings of enmity toward them are common. These attitudes may be difficult for an organization to overcome. Nevertheless, the experience of many companies, as well as a number of academic research projects, indicate that it is possible at least to ameliorate them.

The nature and extent of participation in the budget process is a key factor that affects employee attitudes toward budgets. It is widely recognized today that employees should be closely involved in establishing the goals which they are expected to achieve. Regardless of whether the supervisor or the subordinate makes the initial budget estimates there must be communication between the two as to whether they are realistic. It must be accompanied by a willingness on the part of the supervisor to take into account the views of the subordinate.

Attaining meaningful participation in the budgetary process is not easy. Subordinates may consider it in their interest to negotiate targets that are as modest as possible. By exceeding the readily attainable objectives they will be credited with favorable budgetary variances and they may believe that their performance will be evaluated positively. Mindful of this, supervisors, may tend to press initially for unrealistically demanding goals. Token participation, however, will not do, and if it is intended to deceive employees into thinking that they have had a say in budget estimates it is worse than no participation at all.

Also important are the ways budget variances are communicated, interpreted and reacted to. Reports, for example, should be issued with sufficient frequency to facilitate adjustments to off-target operations. Open discussion between superior and subordinate should take place so that the reasons for the variances are understood by both parties. If a subordinate is to receive a negative evaluation as a consequence of unfavorable deviations from budget estimates, it should be only for those failures over which it was possible to exercise control.

Research into the influence of budgets on individual behavior suggests that the reasonableness of budgeted amounts has a direct impact on results achieved. If budgeted amounts are set at levels which the individual perceives as being beyond his reach, he is likely to reject them as being extreme. He will make no effort to meet the established goals. If they are set so low that he can reach them without effort, they will discourage maximum performance. If, by contrast, they are set at a level beyond the aspirations of the individual, but within a range considered attainable, then they are likely to inspire peak output.

Individuals react to financial information in unpredictable ways. Budgeting, therefore, is not merely a mechanical exercise that can be left to technicians. Budgets will affect employee behavior. The psychological ramifications of budgeting, although unclear at this time, are too important to be overlooked by either managers or accountants.

ZERO-BASE BUDGETING

Periodically, new budgetary "systems" are developed that are intended to add a measure of "rationality" to the budgetary process. One such system is *program budgeting*. Another, closely related, is *zero-base budgeting*.

These new systems inevitably fail to fulfill all of the promises made for them by their proponents. But they are of interest to managers and accountants for a number of reasons. First, they formalize the budgeting process. Many of their elements may be integral to sound management. To organizations that are already well managed they contribute little but at the same time demand little. To those that are not, they provide a framework for rapid improvement. Second, they have been applied with great success in a number of organizations. Where circumstances are favorable, they can have an exceedingly positive effect on organizational performance. Third, as new systems are proposed, managers and accountants must be able to evaluate them in the context of experience with similar systems. Budgeting systems have become fads. Executives rush to adopt them, accepting without question the wildly exaggerated claims made in journal articles and management seminars. Managers must have the perspective to distinguish an effective treatment from a charlatan's panacea.

Zero-base budgeting, although identified most closely with nonprofit organizations, was in fact first reported upon as being used at Texas Instruments, a manufacturer of calculators and other electronic devices, to allocate nonmanufacturing costs.* It has several noteworthy characteristics.

Program Structure

Zero-base budgeting requires that the activities of an organization be grouped into programs. Programs are collections of activities that have similar goals and are targeted toward similar constituencies. Within a state government, examples of programs dealing with the environment are air quality control, water quality control, wildlife preservation, and chemical disposal.

Decision Packages

For each activity that an organizational unit carries out and for which it requests support, the unit must prepare a decision package. A decision package for an air quality control laboratory is presented in Exhibit 19-2. Among the elements of a decision package are:

a. A statement of purpose, in which the objectives of the activity are set forth.

b. An indication of the benefits, in quantifiable terms, that would accrue to the organization or the constituency that it serves assuming various levels of funding. Most organizations that have adopted zero-based budgeting require that the lowest level of funding be one that is considerably below that at which the activity is presently operating.

---

* Peter A. Pyhrr, "Zero-Base Budgeting," *Harvard Business Review*, 48 (November–December 1970) pp. 111–121.

The specific amounts that a unit requests must take into account the relationships between costs and benefits, with specific attention being directed to the incremental costs to be incurred throughout the "relevant range." If substantive benefits can be achieved only by the addition of a complete package of resources, such as an additional training center or research laboratory, it makes little sense to appropriate to the unit sufficient funds for only one-half of a package. Such funds would be wasted; they would not enable the unit to increase output. Implicit in zero-base budgeting is the abandonment of practices whereby the appropriation to a unit is increased by a fixed "across the board" percentage over what it was in a previous year without due regard for the "steps" in its cost function.

c. An indication of alternative means, other than by way of the activity for which funds are being sought, that the objective might be accomplished. This requirement is intended to assure that the unit managers have given thought to other, perhaps more effective ways, of accomplishing their mission.

Ranking

Each increment of funding within a decision package must be ranked in order of priority with similar increments of decision packages for other activities within the same program. The title "zero-base budgeting" is derived from the requirement that all activities for which funds are requested—not only new activities—be incorporated into the rankings and thereby be subject to review. Justification of funds should start from base zero. If an agency wants to be assured of receiving funding for a new activity it would ordinarily have to rank it higher than at least some increments of existing activities. It

EXHIBIT 19-2

(1) Agency	(2) Program Name	(3) Organizational Unit	(4) Date (Mo-Day-Yr)	(5) Prepared By	(150) Agency Code	(160) PGM Code	(170) Activity Code
Air Control Board	Air Quality Control		3/15/74	John Adams			

(1) Activity Name: Air Quality Laboratory

(1) Activity Objective Statement:

Ambient air laboratory analysis must be conducted for identification and evaluation of pollutants by type and by volume. Sample analysis enables engineers to determine effect of control and permits use of an emergency warning system.

(7) Describe Means Of Performing Activity: Level (1 of __3__)

Use a central lab in Austin to conduct all sample testing and analysis; Laboratory Director, 1 Chemist II, 1 Chemist I, 2 Technicians, and 1 Stenographer I. This staff could analyze and report on a maximum of 37,300 samples per year, we would only sample the 5 major urban areas of the State (Houston, Beaumont, El Paso, Dallas, Ft. Worth), which covers 70 percent of the population. These 6 people are required as a minimum to conduct comprehensive sample analysis of even a few samples on a continuous basis.

(9) Describe Means Of Performing Activity: Level (2 of __3__)

Add 1 Chemist II and 1 Clerk II and additional operating expenses at an increased cost of $61,000 to permit the analysis of 17,700 additional samples, thereby determining the air quality for 5 additional urban areas and including 8 other counties chosen on the basis of most severe pollution. The five additional urban areas include Amarillo, San Antonio, Austin, Waco, and Port Arthur. Coverage of 80 percent of the State's population would require analysis of 55,000 samples.

(7A) RESOURCES

	1974 Estimated		1975 Budgeted	
	Personnel	Cost	Personnel	Cost
	8	$ 215,000	8	$ 224,000

(7B) Workload/Performance Measures

	Measures	Measures
Samples analyzed and reported	55,000	55,000
Cost per sample	$ 3.91	$ 4.07
Samples per man hour	3.9	3.9

(8A) Resources

(8C) Rank	This Level	1976 Request		1977 Request	
		Personnel	Cost	Personnel	Cost
3		6	$ 140,000	6	$ 140,000

(8B) Workload/Performance Measures

	Measures	Measures
Samples analyzed and reported	37,300	37,300
Cost per sample	$ 3.75	$ 3.75
Samples per man hour	3.7	3.7

(9A) Resources

(9C) Rank	This Level / Cumulative	1976 Request		1977 Request	
		Personnel	Cost	Personnel	Cost
6	This Level	2	$ 61,000	2	$ 61,000
	Cumulative	8	$ 201,000	8	$ 201,000

(9B) Workload/Performance Measures

	Measures	Measures
Samples analyzed and reported	55,000	55,000
Cost per sample	$ 3.65	$ 3.65
Samples per man hour	3.9	3.9

EXHIBIT 19-2 (continued)

TABLE III: ACTIVITY DECISION PACKAGE

(1) Agency	(2) Program Name		(3) Organizational Unit	(4) Date (Mo.Day.Yr.)	(5) Prepared By	(50) Agency Code	(60) P.I.N. Code	(70) Activity Code
Air Control Board	Air Quality Control			3/15/76	John Adams			

(1) Activity Name: Air Quality Laboratory Level (3 of __3__)

(12) Describe Means Of Performing Activity: Level (3 of __3__)

Add 1 Chemist II and 1 Cleark II and additional operating expenses at a cost of $45,000 for the analysis of 20,000 additional samples. These added samples would cover all counties except rural areas with little or no pollution, which would over 90 percent of the population. There is no need to cover the remaining rural population. A listing of the counties covered by the additional 20,000 samples, plus the counties not covered, is attached.

(10C) Rank	(10A) Resources	1976 Request		1977 Request	
		Personnel	Cost	Personnel	Cost
11	This Level	2	$ 45,000	2	$ 45,000
	Cumulative	10	$246,000	10	$ 246,000

(10B) Workload/Performance Measures

	Measures	Measures
Samples analyzed and reported	75,000	75,000
Cost per sample	$ 3.28	$ 3.28
Samples per man hour	3.9	3.9

(11) Describe Means Of Performing Activity: Level (4 of ____)

(11C) Rank	(11A) Resources		Personnel	Cost	Personnel	Cost
	This Level					
	Cumulative					

(11B) Workload/Performance Measures

	Measures	Measures

(12) Alternative Methods Of Accomplishing This Activity:

Levels
1, 2, and 3

1. Contract sample analysis work to the University of Texas – Cost $6 per sample for a total cost of $224,000 for analyzing 37,300 samples.
2. Conduct sample analysis work entirely in regional locations – Cost a total of $506,000 the first year and $385,000 in subsequent years. Specialized equipment must be purchased in the first year for several locations; lab staffing at several locations at minimum levels which would not fully utilize people.
3. Conduct sample analysis work in central lab for special pollutants only, and set up regional labs to reduce sample mailing costs — Cost a total of $305,000 for analyzing 37,300 samples. Excessive cost would persist due to minimum lab staffing at several locations in addition to the special central lab.

thereby runs the risk that a new activity will be funded only at the expense of an existing one. It is expected that existing activities will be reviewed each budgetary cycle and those that are no longer as effective as proposed new ones will be ranked low and thus receive either little or no funding.

The Contribution of Zero-Base Budgeting

Zero-base budgeting was introduced into the federal government by President Carter. Efforts at implementation ceased, however, with his election defeat. It was adopted in the 1970s by many state and local governmental units and is still being used by them.

Empirical studies have provided no evidence that zero-base budgeting has had a significant effect on the allocation of available resources in the jurisdictions in which it is being used. This is to be expected. Budgeting in organizations, be they government or business, reflects the political desires and powers of their constituents. In jurisdictions in which the constituents have diverse and often conflicting interests and views of what the objectives of the organization ought to be, there is no single "rational" or optimum allocation scheme. Irrespective of how persuasive the decision packages may be, they are unlikely to convince responsible officials or their constituents that the activities underwritten by the organization should be counter to what they would otherwise believe.

The primary contribution of zero-base budgeting is that it institutionalizes practices that should be followed apart from any specific system of budgeting. It requires organizations to establish goals, express benefits in quantifiable terms, analyze costs, consider alternatives and establish priorities. Many organizations need the structure that

it provides in order to develop effective managerial processes. To such organizations the improvements caused by zero-base budgeting can be dramatic.

SUMMARY

Whereas the director of the Office of Management and Budget in the federal government was once regarded as an obscure bureaucrat, in recent years he has come to be recognized as one of the most powerful officials in the government. He determines, subject to the approval of the President and Congress, the extent to which the various federal programs will be funded. The relative influence of those in charge of making budgeting decisions in corporations is no less great. The direction in which a corporation will move is determined in large measure by the amount of funds directed to each of the activities in which it engages.

Budgeting is not merely a technical activity in which an organization and its components must periodically engage; it represents the essence of management. By way of the budgeting process, responsible managers determine organizational objectives, develop strategies and plans, allocate resources, and establish the basis for measuring performance.

Budgets can take many forms. None is inherently preferable to others. The superiority of one form over another depends ultimately on the extent to which it provides the information necessary to carry out the functions of management. The manner in which budgets are prepared and executed can, however, have a significant impact on the attitutes and performance of those affected by them. The "behavioral" effects of budgets may not yet be well understood. Nevertheless, managers and accountants must be sensitive to their potential dysfunctional consequences for the organization and do what they can to ameliorate them.

EXERCISE FOR REVIEW AND SELF-TESTING

Robertson Lighting Fixtures, Inc., has established as an objective for 1984 a 10 percent increase in gross margin (defined as sales revenue minus cost of goods sold). The company estimates that each of the factors which enters into production of its lighting fixtures will increase by 6 percent over what it was in 1983. At the same time, the company believes that it will be able to increase the selling prices of its fixtures by 6 percent.

In 1983, the cost of producing each fixture, based on a volume of 60,000 units was $17, comprising the following elements.

Variable costs		
Direct labor	$6.00	
Raw materials	6.00	
Variable overhead	2.00	$14.00
Fixed costs		
Depreciation	$1.00	
Other fixed costs	2.00	3.00
Total cost per unit		$17.00

Inasmuch as the firm does not intend to acquire new assets in 1984, the charge for depreciation can be expected to remain the same as it was in 1983.

The selling price of the lighting fixtures was $20 per unit in 1983. In 1983 the firm sold as many units as it produced; it expects to do the same in 1984. Operating profit in 1983 was $180,000.

1. How many units must the firm produce and sell in 1984 if it is to meet its objective of a 10 percent increase in gross margin?

2. The firm allows its customers 30 days from date of sale to make payment. Under the assumptions that sales are spread evenly throughout the year and that the firm meets the sales target determined in part 1, how much can the company expect to collect in cash in 1984?

3. How much cash should the company budget to meet production requirements assuming that all production costs (excluding depreciation, of course) are paid for in the year incurred?

4. The firm is taxed at an effective rate of 40 percent. The fixed assets on which depreciation is charged were acquired in January 1983 at a cost of $360,000. Useful life is expected to be 6 years with no salvage value. The firm charges depreciation for general purpose reporting on the straight-line basis, but uses the sum-of-the-years' digits method for tax computations.
   a. How much cash should the firm allocate for the payment of 1984 taxes?
   b. What would be the amount of the tax expense to be reported on its 1984 financial statement? (Assume that the firm incurs no costs other than those indicated.)

QUESTIONS FOR REVIEW AND DISCUSSION

1. Why is it difficult, if not impossible, to prepare a budget without taking into account organizational goals? Why is it also difficult to establish objectives without due regard for the organizational budget?

2. What is meant by "operational" objectives? Why is it particularly important that not-for-profit organizations develop operational objectives?

3. Why may "maximization of profits" be an objective of limited utility for many units of a corporation?

4. What are three broad categories of techniques that can be used to forecast sales?

5. Why is a budget a "political" document, in *both* nonbusiness and business organizations?

6. Why might it be said that the budget is a much more significant document in government organizations that it is in business firms?

7. What is a "master" budget?

8. What are the essential elements of *zero-base* budgeting? What is the significance of the term "zero base"?

9. Why may budgets result in diminished rather than enhanced performance?

10. In what ways can hostility toward budgets be ameliorated?

PROBLEMS

1. Principles of cost behavior are as fundamental to budgeting in the public sector as in the private sector.

The Eyes for the Needy Center, an agency of a State Department of Welfare, provides eyeglasses for children of parents who are receiving government financial assistance. Children are referred to the center after receiving preliminary eye examinations by either school teachers or social workers.

In 1983, its second year of operation, the center served 21,000 children. It gave each child an eye examination and issued 21,000 pairs of eyeglasses. The total cost of operating the center was $1,428,000—approximately $68 per client served—broken down as follows:

Director	$ 48,000
Ophthamologist	80,000
Optometrists (7 @ $46,000)	322,000
Technician	20,000
Secretaries (2 @ $20,000)	40,000
Nurses (7 @ $26,000)	182,000
Maintenance worker	16,000
Department of Welfare charge for overhead (fixed cost)	204,000
Glasses (21,000 @ $20)	420,000
Other supplies (21,000 @ $2)	42,000
Other operating costs ($12,000 + 21,000 @ $2)	54,000
Total operating costs	$1,428,000

The director of the center recently submitted a budget request for 1984 for $1,713,600. This represents a 20 percent ($285,600) increase in costs over the budget for 1983. According to the budget officer, such an increase would allow for the expansion of the program so that 20 percent (4,200) additional children might be served.

Within the range relevant to this problem all costs behave as implied by the data. To the extent that additional employees must be hired, they must be employed full-time.

a. Assume that you are a budget officer of the Department of Welfare and you accept the need for a 20% increase in services provided. How much of an increase in expenditures (both in dollars and percent) would you be willing to approve?

b. Suppose that for the following year, 1985, the director believes it necessary to serve an additional 1,800 clients. What is the dollar amount of a budget increase that you as a budget officer would be willing to approve? Compare the percent increases in services and in costs with those budgeted for 1984.

c. The director of the center has established a policy that one month's supply of glasses should be on hand at all times. The director has estimated that as of December 31, 1983, only 1,400 pair of glasses will be on hand. Of these, 1,000 will have been received in December 1983. The December 31, 1984, inventory will be based on number of glasses to be dispensed in 1984 (i.e., 25,200).

Glasses must ordinarily be paid for within 30 days after they are received. Glasses ordered in 1984 will be received uniformly throughout the year.

How much cash will have to be disbursed to pay for eyeglasses in 1984? Do you think that the budgeted amount for eyeglasses should be based on cost of eyeglasses (1) received, (2) dispensed, or (3) paid for? Explain.

2. Cash disbursements depend on timing of production, purchases, and payments.

LHG Industries assembles electronic devices. It purchases required components in sets.

The firm orders the components twice per month, on the 4th and 19th days of the month. Orders are filled in 10 days. Terms are 2/10, n/30. A 2 percent discount is granted for payment within 10 days; payment is due within 30 days. Invoices are received along with the goods (on the 14th and 29th of the month) and payment is made eight days later (on the 22nd and 7th of the month).

It is the policy of the firm to order a sufficient quantity of components so that it will have on hand on the 1st and 16th of the month, 140 percent of number of sets to satisfy the requirements of the next 15 days. The 40 percent above the actual requirements represents a safety stock in the event of a delay in the receipt of an order.

The firm forecast that the number of devices to be assembled in December 1983 and the first four months of 1984 will be as follows.

December 1983	9,000 units
January 1984	6,000 units
February	5,000 units
March	7,000 units
April	8,000 units

Assembly takes place uniformly throughout the month.

Cost per set of components is $3 after taking into account the cash discount of 2 percent.

a. Compute the number of sets of components that the firm must order each 15-day period in the first three months of 1984.

b. Determine the amount of each cash payment the firm must make during the first three months of 1984. Summarize by month the expected cash disbursements.

3. *Budgeted cost of goods sold may differ substantially from budgeted production costs.*

Aranya, Inc., forecasts that sales for 1984 and first quarter 1985 will be (by quarter and in units):

Quarter	Unit
1984	
I	26,000
II	34,000
III	40,000
IV	80,000
Total, 1984	180,000
1985	
I	26,000

Sales price per unit is $100. Manufacturing costs are expected to be as follows:

| Variable costs per unit | $ 63 |
| Fixed costs, total | $2,514,400 |

Selling and administrative costs are anticipated to be $4,000,000 per year.

The firm has established a policy of maintaining an inventory at the end of each quarter of approximately 10 percent of estimated sales for the coming quarter. However, ending inventory as of December 31, 1983, is expected to be 3,000 units.

Fixed manufacturing costs as well as selling and administrative costs are incurred evenly throughout the year.

a. Prepare a schedule in which you indicate the number of units that should be produced, by quarter, in 1984.

b. Prepare a schedule in which you indicate, by quarter forecasted cash flow for 1984. Assume that collections on sales are made in the quarter in which the sales are made and that all manufacturing, selling, and administrative costs are paid in cash in the quarter in which they are incurred.

c. Prepare a schedule in which you indicate estimated earnings by quarter for 1984. Assume that fixed manufacturing costs are assigned to units produced via an overhead charging rate based on estimated annual production (as determined in part a) and costs. The per unit cost of goods held in inventory on December 31, 1983, is the same as that of the goods to be produced in 1984.

4. *Careful cash budgeting facilitates tight controls over the amounts in interest-free accounts and enables calculation of the opportunity cost associated with average balance requirements.*

Barlev Industries has a weekly payroll of $280,000. It issues checks to its employees each Wednesday. The following schedule indicates the company's estimate, based on past experience, of the percentage of checks that will clear its bank on the days subsequent to that on which they were issued.

Thursday	20%
Friday	30%
Monday	20%
Tuesday	10%
Wednesday	5%
Thursday	5%
Friday	5%
Monday	5%

The company maintains a separate bank account for its payroll transactions. Because its bank does not pay interest on commercial checking accounts, the company maintains no more than the minimum required balance. That minimum, as determined by the company, is the dollar amount of the checks expected to clear on any given day plus a safety stock of $10,000. Each afternoon, just prior to the close of business, the company transfers from an interest-bearing account to the payroll account the funds necessary to satisfy the checks that will clear the following day. The deposit required to meet the checks that will clear on Monday is made on Friday afternoon.

The company is considering accepting a line of credit from the bank. Under the terms of the credit agreement it will be required to maintain an average daily balance in a checking account (the payroll account is acceptable) of $100,000. Average daily balance is based on the amount on deposit at the close of each day.

The company earns interest at the rate of 12 percent per annum on funds on deposit in its interest-bearing account.

a. Prepare a schedule in which you indicate the dollar amount of checks that will clear each day over any period of seven days. Determine the balance required at the start of business of each of the days taking into account the safety stock.

b. Compute the *average* balance that the firm would have to maintain over the period of seven days.

c. Calculate the effective incremental cost to the company of maintaining the balance that would be required under the terms of the line of credit agreement.

5. A cash receipts budget must take into account the timing of collections on sales. (Although the facts in this problem are straightforward, many students may find the solution unexpectedly complex.)

The Paskow Co. sells on terms 2/10, n/30. A 2 percent discount is granted for payment within 10 days; payment is due within 30 days.

Experience indicates the following pattern of collections:

Within the 10-day discount period	60%
Within 11 to 30 days	18%
Within 31 to 60 days	15%
Within 61 to 90 days	5%
Uncollectible	2%
	100%

Sales are made uniformly within a month and collections are made uniformly throughout the intervals indicated. (Thus, for example, of the 60 percent of the sales of December 1 that will be collected within the discount period, uniform amounts will be collected on December 1 through December 10.)

Sales for the month of December were $300,000.

Prepare a schedule in which you indicate the amount of December sales that will be collected in December, January, February, and March. For convenience assume that each month has 30 days.

6. Cash receipts and disbursements can be "modeled" by a series of algebraic equations.

Times Square Industries intends to develop a computer program that will project monthly cash requirements. In order to facilitate the programming, budget analysts must first develop a cash flow "model" that expresses in the form of algebraic equations the influences on cash receipts, cash disbursements, and ending cash balances.

The analysts have identified the following relationships:

Of the sales in a particular month, 75 percent are collected in the month of sale and 25 percent are collected in the following month.

The firm requires an inventory of finished goods equal to 15 percent of the expected sales of the following month. Production each month is equal, therefore, to 85 percent of current sales plus 15 percent of the next month's anticipated sales.

The firm requires an inventory of raw materials equal to 10 percent of the expected production of the following month. Raw materials purchases are equal, therefore, to 90 percent of current production plus 10 percent of next month's anticipated production. Eighty percent of raw materials are paid for in the month of purchase; the remaining 20 percent are paid for in the following month. Three pounds of raw materials are required for each unit of production.

Seventy-five percent of labor costs are paid in the month in which the employees provide their services; the remaining 25 percent are paid for in the following month. Each unit of product requires 0.1 hours of direct labor. Fixed labor costs are $20,000 per month.

Administrative costs are $50,000 per month.

Sales commissions are 3 percent of sales; they are paid on sales of the previous month.

The analysts have agreed on the following notation:

B = cash balance, end of month

R = cash receipts in a month

O = total cash outlays in a month

D = disbursements for raw materials

L = disbursements for labor costs

A = disbursements for administrative costs

C = disbursements for sales commissions

P = production in units

M = purchases of raw materials (in dollars)

S = sales in units

Pr = selling price per unit

H = labor rate per hour

U = raw materials price per pound

Amounts of a previous or subsequent month are to be indicated by the subscript $n - 1$ or $n + 1$. Thus if sales in units for the current month are indicated by S, sales for the past month would be denoted by S_{n-1} and those of the next month by S_{n+1}.

a. Develop a model, consisting of a series of related equations which can be used to determine the cash balance at the end of a month.

b. Applying the model, determine the cash balance that can be anticipated at the end of February 1984. Sales for the first four months of 1984 are expected to be as follows:

January	40,000 units
February	30,000 units
March	50,000 units
April	50,000 units

Other variables are expected to be:

Selling price per unit (Pr)	$10.00
Labor rate per hour (H)	$16.00
Raw materials price per pound (U)	$ 2.00
January production in units (P_{n-1})	38,500 units
January purchases of raw materials (M_{n-1})	$227,700
Cash balance, January 31, (B_{n-1})	$ 8,000

7. *A master budget links together a number of related schedules.*

Vitality Cosmetics, Inc., produces two products, a cologne for men and a cologne for women. Management of the firm forecasts that the balance sheet for the year ending December 31, 1983, will be (in condensed form) as follows:

Statement of Position
(December 31, 1983)

Assets

Cash		$1,500,000
Accounts receivable		1,280,000
Raw materials inventory		200,000
Finished goods inventory		160,000
Plant and equipment	$1,800,000	
Less: Accumulated depreciation	600,000	1,200,000
Total assets		$4,340,000

Liabilities and Owners' Equity

Accounts payable		$ 950,000
Owners' equity		
Common stock	$3,000,000	
Retained earnings	390,000	3,390,000
Total liabilities and owners' equity		$4,340,000

Management has decided that preparation of the 1984 budget will be governed by the following assumptions:

Sales of men's cologne will be 420,000 bottles at $12 per bottle; sales of women's cologne will be 360,000 bottles at $15 per bottle.

Inventory of finished goods at December 31, 1984, should be at a level equal to production of one month (i.e., 35,000 bottles of men's cologne; 30,000 bottles of women's cologne).

Inventory of raw materials at December 31, 1984, should be at a level equal to 10 percent of the production for the year.

The inventory of finished goods at December 31, 1983, comprises 20,000 bottles of men's cologne produced at a cost of $2.70 per bottle and 40,000 bottles of women's cologne produced at a cost of $2.65 per bottle.

Direct labor costs will be $.50 per bottle for both the men's and the women's cologne.

Direct materials costs will be $2 per bottle for the men's cologne and $2.10 per bottle for the women's cologne.

Manufacturing overhead, which is applied to products via an overhead charging rate based on direct labor dollars, will be:

Supplies	$ 40,000
Indirect labor	80,000
Building occupancy costs	34,750
Depreciation	120,000
Total	$274,750

Selling and advertising costs for the year will be $3,200,000. Administration costs will be $1,480,000.

The ending balance in accounts receivable will be equal to 12 percent of dollar sales for the year.

Income taxes are paid at a rate of 40 percent.

The ending balance in accounts payable will be equal to 10 percent of obligations incurred during the year, including those for purchases of raw materials, direct labor, overhead (excluding depreciation), selling and advertising, administration, and income taxes.

Prepare a budget comprising the following schedules:

1. Sales
2. Units to be produced
3. Direct labor costs
4. Direct materials costs
5. Purchases (dollars)
6. Manufacturing overhead
7. Per unit cost of goods manufactured
8. Cost of goods sold
9. Statement of income
10. Cash receipts
11. Cash disbursements
12. Summary of changes in cash balance
13. Statement of Position, December 31, 1984

8. Subjective probabilities can be used in forecasting cash flows and assessing the need for a line of credit. (This problem requires knowledge of "subjective probabilities," a topic often dealt with in courses in statistics. An introduction to subjective probabilities is provided in this text in Chapter 21.)

Quality Brands, Inc., has assigned the following subjective probabilities to sales of 1984 (in millions):

Sales	Probability
$400	.2
500	.5
600	.3

Variable costs are approximately 60 percent of sales revenue. Fixed costs are $180 million per year. In the course of 1984 the firm will have to retire $30 million in long-term debt. It may be assumed that all revenues will be received and all costs will be paid in cash.

The firm expects to have on hand at the start of 1984 zero cash.

a. Determine the anticipated cash balance (or deficit) at year-end 1984 for each level of sales as well as the *expected* value of the cash balance (or deficit).

b. Insofar as the firm has a cash deficit at year-end 1984 it would be required to borrow funds in the amount of the shortage. The period of the loan would be for one year. It is anticipated that interest rates will increase substantially during 1984. The firm has the opportunity to obtain from a bank at the start of 1984 a line of credit. The line of credit would allow the firm to borrow the required funds up to an agreed upon limit at an interest rate of 10 percent regardless of subsequent increases in prevailing rates. The cost of the line of credit would be 1 percent of the funds that are available to the firm for borrowing (i.e., the credit limit less the amount that has already been borrowed). Economists forecast that by the end of 1984 prevailing rates of interest will increase to 16 percent.

Management of Quality Brands is considering whether it should establish a line of credit with a limit equal to the maximum amount that it might have to borrow. If, for example, the maximum cash shortage (as determined in part a) were $100 million, then the cost of establishing the line of credit at the start of 1984 would be $1 million (1 percent of $100 million). In return for this amount, the firm would have the right to borrow up to $100 million at the end of 1984 at the rate of 10 percent. If it did not establish the line of credit, the rate of interest on amounts to be borrowed would be 16 percent.

Should the firm establish a line of credit equal in amount to the *maximum* cash shortage that might exist as of the end of 1984? Explain.

9. *Can academic accountants apply the theories that they espouse?*

The recently appointed chairman of the Department of Accounting of a large midwestern state university gave a presentation on budgeting for nonprofit organizations. He concluded his remarks with the following comment:

"In summary, let me emphasize that the budget must relate to organizational objectives. The budgetary materials must include a statement of *operational* objectives. Such objectives must be specific and quantifiable. If additional funds are requested in the budget, then supporting documents should indicate the resultant benefits to the constituents served by the organization. Such benefits should, of course, be tied directly to the objectives and should, if at all possible, be quantified. At the conclusion of the period covered by the budget it should be possible to measure the extent to which the anticipated benefits were, in fact, realized and the organizational goals achieved."

The mission of an academic department of accounting is, in general terms, threefold:

1. To educate students
2. To conduct research
3. To serve the university, the accounting profession, and the academic community at large

The faculty and the chairman of the department of accounting agree that budgetary allocations from the university administration need to be increased. Additional funds are required to increase faculty salaries, to provide funds so that faculty members can travel to professional conferences, to raise the level of secretarial services, to provide summer research grants for faculty and graduate students, to purchase instructional equipment and materials, to support development of new courses, and to increase the amount of computer time available to students.

The Department of Accounting is in direct competition for funds with other academic departments throughout the University.

a. Prepare the rudiments of a budget request in which you set forth operational goals, specify the benefits to be derived from an increase in the funds allocated to the Department of Accounting and indicate the criteria by which departmental performance can be measured. Draw on your own general knowledge of the goals of an academic department and the activities in which it engages.

b. Comment on the extent to which the objectives you set forth are truly the goals of the Department of Accounting rather than merely factors that can conveniently be quantified. Will it be possible to measure objectively the extent to which the objectives have been realized?

10. *Zero-base budget decision packages highlight the dangers of across-the-board budget reductions.*

As a consequence of an unprofitable year, the chief executive officer of Beauty-Wax, Inc., ordered a minimum 20 percent across-the-board cut in all nonmanufacturing costs for 1984. The budget of Unit A of the firm's research department for 1983 is as follows:

Senior chemist	$ 65,000
Staff chemists (2 @ $45,000)	90,000
Laboratory technician	25,000
Supplies	15,000
Total	$195,000

Unit A is working on the development of a new household wax. Each chemist is researching a different phase of the project. Each phase can be performed concurrently and it is estimated that the project can be completed by the end of 1984 at the present rate of progress. If, however, any one member of the team is eliminated, then that phase will have to be delayed until the other chemists can turn their attention to it upon completion of their other work. Even if two chemists were to work on any one phase, however, the phase could not be completed more rapidly than if a single chemist were to work on it.

If one chemist were eliminated, supply costs could be reduced by $4,000. The work could not be carried out satisfactorily without a laboratory technician.

It is expected that the new product will provide earnings of $500,000 per year.

a. Prepare a zero-base budget decision package (containing the type of information described in the text) for 1984 which includes data for two levels of funding: the current (1983) level and a level that would put the unit in compliance with the order of the chief executive officer (i.e., a reduction in costs of at least 20 percent). Be sure to indicate the consequences of the reduction in funds. Omit consideration of specific work load performance measures and alternative means of carrying out the project.

b. Comment on the dangers of "across-the-board" budget cuts.

11. Budgets, even if only in summary form, must be designed to provide information that is useful to those who will use them.

Exhibit 19-3 is the complete budget summary of the Department of Public Welfare of a large

EXHIBIT 19-3

State Department of Public Welfare
Operating Budget—Statewide Budget Summary

Administration		Rentals		
Personal services		Office and warehouse space	$ 2,277,315	
Board Members' per diem	$ 3,600	Equipment—EDP	1,929,840	
Exempt positions	1,127,500	Other	175,210	
Salaries of classified positions	72,848,166	Employees' insurance premiums	1,366,603	
Seasonal help	41,590	Merit system expenses	226,489	
Planned future program adjustments due to changing	1,948,590	Allocation of federal funds to counties (operating expense fund)	666,025	
Planned food stamp adjustment	1,681,474	Commodity emergency (rider appropriation)	30,000	
Professional educational stipends	225,985	Professional educational services to graduate schools of social work	500,000	
Professional fees and services	1,499,998	Other operating expenses	5,916,641	
Examining and professional fees—medical	831,010	Subtotal, operating expenses	$ 18,283,552	
OASI matching	4,352,439			
Employees' retirement matching	4,621,329	Capital outlay		
		Equipment and furniture	$ 789,666	
Subtotal: Personal services	$ 89,191,681	Land purchased	0	
Less: Estimated salary lapse	(3,051,603)	Land improvements	0	
		Buildings	0	
Total, personal services	$ 86,130,078	Subtotal, capital outlay	$ 789,666	
Travel expense	$ 5,258,427	Total, administration	$110,461,712	
		Assistance payments	235,218,794	
Operating expense		Medical assistance programs	506,448,957	
Printing and office supplies	$ 964,002	Social services programs	35,024,375	
Gas, oil, grease, etc.	24,960	Contract services	9,041,235	
Other supplies and materials	776,127			
Postage	1,790,591	Grand total, Department of Public Welfare	$896,195,073	
Utilities, telephone, and telegraph	1,438,751			
Transportation of things	83,998			
Other repairs	117,000			

southwestern state. It is an actual budget, not merely a textbook illustration.

The budget item "Assistance payments" represents direct grants to various groups of needy, including families with dependent children, the aged, the blind, and the disabled. "Medical assistance programs" include medical services in nursing homes and state institutions for the mentally retarded, diagnostic medical exams, dental services, drugs, and hearing aids. "Social services programs" comprise protective and support services (e.g., counseling) for children, the aged, the blind, and the disabled. "Contract services" are services which the Department contracts out to private parties, such as nursing homes.

A member of the state legislature has many retired persons in his district and, as a consequence, is especially concerned with the commitment of the state to provide services for the aged. He requests that you review the budget summary in order to learn how much the Department of Public Welfare intends to spend on services and direct financial aid to the aged.

a. Review carefully the budget summary. Can you determine how much the Department of Public Welfare intends to spend on services and direct financial aid to the aged?

b. By contrast, can you determine how much the Department of Public Welfare intends to spend on gas, oil, and grease?

c. Which of the two questions is likely to be of greater significance to members of the legislature or citizens of the state?

d. Suppose that you were able to examine the detailed budget, not merely the summary. Why is it likely that you would still be unable to obtain the information requested by the legislator?

e. Based on informatio contained in the budget, as well as on your general knowledge of the activities carried out by a state department of public welfare, indicate how the budget could be recast in order to provide information that would be of greater utility to members of the legislature and citizens of the state.

12. A university budget cannot necessarily be relied on to reveal the extent to which the football team is subsidized.

The following is an excerpt of a letter to the editor of the *Wall Street Journal* (published February 18, 1981) from the President, The University of Texas:

In your Jan. 29 front page article, "Colleges Spend Millions to Modify Buildings for Disabled Students," you quoted a federal bureaucrat as saying, "The University of Texas subsidizes its football team heavily." Not true. The Department of Intercollegiate Athletics for Men, which includes the football team, earns its own way from gate receipts, television income and private benefactions. We do subsidize Women's Intercollegiate Athletics.

a. Suppose that you were the federal bureaucrat referred to in the letter. You are asked to support your assertion that the University of Texas subsidizes its football team heavily. You examine the budget of the Department of Intercollegiate Athletics for men and find that, as the President indicated, the Department receives no University revenues.

Assuming that you have access to the budget of the entire University, how might you go about defending your position? What questions would you want to resolve?

b. Suppose that your investigation reveals that The University of Texas does, in fact, when *all* benefits provided are taken into account, "subsidize" intercollegiate athletics. What deficiencies or limitations does this suggest with respect to University budgeting practices? Are there any changes that you would recommend?

13. Effective budgeting requires that costs be related to objectives. Nevertheless, budgeting remains, to a great extent, a political process.

CASE: HALFWAY HOUSE PROGRAM

A southwestern state operates a program of "halfway houses" for teenagers who have run away from home or have been delinquent (primarily those who have been arrested for minor drug violations). The halfway houses are located throughout the state and teenagers are assigned to a house that is located within or near their county of residence. The centers provide food and lodging for the teenagers. While they are residing at the houses, the teenagers are encouraged to meet, both individually and in groups, with trained counselors, who help them work out their problems and pave the way for a return to their homes and schools. In addition, the program provides that each teenager receives a thorough physical exam and medical counseling to help control any physical problems (such as overweight or poor complexion) that might contribute to his emotional problems.

To date the program has been generally successful. A recent survey indicated that over 75 percent of the teenagers who spent time at the halfway houses returned to their homes, improved their grades at school, abandoned the use of drugs, and did not subsequently run away.

Each center serves approximately 40 teenagers at a time. The average stay is 2 months; hence each house serves approximately 240 teenagers per year.

There are currently 20 halfway houses in operation throughout the state. Since the program began, each of the centers has always been filled to its prescribed capacity of 40. Indeed, there is a considerable waiting list for admission to each of the houses. As a consequence, the administrators of the program see a need to expand the number of teenagers served. They prefer to increase the number of halfway houses, but as an alternative they would increase the prescribed enrollment at each house from 40 to maximum practical capacity of 50. An increase in the number served at existing houses may, of course, decrease the level of service, but the administrators believe that an increase in stated capacity of each house will better serve the people of the state than the existing limitations on number of teenagers served.

The administrators also believe that the program would be considerably more effective if the ratio of counselors to teenagers improved. At present, a ratio of one counselor for each ten teenagers is maintained. The administrators would like to increase that ratio to one counselor for each eight teenagers.

The cost of operating the entire program is $5,240,000 per year; that of operating each of the

EXHIBIT 19-4

Annual Cost of Operating a Halfway House
(Based on Capacity of 40)

Rent	$ 12,000
Director	28,000
Counselors (4 @ $20,000)	80,000
Kitchen and maintenance employee	16,000
Furniture and fixtures[a]	6,000
Food ($2,000 per teenager per year)	80,000
Supplies and miscellaneous costs ($300 per teenager per year)	12,000
Utilities	3,000
Medical and drugs ($400 per teenager per year)	16,000
Central office costs[b]	9,000
Total costs per center	$262,000

Total cost of program: $262,000 × 20 centers = $5,240,000

[a] Total cost of furniture and fixtures is $24,000; useful life is 4 years.
[b] Central office costs are $180,000. They are divided equally among the 20 centers. Of the central office costs, approximately $120,000 are fixed; the remainder vary with the number of centers.

20 centers is $262,000. The cost of maintaining a teenager at the center is, on average, $6,550 per year (or $1,092 for a two-month stay). The breakdown of costs is presented in Exhibit 19-4.

Required:
1. Specify the costs and benefits of increasing capacity of each of the existing 20 centers by 10 teenagers (a total of 1,200 assuming that each teenager stays at a center for one-sixth of a year).
2. Specify the costs and benefits of serving the additional 200 teenagers (1,200 per year) at five *new* centers, each with 40 teenagers. The centers would be located in areas not presently served by the program.
3. Which of the alternatives described above would you recommend? Explain.
4. Specify the costs and benefits of increasing the ratio of counselors to teenagers at each of the existing 20 centers from 1 : 10 to 1 : 8.
5. Suppose that the state was forced to reduce the scope of the program. The administrator of the program was informed that his budget would

be reduced by 15 percent ($786,000). How would you recommend that the cuts be effected? Indicate the reductions in costs and benefits that would result.

SOLUTIONS TO EXERCISE FOR REVIEW AND SELF-TESTING

1. Required number of units to be produced and sold to meet objective of 10 percent increase in gross margin.
   a. Required margin: 110% of 1983 margin of $180,000: thus, $198,000.
   b. Anticipated selling price: 106% of $20.00; thus, $21.20.
   c. Anticipated variable costs: 106% of $14.00; thus, $14.84 per unit.
   d. Anticipated depreciation: no change; $1.00 per unit times 1983 production volume of 60,000 units $ 60,000
   Anticipated other fixed costs: 106% of $2.00 per unit times 1983 production volume of 60,000 units   127,200

   Total anticipated fixed costs $187,200

   e. Revenue − Fixed costs − Variable costs = Required margin
   Let x = number of units required to be produced and sold
   $$\$21.20x - \$187,200 - \$14.84x = \$198,000$$
   $$\$6.36x = \$385,200$$
   $$x = 60,566 \text{ units}$$

2. Anticipated cash collections in 1984
   a. Units sold per month in 1983:
   $60,000 \div 12 = 5,000$
   Units to be sold per month in 1984:
   $60,566 \div 12 = 5,047$
   b. Collections from sales of 1983
   (1 month; 5,000 units @ $20.00) $ 100,000
   Collections from sales of 1984 (11 months; 5,047 units @ $21.20 times 11)   1,176,960

   Total cash collections $1,276,960

3. Anticipated cash disbursements to meet 1984 production requirements

   Anticipated fixed costs, excluding depreciation (per part 1.d.) $ 127,200
   Anticipated variable costs: $14.84 per unit (per part 1.c.) times anticipated production of 60,566 units (per part 1.e.)   898,799

   Total cash disbursements to meet 1984 production requirements $1,025,999

4. a. Required tax payment. Depreciation for tax purposes using sum-of-the-years' digits method (Sum of digits for useful life of 6 years = 21; in 1984, assets have 5 years of useful life remaining): $5/21 \times 360,000 = 85,714$

Sales revenue (60,566 units @ 21.20)		$1,283,999
Less: Cost of goods produced and sold		
Variable costs (60,566 @ $14.84)	$898,799	
Depreciation	85,714	
Other fixed costs	127,200	1,111,713
Taxable income		$ 172,286
Tax rate		× .40
Required tax payment		$ 68,914

   b. Reported tax expense. Depreciation for reporting purposes is computed using the straight-line method and is, as indicated in part 1.d, $60,000 per year. The reported tax expense would be based on reported income.

Sales revenue		$1,283,999
Less: Cost of goods produced and sold		
Variable costs (60,566 @ $14.84)	$898,799	
Depreciation	60,000	
Other fixed costs	127,200	1,085,999
Income before taxes		$ 198,000
Tax rate		× .40
Tax expense		$ 79,200

INCREMENTAL COSTS AND BENEFITS: THE KEY TO MANAGEMENT DECISIONS

In this chapter we shall continue our discussion of the role that accounting can play in facilitating managerial planning. Our purpose shall be to set forth a general approach to deciding among alternative courses of action. We shall center our attention on decisions in which the time value of money is not a significant factor either because the time horizon is too short or because the discounting process will have the same relative effect on each of the alternatives. Our discussion will be constructed around a series of short cases, several of which, although simple, suggest choices that may not be intuitively obvious.

IDENTIFYING COSTS AND BENEFITS

A decision involves a choice between two or more possibilities. Managers must strive to select the course of action that provides the greatest *benefit* with the least amount of *cost*. Although the term *cost–benefit analysis* is one that is conventionally associated with the nonprofit sector, it is equally applicable to commercial organization. In fact, to a great extent, the art of management as it applies to making decisions involves the identification and the assessment of costs and benefits attributable to two or more options. Once the costs and benefits have been identified, measured, and assigned to the possibilities, the preferable courses of action can usually be determined quite readily.

The benefits associated with a course of action stem directly from the objectives of the organization. In making a decision, managers must specify what it is they expect to accomplish. For most corporate decisions the operational objective is maximization of cash inflow. As a consequence the expected benefits are expressed in terms of net cash receipts. The course of action to be selected is that which provides the greatest net cash flow (adjusted for the time value of money) after taking into account all costs. Maximization of income is ordinarily an inappropriate objective because, in the "short term" (any term less than the life of the enterprise), it is tainted by arbitrary choices among accounting principles, estimates, and allocations of costs.

In theory, all benefits and costs, no matter how indirect, should be taken into account in making a decision as long as the cost of obtaining and processing the required information is less than the expected value of any loss that might be incurred by not taking them into account. Not all benefits and costs, however, can be easily identified, quantified and monetarized. Whereas it may be appropriate to exclude from consideration those costs and benefits that are unlikely to affect the outcome of the decision, it is not acceptable to disregard a cost or benefit merely because it cannot be readily measured and expressed in dollars. If, for example, customer goodwill is an important benefit to be derived, it is preferable to attempt to assign a dollar value to it—even if such an amount is nothing more than the most imperfect estimate—than to ignore it and thereby implicitly assign it a value of zero.

In practice, many managers are uncomfortable assigning dollar values to intangible benefits, such as customer goodwill. Therefore, they exclude them from consideration in the quantitative analysis of the various possibilities. In making the final selection among courses of action, however, they temper the quantitative results of the analysis with the intangible costs and benefits and are willing to select an alternative with lesser quantifiable net benefits over one with greater. The analytical techniques described in this text are unfortunately no better than the estimates of costs and benefits to which they are applied. As a consequence management remains very much of an art rather than a science.

FOCUSING ON DIFFERENTIAL COSTS

While the importance of identifying and quantifying the costs and benefits associated with alternative courses of action cannot be minimized, the burden on the analyst or manager is considerably less onerous than it might first appear. A decision model need not incorporate *all* costs and benefits associated with the various choices; it need include only those costs and benefits that will *differ* among the choices. Those costs and benefits that will be unaffected by the choice need not specifically be taken into account. Suppose, for example, that a firm is considering replacing one machine with another. The new machine will enable the firm to reduce its direct labor costs. If the firm can assume that sales and nonlabor operating costs will be unaffected by the change, then the analysis can focus exclusively on the cost to acquire the machine and the savings in labor costs. Materials, maintenance, and power costs may be directly associated with the use of the machines. But, if they will remain the same irrespective of whether the new machine is acquired, they are irrelevant to the replacement decision.

SPECIFYING A TIME HORIZON

A manager must give careful consideration to the period of time over which a decision will have its effect. For some types of decisions the time horizon that should be taken into account is fairly obvious. If a manager is selecting among firms with which to sign a contract to supply a part to be manufactured according to specification, then the appropriate time frame would ordinarily be the length of the contract. At the conclusion of the contract the firm presumably will be free to choose a new supplier, and its choice the second time can be independent of the supplier it selected the first time. For other types of decisions, the period of time over which to evaluate alternative courses of action is far less clear. Assume, for example, that a firm is engaged in collective bargaining with a union representing its employees. It must decide whether to offer an increase in the base wage rate or an improvement in a medical insurance program. Although the contract may be for a period of two years, a benefit once provided cannot usually be retracted except at considerable cost. Moreover, the wage rate in effect at the conclusion of one contract serves as the basis for negotiations on the next contract. And the wage in effect at the conclusion of the next contract in turn affects the subsequent contract.

UNAVOIDABLE COSTS
ARE IRRELEVANT

Costs which a firm cannot avoid regardless of alternative selected are irrelevant and need not—*should* not—be incorporated into an analysis of costs and benefits. Unavoidable costs are often referred to as *sunk* costs. Sunk costs can be costs that have already been incurred. They can also be those that have yet to be incurred if they will be the same under all available courses of action. The cost of an asset already purchased is a sunk cost. It cannot be retrieved. So also are the costs to be paid in the future on an equipment lease that has already been signed, if the lease is noncancellable. The two cases that follow are intended to highlight the irrelevance of costs that have previously been incurred.

CASE: THE FOOLISH OVERHAUL

Recently, a firm spent $5,000 to repair and overhaul its copy machine. The machine makes copies at a cost of approximately $.05 per copy. This amount includes labor, supplies, power, and maintenance, all of which are variable costs.

The office manager of the firm has been approached by a salesman from a leading copy machine company. His company has offered to lease the firm a new, technologically improved, machine at a cost of $.02 per copy. Additional variable costs will bring the total cost per copy to $.04.

The old machine cannot be sold or leased out for a material amount (a reasonable assumption since the lease arrangement on the new machine is available to any prospective customer). For tax purposes the old machine is fully depreciated and has a book value of zero.

The term of the lease on the new machine can be for a period equal in length to the remaining useful life of the old machine.

The office manager has refused to seriously consider leasing the new machine. "We just spent $5,000 to overhaul the old machine," he said, "There's no point in leasing a new machine until we've received some benefit from the expenditure."

Should the firm sign the lease agreement and abandon the machine that has just been overhauled?

In this case, the $5,000 paid to overhaul the old machine is a sunk cost. It cannot be recovered. As the title to the case suggests, in retrospect at least, it was a mistake to spend the $5,000. The issue that the case presents is whether the firm should now compound its error by continuing to use the old machine or whether it should take advantage of an opportunity to reduce future copying costs by $.01 per copy.

The relevant costs in this case are but two: (1) the $.05 per copy required to operate the old machine, and (2) the $.04 per copy required of the new. A comparison of these two amounts clearly indicates that the lease offer should be accepted.

Pointedly omitted from the case is the number of copies that the organization makes. Such amount is irrelevant as long as it is within the capacity of the two machines. The savings attached to the lease agreement are $.01 per copy regardless of the number of copies made. The greater the number of copies made, the greater the amount of the savings, *but there will be savings as long as any copies are made.* If the facts of the case were different and the firm could sell, lease or make use of the machine in some other manner, then the benefits of such actions (net of taxes) would, of course, have to be taken into account.

CASE: THE UNREPORTED LOSS

A firm has an opportunity to replace a machine with one that is more efficient. The new of five years. The old machine will have no salvage value at the end of its useful life. It could be sold today, however, for $7,000. The machine has a reported book value of $25,000, determined as follows:

Original cost	$40,000
Accumulated depreciation (three years @ $5,000)	15,000
Book value	$25,000

Were the machine to be sold today the firm would have to report a loss on sale of $18,000—book value of $25,000 less sales price of $7,000.

The plant manager has rejected the opportunity to replace the old machine with the new, asserting that the annual cash operating savings are not sufficient to cover the cost of the new machine and the loss that will be incurred upon the sale of the old:

Annual cash savings ($6,000 per year for 5 years)			$30,000
Less: Purchase price of new machine		$20,000	
Loss on sale of old machine			
Book value	$25,000		
Less: Sales price	7,000	18,000	(38,000)
Excess of cost of new machine and loss on old machine over annual cash savings on new machine			$ 8,000

machine will enable the firm to realize *cash* operating savings of $6,000 per year.

The cost of the new machine is $20,000. It will have a useful life of five years, with no salvage value at the end of the five years.

The old machine cost $40,000 when it was acquired three years ago. It has a total useful life of eight years and a remaining useful life

Do you agree with the decision of the plant manager?

This case has much in common with "The Foolish Overhaul." The cost of the old machine, like that of the overhaul, is a sunk cost that cannot be recovered. It is therefore irrelevant to the analysis of the alternatives. The relevant factors are the cash flows that would be different if one alternative as opposed to the other were chosen. For an initial outlay of $13,000 ($20,000 purchase price of new machine less the $7,000 sales price of old), the firm can save $6,000 per year for five years—$30,000. Disregarding the time value of money, the acquisition is clearly favorable:*

Cash Flows

Period		Replace	Do Not Replace
0	Sell old machine	$ 7,000	—
0	Purchase new machine	(20,000)	—
1–5	Cash operating savings (total)	30,000	—
	Net cash inflow	$17,000	

The $18,000 loss results because the firm purchased a machine three years earlier with the expectation that it would have a useful economic life of eight years. It has been depreciating—spreading the cost of—the machine over eight years. If it had correctly foreseen the future, the firm would have depreciated the machine over three years down to its salvage value of $7,000. No loss would then have to be reported; the full cost of using the machine over the three-year period would have been incorporated into the depreciation charges. Because the firm was unable to predict with accuracy the useful life and selling price of the old machine, it must now *recognize* a loss. But such loss is

---

* Because the time horizon for this decision is five years, the time value of money *cannot* properly be ignored. It is ignored here in order to concentrate on the key point which the example is designed to make: the cost of the machine to be disposed of is a sunk cost; neither depreciation charges nor losses, both of which represent the allocation of the cost to particular periods, should be incorporated into the replacement analysis.

nothing more than the assignment of a portion of the cost of the asset to the period of sale.

Depreciation to be charged in the future on both the old and new machines has also been excluded from the analysis. Depreciation is nothing more than an allocation among accounting periods of the original purchase price of an asset. Depreciation on the old machine represents an allocation of a sunk—and therefore irrelevant—cost. Depreciation on the new machine, if incorporated into the analysis, would result in double counting because the cost of the asset has been accounted for directly.

To avoid complicating the analysis, the impact of income taxes has been disregarded. Tax considerations will be dealt with in the chapter to follow.

ONLY INCREMENTAL COSTS ARE RELEVANT

The general notion that unavoidable costs are irrelevant can be applied in a number of situations, in each of which the unavoidable costs take a slightly different form. The case that follows pertains to a decision to manufacture and sell additional units of product. The focus is on *incremental* cost—those that will change if production is increased—rather than on unit average costs, which include elements that will remain unchanged.

CASE: ACCEPT OR REJECT AN "UNPROFITABLE" OFFER

Supertype, Inc., manufactures electronic word processors. They are sold to distributors for $3,000 each. Based on annual volume of 1,000 units, production cost is $2,000 per unit:

Rent of plant offices	$ 150,000
Administration and other fixed overhead costs	350,000
Design and engineering costs included in product cost	300,000
Direct labor (1,000 units @ $500)	500,000
Materials (1,000 units @ $700)	700,000
Total costs	$2,000,000
Number of units	1,000 units
Cost per unit	$ 2,000

Radio World, a national chain of electronics stores, has offered to purchase and distribute under its private label 200 units. The contract price would be $1,400 per unit. The sales manager has indicated that the contract with Radio World would have no impact on the quantity of existing sales.

Should Supertype accept the offer from Radio World?

Although the contract price of $1,400 is considerably less than the $2,000 average production cost, the information suggests that only the direct labor and materials costs would increase if the contract were accepted. The remaining costs are fixed and would, therefore, be unaffected by the decision to accept or to reject the contract. If the contract were accepted the firm would receive an additional $1,400 per unit and incur additional costs of only $1,200 per unit ($500 in direct labor plus $700 in direct materials):

Incremental receipts (200 units @ $1,400)	$280,000
Incremental costs (200 units @ $1,200)	240,000
Net incremental receipts	$ 40,000

It is, therefore, in the interests of the firm to accept the offer. Cash inflow, as well as earnings, would be increased by the sale of the additional 200 units at a price less than *average* production cost.

Whereas it may be inviting to assert that only *variable* costs as opposed to *fixed* costs should be taken into account, it is dangerous to do so, unless it is made clear that the costs are being classified as fixed or variable with respect only to the decision at hand. Rent is ordinarily categorized as a fixed cost. Suppose, however, that the capacity of Supertype's plant is only 1,000 units. If the firm were to accept the offer of Radio World, it would have to rent additional space. As a consequence of the increase in volume, rent costs would also increase. In order to avoid running counter to the conventional classification of costs, it is preferable to generalize the analytical guidelines in terms of incremental versus static or unchanging costs rather than fixed versus variable costs: In making decisions about the future only incremental costs should be taken into account; costs that are static and will remain unchanged regardless of the course of action taken need not be brought into the analysis.

MAKE OR BUY DECISIONS

A broad category of decisions which illustrates further the significance of focusing upon incremental costs is known as "make or buy" decisions. Decisions of this category involve a choice whether to manufacture goods or provide services internally or to acquire them from outsiders. In essence, the approach to making this type of decision is similar to that illustrated previously in the chapter; it requires a determination as to which of two courses of action will enable the organization to maximize net benefits, net benefits being defined as cash inflows less cash outflows. The analytical means of resolving make or buy issues can be illustrated with regard to a service organization.

CASE: ENGAGING A CONTRACTOR TO PERFORM A SERVICE AT LESS THAN COST

Homecheck is a division of Texas Home Sales, Inc. Homecheck inspects homes, prior to their sale, for mechanical and structural defects and certifies to the condition of the homes. The certificate of the company is accepted by a buyer of a home for assurance, in lieu of seller warranties, that the home is in the state represented by the seller. The company charges the seller a fee for its service.

Homecheck has never been profitable; it does, however, support the sales division of Texas Home Sales, Inc., and enables it to provide a full range of services to its customers.

For the year 1983 the financial report of Homecheck indicated the following costs:

Revenues		
(2,500 inspections @ $125)		$312,500
Expenses		
Salaries	$228,000	
Automobile rental fees	24,000	
Rent	6,000	
Allocation of home office overhead	30,000	
Other administrative costs	32,000	320,000
Operating profit (loss)		($ 7,500)

Texas Home Sales, Inc., has received an offer from an outside firm to conduct the inspections on its behalf. The outside firm would charge a fee of $120 per inspection, an amount considerably less than the $128 average cost (2,500 inspections at a total cost of $320,000) presently incurred by the firm. Were Texas Home Sales, Inc., to use the services of the outside contractor, it would retain the revenue of $125 per inspection that it derives from its customers. It would be able to eliminate all expenses associated with Homecheck except that it would be able to reduce office overhead by only $4,000. Moreover, instead of giving up the space presently leased by Homecheck at a cost of $6,000 it would move into those offices the accounting department of another division. That division presently pays $8,000 per year in rental costs.

Assuming that volume of inspections and operating costs of 1983 are indicative of those to be incurred in the future, should Texas Home Sales, Inc., continue to permit its Homecheck division to provide the inspection service or should it acquire the service from the outside firm?

Because the revenues will be unaffected by course of action, the analysis need be directed only to differential costs. Salaries, automobile rental fees, and other administrative costs will be incurred only if Homecheck continues to make the inspections, not if they are contracted-out. Of the home office costs, Texas Home Sales, Inc., will continue to incur $30,000 if the inspection services are performed internally, but only $26,000 if they are carried out by the external contractor. If the firm contracts with the outside company, then $30,000 of overhead will no longer be allocated to Homecheck; all but the $4,000 that will be saved will be reallocated to other corporate divisions.

If the firm continues to carry out the inspections itself it will incur $6,000 per year in rent costs for the space occupied by

Homecheck and $8,000 for that occupied by the accounting department of the other division—a total of $14,000. If it contracts with the outside firm it will incur only the $6,000 per year in rent costs. That would be on the office space now occupied by Homecheck but into which the accounting department of the other division would move. The rental costs on both premises are relevant to the decision and must be incorporated into the analysis.

A comparison of differential costs is as follows:

	Accept the Offer from the Outside Firm	Reject the Offer from the Outside Firm
Salaries		$228,000
Automobile rental fees		24,000
Home office costs	$ 26,000	30,000
Other administrative costs		32,000
Rent on space now occupied by Homecheck	6,000	6,000
Rent on space now occupied by accounting department of other division		8,000
Fee paid to outside firm (2,500 inspections @ $120)	300,000	
Total cash outflows	$332,000	$328,000

The net outflow of the relevant costs is less if the firm continues to provide the service itself. It should reject the offer from the outside concern even though the outside company is willing to provide the service at a per unit cost that is less than the "full" cost that the firm must incur to provide the service itself.

ABANDONMENT DECISIONS

The decision to abandon a line of business has many of the same characteristics as that to make or buy. Those costs that the firm will be able to eliminate must be differentiated from those that it will not, and the analysis must focus exclusively on the former.

CASE: DISCONTINUING A LOSING PRODUCT

Green Thumb, Inc., is deciding whether to discontinue the production and sale of a garden tool that it manufactures. Management has determined that at anticipated volume of 10,000 units per year and a competitive selling price of $14 per unit, the firm will lose $2.50 per unit sold:

Selling price			$14.00
Less: Standard manufacturing costs			
Direct labor	$4.00		
Direct materials	6.00		
Overhead ($.75 per direct labor dollar)	3.00	$13.00	
Selling costs		3.50	16.50
Profit (loss) per unit			($ 2.50)

The overhead charging rate of $.75 per direct labor hour was developed as follows:

Overhead costs	
Payroll-related fringe benefits and taxes	$ 6,000
Allocation of plant depreciation	5,000
Allocation of building occupancy costs	8,000
Allocation of factory administration and maintenance costs	2,000
Depreciation of manufacturing equipment	9,000
Total overhead costs	$30,000
Direct labor dollars	÷ $40,000
Overhead charging rate	$ 0.75

tool is discontinued the costs will be spread among the other products.

The manufacturing equipment would have to be abandoned; it has but negligible salvage value.

Were the firm to continue to produce the garden tool, then on average $12,000 of equipment would have to be acquired each year.

Of the overhead costs requiring cash outlays, only the payroll related fringe benefits and taxes could be eliminated if the garden tool were discontinued. The other cash costs (building occupancy, factory administration, and maintenance) would be reallocated to other products.

The analysis that follows indicates those revenues that would be greater and costs that would be less if the product were continued:

	Product Continued	Product Discontinued
Sales revenue (10,000 @ $14)	$140,000	—
Direct labor (10,000 @ $4)	(40,000)	—
Direct materials (10,000 @ $6)	(60,000)	—
Payroll-related fringe benefits and taxes	(6,000)	—
Replacement of manufacturing equipment	(12,000)	—
Selling costs	(5,000)	—
Net inflows (+) or outflows (−)	$ 17,000	—

Management has also made the following additional determinations pertaining to its decision whether to discontinue:

Selling costs amount to $35,000. Of this amount only $5,000 can be associated directly with the garden tool. The remaining $30,000 are costs that are common to other products. If the garden

Despite an apparent loss of $2.50 per unit—a total of $25,000—the firm would be $17,000 better off by continuing the product.

The differential costs that are incorporated into the analysis include manufacturing equipment to be acquired in the future. They exclude the depreciation charges on the existing equipment because those expenses are nothing more than the amortization of past—and therefore irrelevant—costs. Also excluded are the costs that will be reallocated to other departments or products. From the perspective of the company as a whole they will be unaffected by the decision whether to discontinue the garden tool.

As an alternative to the analysis presented, the costs that would be the same under both courses of action (e.g., the costs to be reallocated) could be included in *both* columns. The net difference of $17,000 between continuing and discontinuing would, of course, remain unaffected by the addition of identical amounts to the two columns.

SELL OR PROCESS FURTHER

Another class of decisions in which the analytical focus must be on incremental revenues and costs is whether to sell a product at one stage of production or to continuing processing so that it may be eventually sold at a higher price. In general, the decision rule is simple: continue to process as long as the additional revenues to be earned will be greater than the additional costs to be incurred.

CASE: PROCESS FURTHER DESPITE LOSSES

As a consequence of producing its primary product, a liquid detergent, the Niagara Chemical Company must also produce an industrial solvent. A batch of 10,000 gallons of raw materials will ordinarily produce 6,000 gallons of detergent and 4,000 gallons of solvent. Total cost per batch is $40,000. The policy of the company is to allocate joint costs on the basis of physical units.

The detergent is sold at a price of $6 per gallon. The 4,000 gallons of solvent can be sold as a low-grade solvent for $3 per gallon. Alternatively, it can be processed further, at a cost of $3.75 per gallon and sold as a high-grade solvent at a price of $7 per gallon.

Should the company sell the 4,000 gallons as a low-grade solvent or should it process it further and sell it as a high-grade solvent? Alternatively, should it dispose of the 4,000 gallons as waste and not sell them at all?

As in the previous illustrations, an appropriate analysis focuses on the incremental receipts and costs associated with each of the courses of action to be considered. The costs and receipts associated with the 6,000 gallons of detergent as shown below are not introduced into the analysis as they will be the same regardless of the decision made with respect to the 4,000 gallons of solvent.

The analysis makes it clear that the firm would be best-off by processing further. This course of action would leave it with a $.25 per gallon (a total of 4,000 times that amount, $1,000) advantage over not processing further.

The appropriate choice may seem obvious; indeed, the issue may seem trivial. It is clear there would be no reason to dispose of goods that could be sold, with no incremental cost,

	Do Not Process Further	Process Further	Dispose of as Waste
Receipts per gallon	$3.00	$7.00	$0.0
Additional costs to be incurred	0.00	3.75	0.0
Net incremental receipts	$3.00	$3.25	$0.0

for $3 per gallon; it is equally apparent that a firm should incur an additional $3.75 in costs in order to be able to earn additional revenue of $4 per gallon (the $7 per gallon selling price of high-grade solvent less the $3 per gallon selling price of low-grade solvent).

The analysis is straightforward only, however, because it focused on incremental costs and receipts. From the perspective of the manager concerned with *external reporting*, the $40,000 of common costs—those to produce the 10,000 gallons of both detergent and solvent—would have to be allocated between the two products. If allocated on the basis of physical units, then the cost per gallon of solvent, before additional processing would be:

Share of common costs
   (4,000/10,000 of $40,000) $16,000
Divided by number of
   gallons   ÷ 4,000 gal
    Cost per gallon of solvent
    before additional
    processing $ 4.00

dispose of the product as waste rather than sell it "as a loss." Such a conclusion would clearly be unwarranted; the $40,000 of common costs must be incurred in order to produce the 6,000 gallons of detergent. Inasmuch as they will be incurred regardless of whether the solvent is disposed of as waste, or sold as either low-grade or high-grade solvent, they are irrelevant to the decision at hand.

The irrelevance of the $40,000 common costs to the question of what to do with the 4,000 gallons of solvent can be emphasized further by pointing to the variety of bases, other than physical units, by which they could have been allocated between the two products. One popular basis of allocating joint costs is net realizable value. Net realizable value is the total revenues to be received, less any additional costs to be incurred. If the common costs were allocated on the basis of net realizable value, the per gallon cost of the solvent prior to further processing would be only $2.65 as indicated in the analysis that follows:

	Detergent	Solvent	Total
Total revenues	$36,000[a]	$28,000[b]	$64,000
Costs of additional processing	—	(15,000)[c]	(15,000)
Net realizable value	$36,000	$13,000	$49,000
% of net realizable value	73.47%	26.53%	100%
Share of common costs (% of net realizable value applied to $40,000)	$29,388	$10,612	$40,000
Number of gallons of solvent		÷ 4,000	
Cost per gallon of solvent before additional processing		$ 2.65	

[a] 6,000 gallons @ $6.00.
[b] 4,000 galloons @ $7.00.
[c] 4,000 galloons @ $3.75.

If the cost per gallon were $4.00 and the amount for which it could be sold in an unprocessed state were only $3.00 per gallon, it might appear that the firm should prefer to

Choice of basis is at the discretion of the firm. It is unreasonable to suppose that an arbitrary decision as to how to *allocate* costs among joint products could make it more or less economically desirable to sell or dispose of the products one way as opposed to others. The principles of financial accounting and reporting require that cost of goods sold include a share of all costs needed to manufacture a product. Hence, management *must* select a means of allocating joint costs to the common products. But since the total joint costs incurred will be the same regardless of how allocated, they are irrelevant to decisions as to how best to sell or dispose of any one of the joint products.

PRICING DECISIONS

Decisions pertaining to the prices at which goods are to be sold or services rendered are among the most common made by managers. Without question, "cost" must be a key element of any pricing analysis. Pricing decisions, however, necessarily involve numerous other considerations. Among them, to indicate but a few, are the extent of competition faced by the firm, the regulatory environment in which the organization does business, the shape of the product's demand curve (a graphic depiction of the number of units that can be sold at various prices), the "image" that a firm wants a product to project, and the role played by the product in supporting other products of the firm. Pricing decisions are both complex and cross-disciplinary; they cannot be covered adequately in this text. Nonetheless, because of the importance attached to costs, a few caveats pertaining to "full cost" pricing are in order.

In adopting pricing policies it is common for companies to add a percentage markup to the cost of their products. The cost to which the markup is applied is generally the "full cost." Full cost, as explained in previous chapters, includes direct labor, direct materials, and overhead. Overhead, commonly

assigned by way of an overhead charging rate, includes variable overhead as well as fixed overhead. Fixed overhead may comprise costs, such as those of building occupancy, which have been allocated from service departments.

Inherent Flow in Full-Cost Pricing Policies

Pricing policies that are based on full costs have an inherent flaw: they are based on a factor, full cost, that is not only unstable but is dependent on the amount that is to be determined, price itself. The overhead charging rate is calculated by dividing estimated overhead costs by estimated volume. Hence, the fewer the number of units produced, the greater will be the overhead charging rate and the greater will be the full cost of the product. If price is to be established by adding a percentage markup to full cost, then the fewer the number of units produced, the greater will be the price. For most costs or services, however, the greater the price, the fewer will be the number of units sold. The consequences of adhering rigidly to a policy of adding a percentage markup to full cost can be appreciated by considering a manufacturing concern which, as a result of increases in direct materials, elects to raise the price of its product. The price increase causes a slight decline in sales volume. In response to the reduced sales, the manufacturer reduces output, thereby causing an increase in unit cost. If the manufacturer were to react by further increasing prices to reflect this increase in cost, then a spiral of price increases, volume decreases, and cost increases would be set into motion.

Unnecessary to Always Cover Full Cost

There is no need for a firm to cover full cost on all products at all times. This point was implied earlier in this chapter in the context of the decision as to whether to accept or reject a contract in which the selling price was less than full cost but greater than incremental cost (see the case "Accept or Reject an Unprofitable Offer"). A firm can realize maximum profitability even if it never covers the full cost of some of its products—as long, of course, as it covers the incremental cost of each of its products and the full cost of all of its products combined. The case "Process Further Despite Losses" provided an example of a situation in which the market price for one of the firm's two products was insufficient to cover its full cost. Nonetheless, it was clearly in the interest of the firm to continue to sell the product because the combined revenue from the two products exceeded the combined cost.

Full cost is almost always a function of a number of management decisions as to how to allocate costs that are common to various departments and products. Different allocation decisions would result in different costs. If a pricing scheme based on percentage markups to full cost were truly to result in the establishment of optimum prices, then one arbitrary allocation decision would result in one "optimum" price; another arbitrary allocation decision in a different "optimum" price. It is unreasonable to suspect—and in fact can be easily demonstrated analytically—that optimality of price is independent of management decisions as to how to distribute common manufacturing costs.

Regardless of the pricing policy adopted by a firm, it is essential that management evaluate the impact upon profits that alternative prices will have. Management must estimate the number of units that will be sold at the various prices under consideration and determine the production costs at the volumes required to satisfy demand. Cost–volume–profit analysis, which was discussed in a previous chapter, is one means of assuring that a distinction is made between those costs that will remain fixed as output changes and those that will vary. Because it is so important to determine the contribution that each product is making toward covering fixed costs, some firms employ a form of direct costing to establish prices and evaluate their impact on profits. The "relevant" cost of a product is considered to be the variable cost—direct labor, direct materials, and *variable* overhead only. A percentage markup is added to the variable cost rather than the full cost. Any pricing formula that is entirely cost-cased can be faulted as being simplistic in that it can never result in prices that are optimum in all economic circumstances. But a direct-cost pricing formula is likely to be preferable to a full-cost formula in that it at least assures that the focus of analysis is upon the incremental production costs.

"Accountants' Cost"

Marketing executives have been known to refer disparagingly to the "accountants' cost." By that they invariably mean full cost—that assigned on the financial statements to the goods sold or in inventory. They point out—quite correctly—that such cost is inappropriate for making pricing and other marketing decisions. They err, however, in implying that there is a particular "accountants' cost." Knowledgeable accountants (as well as knowledgeable marketing executives) are well aware of the limitations of full cost and of the importance of including in the determination of cost only those elements that are relevant to the decisions that it will be used to facilitate.

SELECTING THE PRODUCT MIX

Decisions regarding the mix of products that a firm should produce are, like pricing decisions, interdisciplinary. The discussion that follows focuses on accounting aspects of the product-mix question, and avoids issues conventionally considered within the domain of marketing, production, or other nonaccounting specialists. Underlying the illustrations, for example, will be the assumption that the sales volume of the various products produced by a firm are independent of one another. In practice, two or more products may be closely tied. One product may complement another. A manufacturer of shaving equipment may find that the profitability of blades is greater than that of razors. Accounting analyses might indicate that the firm should therefore devote all of its resources to the production of blades. Yet marketing considerations may dictate that in order to support the sale of blades, it must produce and sell razors as well.

CASE: SELECTING THE OPTIMUM PRODUCT MIX

Ceiling Fans, Inc., has the capability of producing two styles of fans: modern and traditional. The following data pertain to each of the two styles:

	Traditional	Modern
Selling price per unit	$120	$145
Variable costs per unit	80	100
Contribution margin (selling price less variable costs) per unit	40	45
Number of direct labor hours required to produce each unit	2 hours	3 hours

The company must decide on a combination of the two styles to produce. It can produce all traditional fans, all modern fans, or a mix of the two.

The modern style is the more profitable of the two styles. Its contribution margin is $45 as opposed to $40 for the traditional style. A sale of one unit of the modern style will add $45 to the profits of the firm while a sale of one unit of the traditional style will add only $40. This is true regardless of the amount of fixed costs or the means of allocating common costs (information on both having been omitted to emphasize their irrelevance to the decision at hand).

One Constraint

Assume that Ceiling Fans, Inc., can sell all the fans that it produces, but that the key factor that limits production is the number of available skilled employees. Direct labor hours is, therefore, the critical *constraint* on production.

When there is only one constraint, a firm can maximize contribution to profit by devoting its resources entirely to the production of the product for which the contribution margin of each unit of the constraining factor is the greatest.

Regardless of the specific number of direct labor hours available to it, the firm could maximize its profits by manufacturing only the traditional style fan. The contribution margin per the constraining factor will be greater for traditional-style than for modern-style fans:

	Traditional	Modern
Contribution margin	$40	$45
Number of direct labor hours required	÷ 2 hours	÷ 3 hours
Contribution margin per direct labor hour	$20	$15

Suppose that Ceiling Fans, Inc., can hire employees to provide a total of 180 direct labor hours per day. With 180 direct labor hours per day, it could produce any number of combinations of traditional- and modern-style fans. At the extremes, however, it could produce 90 traditional fans or 60 modern fans:

combinations of production that would yield a contribution of $720. A contribution of $720 could be achieved, for example, by producing 18 traditional-style fans and zero modern-style fans, zero traditional-style fans and 16 modern-style fans, or 9 traditional-style fans and 8 modern-style fans. Equal contribution line 2 indicates the possible com-

	Traditional	Modern
Number of direct labor hours available	180 hours	180 hours
Number of direct labor hours required to produce each unit	÷ 2 hours	÷ 3 hours
Maximum number of units that could be produced assuming zero hours directed to manufacture of other style	90 units	60 units

If the firm were to produce 90 traditional-style fans, then the contribution to profit would be $3,600—90 times the traditional-style fan contribution margin of $40. If the firm shifted any portion of available direct labor hours—the critical resource—to the manufacture of modern-style fans, then the overall contribution to profits would be decreased.

The combination that maximizes contribution to profit can also be determined graphically. In Exhibit 20-1 the direct labor constraint line indicates the possible combinations of the two styles of fans that could be produced with 180 direct labor hours. Also indicated in Exhibit 20-1 are two lines (dashed), each point on which represents a combination of production that would yield the same contribution to profit as any other point on that line. Each line (said to depict the *objective function* because it is the objective of the firm to maximize contribution to profit) represents a particular dollar contribution to profit. Equal contribution line 1, for example, indicates the possible

binations of production that would yield a contribution of $3,600. The two lines are merely illustrative of an infinite number of other possible lines—all parallel to one another—that represent other contributions to profit. The more distant is a line from the origin, the greater is the contribution to profits that it represents and the greater the amount of resources that is required to achieve that contribution to profits. A firm, however, must operate within the boundaries of its constraints. Equal contribution line 2 is the line that is farthest from the origin and still within (if only at a single point) the area bounded by the labor constraint. At that point, which indicates production of 90 traditional-style fans and zero modern-style fans, the contribution to profits is a maximum—$3,600. Any other point on the graph would be either outside the constraint line (and require the use of more than 180 hours of direct labor) or on an equal contribution line representative of a smaller contribution to profits. Graphically, therefore, the optimum combination is found by locating the

EXHIBIT 20-1

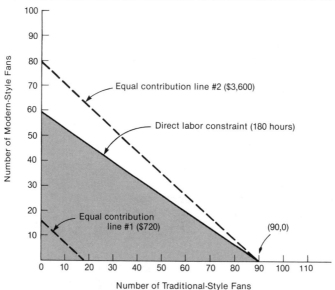

All combinations on equal contribution line #1 contribute $720 to firm profits.

All combinations on equal contribution line #2 contribute $3,600 to firm profits.

All combinations on the direct labor constraint line require 180 direct labor hours.

The shaded area represents all feasible combinations—those which satisfy the constraints.

point that is within the area bounded by the constraint and on the equal contribution line that is farthest from the origin.

Two Constraints

Assume now, in addition to the facts already presented, that each fan must undergo a machining process, the number of hours of which depends on the style:

Style	Required Machine Hours
Traditional	2.0
Modern	1.5

The maximum number of machine hours that are available per day is 150. At the extremes, therefore, the firm could produce either 75 traditional-style fans and zero modern style-fans or 100 modern-style fans and zero traditional-style fans:

	Traditional	Modern
Number of machine hours available	150	150
Number of machine hours required to produce each unit	÷ 2.0	÷ 1.5
Maximum number of units that could be produced assuming zero hours directed to manufacture of other style	75	100

The firm could no longer, under any circumstances, produce the 90 traditional fans that served to maximize contribution to profit when there was only one constraint.

The objective of the firm is to maximize contribution to profits, subject to two constraints. Algebraically, the contribution to profits (CP) can be expressed as:

$$\$40T + \$45M = CP$$

where T and M represent, respectively, the number of traditional and modern fans. The two constraints can be expressed as:

1. Labor hours constraint $2T + 3M \leq 180$
2. Machine hours constraint $2T + 1.5M \leq 150$

When expressed in this form, the problem can readily be solved using a quantitative technique known as *linear programming*. Linear programming is described in standard texts on operations research. Diagrammatically, the product mix that maximizes contribution to profit can be determined in the same manner as was illustrated with a single constraint.

Exhibit 20-2 incorporates two lines representing constraints, as opposed to only one in Exhibit 20-1. The area bounded by the constraints (the shaded area) represents the feasible solution. The firm can produce any

EXHIBIT 20-2

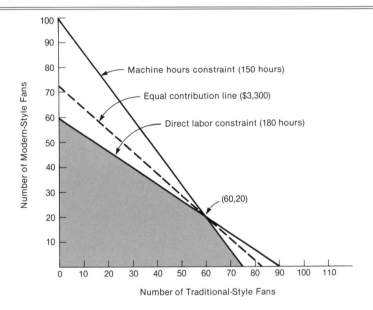

All combinations on the equal contribution line contribute $3,300 to firm profits.

All combinations on the machine hours constraint line require 150 machine hours.

All combinations on the direct labor constraint line require 180 direct labor hours.

The shaded area represents all feasible combinations—those which satisfy the two constraints.

combination within that region. The combination that maximizes contribution to profit, however, is the one which lies on the equal contribution line farthest from the origin yet is still within the feasible region. The equal contribution line drawn in Exhibit 20-2 is, as in Exhibit 20-1, but one in a series of possible parallel lines, each of which represents a particular contribution to profits. It was drawn by first selecting a convenient dollar amount (e.g., $3,600) and plotting the two extreme combinations of products that would provide this contribution to profit. A line (not shown) connecting these points was drawn. A ruler was then placed on the line and moved downward to the corner of the feasible region where the two constraint lines intersect (point 60, 20) and a second line, parallel to the first was drawn. This second line is the equal contribution line that is farthest from the origin and still within the feasible region. It is within the feasible region at only one point, that representing a combination of 60 traditional-style fans and 20 modern-style fans. It is this combination, therefore, that satisfies the two constraints and yields the maximum contribution to profit. Since the contribution margin of traditional-style fans is $40 and that of modern-style fans is $45, the total contribution of this combination would be $3,300:

$$\$40T + \$45M = CP$$

$$\$40(60) + \$45(20) = \$3,300$$

The graphic solution can be generalized to take into account any number of constraints. The optimum solution will be on the corner of the feasible region that is tangent to the equal contribution line located farthest from the origin but which still has a feasible combination on it.

SUMMARY

In Chapter 17 we set forth several themes for the section of the text pertaining to "management" accounting. Two of them were:

1. For virtually all decisions managers are called on to make, only future receipts and costs matter and should properly be taken into account. Past receipts and costs are relevant only to the extent that they serve as a guide to or affect the determination of those of the future.

2. Insofar as it is the objective of a manager to maximize the economic well-being of an organization then only *cash*—not income—matters. In evaluating the effect of decisions, a manager must focus on anticipated inflows and outflow of cash.

This chapter has served to develop these themes. In presenting the examples we have emphasized the need to identify the incremental cash receipts and disbursements that will be associated with a course of action. Depreciation and gain or loss on sale, we pointed out, while they might appear to be outlays of the future, are in fact allocations of costs previously incurred. Generally, therefore (except to the extent that they may have an impact on future tax liabilities) they are irrelevant to most decisions that managers are called on to make. Similarly, allocations of factory, administrative, or other costs that will remain unchanged in total regardless of course of action selected need not be explicitly incorporated into an analysis of the choices faced by a manager.

A third theme set forth in Chapter 17 was that in evaluating cash flows, both the time value of money and the uncertainty surrounding the cash flows must be taken into account. In this chapter, however, the examples were structured so that the significance in differences in the timing of cash flows between alternative courses of action was minimized. In all cases we assumed that cash flows could be estimated with certainty. Moreover, in an effort to focus on a small number of concepts, we failed to take into account the income tax consequences of the decisions analyzed. Each of these gaps will be closed in the forthcoming chapter.

EXERCISE FOR REVIEW AND SELF-TESTING

Pottsdam Paper, Inc., manufactures and sells to retailers a line of quality stationery. The firm also sells its products directly to consumers, soliciting mail orders through magazine advertisements. The stationery sold to retailers is not personalized; that sold directly to consumers is. Pottsdam maintains a small printshop, which imprints the stationery with a name and address as ordered by the customer. The company does not own a printing press; it rents one under a long-term lease arrangement. The lease agreement can be canceled by the lessee at any time.

The firm estimates that the cost of producing a single box of stationery, without printing is $16. Printing adds an additional $4.25 per box. The company sells approximately 10,000 boxes of personalized stationery per year. Per box, as well as annual, printing costs are as follows:

	Per Box	Annual (10,000 boxes)
Direct labor	$3.00	$30,000
Ink and other supplies	.25	2,500
Lease of printing press	.40	4,000
Allocation of plant overhead	.60	6,000
Total	$4.25	$42,500

The company is considering discontinuing its printing operation and contracting the work to an outside firm. It would continue, however, to carry out all other phases of its mail order business. Were the firm to discontinue the printing operation, it could rent the space to outsiders at an annual rental charge of $3,000. The tenant would provide its own heating and air conditioning, thereby enabling Pottsdam to reduce its plant overhead by $1,000. The print shop is presently operated by a single employee, who earns $30,000 per year in salary. Were the printing operation to be discontinued, he would be transferred to another department and would draw his present salary. He would, however, be filling a position that is classified for a considerably lower salary—$24,000—and would ordinarily be filled with an employee who would be paid at that rate. What is the maximum price per box that Pottsdam should be willing to pay an outsider contractor to perform the printing services? To simplify the analysis, income tax considerations may be ignored.

1. What, in general terms, is the most the company should pay to have a service performed by outsiders?

2. Would either revenues or the costs of manufacturing the stationery, excluding printing and other costs described previously, be affected by the decision to contract-out the printing? Are such revenues and costs relevant to the determination of the price to be paid to an outside contractor?

3. Indicate for each of the following the relevant amounts to be paid or received under the alternative assumptions that the firm continues to personalize the stationery itself and that it contracts the service to an outside printer.
   a. Ink and other supplies.
   b. Labor (taking into account any "extra" costs that the firm would incur in other departments if it were to abandon the printshop, transfer the printshop employee to another department, and pay him a premium above the rate at which it would have to compensate a different employee carrying out the same assignment.
   c. Rent on printing press.
   d. Air conditioning and heating costs.
   e. Other plant overhead.
   f. Rent received from tenant.

4. Summarize the differences in costs and revenues and indicate the per box savings—the amount

the company would be willing to pay to an outside contractor—that would be realized by discontinuing the printing operations.

5. Suppose that the company owned rather than leased its printing press. Book value (original cost less accumulated depreciation) of the press was $15,000. It could be sold for $10,000 cash. Annual depreciation was $5,000. Explain how the opportunity to sell the press would affect the analysis.

QUESTIONS FOR REVIEW AND DISCUSSION

1. The costs and benefits associated with possible courses of action must be related to the objectives of the organization. What do managers ordinarily assume to be the objectives of a corporation? Why is maximization of *income* ordinarily an inappropriate objective for most types of decisions?

2. Why is it ordinarily unnecessary for a manager to identify and quantify *all* costs and benefits associated with alternative courses of action?

3. Why is the time horizon of a course of action sometimes uncertain or difficult to determine? Provide an example.

4. Why are *loss on sale of equipment* and *depreciation expense* generally irrelevant to most decisions (except insofar as they affect a firm's tax liability)?

5. In determining whether to make or to buy a product, how should administrative and factory costs that are common to more than one product be taken into account?

6. Why is the *average* unit cost of a product generally irrelevant in decisions as to whether a product should be discontinued, processed further, or sold at a "loss?"

7. It is the policy of a company to sell all goods that it produces at a price 20 percent above "full" cost? What is "full" cost and what are the limitations of such a policy?

8. "*Accountants*' cost is inappropriate for most marketing decisions." Comment.

9. "In determining optimum product mix, it is generally to the advantage of the company to produce the maximum number of units possible of the product with the greatest contribution margin." Do you agree? Explain.

10. If optimum product mix is to be determined graphically, what point on the graph would represent optimum product mix? Explain.

PROBLEMS

1. *In deciding which of two or more products should be produced, only incremental revenues and costs are relevant.*

Artform Printers, Inc., had planned to publish a calendar containing quality prints. The firm established that it would be able to sell 5,000 of the calendars at a price of $13 per calendar. It had already incurred $20,000 in art and design costs. It estimated that it would be able to earn a profit on the calendars of $18,150 ($3.63 per unit) computed as follows:

Sales revenue (5,000 @ $13.00)			$65,000
Cost of goods sold			
Direct labor (360 hours @ $15.00)		$ 5,400	
Direct materials ($.75 per unit)		3,750	
Overhead			
Fixed ($5.00 per direct labor hour; 360 hours @ $5.00)	$1,800		
Variable ($2.50 per direct labor hour; 360 hours @ $2.50)	900	2,700	
Art and design costs		20,000	31,850
Gross margin			33,150
Selling and advertising costs			15,000
Income			$18,150

As the company was about to print the calendars, it received a special order to print 10,000 posters at a contract price of $30,000. The firm estimates the cost of the posters to be $10,750 ($1.075 per unit) determined as follows:

Direct labor (300 hours @ $15.00)		$ 4,500
Direct materials ($.40 per unit)		4,000
Overhead		
Fixed ($5.00 per direct labor hour; 300 hours @ $5)	$1,500	
Variable ($2.50 per direct labor hour; 300 hours @ $2.50)	750	2,250
Total cost		$10,750

Thus, its estimated profit on the posters will be $19,250—revenue of $30,000 less costs of $10,750. The order for the posters is "special rush"; the posters must be given priority over the calendars. However, if the firm postpones printing the calendars, it will be too late to distribute them on a timely basis and customers will refuse to accept them.

In light of the costs already incurred to produce the calendars, should the firm accept the order for the posters? Explain, show all calculations, and specifically identify the revenues and costs that are relevant to your analysis.

2. Incremental costs can be greater rather than less than average costs.

Winter Sports, Inc., manufactures a line of fiberglass skis. Based on annual volume of 5,000 pairs, cost per pair is $185:

Direct labor ($75 per pair)		$375,000
Direct materials ($60 per pair)		300,000
Overhead		
Fixed	$100,000	
Variable ($.40 per direct labor dollar)	150,000	250,000
Total costs		$925,000
Annual volume		÷ 5,000 pairs
Cost per pair		$ 185

Winter Sports, Inc., sells its skis to retailers at a price of $225 per pair.

Sports Palace, Inc., a discount sporting goods store, has asked Winter Sports, Inc., to sell to it 1,000 pairs of skis, under a private brand, at a price of $200 per pair. The skis would be identical to those normally sold for $225.

Winter Sports has estimated that if it accepted the order, then Sports Palace, Inc., would reduce its usual order by 500 pairs and these sales could not be recouped elsewhere. It has also determined that in order to manufacture the additional skis that would result from accepting the order, all of the resultant direct labor hours would have to be compensated at overtime rates, which are $1\frac{1}{2}$ times the base rates. Overtime premium is charged to an overhead account rather than to direct labor; variable overhead is based on direct labor dollars, excluding overtime premiums.

Should Winter Sports, Inc., accept the special order from Sports Palace, Inc.? Prepare a supporting analysis.

3. Further processing may result in lower reported profits than sales without further processing but may nevertheless be in the best interests of the company.

Real Timepiece Co. manufactures several lines of watches. The cost to manufacture one type of digital watch is $212:

Direct labor		$ 40.00
Direct materials		150.00
Overhead		
Fixed	$16.00	
Variable	6.00	22.00
Total cost per unit		$212.00

Fixed overhead is applied at the rate of $0.40 per direct labor dollar; variable overhead at the rate of $0.15 per direct labor dollar.

The company manufactured 10,000 units of this type of watch and has sold 9,000 of them at a price of $250. Owing to technological improvements in the industry and increased competition from other firms, the firm will have considerable difficulty in selling the remaining 1,000 units at the "standard" price of $250 unless it is willing to undertake an extensive advertising and sales campaign. Such a campaign would cost approximately $60,000. The firm is unwilling to reduce the price of the watch for fear that it would tarnish its image as a manufacturer of high-quality timpieces and thereby have a deleterious effect on sales of other products.

The firm has had an offer from a marketing concern that sells specialty items to university alumni associations. The concern would buy 1,000 watches at a price of $225 per watch if the firm would customize the watches with the crest of a particular university. Real Timepiece estimates that the customizing work would require $20 per watch in direct labor, $10 in direct materials, and $.15 per direct labor dollar in variable overhead. Consistent with company policies, overhead would be applied to the extra work at the standard overhead rates of $.40 (fixed) and $.15 (variable) per direct labor dollar.

a. The company is concerned about the negative effect that both of the alternatives (conducting the costly advertising campaign and selling without customizing, or selling after customizing) would have upon the quarterly income that it will be required to report. Which of the alternatives would have the more negative impact on earnings? Show all computations. (Do not include in your calculations any adjustments for under- or overabsorbed overhead; assume that they are made only at year end.)

b. Which of the alternatives would you recommend to the company if the selection criterion is to be net incremental revenue?

c. Suppose that the marketing concern offered the company only $50 per watch and that the firm's best other option was to sell the watches to a salvage dealer for $10 per watch. Should the company accept the offer from the marketing concern, assuming that it will have no effect on the prices at which other lines of watches are sold? What are the relevant revenues and costs for such a decision?

4. *The decision to make or buy may be influenced by volume.*

Empire Engines is considering purchasing a part that it currently manufactures. Annual costs asso-

ciated with the production of the part are as follows:

Variable		
Materials	$130,000	
Direct labor	90,000	
Supplies	4,000	
Power	3,000	
Other variable costs	16,000	$243,000

Fixed		
Indirect labor	30,000	
Depreciation	15,000	
Allocation of factory and administrative costs from other departments	20,000	
Other fixed costs	6,000	71,000
Total costs		$314,000

All fixed costs, with the exception of the allocated costs, are associated directly with the production of the part and could be eliminated if the firm ceased to manufacture it. Depreciation charges are approximately equal to annual expenditures required to replace plant and equipment.

Annual production of the part is 5,000 units.

An outside supplier has agreed to furnish the part for $55 per unit.

a. Determine the "full" cost of the part.

b. Prepare a schedule which compares the relevant costs of buying the part with those of manufacturing it. Should the company buy or manufacture the product?

c. Suppose that the annual production volume of the part was 10,000 units. Would your recommendation be the same? Explain and show any relevant computations.

5. *Only future costs are relevant to the decision whether to discontinue a business segment.*

Multiproducts, Inc., is considering selling the assets associated with one segment of its business. It would also retire the bonds for which the assets serve as collateral.

The assets and the bonds are reported on the firm's balance sheet as follows:

Plant and equipment	$6,000,000	
Less: Accumulated depreciation	(2,000,000)	$4,000,000
Patents and licensing agreements	$ 800,000	
Less: Accumulated amortization	(300,000)	500,000
Total assets		$4,500,000
Bonds payable	$1,000,000	
Add: Unamortized bond premium	70,000	1,070,000
Net book value of assets to be sold and bonds retired		$3,430,000

The firm anticipates that the reported income of the segment that would be discontinued would be approximately $420,000 per year comprising the following elements:

Sales revenue			$5,713,000
Less: Expenses			
Labor, material and other manufacturing costs associated with the segment		$4,640,000	
Depreciation		500,000	
Amortization of patents and licensing agreements		100,000	
Interest on bonds	$60,000		
Less: Amortization of bond premium	(7,000)	53,000	5,293,000
Income of segment that would be discontinued			$ 420,000

The firm estimates that annual cash outlays of $800,000 would be required to replace and renew plant equipment, patents, and licensing agreements.

The firm has been offered $3,500,000 for the plant and equipment and $600,000 for the patents and licensing agreements. It would be able to redeem the bonds at their face value of $1 million.

Were the firm to sell the assets and retire the bonds, it would invest the net proceeds of $3,100,000 in securities that will provide an annual return of $465,000 (15 percent).

a. Determine the amount of net gain or loss that the firm would have to report at the time the assets were sold and the bonds retired if it elected to discontinue the business segment. For simplicity of analysis, ignore the impact of income taxes.

b. Prepare an analysis which would aid management in deciding whether to discontinue the business segment. Be sure that you identify the revenues and costs that are relevant to the decision at hand. Assume that all revenues and ex-penses associated with the segment would continue at their same level indefinitely. Of what relevance is the net gain or loss determined in Part a?

6. *The decision to add a business segment, like that to discontinue one, requires incremental analysis.*

Fashion Shoes, Inc., manufactures quality men's shoes. The shoes are sold to retailers at $90 per pair; annual volume is 30,000 pairs. The cost to manufacture each pair of shoes is $72:

Direct labor		$40
Direct materials		10
Overhead		
Fixed	$14	
Variable	8	22
Total cost		$72

Fixed overhead, which totals $420,000, is applied at the rate of $.35 per direct labor dollar; variable overhead, which totals $240,000, is applied at the rate of $.20 per direct labor dollar.

The firm is considering adding a line of men's boots. It estimates that it could sell 5,000 pairs per year at a price of $130.

The company has determined that for the boots direct labor would be $70 per pair and direct materials would be $30 per pair. Variable overhead would remain proportional to direct labor costs ($.20 per direct labor dollar), but owing to the addition of new facilities fixed overhead would increase by $45,000 to $465,000. Correspondingly, the fixed portion of the overhead charging rate would change to take into account the additional fixed overhead as well as the additional direct labor dollars.

Some managers of the firm have opposed adding the new product line, contending that cost per unit would exceed the selling price of $130.

a. Prepare an income statement for the existing line of *shoes*, assuming that the firm does *not* add the line of boots.

b. Determine the per unit cost, including both fixed and variable overhead, of manufacturing each pair of *boots*.

c. Prepare a statement of income for the line of boots.

d. Do you think that the company should add the line of boots, even if it would have to sell the boots at less than full cost? Explain and support your response with appropriate calculations.

e. Prepare an income statement for the two products combined. Include one column for shoes, one for boots, and one for the total of the two lines. In calculating cost of the *shoes* sold, be sure to use the revised overhead charging rate. Is the difference in income between that reported in the combined statement and that determined for the shoes alone (part a) consistent with your response to part d?

7. *Choice of depreciation method is irrelevant (ignoring taxes) to a decision as to whether to replace an asset.*

Nova, Inc., is presently using a stamping machine that it acquired two years ago at a cost of $40,000. The total estimated useful life of the machine is five years; estimated salvage value at the end of five years is $10,000. The firm charges depreciation using the double-declining balance method and book value of the machine, with three years of useful life remaining, is $14,400. The machine could be sold today for $12,000.

Nova, Inc., has the opportunity to sell the old machine and replace it with a new one. The new machine would enable it to effect cash savings of $12,000 per year. The new machine would cost $30,000 and have a useful life of three years—same as the remaining useful life of the old machine. The company would charge depreciation on the new machine using the double-declining balance method. It estimates that the new machine would have zero salvage value at the end of its useful life. The full amount of the remaining book value of the new machine would be charged off as depreciation in the third and final year of useful life.

The company is reluctant to replace the old machine with the new because the new machine is almost fully depreciated. Nova, Inc., is a nonprofit organization and pays no income taxes.

a. Prepare a schedule in which you indicate the differences in *earnings* that would be reported during each of the next three years, as well as the three years combined, if the company were to replace the old machine with the new as compared to if it did not. Remember that depreciation should not be charged beyond the point at which the book value of an asset has been reduced to its salvage value. Be sure to take into account any gain or loss on the sale of the old machine if it were replaced with the new.

b. Prepare a schedule in which you indicate the differences in cash flows that would result over the period of three years if the firm were to replace the old machine with the new as opposed to if it did not.

c. Should the firm replace the old machine with the new? Explain.

d. Suppose that the firm used the straight-line method instead of the double-declining method. How would that affect the schedules which you prepared? Would it change your decision as to whether the machine should be replaced? Explain.

8. *Orders should not necessarily be filled at the plant with the lower apparent cost.*

Shore Industries, Inc., has two plants, one in Texas, and one in Michigan. Inasmuch as the Texas plant is considerably newer than the Michigan plant, fixed production costs in Texas are higher, but variable costs lower. Per unit costs at a volume of 8,000 units per month, the volume at which both plants are presently operating, are as follows:

	Per Unit Cost	
	Texas Plant	Michigan Plant
Fixed manufacturing costs	$ 50	$ 25
Variable manufacturing costs	55	80
Total	$105	$105

The firm has accepted an order from a customer in Ohio. Transportation costs of filling the order from the plant in Michigan would be $10 per unit; from that in Texas, $15 per unit. Both plants are presently operating at substantially less than full capacity.

a. What would be the per unit cost of manufacturing the product at each of the two plants? Consider "cost" to be the *full* cost—that which would be reflected in cost of goods sold.
   1. Assume that the order was for 1,000 units.
   2. Assume alternatively that the order was for 4,500 units.

b. At which of the two plants should the order be filled?
   1. Assume that the order was for 1,000 units.
   2. Assume that the order was for 4,500 units.

9. Incremental analysis can be used to estimate strike losses.

Sturdman Valve Co. carries a strike insurance policy. The policy provides for reimbursement of all losses attributable to strikes. Losses are defined as the amount by which the excess of incremental revenues over incremental costs is less during the period of the work stoppage than it would have been had there been no strike.

In June 1983, the manufacturing operations of one division of Sturdman were discontinued because of a strike. Management estimates that on account of the strike its production was reduced by 4,000 units, each of which could have been sold for $80. Cost of manufacturing each unit would have been $61 composed of the following costs:

Direct labor		$20
Direct materials		19
Overhead		
Fixed	$17	
Variable	5	22
Cost per unit		$61

Monthly fixed manufacturing overhead consists of the following:

Supervision	$16,000
Depreciation	17,000
Allocation of home office costs	3,000
Heat and power	8,000
Maintenance	21,000
Supplies	3,000
Total fixed overhead	$68,000

Variable overhead depends entirely upon the use of direct labor.

During the strike, supervisors reported to work and performed essential maintenance operations; they were paid their normal salaries. Heat and power costs during the strike were $4,000. Supply costs were $500. All nonmanufacturing activities were carried on as normal, with the exception that the firm canceled magazine ads which would have cost $2,500.

Determine the amount of the claim that Sturdman should submit to its insurer.

10. Incremental cost analysis is appropriate for the decision as to the number of hours a supermarket should remain open.

Save-More Supermarket is contemplating increasing the number of its business hours. Save-More is presently open from 9 a.m. to 8 p.m. Two proposals are under consideration. The first would extend the business hours until 1 a.m. The second would extend the hours until 9 a.m.; the store would be open 24 hours per day.

Management estimates that sales between 8 p.m. and 1 a.m. would be approximately $6,000; those between 1 a.m. and 9 a.m. would be $4,000. It believes that of the customers who would shop during the proposed new hours, 40 percent would make their purchases during the standard daytime hours if the store did not remain open; the other 60 percent would shop at other stores that were open at night.

On average, per the firm's annual report, net income is approximately 2 percent of sales. Of the merchandise that would be sold during the period 8 p.m. to 1 a.m., management estimates that the average markup from cost would be 15 percent. On that sold from 1 a.m. to 9 a.m. it would be 20 percent. The difference in markup can be explained by differences in product mix; purchases in the early morning hours tend to be specialty items.

During the period from 8 p.m. to 1 a.m. the store would require the services of 10 employees. Three of these ten, however, would ordinarily have to be in the store during those hours even if the store were to be closed for business, in order to restock the shelves. During the period 1 a.m. to 9 a.m. the store would have to be staffed by only three employees, inasmuch as certain services can be reduced. None of these three would otherwise be in the store. The average wage rate for the employees is $10 per hour.

Management estimates that by staying open from 8 p.m. to 1 a.m. it would incur $150 in additional electricity, air conditioning, heating, and miscellaneous costs; from 1 a.m. to 9 p.m. it would incur $200 in additional costs.

Were the store to remain open for 24 hours per day, it would no longer require the services of a security service. The cost of the security service is $60 per night. The firm would *not* be able to engage the security service for only a portion of the night at a fraction of the standard rate. If it remained open only until 1 a.m., it would still be required to engage the security service.

Based on the information provided, should the supermarket:

1. Extend its hours to 1 a.m.?
2. Extend its hours to 9 a.m.?
3. Not extend its hours?

Support your response with an appropriate analysis.

11. *Incremental analysis facilities pricing decisions.*

Kitchen Products, Inc., manufactures a large number of household items. Among them are items 150 and 285. Both cost $15.20 to manufacture:

	Item 150	Item 285
Direct labor	$ 4.00	$ 8.60
Direct materials	10.00	4.02
Variable overhead	.40	.86
Fixed overhead	.80	1.72
Total cost	$15.20	$15.20

Fixed overhead is applied at a rate of $.20 per direct labor dollar; variable overhead is applied at the rate of $.10 per direct labor dollar.

It is the policy of the firm to price all items at an amount 25 percent above cost. Thus, both items are sold for $19.00.

a. Which of the two items contributes the greater amount to the profitability of the firm in both absolute dollars and as a percentage of selling price? Explain and show relevant calculations.

b. Suppose alternatively the firm had a policy of pricing all products at an amount 32 percent above *variable* cost. What would be the price at which each of the two products would be sold? What would be the contribution of each to the profitability of the firm? What would be the contribution of each as a percentage of selling price?

c. The salesmen of the firm receive a commission equal to 10 percent of dollar sales. Suppose that the price of item 150 was established at $19.00; that of 285 at $18.50. Which of the two products would the salesmen have the greater incentive to promote? Compare the contributions to profits that would result from the sale of each of the two products. Comment on possible dysfunctional consequences of basing salesmen's commissions on dollar sales.

12. *Allocations of joint costs may confound the decision as to whether to process further.*

The Salt Sea Chemical Works engages in a process that yields two chemicals, QX1 and QX2, from common raw materials. Joint costs of producing the two chemicals up to the split-off point are $24,000 per batch.

If processed beyond the split-off, at additional costs of $64,000 per batch, then QX1 can be sold to industrial customers for $70,400 per batch. If not processed further then it has no value.

QX2, by contrast, can be sold to industrial customers without further processing for $25,600 per batch. If, however, it is processed further, then it can be sold as a consumer product for $121,600 per batch. The incremental processing costs would be $60,000 per batch, but in addition, the firm would be required to incur $35,000 in advertising and selling costs.

The firm allocates joint costs in proportion to net incremental revenues beyond the split-off point. Net incremental revenues are defined as the selling price of the product less the additional *processing* costs (*excluding* advertising and selling costs). For example, assuming that QX1 is processed further but that QX2 is not, the $24,000 of common costs would be allocated as follows:

	QX1	QX2	Total
Selling price	$70,400	$25,600	$96,000
Less: Additional processing costs	64,000	-0-	64,000
Net incremental revenue	$ 6,400	$25,600	$32,000
Percent of net incremental revenue	20%	80%	100%
Proportionate share of $24,000 of common costs	$ 4,800	$19,200	$24,000

a. Determine the income, per batch, that would be attributable to QX2, assuming that it *is not* processed beyond the split-off point and is instead sold to industrial customers.

b. Determine the income attributable to QX2, assuming that it *is* processed further and sold as a consumer product. Be sure to recalculate the allocation of common costs.

c. Do you think that the company should sell the QX2 at the split-off point or should process it further even if further processing results in a decrease in the apparent profitability of the product? Explain and support your response with specific data.

13. *Selection of product mix is guided by the critical constraint.*

Calculators Ltd. manufactures specialized calculators. It has recently developed three new types of calculators; for joggers, for auto race fans, and for dieters. The company has limited capacity. It has work stations for only 25 assemblers. It is certain, however, that it can sell all the calculators that it produces regardless of type. The following data pertain to the three types of calculators:

	Joggers	Race Fans	Dieters
Selling price	$17.00	$12.00	$24.00
Direct materials cost	3.20	2.80	7.20
Direct labor cost (assemblers)	5.00	2.50	5.00
Variable overhead ($.25 per direct materials dollar)	.80	.70	1.80
Required hours of assembly time	.50 hour	.25 hour	.50 hour

Because of the limitation in number of work stations, the company has available a maximum of 200 hours of assembly time per day. Fixed manufacturing costs are $3,500 per day. It is company policy to allocate fixed manufacturing costs on the basis of direct labor dollars.

The firm can produce any combination of the three types of calculators.

If it is the objective of the firm to maximize contribution to profits, how many of each type of calculator should it produce per day?

14. *Optimum product mix with two constraints can be determined graphically.*

Plas-Tec, Inc., is faced with the problem of determining the optimum mix of its two products, toy trucks and toy dolls. Both types of toys must be processed in a molding department and an assembly department. The following data pertain to the two products (based on batches of 100 units):

	Trucks	Dolls
Contribution margin	$100	$80
Required hours in molding department	2	3
Required hours in assembly department	4	2

The manufacturing facilities of Plas-Tec, Inc., including both the molding and assembly departments, are in operation 40 hours per week.

a. Prepare a graph, the horizontal axis of which represents the number of batches of trucks and the vertical axis of which represents the number of batches of dolls that can be produced each week. Scale the axes from zero to 20.

b. Draw lines representing the two constraints on production—the available hours in the molding and the assembly departments. Shade-in the region of feasible combinations.

c. Add to the graph a line representing all combinations of the two products that would provide a contribution margin of a convenient dollar amount—$800, for example. Draw a second line, parallel to the first, that is as far from the origin of the graph as possible yet still within the region of feasible combinations (at one point at least).

d. What is the combination of products that maximizes contribution to profit? What is the total contribution to profits of that combination? Test your answer by shifting resources from one product to the other. If the shift serves to increase the contribution to profit and does not cause the constraints to be violated, then your answer must be in error.

15. *A graphic determination of optimum product mix is feasible even with three or more constraints.*

Electronic Gadgets, Inc., has the capability of manufacturing in one of its plants two products: a digital bathroom scale and a digital household thermometer. The contribution margin of the scale is $15 per unit; that of the thermometer is $10 per unit. An important component of both products is Type B silicone chips. The scale requires two such chips; the thermometer one such chip. Owing to shortages in such chips, the company is able to acquire only 140 chips per day.

a. If it is the objective of the firm to maximize contribution to profits, what combination of the two products do you recommend be manufactured each day? Prepare a graph (with units from zero to 150) in which the horizontal axis represents number of scales and the vertical axis represents number of thermometers. Draw one line that depicts the critical production constraint and another which connects all possible combinations of products that will provide the same contribution to profits as the combination that you recommend be manufactured.

b. Suppose that the firm has available each day a maximum of 120 hours of assembly labor. Each scale requires 1.2 hours of assembly time; each thermometer requires 1.5 hours. Add to your graph an additional line representing the assembly labor constraint. What, per your graph, is the optimum product mix taking into account the additional constraint?

c. Suppose that the firm can sell no more than 40 scales per day. Add to your graph a line representing this third constraint. What, per your graph, is now the optimum product mix.

d. Suppose alternatively that the firm could sell no more than 60 scales per day. What impact would this constraint have on product mix?

SOLUTIONS TO EXERCISE FOR REVIEW AND SELF-TESTING

1. The maximum price per box that Pottsdam should be willing to pay an outside contractor is the amount that it could save by discontinuing the printing operation. Thus, if it could truly save $4.25 per box, then it should be willing to pay up to $4.25 per box to an outside contractor.

2. Sales revenues and costs of manufacturing the stationery (except as noted in part 3) would be the same regardless of whether the printing is done within the company or outside. They are, therefore, irrelevant to the decision at hand.

3. a. The firm would have to incur $2,500 in ink and other supplies if it continued the printing operations; zero if it discontinued.

   b. It would incur $30,000 in labor costs if it continued the printing operations. It would, however, incur $6,000 in costs if it discontinued. The $6,000 (the excess of the $30,000 to be paid over the $24,000 that the job is worth) represents a cost that the firm elects to incur in order to satisfy an obligation—perhaps "moral," perhaps "legal"—to retain the print-shop employee and pay him his printshop salary even if he were to work at a job that usually commands a lesser salary.

   c. Rent expense of $4,000 would be incurred only if the printing operation were continued.

   d. If the firm were to continue the printing operations it would incur $1,000 more in heating and air conditioning costs than if it discontinued. The remaining heating and air conditioning costs would be the same under each alternative and are therefore irrelevant.

   e. Other plant overhead costs would be the same regardless of alternative selected. If the printing operations were discontinued, the amounts *allocated* to the remaining departments would increase since the departments would have to bear among them the costs previously allocated to the printing operation.

   f. Rent revenue would be $3,000 if the printing operation were discontinued; zero if it were continued.

4. (+ = inflow; − = outflow)

	Printshop Continued	Printshop Discontinued	Saving if Printshop Discontinued
Ink and other supplies	− $ 2,500	—	$ 2,500
Labor costs	− 30,000	− $6,000	24,000
Rent expense	− 4,000	—	4,000
Heating and air conditioning	− 1,000	—	1,000
Rent revenue	—	+ 3,000	3,000
Total	− $37,500	− $3,000	$34,500
Number of boxes per year			÷ 10,000 boxes
Savings per box			$ 3.45

The firm would be willing to pay no more than $3.45 per box to a printing contractor—considerably less than the apparent print cost per box of $4.25.

5. If the company owned the printing press, then the cash inflow—and only the cash inflow—resulting from the sale of the press should be taken into account. The amount to be realized upon the sale represents a *future* cash flow, one that would be affected by the decision to discontinue or continue printing operations. By contrast, both depreciation and loss on sale represent the allocation of a previously incurred cost to a particular accounting period. Neither depreciation expense nor loss on sales involves an outflow of cash and needs be incorporated into the analysis of the decision.

Capital Expenditure Decisions 21

The focus of this chapter will be on capital expenditure decisions. Capital expenditure decisions are those that involve an investment of capital made in the expectation of returns in the future. The characteristic of capital expenditures which warrants special attention is that the cash receipts and outlays associated with an investment can occur over an extended period of time. In order to give recognition to the differences in value between dollars received or paid in different years, it is necessary to "discount" back to the present all anticipated cash receipts and disbursements. Prominent among capital expenditure decisions are those to acquire or replace long-lived assets by purchase or construction. The approaches to capital expenditure analysis described in this chapter are generalizable, however, to virtually all courses of action in which receipts or disbursements will take place at different times.

The foundation for analysis of capital expenditure decisions has been firmly established in earlier chapters of this text. Chapter 6 set forth the concepts of time value and money and described the techniques whereby dollars to be paid or received in the future can be equated to those to be paid or received in the present. Chapter 20 stressed the importance and illustrated the means of identifying incremental cash flows associated with alternative courses of action.

The general approach to capital expenditure analysis, which will be termed the present value technique, is straightforward:

1. Identify the incremental cash flows of each course of action—that is, those cash flows which would be different if one alternative as opposed to the other were selected.
2. Discount all cash receipts and disbursements back to the present. Sum the discounted cash receipts and disbursements for each alternative.
3. Select the course of action with the largest net cash inflow (or smallest net cash outflow). If the choice is merely to accept or reject a particular investment project, accept it if the net discounted cash flow is zero or positive; reject it if it is negative.

The present value technique can be illustrated using a simple example.

Example: Decision to Acquire a Machine

A firm has the opportunity to acquire a machine that would enable it to reduce operating costs by $10,000 per year. The cost of the machine is $35,000. The firm estimates that after four years, the end of its useful life, the machine could be sold for $8,000. The discount rate used by the firm to evaluate investments is 10 percent.

The table that follows indicates the actual as well as the discounted cash receipts and disbursements associated with the machine. Cash savings are accounted for as if they were cash receipts. For computational convenience (in order that the standard present value tables or formulas can be applied) it shall be assumed in this and subsequent examples, that the cash receipts or disbursements occur at the *end* of an accounting period. Slight modifications to the present value formulas presented in Chapter 6 or the tables in the Appendix would be required to reflect a more realistic pattern in which operating savings occur uniformly throughout a period.

The present value of the cash receipts exceeds the present value of the cash disbursements by $2,162; hence the company should acquire the machine. The acquisition of the machine will provide the firm with a return on its invested capital (the cost of the machine) of an amount greater than 10 percent. Implicit in the selection of the discount rate is the assumption that the firm will accept a proposed investment project if it will provide a return equal to or greater than that. If, in the example, the net cash receipts were zero, then the return on the investment of $35,000 would have been exactly 10 percent—enough to justify acceptance of the project. If the net cash receipts were less than zero (negative), then the return on investment would be less than 10 percent and the project would not meet the return criterion established by the firm.

In this particular example, it would not be necessary to discount individually the savings of each year. The operating savings can be interpreted as an annuity of $10,000 per year for four years. The present value of an annuity of $10,000 for four years discounted at 10 percent is, per Table 4 (Present Value of

	Discounted (Present) Value of Cash Flows	Present Value of $1[a]	Relevant Cash Flows in Year:				
			0	1	2	3	4
Acquire machine	($35,000)	$1.0000	($35,000)				
Operating savings							
Yr. 1	9,091	.9091		$10,000			
Yr. 2	8,264	.8264			$10,000		
Yr. 3	7,513	.7513				$10,000	
Yr. 4	6,830	.6830					$10,000
	5,464	.6830					$ 8,000
Present value of net cash receipts	$2,162						

[a] At a discount rate of 10 percent, per Table 2.

an Annuity of $1 in Arrears), $10,000 ×
3.1699—$31,699. The present value of the
$8,000 to be received at the end of the useful
life of the asset is, per Table 2, $8,000 ×
.6830—$5,464. The sum of these two
amounts, $37,163, is $2,163 greater than the
initial investment of $35,000.

DETERMINING THE DISCOUNT RATE

A critical element in the analysis of investment opportunities is the rate of discount.
The appropriate means of determining the
rate of discount is the subject of ongoing
controversy among economists and specialists in finance.

Many experts assert that the discount rate
for all projects should reflect the *weighted
average* of a firm's *cost of capital*. Cost of
capital comprises the costs of bonds and
other debts, common and preferred stock,
and retained earnings. Because there are no
required payments associated with common
stock and retained earnings, intricate formulas have been developed to estimate the costs
associated with these components of capital.

The literature of finance and economics of
recent years, however, favors using a different
rate of discount for each project under
consideration. The rate selected would be
dependent on the degree of risk associated
with the project. The higher the risk, the
higher the rate of discount. Support for a
risk-related rate rests to a considerable
extent on research pertaining to the value of
investments (particularly stocks and bonds),
and the selection of "portfolios" of assets
that maximize returns at specified levels of
risk.

In practice it is not uncommon for
managers to use a discount rate representing
a target rate of return. Such rate would be
based on executive judgment as to the
minimum return that is expected of all
investments.

Owing to its complexity, the issue of
appropriate rate of discount is beyond the
scope of this text. We can do no more than
demonstrate how the discount rate can be
applied in capital investment analysis.

IMPACT OF TAXES ON CASH FLOWS

In previous sections we emphasized that only
incremental cash receipts and disbursements
should be taken into account in assessing
the desirability of alternative courses of
action. Neither depreciation expense nor
gains or losses on the sale of assets can be
included among the receipts or disbursements
of cash. They represent the mere assignment
of the cost of the assets to particular account
periods. It may be recalled from Chapter 14
relating to statements of funds that depreciation as well as losses on sales of assets must
be "added back" to reported income to
obtain cash (or working capital) provided by
operations.

Both depreciation and gains or losses on
the sale of assets are items of revenue and
expense that enter into the determination of
taxable earnings and, hence, the amount that
will be *disbursed* to the taxing authorities.
The example that follows is intended to
emphasize that depreciation (or amortization) as well as gains or losses are not themselves cash items but do have a bearing on
the net *after-tax* receipts or disbursements
associated with a project.

Example: Acquire a New Machine

A firm is deciding whether to replace an
old machine with a new. The new machine

will enable the firm to increase output. The data that follow relate to the new machine and the one that it will replace.

New Machine	
Cost	$180,000
Useful life	3 years
Salvage value	$30,000
Annual fixed operating costs, excluding depreciation	$27,000
Contribution margin on additional units that can be produced by the new machine (sales revenue less variable costs)	$82,000
Annual depreciation charges (straight-line method)	$50,000

Old Machine	
Amount for which machine could be sold if replaced by new	$70,000
Book value	60,000
Remaining useful life of old machine	3 years
Salvage value at the end of useful life	-0-
Annual fixed operating costs, excluding depreciation	$10,000
Annual depreciation charges (straight-line method)	$20,000
Tax and discount rates	
Tax rate on income	40%
Tax rate on gains on sale of plant and equipment	25%
Discount rate for evaluating purchases of equipment	12%

Exhibit 21-1 indicates the incremental cash flows associated with the purchase of the new machine. Year 0 represents the date at which the new machine would be purchased and the old one sold. All other cash receipts or disbursements are assumed to occur at the *end* of the respective years. A few explanatory comments may be helpful.

1. All receipts and disbursements that would be the same regardless of whether the new machine is acquired are excluded from the analysis; they would be unaffected by the purchase decision.

2. The analysis could have been separated into two tables. In one would be indicated the cash flows associated with the purchase of the new machine; in the other, those associated with the retention of the old. The alternative in which the present value of the net cash inflows was the greater would be selected.

3. The tax on the sale of the old machine was calculated as follows:

Amount for which old machine could be sold	$70,000
Less: Book value of old machine	60,000
Gain on sale of machine	$10,000
Tax rate on gains on sale of plant and equipment	× .25
Tax	$ 2,500

4. The additional tax expense for each of the three years during which the new machine will be used was determined as follows:

Contribution margin on additional units to be produced by new machine		$82,000
Less: Additional fixed operating costs ($27,000 − $10,000)	$17,000	
Additional depreciation ($50,000 − $20,000)	30,000	47,000
Additional income before taxes		$35,000
Tax rate		× .40
Additional tax expense		$14,000

EXHIBIT 21-1

**Incremental Net Cash Receipts from
Replacing Old Machine with New**

	Present Value of Cash Flows	*Present Value of $1 at 12%*	*Relevant Cash Flows in Year:*			
			0	*1*	*2*	*3*
Disbursement for new machine			($180,000)			
Receipt from sale of old machine			70,000			
Tax on gain on sale of old machine			(2,500)			
Contribution margin on additional sales				$82,000	$82,000	$82,000
Additional fixed operating expenses ($27,000 – $10,000)				(17,000)	(17,000)	(17,000)
Additional tax expense				(14,000)	(14,000)	(14,000)
Receipt upon sale at end of useful life						30,000
Net disbursement, year 0	($112,500)	1.000	($112,500)			
Net receipts, year 1	45,538	.8929		$51,000		
Net receipts, year 2	40,657	.7972			$51,000	
Net receipts, year 3	57,656	.7118				$81,000
Present value of net receipts	$ 31,351					

5. The rate by which the cash flows are discounted must be an *after-tax* rate. It should be indicative of the minimum acceptable return *after* allowance for tax expenditures. Clearly, the minimum acceptable return after taxes will be less than that before taxes.

The present value of the net receipts to be generated by replacing the old machine with the new ($31,351) is positive. Hence, it is to the advantage of the firm to undertake the proposed capital investment.

IMPACT OF FINANCING CHARGES

The means by which payments relating to the financing of a project should be incorporated in the analysis of cash flows are invariably a source of confusion among practitioners of capital budgeting.

As a general rule it is preferable not to include in a capital expenditure analysis any of the receipts or disbursements associated with financing a proposed project. The amount borrowed to acquire an asset, the interest payments, and the liquidation of the balance of the loan should be excluded. Instead, the project should be evaluated on its own merits, apart from the means by which it will be financed. Implicitly, of course, costs of financing are taken into account via the discounting process; there is, therefore, no need to take them into account again.

Nonetheless, as an alternative, financing costs can be explicitly incorporated into the analysis as long as *all* financial cash flows—amounts borrowed, amounts repaid, and interest charges—are taken into account. Consider a simple investment proposal.

A firm has the opportunity to invest $10,000 in a project. The project will return $12,000 at the end of one year. The firm will finance the project by borrowing the $10,000. It will repay the $10,000 plus interest at the rate of 10 percent ($1,000) at the end of the year. The firm uses a discount rate of 10 percent to evaluate all investment proposals.

Excluding financing charges, the analysis would take the following form:

	Present Value of Cash Flows	Present Value of $1 @ 10%	Relevant Cash Flows in Year:	
			0	1
Initial outlay	($10,000)	1.0000	($10,000)	
Returns	10,909	.9091		$12,000
Net present value	$ 909			

The proposal should be accepted inasmuch as the present value of the net receipts is positive, $909.

Including all flows associated with financing the project, the present value of the net receipts would also be $909:

	Present Value of Cash Flows	Present Value of $1 @ 10%	Relevant Cash Flows in Year:	
			0	1
Loan for cost of project	$10,000	$1.0000	$10,000	
Initial outlay	(10,000)	1.0000	(10,000)	
Returns	10,909	.9091		$12,000
Repayment of loan	(9,091)	.9091		(10,000)
Interest on loan	(909)	.9091		(1,000)
Net present Value	$ 909			

The two approaches will always lead to the same outcome as long as the actual interest rate is equal to the discount rate. The approach whereby financing costs are excluded is generally preferable because it is often improper to associate specific financing costs with particular projects. A firm usually finds it desirable to obtain capital from a mix of sources. It may be able to finance some projects with relatively low-cost capital only because it has financed others with high-cost capital. The decision to undertake a specific project should not be influenced by the particular source of funds to which it has been assigned.

There are investment opportunities, however, for which it may be difficult or impossible to distinguish between the cash flows inherent in the opportunity itself and those associated with the financing arrangements. Suppose, for example, a firm is considering acquiring the use of an asset by lease rather than purchase. As discussed in Chapter 10, many leases are, in essence, purchase/borrow arrangements. It is desirable that the firm first determine what the asset would cost if it acquired it outright and whether, in light of the present value of the incremental earnings or savings that can be attributed to it, it is a worthwhile investment. Having decided to acquire it, the firm should then consider whether the leasing arrangement is the optimum means of financing it. Sometimes, however, particularly when the lessor is to provide services (e.g., maintenance and repairs) along with the right to use the asset, it becomes exceedingly difficult to decompose each of the lease payments into its elements—a repayment of principal on the "loan" balance, a payment of interest and a charge for the services rendered. In such a case, it may be necessary to incorporate *all* cash flows, including financing costs, into the analysis.

INTERNAL RATE OF RETURN

A variation of the net present value criterion of evaluating investment proposals is internal rate of return. Internal rate of return represents the rate, which when used to discount each of the cash receipts and disbursements associated with a project, would result in a net present value of zero. The higher the internal rate of return, the more desirable a project.

Internal rate of return, as does net present value, explicitly takes into account incremental cash flows as well as the time value of money. In calculating internal rate of return, however, it is unnecessary to specify a discount rate. Instead, one computes the rate itself. This rate, when applied to each of the cash inflows and outflows would cause the sum of the *present values* of the inflows to be equal to the sum of the present values of the outflows.

If the cash flows are uniform, then it is possible to determine algebraically the internal rate of return. If they are not, then it is necessary to resort to a trial and error process.

Example: Uniform Cash Flows

A firm has the opportunity to make an investment of $47,912 that will provide net cash receipts, after taxes of $12,000 per year for five years. What is the internal rate of return?

The present value of the single cash outflow, inasmuch as it takes place at time zero, is $47,912 regardless of discount rate. The internal rate of return, therefore, is that rate which when used to discount the inflows—an annuity of $12,000 for five years—is exactly equal to $47,912. If x equals the internal rate of return, then

$47,912 = $12,000 times the present value of an annuity of $1 for 5 years at $x\%$

and

$$\frac{\$47,912}{\$12,000} = \text{the present value of an annuity of \$1 for 5 years at } x\%$$

$3.9927 = the present value of an annuity of $1 for 5 years

Per Table 4, 3.9927 is equal to the present value of an annuity for five years at a discount rate of 8 percent. This rate can be determined by reading along the row for five periods until 3.9927 is reached; 3.9927 is under the column for 8 percent. The internal rate of return is therefore 8 percent. If the amount to be found fell between two rates of discount indicated in the table, then it would be necessary to estimate the internal rate of return by way of interpolation (see the next example).

there are nonuniform cash flows, the trial and error method will have to be used. Owing to the additional cash receipt at the end of the fifth year, the internal rate of return is obviously greater than the 8 percent calculated in the previous example. The following table indicates the present value of the cash flows discounted at a trial rate of 14 percent:

Present Value of Cash Flows at 14 Percent

	Present Value	Discount Factor, 14%	Cash Flow
Initial investment, year 0	($47,912)	1.0000	($47,912)
Annual returns, years 1 through 5 (an annuity)	41,197	3.4331	12,000
Sale of interest in investment at end of year 5	5,194	.5194	10,000
Net present value	($ 1,521)		

Example: Nonuniform Cash Flows

Assume the same facts as in the previous example with the addition that at the end of the fifth year the firm will sell its interest in the investment for $10,000. Thus, the internal rate of return is that rate of discount which

The objective is to determine a discount rate such that the net present value is zero. Since the net present value at 14 percent is negative, the trial rate of 14 percent is too high. The following table indicates the present value of cash flows discounted at a second trial rate of 12 percent:

Present Value of Cash Flows at 12 Percent

	Present Value	Discount Factor, 12%	Cash Flow
Initial investment, year 0	($47,912)	1.0000	($47,912)
Annual returns, years 1 through 5 (an annuity)	43,258	3.6048	12,000
Sale of interest in investment at the end of year 5	5,674	.5674	10,000
Net present value	$ 1,020		

will equate the present value of a cash outflow of $47,912 in period zero with an annuity of $12,000 for five years and a single payment of $10,000 at the end of year five.

Because there is no simple algorithm to determine the internal rate of return when

The net present value at 12 percent is positive; therefore, the desired present value of zero is between 12 and 14 percent. The approximate internal rate of return is proportionately as far from 12 percent as the desired present value of zero is from the present value at 12 percent of $1,020. Thus, by way of interpolation, if x = the unknown actual internal rate of return:

$$\frac{\text{High rate} - \text{Low rate}}{\left(\begin{array}{c}\text{Net present value} \\ \text{at high rate}\end{array}\right) - \left(\begin{array}{c}\text{Net present value} \\ \text{at low rate}\end{array}\right)}$$

$$= \frac{x - \text{Low rate}}{0 - \text{Net present value at low rate}}$$

$$\frac{.14 - .12}{(-1,521) - 1,020} = \frac{x - .12}{0 - 1,020}$$

$$\frac{.02}{(-2,541)} = \frac{x - .12}{-1,020}$$

By cross multiplying, we get

$$-20.4 = -2,541x + 304.92$$

$$2541x = 325.32$$

$$x = .128$$

The appropriate internal rate of return is 12.8 percent.

NET PRESENT VALUE VERSUS INTERNAL RATE OF RETURN

If the useful lives of two or more investment projects under consideration are the same, then the net present value and the internal rate of return procedures will serve to rank projects in the same order of preferability. If, however, the useful lives of projects are different, then the order of preferability may also be different. Consider two investment proposals between which a firm must select.

	Project A	Project B
Initial investment	$100,000	$100,000
Life of project	1 year	5 years
Annual cash returns	$20,000	$15,000
Return of investment at the end of project life	$100,000	$100,000

The internal rate of return that will be provided by Project A is 20 percent; that which will be provided by Project B is 15 percent. If internal rate of return were the decision criterion, the firm would select Project A over Project B.

By contrast, suppose the firm uses a discount rate of 10 percent to evaluate investment opportunities. The net present value of the cash receipts and disbursements associated with Project A, discounted at a rate of 10 percent is $9,091; that of Project B is $18,954. If present value of net cash receipts were the decision criterion, the firm would select Project B over Project A.

The different rankings are a consequence of the differences in project life. Project A offers a higher rate of return, but for a shorter period of time than does Project B. The important question that management must address is what will the firm do with the funds that are returned to it at the end of one year, the conclusion of the life of Project A. If it were able to reinvest the principal of $100,000 in another project that would provide a return of $20,000 per year for four additional years, then it would be better off selecting Project A over Project B, which provides a return of only $15,000 per year. But if it were able to reinvest the principal in a project that will provide a return of only $10,000—that suggested by the discount rate of 10 percent—then Project A would be preferable. If a firm were to select Project A over Project B on account of Project A's higher internal rate of return, then it would be assuming implicitly that the reinvestment rate of Project A subsequent to its termination was equal to that earned on the project during its life. If, however, it were to select Project B over Project A on account of Project B's greater net present value, then it would be assuming implicitly that the funds invested in Project A were, upon its termination, returned to the parties which provided them. The firm would no longer incur a cost of the capital; it would no longer earn a return on it.

Because both implicit assumptions may be contrary to the intentions of, or opportunities available to, the firm, it is best to avoid the dilemma of having to choose between the two techniques in circumstances in which they will provide different rankings. The firm should make every effort to equalize the useful lives of each competing proposal. This can be accomplished by making explicit reinvestment assumptions. Suppose, for example, that the $100,000 principal that will be returned to the firm at the expiration of Project B could be used to acquire marketable securities that would pay dividends and interest at a rate of 13 percent ($13,000) per year. The firm could incorporate into the cash flows of the project annual returns of $13,000 in years two through five and $100,000 at the end of year five. For analytical convenience, it would assume that the securities would then be sold.

OTHER CRITERIA FOR EVALUATING INVESTMENTS

Payback Period

A popular "rule of thumb" guide to investment profitability is *payback period*. Payback period indicates the number of years required to recover an initial outlay.

Payback period is conventionally calculated by dividing the initial investment outlay by the annual *cash* returns:

$$\text{Payback period} = \frac{\text{Investment outlay}}{\text{Annual net cash receipts}}$$

Previously in the chapter we considered an investment of $47,912 that provided a return after taxes of $12,000 per year for five years. At the conclusion of the fifth year, the firm was able to sell its interest in the project for $10,000. The payback period would be 3.99 years:

$$\frac{\$47,912}{\$12,000} = 3.99 \text{ years}$$

It would take the firm 3.99 years to get back its outlay of $47,912.

If the cash flows are not uniform in the years prior to that in which the initial outlay is recovered, then the cash flows of each year can be summed until an amount equal to the initial outlay is reached. If, for example, an investment required an initial outlay of $10,000 and the net cash receipts were $5,000 in year one, $4,000 in year two, and $3,000 in year three, then the payback period would be $2\frac{1}{3}$ years; it would take the cash receipts in years one and two, plus one-third of the receipts in year three to "pay-off" the investment.

The payback period is useful when nothing more than an imprecise measure of the earnings potential of an investment is required. The shorter the payback period, the more desirable the investment. It is easily computed and understood, and it is particularly serviceable when managers are concerned with the length of time that funds will be "at risk."

The limitation of the payback period is that it does not take into account cash flows beyond the point where the initial investment has been recovered and the time value of money. In the example presented, neither the cash receipts of year five nor the amount for which the interest in the investment could be sold at the end of five years was incorporated into the analysis.

Suppose that a real estate developer had to select between two office complexes in which it could invest:

	Complex A	Complex B
Initial investment	$1,000,000	$1,000,000
Number of years that complex will be held	3 years	10 years
Estimated sale price when complex will be sold	$100,000	$1,000,000
Annual net cash receipts	$333,000	$250,000

The payback period for the investment in Complex A is three years—$1,000,000 ÷ $333,000; that for the investment in Complex B is four years—$1,000,000 ÷ $250,000. If payback were the decision criterion, then Complex A would be the more desirable. Yet internal rate of return, net present value

and common sense point to Complex B as preferable.

The payback period has been discredited by academics and others concerned with the theory of capital budgeting. Over the last four decades there has been a decided shift in practice away from the payback period and toward net present value and internal rate of return as investment decision criteria. Nevertheless, payback period remains in widespread use today.

Within the last several years, however, academic revisionists have come to view the payback period as not so bad after all. They have demonstrated analytically that for investments with certain characteristics the *payback reciprocal* approximates the internal rate of return. *Payback reciprocal*, is nothing more than the reciprocal of the payback formula; that is, annual net cash receipts divided by investment outlay, or 1 divided by

payback period. For example, the payback reciprocal for a project with a payback of five years would be 1 divided by 5—20 percent. Payback reciprocal can be used as a surrogate for internal rate of return when the duration of the investment is at least twice the payback period and when the cash flows are uniform. It approaches internal rate of return as both the duration of the investment and the true internal rate of return increase.

Average Return on Investment

Another popular criterion for evaluating investment proposals is average return on investment. Average return on investment relates average net cash receipts after taxes *less* average depreciation to average lifetime investment:

$$\text{Average return on investment} = \frac{\text{Average annual net cash receipts} - \text{Average annual depreciation}}{\text{Average investment}}$$

If straight-line depreciation is charged, average investment would be

$$\frac{\text{Initial investment} - \text{Salvage value (or other recoverable amount)}}{2}$$

The average investment on the previously presented investment of $47,912 that provided annual net cash receipts of $12,000 and allowed for the recovery of $10,000 upon termination of the project at the end of five years would be

$$\frac{\$47,912 - \$10,000}{2} = \$18,956$$

(If accelerated depreciation were charged, this formula for computing average investment would be inappropriate inasmuch as the remaining book value of the investment would be less in each year of project life than if straight-line depreciation were charged.

It would be necessary to determine the remaining book value of the investment at the end of each year and calculate the average book value over the life of the asset.) Using the straight-line method, annual depreciation charges would be

$$\frac{\$47,912 - \$10,000}{5 \text{ years}} = \$7,582$$

Average return on investment would be, therefore,

$$\frac{\$12,000 - \$7,582}{\$18,956} = 23\%$$

Average return on investment, unlike payback period, *does* take into account amounts received throughout the life of an investment. It is computationally convenient and, because it incorporates depreciation into the calculation, it is reflective of rate of return as it would be determined on the basis of data reported in financial statements intended for investors. The primary deficiency of average rate of return as an investment criterion is that like payback period it does not give effect to the time value of money. Cash flows that occur early in the life of the project, and which are thereby of greater value to an organization, are weighted the same as those that occur later. Average rate of return tends, however, to approach the internal rate of return as both the investment period and the rate of return decrease.

UNCERTAINTY

Characteristic of most expenditure decisions is risk—uncertainty about the outcome of the possible courses of action. The effectiveness of even the most sophisticated decision models is limited by the reliability of the underlying predictions of cash flows. There is available an extensive body of literature on the subject of decision making in the face of uncertainty. Regrettably, it does not provide the guidance necessary for ordinary managers to become clairvoyant. It does, however, provide insight into how statistical probability, as well as managerial experience, "judgment" or "intuition" can be explicitly incorporated into an evaluation of options under consideration.

Management decisions can be characterized by the number of independent events which determine the outcome of the course of action selected. When the outcome depends on a large number of independent events, management is able to benefit from the "certainty" that results from combining a large number of events, each of which individually is uncertain. In evaluating the cost of a proposed employee insurance plan, for example, a manager has no way of predicting whether a particular employee will die during the period of coverage. But provided with sufficient demographic data about the employee population, an actuary could forecast with considerable accuracy the *total* number of employees who will pass away. By contrast, when the overall result depends on but a single event, the "laws" of large numbers cannot be applied. A predictable number of favorable occurrences is not available to offset a predictable number of unfavorable occurrences. When an aircraft manufacturer undertakes the development of a unique commercial aircraft there is no population of similar projects to support statistically defensible predictions of success. The project stands alone. Success in some projects cannot be counted upon to offset failures in others.

If the return on an investment project will depend on the outcome of numerous independent events, then it is possible to compute an *expected value* of the return. The expected value is an average of the possible outcomes, weighted by the probability that each will occur. Suppose that a real estate developer is considering purchasing a resort complex that comprises a large number of apartments. The apartments are rented by the week. The cash flow for any individual month depends on the number of weeks that an apartment is rented. The firm has had extensive rental experience with similar properties and has been able to determine the probabilities of apartments being occupied for varying periods of time. The weekly rental charge is $300. The following table summarizes the probabilities of possible rental periods and the associated cash receipts:

If, on the other hand, the return on an investment depends on a single outcome, then the "laws" of probability cannot be relied on to produce an expected *average* outcome. The "average" outcome will be the actual outcome. Nevertheless, managers can incorporate uncertainty into an analysis *as if* there were a large number of recurring events by assigning to the outcomes *subjective probabilities*. Subjective probabilities represent a particular individual's assessment of the likelihood of a particular outcome. They may be developed on the basis of past ex-

Number of Weeks per Month of Occupancy	Percentage of Apartments Likely to Be Rented for Such a Period	Rental Receipts per Apartment if Apartment Is Rented for Such a Period (Number of Weeks Times $300)
4 weeks	20	$1,200
3 weeks	35	900
2 weeks	30	600
1 week	10	300
0 weeks	5	0
	100%	

The expected value (EV) of the rent receipts for any one apartment is the average of the possible rent receipts, weighted by the related probabilities. Thus,

$$EV = .20(\$1,200) + .35(\$900) + .30(\$600) + .10(\$300) + .5(\$0)$$

$$= \quad \$240 \quad + \quad \$315 \quad + \quad \$180 \quad + \quad \$30 \quad + \quad \$0$$

$$= \quad \$765$$

To the extent that the past experience of the real estate firm is relevant to the future it can use the expected value of the per apartment receipts to approximate the total receipts for the entire project. Obviously, no one apartment can be expected to provide receipts of $765, but *on average* the receipts of the entire complex can be expected to be near $765 per apartment. The greater the number of apartments, the smaller will be the deviation from the expected mean (average) of $765.

perience, judgment, or merely "hunch." Based on subjective probabilities derived from its past experience, for example, the aforementioned real estate firm might assert that the subjective probabilities of any *single* apartment being occupied for four weeks is 20 percent; for three weeks 35 percent; and so on. Then, by weighting the possible outcomes by the subjective probabilities, it could compute an expected value of the rental receipts for a particular month. The expected value would, of course, be the same $765 as determined previously.

But such expected value has to be interpreted with care. If the developer were to acquire 100 apartments, then it could assert with reasonable assurance the total receipts would be approximately $76,500 ($765 × 100 apartments). It might be somewhat

executives consider that amount to be more of a goal than a prediction.

The financial planners have assigned the following probabilities to costs and revenues:

	Costs		Revenues			
		Amount		Amount (millions)		
State	Probability	(millions)	Probability	Year 1	Year 2	Year 3
Unfavorable	.5	$40	.3	$15	$ 6	$ 2
Neutral	.4	30	.5	25	15	5
Favorable	.1	20	.2	30	20	10

greater or less, but if the past experience on which it developed its probabilities was both reliable and relevant, then the deviation from an average of $765 per apartment should not be great. By contrast, if the developer were to acquire but a single apartment, then the actual cash receipts *cannot* be $765. They may be $0, $300, $600, $900 or $1,200. The expected value of $765 represents merely a weighted average of possible outcomes.

Subjective probabilities can be incorporated into an evaluation of capital projects by computing the *expected value* of their cash flows. The following example illustrates how this can be accomplished.

Example: Evaluating a Project in the Face of Uncertainty

A motion picture studio must decide whether to produce a film, the temperamental director of which, although creative, has little regard for accountants, their budgets and their financial controls. The cost of the film is planned initially to be $20 million, but experienced studio executives view that amount with suspicion. If the film is successful, it could generate $60 million in film rentals, over a three-year period. Studio

The costs, it may assumed, will have to be paid at the end of the first year after production begins. The revenues will be received at the end of the years indicated. The company applies a discount rate of 14 percent to all investment proposals. The table on the next page indicates the *expected* present value of the net cash receipts.

The expected present value of the cash receipts exceeds that of the cash disbursements by $6.66 million. Consistent with the criterion of expected present value of cash receipts, the company should undertake the production of the film.

An actual distribution of possible outcomes may contain an infinite number of points. In the example, however, the distribution was described by only three points (unfavorable, neutral, favorable). The company executives could obtain greater precision in the computation of expected value by assigning probabilities to other possible outcomes (e.g., receipts of $25 or $35 million).

There is considerable risk to management in focusing exclusively on the "bottom line" of the table, the expected present value of net cash receipts ($6.66 million). Such amount represents only a weighted average of possible outcomes. Management should properly consider also the shape of the distribution of possible outcomes. A broad distribution of

Unadjusted Cash Flows (millions)

	Year 1	Year 2	Year 3	Total	Probability	Expected Value
Receipts						
Unfavorable outcome						
Unadjusted	$15.00	$ 6.00	$ 2.00			
Present value of $1 @ 14%	.8772	.7695	.6750			
Adjusted	$13.16	4.62	1.35	$19.13	.3	$ 5.74
Neutral outcome						
Unadjusted	$25.00	$15.00	$ 5.00			
Presented value of $1 @ 14%	.8772	.7695	.6750			
Adjusted	$21.93	$11.54	$ 3.38	$36.85	.5	$18.43
Favorable outcome						
Unadjusted	$30.00	$20.00	$10.00			
Present value of $1 @ 14%	.8772	.7695	.6750			
Adjusted	$26.32	$15.39	$ 6.75	$48.46	.2	$ 9.69
Total receipts						$33.86
Disbursements						
Unfavorable outcome						
Unadjusted	$40.00					
Present value of $1 @ 14%	.8772					
Adjusted	$39.09			$35.09	.3	$10.53
Neutral outcome						
Unadjusted	$30.00					
Present value of $1 @ 14%	.8772					
Adjusted	$26.32			$26.32	.5	$13.16
Favorable outcome						
Unadjusted	$20.00					
Present value of $1 @ 14%	.8772					
Adjusted	$17.54			$17.54	.2	$ 3.51
Total disbursements						$27.20
Expected present value of net cash receipts (receipts less disbursements)						$ 6.66

possible outcomes might suggest that the project is one of high risk; the net cash receipts could be considerably higher or lower than the expected average. A narrow distribution would suggest a project of less risk; the actual outcome is likely to be in the vicinity of the expected average. Management should take into account also the consequences of the possible outcomes, particularly the highly unfavorable ones. In the example, there is a 30 percent chance that the present value of the costs will be $35.09 and a

30 percent chance that the present value of the receipts will be only $19.13. There is, therefore, a combined probability of .09 (.30 times .30) that the company will incur a loss of $15.96. Corporate executives must question whether the firm could withstand a loss of this magnitude. If it could not, then the project should be rejected, even though "on average" it can be anticipated that the project will be profitable. The section that follows elaborates on factors that affect a firm's attitude toward risk.

ATTITUDES TOWARD RISK

Corporations like individuals have personalities. Some are willing to assume risks; others are "risk adverse." Inasmuch as capital projects are inherently uncertain, it is especially important that the attitudes toward risk of the individual managers that will make the expenditure decisions are in harmony with those of the corporation as a whole. Attitudes toward risk are not merely a matter of subjective emotions. It may be perfectly rational and in their respective self-interests for individual managers and their companies to be willing to assume different levels of risk.

Suppose that a corporation is offered the opportunity to spend $50,000 on a project that would provide a 50 percent chance of a total return of $0 and a 50 percent chance of a total return of $105,000. The expected value of the project would be $2,500:

Expected value of receipts	$52,500
.50($0) + .50($105,000)	
Less: Expected value of	
disbursement 1.0($50,000)	50,000
Expected value of project	$ 2,500

Because the expected value is positive, the decision model that has been presented in the preceding section would indicate that the investment is one that should be taken advantage of.

The analysis to this point, however, fails to take into account what would be gained or lost in terms of overall corporate well-being. If the outcome is successful, the corporation may achieve a significant increase in earnings which would allow for an increase in its dividend rate. If it is unsuccessful, it might be forced to terminate operations. If the termination of business is of more "value" than the increase in earnings, then the investment opportunity may not, in fact, be as propitious as it first appeared. The *utility* of the dollars lost may be greater than those of the dollars to be gained.

As a rule, the more dollars a party has or stands to gain, the less the utility (i.e., value) of each incremental dollar. If the wealth of an individual or corporation is negligible, then a small number of additional dollars may facilitate substantial improvements in quality of life. If, however, the party is already affluent, then the same number of dollars would have but an insignificant impact on its well-being.

Whether or not the investment opportunity just referred to is advantageous will depend on the characteristics and objectives of the particular company to which it was offered. Of pervasive importance is likely to be the size of the company. If the company were large—several million dollars in earnings—then the proposal would probably represent a sound business risk. The consequences of losing $50,000 would not be substantial; the expected value of the possible increase in overall well-being would exceed the expected value of the potential decrease. By contrast, if the firm were a small business with earnings of only several thousand dollars, the consequences of failure may far outweigh the benefits of success. The expected value of the investment project in terms of well-being may well be negative and, hence, an unsound business risk.

In any organization, particularly a large one in which the managers are not owners, it is possible—perhaps even likely—that the managers who must make capital expenditure decisions will assess the "value" of potential gains and losses in the context of their own character traits and objectives rather than those of the corporation. As indicated, the aforementioned investment project may well represent a sound business risk from the perspective of a large corporation but not necessarily a small one. The manager of one unit of the corporation, however, could quite reasonably reject the proposal because the consequences of failure would be severe both to his unit and to him personally. At an extreme, for example, a substantial decrease in earnings could cause the demise of his unit and the termination of his own position.

Procedures have been developed to explicitly incorporate into capital expenditure analysis the *utility* of incremental dollars to a particular company.* In essence, these techniques require that dollars be translated into a measure of utility (e.g., "utiles") and that expected value be computed in terms of such measure rather than dollars. For example, selected dollar amounts may be expressed in utiles as follows:

Dollars	Utiles
$ 0	0
25,000	2,400
50,000	4,600
100,000	8,700
105,000	9,100

* See, for example, Ralph O. Swalm, "Utility Theory—Insights into Risk Theory," *Harvard Business Review*, vol. 44, No. 6 (November–December), 1966, pp. 123–136. Swalm describes techniques of eliciting from an individual his valuations of dollars in terms of utiles.

This table suggests that to a particular firm, $100,000 is "worth" not four times more than $25,000, but only 3.6 times (8,7000 utiles divided by 2,400 utiles).

If a corporation is offered the opportunity to spend $50,000 on a project that would provide a 50 percent chance of a total return of $0 and a 50 percent chance of a total return of $105,000, then the expected return in utiles would be negative, indicating that the opportunity should be forgone:

Expected value of receipts .50(0 utiles) + .50(9,100 utiles)	4,550 utiles
Expected value of disbursement 1.0(4,600 utiles)	4,600 utiles
Expected value of project	(50 utiles)

Reference to this type of utility analysis is made in this text not because of its wide use in practice. In fact, it has proven difficult to implement and, as a consequence, is by no means a generally accepted managerial procedure. Awareness of it, however, should serve to sensitize a manager to the limitations of the conventional means of incorporating uncertainty into expenditure analysis. Monetary units, such as dollars, are an inadequate expression of either corporate or individual well-being. Merely because an investment has a positive expected dollar value it is not necessarily likely to enhance the overall utility of the party assuming the risk.

SUMMARY

The essence of capital expenditure analysis is a comparison of cash inflows with cash outflows. Gains and losses, as well as depreciation, are elements of income that do not reflect either the receipt or disbursement of cash. They do, however, enter into the determination of income taxes, an expenditure which does require a disbursement of cash.

Cash receipts and disbursements take place at different times throughout the life of a project. Owing to the "time value of money" they must be discounted back to the present if they are to be expressed in a monetary unit of common worth. Both the present value and the internal rate of return methods of evaluating investment projects focus on cash flows and explicitly take into account the time value of money. Other techniques, such as payback period and average return on investment, have little theoretical support, but they are useful rules of thumb and under specific conditions can be relied upon to produce the same results as the preferred methods.

Characteristic of all cash flows is uncertainty. Uncertainty can be incorporated into an analysis of a project by assigning probabilities to the various possible outcomes. The expected value of any particular receipt or disbursement would represent an average, weighted by the probabilities, of the possible receipts or disbursements. In general, a proposal should be accepted if the expected value of the net discounted cash receipts is positive. However, the consequences of the possible gains and losses must also be taken into account. Even though the expected value of a project is positive, the utility of the potential losses may exceed that of the expected gains.

EXERCISE FOR REVIEW AND SELF-TESTING

A company has the opportunity to replace an old machine with a new. The following data pertain to the two machines:

	New Machine	Old Machine
Purchase price	$200,000	
Original cost		$120,000
Accumulated depreciation		$30,000
Remaining useful life	5 years	5 years
Amount for which machine could be sold today		$80,000
Salvage value in five years	$50,000	$40,000
Annual depreciation charges	$30,000	$10,000

The old machine will require $92,000 in cash per year to operate. Company engineers believe that there is a 60 percent probability that the new machine will require $70,000 and a 40 percent chance that it will require only $50,000 per year in cash to operate.

The company evaluates investment proposals using a discount rate of 12 percent. Gains on the sale of equipment are taxed at a rate of 20 percent; ordinary income is taxed at a rate of 46 percent. The firm expects to sell other equipment at a gain during the year; any losses incurred on the sale of the old machine could be used to offset those gains.

1. If the company elects to replace the old machine with the new, what would be the required initial outlay, taking into account the reduction in taxes owing to the loss on the sale of the old machine?

2. What is the expected value of the annual operating costs of the new machine prior to taking into account income taxes?

3. What are the expected values of the annual operating costs of the new machine and the old machine after taking into account the tax reductions associated with both the direct operating costs and the charges for depreciation? What are the *present* values of these amounts?

4. What are the present values of the amounts to be received upon the sale of both the new machine and the old machine at the end of their useful lives?

5. What are the net present values of the disbursements associated with the two alternatives? Based on the criteria of net present value, should

the company replace the old machine with the new?

6. Determine the after-tax internal rate of return of the proposed expenditure. The cost of the new machine can best be represented by the net required outlay (as calculated in part 1). The annual return would be the difference between the per year after-tax operating costs of the new machine and the old (the cost indicated in part 3, prior to discounting). The relevant salvage value would be the difference between what would be received upon the sale of the new machine and the old. In attempting to find the rate that equates the present values of the inflows to the present value of the outflows, first try a rate of 4 percent.

QUESTIONS FOR REVIEW AND DISCUSSION

1. What is current thinking as to the most appropriate means of determining an appropriate rate of discount?

2. Depreciation is a noncash expense. Yet it is an element to be considered in calculating the net present value of an investment project. Why, and to what extent, must depreciation be taken into account in determining the net present value of a project?

3. In calculating the net present value of an investment project, how should the interest payments associated with the loans made to finance the project be taken into account?

4. Suppose that a firm must choose between two projects, one of which would provide a substantially greater internal rate of return than the other. Both projects entail the same degree of risk. Why might it be in the interest of the firm to select the project with the *lower* internal rate of return? Why might the project that provides the greater rate of return have the smaller net present value?

5. What is the common deficiency of both payback period and accounting rate of return as means of evaluating investment proposals? How can the use of either be defended?

6. What are *subjective probabilities?* What is subjective about them? Why must they be resorted to?

7. What is a significant limitation of *expected value* as a decision criterion? Indicate by way of an example how two proposals could have the same expected value, yet one would clearly be more consistent with a firm's objectives than the other.

8. A gambler has an opportunity to place two bets. The first would require an outlay of $45. There would be a .5 probability of a return of zero and a .5 probability of return of $100. The second would require an outlay of $45,000. There would be a .5 probability of a return of zero and a .5 probability of a return of $100,000. Why might he (quite rationally) accept the former and reject the latter.

9. Why is it generally preferable that a firm separate the decision to acquire an asset from that as to whether it should purchase or lease it; that is, why should a firm first decide whether to acquire an asset, based on the cash price, and then determine whether a lease arrangement is preferable to an outright purchase?

PROBLEMS

1. Tax expenditures and savings must be taken into account in evaluating investment proposals.

Mifflin Co. has the opportunity to acquire a new machine that would replace an old one. The machine would cost $80,000 and would have a useful life of 10 years with no salvage value. Acquisition of the new machine would necessitate special training for the operators at a cost of $7,000. It would enable the firm to reduce annual cash operating costs by $8,000.

The old machine has a remaining useful life of 10 years and it is estimated that there will be no salvage value at the end of its life. The book value of the machine is presently $50,000 and annual depreciation charges are $5,000. If the new machine were purchased, the old machine would be sold for $30,000.

The tax rate is 40 percent on ordinary income and 20 percent on the sale of plant and equipment.

The new machine would be eligible for an investment tax credit of 10 percent. The training costs would be amortized over the life of the asset, but for tax purposes they would be deductible immediately. The company takes depreciation on a straight-line basis. The firm has sufficient ordinary income and gains on the sale of plant and equipment to offset (and thereby benefit from) any taxable losses associated with the sale of the old machine and the acquisition of the new.

The firm accepts expenditure proposals only if they provide an after-tax return of 10 percent or greater.

a. Determine the net after-tax cash outlay (including training costs) that would be required if the machine were purchased.
b. Determine the annual net after-tax cash savings.
c. Determine whether the machine would provide an after-tax return on investment of 10 percent or more.

2. *Accelerated methods of depreciation, relative to the straight-line method, provide an investment incentive.*

Trans Texas Trucking Co. is considering the purchase of a new truck. The cost of the truck will be $100,000. It will have a useful life of four years and an estimated salvage value of $20,000. The firm estimates that the new truck would enable it to increase annual cash earnings, prior to depreciation and taxes, by $35,000. The firm would only purchase the truck if it would provide a return, after taxes, of 12 percent. The marginal rate of income tax for the firm is 46 percent.

a. Suppose that Internal Revenue Service regulations require that the firm use the straight-line method of depreciation. Should the firm accept the proposal to acquire the new truck?
b. Suppose, alternatively, that regulations permit the use of the double-declining balance method of depreciation. Should the firm accept the proposal to acquire the new truck?

3. *This exercise contrasts four means of evaluating investment proposals. Note particularly how the different criteria result in different rankings.*

A firm is evaluating three investment proposals. Each requires an initial outlay of $80,000. The net cash inflows associated with each are as follows:

Net Cash Receipts under Proposal:

Year	A	B	C
1	$25,000	$10,000	$40,000
2	25,000	20,000	30,000
3	25,000	30,000	20,000
4	25,000	50,000	10,000

For each of the proposals compute the measures of return indicated. Determine the order of preferability of the proposals using each of the measures as a criterion.

a. Payback period
b. Accounting rate of return
c. Net present value
   1. Using a discount rate of 15 percent
   2. Using a discount rate of 2 percent
d. Internal rate of return (within 1%). For convenience, in computing the rates of return of Proposals B and C interpolate between the rates of 15 percent and 2 percent.

4. *Different investment criteria—including net present value and internal rate of return which are similar in nature—may result in different rankings of proposals.*

Bexar Investment Co. is considering three mutually exclusive investment proposals.

Proposal A requires an initial outlay of $100,000 and provides a return of $26,380 for each of five years.

Proposal B requires an initial outlay of $50,000 and provides a return of $13,870 for each of five years.

Proposal C requires an initial outlay of $100,000 and provides returns as follows:

Year 1	$50,000	Year 4	$7,000
Year 2	40,000	Year 5	4,400
Year 3	10,000		

The firm's after-tax cost of capital is 5 percent.

a. For each of the three proposals, calculate:
   1. Net present value
   2. Internal rate of return
   3. Payback period
b. Rank the proposals according to each of the three criteria.

c. Comment on why Proposal A has a greater net present value but lower internal rate of return than does Proposal B. Suppose that Proposal A and Proposal B were mutually exclusive. How should the firm decide between the two proposals? What other information must be incorporated into the analysis?

5. *Investment projects that have a positive net present value may not always be "profitable."*

Amerex, Inc., is evaluating a proposal to modernize its plant by acquiring new equipment. The equipment that it is considering would cost $600,000. It would have a useful life of four years and a salvage value of $200,000. It would result in cash savings, before financing costs and taxes, of $150,000 per year.

Amerex, Inc., uses the double-declining balance method of depreciation for tax purposes. The equipment to be purchased is eligible for an investment tax credit of 10 percent of cost. It may be assumed that the firm will reap the benefit of the tax credit at the date of purchase. The incremental rate at which the firm pays income taxes is 40 percent.

The firm estimates that its average cost of capital, after taxes, is 9 percent.

a. On the basis of the net present value criterion would you recommend that the equipment be acquired?

b. Were the firm to acquire the equipment, it would borrow the required cash ($540,000, after taking into account the investment tax credit of $60,000) at an annual rate of 15 percent (which is the equivalent of 9 percent after taxes). For financial reporting purposes, the firm charges depreciation on the straight-line basis and amortizes the investment tax credit over the expected useful life of the equipment acquired. Determine the impact of the acquisition on earnings of the first year.

c. In light of your results in parts a and b, comment on why application of generally acceptable accounting principles may discourage investment decisions that are in the best interests of a company.

6. *"Artificial" assumptions must sometimes be made to equalize project lives.*

Downtown University is in need of additional classroom space for its College of Business. Classes are presently conducted in a building that the University leases at an annual cost of $800,000. The required additional space could be rented for a 10-year period in a nearby building for $700,000 per year.

The University is studying the possibility of constructing a new building which would eliminate entirely the need to rent from outsiders. It would be located on land which the University owns and which is presently being operated as a commercial parking lot. The cost of constructing the new building would be $10 million. Annual operating costs would be $200,000. The useful life of the building would be 50 years (no salvage value).

The parking lot on which the new building would be constructed generates $250,000 in revenue each year; operating costs are $75,000 per year. The land could be sold today for $2 million cash.

The lease on the building that the University presently uses has 10 years remaining until expiration. The owners of the building have agreed, however, to terminate the lease upon completion of the new building, for a cash payment of $1,200,000.

University planners predict that after 10 years (the period remaining until expiration of the lease) the new building including the land, could be sold for $8.5 million. The land alone, if the building were not constructed, could be sold for $2.5 million.

The University would construct the new building only if it would provide a "return" of 8 percent. Assume, for convenience, that construction of the building could be both started and completed in period 0.

Based on the criteria of net present value, should the University construct the building or, alternatively, should it continue to occupy the present quarters and lease additional space? Over how many years did you carry out the analysis? What assumptions did you make with respect to the disposition of the new building and land at the end of the period covered by the analysis? Is such assumption reasonable?

7. *How sensitive is present value analysis to errors of estimate and prediction?*

An executive of a company indicated that he prefers "rules of thumb" evaluative techniques to net present value because of the unreliability of the estimates and predictions required by the net present value technique. He cited, in particular, estimates of cost of capital and predictions of cash flows and asset lives.

Assume that a firm is considering the acquisition of an asset that has an estimated useful life of 10 years and will provide cash receipts of $100,000 per year. The firm uses a discount rate of 10 percent.

a. Determine the present value of the cash receipts.
b. Suppose that the firm made the misestimates that follow. For each, indicate the percentage difference between the present value as computed in part a and the present value that would be computed based on the misestimates.
   1. The firm estimated that cash receipts in years 6 through 10 would be 25 percent greater than they actually were (i.e., $125,000).
   2. It used a discount rate 20 percent greater than was appropriate (i.e., 12 percent).
   3. It predicted the useful life of the asset to be 20 percent longer than it actually will be (i.e., 12 years).
   4. It predicted the useful life of the asset to be 100 percent longer than it actually will be (i.e., 20 years).
c. Based on your computations what assertation

	Number of Years		
Net Cash Inflow	4	12	20
$30,159			
$26,262			

a. For each cell in the table, determine:
   1. Internal rate of return (within 1 percent)
   2. Payback reciprocal
   3. Average return on investment (assume straight-line depreciation and zero salvage value)
b. Despite their theoretical limitations, both payback reciprocal and average return on investment can, if the investment proposals have certain characteristics, be used as appropriate surrogates for internal rate of return. Based on the data that you calculated, under what circumstances (e.g., length of investment period, internal rate of return) would payback reciprocal provide a reasonable approximation of internal rate of return; under what circumstances would average return on investment provide a reasonable approximation?

The following represents the present value of an annuity of $1 discounted at rates that are not included in Table 4 of the Appendix:

	Rate						
Periods	24%	25%	26%	27%	28%	29%	30%
12	3.8514	3.7251	3.6059	3.4933	3.3868	3.2859	3.1903
20	4.1103	3.9539	3.8083	3.6726	3.5458	3.4271	3.3158

might you make in defense of the net present value technique?

8. *Both payback reciprocal and average return on investment can be used in certain circumstances as surrogates for internal rate of return.*

The table that follows represents six independent investment projects, each of which provides the indicated net cash flow for the indicated number of years. Each of the projects requires an initial outlay of $100,000.

9. *The financing decision must be distinguished from the acquisition decision.*

Deborah, Inc., is contemplating the acquisition of a new machine. The machine would enable the company to realize manufacturing savings, after taxes, of $67,500 per year. The machine has an estimated useful life of five years (no salvage value). The machine could be purchased for $250,000.

Deborah, Inc., uses a discount rate of 12 percent. It could, however, obtain financing for the new machine from either a bank or the manufacturer at the current prime rate of 10 percent.

a. Based on the net present value criteria, should the firm acquire the new machine?

b. Suppose, alternatively, that the equipment manufacturer agreed to lease the machine to Deborah, Inc., for a period of five years (the useful life of the machine). The annual rental charge would be $65,950. Annual after-tax manufacturing savings would be the same as if the machine were purchased outright ($67,500). Using as a criterion the net present value of all anticipated cash inflows and outflows, should the company lease the machine?

c. Are your two answers in conflict? If so, explain the conflict and point to any flaws in your analysis.

10. *The time value of money can readily be incorporated into break-even analysis; it may alter significantly the break-even point.*

Danco, Inc., must decide whether to purchase conventional or technologically advanced equipment. The conventional equipment would cost $4 million; the technologically advanced, $10 million. The useful lives of both are 10 years, with no anticipated salvage value.

The firm manufactures a product that it sells for $400 per unit. If the conventional equipment is acquired, variable manufacturing costs would be $300 per unit; if the technologically advanced equipment is purchased, then variable costs would be $200 per unit. The only fixed cost that need be considered is depreciation, which is charged on a straight-line basis.

The firm uses a discount rate of 12 percent to evaluate equipment acquisitions.

a. Ignoring the time value of money, determine the number of units that will have to be manufactured and sold each year for the firm to break even assuming the purchase of, first, the conventional equipment and, second, the technologically advanced equipment. Use conventional break-even analysis, considering the fixed costs to be annual depreciation.

b. Suppose that the firm expects to produce and sell 5,000 units per year over a 10-year period. If net present value is the decision criterion, can

the acquisition of either type of equipment be justified? If one type must be acquired, which is preferable?

c. Using net present value as a criterion, what is the minimum number of units that must be produced and sold each year to justify acquisition of the *technologically advanced* equipment?

11. *Owing to accelerated depreciation as well as to "leverage," investments in real estate can provide high rates of return even if appreciation in value is small and before-tax payments exceed rental receipts.*

Speculative Realty, Inc., is evaluating the earnings potential of an apartment complex. The firm can acquire the complex at a price of $5 million. The firm would be required to pay $500,000 cash and would assume a 12 percent 20-year mortgage for the balance.

The firm estimates that annual rent receipts would be $600,000 per year. Property taxes, insurance, and other cash operating costs would be $140,000 per year.

The firm plans to hold the property for three years and then sell it. Annual mortgage payments during each of the three years would be $602,455, divided between principal and interest as follows:

Year	Principal	Interest
1	$ 62,455	$ 540,000
2	69,950	532,505
3	78,344	524,111
Total	$210,749	$1,596,616

The firm estimates that at the end of three years it could sell the property for $5,200,000 (an amount reflecting an annual compound increase in value of only 1.3 percent). At the time of sale, the firm would repay the outstanding mortgage balance, which would then be $4,289,251.

The tax rate on ordinary income is 46 percent; that on gains resulting from the sale of property is 23 percent. The company will charge depreciation using the double-declining balance method assuming a useful life of 20 years and no salvage value. Internal Revenue Service regulations provide that when real property is sold for more than its book value, the "excess" depreciation resulting from the use of accelerated depreciation methods must be "recaptured" and taxed at ordinary, rather than capital gains, rates. According to the regulations, the total gain subject to tax is the difference between selling price of the asset and book value (cost less accumulated depreciation). That portion of the gain which represents the difference between the actual book value and what the book value would have been if the firm had used the straight-line method of depreciation rather than the accelerated method would be taxed at a rate of 46 percent. The remaining part of the gain would be taxed at a rate of only 23 percent. Speculative Realty has sufficient income from other properties to offset any tax losses attributable to the apartment complex that it is considering purchasing. Hence, any "negative" tax obligations can be viewed as cash receipts.

The firm will acquire the property only if it will provide an after-tax return on its required initial investment ($500,000 cash) of 15 percent.

a. Determine the net after-tax cash receipts (excluding those from the sale of the property) during each of the three years. Depreciation, property taxes, insurance, other operating costs, and that portion of the mortgage payment representing interest are expenses that are deductible for tax purposes. Calculate the present value of the net receipts.

b. Determine the net cash receipts upon sale of the property, and payment of both the balance on the mortgage and the required taxes on the resultant gain. Compute the present value of the net receipts.

c. Should the firm acquire the complex? Explain.

12. Subjective probabilities may be assigned to possible useful lives.

Posthaste Co. has decided to acquire a new delivery vehicle. The vehicle can be acquired outright for $72,000 or it can be leased for $20,000 per year. The minimum term of the lease is only one year. At the end of one year, the company has the right to extend the lease on a month to month

basis for as long as it wishes at the same rental rate. Per terms of the lease agreement, Posthaste is responsible for all insurance and maintenance costs.

Posthaste managers are unsure of the useful life of the vehicle. They have assigned the following subjective probabilities to various possibilities:

Years of Useful Life	Probability
3	.10
4	.20
5	.25
6	.20
7	.15
8	.10
	1.00

Posthaste evaluates all expenditure proposals using a discount rate of 12 percent.

Ignoring the impact of income taxes, should the company buy the vehicle or lease it?

13. Subjective probabilities can be assigned to anticipated receipts and disbursements to determine their expected values.

Keys, Inc., manufactures a household product that sells for $40 per unit. Annual fixed manufacturing costs are presently $600,000; variable costs are $26 per unit.

The firm has the opportunity to acquire a new machine which would cause variable costs to be reduced by $2 per unit. The machine can be purchased for $200,000. It has a useful life of three years and no salvage value.

The firm has assigned subjective probabilities to annual sales for the next three years:

Probability	Sales per Year (units)
.20	40,000
.50	46,000
.30	48,000

The firm uses a discount rate of 10 percent to evaluate purchases of plant and equipment.

a. Using net present value as a criterion, should the firm acquire the new machine?

b. Suppose alternatively that company engineers estimate that there is a 10 percent probability that the machine will not perform satisfactorily. The firm will be able to determine whether the machine is acceptable immediately after it is installed. If it is unacceptable, the manufacturer will permit the firm to return the machine and will refund 85 percent of the purchase price. What is the maximum amount that the firm should be willing to pay for the machine assuming cost savings and estimated sales as presented?

14. *Expected value of net receipts is not, by itself, a definitive decision criterion.*

A company has the opportunity to invest in a mining project. The amounts of both the required investment and the expected returns are uncertain.

The amount to be invested depends on excavation costs. Geologists and engineers have indicated that there is an .8 probability that the excavation costs will be $5 million and a .2 probability that they will be only $2 million.

The return on the investment depends on the price at which the mine can be sold. Company specialists believe that there is a .7 probability that it can be sold for $6 million and a .3 probability that it can be sold for only $4 million.

Any funds that the company does not invest in the project would be kept in government securities that return 6 percent per year. Thus, if the cost of the project is only $2 million, then the $3 million difference between such cost and the maximum cost of $5 million would be placed in the government securities.

The time span between the date of investment and the sale of the mine will be approximately one year. For computational convenience, it may be assumed that the anticipated receipts from the sale of the mine are expressed in dollars of the present; hence, there is no need to discount them.

a. Assuming that the decision criterion is expected value of net receipts, should the company invest in the mining project?

b. Suppose alternatively that the company wishes to maximize the expected value of net receipts subject to avoiding any possibility of a loss on its investment. Should it invest in the project?

15. *The expected value criterion fails to take into account the "worth" of dollar to be gained or lost.*

Gamble, Inc., must decide which of two versions of a new product to introduce. Version A is similar to other products currently on the market. Version B has several features which make it unique. The initial cost of introducing the two versions will be the same, $33 million. The firm has assigned the following subjective probabilities to the potential net cash receipts during each of the next 10 years:

Version A		Version B	
Probability	Annual Net Cash Receipts (millions)	Probability	Annual Net Cash Receipts (millions)
.05	$3.0	.20	$ 0.0
.25	4.0	.25	4.0
.40	5.0	.25	6.0
.25	6.0	.15	10.0
.05	7.0	.05	20.0

The firm uses a discount rate of 10 percent to assess investment proposals.

1. Based on the information provided, should the firm introduce either of the two versions? If it had to choose one, which would it prefer? Which provides the opportunity of the greater gain? Which allows for the greater loss?

2. Suppose that the company recognizes that the more dollars it has, or is able to acquire, the less valuable is each incremental dollar. To account for this explicitly, it has developed a table in which various dollar amounts are translated into a measure of value, which it refers to as utiles. The following are selected excerpts from the table:

Dollars (millions)	Utiles
$ 0.0	0
3.0	320
4.0	400
5.0	477
6.0	550
7.0	622
10.0	830
20.0	1,430
33.0	2,080

Notice how as the dollar amounts increase, the value per dollar, in utiles, decreases.

Recompute the expected present value of the two versions of the product using utiles instead of dollars. That is, in place of each dollar amount substitute the equivalent number of utiles. Taking into account the additional information, should the firm introduce either of the two versions? Which should it prefer?

SOLUTIONS TO EXERCISE FOR REVIEW AND SELF-TESTING

1. **Tax Savings from Sale of Old Machine**

Sales price of old machine		$ 80,000
Less: Book value of old machine		
Original cost	$120,000	
Accumulated depreciation	(30,000)	90,000
Loss on sale of old machine		$ 10,000
Tax rate on sale of equipment		× .20
Savings in taxes		$ 2,000

Required Outlay

Outlay to purchase new machine		$200,000
Less:		
Proceeds from sale of old machine	$ 80,000	
Savings in taxes owing to loss on sale of old machine (per previous computation)	2,000	82,000
Required net outlay		$118,000

2. Expected value = .60($70,000) + .40($50,00)
Expected value = $62,000

3.

	New Machine	Old Machine
Expected value of annual operating costs	$62,000	$ 92,000
Depreciation charges	30,000	10,000
Total deductible costs	92,000	102,000
Tax rate on ordinary income	× .46	× .46
Tax saving	$42,320	$ 46,920
Expected value of annual operating costs	$62,000	$ 92,000
Less: Tax saving	42,320	46,920
Expected value of annual operating costs after taxes	19,680	45,080
Present value of an annuity of $1 for 5 years discounted at 12 percent	× 3.6048	× 3.6048
Present value of expected annual operating costs	$70,942	$162,504

4.

	New Machine	Old Machine
Amount to be received upon salvage	$50,000	$40,000
Present value of $1 to be received in 5 years discounted at 12 percent	.5674	.5674
Present value of salvage proceeds	$28,370	$22,696

5.	New Machine	Old Machine
Net outlay upon acquisition of new machine (per part 1)	$118,000	
Present value of net operating costs (per part 3)	70,942	$162,504
Present value of salvage proceeds (per part 4)	(28,370)	(22,696)
Present value of net cash disbursements	$160,572	$139,808

Inasmuch as the present value of the net cash disbursements would be greater if the new machine were acquired than if it were not, the new machine should *not* be acquired.

6.		4%		5%	
	Amount	Discount Factor	Present Value	Discount Factor	Present Value
Initial outlay	($118,000)	1.000	($118,000)	1.0000	($118,000)
Difference in operating costs (annuity for 5 years)	25,400(a)	4.4518	113,076	4.3295	109,969
Difference in salvage value (single payment in 5 years)	10,000	.8219	8,219	.7835	7,835)
Net present value			$ 3,295		($ 196)

(a) Per part 3, expected value of annual operating costs after taxes:

Old machine	$45,080
New machine	19,680
Difference	$25,400

The internal rate of return will be that rate which provides a net present value of zero. Since 4 percent results in a net present value greater than zero, a slightly greater rate, 5 percent, was tried. Because 5 percent provides a net present value less than zero, the actual rate of return must be between 4 percent and 5 percent. Interpolation would indicate a rate of 4.9 percent.

CONTROLLING AND REPORTING 22
ON PERFORMANCE

Control may be defined as the policies and practices of an organization intended to assure that its plans are fulfilled. Systems of control should be designed so that the activities of an organization are monitored, analyzed, and reported on to responsible managers. They should highlight the need for adjustments in operations to make certain that overall objectives are realized to the fullest extent possible.

Central to a system of control are accounting and reporting procedures that provide management with information of any deviations from what was planned. The information should allow for inferences as to the reason for the deviation and, insofar as possible, should affix responsibility for it. A report that indicates that the manufacturing cost of a product was $4 instead of the planned $3.50 may serve as a warning to management that something is amiss, but it is neither illuminating as to the cause of the variance or suggestive of what corrective actions, if any, are appropriate. The first part of this chapter will be devoted primarily to the use of *standard costs* as a means of controlling both direct and overhead costs. A *standard cost system*, when properly designed and implemented, directs attention to variations in cost from what was planned, provides insights as to their underlying causes and identifies the parties to be held accountable for them.

Standard cost systems will be discussed in the context of manufacturing firms. The presentation is intended, however, to provide an introduction to control procedures in all types of organizations.

The second part of the chapter will focus on reports of performance to managers. Performance reports are a key element in an overall system of planning and control. They provide the link between what has taken place in the past and what can be accomplished in the future.

The primary concern of this chapter will be on systems of control and reporting intended to facilitate the fulfillment of *operational* or *routine* plans—those which relate to the day-to-day, month-to-month, or even quarter-to-quarter activities of a firm. These types of plans can be distinguished from *strategic* and *long-term plans*, which commonly involve a longer time perspective and have a more global impact on the way a firm acquires and uses its resources.

DEFINITION AND ADVANTAGES OF STANDARD COSTS

A *standard* cost is a planned or allowable cost. The standard cost of a particular unit, be it a unit of input such as direct labor or materials, or a unit of output, such as a product manufactured, can be viewed as the amount budgeted for that unit. A *standard cost system* is one in which units are recorded at *predetermined—standard*—costs as opposed to actual costs incurred.

The introduction of standard costs enriches a management planning and control system in at least three ways:

1. Budgeting and planning are facilitated in that a planner can readily determine the number of units of input that should be required to produce a specific number of units of output. He can then easily estimate costs of production.

2. The accounting system can be designed so that deviations from standards are automatically calculated and reported to responsible managers.

3. The recording process can be simplified because transfers from one account to another can be made on the basis of fixed, predetermined amounts rather than actual costs which, of course, are subject to continual change.

In a previous chapter pertaining to characteristics of costs, the advantages of applying overhead by way of a predetermined—a standard—rate were demonstrated. In this section the benefits to be derived from applying also direct labor and direct materials at standard costs will be discussed.

TYPES OF STANDARDS

At least four types of standards may be identified.

First, standards may represent an ideal level of performance—one which could be attained only under the most favorable of circumstances. Often ideal standards are engineered standards and once they have been established they remained fixed until there is a change in product, manufacturing process, materials prices, or labor rates. Ideal standards generally do not take into account the frailties and imperfections of either man or machine.

Second, standards may represent reasonably attainable goals. These standards may be less demanding than ideal standards, and they are set at a level intended to bring forth the best efforts on the part of those whose performance will be measured against them. They are *motivational* in purpose. They will not be so rigorous as to discourage attainment, but at the same time will not be so lax as to be met without maximum effort.

Third, standards may indicate what is anticipated over an extended period of time, usually a year. Such standards are referred to as *normal* standards. They are established with reference to past experience. They indicate what is *expected*, not necessarily what is desired. They are readily attainable over the period that they are designed to cover, but within shorter time spans there likely will be both favorable and unfavorable deviations.

Fourth, standards may be based on what is expected within the *immediate future*. These standards take into account current operating conditions and are revised with frequency. It is expected that they will be attained.

DIRECT MATERIAL COSTS

There are two primary reasons why the cost of materials used in the manufacture of a product may be different from what was planned. First, the *price* paid for materials used may have been higher or lower than standard; second, the *quantity* of materials used may have been greater or less than standard. Each of these reasons suggests a type of variance about which it is critical for management to be informed on a timely basis. The difference between actual and standard price forms the basis of a *price variance;* that between actual and standard quantity forms the basis of a *quantity* or *usage* variance. Both of these variances can be calculated and recorded as materials are purchased and used.

Suppose that a firm has adopted the following standards and achieved during a month the following results:

Standard amount of raw material for *one* unit of product	100 lb.
Standard cost per lb of raw materials	$1.00
Actual results for month	
Units produced	2,000 units
Raw materials purchased and used	240,000 lb
Cost of raw materials ($1.05 per lb)	$252,000

The standard materials cost of producing 2,000 units would be $200,000 (200,000 lb @ $1.00). The total materials variance is, therefore, $52,000 (unfavorable):

Actual materials cost of producing 2,000 units (240,000 lb @ $1.05)	$252,000
Standard materials cost of producing 2,000 units (2,000 × 100 lb @ $1.00)	200,000
Total materials variance	$ 52,000 U

Price Variance

The price variance can be determined by comparing the actual cost of the materials *acquired* with their standard cost:

Materials price variance

= Actual cost of materials acquired
   − Standard cost of materials acquired

or

Materials price variance

= (Actual price − Standard price)

   × Actual number of units of material acquired

In the example the materials price variance is $12,000 (unfavorable):

(Actual price − Standard price)

   × Actual number of units acquired

($1.05 − $1.00) × 240,000 lb = $12,000

One means of recording the acquisition of materials so that the price variation is isolated immediately is to enter the raw materials inventory at standard prices and charge the amount paid in excess of standard to a special variance account. Thus:

Raw materials (240,000 lbs @ $1.00)	$240,000	
Materials price variance (240,000 lb @ $.05)	12,000	
Accounts payable (240,000 lb@ $1.05)		$252,000

To record the acquisition of raw materials.

In many companies, raw materials are charged initially at actual rather than standard prices. When used, they are added to work in process at standard cost, and the price variance is recorded at that time. The advantage of isolating the variance at the time the goods are acquired (the procedure illustrated) instead of when they are used is that management is made aware of the deviation at an earlier date and can take corrective action more promptly. With regard to the purchase of some types of raw material, there is little that management can do to eliminate an unfavorable price variance. Prices may be established in a free market and the company can do no more than pay the price at which items are offered. The prices paid for other types of raw materials, however, may be more susceptible to negotiation or careful buying practices.

Quantity Variance

The materials quantity variance can be expressed as the difference between the amount of materials *actually* used and the *standard* amount that should have been used, both amounts being valued at *standard prices*. Thus:

Materials quantity variance

= Standard value of actual amount
  of materials used

  − Standard value of standard
    amount of materials

or

Materials quantity variance

= (Actual units of materials
  − Standard units of materials)
  × Standard price per unit of materials

In the case at hand the materials quantity variance is $40,000 (unfavorable):

(Actual units of materials

  − Standard units of materials)

  × Standard price per unit of materials

  (240,000 lb − 200,000 lb) × $1.00 = $40,000

The materials quantity variance can be identified and recorded at the time the materials are put into process by charging work in process with only the standard number of units required for the actual output. Any extra materials used would be charged to a quantity variance account:

Work in process	
(2,000 units ×	
100 lb @ $1)	$200,000
Materials quantity	
variance (40,000	
extra lb @ $1)	40,000
Raw materials	
(240,000 lb @ $1)	$240,000

To record the use of 240,000 pounds of material to manufacture 2,000 units of product. The 2,000 units of product should have required the use of only 200,000 pounds of raw materials.

Alternatively, under some systems, actual amounts of raw materials are recorded in work in process. The variance is then computed and recorded when completed goods are transferred to finished goods inventory. The advantage of the procedure illustrated, as with the price variance, is earlier recognition of the variance and, as a consequence, the opportunity for more prompt action to rectify unfavorable deviations.

The price and the usage variances can be depicted graphically as shown in Exhibit 22-1.

EXHIBIT 22-1   Materials Variances: Price and Usage

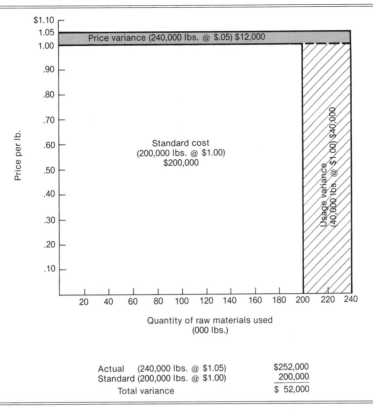

Actual	(240,000 lbs. @ $1.05)	$252,000
Standard	(200,000 lbs. @ $1.00)	200,000
	Total variance	$ 52,000

DIRECT LABOR COSTS

Labor costs can be accounted for in a way that closely corresponds to material costs. As with materials, there are two fundamental reasons why actual labor costs may vary from standard: the rate (the price) actually paid may be different from the standard rate; the efficiency with which labor was used (the quantity) may be different from standard.

Assume the following standards and actual results:

Standard amount of direct labor for *one* unit of product	5 hours
Standard labor rate per hour	$12.00
Actual results for month	
Units produced	2,000 units
Direct labor hours used	9,750 hours
Cost of direct labor ($12.40 per hour)	$120,900

The total labor variance is, therefore, $900 (unfavorable):

Actual labor cost of
   producing 2,000 units
   (9,750 hours @ $12.40) $120,900
Standard labor cost of
   producing 2,000 units
   (2,000 units × 5 hours
   @ $12)   120,000
      Total labor variance $ 900 U

Rate Variance

The labor rate variance may be calculated by comparing *actual labor costs* with *actual hours valued at standard rates:*

Labor rate variance

   = Actual labor costs

     − Standard cost of labor hours actually used

or

Labor rate variance

      = (Actual rate − Standard rate)

        × Actual number of hours worked

In the illustration the labor rate variance is $3,900 (unfavorable):

(Actual rate − Standard rate)

       × Actual number of hours worked

    ($12.40 − $12.00) × 9,750 = $3,900

Efficiency Variance

The labor efficiency variance represents the difference between the number of hours *actually* used and the *standard* number of hours that should have been used, both numbers of hours being stated at *standard rates*. Thus:

Labor efficiency variance

  = Standard value of actual number of hours used

    − Standard value of standard number of hours

or

Labor efficiency variance

      = (Actual hours − Standard hours)

        × Standard rate

In the case at hand the variance, this time favorable, is $3,000:

(Actual hours − Standard hours) × Standard rate

    (9,750 − 10,000) × $12.00 = $3,000

Inasmuch as direct labor, unlike materials, is added to work in process as it is "acquired," the entries to record the variances may be made concurrently. First, direct labor is charged with number of hours actually used, valued at standard rates, and a liability account is credited with the amount actually to be paid to the employees. The difference is charged (or credited) to a variance account:

Direct labor (9,750
   hours @ $12.00) $117,000
Labor rate variance
   (9,750 hours @
   $.40)   3,900
    Payroll liability
     (9,750 hours @ $12.40) $120,900
To record payroll liability.

Then, the standard number of direct labor hours, valued at standard rates, is added to work in process. The difference between that amount and the amount initially charged to direct labor is recognized as the labor efficiency variance:

Work in process
   (10,000 hours
   @ $12) $120,000
    Direct labor
     (9,750 hours @ $12) $117,000
    Labor efficiency variance
     (250 hours @ $12)   3,000

EXHIBIT 22-2

Summary of Price and Quantity Variances[a]

	Actual Quantity × Actual Price or Rate	Actual Quantity × Standard Price or Rate	Standard Quantity × Standard Price or Rate
Materials	240,000 lb × $1.05 = $252,000	− 240,000 lb × $1.00 = $240,000	− 200,000 lb × $1.00 = $200,000
	Price variance = $12,000 U	Quantity variance = $40,000 U	
Labor	9,750 hours × $12.40 = $120,000	9,750 hours × $12.00 = $117,000	− 10,000 hours × $12.00 = $120,000
	Rate variance = $3,900 U	Efficiency variance = ($3,000)F	

[a] F, favorable variance; U, unfavorable variance.

To record the use of 9,750 direct labor hours to manufacture 2,000 units of product. The 2,000 units of product should have required the use of 10,000 direct labor hours.

As with materials, under some systems the number of labor hours actually used is added to work in process and the efficiency variance is recorded when the completed units are transferred to finished goods inventory. The entries illustrated provide for more timely recognition of the variances.

The price (rate) and quantity (efficiency) variances for both labor and materials are summarized in Exhibit 22-2.

DECISION TO TAKE CORRECTIVE ACTION

It stands to reason that *all* reported variances should be reviewed by management. Other-wise, there would be no point in calculating and reporting them. But whether corrective action should be taken or whether even a comprehensive investigation into the cause of the variance should be made depends on a number of considerations. Among them are:

1. The appropriateness of the standards. As implied by the preceding paragraphs, standards may be so rigorous that it is not expected that they will be met. Unfavorable variances may be indicative of performance short of perfection, but nevertheless adequate and not in need of management intervention. Standards that exceed expectations may well serve to motivate, but their utility as a means of control is limited. Management can circumvent the deficiencies of unduly rigorous standards by establishing a variance threshold such that variances will be investigated

only when they exceed a permissible level. The practical effect of establishing a variance threshold would be to create a dual set of standards, one for motivation, the other for control.

2. The probability that the variance is significant. Virtually all production processes are subject to random fluctuations. Standards are point estimates. Most processes, however, can be properly described only by probability distributions. A standard may require that an operation be completed in 30 minutes. But regardless of how efficient the employees, very rarely will the operation be done in exactly 30 minutes. Sometimes it will be done in 29 minutes; sometimes in 32 minutes. A series of several jobs could be characterized by unfavorable labor efficiency variances. Both the process, as well as the workers, could nevertheless be operating efficiently. The deviations could be nothing more than random fluctuations from the mean (average) expected operating time. Statistical tests can be applied to determine the probability that a sample of variances represents a true operating inefficiency or merely a normal operating fluctuation. These tests are described in many standard texts on production quality control.

3. The materiality of the variance. The larger a variance the less the probability that it is a mere statistical aberation and the greater the probability that it warrants investigation and corrective action. As a substitute for elaborate statistical quality control guidelines, many organizations use materiality guidelines—whenever a variance is greater than a fixed percentage of standard the variance must be investigated and appropriate corrective measures taken.

4. The cost to investigate and, if necessary, correct. In some productive processes, the cost to investigate, and, if necessary, correct variances may be substantial. Production lines may have to be shut down, experts may have to be called in, chemical tests may have to be performed. It is in the interest of management to incur the investigative and corrective outlays only when it is probable that they will be less than any resultant savings in operating costs. The literature of both cost accounting and quality control contains descriptions of statistical models that can facilitate a determination as to when investigation and correction is worthwhile.

5. The interrelationship among variances. A single unfavorable variable, even if statistically significant, is not necessarily a sign of inefficiency. A firm can make trade-offs among the four factors (the prices and quantities of both labor and materials) which are described by the variances illustrated. Suppose, for example, that in determining labor standards, it was assumed that the work would be performed by employees with a particular degree of skill and experience. In a particular period the firm may be required, or may have the opportunity, to substitute employees with less skill or less experience who are in a lower pay classification. The consequence of the substitution may be an unfavorable labor efficiency variance, offset by a favorable labor rate variance. Similarly, a firm may elect to substitute a lower quality material for that on which the standard is based. This material may cause a greater number of units than standard to be rejected. The result may be a favorable materials price variance but unfavorable quantity variances for materials as well as for labor.

The four basic variances illustrated in this section may be further refined to account for changes in the mix of the factors of production. The refinements serve to formalize and quantify a necessary element in the interpretation of variances—the analysis of the variances in combination with, rather than in isolation of, one another.

6. The controllability of variances. Although the operations of a firm may be at variance with standard, there may be little that management can do by way of corrective action—at least in the short run. Materials price variances, for example, may be beyond the ability of management to eliminate, particularly if the firm acquires the materials in a competitive market and can make no substitutions. This is not to suggest that variances which are not subject to immediate correction should be of no concern to management. Given sufficient time, management can adjust all factors of production and variances serve to put management on notice that certain costs may be "getting out of line."

LEARNING CURVES

In establishing prices, in bidding on contracts, and in setting standards it is necessary for management to estimate the labor time necessary to complete each phase of a production process. When new products or processes are being introduced, however, it may be difficult to make the required estimate because the labor time demands are in a state of change. The literature of production management provides descriptions of a number of estimation techniques. One, based on *learning curves*, is widely used and, as a consequence both accountants and managers who may be involved in the process of making, interpreting, or using cost estimates should be familiar with it.

Learning curves give quantitative or graphic expression to an intuitively obvious phenomenon; as workers gain production experience, their productivity increases—at least up to a point. Each batch of units produced will take less time to complete than previous batches. Per the theory on which learning curves are based, whenever the *cumulative* production output is *doubled*, the *average* time to produce each unit of *cumulative* production will be a certain percentage of the time required to produce the units up to that point. The particular percentage will vary from process to process, but usually it is between 60 and 90 percent.

Suppose for example it requires 10,000 minutes to produce the first 1,000 units of product—an average of 10 minutes per unit. If an 80 percent learning curve is appropriate, then it would take 16,000 minutes, an average of 8 minutes per unit (80 percent of 10 minutes) to produce a *cumulative* total of 2,000 units (double 1,000 units) and 25,600 minutes, an average of 6.4 minutes per unit (80 percent of 8 minutes) to produce a cumulative total of 4,000 units (double 2,000 units). Exhibit 22-3 provides a more detailed illustration of an 80 percent learning curve given the assumptions regarding the time required to produce the initial batch.

Exhibit 22-4 displays graphically the effect of learning on the average cumulative times needed for production. The curve makes clear that the improvements to be expected as a consequence of experience are great at first, but they are quickly reduced as the production process achieves a "steady state."

The phenomenon of the learning curve must be taken into account in establishing standards and in making related forecasts of expenditures. Management must recognize that standards based experiences represented by the rapidly declining section of the curve will prove to be unnecessarily lax as operations move toward a steady state. Correspondingly, those based on expectations of

EXHIBIT 22-3

Eighty Percent Learning Curve

Number of Units in Batch	Cumulative Production (units)	Cumulative Average Time per Unit (minutes)	Total Time Accumulated (minutes)	Average Time per Unit in Particular Batch[a] (minutes)	Number of Units Produced per Hour[b]
1,000	1,000	10.00	10,000	10.00	6.00
1,000	2,000	8.00	16,000	6.00	10.00
2,000	4,000	6.40	25,600	4.80	12.50
4,000	8,000	5.12	40,960	3.84	15.63
8,000	16,000	4.10	65,600	3.08	19.48
16,000	32,000	3.28	104,960	2.46	24.39
32,000	64,000	2.62	167,680	1.96	30.61

[a] Difference in total time accumulated between a particular batch and the previous batch divided by number of units in the batch [e.g., for the second batch, $(16,000 - 10,000) \div 1,000 = 6.00$ minutes].

[b] 60 minutes divided by average time per unit.

EXHIBIT 22-4   Eighty Percent Learning Curve

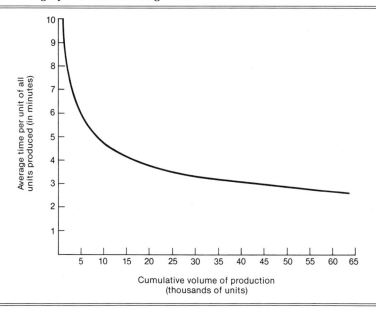

operations at a steady state will be unduly rigorous when the learning process has just begun.

OVERHEAD COSTS

Overhead costs are commonly of substantial magnitude and must thereby be subject to controls that are as rigorous as those applied to direct labor and materials. In fact, reports to management which focus on variances in direct labor and materials can easily be adapted to incorporate variances in overhead costs as well.

Characteristics

In previous chapters two characteristics of overhead costs were described that are directly pertinent to the control of overhead costs.

First, overhead costs often have both fixed and variable elements. The fixed element is not, of course, unchanging; it is fixed only in relation to level of activity. The variable element, by contrast, varies in relation to a selected measure of production volume. The measure of production volume is usually an input measure, such as number of direct labor hours worked. As a consequence of the variability of overhead, total overhead costs incurred may be affected by factors outside of the department responsible for providing the overhead services. For example, insofar as maintenance costs contain an element that is variable in relation to number of machine hours, the variable portion of maintenance costs—and thus total maintenance costs—will be affected by both the department responsible for machine usage as well as the department in charge of machine maintenance.

Second, overhead costs are not usually applied *directly* to specific jobs or units of product. Instead they are *absorbed* by means of an overhead charging rate, preferably one that is predetermined. The overhead charging rate is calculated by dividing expected overhead costs by expected units of activity. The amount of overhead absorbed is determined by multiplying the overhead charging rate by units of activity.

Absorption Based on Standard Units of Activity

In the examples of a preceding chapter related to overhead absorption, the amount of overhead absorbed was calculated by multiplying the overhead charging rate by the *actual* number of units of activity. If, for example, the overhead charging rate were based upon direct labor hours, then the amount of overhead absorbed was determined by multiplying the overhead charging rate by the *actual* number of direct labor hours associated with a job or product.

In an earlier section of this chapter it was pointed out that in a standard cost system, both *direct* labor and *direct* materials are charged to a job or product in accordance with preestablished standards rather than actual costs incurred. Thus, regardless of by how much actual costs differ from standard costs, the amount assigned to the job or product will be the standard direct cost.

If consistency is to be maintained, overhead must be *absorbed* into the job or product on the basis of *standard* units of activity. Thus, under most standard cost systems, the amount of overhead absorbed is calculated by multiplying the predetermined burden rate by the *standard* number of units of materials or direct labor hours or dollars.

Once the predetermined overhead charging rate and the direct labor and materials standards have been established the amount of overhead absorbed will depend *entirely* on the number of units of product produced. Variations in either the price of the various factors of production—labor, materials, and overhead—or in the efficiency with which they are used will have no impact on the amount of overhead assigned to jobs or products.

Three Reasons for Overhead Variances

The nature of overhead costs and the manner in which they are absorbed into products suggest that there are three primary reasons why actual overhead costs incurred in a period may differ from the amount of overhead absorbed.

First, production volume may be greater or less than normal. If it were greater than normal—and the company is making more effective use of its facilities than anticipated— then other factors being equal overhead would be overabsorbed; if it were less than normal—and the firm is not getting full benefit from its "fixed" or "capacity" costs— then overhead would be underabsorbed. The variance suggested by this difference is known as a *volume, capacity* or *denominator* variance.

Second, the amount of direct labor or materials—or whatever input factor drives the variable portion of overhead—may be greater or less than standard. The variable portion of the overhead is dependent on the level of activity as measured by *inputs* to the manufacturing process rather than on number of units produced. Any inefficiency in the use of direct labor or materials (or other appropriate factor) will require greater use of the services represented by the overhead costs. It will thereby result in a variance in the variable portion of overhead costs. The variance that can be attributed to deviations in the use of direct labor or materials is known as the *overhead* efficiency variance.

Third, the services represented by the overhead costs may have been performed at greater or less cost than anticipated, even after taking into account unanticipated changes in volume or variances in direct labor or materials. For example, the maintenance department may have used more labor hours or paid higher wages than anticipated to perform routine maintenance. Or, owing to unusually cold weather, heating costs may have been greater than planned. The variance that can be attributed to greater or less than usual overhead costs *after* taking into account the factors which explain the other two variances, is known as a *budget* or *spending* variance.

Each of these three variances may be illustrated by way of an example.

The following data pertain to operations of a particular month:

Number of units produced	2,000 units
Standard direct labor hours for 2,000 units (5 per unit)	10,000 hours
Actual number of direct labor hours used	9,750 hours
Normal production volume per *month* (26,400 per *year*)	2,200 units

Overhead costs for a month are budgeted on the basis of the following estimates:

Fixed portion of overhead	
Depreciation	$ 4,000
Supervision	20,000
Maintenance employee wages	35,000
Allocations from other cost centers	7,000
Total fixed overhead	$66,000

Variable portion of overhead
(per direct labor hour)

Fringe benefits and other payroll costs	$3.20
Rework and inspection	.80
Supplies and miscellaneous	1.00
Allocations from other cost centers	2.00
Total variable overhead	$7.00

Actual overhead costs incurred during the month were:

Fixed overhead	$ 68,000
Variable overhead	71,000
Total overhead costs	$139,000

Flexible Budgets

Central to the analysis—and therefore the control—of overhead costs is the concept of a *flexible budget*. As previously discussed, the total of variable overhead costs incurred by a firm may be influenced by factors beyond the control of the departments responsible for providing the overhead services. Therefore, the performance of those departments cannot be measured by simply comparing actual costs with those budgeted for a predetermined level of output. In the case at hand, for instance, overhead costs are affected by the number of direct labor hours used. The efficiency with which overhead services were rendered cannot be evaluated until the number of direct labor hours actually used is known.

A flexible budget indicates the expected overhead costs that should be incurred at various levels of activity. It explicitly distinguishes between the fixed and variable portions of overhead. A flexible budget based on fixed costs of $66,000 and variable costs of $7.00 per direct labor hour is presented in Exhibit 22-5. In order to highlight the relationship between the overhead charging rate and the flexible budget, the calculation of the overhead charging rate is shown as an addendum to the budget. The budget itself is shown in condensed form since the component elements of both fixed and variable costs are each summarized in a single amount.

EXHIBIT 22-5

Flexible Budget for Overhead

Level of Activity in Direct Labor Hours

	9,750	10,000	Normal 11,000	12,000	13,000
Fixed overhead costs	$ 66,000	$ 66,000	$ 66,000	$ 66,000	$ 66,000
Variable overhead costs @ $7 per direct labor hour	68,250	70,000	77,000	84,000	91,000
Total overhead costs	$134,250	$136,000	$143,000	$150,000	$157,000
Normal level of activity (direct labor hours)			÷ 11,000		
Overhead charging rate			$ 13[a]		

[a] The overhead charging rate is conventionally based on annual rather than monthly estimates of costs and activity. It is assumed in this example that normal monthly costs and activity are $\frac{1}{12}$ of the estimated annual amounts.

The overhead charging rate comprises two elements:

A fixed element ($66,000 divided by
the 11,000 direct labor hours) $ 6
A variable element (the budgeted
variable costs per direct labor hour)   7
        Overhead charging rate $13

At the normal level of activity—and only at that level—the overhead charging rate times the number of direct labor hours is equal exactly to the total budgeted overhead costs. At that level also, the amount of costs

actual number of direct labor hours used (9,750, per data provided) was only $134,250. The difference of $4,750 between the two amounts represents the *budget* or *spending* variance. A spending variance indicates the difference between actual overhead costs and those budgeted per the flexible budget for the inputs *actually* used.

Since either fixed costs or variable costs can vary from the standard provided by the flexible budget, the budget variance has both a fixed and a variable element. In our example, both are unfavorable:

	Fixed Element	Variable Element	Total
Actual overhead costs incurred (per data provided)	$68,000	$71,000	$139,000
Overhead budgeted, per flexible budget for *actual* number of direct labor hours (9,750)	66,000	68,250	134,250
Budget variance	$ 2,000 U	$ 2,750 U	$ 4,750 U

absorbed into a product would be equal to costs that were budgeted. At activity levels less than normal, budgeted costs would exceed amounts absorbed; at activity levels greater than normal, amounts absorbed would exceed budgeted costs.

Budget or Spending Variance

The budget or spending variance compares actual overhead costs with those budgeted for the actual level of activity. It focuses on variances from budget *after* taking into account deviations from normal in both the number of units produced and the amount of input (such as direct labor hours) required to produce that output. Actual total overhead costs per the data provided, were $139,000. Yet the overhead that would have been budgeted (per the flexible budget) for the

The budget variance is solely the *responsibility* of the departments in charge of providing the overhead services. An unfavorable variance, may of course signify inadequate control over costs. In the example, the variance in fixed costs may represent overtime paid to maintenance employees for work that could have been performed during regular working hours had job assignments been properly scheduled. At the same time, however, an unfavorable variance may be the consequence of factors beyond the control of the department with which it is associated. The overtime wages paid to the maintenance employees may have been necessitated by a power outage which prevented them from performing required services in the course of their normal working hours. The purpose of the budget variance, as well as *all* variances, is *not to affix blame*. Rather, it is *to assign responsibility* for explanation.

Efficiency Variance

As indicated by the data, the firm was efficient in its use of direct labor. The standard for the actual output of 2,000 units is 10,000 direct labor hours. The firm used only 9,750 hours. The saving to firm was greater than merely the wages for 250 hours, however. Variable overhead costs are directly affected by the number of direct labor hours used. The greater the use of labor, the higher the costs for fringe benefits, rework, inspection, and supplies. Indeed, because as each hour of direct labor results in $7 of overhead costs, the 250 direct labor hours saved caused a reduction in variable overhead costs of $1,750. By contrast, the efficient use of direct labor had no impact on fixed overhead costs. By nature, fixed costs are unaffected by changes in level of activity.

The overhead efficiency variance indicates the difference between the overhead that is budgeted for the actual number of direct labor hours used and the overhead that would be budgeted for the *standard* number of direct labor hours required to produce the actual output:

in variable overhead attributable to the inefficient use of direct labor.

Volume or Capacity Variance

Per the information presented, the firm produced at a volume less than normal— 2,000 units were produced instead of the expected 2,200. As a consequence, the firm did not fully utilize its capacity. An indication of the cost of the wasted capacity may be obtained by comparing the budgeted overhead costs for the actual output with the costs that were absorbed into the product. The purpose of the volume variance is to focus attention on the cost attributable to the reduced production volume. Therefore, the amounts that are both budgeted and absorbed are based on *standard* number of direct labor hours for the actual output. Production inefficiencies thereby have no impact on the variance. The volume variance pertains only to fixed costs. At any specified level of output, the budgeted variable costs (e.g., $7 per direct labor hour) will always be equal to the amount of variable costs absorbed (also $7 per direct labor hour). The volume

	Fixed Element	Variable Element	Total
Overhead, budgeted per flexible budget for *actual* number of direct labor hours (9,750)	$66,000	$68,250	$134,250
Overhead budgeted, per flexible budget, for standard number of direct labor hours (10,000) required to produce the actual output of 2,000 units	66,000	70,000	136,000
Efficiency variance	$ -0-	($ 1,750)F	($ 1,750)F

The efficiency variance is solely the responsibility of the department accountable for direct labor. It measures the cost to the firm

variance, in this example, indicates the "cost" of operating at a volume of 2,000 units (10,000 direct labor hours) when there is capacity for 2,200 units (11,000 direct labor hours):

	Fixed Element	Variable Element	Total
Overhead budgeted, per flexible budget, for standard number of direct labor hours (10,000) required to produce the actual output of 2,000 units	$66,000	$70,000	$136,000
Overhead absorbed by the standard number of direct labor hours (10,000). Fixed portion of the overhead charging rate is $6 per direct labor hour; variable portion is $7 per direct labor hour	60,000	70,000	130,000
Volume variance	$ 6,000 U	$ -0-	$ 6,000 U

Alternatively, the volume variance can be calculated as follows:

Standard labor hours for normal output (2,200 units @ 5 direct labor hours)	11,000	
Less: Standard labor hours for actual output (2,000 units @ 5 direct labor hours)	10,000	1,000
Multiplied by *fixed* portion of overhead charging rate		× $6
Volume variance		$6,000 U

The utility of the volume variance in controlling overhead costs is limited. Unlike both the budget and efficiency variances, the volume variance does not indicate an actual out-of-pocket cost incurred by a firm. Instead, it indicates the opportunity cost of not fully utilizing capacity. It signifies a failure to fully absorb fixed costs. The volume variance is generally controllable not by manufacturing departments, but by a sales department. In the main, it is attributable to inadequate production, which is commonly the result of inadequate sales. The performance of sales departments can almost always be more effectively evaluated and controlled from sales reports directly rather than from manufacturing reports.

The three overhead variances may be summarized in two forms, tabular (Exhibit 22-6) and diagrammatic (Exhibit 22-7), each of which highlights their common components.

In journal entry form, the overhead costs can be added to work in process and the variances recorded, as follows:

Overhead control	$139,000	
Various overhead accounts (depreciation, supervision, maintenance, etc.)		$139,000

To summarize overhead costs in the overhead control account.

Work in process	$130,000	
Budget variance	4,750	
Volume variance	6,000	
Efficiency variance		$ 1,750
Overhead control		139,000

To transfer overhead costs to work in process and record overhead variances.

EXHIBIT 22-6

	Summary of Overhead Variances[a]		
	Fixed Element	*Variable Element*	*Total*
Actual overhead costs	$68,000	$71,000	$139,000
Overhead budgeted, per flexible budget, for actual input (9,750 direct labor hours)	66,000	68,250	134,250
Budget variance	$ 2,000 U	$ 2,750 U	$ 4,750 U
Overhead, per flexible budget, for actual input (9,750 direct labor hours)	$66,000	$68,250	$134,250
Overhead budgeted for standard input (10,000 direct labor hours) required to produce actual output (2,000 units)	66,000	70,000	136,000
Efficiency variance	$ -0-	($ 1,750)F	($ 1,750)F
Overhead budgeted for standard input (10,000 direct labor hours) required to produce actual output (2,000 units)	$66,000	$70,000	$136,000
Overhead absorbed at standard input (10,000 direct labor hours) required to produce actual output (2,000 units)	60,000	70,000	130,000
Volume variance	$ 6,000 U	$ -0-	$ 6,000 U
Total variance	$ 8,000 U	$ 1,000 U	$ 9,000 U

[a] F, favorable variance; U, unfavorable variance.

EXHIBIT 22-7 *Summary of Overhead Variances*

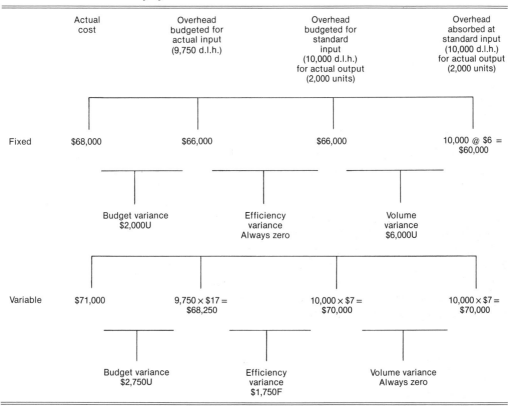

STANDARD COSTS AND EXTERNAL FINANCIAL REPORTS

Generally accepted accounting principles require that financial reports intended for parties external to the organization incorporate *actual* as opposed to estimated costs. Standards and predetermined charging rates necessarily reflect management estimates rather than actual costs. As a consequence, when the accounting procedures described in this and other chapters are applied, both cost of goods sold and ending inventory accounts (raw materials, work in process, and finished goods) must be translated from estimated or standard amounts to actual. Although most record-keeping processes do not provide sufficient information for the firm to adjust the accounts item by item or job by job they do permit it to do so by account–cost of goods sold and the major groupings of inventory. Seldom is there need for greater detail.

can be accomplished by prorating the balances in the variance or overhead control accounts on the basis of the production factor out of which the discrepancy arose. Materials and labor variances would be distributed in proportion to the amounts of raw materials or labor costs incurred. Overhead variances (or under- or over-absorbed overhead) would be distributed in proportion to the production factor on which the initial application of overhead was made.

The following two tables, using the data from the examples in this chapter, are illustrative of the calculations required. It will be assumed that of the 2,000 units produced during the period 1,500 (75 percent) were sold and 500 (25 percent) remain in finished goods inventory.

The first table indicates the percentages of the materials- and labor-related variances that will be allocated to the appropriate accounts:

Costs Applied During Period (at Standard)

| Factor of Production | Total | Portion Charged to (or Remaining in Accounts) | | | | |
| | | Finished Goods Inventory | | Cost of Goods Sold | |
		Amount	%	Amount	%
Materials	$200,000	$50,000	25	$150,000	75
Labor	$120,000	$30,000	25	$ 90,000	75

In standard cost systems, the differences between actual costs and standard costs are accumulated in variance accounts. In systems in which direct labor and materials are applied in actual amounts but overhead is charged by way of an overhead charging rate, the difference between actual overhead and that which has been applied remains at year-end in the overhead control account. The transformation of the records so that they indicate actual rather than estimated costs

The proration in this instance is relatively simple because all of the raw materials purchased were used and all of the goods started were completed. As a result the allocation percentages are the same for both labor and materials. If this were not the case, it would be necessary to prorate the variances among raw materials inventory and work in process as well as finished goods inventory and cost of goods sold. Different allocation percentages would then have to be applied.

The second table indicates the allocation of the variances based on the percentages shown in the first table:

they charge or credit the entire amount to cost of goods sold or some other expense account. Such approach fails to make a com-

| | | | Proration | |
| | | | --- | --- |
Variance	Basis of Proration	Amount of Un-favorable (Fav-orable) Variance	Finished Goods Inven-tory (**25**%)	Cost of Goods Sold (75%)
Materials price	Materials	$12,000	$ 3,000	$ 9,000
Materials quantity	Materials	40,000	10,000	30,000
Labor rate	Labor	3,900	975	2,925
Labor efficiency	Labor	(3,000)	(750)	(2,250)
Overhead volume	Labor	6,000	1,500	4,500
Overhead budget	Labor	4,750	1,187	3,563
Overhead efficiency	Labor	(1,750)	(437)	(1,313)
Total variances		$61,900	$15,475	$46,425

The journal entry to effect the proration would be:

Finished goods inventory	$15,475	
Cost of goods sold	46,425	
Labor efficiency variance	3,000	
Overhead efficiency variance	1,750	
Materials price variance		$12,000
Materials quantity variance		40,000
Labor rate variance		3,900
Overhead volume variance		6,000
Overhead budget variance		4,750

TO PRORATE VARIANCES

The data in this illustration were for a month. Generally, however, variances are closed out only annually. In practice, many firms do not prorate either variances or under- or overabsorbed overhead. Instead

plete transformation from estimated to actual costs; at best, it may be overlooked when the amounts involved are not material.

PART II: PERFORMANCE REPORTS

INTERNAL REPORTING SYSTEMS

A reporting system within an organization must provide the information that will enable the employees and members of that organization to carry out efficiently and effectively the activities for which they are responsible. The reporting system should be designed to facilitate not only routine decisions, but unusual, strategic decisions as well. A reporting system encompasses the entire accounting system of an organization—the procedures designed to accumulate, record, and summarize data relating to the goods or services that it provides or sells. Because reports intended to facilitate *strategic* decisions must be unique to the question at hand, this section shall focus only on *performance* reports. Performance reports are those designed to facilitate *management control* and, as the name implies, to evaluate the accomplishments of managers and the activities for which they are accountable. They compare actual results with those that were planned and, to the extent possible, explain any differences. They serve as the basis for correcting off-target operations and for developing plans for the future.

Performance reports are primarily a means of communicating to responsible parties the results of operations. But they are much more than that. They are implicit expressions of the objectives of the units being reported on and the criteria by which their performance will be evaluated. They indicate which of the activities engaged in by the units are sufficiently important to measure and inform managers about.

SIGNIFICANCE OF FORM AS WELL AS OF SUBSTANCE OF INFORMATION PRESENTED

The significance of decisions as to what specific information should be included in reports cannot be minimized. Managers have neither the time nor the mental capacity to accumulate and process *all* data that might be pertinent to their responsibilities. In evaluating possible courses of action they establish a limited number of criteria and focus on a subset of the facts that bear upon those criteria. As long as the reports available to them contain a satisfactory amount of relevant information, they are unlikely to seek out additional data. To a considerable extent, therefore, the information provided in the reports may determine the decisions made.

The *form* in which information is presented is also important and may have a direct bearing upon the messages that are conveyed by a report. As pointed out in earlier chapters, account balances by themselves have little meaning. Only when associated with other data by way of ratios and trends over time do they become of consequence. A report which indicates sales on one page and costs of goods sold on another may contain the same basic raw data as one which, in a single table, relates sales to fixed costs and variable costs. But the signals conveyed by the latter may be much more forceful than those by the former.

The perceptions of managers, like those of all human beings, are affected by subtle, subliminal, factors of which they may not be aware. A graphic presentation, for example, may bring forth relationships that would go undetected if the same data were set forth in tabular form. Moreover, a graph in which a scale is compressed may lead to different inferences than one in which it is expanded. Even the use of one color as opposed to another on a graph or table may alter the perceptions of the reader.

WORTHWHILE CHARACTERISTICS OF PERFORMANCE REPORTING SYSTEMS

Systems of reporting are likely to undergo radical changes in the next decade as the use of real-time computer systems accelerates. The concept of *periodic* reports may give way to that of continually updated, always available, information. Managers at all levels may have at their desks video display terminals which they can use to summon data on any aspect of operations within their control.

The discussion that follows sets forth several characteristics that a system of performance reporting should possess. They are general in nature and are applicable to on-line as well as to periodic reports.

Should Be Tailored to Organizational Structure

A reporting system must be designed to serve the needs of a specific organization and

EXHIBIT 22-8   Excerpts from an Organization Chart

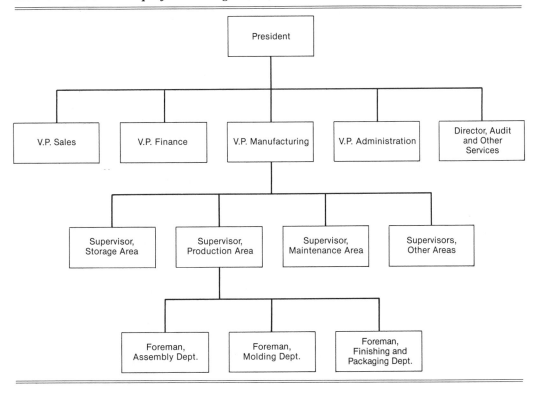

should be reflective of its organization chart. Information should be accumulated and reported for each *responsibility center*. A responsibility center is a segment of an organization responsible for specific activities which must be planned for, controlled, reported on, and evaluated.

A reporting system should be integrated. The total of costs and revenues of one unit should tie into the report of the unit by which it is supervised. Exhibit 22-8 illustrates the organizational chart of a manufacturing concern. Exhibit 22-9 illustrates the framework of a cost reporting system tailored to the specific hierarchy of responsibility centers. The costs flow upward from the lowest responsibility center to the highest (the office of the president).

Should Be Tailored to the Individual Recipients

Reports should be tailored to individual recipients. Internal reports need not be bound by the same constraints as those intended for outsiders. Firms are free to base them on any accounting principles and present them in any form that their managers find useful.

Reports should be simple and understandable. They should contain information that is relevant to the responsibilities of the parties

EXHIBIT 22-9

Illustration of Hierarchical Cost Relationships

Monthly Costs

	Actual	Budgeted	Variance: Unfavorable (Favorable)
Report to the President			
Selling	$ 453,710	$ 430,600	$23,110
Finance	42,900	42,300	600
Manufacturing	910,576	928,600	(18,024)
Administration	108,100	106,000	2,100
Other	132,856	130,500	2,356
Total	$1,648,142	$1,638,000	$10,142
Report to the Vice-President of Manufacturing			
Production	$ 781,890	$ 803,100	($21,210)
Storage	20,710	21,000	(290)
Maintenance	92,856	90,000	2,856
Other	15,120	14,500	620
Total	$ 910,576	$ 928,600	($18,024)
Report to the Production Supervisor			
Molding Department	$ 250,124	$ 250,000	$ 124
Assembly Department	350,890	358,100	(7,210)
Finishing and Packaging Department	180,876	195,000	(14,124)
Total	$ 781,890	$ 803,100	($21,210)
Report to the Assembly Department Foreman			
Direct labor	$ 125,230	$ 123,000	$ 2,230
Direct materials	137,890	148,000	(10,110)
Total direct costs	$ 263,120	$ 271,000	($ 7,880)
Controllable overhead			
Supervision	$ 40,600	$ 40,600	$ -0-
Setup time	6,240	6,000	240
Employee benefits	25,111	24,500	$ 611
Maintenance	15,819	16,000	($ 181)
Total controllable overhead	$ 87,770	$ 87,100	$ 670
Total	$ 350,890	$ 358,100	($ 7,210)

that will use them. They should be uncluttered by extraneous data.

Insofar as reports are to be used by more than one individual, it is obviously not feasible to design statements that satisfy completely each party's needs. Compromises must be made. The capability of computers in permitting reporting flexibility is increasing rapidly and there is no reason for managers to be wedded to existing types of reports. They must constantly be looking for new ways to reduce the gap between information that they would like and that which is available to them.

For some individuals, data displayed graphically are more understandable than those presented in table form. Until recently, the cost of translating more than a very few numerical tables into graphs was prohibitive for most companies. Accountants, after all, are not artists and their time cannot justifiably be expended on the preparation of pictures. Today, however, software packages are available which enable information to be depicted as economically in graphic as in tabular form. Exhibit 22-10 provides illustrations of graphs that can readily be produced on cathode ray tubes or regular paper.

Should Provide Timely Information

Reports should be prepared as often as is cost justified. The length of a reporting cycle depends on the activity being reported upon. Some processes, especially those in industrial plants can be monitored on an ongoing basis, and any corrective action can have an instantaneous effect. The benefits to be derived from frequent reports—several per day or even per hour—may outweigh their costs. Obviously, such reports would not be comprehensive; they would focus exclusively on specific phases of a process, such as the number of gallons flowing through a particular line. Other operations—those of an accounting department, for example—cannot be controlled with such precision. The operating cycle of an accounting department may be monthly or quarterly. Control reports at more frequent intervals might provide little or no information that can be acted upon effectively.

Irrespective of how frequently reports are compiled, they should be made available to responsible officials as soon after the end of the period covered as possible. The longer the delay, the longer an aberrant condition will be permitted to exist. The contribution of the computer with regard to timely reporting is that it reduces the cost of report preparation and allows reports to be prepared more frequently as well as more rapidly.

Should Highlight Variances from Budgets and Standards

Performance reports should highlight deviations from budgets and standards. They should facilitate the practice of "management by exception." The emphasis of this chapter has been on the interpretation of differences between plans and results. Performance reports should not only indicate the differences between budgeted and actual amounts but should explain them by way of variance analysis. Budgeted amounts should be derived from flexible rather than fixed budgets. Flexible budgets, not fixed budgets, allow for the decomposition of deviations into their elements: budget or spending variance; efficiency variance; volume variance.

A common type of performance report is that illustrated previously in Exhibit 22-9. It compares actual and budgeted costs and indicates the variances from budget. Often it contains three additional columns for year-to-date amounts. This type of report is satisfactory as a means of summarizing total discrepancies. But if not used with discretion it can do as much to mislead as to elucidate. Because costs are presented as budgeted for the *anticipated* volume of production the report provides no indication of what they should have been at the *actual* volume. The magnitude of the budget variances shown are inappropriate measures of performance.

Quantitative data contained in reports should always be supplemented by written or oral comments by the individuals who are accountable for the operations covered.

EXHIBIT 22-10

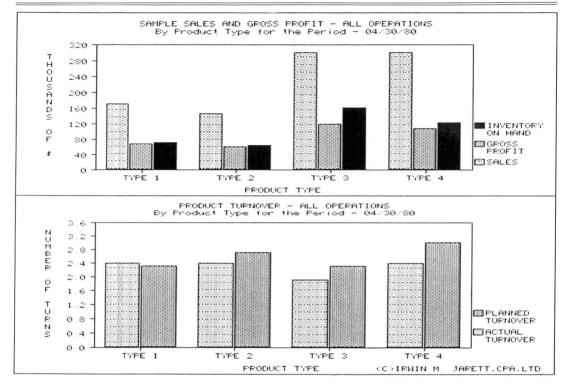

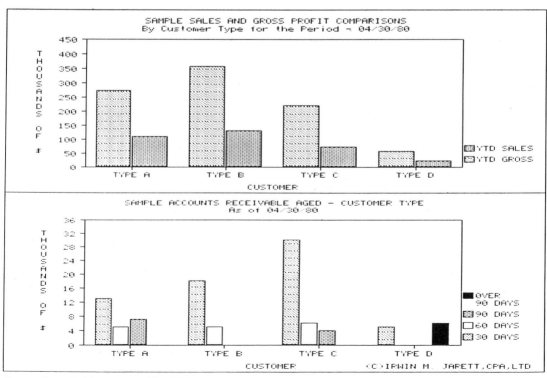

Reports generated by computers, no matter how detailed, can never substitute entirely for personal accounts.

Should Focus on Costs That Are Controllable

Reports on the performance of a unit should focus on costs over which the unit has control. As indicated in this as well as previous chapters, a unit seldom has control over all costs for which it is charged. In order to determine the "full" costs of a product—costs which must be incorporated into external financial reports—overhead, such as factory rent and heat, must be allocated to the various production departments. They may be apportioned on the basis of factors, such as amount of floor space, over which the production departments have no control and, therefore, for which they should not be held accountable. To be sure, it may be desirable to include such costs on unit cost summaries in order to make the managers aware that costs are being incurred on behalf of their departments. But noncontrollable costs should be clearly segregated from those that are controllable; the emphasis of the reports should be on the controllable costs.

Should Relate to Objectives

Performance reports should relate to objectives. Objectives are statements of what it is an organization intends to accomplish. It stands to reason that performance reports should indicate the extent to which the objectives have been realized.

In the chapter pertaining to budgeting, it was emphasized that although profit maximization is often assumed to be the ultimate objective for a business, it is, in fact, an unsatisfactory *operational* goal. Units of a firm are not usually *profit centers;* they have responsibility for only a limited number of the elements which enter into the determination of income. Production units, for example, have responsibility for output only; they have no control over sales. The operational goal of a production unit, such as an assembly department, may be to manufacture a requested number of goods at a cost equal or less than standard. This goal may be decomposed into subobjectives dealing with labor, materials, and overhead costs. A report on the performance of such a unit would, in essence, be an analysis of the production variances described in this chapter.

As the segments of a business become wider in scope and approach the divisional level, the objectives become more comprehensive and the subobjectives more numerous. Ratios which relate diverse accounts (turnover ratios, for example) take on increasing significance. Overall measures of profitability become more appropriate, and the perspective of top management becomes nearly the same as that of external investors.

In the first part of this text, that dealing with external reporting, numerous ratios were described by which the performance of a firm as a whole could be evaluated. These ratios were grouped into three categories: profitability and activity ratios; liquidity ratios; financing ratios. The most comprehensive of the profitability ratios is return on investment (ROI). ROI as a measure of performance was evaluated in Chapter 16. Part of the discussion was directed specifically to ROI as it can be applied to business segments. Measures of performance supplementary to ROI were also set forth. Readers are strongly advised to conclude their study of Part II of this text by rereading Chapter 16. Much of the material covered is as appropriate as a capstone to Part II of this text as for Part I.

SUMMARY

This chapter has focused on the control of manufacturing operations. Its purpose, however, was not to present a great deal of technical material of concern exclusively to managers or accountants of manufacturing concerns. Instead, it was intended to provide an approach to understanding and controlling costs in any type of organization.

A central theme of the chapter was that deviations from plans must be evaluated in terms of the variables that serve to explain them. A mere comparison between planned and actual results may prove deceptive as to the character as well as the cause of a deviation. Seemingly unfavorable overhead variances, for example, may actually be favorable when the volume of production is taken into account. The ultimate cause of a discrepancy between actual and planned overhead costs may be the excessive use of direct labor or materials—factors beyond the control of the departments responsible for controlling overhead costs.

Variance analysis can seldom, by itself, serve to affix blame for deviations from plans. It can, however, point to a need for explanations and identify the parties who should be called upon to make them. It is but a preliminary, though nevertheless essential, step in the process of determining whether the deviations warrant corrective action.

The second part of the chapter sets forth several characteristics that internal reports should possess if they are to facilitate the process of management. They must be tailored to the structure of the organization as well as to the needs of the managers who will receive them. They should be timely, should highlight variances from budgets and should focus on costs that are controllable. Perhaps most important, they should indicate the extent to which the units being reported upon have achieved their objectives. Although reports tell what has transpired in the past, they should provide guidance for decisions that will affect the future.

EXERCISE FOR REVIEW AND SELF-TESTING

The property department of a corporation is responsible for processing documents pertaining to real estate owned by the company. According to standards established by the firm, each document should take two hours to complete. Clerical employees who work on the documents are called documentation clerks and are of classification Clerk III. They receive wages of $8 per hour. In a typical month the department processes 250 documents.

Each document processed requires, in addition to the direct labor of the documentation clerks, services provided by a service pool. These services include typing, copying, and verification. Monthly fixed costs of the service pool are $1,000. Variable costs of the service pool have been found to be closely associated with the number of hours worked by the documentation clerks. They approximated $1.50 for each hour worked by the documentation clerks.

The costs of the service pool are charged to the property department by way of a predetermined overhead charging rate. The rate is related to number of hours worked by the documentation clerks. It is based on estimates of fixed costs of $1,000 per month, of variable costs of $1.50 per hour of labor performed by the documentation clerks and of volume of 250 documents (500 hours of documentation clerk labor) per month.

In the month of June, owing to filing delays on the part of corporate regional offices, the property department was required to process only 220 documents. Instead of assigning employees of Clerk III classification to the processing work, the department assigned employees of Clerk IV classification. The wage rate of Clerk IV employees is only $7 per hour. Owing to their inexperience, the Clerks IV took an average of 2.4 hours to process each of the 220 documents; they worked a total of 528 hours and were paid a total of $3,696.

The service pool incurred total costs of $1,740.

1. Evaluate the efficiency of the property department in using the "direct labor" of the documentation clerks.

   a. Determine the amount saved by compensating each hour of labor at a wage rate lower than standard (i.e., the labor rate variance).

   b. Determine the value, at standard rates, of the additional hours of labor that were required (i.e., the labor efficiency variance).

   c. Determine the total direct labor variance.

2. Analyze the costs incurred by the service pool.

   a. Determine the "opportunity costs" (i.e., the *volume* variance) of employing service pool capacity to process 220 documents instead of the usual 250 documents.

      1. Calculate the fixed portion of the overhead charging rate based on the standard number of direct labor hours required to process 250 documents.

      2. Indicate the fixed overhead that should be budgeted to support a volume of 250 documents.

      3. Calculate the fixed overhead that would be absorbed, assuming that only 220 documents were processed with standard efficiency.

      4. Determine the difference between items 2 and 3.

   b. Determine the additional costs incurred by the service pool owing to the inefficiency in the use of the direct clerical labor (i.e., the overhead *efficiency* variance).

      1. Compute the amount that the service pool should budget for the *standard* number of direct labor hours required to process 220 documents.

      2. Compute the amount that the service pool should budget for the *actual* number of direct labor hours used to process 220 documents.

      3. Calculate the difference between items 1 and 2.

   c. Determine the deviation from planned costs incurred by the service pool attributable to

its own apparent efficiency or inefficiency (i.e., the *budget* or *spending* variance).

      1. Indicate the amount (previously computed) that the service pool should budget for the actual number of direct labor hours for which support was provided.

      2. Indicate the costs that were actually incurred.

      3. Compute the difference between items 1 and 2.

QUESTIONS FOR REVIEW AND DISCUSSION

1. What are standard costs? How do they facilitate control?

2. Why is it important that variances be analyzed in conjunction with one another rather than independently?

3. Under one record-keeping system efficiency variances are identified and recorded at the time resources are added to work in process. Under another they are identified and recorded as goods are transferred from work in process to finished goods. What is the advantage of the former system?

4. "Standards should represent an ideal level of performance, one that employees should strive to attain but should seldom be able to do so." Do you agree? Explain.

5. "An unfavorable variance indicates the need for corrective action on the part of management." Do you agree? Explain.

6. Explain why there is likely to be a direct connection between either a direct labor or materials variance and the overhead efficiency variance.

7. What is the key advantage of a *flexible* over a *fixed* budget in controlling overhead costs?

8. What does the volume variance represent and why is it of limited usefulness in controlling overhead costs?

9. Why does the overhead budget or spending variance contain both fixed and variable elements whereas the efficiency variance contains only a variable element?

10. What is a *learning curve* and how can it contribute to improved control over labor costs?

11. Why can't standard costs be incorporated into general-purpose reports intended for external users? What adjustments must be made to standard cost accounts so that they can be used in general-purpose reports?

12. Why must management give careful attention to the type of information that is included in performance reports. Why must it be concerned with the form of such reports?

PROBLEMS

1. Variances can be isolated through the normal recording process.

Hall Office Equipment manufactures desk trays at a standard cost of $8.40 per set determined as follows:

Materials (3 feet of sheet metal @ $2)	$6.00
Labor (.4 hour @ $6)	2.40
Total cost per unit	$8.40

In a particular period the company purchased 600 feet of sheet metal for $1,260 ($2.10 per foot). It produced 180 sets of trays using 520 feet of sheet metal and 75 direct labor hours. The labor hours were compensated at a total cost of $465 ($6.20 per hour).

The company records manufacturing variances as soon as they are identified. That is, price or rate variances are recorded at the time goods or services are acquired; quantity or efficiency variances at the time goods or services are added to work in process.

Prepare journal entries to record the purchase of the raw materials and the manufacture of 180 sets of desk trays.

2. Actual and standard costs can be derived from entries to selected manufacturing accounts.

The Strauss Corp. manufactures refrigeration systems. In one department, plastic tubing is shaped into required configurations.

The operations of the department are accounted for by a standard cost system. Both direct labor and materials (measured in feet of tubing) are added to work in process in standard quantities valued at standard prices. Assume, for simplicity that no overhead is added.

Total debits and credits (not balances) to selected manufacturing accounts for the month of April were as follows:

	Debits	Credits
Materials (plastic tubing)	$12,600	$ 9,240
Accounts payable (for materials only)	5,000	?
Materials price variance	600	
Materials quantity variance	840	
Direct labor	5,850	5,850
Wages payable	5,500	?
Labor rate variance	156	
Labor efficiency variance		150
Work in ⎰Labor	6,000	
process ⎱Materials	8,400	14,400
"Finished" goods (units completed and available for transfer to other departments)	14,400	14,400

During the month the department started and completed 500 units. There were no beginning of month inventories of materials. The department purchased (but did not necessarily use) 3,000 feet of tubing, and it used 780 hours of direct labor.

Determine the *actual* and *standard* cost (divided into direct labor and materials) of completing each unit of product. You might find it helpful to reconstruct, in summary form, each of the journal entries that was made during the month.

3. A flexible budget forms the basis for analysis of overhead variances.

Lamar Tool Corp. has found that manufacturing overhead is most closely associated with *direct labor dollars.* Monthly fixed overhead is $18,000; variable overhead is $.12 per direct labor dollar.

Manufacturing standards indicate that standard *direct* labor cost is $20 per unit. Normal monthly output is 3,000 units ($60,000 in direct labor costs).

a. Prepare a flexible overhead budget for each of the following levels of activity, as expressed in direct labor dollars: $50,000; $55,000; $60,000; $65,000; $70,000.

b. Determine the overhead charging rate based on normal monthly activity of $60,000 direct labor hours.

c. Determine the amount of overhead that would be *absorbed* into work in process at each level of activity indicated in the flexible budget (i.e., $50,000, $55,000, etc.).

d. Assuming that direct labor costs incurred during a month conformed to standard, which overhead variance would be indicated by the difference, at each level of activity, between the overhead budgeted and the overhead absorbed.

e. Suppose that direct labor costs of $57,000 were incurred to produce 2,750 units of output. Determine the *volume* variance.

f. Assume that the firm incurred (as per standard) direct labor costs of $70,000 to produce 3,500 units of product. It also incurred fixed overhead costs of $19,000 and variable overhead costs of $8,600. Determine the *budget* or *spending* variance. Determine also the *volume* variance.

g. Assume that the firm incurred direct labor costs of $65,000.

  1. Indicate the amount of *overhead* that the firm must incur for there to be zero overhead *efficiency* variance.

  2. Indicate the number of *units* that the firm must produce for there to be zero overhead *efficiency* variance.

  3. Indicate the number of *units* that the firm must produce for there to be zero volume variance.

4. The purpose of variance analysis is to assign responsibility, not to affix blame.

Luxury Leathers, Inc., has established the following standards for the manufacture of belts:

Materials (.5 lb of leather @ $6)	$3.00	
Direct labor (.25 hour @ $8)	2.00	
Overhead ($1 per unit)	1.00	
Total	$6.00	

Overhead is applied on the basis of a predetermined charging rate of $4 per direct labor hour based on normal monthly volume of 1,000 units (250 direct

labor hours). Fixed overhead per month is estimated at $600; variable overhead at $1.60 per direct labor hour.

In September 1984 the company produced 1,100 belts. Actual costs were:

Materials purchased and used		
(580 lb of leather @ $6.20)		$3,596
Direct labor (290 hours @ $8.30)		2,407
Overhead		
Fixed	$700	
Variable	435	1,135
Total costs incurred		$7,138

Fixed overhead comprises primarily depreciation of equipment, repair and maintenance costs, and building occupancy costs. Variable overhead is mostly payroll-related costs.

1. To the extent that the data permit, explain the differences between actual and standard costs in terms of materials, labor, and overhead variances.

2. Indicate in a general way the departments which should most likely be held responsible for explaining each of the variances.

5. The volume variance has only a fixed element; the efficiency variance only a variable element; the budget variance both a fixed and variable element.

Housewares, Inc., estimates that its annual fixed overhead costs are $720,000 ($60,000 per month). Variable overhead costs are $1 per direct labor hour. Estimated production volume is 120,000 units per year (10,000 per month). Per company standards, each unit requires 2 hours of direct labor.

In June 1983 actual overhead costs were $80,000—$61,200 fixed and $18,800 variable. The firm used 18,000 direct labor hours in producing 8,800 units.

The firm applies overhead to the product by means of a predetermined charging rate.

1. Determine the overhead charging rate. Distinguish between the fixed and variable portions.

2. Compare actual overhead costs incurred with those that the firm would have budgeted for the month had it known that it would operate at an activity level of 18,000 direct labor hours. Compare separately the fixed and variable elements

of the costs. Comment briefly on why the *budget* or *spending* variance that you calculated can have both fixed and variable elements even if "fixed" costs are truly fixed.

3. Compare the overhead costs that the firm would have budgeted had it known that it would operate at an activity level of 18,000 direct labor hours with those that should be budgeted to produce 8,800 units using the standard number of direct labor hours. Compare separately the fixed and variable portions of the costs, and comment briefly on why the *efficiency* variance that you calculated has only a variable element.

4. Compare the overhead costs that the firm would have budgeted in order to produce 8,800 units using the standard number of direct labor hours with the amount of overhead that would be *absorbed* at a volume of 8,800 units using the standard number of direct labor hours. In addition, compare the fixed overhead that would be *absorbed* at the normal volume of 10,000 units with that which would be *absorbed* at the actual volume of 8,800 units. Comment briefly on why the *volume* variance that you calculated has only a fixed element.

6. *Overhead variances can be depicted graphically.*

The Stern Company estimates that fixed overhead is $9,000 per month and variable overhead is $5 per direct labor hour. Per the company's standards, one direct labor hour is required for each unit of product. Normal monthly volume is 3,000 units of product (also 3,000 direct labor hours).

In a particular month, the firm incurred actual overhead costs of $25,000. It used 2,000 direct labor hours to produce 1,600 units of output.

a. Determine the overhead charging rate, based on 3,000 direct labor hours per month.

b. Prepare a graph in which the horizontal axis represents level of activity expressed in terms of direct labor hours (0 to 5,000) and the vertical axis represents overhead costs ($0 to $35,000). Draw two lines: the first representing the amount of overhead that would be *absorbed* (based on the overhead charging rate) at various levels of activity; the second indicating the amount of

overhead that should be budgeted for the various levels of activity.

c. Show by a point the actual overhead costs incurred. Indicate the amount of overhead that would be budgeted for actual number of direct labor hours used (2,000). Denote the budget or spending variance.

d. Indicate the amount of overhead that would be budgeted for the *standard* number of direct labor hours that should have been used to produce the actual output of 1,600 units. Indicate also the amount of overhead that would have been absorbed at that level of activity. Denote the *volume* variance.

e. Compare the amount of overhead that would be budgeted for the actual number of direct labor hours used with the amount that would be budgeted for the standard number of direct labor hours required to produce the actual output of 1,600 units. Denote the overhead efficiency variance.

7. *The volume variance differs in concept from both the budget and efficiency variances.*

The Davies Corp. estimates that fixed overhead per month is $40,000 and variable overhead is $3 per direct labor hour. In a normal month, the firm produces 1,000 units of output, each of which requires, per standard, 4 hours of direct labor. The company charges overhead to work in process using a predetermined charging rate of $13 per direct labor hour. The charging rate was calculated on the assumption that in a typical month the firm would use 4,000 direct labor hours and incur $40,000 of fixed overhead costs and $12,000 of variable overhead costs.

In July 1984 the firm produced only 900 units of output. It used 3,780 hours of direct labor and incurred total overhead costs of $53,000. All costs were paid as incurred.

1. Determine the overhead budget variance. Indicate the *incremental cash per unit* that the firm was required to expend as a consequence of incurring greater overhead costs than were budgeted for the actual number of direct labor hours used.

2. Determine the overhead efficiency variance. Indicate the *incremental cash per unit* that the

firm was required to expand as a consequence of using a greater number of labor hours than is standard for the actual number of units produced.

3. Determine the overhead volume variance. Indicate the *incremental cash per unit* of additional cash that the firm was required to expend as a consequence of producing at a volume different than planned.

4. Comment on the utility of the volume variance in controlling overhead costs. To which department in an organization can responsibility for the volume variance ordinarily be attributed? Why does the volume variance provide information that is of limited usefulness to management?

8. *Estimates of volume can affect reported product cost.*

Industrial Products has determined that the fixed portion of its overhead costs is $720,000 and the variable portion is $4 per direct labor hour. One direct labor hour is required for each unit of product.

The firm bases its predetermined overhead charging rate on estimated annual volume of 240,000 units.

1. Determine the overhead charging rate.

2. Suppose that actual volume was only 200,000 units. Indicate the per unit amount of overhead that would be applied to the product and calculate the total amount that would be applied.

3. Suppose alternatively that the firm was better able to forecast volume and based its overhead charging rate on estimated volume of 200,000 units.

   a. Determine the overhead charging rate.

   b. Indicate the per unit amount of overhead that would be applied to the product and calculate the total amount that would be applied.

4. The impact of arbitrary estimates on amounts reported in external financial reports must be minimized. Assume that actual volume was 200,000 units but that the overhead charging rate was based on 240,000 units. Of the 200,000 units produced 160,000 were sold; the other 40,000 remained in inventory. Prepare a journal entry so that the accounts will reflect actual

overhead costs rather than those which were applied on the basis of an arbitrary estimate of volume.

9. *The issue of how to account for variances in interim reports points to conceptual differences between the volume variance and other variances.*

Adult Games, Inc., a manufacturer of electronic games, engages in operations that are highly seasonal. Production volume in the first quarter of a year can be expected to be considerably less than in other quarters. Anticipated volume for 1984 is 12,000 units.

Budgeted fixed overhead for the year is $96,000; per quarter it is $24,000. Variable overhead is $1 per direct labor hour. Standard overhead per unit is $11.

Standard labor cost is $21 (3 hours @ $7) and standard materials cost is $30. Total standard cost per unit is $62.

In the first quarter of the year the firm produced and sold 1,500 electronic games. Actual labor costs were $32,200 (4,600 hours @ $7). Actual materials costs were $45,000. Actual overhead costs were $29,000.

At the end of the first quarter the accounts of the firm revealed the variances that follow; there were no other variances:

Labor efficiency	$ 700
Overhead spending	400
Overhead efficiency	100
Overhead volume	12,000

1. Show how each of the variances was determined.

2. The firm is required to prepare interim financial reports to stockholders and regulatory authorities after the first quarter. What amount do you think should be reported as cost of goods sold?

3. Do you think that the volume variance (which represents underabsorbed overhead) should be accounted for differently than the other variances in determining interim cost of goods sold. Explain, directing specific attention to any conceptual differences between the volume variance and other variances. Can the volume variance be expected to be eliminated by year end?

10. *Employees may be entitled to a cost-saving bonus despite unfavorable variances.*

Industrial Generators, Inc., contracted with employees of selected production departments to provide them a bonus equal in amount to 20 percent of any savings in costs that are within their control. The amount of the savings will be determined by comparing actual costs with standard costs.

The standard cost of overhauling a Type I generator is $126;

Direct labor (4 hours @ $10)	$ 40
Parts (1.1 sets @ $60)	66
Overhead ($5 per direct labor hour;	
4 hours @ $5)	20
Standard cost per unit	$126

In fact, only one set of parts is required for each generator. The standard of 1.1 sets takes into account normal waste and breakage.

The overhead charging rate of $5 per direct labor hour assumes a volume of 4,500 generators (18,000 direct labor hours) and was determined as follows:

Fixed overhead costs	$54,000
Variable overhead costs ($2 per direct labor; 4,500 units × 4 direct labor hours × $2)	36,000
Anticipated overhead costs	$90,000
Anticipated activity (direct labor hours)	÷ 18,000
Charging rate per direct labor hour	$ 5

At the end of the first year of the bonus plan, the following data were compiled and presented to the employees responsible for overhauling Type I generators.

Actual number of units overhauled	4,200 units
Direct labor hours (an average of 3.7 per unit)	15,540 hours
Direct labor cost ($10 per hour)	$155,400
Number of sets of parts purchased and used (an average of 1.05 per generator)	4,410 sets

Cost of parts (an average of $70 per set)		$308,700
Overhead		
Fixed	$56,000	
Variable (an average of $2.10 per direct labor hour)	32,634	$ 88,634
Total manufacturing costs (an average of $131.60 per unit)		$552,734

Inasmuch as the standard cost of overhauling 4,200 units is, at $126 per unit, only $529,200, management informed the employees that they would receive no bonus for the year.

The number of units overhauled is determined by management, not the employees eligible for the bonus. Manufacturing overhead is also beyond the control of the employees, except insofar as it is influenced by number of direct labor hours. All acquisitions of parts are made by a corporate purchasing department.

Contrary to the determination of management, the employees believe that they are entitled to a bonus. Assume that they have engaged you to represent them in negotiations with management.

1. Prepare an analysis in which you account, as far as permitted by the data available, for the unfavorable variance of $23,535 between actual costs ($552,734) and standard costs ($529,200) for output of 4,200 units.

2. Determine the amount of the bonus to which the employees should be entitled if it is truly to be based on savings in costs over which they have control. Justify your analysis.

11. *Dollars saved may not be dollars earned.*

A purchasing agent recently entered into a contract for which he believes he deserves commendation from corporate management. The agent was able to acquire electronic components from a new supplier at a price of $.80 less than that which the company pays to its usual supplier.

The components are used in the manufacture of electronic test equipment.

Because the equipment has to be constructed with precision, a considerable number of units must be rejected after they have been completed. In fact, production standards have been set that allow for the production of 105 units for every 100 that are able to pass final inspection.

Each unit of equipment produced requires one set of components and .5 hours of labor. The standard labor rate is $8 per hour.

Budgeted fixed overhead is $18,000 per month. Variable overhead is $1.90 per direct labor hour. In a normal month production employees work 3,150 direct labor hours. This is the number of hours that are required to produce a total of 6,300 units, of which 6,000 ($6,300 \times 100/105$) should be sufficiently free of defects so that they can be shipped.

The purchasing agent was able to obtain the components from the new supplier at a price of $5.20 per unit rather than the standard $6.00. He recognized that the components were not of the same quality as those obtained from the usual supplier but he believed that the substantial saving in price would more than offset the cost of any additional units that would have to be rejected. He estimated—an estimate that proved to be accurate—that using the components from the new supplier, 115 units of equipment would have to be manufactured in order to produce 100 units that passed inspection. As a consequence, in order to satisfy the monthly demand for 6,000 units suitable for shipment, he purchased 6,900 ($6,000 \times 115/100$) components.

Based on the information provided, did the purchasing agent enter into a contract that could be justified economically? Assume that in the month that the substandard components are used, production will be "at standard," except insofar as the inferior components cause the standards to be violated. Assume also that the completed units that are rejected have no value.

a. Calculate the standard costs of producing 6,000 acceptable units and compare it with cost that would be incurred using the substandard components.

b. Analyze the difference between actual and standard costs in terms of the following variances:
 1. Materials price
 2. Materials quantity
 3. Labor rate
 4. Labor quantity

5. Volume (based on number of *acceptable* units)
6. Overhead efficiency
7. Overhead spending

c. Comment on whether the contract entered into by the purchasing agent merits a commendation.

12. *Reports which compare actual and standard costs should serve to explain, as far as possible, the reasons for any variances.*

Queens Shirts, Inc., has established the following standards for each shirt manufactured:

Material: 2 yards @ $6	$12
Labor: .3 hour @ $9	3
Total	$15

In March 1983 the company produced and shipped 4,000 shirts. In addition, it was forced to reject and discard a batch of 300 shirts in midproduction upon discovering an error in a pattern. The company had applied 450 yards of material and 55 hours of labor to the defective units.

In March the company purchased and used 9,000 yards of material at a cost of $5.85 per yard. It applied to production 1,300 hours of labor at a cost of $12,408.

The labor standards do not take into account a wage increase of $.40 per hour, effective March 1. In order to make up for the loss in production owing to the defective pattern, the firm was required to schedule 40 hours of overtime (included in the 1,300 hours of labor) which were compensated at time and a half.

Prepare a report in which you explain, to the extent the data permit, the difference between actual costs and standard costs for a volume of 4,000 shirts. Be sure to indicate the portions of the variance attributable to the defective pattern and the wage increase.

13. *Standard costs are inappropriate for external financial reports.*

The Hall Corporation maintains the accounts for its manufacturing operations on a standard cost system. Both labor and materials are recorded in work in process at standard quantities valued at standard prices. Raw materials are stated at actual quantities valued at standard prices.

As of December 31, 1983, the firm's trial balance reflected the following amounts (all debits):

Raw materials inventory	$ 40,000
Work in process inventory	97,200
Finished goods inventory	48,600
Cost of goods sold	972,000
Raw materials price variance	30,704
Raw materials quantity variance	22,080
Labor rate variance	21,390
Labor efficiency variance	18,860

The standard cost of each unit of product is $48.60;

Labor (3 hours @ $8.20)	$24.60
Materials (6 lb @ $4)	24.00
Total standard cost	$48.60

For convenience, it may be assumed that overhead is applied as a percentage of direct labor and that the labor rate of $8.20 includes an element of overhead. For purposes of this problem there is no need to deal with overhead independently of labor.

As of the start of 1983 there were zero balances in all of the accounts indicated.

Work in process represents goods that are one-half complete with respect to both labor and materials; thus for purposes of determining productivity for the year, it contains a number of units equivalent to one-half the number actually in process.

The company needs to adjust the inventory and cost of goods sold balances indicated in the trial balance so that actual costs can be reflected in the financial statements to be included in the firm's annual report.

a. Determine the number of units of output represented by the balances in cost of goods sold, finished goods, and work in process. Determine also the number of pounds of raw materials held in inventory.

b. Using the variances indicated in parentheses, derive the following actual amounts:
   1. Pounds of materials used (materials quantity)
   2. Price of materials purchased (materials price, based on number of pounds purchased rather than used)
   3. Number of hours of direct labor (labor efficiency)
   4. Hourly labor rate (labor rate)

c. Determine the actual materials and labor cost per unit.

d. Determine the amounts that should be reported in the raw materials, work in process, finished goods, and cost of goods sold accounts in the financial statements. Prepare a journal entry to adjust the amounts indicated in the trial balance and to assign the variances to these accounts.

14. Year-end proration of under- or overabsorbed overhead serves to correct for "errors" in the predetermined overhead charging rate.

Sherwood Company uses a job order costing system. Overhead is applied by means of a predetermined rate based on direct labor dollars. Records for 1984 indicate the following:

Budgeted factory overhead	$400,000
Actual factory overhead	369,000
Budgeted direct labor dollars	800,000
Actual direct labor dollars	820,000

All jobs that were worked on during the year, with the exception of two, were completed and sold. Job 68 has been completed but has not yet been sold; job 69 is still in process. At year end, there were no other jobs in process or in inventory. Direct labor and materials costs applicable to these two jobs are:

	Direct Labor	Direct Materials
Job 68 (in finished goods inventory)	$60,000	$50,000
Job 69 (in work in process inventory)	40,000	20,000

a. Determine the cost of job 68 prior to any reallocation of under- or overabsorbed overhead.

b. At year end the firm prorates under- or overabsorbed overhead to work in process, finished goods inventory, and cost of goods sold based on the direct labor dollars included in each of the accounts. Determine the balance in finished goods inventory (job 68) after the proration of under- or overabsorbed overhead.

c. Suppose that the company had perfect foresight and was able, at the start of the year, to accurately predict both factory overhead and direct labor cost. Determine, first, what the overhead charging rate would have been and, second, what the total charges to job 68, including direct labor, direct materials and overhead would have been. Compare the total amount that would have been charged to job 68 with that charged per part b.

15. Standards must reflect reductions in time owing to experience.

Electronic Controls, Inc., is about to begin production of a new control device. It is attempting to develop labor cost standards that can be incorporated into a standard cost accounting system.

The firm's engineers have estimated that the first batch of 200 control devices will require 2,000 direct labor hours—an average of 10 hours per unit. Thereafter, the time required to complete subsequent units will reflect an 80 percent learning curve.

The standard hourly wage rate paid by the firm is $8. The combined standard work-month for all employees assigned to production of the control device is a total of 2,000 labor hours.

a. Prepare a table in which you indicate the average number of direct labor hours required to manufacture various "batches" of control devices, up to a cumulative total of 12,800 units.

b. Suppose that the firm adjusts its standards each month.
1. What should be the standard labor cost of producing a single unit during the first month?
2. What should be the standard labor cost of producing a single unit during the fourth month? (In this and subsequent parts of this problem, you need not interpolate between points on the learning curve. For convenience, where a range of production is between two points on the curve, use the point representing the lesser amount of time.)

c. Suppose that the firm adjusts its standards quarterly. What should be the standard labor cost of producing a single unit during the first quarter (the first 8,000 hours)?

d. Suppose that the firm adjusts its standards annually. What should be the standard labor cost of producing a single unit during the first year (the first 24,000 hours)?

16. The cost assigned to particular units of production depends on the extent to which data are aggregated.

Lincoln-Douglas Aircraft Co. is negotiating with the military for the production of a new jumbo transport plane. The military wishes to acquire 160 aircraft.

Having developed the plane for the military, Lincoln-Douglas will then be able to produce and sell a slightly modified version to civilian airlines. The company estimates that sales of the civilian version will be approximately 160 units.

The firm has calculated that the cost of producing the first batch of 20 planes will be $800 million ($40 million per plane). The cost of subsequent planes will be less; the pattern of cost reductions will be consistent with a 90 percent learning curve. The learning curve is based on costs, rather than time as illustrated in the chapter. Each time cumulative production is doubled, the average cost of the cumulative units produced will be 90 percent of the cost to produce the units up to that point.

The price at which the planes are sold to the military will be cost based.

a. Suppose that you are a negotiator for the military. What cost per unit would you assert should serve as the basis for price determination for the 160 units to be acquired? What cost per unit do you think the negotiators for the company would favor? Explain.

b. Suppose instead that you were a negotiator for a foreign airline which intends to acquire 10 aircraft. The purchase price will also be cost based. The foreign airline is scheduled to receive the 291st through 300th aircraft produced. What cost per unit would you now assert should serve as the basis for price determination?

c. The issue raised by this problem is similar to that of the appropriate drilling costs to assign to successful oil wells in situations in which a company has had to drill several unsuccessful wells in order to strike oil. Do you see the connection between the two issues? Explain.

17. "Typical" reports that compare actual to budgeted costs may be inadequate for purposes of evaluation and control.

Fowler, Inc., employs a "responsibility accounting" system. Each month reports are prepared which compare actual costs with those that have been budgeted. The reports are of the form illustrated in Exhibit 22-9 of the text. The report to the president indicates costs by major functional areas (manufacturing, marketing, administration, etc.); that to the vice-president of manufacturing shows the costs of the various manufacturing units (e.g., direct production, warehousing, plant maintenance, etc.); that to the direct production supervisor enumerates the costs of the direct production departments (assembly, molding, finishing). The report to the foreman of the molding department for the month of February is, in summary form, as follows:

costs. The allocation from other departments is budgeted as a fixed percentage of the expected costs of several other cost centers. The amount charged each month is equal to a fixed percentage of *actual* costs incurred by the other cost centers. The budget for February is based on anticipated output of 10,000 units. In fact, actual output was 11,000.

a. Indicate the deficiency of the reporting system as a means of providing the information necessary to evaluate efficiency of production.

b. Prepare a report that compares actual costs with those that should have been incurred at the actual volume of production.

	Actual Costs	Budgeted Costs	Variance: Unfavorable (Favorable)
Direct costs			
Direct labor	$ 88,600	$ 80,000	$ 8,600
Direct materials	73,100	70,000	3,100
Overhead			
Supervision (labor)	8,450	8,400	50
Setup time (labor)	1,300	1,500	(200)
Maintenance (labor)	2,100	2,000	100
Employee benefits	15,045	14,190	855
Allocations from			
other cost centers	4,350	4,000	350
Total	$192,945	$180,090	$12,855

The report to the president for February indicated a substantial variance in manufacturing costs. Deciding to investigate, he obtained all the supporting reports, including that of the molding department. Since the variance in the molding department accounted for a sizable portion of the total manufacturing variance, he demanded that the vice-president of manufacturing explain the apparent inefficiencies in that department.

Among the overhead costs in the molding department, supervision is considered to be fixed. Setup time is budgeted at $150 per production run; a production run is ordinarily 1,000 units of output. Maintenance is budgeted at $1,500 plus $.05 per unit of output. Employee benefits are budgeted at $5,000 plus 10 percent of all departmental labor

c. Prepare a schedule in which you indicate for each cost the total variance, that portion of the total variance explained by the additional volume, and that portion explained by inefficiencies or other factors.

SOLUTIONS TO EXERCISE FOR REVIEW AND SELF-TESTING

1. a. Actual direct labor hours at
actual rate (528 hours @ $7) $3,696
Actual direct labor hours at
standard rate (528 hours @ $8)   4,224
Labor rate variance
(favorable)   ($ 528)

b. Actual direct labor hours at
standard rate (528 hours @ $8) $4,224
Standard direct labor hours at
standard rate (440 hours @ $8)   <u>3,520</u>
    Labor efficiency variance   <u>$ 704</u>

c.   Total direct labor variance $ 176

2. a. 1. Fixed portion of overhead charging rate

$$= \frac{\text{Fixed costs}}{\begin{array}{c}\text{Number of hours required}\\\text{to process 250 documents}\end{array}} = \frac{\$1,000}{500}$$

   = $2 per direct labor hour

2. Fixed costs budgeted for 250 (or any number) of documents would be $1,000.

3. Overhead absorbed at production volume of 220 documents at standard efficiency (i.e., 440 direct labor hours)

    Standard number of hours   440
    Fixed portion of overhead
      charging rate   ×2.00
      Overhead absorbed $880

4. Budgeted fixed costs [per (2)] $1,000
Less: Fixed costs absorbed at
    standard number of
    hours to process actual
    number of documents
    [per (3)]   880
      Volume variance $ 120

b. 1. Budget for standard (440) hours to process 220 documents:

Fixed costs	$1,000
Variable costs	
(440 hours @ 1.50)	660
Total overhead budget	$1,660

2. Budget for actual (528) hours used to process 220 documents:

Fixed costs	$1,000
Variable costs	
(528 hours @ $1.50)	792
Total overhead budget	$1,792

3. Overhead budgeted for actual
hours [per (2)] $1,792
Less: Overhead budgeted for
    standard hours
    [per (1)]   1,660
      Overhead efficiency variance $ 132

c. 1. Budget for actual number of direct labor hours [per b(2)] × = $1,792

2. Actual costs incurred = $1,740

3. Actual costs incurred [per (2)] $1,740
Less: Budget for actual
    number of direct
    labor hours [per (1)]   1,792
    Budget or spending variance
    (favorable)   ($ 52)

Appendix

table 1

Future Value of $1 $F_n = P(1 + r)^n$

No. of periods	2%	3%	4%	5%	6%	7%	8%
1	1.0200	1.0300	1.0400	1.0500	1.0600	1.0700	1.0800
2	1.0404	1.0609	1.0816	1.1025	1.1236	1.1449	1.1664
3	1.0612	1.0927	1.1249	1.1576	1.1910	1.2250	1.2597
4	1.0824	1.1255	1.1699	1.2155	1.2625	1.3108	1.3605
5	1.1041	1.1593	1.2167	1.2763	1.3382	1.4026	1.4693
6	1.1262	1.1941	1.2653	1.3401	1.4185	1.5007	1.5869
7	1.1487	1.2299	1.3159	1.4071	1.5036	1.6058	1.7138
8	1.1717	1.2668	1.3686	1.4775	1.5938	1.7182	1.8509
9	1.1951	1.3048	1.4233	1.5513	1.6895	1.8385	1.9990
10	1.2190	1.3439	1.4802	1.6289	1.7908	1.9672	2.1589
11	1.2434	1.3842	1.5395	1.7103	1.8983	2.1049	2.3316
12	1.2682	1.4258	1.6010	1.7959	2.0122	2.2522	2.5182
13	1.2936	1.4685	1.6651	1.8856	2.1329	2.4098	2.7196
14	1.3195	1.5126	1.7317	1.9799	2.2609	2.5785	2.9372
15	1.3459	1.5580	1.8009	2.0789	2.3966	2.7590	3.1722
16	1.3728	1.6047	1.8730	2.1829	2.5404	2.9522	3.4259
17	1.4002	1.6528	1.9479	2.2920	2.6928	3.1588	3.7000
18	1.4282	1.7024	2.0258	2.4066	2.8543	3.3799	3.9960
19	1.4568	1.7535	2.1068	2.5270	3.0256	3.6165	4.3157
20	1.4859	1.8061	2.1911	2.6533	3.2071	3.8697	4.6610
21	1.5157	1.8603	2.2788	2.7860	3.3996	4.1406	5.0338
22	1.5460	1.9161	2.3699	2.9253	3.6035	4.4304	5.4365
23	1.5769	1.9736	2.4647	3.0715	3.8197	4.7405	5.8715
24	1.6084	2.0328	2.5633	3.2251	4.0489	5.0724	6.3412
25	1.6406	2.0938	2.6658	3.3864	4.2919	5.4274	6.8485
26	1.6734	2.1566	2.7725	3.5557	4.5494	5.8074	7.3964
27	1.7069	2.2213	2.8834	3.7335	4.8223	6.2139	7.9881
28	1.7410	2.2879	2.9987	3.9201	5.1117	6.6488	8.6271
29	1.7758	2.3566	3.1187	4.1161	5.4184	7.1143	9.3173
30	1.8114	2.4273	3.2434	4.3219	5.7435	7.6123	10.0627
31	1.8476	2.5001	3.3731	4.5380	6.0881	8.1451	10.8677
32	1.8845	2.5751	3.5081	4.7649	6.4534	8.7153	11.7371
33	1.9222	2.6523	3.6484	5.0032	6.8406	9.3253	12.6760
34	1.9607	2.7319	3.7943	5.2533	7.2510	9.9781	13.6901
35	1.9999	2.8139	3.9461	5.5160	7.6861	10.6766	14.7853
36	2.0399	2.8983	4.1039	5.7918	8.1473	11.4239	15.9682
37	2.0807	2.9852	4.2681	6.0814	8.6361	12.2236	17.2456
38	2.1223	3.0748	4.4388	6.3855	9.1543	13.0793	18.6253
39	2.1647	3.1670	4.6164	6.7048	9.7035	13.9948	20.1153
40	2.2080	3.2620	4.8010	7.0400	10.2857	14.9745	21.7245
41	2.2522	3.3599	4.9931	7.3920	10.9029	16.0227	23.4625
42	2.2972	3.4607	5.1928	7.7616	11.5570	17.1443	25.3395
43	2.3432	3.5645	5.4005	8.1497	12.2505	18.3444	27.3666
44	2.3901	3.6715	5.6165	8.5572	12.9855	19.6285	29.5560
45	2.4379	3.7816	5.8412	8.9850	13.7646	21.0025	31.9204
46	2.4866	3.8950	6.0748	9.4343	14.5905	22.4726	34.4741
47	2.5363	4.0119	6.3178	9.9060	15.4659	24.0457	37.2320
48	2.5871	4.1323	6.5705	10.4013	16.3939	25.7289	40.2106
49	2.6388	4.2562	6.8333	10.9213	17.3775	27.5299	43.4274
50	2.6916	4.3839	7.1067	11.4674	18.4202	29.4570	46.9016

9%	10%	11%	12%	13%	14%	15%
1.0900	1.1000	1.1100	1.1200	1.1300	1.1400	1.1500
1.1881	1.2100	1.2321	1.2544	1.2769	1.2996	1.3225
1.2950	1.3310	1.3676	1.4049	1.4429	1.4815	1.5209
1.4116	1.4641	1.5181	1.5735	1.6305	1.6890	1.7490
1.5386	1.6105	1.6851	1.7623	1.8424	1.9254	2.0114
1.6771	1.7716	1.8704	1.9738	2.0820	2.1950	2.3131
1.8280	1.9487	2.0762	2.2107	2.3526	2.5023	2.6600
1.9926	2.1436	2.3045	2.4760	2.6584	2.8526	3.0590
2.1719	2.3579	2.5580	2.7731	3.0040	3.2519	3.5179
2.3674	2.5937	2.8394	3.1058	3.3946	3.7072	4.0456
2.5804	2.8531	3.1518	3.4785	3.8359	4.2262	4.6524
2.8127	3.1384	3.4985	3.8960	4.3345	4.8179	5.3503
3.0658	3.4523	3.8833	4.3635	4.8980	5.4924	6.1528
3.3417	3.7975	4.3104	4.8871	5.5348	6.2613	7.0757
3.6425	4.1772	4.7846	5.4736	6.2543	7.1379	8.1371
3.9703	4.5950	5.3109	6.1304	7.0673	8.1372	9.3576
4.3276	5.0545	5.8951	6.8660	7.9861	9.2765	10.7613
4.7171	5.5599	6.5436	7.6900	9.0243	10.5752	12.3755
5.1417	6.1159	7.2633	8.6128	10.1974	12.0557	14.2318
5.6044	6.7275	8.0623	9.6463	11.5231	13.7435	16.3665
6.1088	7.4002	8.9492	10.8038	13.0211	15.6676	18.8215
6.6586	8.1403	9.9336	12.1003	14.7138	17.8610	21.6447
7.2579	8.9543	11.0263	13.5523	16.6266	20.3616	24.8915
7.9111	9.8497	12.2392	15.1786	18.7881	23.2122	28.6252
8.6231	10.8347	13.5855	17.0001	21.2305	26.4619	32.9190
9.3992	11.9182	15.0799	19.0401	23.9905	30.1666	37.8568
10.2451	13.1100	16.7386	21.3249	27.1093	34.3899	43.5353
11.1671	14.4210	18.5799	23.8839	30.6335	39.2045	50.0656
12.1722	15.8631	20.6237	26.7499	34.6158	44.6931	57.5755
13.2677	17.4494	22.8923	29.9599	39.1159	50.9502	66.2118
14.4618	19.1943	25.4104	33.5551	44.2010	58.0832	76.1435
15.7633	21.1138	28.2056	37.5817	49.9471	66.2148	87.5651
17.1820	23.2252	31.3082	42.0915	56.4402	75.4849	100.6998
18.7284	25.5477	34.7521	47.1425	63.7774	86.0528	115.8048
20.4140	28.1024	38.5749	52.7996	72.0685	98.1002	133.1755
22.2512	30.9127	42.8181	59.1356	81.4374	111.8342	153.1519
24.2538	34.0039	47.5281	66.2318	92.0243	127.4910	176.1246
26.4367	37.4043	52.7562	74.1797	103.9874	145.3397	202.5433
28.8160	41.1448	58.5593	83.0812	117.5058	165.6873	232.9248
31.4094	45.2593	65.0009	93.0510	132.7816	188.8835	267.8635
34.2363	49.7852	72.1510	104.2171	150.0432	215.3272	308.0431
37.3175	54.7637	80.0876	116.7231	169.5488	245.4730	354.2495
40.6761	60.2401	88.8972	130.7299	191.5901	279.8392	407.3870
44.3370	66.2641	98.6759	146.4175	216.4968	319.0167	468.4950
48.3273	72.8905	109.5302	163.9876	244.6414	363.6791	538.7693
52.6767	80.1795	121.5786	183.6661	276.4448	414.5941	619.5847
57.4176	88.1975	134.9522	205.7061	312.3826	472.6373	712.5224
62.5852	97.0172	149.7970	230.3908	352.9923	538.8065	819.4007
68.2179	106.7190	166.2746	258.0377	398.8813	614.2395	942.3108
74.3575	117.3909	184.5648	289.0022	450.7359	700.2330	1083.6574

table 2

Present Value of $1 $P = F_n \dfrac{1}{(1 + r)^n}$

No. of periods	2%	3%	4%	5%	6%	7%	8%
1	.9804	.9709	.9615	.9524	.9434	.9346	.9259
2	.9612	.9426	.9246	.9070	.8900	.8734	.8573
3	.9423	.9151	.8890	.8638	.8396	.8163	.7938
4	.9238	.8885	.8548	.8227	.7921	.7629	.7350
5	.9057	.8626	.8219	.7835	.7473	.7130	.6806
6	.8880	.8375	.7903	.7462	.7050	.6663	.6302
7	.8706	.8131	.7599	.7107	.6651	.6227	.5835
8	.8535	.7894	.7307	.6768	.6274	.5820	.5403
9	.8368	.7664	.7026	.6446	.5919	.5439	.5002
10	.8203	.7441	.6756	.6139	.5584	.5083	.4632
11	.8043	.7224	.6496	.5847	.5268	.4751	.4289
12	.7885	.7014	.6246	.5568	.4970	.4440	.3971
13	.7730	.6810	.6006	.5303	.4688	.4150	.3677
14	.7579	.6611	.5775	.5051	.4423	.3878	.3405
15	.7430	.6419	.5553	.4810	.4173	.3624	.3152
16	.7284	.6232	.5339	.4581	.3936	.3387	.2919
17	.7142	.6050	.5134	.4363	.3714	.3166	.2703
18	.7002	.5874	.4936	.4155	.3503	.2959	.2502
19	.6864	.5703	.4746	.3957	.3305	.2765	.2317
20	.6730	.5537	.4564	.3769	.3118	.2584	.2145
21	.6598	.5375	.4388	.3589	.2942	.2415	.1987
22	.6468	.5219	.4220	.3418	.2775	.2257	.1839
23	.6342	.5067	.4057	.3256	.2618	.2109	.1703
24	.6217	.4919	.3901	.3101	.2470	.1971	.1577
25	.6095	.4776	.3751	.2953	.2330	.1842	.1460
26	.5976	.4637	.3607	.2812	.2198	.1722	.1352
27	.5859	.4502	.3468	.2678	.2074	.1609	.1252
28	.5744	.4371	.3335	.2551	.1956	.1504	.1159
29	.5631	.4243	.3207	.2429	.1846	.1406	.1073
30	.5521	.4120	.3083	.2314	.1741	.1314	.0994
31	.5412	.4000	.2965	.2204	.1643	.1228	.0920
32	.5306	.3883	.2851	.2099	.1550	.1147	.0852
33	.5202	.3770	.2741	.1999	.1462	.1072	.0789
34	.5100	.3660	.2636	.1904	.1379	.1002	.0730
35	.5000	.3554	.2534	.1813	.1301	.0937	.0676
36	.4902	.3450	.2437	.1727	.1227	.0875	.0626
37	.4806	.3350	.2343	.1644	.1158	.0818	.0580
38	.4712	.3252	.2253	.1566	.1092	.0765	.0537
39	.4619	.3158	.2166	.1491	.1031	.0715	.0497
40	.4529	.3066	.2083	.1420	.0972	.0668	.0460
41	.4440	.2976	.2003	.1353	.0917	.0624	.0426
42	.4353	.2890	.1926	.1288	.0865	.0583	.0395
43	.4268	.2805	.1852	.1227	.0816	.0545	.0365
44	.4184	.2724	.1780	.1169	.0770	.0509	.0338
45	.4102	.2644	.1712	.1113	.0727	.0476	.0313
46	.4022	.2567	.1646	.1060	.0685	.0445	.0290
47	.3943	.2493	.1583	.1009	.0647	.0416	.0269
48	.3865	.2420	.1522	.0961	.0610	.0389	.0249
49	.3790	.2350	.1463	.0916	.0575	.0363	.0230
50	.3715	.2281	.1407	.0872	.0543	.0339	.0213

9%	10%	11%	12%	13%	14%	15%
.9174	.9091	.9009	.8929	.8850	.8772	.8696
.8417	.8264	.8116	.7972	.7831	.7695	.7561
.7722	.7513	.7312	.7118	.6931	.6750	.6575
.7084	.6830	.6587	.6355	.6133	.5921	.5718
.6499	.6209	.5935	.5674	.5428	.5194	.4972
.5963	.5645	.5346	.5066	.4803	.4556	.4323
.5470	.5132	.4817	.4523	.4251	.3996	.3759
.5019	.4665	.4339	.4039	.3762	.3506	.3269
.4604	.4241	.3909	.3606	.3329	.3075	.2843
.4224	.3855	.3522	.3220	.2946	.2697	.2472
.3875	.3505	.3173	.2875	.2607	.2366	.2149
.3555	.3186	.2858	.2567	.2307	.2076	.1869
.3262	.2897	.2575	.2292	.2042	.1821	.1625
.2992	.2633	.2320	.2046	.1807	.1597	.1413
.2745	.2394	.2090	.1827	.1599	.1401	.1229
.2519	.2176	.1883	.1631	.1415	.1229	.1069
.2311	.1978	.1696	.1456	.1252	.1078	.0929
.2120	.1799	.1528	.1300	.1108	.0946	.0808
.1945	.1635	.1377	.1161	.0981	.0829	.0703
.1784	.1486	.1240	.1037	.0868	.0728	.0611
.1637	.1351	.1117	.0926	.0768	.0638	.0531
.1502	.1228	.1007	.0826	.0680	.0560	.0462
.1378	.1117	.0907	.0738	.0601	.0491	.0402
.1264	.1015	.0817	.0659	.0532	.0431	.0349
.1160	.0923	.0736	.0588	.0471	.0378	.0304
.1064	.0839	.0663	.0525	.0417	.0331	.0264
.0976	.0763	.0597	.0469	.0369	.0291	.0230
.0895	.0693	.0538	.0419	.0326	.0255	.0200
.0822	.0630	.0485	.0374	.0289	.0224	.0174
.0754	.0573	.0437	.0334	.0256	.0196	.0151
.0691	.0521	.0394	.0298	.0226	.0172	.0131
.0634	.0474	.0355	.0266	.0200	.0151	.0114
.0582	.0431	.0319	.0238	.0177	.0132	.0099
.0534	.0391	.0288	.0212	.0157	.0116	.0086
.0490	.0356	.0259	.0189	.0139	.0102	.0075
.0449	.0323	.0234	.0169	.0123	.0089	.0065
.0412	.0294	.0210	.0151	.0109	.0078	.0057
.0378	.0267	.0190	.0135	.0096	.0069	.0049
.0347	.0243	.0171	.0120	.0085	.0060	.0043
.0318	.0221	.0154	.0107	.0075	.0053	.0037
.0292	.0201	.0139	.0096	.0067	.0046	.0032
.0268	.0183	.0125	.0086	.0059	.0041	.0028
.0246	.0166	.0112	.0076	.0052	.0036	.0025
.0226	.0151	.0101	.0068	.0046	.0031	.0021
.0207	.0137	.0091	.0061	.0041	.0027	.0019
.0190	.0125	.0082	.0054	.0036	.0024	.0016
.0174	.0113	.0074	.0049	.0032	.0021	.0014
.0160	.0103	.0067	.0043	.0028	.0019	.0012
.0147	.0094	.0060	.0039	.0025	.0016	.0011
.0134	.0085	.0054	.0035	.0022	.0014	.0009

table 3

Future Value of an Annuity of $1 in Arrears

$$F_A = \frac{(1 + r)^n - 1}{r}$$

No. of periods	2%	3%	4%	5%	6%	7%	8%
1	1.0000	1.0000	1.0000	1.0000	1.0000	1.0000	1.0000
2	2.0200	2.0300	2.0400	2.0500	2.0600	2.0700	2.0800
3	3.0604	3.0909	3.1216	3.1525	3.1836	3.2149	3.2464
4	4.1216	4.1836	4.2465	4.3101	4.3746	4.4399	4.5061
5	5.2040	5.3091	5.4163	5.5256	5.6371	5.7507	5.8666
6	6.3081	6.4684	6.6330	6.8019	6.9753	7.1533	7.3359
7	7.4343	7.6625	7.8983	8.1420	8.3938	8.6540	8.9228
8	8.5830	8.8923	9.2142	9.5491	9.8975	10.2598	10.6366
9	9.7546	10.1591	10.5828	11.0266	11.4913	11.9780	12.4876
10	10.9497	11.4639	12.0061	12.5779	13.1808	13.8164	14.4866
11	12.1687	12.8078	13.4864	14.2068	14.9716	15.7836	16.6455
12	13.4121	14.1920	15.0258	15.9171	16.8699	17.8885	18.9771
13	14.6803	15.6178	16.6268	17.7130	18.8821	20.1406	21.4953
14	15.9739	17.0863	18.2919	19.5986	21.0151	22.5505	24.2149
15	17.2934	18.5989	20.0236	21.5786	23.2760	25.1290	27.1521
16	18.6393	20.1569	21.8245	23.6575	25.6725	27.8881	30.3243
17	20.0121	21.7616	23.6975	25.8404	28.2129	30.8402	33.7502
18	21.4123	23.4144	25.6454	28.1324	30.9057	33.9990	37.4502
19	22.8406	25.1169	27.6712	30.5390	33.7600	37.3790	41.4463
20	24.2974	26.8704	29.7781	33.0660	36.7856	40.9955	45.7620
21	25.7833	28.6765	31.9692	35.7193	39.9927	44.8652	50.4229
22	27.2990	30.5368	34.2480	38.5052	43.3923	49.0057	55.4568
23	28.8450	32.4529	36.6179	41.4305	46.9958	53.4361	60.8933
24	30.4219	34.4265	39.0826	44.5020	50.8156	58.1767	66.7648
25	32.0303	36.4593	41.6459	47.7271	54.8645	63.2490	73.1059
26	33.6709	38.5530	44.3117	51.1135	59.1564	68.6765	79.9544
27	35.3443	40.7096	47.0842	54.6691	63.7058	74.4838	87.3508
28	37.0512	42.9309	49.9676	58.4026	68.5281	80.6977	95.3388
29	38.7922	45.2189	52.9663	62.3227	73.6398	87.3465	103.9659
30	40.5681	47.5754	56.0849	66.4388	79.0582	94.4608	113.2832
31	42.3794	50.0027	59.3283	70.7608	84.8017	102.0730	123.3459
32	44.2270	52.5028	62.7015	75.2988	90.8898	110.2182	134.2135
33	46.1116	55.0778	66.2095	80.0638	97.3432	118.9334	145.9506
34	48.0338	57.7302	69.8579	85.0670	104.1838	128.2588	158.6267
35	49.9945	60.4621	73.6522	90.3203	111.4348	138.2369	172.3168
36	51.9944	63.2759	77.5983	95.8363	119.1209	148.9135	187.1021
37	54.0343	66.1742	81.7022	101.6281	127.2681	160.3374	203.0703
38	56.1149	69.1594	85.9703	107.7095	135.9042	172.5610	220.3159
39	58.2372	72.2342	90.4091	114.0950	145.0585	185.6403	238.9412
40	60.4020	75.4013	95.0255	120.7998	154.7620	199.6351	259.0565
41	62.6100	78.6633	99.8265	127.8398	165.0477	214.6096	280.7810
42	64.8622	82.0232	104.8196	135.2318	175.9505	230.6322	304.2435
43	67.1595	85.4839	110.0124	142.9933	187.5076	247.7765	329.5830
44	69.5027	89.0484	115.4129	151.1430	199.7580	266.1209	356.9496
45	71.8927	92.7199	121.0294	159.7002	212.7435	285.7493	386.5056
46	74.3306	96.5015	126.8706	168.6852	226.5081	306.7518	418.4261
47	76.8172	100.3965	132.9454	178.1194	241.0986	329.2244	452.9002
48	79.3535	104.4084	139.2632	188.0254	256.5645	353.2701	490.1322
49	81.9406	108.5406	145.8337	198.4267	272.9584	378.9990	530.3427
50	84.5794	112.7969	152.6671	209.3480	290.3359	406.5289	573.7702

9%	10%	11%	12%	13%	14%	
1.0000	1.0000	1.0000	1.0000	1.0000	1.0000	
2.0900	2.1000	2.1100	2.1200	2.1300	2.1400	
3.2781	3.3100	3.3421	3.3744	3.4069	3.4396	
4.5731	4.6410	4.7097	4.7793	4.8498	4.9211	
5.9847	6.1051	6.2278	6.3528	6.4803	6.6101	
7.5233	7.7156	7.9129	8.1152	8.3227	8.5355	8.7537
9.2004	9.4872	9.7833	10.0890	10.4047	10.7305	11.0668
11.0285	11.4359	11.8594	12.2997	12.7573	13.2328	13.7268
13.0210	13.5795	14.1640	14.7757	15.4157	16.0853	16.7858
15.1929	15.9374	16.7220	17.5487	18.4197	19.3373	20.3037
17.5603	18.5312	19.5614	20.6546	21.8143	23.0445	24.3493
20.1407	21.3843	22.7132	24.1331	25.6502	27.2707	29.0017
22.9534	24.5227	26.2116	28.0291	29.9847	32.0887	34.3519
26.0192	27.9750	30.0949	32.3926	34.8827	37.5811	40.5047
29.3609	31.7725	34.4054	37.2797	40.4175	43.8424	47.5804
33.0034	35.9497	39.1899	42.7533	46.6717	50.9804	55.7175
36.9737	40.5447	44.5008	48.8837	53.7391	59.1176	65.0751
41.3013	45.5992	50.3959	55.7497	61.7251	68.3941	75.8364
46.0185	51.1591	56.9395	63.4397	70.7494	78.9692	88.2118
51.1601	57.2750	64.2028	72.0524	80.9468	91.0249	102.4436
56.7645	64.0025	72.2651	81.6987	92.4699	104.7684	118.8101
62.8733	71.4027	81.2143	92.5026	105.4910	120.4360	137.6316
69.5319	79.5430	91.1479	104.6029	120.2048	138.2970	159.2764
76.7898	88.4973	102.1742	118.1552	136.8315	158.6586	184.1678
84.7009	98.3471	114.4133	133.3339	155.6196	181.8708	212.7930
93.3240	109.1818	127.9988	150.3339	176.8501	208.3327	245.7120
102.7231	121.0999	143.0786	169.3740	200.8406	238.4993	283.5688
112.9682	134.2099	159.8173	190.6989	227.9499	272.8892	327.1041
124.1354	148.6309	178.3972	214.5828	258.5834	312.0937	377.1697
136.3075	164.4940	199.0209	241.3327	293.1992	356.7868	434.7451
149.5752	181.9434	221.9132	271.2926	332.3151	407.7370	500.9569
164.0370	201.1378	247.3236	304.8477	376.5161	465.8202	577.1005
179.8003	222.2515	275.5292	342.4294	426.4632	532.0350	664.6655
196.9823	245.4767	306.8374	384.5210	482.9034	607.5199	765.3654
215.7108	271.0244	341.5896	431.6635	546.6808	693.5727	881.1702
236.1247	299.1268	380.1644	484.4631	618.7493	791.6729	1014.3457
258.3759	330.0395	422.9825	543.5987	700.1867	903.5071	1167.4975
282.6298	364.0434	470.5106	609.8305	792.2110	1030.9981	1343.6222
309.0665	401.4478	523.2667	684.0102	896.1984	1176.3378	1546.1655
337.8824	442.5926	581.8261	767.0914	1013.7042	1342.0251	1779.0903
369.2919	487.8518	646.8269	860.1424	1146.4858	1530.9086	2046.9539
403.5281	537.6370	718.9779	964.3595	1296.5289	1746.2358	2354.9969
440.8457	592.4007	799.0655	1081.0826	1466.0777	1991.7088	2709.2465
481.5218	652.6408	887.9627	1211.8125	1657.6678	2271.5481	3116.6334
525.8587	718.9048	986.6386	1358.2300	1874.1646	2590.5648	3585.1285
574.1860	791.7953	1096.1688	1522.2176	2118.8060	2954.2439	4123.8977
626.8628	871.9749	1217.7474	1705.8838	2395.2508	3368.8380	4743.4824
684.2804	960.1723	1352.6996	1911.5898	2707.6334	3841.4753	5456.0047
746.8656	1057.1896	1502.4965	2141.9806	3060.6258	4380.2819	6275.4055
815.0836	1163.9085	1668.7712	2400.0182	3459.5071	4994.5213	7217.7163

Present Value of an Annuity of $1 in Arrears $P_A \dfrac{1 - (1 + r)^{-n}}{r}$

No. of periods	2%	3%	4%	5%	6%	7%	8%
1	.9804	.9709	.9615	.9524	.9434	.9346	.9259
2	1.9416	1.9135	1.8861	1.8594	1.8334	1.8080	1.7833
3	2.8839	2.8286	2.7751	2.7232	2.6730	2.6243	2.5771
4	3.8077	3.7171	3.6299	3.5460	3.4651	3.3872	3.3121
5	4.7135	4.5797	4.4518	4.3295	4.2124	4.1002	3.9927
6	5.6014	5.4172	5.2421	5.0757	4.9173	4.7665	4.6229
7	6.4720	6.2303	6.0021	5.7864	5.5824	5.3893	5.2064
8	7.3255	7.0197	6.7327	6.4632	6.2098	5.9713	5.7466
9	8.1622	7.7861	7.4353	7.1078	6.8017	6.5152	6.2469
10	8.9826	8.5302	8.1109	7.7217	7.3601	7.0236	6.7101
11	9.7868	9.2526	8.7605	8.3064	7.8869	7.4987	7.1390
12	10.5753	9.9540	9.3851	8.8633	8.3838	7.9427	7.5361
13	11.3484	10.6350	9.9856	9.3936	8.8527	8.3577	7.9038
14	12.1062	11.2961	10.5631	9.8986	9.2950	8.7455	8.2442
15	12.8493	11.9379	11.1184	10.3797	9.7122	9.1079	8.5595
16	13.5777	12.5611	11.6523	10.8378	10.1059	9.4466	8.8514
17	14.2919	13.1661	12.1657	11.2741	10.4773	9.7632	9.1216
18	14.9920	13.7535	12.6593	11.6896	10.8276	10.0591	9.3719
19	15.6785	14.3238	13.1339	12.0853	11.1581	10.3356	9.6036
20	16.3514	14.8775	13.5903	12.4622	11.4699	10.5940	9.8181
21	17.0112	15.4150	14.0292	12.8212	11.7641	10.8355	10.0168
22	17.6580	15.9369	14.4511	13.1630	12.0416	11.0612	10.2007
23	18.2922	16.4436	14.8568	13.4886	12.3034	11.2722	10.3711
24	18.9139	16.9355	15.2470	13.7986	12.5504	11.4693	10.5288
25	19.5235	17.4131	15.6221	14.0939	12.7834	11.6536	10.6748
26	20.1210	17.8768	15.9828	14.3752	13.0032	11.8258	10.8100
27	20.7069	18.3270	16.3296	14.6430	13.2105	11.9867	10.9352
28	21.2813	18.7641	16.6631	14.8981	13.4062	12.1371	11.0511
29	21.8444	19.1885	16.9837	15.1411	13.5907	12.2777	11.1584
30	22.3965	19.6004	17.2920	15.3725	13.7648	12.4090	11.2578
31	22.9377	20.0004	17.5885	15.5928	13.9291	12.5318	11.3498
32	23.4683	20.3888	17.8736	15.8027	14.0840	12.6466	11.4350
33	23.9886	20.7658	18.1476	16.0025	14.2302	12.7538	11.5139
34	24.4986	21.1318	18.4112	16.1929	14.3681	12.8540	11.5869
35	24.9986	21.4872	18.6646	16.3742	14.4982	12.9477	11.6546
36	25.4888	21.8323	18.9083	16.5469	14.6210	13.0352	11.7172
37	25.9695	22.1672	19.1426	16.7113	14.7368	13.1170	11.7752
38	26.4406	22.4925	19.3679	16.8679	14.8460	13.1935	11.8289
39	26.9026	22.8082	19.5845	17.0170	14.9491	13.2649	11.8786
40	27.3555	23.1148	19.7928	17.1591	15.0463	13.3317	11.9246
41	27.7995	23.4124	19.9931	17.2944	15.1380	13.3941	11.9672
42	28.2348	23.7014	20.1856	17.4232	15.2245	13.4524	12.0067
43	28.6616	23.9819	20.3708	17.5459	15.3062	13.5070	12.0432
44	29.0800	24.2543	20.5488	17.6628	15.3832	13.5579	12.0771
45	29.4902	24.5187	20.7200	17.7741	15.4558	13.6055	12.1084
46	29.8923	24.7754	20.8847	17.8801	15.5244	13.6500	12.1374
47	30.2866	25.0247	21.0429	17.9810	15.5890	13.6916	12.1643
48	30.6731	25.2667	21.1951	18.0772	15.6500	13.7305	12.1891
49	31.0521	25.5017	21.3415	18.1687	15.7076	13.7668	12.2122
50	31.4236	25.7298	21.4822	18.2559	15.7619	13.8007	12.2335

9%	10%	11%	12%	13%	14%	15%
.9174	.9091	.9009	.8929	.8850	.8772	.8696
1.7591	1.7355	1.7125	1.6901	1.6681	1.6467	1.6257
2.5313	2.4869	2.4437	2.4018	2.3612	2.3216	2.2832
3.2397	3.1699	3.1024	3.0373	2.9745	2.9137	2.8550
3.8897	3.7908	3.6959	3.6048	3.5172	3.4331	3.3522
4.4859	4.3553	4.2305	4.1114	3.9975	3.8887	3.7845
5.0330	4.8684	4.7122	4.5638	4.4226	4.2883	4.1604
5.5348	5.3349	5.1461	4.9676	4.7988	4.6389	4.4873
5.9952	5.7590	5.5370	5.3282	5.1317	4.9464	4.7716
6.4177	6.1446	5.8892	5.6502	5.4262	5.2161	5.0188
6.8052	6.4951	6.2065	5.9377	5.6869	5.4527	5.2337
7.1607	6.8137	6.4924	6.1944	5.9176	5.6603	5.4206
7.4869	7.1034	6.7499	6.4235	6.1218	5.8424	5.5831
7.7862	7.3667	6.9819	6.6282	6.3025	6.0021	5.7245
8.0607	7.6061	7.1909	6.8109	6.4624	6.1422	5.8474
8.3126	7.8237	7.3792	6.9740	6.6039	6.2651	5.9542
8.5436	8.0216	7.5488	7.1196	6.7291	6.3729	6.0472
8.7556	8.2014	7.7016	7.2497	6.8399	6.4674	6.1280
8.9501	8.3649	7.8393	7.3658	6.9380	6.5504	6.1982
9.1285	8.5136	7.9633	7.4694	7.0248	6.6231	6.2593
9.2922	8.6487	8.0751	7.5620	7.1016	6.6870	6.3125
9.4424	8.7715	8.1757	7.6446	7.1695	6.7429	6.3587
9.5802	8.8832	8.2664	7.7184	7.2297	6.7921	6.3988
9.7066	8.9847	8.3481	7.7843	7.2829	6.8351	6.4338
9.8226	9.0770	8.4217	7.8431	7.3300	6.8729	6.4641
9.9290	9.1609	8.4881	7.8957	7.3717	6.9061	6.4906
10.0266	9.2372	8.5478	7.9426	7.4086	6.9352	6.5135
10.1161	9.3066	8.6016	7.9844	7.4412	6.9607	6.5335
10.1983	9.3696	8.6501	8.0218	7.4701	6.9830	6.5509
10.2737	9.4269	8.6938	8.0552	7.4957	7.0027	6.5660
10.3428	9.4790	8.7331	8.0850	7.5183	7.0199	6.5791
10.4062	9.5264	8.7686	8.1116	7.5383	7.0350	6.5905
10.4644	9.5694	8.8005	8.1354	7.5560	7.0482	6.6005
10.5178	9.6086	8.8293	8.1566	7.5717	7.0599	6.6091
10.5668	9.6442	8.8552	8.1755	7.5856	7.0700	6.6166
10.6118	9.6765	8.8786	8.1924	7.5979	7.0790	6.6231
10.6530	9.7059	8.8996	8.2075	7.6087	7.0868	6.6288
10.6908	9.7327	8.9186	8.2210	7.6183	7.0937	6.6338
10.7255	9.7570	8.9357	8.2330	7.6268	7.0997	6.6380
10.7574	9.7791	8.9511	8.2438	7.6344	7.1050	6.6418
10.7866	9.7991	8.9649	8.2534	7.6410	7.1097	6.6450
10.8134	9.8174	8.9774	8.2619	7.6469	7.1138	6.6478
10.8380	9.8340	8.9886	8.2696	7.6522	7.1173	6.6503
10.8605	9.8491	8.9988	8.2764	7.6568	7.1205	6.6524
10.8812	9.8628	9.0079	8.2825	7.6609	7.1232	6.6543
10.9002	9.8753	9.0161	8.2880	7.6645	7.1256	6.6559
10.9176	9.8866	9.0235	8.2928	7.6677	7.1277	6.6573
10.9336	9.8969	9.0302	8.2972	7.6705	7.1296	6.6585
10.9482	9.9063	9.0362	8.3010	7.6730	7.1312	6.6596
10.9617	9.9148	9.0417	8.3045	7.6752	7.1327	6.6605

Index

Index

Debentures, 290
Debits, 61
Debt to equity ratio, 335
Decision packages, 574
Deferral method (investment tax credit), 310
Deferred charges, 33
Deferred credits, 35
Deferred income taxes; *See* Income taxes
Depletion, 259, 275, 412
Depreciation, 33, 103, 109, 259, 267–70
  accelerated methods, 268
  double-declining balance, 269
  location-specific equipment, 275
  straight-line, 268
  sum-of-the-years' digits method, 268
Differential costs, 590; *See also* Incremental costs
Dilution (earnings per share), 359
Direct costing, 543–46
Direct costs, 118, 504, 529; *See also* Direct costing
  standard cost variances, 649–55
Direct write-off method (uncollectible accounts receivable, 196
Discount (bonds), 291, 294–98
Discounted cash flows, 179; *See also* Present value of cash flows
Discount note, 207
Discount rate, 174, 207, 621
Discounts, cash 202
Dividends, 28, 39, 76, 100, 349–54
  accounting entries, 350
  declaration of, 349
  in kind, 351
  intercorporate, 377–80
  stock, 352–54
Double-entry record keeping system, 28
Dun and Bradstreet, 42

E

Earned surplus, 350
Earnings per share, (EPS), 42, 358–63
Earnings process, 137; *See also* Income
Economic models, 563
Economists (view of costs), 508
Efficiency variance (direct labor), 652
Efficiency variance (overhead), 661

Eisner v. Macomber, 353n
Employment stock options, 355–58
Equities, 26
Equity method (intercorporate investments), 376, 378–80
Equivalent units (process costing), 535
Errors, 114
Exchange prices, 153
Exercise price (employee stock options), 356
Expected value, 630–35
Expenses, 66
  budgeting of, 564
  closing entries, 74
  defined, 29, 69
  means of accounting for, 104
  overview of recognition issues, 152
  selected industry problems, 151
  timing of, 151
Extraordinary gains and losses, 37, 358

F

Fair market value; *See* Market value
FASB; *See* Financial Accounting Standards Board
Federal Insurance Contribution Act, 213
FICA; *See* Federal Insurance Contribution Act
FIFO; *See* First in, first out method
Financial accounting defined, 2
Financial Accounting Standards Board (FASB), 17
  contingent losses, 355, 473
  current values, 170, 247, 263, 438, 452
  definitions of terms, 69n
  leases, 304
  lines of business, 474
  lower of cost or market rule, 185
  marketable securities, 377n
  objectives of financial reporting, 467
  oil drilling costs, 277
  research and development costs, 278
Financial ratios; *See* Ratios
Financial reporting, 467–82; *See also* Accounting
  limitations of for managers, 471
  management explanations, 474
  objectives of, 467